Intellectual Culture in Medieval Paris

In the thirteenth century, the University of Paris emerged as a complex community with a distinctive role in society. This book explores the relationship between contexts of learning and the ways of knowing developed within them, focusing on twelfth-century schools and monasteries, as well as the university. By investigating their views on money, marriage and sex, Ian Wei reveals the complexity of what theologians had to say about the world around them. He analyses the theologians' sense of responsibility to the rest of society and the means by which they tried to communicate and assert their authority. In the late thirteenth and early fourteenth centuries, however, their claims to authority were challenged by learned and intellectually sophisticated women and men who were active outside as well as inside the university, and who used the vernacular – an important phenomenon in the development of the intellectual culture of medieval Europe.

IAN P. WEI is Senior Lecturer in History at the University of Bristol. His publications include two co-edited volumes, *Authority and Community in the Middle Ages* (with Don Mowbray and Rhiannon Purdie, 1999) and *Medieval Futures: Attitudes to the Future in the Middle Ages* (with John Burrow, 2000).

Intellectual Culture in Medieval Paris

Theologians and the University c. 1100–1330

Ian P. Wei

CAMBRIDGE
UNIVERSITY PRESS

University Printing House, Cambridge CB2 8BS, United Kingdom

Cambridge University Press is part of the University of Cambridge.

It furthers the University's mission by disseminating knowledge in the pursuit of education, learning and research at the highest international levels of excellence.

www.cambridge.org
Information on this title: www.cambridge.org/9781107460362

First published 2012
First paperback edition 2014

A catalogue record for this publication is available from the British Library

Library of Congress Cataloguing in Publication data
Wei, Ian P.
Intellectual culture in medieval Paris : theologians and the university, c.1100-1330 / Ian P. Wei.
pages cm
Includes bibliographical references and index.
ISBN 978-1-107-00969-1
1. Education, Higher–France–Paris–History–To 1500.
2. Church and college–France–Paris–History–To 1500.
3. Université de Paris–History–To 1500. 4. Paris (France)–Intellectual life–History–To 1500. I. Title.
LA698.W43 2012
378.443′610902–dc23
2011052386

ISBN 978-1-107-00969-1 Hardback
ISBN 978-1-107-46036-2 Paperback

For Betty R. Wei and Teh-Hsing Wei

Contents

Preface *page* ix
Acknowledgements xii
List of abbreviations xiii

Introduction 1

1 The twelfth-century schools of northern France 8
Competition, student power and the emergence of a new career 9
The lure of logic 17
Texts: interpreting authorities 33
Sense perception 37
Myth and poetry 40
Diversity and conflict 44
Towards universities 47

2 The twelfth-century monasteries and Hugh of Saint Victor 52
Anselm of Bec and Canterbury 53
Bernard of Clairvaux 59
William of Saint Thierry 65
Hildegard of Bingen 68
Conflict between monks and schoolmen 72
Hugh of Saint Victor 78

3 The University of Paris in the thirteenth century 87
Institutionalization, cultural identity and a new discourse of learning 87
Bonaventure 124
Aquinas 143
Conflict and condemnation 161

4 Communication and control 170
Self-image 174
Generating a need for masters of theology and their judgements in Christian society 184
Means of communication 228
Conclusion 245

5 Sex and marriage 247
The nature of men and women 248
Marriage 250
Marital sex 260
Marital problems 272

6 Money 293
Exchange 296
Usury 306
Annuities: a case study 323
Living with usury: tolerating a lesser evil 345
Living with usury: usurious money 348
Conclusion 353

7 Anti-intellectual intellectuals in the late thirteenth and early fourteenth centuries: a new context 356
Jean de Meun and the *Romance of the Rose* 357
Marguerite Porete and *The Mirror of Simple Souls* 374
Eckhart 392
Conclusion 408

Bibliography 415
Index 437

Preface

The arguments that I present in this book have been developed in the course of both teaching and research. I owe a great debt to successive generations of students at the universities of Edinburgh and Bristol in whose company my thinking has developed. I hope that former students who read this book will hear echoes of the passionate debates in which they helped me to refine my ideas and find the best way to present them. Although the students who have contributed to my work are too numerous to mention by name, I must offer very special thanks to those whose research at doctoral level has greatly enriched my understanding of medieval intellectual culture: Helen Casey, Mark Kauntze, Richard Lambert and Don Mowbray. I must also express my thanks to colleagues at the universities of Edinburgh and Bristol. I began my teaching career at the University of Edinburgh and I will always be immensely grateful to my former colleagues for showing me how the job should be done, especially Michael Angold, Tom Brown, Gary Dickson, Ken Fowler, Tony Goodman, Angus Mackay, Nicholas Phillipson and John Stephens. I must also offer heartfelt thanks to former and current colleagues at the University of Bristol who have commented on my work and stimulated my thinking. In the Centre for Medieval Studies, I would like to thank especially Elizabeth Archibald, Kenneth Austin, Marcus Bull, Fernando Cervantes, Gillian Clark, James Clark, Emma Dillon, George Ferzoco, Anke Holdenried, David Hook, Evan Jones, Pam King, Carolyn Muessig, Ad Putter, Anne Simon, Brendan Smith, Denys Turner, Carol Meale and Beth Williamson. I have, however, received support and encouragement from many quarters in the university, and I am especially grateful to Bernard Alford, Robert Bickers, Bill Doyle, Bob Fowler, Ronald Hutton, Michael Liversidge, Chris McLeod, Josie McLellan, Kirsty Reid, Philip Richardson, Richard Sheldon, Eric Thomas and James Thompson. A list of medievalists from other universities to whom I am indebted for advice would extend over many pages, but I am especially grateful to David d'Avray, Alan Bernstein, Peter Biller, Mishtooni Bose, Laura Cleaver (who helped me find an image for the cover), Anne Cobby, David Ditchburn, Jean Dunbabin, Fionnuala Sinclair, Spencer Young and Nicolette Zeeman. I must also thank those who read the book on behalf of Cambridge University Press for excellent advice; two readers remained anonymous, but Peter Denley revealed his identity when offering specific help on Italian universities.

In recent years my work on medieval universities has been greatly enriched by collaboration with colleagues in the Ideas and Universities project which runs as part of the Worldwide Universities Network and compares universities in different cultures and periods. I must thank especially Isobel Howe, Susie Jim, Glen Jones, Lisa Lucas, David Shepherd, John Taylor, Tony Welch and Xu Xiaozhou.

In 2009–10 I enjoyed the huge privilege of being a member of the School of Social Science at the Institute for Advanced Study in Princeton. I am extremely grateful to Danielle Allen for inviting me to work in an immensely stimulating environment, and for the intellectual and personal generosity with which she received my work. She and her colleagues, Didier Fassin, Joan Scott and Michael Walzer, were endlessly perceptive and encouraging in their comments. As if this were not enough, Caroline Bynum and Giles Constable made me equally at home in the School of History and generously took a lively interest in this book. In both schools extraordinarily brilliant scholars had been gathered together, and I am grateful to all of them for the atmosphere of intellectual excitement in which I had the opportunity to rework the final draft of this book.

This book would not have reached fruition without the help and encouragement of staff at Cambridge University Press. Michael Watson waited patiently for this book for a long time, gently enquiring how it was coming along, but always careful to make it clear that it must be the book that I wanted it to be. Once I had submitted the book, Liz Friend-Smith oversaw crucial rewriting and her sound judgement has been of immense value. Chloe Howell has guided me through the production of the book with great care and kindness.

I must express my particular gratitude to some very special friends whose relentless kindness and intellectual energy have turned moments of intellectual uncertainty into passionate conversations that have shaped my work: Julie Cooper, Rita Copeland, Rosemary Deem, Marilynn Desmond, Ka Ho Mok, Adam Nelson, Matt Nelson, Miri Rubin and David Wallace.

My greatest intellectual debt is to two wonderful teachers. Peggy Brown 'adopted' me when I was a graduate student in Paris, decided that I had something worth saying when others might reasonably have had their doubts, and has been unwavering in her support for over twenty-five years. Her intellectual power and generosity have been the making of many of us, and the challenge has always been to live up to her expectations. The late Jeff Denton introduced me to medieval history when I was an undergraduate at the University of Manchester. He had the extraordinary gift of making every single student feel as if she or he were embarking on a personal mission to understand the past in a new way. He combined intellectual rigour with a free spirit of great generosity and enthusiasm. He pointed me in many of the directions that I have subsequently followed and, though I miss him, I hear his voice whenever I read his work.

I must conclude by thanking my family. They have lived with this book for a long time, whether or not they were aware of it, and they give meaning to everything that I do. I offer many thanks to my sister and her family: Anne, Phil, Alex and Beth. My final, greatest and most important thanks go to my mother and father. They taught me to value education and appreciate university culture in its many forms. They are my closest friends, on whose love and support I have always depended. It is to Betty R. Wei and Teh-Hsing Wei that I dedicate this book.

Acknowledgements

I am grateful to the publishers of the following articles for permission to re-use material in this book: 'The self-image of the masters of theology at the university of Paris in the late thirteenth and early fourteenth centuries', *Journal of Ecclesiastical History* 46 (1995): 398–431; 'Intellectuals and money: Parisian disputations about annuities in the thirteenth century', *Bulletin of the John Rylands University Library of Manchester* 83, no. 3 (2001), a special edition further titled P. D. Clarke (ed.), *Owens's Historical Essays in Honour of Jeffrey H. Denton*, pp. 71–94; 'Gender and sexuality in medieval academic discourse: marriage problems in Parisian quodlibets', *Mediaevalia* 31 (2010): 5–34; 'From twelfth-century schools to thirteenth-century universities: the disappearance of biographical and autobiographical representations of scholars', *Speculum* 86 (2011): 42–78.

Abbreviations

Chartularium	*Chartularium Universitatis Parisiensis*, ed. H. Denifle and E. Chatelain, 4 vols. (Paris, 1889–97)
B. N. lat.	Paris, Bibliothèque Nationale, latin
Peter Lombard, *Sententiae*	Peter Lombard, *Sententiae in IV libris distinctae*, Spicilegium Bonaventurianum 4 and 5 (Grottaferrata, 1971 and 1981)
PL	*Patrologia cursus completus, series Latina*, ed. J.-P. Migne, 221 vols. (1844–61)
ST	Thomas Aquinas, *Summa Theologiae: Latin Text and English Translation*, ed. T. Gilby *et al.*, 61 vols. (London, 1964–80). With volume and page numbers in brackets
University Records	L. Thorndike, *University Records and Life in the Middle Ages* (New York, 1944)

Introduction

This book is an introduction to the intellectual culture that developed in Paris from the early twelfth century, and it focuses in particular on the theologians. The international standing of Paris and its theologians, who came to Paris from all over Europe and left to hold important jobs on an equally wide scale, makes this study relevant to medieval intellectual culture more generally. The book has also been conceived so as to cut across categories and conceptual boundaries that have separated various fields of study and thus framed most existing works. First, intellectual history and institutional history have generally been treated separately. There are many outstanding studies of medieval thought, but they have not been primarily concerned with the contexts in which thinking took place; such information has been presented merely as background. There are also excellent institutional histories of schools, monasteries and universities, but they have tended not to dwell on the scholarly work that took place in them. This book, however, examines the relationship between ways of thinking and contexts. In part this reflects a methodological principle that ideas can only be understood historically if placed in context, but it was also an issue that medieval scholars themselves considered, and their views on the matter were fundamentally important to their sense of identity and authority. Second, the history of abstract philosophy and theology and the history of ethics and moral theology have also been studied separately, and often by different historians. The work of theologians who operated in both fields is only rarely analysed as a whole, and those who were preoccupied with ethics and pastoral theology are sometimes dismissed as second-rate thinkers by intellectual historians. This is to miss the place that medieval theologians themselves accorded to ethics and moral theology, the sense of pastoral mission that underpinned much of their apparently abstract work, and the institutional significance of attitudes to virtue and pastoral mission. Third, existing histories of medieval thought have generally ignored the intellectual work of women, while learned women have received separate treatment as individuals, in studies of women, or in histories of 'mysticism'. This book only begins the work of synthesis and re-conceptualization that will be required to produce a general history of ideas and gender, but at least the inclusion of Hildegard of Bingen and Marguerite Porete points up the masculinity of Parisian intellectual culture.

This book also includes much more extended textual analysis than is usual in outline intellectual histories of the period. The disadvantage of this approach is that many significant figures and many themes have to be omitted lest the book assume unmanageable proportions. Many existing histories of medieval thought therefore offer much fuller coverage, but their brief references and compressed accounts of key arguments surely mean more to specialists than to general readers. Students can repeat the account of an argument, but they are in no position to engage with it critically, or to place it with any confidence in any broader analysis of their own. Moreover, they are not prepared effectively to read the primary texts for themselves. Given the current trend in universities towards independent learning and the writing of long essays and dissertations, it is essential to train students to make sense of texts that raise complex intellectual problems in unfamiliar and technical terms, and this requires close textual reading of substantial passages. This emphasis also facilitates the kind of interdisciplinary work that is flourishing in centres of medieval studies. Wherever possible, use is made of texts that are available in translation. Unfortunately this skews the selection of material since the work of translation has sometimes been driven by confessional as well as scholarly concerns. Different styles of translation can also create misleading impressions of, for example, similarity or difference between two figures, and it has been necessary to make adjustments where translators have sought to use modern terms in order to force an engagement between medieval texts and modern philosophical debates. The great advantage of using the most readily available translations, however, is that it permits non-specialist readers to test the analysis on the basis of their own reading beyond the quoted passages.

It will perhaps be helpful briefly to set out the structure of the book. The first three chapters look at three different contexts of learning and the ways of knowing that were cultivated within them. The schools of northern France, discussed in Chapter 1, were institutionally fluid, highly competitive, and offered a new type of career to masters who were able to cultivate their reputations and attract students. The intellectual methods developed in the schools were highly diverse. Scholars developed new methods of textual interpretation, and sought to understand the physical world partly through sense perception but chiefly through poetry and myth. Increasingly, however, the schools came to be dominated by the study of logic which offered its exponents a powerful form of argument that could be deployed in all subjects, a way into major philosophical issues, the promise that divine mysteries could be opened up to human understanding, and a process of initiation creating an intellectual elite. The plethora of intellectual approaches caused heated debate about what was true and appropriate. Nevertheless, the second half of the century witnessed developments that were to underpin the emergence of a university in Paris: a growing consensus about what should be studied and how, support for schools from major political authorities, and the emergence of a limited number of places as key centres of learning.

Chapter 2 focuses on the equally dynamic world of the twelfth-century monasteries, exploring their ways of knowing through the work of Anselm, Bernard of Clairvaux and William of Saint Thierry. They stressed the importance of personal experience, self-knowledge, prayer and love. Invariably they granted a critical role to God, as Hildegard's visionary experiences made especially clear. Crucially, they insisted that it was necessary to live a life of virtue, and that only an elite audience in a religious house could properly receive the more advanced ideas. In the late eleventh and early twelfth centuries, Anselm was keen to include reason and logic amongst many ways to know God, but a generation later Bernard and William reacted against the schools and their emphasis on logic, criticizing their intellectual methods, their way of life and their attitude to their audience. Despite instances of dramatic conflict, however, some saw a way forward through synthesis of the different approaches. Hugh of Saint Victor shared the fundamental monastic values and was highly critical of the schoolmen, but while emphasizing that a life of learning had to be a life of virtue, he offered a theory of knowledge and valued the liberal arts. Crucially, he found a place for study in the ascent to God, requiring those who moved beyond study to continue to practise scholarship on its own terms, an approach that was to underpin the ideology of the new university.

Chapter 3 explores the University of Paris in the thirteenth century. The statutes of 1215 and the papal bull *Parens scientiarum* of 1231 articulated a public vision that was shaped by key monastic ideals: the university was to be a properly regulated environment in which the virtuous behaviour necessary for achieving knowledge was required, and in which masters would take responsibility for the impact of their teaching on their audience. The university would therefore be immune to the criticisms that had been directed at the twelfth-century schools. *Parens scientiarum* also declared that the fundamental purpose of the university was to transform men into preachers, tying the university into the pastoral mission of the church. A process of institutionalization turned the university into a permanent locus of authority, with masters now dominating the students. The university was, however, extremely complex; it was a community made up of many other communities, offering masters and students a range of identities, and sometimes causing dissension within the university. There were also striking intellectual differences in approaches to knowing. Bonaventure and Thomas Aquinas, for example, were very different in their assessments of sense perception and innate ideas, and therefore in their reception of Aristotle. The most dramatic controversies arose, however, when members of the faculty of arts considered the unity of the intellect and the eternity of the world. Despite the condemnations that ensued, and the involvement of external authority on these occasions, these conflicts were largely played out within the university. Moreover, there was a general consensus that it was possible to know truths with certainty, and that the learned exposition of truth underpinned the authority of the university and especially the masters of theology.

The fourth chapter occupies a pivotal position in the book because it explains the sense of responsibility that Parisian masters of theology felt towards the rest of society and the ways in which they endeavoured to communicate their views to others and assert their authority over them. The masters had been taught ethics and moral theology when they studied grammar and rhetoric as young students, and they regarded ethics and moral theology as the culmination of study. Moreover, they considered themselves to be at the summit of a hierarchy of learning, and justified their continued study and their high status in terms of their social functions. This led them to claim an immediate authority as academic theologians at the University of Paris, an authority that might even set them over prelates of the church. Moreover, they developed a number of ideas that served to generate a universal need for the masters' judgements on every aspect of human life. Ideas about purgatory, the ethic of intention and the devil threw responsibility onto each individual for his or her own fate after death, raising the stakes by inspiring both hope of salvation and fear of pain. At the same time, the issues involved in achieving salvation were presented as so challenging and complex that no individual could reasonably hope to cope alone, hence the need for the masters' authoritative guidance. This guidance was communicated through disputations, sermons and confession, practices about which the masters theorized and to which they were heavily committed.

The next two chapters explore what Parisian theologians actually had to say about two fundamental aspects of human life. The theologians discussed and wrote about a vast range of issues. In addition to matters of doctrine and the basis for religious belief, they analysed Christian society from every angle because the potential for sin was ever present and correct behaviour had always to be defined. It would therefore be possible to examine their views on any number of themes: the nature of the church as an institution, including the positions of the pope and bishops; or the powers and responsibilities of secular rulers; or the relationship between ecclesiastical and secular authorities; and so on. The themes of these two chapters have been chosen because they demonstrate the engagement of Parisian theologians with matters that directly or indirectly concerned the overwhelming majority of the population, and also show a response to profound changes taking place in western European society. Thus Chapter 5 concerns their views on sex and marriage, especially the consistency of their message, the language that they used when discussing marital problems, and the issue of misogyny. They were generally consistent on a whole range of matters including the binary opposition between the active male and the passive female, male dominance, the purpose of marriage, the importance of free consent, the theory of conjugal debt, how and when sexual activity should occur, and the power of women to persuade with words because there were specifically feminine forms of knowledge. Individual masters could be inconsistent, however, when discussing women: they expressed very different views depending on whether they were considering the nature of women directly or extolling the value of marital affection. There were also disagreements between theologians. What established a valid marriage caused problems for some time, but they were largely resolved. Disagreements were never settled, however, with regard to sexual pleasure and the extent to which marital sex was sinful, and with regard to the property rights of wives. While much of their thinking about women is bound to strike the twenty-first-century reader as misogynistic, it is important to avoid oversimplification: they insisted on equality in a number of respects, and their treatment of practical marriage problems shows that they were willing to address moral problems that their basic values created for women, while also taking into account social realities such as custom and personality. The complexity of their attitude to women is perhaps most tellingly revealed by the instability of their discourse when treating what we would call gender issues.

Chapter 6 considers the theologians' treatment of money and urban culture. The university was deeply embedded in the city, its very existence unthinkable without the urban growth of the period. While the masters did not model themselves on artisans and merchants, as has been suggested, they undertook to give townspeople moral direction. Although slower to accept responsibility for financial life than for sexual activity, they came to devote much attention to the effects of the flourishing economy. Their thinking was ambivalent in many respects. They expressed a traditional hostility to trade while also largely justifying trade and the work of the merchant. In performing the latter task, they stressed the importance of justice in exchange, with the just price taken to be the current market price. They unanimously condemned usury, but went beyond the traditional authorities to develop a range of new arguments to support the condemnation, some contradicting older arguments. They then deployed these new arguments when scrutinizing types of contract and discovering that they were licit, thus in effect legitimating specific ways of charging for credit. They also found reasons to tolerate usury as a lesser evil, thus acknowledging the benefits of charging for credit. Furthermore, they used conceptions of money developed in arguing against usury to discover that it was morally safest to do business in money because it was less likely to change hands with an obligation to make restitution attached. Embedded within their arguments were new assumptions: the money economy was autonomous, no longer dependent on agrarian society or traditional forms of political authority for legitimacy; time was infinite and measurable, and experts could make predictions about what would probably happen in the market. These profound shifts remained understated or implicit, however, permitting traditional prohibitions and the church's pastoral strategy to remain intact, while much of what was happening in the marketplace became acceptable.

The final chapter argues that in the late thirteenth and early fourteenth centuries anti-intellectual intellectuals, as I have called them, presented a profound challenge to the authority and identity of the University of Paris and especially its masters of theology. Deeply learned and intellectually sophisticated men and women, operating both inside and outside the university but nevertheless connected with the university and its theologians, expressed their ideas in vernacular languages. Jean de Meun, Marguerite Porete and Eckhart were perhaps the key figures. In different ways they called into question the value of reason, and undermined the idea that language could be used to convey definite meaning, implying that truths could not be known and communicated with certainty. They also challenged the link between living virtuously and knowing correctly. They cast doubt on the worth of the pastoral strategies and the devotional practices of the church. They did not seem interested in how they themselves might be understood or misunderstood, and what effect they might have on many who received their ideas. They deployed the language and imagery of nobility in association with worthwhile knowledge, thus favouring a social category that had its roots outside the university. The wider context in which the theologians worked was now very different: they no longer had a monopoly of higher theological learning. Moreover, the public discourse that had generated the university's sense of purpose and permitted successful negotiation of its privileged status in society was threatened. The masters' ability to generate certain knowledge and to communicate that knowledge with authority was called into question. The University of Paris did not decline or fade in importance as a result, but a fundamental change was taking place, suggesting that a process of reinvention and renegotiation would be required. Historians have pointed to many changes in the intellectual culture of the fourteenth century, and this is perhaps one more strand that needs to be considered as research continues.

1 The twelfth-century schools of northern France

The masters of the twelfth-century schools in northern France lived, taught and wrote as if they were always on to something new. Many younger scholars were certain that they had access to truths that had been beyond their predecessors, whom they did not hesitate to insult and to try to supplant. Those who reacted with horror to the schools accepted that their endeavours had novel qualities, and indeed this was a large part of what they disliked. It is important, however, to step back from twelfth-century polemic and to note the debt that the masters owed to the past. The work of medieval scholars depended on analysis of ancient Greek and Roman texts, of the Bible, and of early Christian writers. Owing to common interests and the means by which the schoolmen came into possession of classical works, the more recent works of Muslim and Jewish thinkers were also highly influential. But this body of material did not exist in its entirety at the beginning of the twelfth century. On the contrary, by a complex process of transmission and translation, more and more of the work of the ancient world became available during the twelfth and thirteenth centuries. Paradoxically, therefore, to study the oldest texts was in a sense to study the newest material. The continual supply of new material had an important effect: it meant that existing scholarship was always going out of date. A student did not have to consider himself a genius to feel that his work was bound to make a worthwhile contribution and indeed surpass that of his teachers. Furthermore, much scholarly effort was directed towards the process of interpreting texts, so that even texts that had long been available could be subjected to new techniques and again a degree of originality was easily attained. It is hard to imagine a greater incentive to intellectual endeavour.

Schools were certainly not, however, a completely new invention of the twelfth century. Monastic schools had existed across western Europe for centuries, and they were chiefly responsible for the survival of those authoritative texts which were available at the start of our period. Cathedral schools had also flourished in many parts of western

Europe in the eleventh century and they did much to provide the framework within which twelfth-century masters operated. It is extremely difficult, however, to establish the relationship between eleventh- and twelfth-century cathedral schools because so little scholarly work by eleventh-century masters survives. It has been convincingly argued that the eleventh-century masters simply did not write a great deal, or attached little importance to what they wrote, because their aim was the ethical formation of men who would go on to serve in ecclesiastical and secular government, and their teaching technique was to offer themselves as living models.[1] These concerns were not entirely lost, but the twelfth-century schools of northern France clearly represented a significant departure from the prevailing pattern in western Europe, with much greater emphasis on texts.[2] Paris was by no means the only place in which schools took on a new character, and the schools of Chartres, Laon, Rheims and Orléans, for example, were just as eminent. The first part of this chapter will identify the characteristics that set a number of northern French schools apart from previous contexts of learning. It will then consider what drew young men to study there, and explore the diverse ways of thinking that were practised. This diversity caused great debate and controversy, and this too must be examined. Finally, we must consider developments that took place in the second half of the twelfth century and that, with hindsight, can be seen to take us towards the formation of a university in Paris.

Competition, student power and the emergence of a new career

We are fortunate in that twelfth-century scholars were strongly inclined to reflect on themselves and their world, with the result that a number of accounts of the twelfth-century schools survive. Peter Abelard, for example, left a vivid and telling description in his autobiographical letter, the *Historia Calamitatum*, or 'History of my Misfortunes'. Peter Abelard was probably the most famous and controversial scholar of the first half of the twelfth century. He was born in 1079, the son of a Breton knight. He came to study in Paris in about 1100 and subsequently studied and

[1] C. S. Jaeger, *The Envy of Angels: Cathedral Schools and Social Ideals in Medieval Europe, 950–1200* (Philadelphia, 1994).

[2] On the shift from the oral to the textual, see C. J. Mews, 'Orality, literacy, and authority in the twelfth-century schools', *Exemplaria* 2 (1990): 475–500; L. Smith, *The Glossa Ordinaria: The Making of a Medieval Bible Commentary* (Leiden, 2009), pp. 5–12, 37; B. Stock, *The Implications of Literacy: Written Language and Models of Interpretation in the Eleventh and Twelfth Centuries* (Princeton, 1983).

taught in various places in northern France, frequently benefiting from the political patronage of Stephen of Garlande, an archdeacon of Paris and a powerful figure at the French royal court. Several aspects of his intellectual achievements will be discussed later, but he was equally well known for his affair with Heloise. When established as the master of the cathedral school of Notre Dame in Paris, he was employed as private tutor to Heloise, the niece of Fulbert, one of the canons of Notre Dame. The affair between Heloise and Abelard has long been the stuff of legend, their story subject to reinvention in every age. Until recently, Heloise was thought to be about seventeen when the relationship began, with Abelard in his late thirties. Now she is more commonly placed in her twenties, at least in her early twenties and perhaps even her late twenties, and she is presented as Abelard's intellectual equal with distinctive views that influenced Abelard's work. However we imagine their affair, it resulted in the birth of a son and secret marriage. When Abelard lodged her in a nunnery, Fulbert supposed that he was repudiating her, and had his men attack Abelard as he slept at night and castrate him. Heloise obeyed Abelard's command to enter a convent, and he too entered religion at the abbey of Saint Denis. Abelard was condemned for heresy at the Council of Soissons in 1121 and became abbot of Saint Gildas in Brittany about 1126. He was once more condemned for heresy at the Council of Sens in 1140 and died, a monk of Cluny, in 1142.[3] The letters of Abelard and Heloise were written in the early to mid 1130s. The first letter in the collection was written by Abelard to an unnamed and probably imaginary friend to offer consolation. In this it conforms to a set rhetorical model, the *epistola consolatoria*, and the gist is that the friend's troubles are nothing compared to Abelard's. The letter tells of Abelard's early career as student and master, his affair with Heloise, their entry to religion, his trial at Soissons, and his subsequent career as monk and teacher.[4]

[3] For the life of Abelard, see R.-H. Bautier, 'Paris au temps Abélard', in J. Jolivet (ed.), *Abélard en sons temps. Actes du colloque international organisé à l'occasion du 9e centenaire de la naissance de Pierre Abélard (14–19 mai 1979)* (Paris, 1981), pp. 21–77; M. T. Clanchy, *Abelard: A Medieval Life* (Oxford, 1997); J. Marenbon, *The Philosophy of Peter Abelard* (Cambridge, 1997), pp. 7–35; C. J. Mews, *Peter Abelard* (Aldershot, 1995), pp. 1–20. For reassessment of Heloise's age and her influence on Abelard, see Clanchy, *Abelard*, pp. 173–4, 275, 330; C. J. Mews, *The Lost Love Letters of Heloise and Abelard: Perceptions of Dialogue in Twelfth-Century France* (New York, 1999), p. 32.

[4] On the nature of the letters of Abelard and Heloise, see Clanchy, *Abelard*, pp. 15–16, 122–5, 154–5, 327–9; D. E. Luscombe, 'From Paris to the Paraclete. The correspondence of Abelard and Heloise', *Proceedings of the British Academy* 74 (1988): 247–83; Marenbon, *Philosophy of Peter Abelard*, pp. 82–93; Mews, *Peter Abelard*, pp. 20–6; Mews, *The Lost Love Letters of Heloise and Abelard*; B. Newman, 'Authority, authenticity

Having described the care which his father took to see that he was instructed in letters before he received a knightly training, Abelard explained his decision to adopt a different path:

For my part, the more rapid and easy my progress in my studies, the more eagerly I applied myself, until I was so carried away by my love of learning that I renounced the glory of a military life, made over my inheritance and rights of the eldest son to my brothers, and withdrew from the court of Mars in order to be educated in the lap of Minerva. I preferred the weapons of dialectic to all the other teachings of philosophy, and armed with these I chose the conflicts of disputation instead of the trophies of war. I began to travel about in several provinces disputing, like a true peripatetic philosopher, wherever I had heard that there was keen interest in the art of dialectic.[5]

Abelard gave up his prospects as an oldest son and the life of a knight in order to study. It is clear that he took with him the knightly taste for combat, and the martial imagery conveys the extent to which scholarly competition was a substitute for battle. The passage also illustrates two other characteristics of twelfth-century learning: the use of classical pagan literature, in this case to describe a crucial point of transition, and the itinerant nature of scholarly life.

Eventually Abelard arrived in Paris to study under William of Champeaux. As he presented it, this was the start of a vicious fight during which Abelard's intellectual superiority brought him success, while William could only resort to acts of jealousy and spite. Apparently William initially welcomed his new student, but it did not last long:

he soon took a violent dislike to me because I set out to refute some of his arguments and frequently reasoned against him. On several occasions I proved myself his superior in debate.[6]

William's leading students also took exception to the newcomer's displays, and Abelard responded by setting up his own school at Melun. Crucially Abelard measured his triumph in terms of reputation:

Thus my school had its start and my reputation for dialectic began to spread, with the result that the fame of my old fellow-students and even that of the master himself gradually declined and came to an end.[7]

and the repression of Heloise', *Journal of Medieval and Renaissance Studies* 22 (1992): 121–57, reprinted in B. Newman, *From Virile Woman to WomanChrist: Studies in Medieval Religion and Literature* (Philadelphia, 1995), pp. 46–75; R. W. Southern, 'The letters of Abelard and Heloise', in *Medieval Humanism and Other Studies* (Oxford, 1970), pp. 86–104.

[5] *Historia Calamitatum* in *The Letters of Abelard and Heloise*, trans. B. Radice, revised M. T. Clanchy (London, 2003), p. 3.

[6] *Ibid.*, p. 4. [7] *Ibid.*

Abelard therefore moved his school closer to Paris where he 'could embarrass him [William] through more frequent encounters in disputation'.[8]

Illness forced Abelard to go back to Brittany, but he returned some years later to tackle William once more. William had joined the canons regular and founded the abbey of Saint Victor, just outside Paris, but Abelard's tactics remained the same. His aim was to discredit William's intellectual achievements and steal his students.

> My own teaching gained so much prestige and authority from this that the strongest supporters of my master who had hitherto been the most violent among my attackers now flocked to join my school.[9]

Eventually William gave up and retired.

These battles suggest the ease with which it was possible to set up a school without institutional backing. To succeed, it was essential to establish a reputation because the students made up their own minds where to go. This did more than flatter the successful master: it brought him a living. As Abelard repeatedly made clear, 'wealth and fame' went together. In short, the early twelfth-century schools had little institutional structure, were highly competitive, and allowed the students a decisive say in the process by which masters rose and fell. For those brave enough to enter this arena, a new type of career was on offer.[10]

This view is confirmed by Rupert of Deutz's account of his encounter with masters and students in the schools. Rupert was given as a child to the Benedictine house of Saint Lawrence, near Liège. He became abbot of Deutz, near Cologne, in 1120 and wrote his *Apologia* in 1125. His great protector and patron, Cuno, abbot of Siegburg, had asked him to write a treatise that tackled questions about which the various orders of monks disagreed. The result was a *Commentary on the Benedictine Rule* in four books, in the first of which, his *Apologia*, Rupert reviewed his scholarly life thus far. He examined four controversies in which he had been involved: whether or not God willed evil; the role of the Holy Spirit; the creation of angels; and the eucharist. In each case he presented his version of events and then interpreted what he saw as the key authoritative texts to establish the validity of his position.[11] The gist of

[8] *Ibid.* [9] *Ibid.*, p. 5.

[10] On the entrepreneurial spirit of twelfth-century masters, see J. Le Goff, *Intellectuals in the Middle Ages*, trans. T. L. Fagan (Oxford, 1993), pp. 61–4.

[11] On the nature of the *Apologia* and the circumstances in which it was written, see J. H. Van Engen, *Rupert of Deutz* (Berkeley, 1983), pp. 176–7, 313–14, 346–50. On the four theological controversies, see *ibid.*, pp. 95–220.

it was that he had been treated appallingly, which was especially galling because he had invariably been right.

He opened by quoting Ecclesiasticus 13.23: 'When the poor man speaks they say, "Who is this fellow?" And should he stumble, they even push him down.' This text came to mind, he explained, because it applied to him: 'For I spoke, and because I spoke they said: "Who is this fellow?"'[12] He complained bitterly that he was seen in this light because he had been a monk since childhood, shut away in the cloister – 'I did not travel across sea and land like those rich merchants in whose thoughts I am a poor man' – and they presumed to think that the parable in Matthew 13.45–6 applied to them. He cited the passage: 'Again, the kingdom of heaven is like a merchant in search of fine pearls, who, on finding one pearl of great value, went and sold all that he had and bought it.'[13] Rupert continued:

For they went long distances, and journeyed to celebrated masters. And after they found many pearls that seemed good, the pearls of poets and philosophers, they found one truly good and valuable pearl, the pearl of holy and divine scripture, which they bought for a great price in vigilance and anxiety, if only they could find it perfectly and keep it into eternity! I did not do this, but like simple Jacob with his mother Rebecca, I lived at home. Consequently I am a poor and contemptible man in their minds, and they say: 'Who is this? For he writes and speaks, speaks and writes, a man who was not worthy even to set eyes on our masters and teachers.'[14]

In a final burst of self-pity, Rupert explained that he really had been poor, barely able to get hold of notebooks in which to write.[15] Rupert, however, reckoned that he had the last laugh:

But I saw the wisdom of God, in a certain way I saw the word incarnate, Christ the son of God, all golden, his whole body as if made from the finest gold, and from it the living waters flowing forcefully into me, rushing everywhere out of his body through many holes.[16]

This was perhaps an allusion to the visionary and mystical experiences that he believed informed his interpretations of scripture, although he did not explicitly make this claim until two years later.[17] Rupert sometimes sounded like the most self-confident of schoolmen, repeatedly

[12] Rupert of Deutz, *Apologia*, PL vol. 170, col. 480.
[13] *Ibid.* In my translation I have supplied more of the biblical text for the sake of clarity.
[14] *Ibid.* [15] *Ibid.* [16] *Ibid.*
[17] Van Engen, *Rupert of Deutz*, pp. 346, 349–52. On Rupert's visions, see B. McGinn, *The Growth of Mysticism*, The Presence of God: A History of Western Mysticism 2 (London, 1994), pp. 328–33.

asserting his independence as a scriptural exegete, even when he found himself in disagreement with the Fathers. As a result, he was sometimes subjected to much the same criticism as leading secular masters.[18] Ultimately, however, his was a way of knowing that made sense in monastic context.[19]

So who were Rupert's oppressors, and what actually happened? Sometimes he fell out with schoolmen, sometimes with monks. The account of his first controversy is especially rich and revealing. Very briefly, Anselm of Laon had distinguished between an 'approving' will and a 'permitting' will in God, concluding that God willed evil in the sense that he permitted it. Rupert considered it outrageous to accuse God of willing evil in any sense at all, and he was therefore accused of denying the omnipotence of God.[20] In his *Apologia* he complained that 'great masters and celebrated teachers, brilliant lights of all Francia' advanced the view that God willed evil, and they not only failed to listen to his view on the matter but condemned it as stupid.[21] What Rupert did not say was that in 1116 he was tried for heresy, for his views on both this matter and the eucharist. Although he was cleared, he found it necessary to take refuge in the monastery of Siegburg. He then wrote a whole work on the omnipotence of God, but still he found no favour.[22]

The men whose views mattered most were Anselm of Laon and William of Champeaux, now bishop of Châlons-sur-Marne. In 1117 Rupert decided to take action: 'I went to Francia to engage in a great battle of disputation against those masters whose authority was set so much above and against me.'[23] He wondered at the sight he had presented, 'alone, sitting on a humble ass, a youngster, attended by just one boy', going to distant cities to attack men whom he knew to be brilliant and to enjoy dignity both of office and in teaching. He was met by a crowd of masters and students, 'like a substantial army', who had turned out to hear and conquer him.[24] Extraordinarily, however, immediately after Rupert entered Laon, Anselm died. Rupert therefore went on to Châlons-sur-Marne where he had a 'violent clash' with William,

[18] Van Engen, *Rupert of Deutz*, pp. 214, 342, 345–6.
[19] J. Leclercq, *The Love of Learning and the Desire for God: A Study of Monastic Culture*, trans. C. Misrahi (London, 1978), p. 272; Van Engen, *Rupert of Deutz*, p. 352.
[20] For an account of this controversy, see Van Engen, *Rupert of Deutz*, pp. 181–216, with the arguments in the *Apologia* at pp. 212–14.
[21] Rupert of Deutz, *Apologia*, PL vol. 170, col. 482.
[22] Van Engen, *Rupert of Deutz*, pp. 200–11.
[23] Rupert of Deutz, *Apologia*, PL vol. 170, col. 482.
[24] *Ibid.*, cols. 482–3.

after which Rupert did not know 'whether he survived a whole year'.[25] Actually all this took place in 1117 and William died in 1122, but the sense is clear: one opponent fell dead at the prospect of fighting Rupert, while the other was mortally wounded in active disputation. Rupert claimed that the view that God willed evil had always been opposed by 'many religious and learned men', but they had kept their silence while Anselm and William were alive. Now, however, they were free to air their criticisms, and this controversy was over, although he himself was much hated by those with whom he had contended, and their desire for revenge came into play in later struggles.[26] Rupert thus recalled a life that had apparently been profoundly scarred by his conflicts with masters and their students.

Another example can be found in the *Life of Saint Goswin*. It describes how many students had come to hear Peter Abelard teach publicly in the cloister of Sainte Geneviève where he was 'the inventor and assertor of unheard-of novelties'.[27] Men of greater wisdom were deeply shocked and wanted to do something about it, so they looked for someone to take on Abelard in disputation. They had little difficulty in persuading the young Goswin to rise to the occasion, despite the objections of his master Jocelin that Abelard went in for mocking rather than disputation, and was more of a jester than a teacher.[28] Giving no thought to his own inexperience, or to the fact that Abelard was 'an extremely warlike man, used to victory', Goswin climbed Monte Sainte Geneviève like David taking on Goliath.[29] Goswin proceeded to interrupt Abelard in mid lecture, ignoring his instruction to be quiet. Apparently Abelard did not deign to reply, but his students said that they knew Goswin to be astute in disputation and learned, and insisted that it would not be improper to engage with him, whereas it would be extremely improper to go on refusing. Abelard therefore let Goswin have his say.[30] The *Life*

25 *Ibid*., col. 483. 26 *Ibid*.

27 'Ex Vita B. Gosvini Aquicinctensis Abbatis', ed. M.-J.-J. Brial, in *Recueil des Historiens des Gaules et de la France* 14 (1806): 442. As Brial's edition consists of excerpts which are not always clearly distinguished from each other, references will also be given to the edition from which they were taken: *Beati Gosvini Vita celeberrimi Aquicinctensis monasterii abbatis septimi a duobus diversis eiusdem coenobii monachis separatim exarata, e veteribus ms*, ed. R. Gibbons (Duaci, 1620), 1.4, p. 12.

28 'Ex Vita B. Gosvini', pp. 442–3; *Beati Gosvini Vita*, 1.4, pp. 12–14. On Abelard's skill 'in the art of repartee' causing fear amongst his contemporaries, see Mews, 'Orality, literacy, and authority', p. 484. For his use of jokes, see also M. T. Clanchy, 'Abelard's mockery of St Anselm', *Journal of Ecclesiastical History* 41 (1990): 1–23.

29 'Ex Vita B. Gosvini', p. 443. *Beati Gosvini Vita*, 1.4, p. 14. See also the account in Clanchy, *Abelard*, pp. 91–3.

30 'Ex Vita B. Gosvini', p. 443. *Beati Gosvini Vita*, 1.4, pp. 15–16.

does not reveal what they argued about, but apparently Goswin gave a magisterial performance in the art of disputation, 'assuming that and affirming this, and by his affirmations not now wholly contradicting that', until in the end Abelard was forced to admit that his position was unreasonable.[31]

The result of Goswin's victory was that 'many flocked to him, placing themselves under his teaching'.[32] He had defeated a renowned master, and his career was made. Goswin subsequently entered religion, becoming a leading monastic reformer. As claustral prior of the abbey of Saint Médard, he encountered Abelard once again when the latter was briefly placed in his hands after his trial at the Council of Soissons in 1121.[33] His *Life* offers yet another account of a student attacking a master and thereby establishing an academic career.

The persistence of these conditions through to the middle of the century is confirmed by John of Salisbury in his *Metalogicon*, or 'Defence of Logic'. John was born between 1115 and 1120, and he went to France to pursue his studies in 1136. Later he served at the papal court before becoming secretary to successive archbishops of Canterbury, Theobald and Thomas Becket. John became bishop of Chartres in 1176 and died in 1180. The *Metalogicon* was presented to Thomas Becket in 1159, when he was still Henry II's chancellor.[34]

In the *Metalogicon*, John recalled with nostalgia the orderly world which had been challenged by the likes of Abelard. He wrote an idealised portrait of Bernard of Chartres, 'the greatest font of literary learning in Gaul in recent times',[35] who gave his pupils a measured and

31 'Ex Vita B. Gosvini', p. 443. *Beati Gosvini Vita*, 1.4, pp. 16–17. I have borrowed Clanchy's particularly fine translation of this passage; Clanchy, *Abelard*, p. 92.

32 'Ex Vita B. Gosvini', p. 443. *Beati Gosvini Vita*, 1.5, p. 19.

33 'Ex Vita B. Gosvini', p. 445. *Beati Gosvini Vita*, 1.18, pp. 78–81. See also Clanchy, *Abelard*, p. 231.

34 On John of Salisbury's life and especially his account of his studies in the *Metalogicon*, see S. C. Ferruolo, *The Origins of the University: The Schools of Paris and their Critics, 1100–1215* (Stanford, 1985), pp. 133–4, 140–56; P. Godman, *The Silent Masters: Latin Literature and Its Censors in the High Middle Ages* (Princeton, 2000), pp. 150–4; K. S. B. Keats-Rohan, 'John of Salisbury and education in twelfth century Paris from the account of his *Metalogicon*', *History of Universities* 6 (1986–7): 1–45; D. D. McGarry, 'Introduction', in John of Salisbury, *The Metalogicon of John of Salisbury: A Twelfth-Century Defense of the Verbal and Logical Arts of the Trivium*, trans. D. D. McGarry (Berkeley, 1955), pp. xvi–xix; R. L. Poole, 'The masters of the schools of Paris and Chartres in John of Salisbury's time', *English Historical Review* 35 (1920): 321–42; P. Riché, 'Jean de Salisbury et le monde scolaire du xiie siècle', in M. Wilks (ed.), *The World of John of Salisbury* (1984, repr. Oxford, 1994), pp. 39–61; O. Weijers, 'The chronology of John of Salisbury's studies in France (*Metalogicon*, II.10)', in Wilks (ed.), *World of John of Salisbury*, pp. 109–16.

35 John of Salisbury, *Metalogicon*, p. 67.

thorough education in grammar. Some he would exhort, and others he would flog. All were required to memorize, recite and compose, while the master also fostered faith and morals. In this world a challenge to the master was unthinkable. But John had little experience of this world himself; Bernard had taught at the cathedral school of Chartres from 1114 to 1119, was chancellor there from 1119 until at least 1124, and died before 1130. By the time John reached France, men who taught like Bernard were being forced into retirement. Indeed John says that two of his grammar teachers, William of Conches and Richard l'Evêque, 'were overwhelmed by the onslaught of the ignorant mob, and retired'.[36] Whatever warmth he professed for the old ways, John himself lived the life of the modern student. His first master was Peter Abelard, from whom he learned the basic principles of dialectic, 'drinking in, with consuming avidity ... every word that fell from his lips'.[37] Over the next twelve years (1136–48) John studied under a succession of at least a dozen masters.[38] Sometimes he had to switch when a master left, and sometimes he took advice, but chiefly he pursued his education as he himself saw fit. At various times John himself earned his living as a teacher.[39] But eventually John left the schools to pursue a career in ecclesiastical government which culminated in his appointment to the see of Chartres. This at least the twelfth-century schools had in common with their predecessors: education could lead to administrative careers and high office, and some men went to the schools for that very reason.

The lure of logic

Whatever the career opportunities that education opened up, however, Peter Abelard and John of Salisbury were passionate about their studies, and so were many others. What were they doing and on what terms were masters competing to attract students? It is difficult to identify the major intellectual trends in the schools because their work was extremely varied. Moreover, twelfth-century scholars themselves did not agree on the meanings of the terms that they used to describe and categorize their work, nor did these terms always relate to actual programmes of study. The basic vocabulary was supplied by the classical programme of the seven liberal arts, which were divided into two groups: the trivium, consisting of grammar, dialectic and rhetoric, and the quadrivium, made up of arithmetic, geometry, astronomy and

36 *Ibid.*, p. 71. 37 *Ibid.*, p. 95.
38 *Ibid.*, p. 95–9. 39 *Ibid.*, p. 98–9.

music. These provided a frame of reference, but not necessarily a formal curriculum.

It will already be apparent that dialectic, or logic, as contemporaries were equally happy to call it, was a major attraction. Both Abelard and John of Salisbury had commenced their travels in pursuit of this kind of learning. The study of dialectic centred upon the logical works written by Aristotle in the fourth century BC and mostly translated by Boethius in the early sixth century. The body of material available at the start of the twelfth century, known as the 'old logic', was gradually supplemented by the remaining works, known as the 'new logic', until the full corpus was in circulation by the end of the 1150s. The 'old logic' consisted of the *Categories* and *On Interpretation* by Aristotle, and the *Isagoge*, an introduction to the *Categories* written by Porphyry in the third century. Various commentaries and independent works by Boethius were also influential. The 'new logic' was made up of Aristotle's *Topics*, *De Sophisticis Elenchis*, *Prior Analytics* and *Posterior Analytics*.

What did medieval scholars find in these works? Why would men like Abelard make sacrifices and take risks to engage with it? The *Categories* looked at the ways in which individual words could refer to the world. The first 'category' was substance, a term that was not to be understood in a physical or material sense. It could refer to an individual thing (Socrates) or to a type of thing (human being). Only this first category could exist on its own. All the others, termed 'accidents', had to be predicated (or said) of a substance, and they were: quantity, quality, relation, location, time, posture, state, activity and passivity. *On Interpretation* looked at different types of propositions that could be formed with words. The *Topics* surveyed different types of argument, while the *De Sophisticis Elenchis* catalogued fallacious arguments. The *Prior Analytics* and the *Posterior Analytics* expounded the syllogism.

A sense of what it meant to begin to study logic can be gained from Porphyry's introduction to Aristotle's *Categories*. Porphyry's *Isagoge* explained the basic meaning and significance of five key terms: genus (the plural is 'genera'), species, difference, property and accident. Porphyry acknowledged that these terms could have several meanings, but he focused on the meanings that were of concern to philosophers. One of his fundamental opening points was that they were all terms that could be predicated (or said) of many things and not just one thing: 'For some predications are said of only one thing, as individual terms like "Socrates", "this" man, and "this" object; but others are said of many things, such as genera, species, differences, properties and accidents that occur jointly in many and not uniquely in some one thing.'[40] These terms came into play when individual things were grouped within classes along with other individual things of the same kind. Thus the individual Socrates could be placed in the class 'man' with other individual men. The collective term 'man' could then be predicated of Socrates ('Socrates is a man') and of other particular men. Some classes, however, could be regarded as sub-classes of larger classes. Thus 'man' could be placed within the class 'animal', along with other sub-classes like 'horse'. The first collective term under which individual things might be grouped was the 'species'. A collective term embracing several species was the 'genus'. Genus could therefore be defined as 'that to which the species is subordinate'[41] and 'that predicated essentially of many things which differ in species, as animal, for example'.[42] Porphyry further explained the distinction between genus and species as follows:

> Genera, therefore, differ from those terms which are predicated of only one thing because they are explained as being predicated of many things. They differ from species which are predicated of many things. Although species are predicated of many things, the many do not differ in species but in number. For example, man, as species, is predicated of Socrates and Plato, who do not differ from one another in species but in number; but animal, a genus, is predicated of man, ox, and horse, which differ from one another in species as well as in number.[43]

Species could therefore be defined as 'what is ordered under the genus and what the genus is predicated of essentially'.[44]

The matter was complicated, however, because a class containing sub-classes could itself be a sub-class of another class, which could be a sub-class of yet another class, and so on until an all-embracing class was reached. In this structure, the all-embracing class at the top would be just a genus, the lowest class containing only individual things and no other classes would be just a species, while all the other intermediate classes would be both genera and species, each one a genus in relation to its sub-classes and a species in relation to the class of which it was itself a sub-group:

> In each category there are the highest classes, the lowest classes, and some which are between the highest and the lowest. There is a highest genus beyond which there can be no other superior genus; there is a lowest species after which there can be no subordinate species; and between the highest genus and the lowest species there are some classes which are genera and species at the

[40] Porphyry the Phoenician, *Isagoge*, trans. E. D. Warren (Toronto, 1975), pp. 30–1.
[41] *Ibid.*, p. 29. [42] *Ibid.*, p. 30.
[43] *Ibid.*, pp. 31–2. [44] *Ibid.*, pp. 34–5.

same time, since they are comprehended in relation to the highest genus and to the lowest species.[45]

Such a structure has become known as 'Porphyry's tree', and he elaborated a specific example with substance as the all-embracing genus at the top and individual men at the bottom:

Substance is itself a genus; under this is body; and under body animate body, under which is animal; under animal is rational animal, under which is man; under man are Socrates, Plato, and particular men. Of these substance is the highest genus, and it is a genus only, while man is the lowest species, and it is species only. Body is a species of substance but a genus of animate body. Animate body is a species of body but a genus of animal. Animal is a species of animate body, but a genus of rational animal. Rational animal is a species of animal, but a genus of man. Man is a species of rational animal, but it is not also a genus of particular men. It is a species only. Every species which is predicated immediately prior to individuals will be a species only, never a genus. Just as, then, substance is highest because there is nothing superior to itself and is the highest genus, so too man is a species after which there is no species nor anything able to be divided into species. Of individuals (Socrates, Plato, and 'this white' are individuals) there can only be a species, namely the last species and, as we said, the lowest species. The intermediate classes will be species of prior classes but genera of posterior classes.[46]

The third term that Porphyry considered was difference. He discussed various kinds of difference but the most important was what he called specific difference. Specific differences were those 'which make another essence' rather than those which merely produced differences in quality.[47] Thus 'the difference "rational" added to animal makes another essence, but the difference "moving" only makes something qualitatively different from resting, so that the one makes a difference-in-essence, the other only a difference-in-quality'.[48] Such essential differences were vital because they differentiated the various species within any one genus. The difference 'rational', for example, marked out 'man' as distinct from other species such as 'horse' within the genus 'animal': 'Man and horse do not differ in genus, for we are mortal animals and also irrational; but rational, when added, distinguishes us from them.'[49] Porphyry further distinguished between separable and inseparable differences. Examples of separable differences were 'moving, resting, being healthy, being ill', while examples of inseparable differences were 'being hook-nosed, snub-nosed, rational, or irrational'. Inseparable difference could exist either *per se* or accidentally. 'Rational, mortal, and being

[45] *Ibid.*, p. 35. [46] *Ibid.*, pp. 35–6.
[47] *Ibid.*, p. 42. [48] *Ibid.*, pp. 42–3.
[49] *Ibid.*, p. 47.

capable of knowledge belong to man *per se*, but hook-nosed or snub-nosed belong accidentally and not *per se*.'[50] Specific differences were inseparable differences existing *per se*, which is why they marked out essence. Such differences were especially valuable because they could be used to construct definitions of things. Definitions consisted of 'a genus and such differences'.[51] Man was therefore defined as a rational animal, 'animal' being the genus, and 'rational' the specific difference distinguishing the species 'man' from other species of animal.

Porphyry spent less time on the last two terms, property and accident. A property was a characteristic shared by all members of a species, but which did not form part of its essence or definition even though no other species possessed that characteristic. An example was 'the capacity to laugh in man', 'For even if a man does not always laugh, still he is said to be capable of laughing, not because he is always laughing but because it is natural for him to laugh.'[52] An accident was a characteristic that could be possessed by members of more than one species, and which could appear and disappear without fundamentally changing whatever temporarily possessed the characteristic: 'What comes into being and passes away apart from the destruction of the substratum is an accident.'[53] Accidents could be 'separable' or 'inseparable': 'Sleeping is a separable accident, while being black occurs inseparably in the crow and the Ethiopian.'[54] In the case of inseparable accidents, what mattered was the limited significance of the characteristic to the conception of whatever possessed it: 'It is possible … to conceive of a white crow and of an Ethiopian who has lost his colour apart from the destruction of the substratum.'[55] Having explained each of the five terms, Porphyry completed his work by comparing each term with every other term, describing for each pair the common characteristics that they shared and the differences between them. This permitted him to repeat his previous points with different phrasing.

Why was Porphyry's *Isagoge* adopted as a key introductory text? A firm grasp of the five terms that he explained was essential to understanding Aristotle's *Categories* not only because Aristotle deployed the terms, but also because he claimed that his ten categories were the ten highest genera, the only genera which were just genera and not also species within a higher genus. To put it another way, there were only ten distinct Porphyrian trees, each headed by one of Aristotle's ten categories. As Peter Abelard explained in his glosses on Porphyry: 'Knowledge

[50] *Ibid.*, p. 43. [51] *Ibid.*
[52] *Ibid.*, p. 48. [53] *Ibid.*
[54] *Ibid.*, pp. 48–9. [55] *Ibid.*, p. 49.

of genus pertains to the categories because Aristotle there sets forth the ten supreme genera of all things, in which categories he comprehends the infinite meanings of the names of all things.'[56] Furthermore, Porphyry's analysis began to address the issue of what constituted a sound argument because it could be used to identify valid and invalid statements:

The genus is always predicated of the species and all the higher of the lower, but the species is predicated neither of its own proximate genus nor of the higher ones. There is no convertibility of genus and species, for equals must be predicated of equals, as neighing of horse, or the greater of the lesser, as animal of man, but never the lesser of the greater. You may never say that animal is a man, as you may say man is an animal. Necessarily, too, the genus of the species and the genus of the genus up to the highest genus will be predicated of whatever things the species is predicated. If it is true to say that Socrates is a man, that man is an animal, and that animal is a substance, then it is also true to say that Socrates is an animal and a substance.

Since, therefore, the higher is always predicated of the lower, (1) the species will be predicated of the individual, (2) the genus both of the species and of the individual, and (3) the highest genus of the genus or genera (if there be very many subordinate intermediates), of the species, and of the individual. The highest genus is predicated of all the subordinate genera, species, and individuals; the genus prior to the lowest species of all the lowest species and individuals; the species alone of all the individuals; but the individual term of one only of the particulars.[57]

Thus, if the individual Socrates belonged to the species man, and the species man was part of the genus animal, it followed that some statements would be valid and some invalid. It would be correct to say that 'Socrates is a man' (the species predicated of the individual), that 'man is an animal' (the genus predicated of the species), and that 'Socrates is an animal' (the genus predicated of the individual). But it would be false to say that 'animal is man' (the species predicated of the genus), 'animal is Socrates' (the individual predicated of the genus), or 'man is Socrates' (the individual predicated of the species). Rules for identifying valid and invalid statements were thus established. Put most simply, having set up one of Porphyry's trees, the higher could always be predicated of the lower, while the lower could never be predicated of the higher. To give just one further instance, Porphyry offered the general rule that 'the property is predicated convertibly with its species, while the genus is convertible with nothing'. This meant that it was legitimate

[56] 'The glosses of Peter Abailard on Porphyry', in R. McKeon (ed. and trans.), *Selections from Medieval Philosophers*, 2 vols. (New York, 1929), vol. 1, pp. 208–58 at 215.

[57] Porphyry, *Isagoge*, pp. 40–1.

to state that 'if there is man, there is the capacity to laugh' and 'if there is the capacity to laugh, there is man'; here the property was being predicated convertibly with its species. It was not, however, correct to state that 'if there is animal, there is man' or 'if there is animal, there is the capacity to laugh'; these false assertions illustrated why the genus was convertible with nothing.[58]

The *Isagoge*'s relevance to the construction of arguments was readily apparent to men like Abelard:

> If the parts of logic have first been distinguished carefully, it is seen at once what is the part through which the science of the present work leads to logic. On the authority of Cicero and Boethius there are two parts of which logic is composed, namely, the science of discovering arguments and of judging them, that is, of confirming and proving the arguments discovered. For two things are necessary to one who argues, first to find the arguments by which to argue, then if any should criticize the arguments as defective or as insufficiently firm to be able to confirm them. Wherefore Cicero says that discovery is by nature prior. The present science, however, is concerned with both parts of logic, but most of all with discovery. And it is a part of the science of discovering. For how can an argument be deduced from genus or species or the others, if the things which are here treated are not known? ... But since an argument is confirmed from the same considerations from which it is discovered, this science is not unrelated to judgment. For, as an argument is derived from the nature of genus and species, so, once derived, it is confirmed from the nature of genus and species. For considering the nature of species in man, so far as it is related to animal, I find at once from the nature of the species the argument for proving animal. But if any one should criticize the argument, I show that it is suitable immediately by indicating the nature of the species and the genus in both, so that from the same conditions of the terms the argument may be found and when it has been found it may be confirmed.[59]

The most advanced work on argument focused on the syllogism, which was most fully treated in the new logic, especially Aristotle's *Prior Analytics*.[60] Aristotle defined the syllogism as 'discourse in which, certain things being stated, something other than what is stated follows of

[58] *Ibid.*, p. 53.

[59] 'The glosses of Peter Abailard on Porphyry', pp. 211–12; see also p. 217.

[60] For basic introductions to syllogistic argument in Aristotle and medieval work, to which I am indebted in the following account, see H. Lagerlund, *Modal Syllogistics in the Middle Ages* (Leiden, 2000), pp. 3–18; J. Marenbon, *Later Medieval Philosophy (1150–1350)* (London, 1987, repr. 1996), pp. 38–41; P. V. Spade, *Thought, Words and Things: An Introduction to Late Mediaeval Logic and Semantic Theory* (Version 1.1, 2002; www.pvspade.com/Logic/docs/thoughts1_1a.pdf). For more extended introductions, see A. Broadie, *Introduction to Medieval Logic*, 2nd edn (Oxford, 1993); I. M. Bochenski, *A History of Formal Logic*, trans. I. Thomas (Notre Dame, IN, 1961), pp. viii–xiii, 40–99, 148–251.

necessity from their being so'.[61] It was made up of two premises and a conclusion. For example:

1. All people are mortal;
2. all Scots are people;
3. therefore all Scots are mortal.

The major premise (1 in the above example) contained the major term, which was the predicate in the conclusion ('mortal' in the above example). The minor premise (2) contained the minor term, which was the subject of the conclusion ('Scots'). The term shared by the two premises, and which did not occur in the conclusion, was the middle term ('people'). Aristotle explored the nature of syllogistic argument by classifying syllogisms in three ways, the third combining the first two.

First, Aristotle classified syllogisms by identifying four different types of proposition, which were later referred to by letters. 'All X are Y' was a universal affirmative, signified by the letter A. 'No X is Y' was a universal negative, labelled E. 'Some X is Y' was a particular affirmative, labelled I. 'Some X is not Y' was a particular negative, allotted the letter O. The letters were not randomly chosen. A and I, attached to the two types of affirmative proposition, were the first two vowels in 'affirmo', meaning 'I affirm', while E and O, given to the two types of negative proposition, were the vowels in 'nego', meaning 'I deny'. Using this system of classification, the example given above consisted of three universal affirmatives, AAA. Another syllogism would be:

1. No human being is perfect;
2. all historians are human beings;
3. therefore no historian is perfect.

Here the major premise is E (universal negative), the minor premise is A (universal affirmative), and the conclusion is E (universal negative): EAE.

Second, further classification was possible when account was taken of how the middle term was positioned in the two premises: in each premise the middle term could be either the subject or the predicate. Four combinations or 'figures' were therefore possible.

> Figure 1: The middle term is the subject in the major premise and the predicate in the minor premise.

61 Aristotle, *Prior Analytics*, 1.1 in *The Basic Works of Aristotle*, ed. R. McKeon (New York, 1941, repr. 2001), p. 66.

Figure 2: The middle term is the predicate in both the major and the minor premises.
Figure 3: The middle term is the subject in both the major and the minor premises.
Figure 4: The middle term is the predicate in the major premise and the subject in the minor premise.

In fact Aristotle only listed the first three figures, while considering instances of the fourth, and he was often followed by medieval scholars in this regard. Reverting to the first example above, where the middle term is 'people', we have:

1. All people (middle term) are mortal;
2. all Scots are people (middle term);
3. therefore all Scots are mortal.

In the major premise, the middle term is the subject. In the minor premise, the middle term is the predicate. So this is an example of the first figure. In the second example above, the middle term is 'human being':

1. No human being (middle term) is perfect;
2. all historians are human beings (middle term);
3. therefore no historian is perfect.

In the major premise, the middle term is again the subject. In the minor premise, the middle term is again the predicate. So this is another example of the first figure. Any syllogism could be placed in one of the figures in this way.

A third type of classification was generated by combining the first two, the four types of proposition and the four figures. In each of the four figures it was possible to envisage every possible combination of types of proposition within the syllogistic form, each combination being called a 'mood'. Thus in the first example above the major premise is a universal affirmative, the minor premise is a universal affirmative, and the conclusion is a universal affirmative, giving us AAA in the first figure. In the second example, however, the major premise is a universal negative, the minor premise is a universal affirmative, and the conclusion is a universal negative, giving us EAE in the first figure. All the possible combinations of types of proposition could be repeated in each of the four figures, which gave 256 moods in total. Not all moods, however, were deemed valid. Aristotle identified fourteen valid moods in his three figures, and he discussed a further five that can be placed in the fourth figure. In the middle ages each valid mood was given a mnemonic name, and they can be listed within each figure along with the types of proposition to be found in the major premise, the minor premise and the conclusion in each case:

First figure

AAA	Barbara
EAE	Celarent
AII	Darii
EIO	Ferio

Second figure

AEE	Camestres
EAE	Cesare
EIO	Festino
AOO	Baroco

Third figure

AAI	Darapti
EAO	Felapton
IAI	Disamis
AII	Datisi
OAO	Bocardo
EIO	Ferison

Fourth figure

AAI	Bramantip
AEE	Camenes
IAI	Dimaris
EAO	Fesapo
EIO	Fresison

Embedded within these strange names were two sets of information. First, the vowels indicated the types of proposition taken by the major premise, the minor premise and then the conclusion in the mood to which the name had been applied. Thus B*a*rb*a*r*a* was A (universal affirmative in the major premise), A (universal affirmative in the minor premise) and A (universal affirmative in the conclusion). C*e*l*a*r*e*nt was E (universal negative in the major premise), A (universal affirmative in the minor premise) and E (universal negative in the conclusion). The figure was not encoded in the names, so one just had to remember that Barbara and Celarent were in the first figure. The two examples used repeatedly above are AAA and EAE, and both in the first figure, so they are instances of the moods Barbara and Celarent respectively. The second set of information concerned the relationship between moods in the first figure and moods in the other figures. Aristotle deemed the syllogisms in the first figure to be obviously valid, whereas the syllogisms in the other figures required proof. They could be proved by being restated as syllogisms in the first figure, a process termed 'reduction', and involving rules of conversion that Aristotle carefully set out. The letters other than the vowels in the mnemonic names indicated how this process was to be conducted. To give just one example, the first letter of the name was the same as the first letter of the mood in the first figure to which the syllogism was to be reduced. Thus Darapti in the third figure should be reduced to Darii in the first figure. Other letters indicated the technical procedures that were to be followed, leaving only a few that simply made up the name.[62] This is just to scratch the surface, but the syllogism became a basic technique of the schools and subsequently of the universities. This form of argument was used in most of the writings produced in these contexts. Because the premises and the conclusion are not usually identified and systematically laid out, the syllogistic form is often difficult for the modern reader to appreciate, but the medieval scholar could spot and classify a syllogism at a glance.

Logic, or dialectic, therefore enabled a scholar to understand the way in which language could be used to construct arguments, and above all to distinguish between valid arguments and fallacies. It offered an approach to truth which was both precise and systematic. To many it therefore represented a key to all other branches of knowledge. John of Salisbury declared that logic 'organizes and vivifies' other studies,[63] continuing:

> while each study is fortified by its own particular principles, logic is their common servant, and supplies them all with its 'methods' or principles of expeditious reasoning. Hence logic is most valuable, not merely to provide exercise [for our faculties], but also as a tool in argumentative reasoning and the various branches of learning that pertain to philosophy.[64]

But there were many others who found dialectic fascinating in itself, or did not so easily see the divisions between the branches of learning. This was not least because the authoritative texts in dialectic raised but did not settle further philosophical problems.

The question of universals was a case in point. The nature of the problem is easily grasped, even if the various possible solutions are not. I am sitting at a table, 'this table'. On the other side of the room there is another table, 'that table'. The collective term 'table' is applied both to 'this table' and to 'that table', and indeed to all other individual tables. Similarly the collective term 'chair' is applied to the particular chair on which I am sitting, 'this chair', and to every other individual chair. All

[62] For full details, see Spade, *Thought, Words and Things*, p. 22
[63] John of Salisbury, *Metalogicon*, p. 101.
[64] *Ibid.*, p. 103.

the particular tables and all the particular chairs could also be included under the collective term 'furniture'. All these collective terms, 'table', 'chair' and 'furniture', are universals. As already observed in Porphyry's *Isagoge*, the particular objects, such as 'this table', were termed 'individua', or 'individual things'. The first collective term under which individual things might be grouped, for example 'table', was called the 'species'. A collective term which embraced several species, for example 'furniture', was called a 'genus'. The problem is to understand the nature of universals. Do universals exist independently of individual things? The labels 'realist' and 'nominalist' are used to refer to the two basic directions which can be taken in answer to this question. The realist argues that in some way universals exist independently of individual things, that 'table', or one might say 'tableness', exists whether or not any particular tables exist, and that all individual tables reflect or partake of 'table' or 'tableness' in a manner to be determined. The nominalist maintains that universals are just words which we use to group individual things together, and that only the individual things truly exist.

The study of dialectic led twelfth-century scholars to tackle universals because the problem was raised in texts which formed part of the 'old logic'. Thus Porphyry, at the start of the *Isagoge*, framed the question explicitly while declining to offer a solution:

> I shall put aside the investigation of certain profound questions concerning genera and species, since such an undertaking requires more detailed examination: (1) whether genera or species exist in themselves or reside in mere concepts alone; (2) whether, if they exist, they are corporeal or incorporeal; and (3) whether they exist apart or in sense objects and in dependence on them.[65]

In the rest of the *Isagoge* it was indeed very unclear whether Porphyry was talking about words alone or about words and things.[66] Debate was further stimulated by Boethius' second commentary on the *Isagoge* in which he discussed the relevant views of both Plato and Aristotle.

The issue of universals was discussed in the eleventh century, but it was in the first half of the twelfth century that it became the subject of frequent and heated debate. John of Salisbury vividly described the plethora of theories which were advanced.[67] One of the earliest masters to become well known for his views on the matter was Roscelin of Compiègne. Roscelin lived from about 1050 to 1125, was a canon

[65] Porphyry, *Isagoge*, pp. 27–8. See also P. V. Spade (trans. and ed.), *Five Texts on the Mediaeval Problem of Universals* (Indianapolis, 1994), p. 1.

[66] See the comments of Marenbon, *Philosophy of Peter Abelard*, pp. 105–8.

[67] John of Salisbury, *Metalogicon*, pp. 112–41.

of Compiègne, taught at Loches and was Abelard's master.[68] Little of Roscelin's work survives, but according to his critics he took an extreme nominalist position, maintaining that universals were merely words or sounds. As John of Salisbury cuttingly put it:

One [man] holds that universals are merely word sounds, although this opinion, along with its author Roscelin, has already almost completely passed into oblivion.[69]

An extreme realist position was maintained by William of Champeaux and, according to Abelard, it was this which finally gave Abelard the chance to destroy William's standing and reputation:

I returned to him to hear his lectures on rhetoric, and in the course of our philosophic disputes I produced a sequence of clear logical arguments to make him amend, or rather abandon, his previous attitude to universals. He had maintained that in the common existence of universals, the whole species was essentially the same in each of its individuals, and among these there was no essential difference, but only variety due to multiplicity of accidents. Now he modified his view in order to say that it was the same not in essence but through non-difference ... Consequently, when William had modified or rather been forced to give up his original position, his lectures fell into such contempt that he was scarcely accepted on any other points of dialectic, as if the whole subject rested solely on the question of universals.[70]

If Abelard is representing William fairly, and William's own work on the matter does not survive, William argued first that every individual member of a species was essentially identical, in other words that the universal was equally present in each individual thing, and that differences between individual members of a species were merely accidental. Thus he would have accepted that the universal 'humanity' was entirely and identically present in all people, and differences were accidental. Abelard was able to point to the absurd consequences of this position. If two people had the same essence, they were the same person. If the two people were in two places, the same person was in two places at once. William then retreated to the position that the universal existed in each individual member of a species without difference. Whatever ideas lay behind this shift, Abelard seemed to imply that it was just a desperate, but fundamentally meaningless, change of words.[71] Abelard's ideas about universals developed over time, and he wrote a great deal on the

[68] Clanchy, *Abelard*, pp. 75–6; M. Haren, *Medieval Thought: The Western Intellectual Tradition from Antiquity to the Thirteenth Century*, 2nd edn (Toronto, 1992), p. 91.
[69] John of Salisbury, *Metalogicon*, p. 112.
[70] *Historia Calamitatum*, in *Letters of Abelard and Heloise*, p. 60.
[71] On this episode, see Clanchy, *Abelard*, p. 83; F. C. Copleston, *A History of Medieval Philosophy* (London, 1972), p. 81.

subject. He was clear, however, that universals were words. He did not mean words as sounds, but words as expressions that carried meaning. Universals were words that bore meanings that had been abstracted by the human mind, words which signified concepts.[72]

It will by now be clear that the men who rushed to study logic were going to acquire the ability to construct arguments and distinguish between truth and falsehood. Whereas today we largely operate with an intuitive sense that an argument works or fails, the medieval schoolmen could say exactly why an argument worked or failed because they could break the argument down into its constituent parts and name every one. More than that, they acquired detailed knowledge of relatively short authoritative texts that raised huge philosophical questions and were dense in potential meaning, which is perhaps to say that their core texts were unclear on some of the most fundamental issues and therefore invited a range of different interpretations. Furthermore, all of this required the acquisition of a specialist vocabulary that was utterly mystifying to anyone who had not received the complex and highly technical training that the schools provided. The uninitiated could not hear or read their work and expect to get anywhere at all with it. When a man entered the schools he became an insider, with a powerful claim to knowledge and understanding that was denied to others.[73]

While it is extremely difficult for us to follow the work of the schoolmen without their training, their sense of excitement and spirit of enquiry are much easier to appreciate. There was huge confidence in human capacity to understand and a belief in the value of asking questions to gain knowledge and insight. This is readily apparent from Abelard's reaction to Anselm of Laon, the master to whom he turned after William of Champeaux retired.

> I therefore approached this old man, who owed his reputation more to long practice than to intelligence or memory. Anyone who knocked at his door to seek an answer to some question went away more uncertain than he came. Anselm could win the admiration of an audience, but he was useless when put

[72] See Copleston, *History of Medieval Philosophy*, pp. 81–3; K. Jacobi, 'Philosophy of language', in J. E. Brower and K. Guilfoy (eds.), *The Cambridge Companion to Abelard* (Cambridge, 2004), pp. 126–57 at 134–7; J. Marenbon, *Early Medieval Philosophy (480–1150)* (London, 1983), pp. 135–6; Marenbon, *Philosophy of Peter Abelard*, pp. 174–201; Spade (trans. and ed.), *Five Texts on the Mediaeval Problem of Universals*, pp. 29–33; M. M. Tweedale, *Abailard on Universals* (Amsterdam, 1976).

[73] R. M. Karras, *From Boys to Men: Formations of Masculinity in Late Medieval Europe* (Philadelphia, 2003), p. 93 refers to logic as 'a private language' when discussing disputation as 'a bonding mechanism' that helped form masculinity in universities of the fourteenth and fifteenth centuries. See also *ibid.*, p. 91.

to the question. He had a remarkable command of words but their meaning was worthless and devoid of all sense.[74]

By 'memory' Abelard did not mean what one could recall from the past; that was really what he condemned as 'long practice', or 'usus'. 'Memory' meant what one could discover by looking inward, by thinking about thinking. This and 'intelligence', or 'ingenium', were the qualities which Abelard valued in himself and others. Moreover, in his view, they were qualities which should be applied not merely to dialectic and the liberal arts, but also to theology. Indeed it was specifically because he wanted to study theology that he sought out Anselm who was 'then the greatest authority' in this field.[75]

Abelard's confidence in his own intellectual abilities did not endear him to Anselm. When Abelard's attendance at classes declined, Anselm's leading students took offence and pointedly asked him what he thought about studying the Bible when all his previous training had been in philosophy. Abelard replied that he 'found it most surprising that for educated men the writings or glosses of the Fathers themselves were not sufficient for interpreting their commentaries without further instruction'.[76] Challenged to interpret a commentary on an obscure prophecy of Ezekiel, Abelard not only accepted but brushed aside those who urged him to take time to prepare:

I replied indignantly that it was not my custom to benefit by practice, but I relied on my own intelligence.[77]

According to the *Historia Calamitatum*, Abelard was so successful that he ended up giving a series of lectures, only for the jealous Anselm to ban him from teaching further.

But Abelard brought more than intellectual confidence to theology: he also used the methods of dialectic. Having become a monk, and having withdrawn from the abbey of Saint Denis to a priory in Champagne, he was able to develop his theological project in full:

Now it happened that I first applied myself to lecturing on the basis of our faith by analogy with human reason, and composed a theological treatise on divine unity and trinity for the use of my students who were asking for human and logical reasons on this subject, and demanded something intelligible rather than mere words. In fact they said that words were useless if the intelligence could not follow them, that nothing could be believed unless it was first understood.[78]

74 *Historia Calamitatum*, in *Letters of Abelard and Heloise*, p. 7.
75 *Ibid.* 76 *Ibid.* 77 *Ibid.*, p. 8.
78 *Ibid.*, p. 20.

Evidently the theological application of logic found an enthusiastic audience. Even more striking is the view that an understanding based on logic was necessary for belief.

Abelard's work on the Trinity was perhaps his most controversial. He began one treatise:

> Christ the Lord, who is the wisdom of God incarnate, has diligently distinguished the perfection of the highest good, which is God, by describing it with three names ... He called the divine substance 'the Father', 'the Son' and 'the Holy Spirit' for three causes. He called it 'the Father' in accordance with that unique power of His majesty which is omnipotence, by which He can effect whatever He wills as nothing is able to resist Him. The same divine substance He said is 'the Son' in accordance with the distinction of His own wisdom, by which He can truly judge and discern all things so that nothing can lie hidden by which He is deceived. He likewise called that substance 'the Holy Spirit' in accordance with the grace of His goodness ... This therefore is how God is three persons, that is, 'the Father', 'the Son' and 'the Holy Spirit'. And so we say the divine substance is power, wisdom and goodness; indeed, it even is power itself, wisdom itself and goodness itself.[79]

Abelard thus distinguished between substance and the different names that could be given to that substance. He further associated each person in the Trinity with a different quality, the Father with power, the Son with wisdom, and the Holy Spirit with goodness. This was theologically dangerous because it might seem that each person in the Trinity was just a name, or that, for example, Christ was not as powerful as the Father. The whole point of Abelard's strategy, however, was to open up approaches that would allow him to apply reason further. In another work he used the distinction between substance and names to work out an analogy to explain how the Trinity was both three and one. Abelard said that the divine substance was designated by three names, and this was like Marcus Tullius Cicero who had three names all designating the same substance:

> Very rightly the Father is believed to be God and the Son and the Holy Spirit, but they are not considered as several gods, since these are three names designating the divine substance. So likewise Tullius is truly said to be a man and so is Cicero and Marcus also is called a man. Yet in no way are Marcus and Tullius and Cicero [different] men, since these are words designating the same substance. Indeed, several things differ from each other only in expression and not in substantial meaning.[80]

Against this it could easily be objected that orthodox belief had the three names designating three persons, whereas the names of Cicero designated just one. Abelard was aware that the analogy was imperfect,

[79] Peter Abelard, *Theologia Summi Boni*, as quoted by Clanchy, *Abelard*, p. 270.

[80] Peter Abelard, *Dialectica*, as quoted by Clanchy, *Abelard*, p. 109.

but thought it worth making.[81] Putting the emphasis on the qualities of power, wisdom and goodness allowed him to argue that these were the qualities that should be attributed to a perfect being on rational grounds, and then to try to show that Old Testament figures and ancient philosophers had known of the Trinity.[82] Logic was very much the modern way to explore traditional problems, and to many it seemed to hold out limitless possibilities. Not only did it confer the power to argue, a way into philosophical debate, and a form of initiation into an intellectual elite, but it also seemed to promise new understanding of divine mysteries.

Texts: interpreting authorities

It is important, however, not to overstate the extent to which men like Abelard were rejecting past traditions. Crucially, Abelard did not mean to undermine the status of authoritative texts. At the Council of Soissons in 1121, Alberic, a former student of Anselm of Laon, queried a passage in Abelard's writings about the nature of God. When Abelard offered to explain, Alberic snapped: 'We take no account of rational explanation ... nor of your interpretation in such matters; we recognize only the words of authority.' But Abelard had cited an authority and could reply, 'Turn the page ... and you will find the authority.'[83]

Indeed, far from rejecting authorities, Abelard was deeply concerned about methods of interpreting them. One of his most significant works regarding textual interpretation was the *Sic et Non*, meaning 'Yes and No', or 'For and Against'. Composed during the 1120s, this book contained 158 headings, each of which raised a theological issue. The issues ranged from the nature of God to matters of practical morality. Under each heading Abelard placed quotations from the Church Fathers. These quotations were selected because they offered contradictory views on the theological issue raised in the heading. No attempt was made to resolve any of the contradictions or to express a clear view on any of the 158 issues. This in itself made the point that authorities could not be used unless they were interpreted. But Abelard went further: the prologue to the *Sic et Non* outlined a method of interpretation which

81 See Clanchy, *Abelard*, p. 109.

82 *Ibid.*, pp. 270–2; Marenbon, *Philosophy of Peter Abelard*, pp. 55–7. For the important argument that concern with the Trinity led to significant developments in Abelard's study of logic, see J. E. Brower, 'Trinity', in Brower and Guilfoy (eds.), *The Cambridge Companion to Abelard*, pp. 223–57; Marenbon, *Philosophy of Peter Abelard*, pp. 155–8.

83 *Historia Calamitatum*, in *Letters of Abelard and Heloise*, p. 21.

would make it possible to reconcile the contradictions and establish a coherent view supported by the authorities.

Abelard began the prologue by urging respect for authorities, despite the contradictions to be found between them:

> Although, amid so great a mass of verbiage, some of the sayings even of the saints not only seem to differ from but also actually to contradict one another, we must not be so bold as to judge those by whom the world itself must be judged ... Let us not presume to denounce them as liars or despise them as mistaken ... Reflecting upon our own feebleness, let us suppose that we lack the gift of understanding rather than that they had no gift for writing.[84]

After the relentless bragging of the *Historia Calamitatum*, these expressions of humility can come as a surprise. The rest of the prologue can be treated in three parts.

First, Abelard urged an essentially historical approach. It was necessary to appreciate the usage of words: 'A particular bar to understanding is the unfamiliar language and the different meaning of a great many identical words, since the same word is used sometimes with one and sometimes with another meaning.'[85] A genuine and accurate text was equally important: 'We should also ... take great care that we are not being deceived by a false attribution or by corruption of the text itself.'[86] The whole corpus of an individual's work had also to be considered since he might have altered his position: 'I think that we should no less consider whether these extracts produced from the writings of the saints are among those which were retracted by them in another place, and were corrected when the truth later became known.'[87] It was also important not to assume that a writer accepted all the views which he described: 'We should also consider whether the saints were making a pronouncement according to the opinion of others rather than according to their own.'[88] The writer's intention was crucial: 'When different things are said about the same matter, it is necessary to discuss thoroughly what is intended as a binding precept and what as a dispensation relaxing the law or an exhortation to perfection, so that we may seek to resolve the conflict by taking into account the difference of intentions.'[89] Finally, the context had to be considered: 'It is necessary to bear in mind the occasion and the reasons for dispensations, because what is permitted at one time is often found to be prohibited

[84] Abelard, Prologue to the *Sic et Non*, in B. Pullan, *Sources for the History of Medieval Europe from the Mid-Eighth Century to the Mid-Thirteenth Century* (Oxford, 1966), p. 99.

[85] *Ibid.* [86] *Ibid.*, p. 100.

[87] *Ibid.* [88] *Ibid.* [89] *Ibid.*, p. 101.

at another.'[90] Abelard's first approach therefore depended on various forms of historical analysis.

Second, Abelard outlined another approach to be used if the first one failed. This involved comparing the authorities and preferring those that occupied a higher place in a set hierarchy. The middle position in this hierarchy was occupied by the Church Fathers amongst whose writings 'there appear to be certain things which have been propounded and written down erroneously'.[91] At the top of the hierarchy were the scriptures:

> The outstanding canonical authority of the Old and New Testaments is in a different category from the books of later writers. If anything in the Bible strikes you as absurd, it is not permissible to say: 'The author of this book did not uphold the truth', but that either the manuscript is false, or the translator made a mistake, or that you do not understand it.[92]

At the bottom of the hierarchy were recent scholars. Unless their arguments were established by reason or superior authority, one was free to judge 'the little works of later men' as one saw fit.[93]

Third, Abelard indicated the pedagogical function of the *Sic et Non* and the way of thinking which he wanted to inculcate. He had gathered apparently contradictory authorities to 'arouse inexperienced readers to the most vigorous activity in seeking out the truth'.[94] So this was an exercise book for students, and the contradictions were left unresolved to stimulate students to think in certain ways. First, as we have seen before, they had to ask questions, '[f]or assiduous and frequent asking of questions is termed the first key to wisdom'.[95] Second, they had to doubt, 'for by doubting we come to inquiry and by inquiring we perceive the truth'.[96] Abelard liked to be provocative and, bearing in mind the issues which the *Sic et Non* raised, urging 'inexperienced readers' to experience doubt was one of his most provocative statements.

The historical approach to textual analysis of authorities was not, however, unique to Abelard and he did not invent it. Indeed, many of the principles articulated in the prologue to the *Sic et Non* had been practised earlier by Anselm of Laon and his students, a reminder that Abelard's judgements of other scholars should not be accepted too readily.[97] Moreover, collecting authorities which contradicted each other with regard to theological issues did not have to be a contentious exercise. A generation later, another such collection became a far more successful

[90] *Ibid.* [91] *Ibid.*, p. 102.
[92] *Ibid.* [93] *Ibid.*
[94] *Ibid.*, p. 103. [95] *Ibid.* [96] *Ibid.*
[97] M. L. Colish, *Peter Lombard*, 2 vols. (Leiden, 1994), vol. 1, p. 44.

textbook than the *Sic et Non*. It was written by Peter Lombard who was born in the region of Novarra in Lombardy, between 1095 and 1100. Having studied at Rheims, he came to Paris in 1136 where he emerged as a master in the 1140s and taught at the cathedral school of Notre Dame. He became bishop of Paris in 1159 and died the following year. The final version of his *Four Books of the Sentences* appeared between 1155 and 1157, and it became the single most important textbook in theology for the rest of the middle ages. Like the *Sic et Non*, it raised theological issues and in each case provided extracts from authoritative texts. But unlike Abelard, Peter Lombard applied the methods which Abelard had championed and gave a judgement. He thus demonstrated that it was possible to use dialectic in theology and to examine authoritative texts critically without raising doubts in the minds of the young and inexperienced.[98]

A similar concern to collect and analyse authoritative texts lay at the heart of the development of legal studies in the twelfth century. Collections of canons had a long history as churchmen wrestled with the mass of material from the Bible, the Fathers, church councils and papal decrees which constituted the law of the church. But in the late eleventh and early twelfth centuries, methods for dealing with these texts were put forward. An influential example was produced by Ivo of Chartres, who died in 1115. He made two collections of canons, a huge one entitled the *Decretum* and a shorter one called the *Panormia*. The latter was widely used in Europe and its prologue outlined a method for interpreting contradictory texts. In many respects Ivo anticipated Abelard in his historical approach. Contradictions might be resolved through examination of context and authenticity. Failing this, there was a hierarchy of ecclesiastical jurisdictions against which the texts could be tested, with, for example, general councils taking precedence over provincial councils; this made it possible to accept one law rather than another. The key developments, however, took place in Italy where the reputation of Irnerius for the study of Roman law had helped Bologna to become Europe's most important centre for legal studies in the first half of the twelfth century. In Bologna the legal equivalent of Peter Lombard's *Sentences* is referred to as Gratian's *Decretum*, or the *Concordia discordantium canonum*, which can be translated as 'A Harmony of Conflicting Canons'. It is now known, however, that a first recension was probably produced by Gratian, about whom little is known, except that he is generally held to have been a monk, and a second recension by at least one

[98] For the life of Peter Lombard, see *ibid.*, vol. 1, pp. 15–23; P. W. Rosemann, *Peter Lombard* (Oxford, 2004), pp. 34–53.

other lawyer. Looking at one problem after another, the *Decretum* cited contradictory laws and then used the kind of method that had been advocated by Ivo and others to argue to a solution, and it very quickly became the basic medieval textbook of canon law.[99]

Sense perception

Thus far it would seem that twelfth-century scholars pursued knowledge without reference to sense perception. Dialectic and the interpretation of authoritative texts depended on analysis of words, reflection on the processes of thought and attention to historical context. What about knowledge of the physical universe? Was no value ever attached to knowledge based on sense perception? In this regard historians looking for the origins of modern science have turned to the work of Adelard of Bath. A layman who lived from about 1080 to 1152, Adelard grew up in Bath and studied at Tours and Laon before embarking on travels which took him to Southern Italy, Sicily, Syria and Palestine. He travelled in search of the learning of the Arabs and indeed he translated many works from Arabic.[100] His *Questiones Naturales*, or 'Natural Questions', addressed seventy-six questions. The first group were about plants and animals, including 'The reason why plants grow without a seed being sown beforehand' (q. 1) and 'Why some brute animals chew the cud, but others not' (q. 7). The second set were about human beings, beginning with 'Why men do not have innate horns or other armour' (q. 15) and 'By what observation the web of nerves and blood-vessels is detected' (q. 16). The final group of questions concerned earth, water, air and fire, starting with 'Why, or by what nature, the globe of the earth is held up in the middle of the air' (q. 48) and 'Where, if the globe of the earth were bored through, a rock thrown into the hole would end up' (q. 49).[101] The *Questiones Naturales* was written as a dialogue between Adelard and his nephew in which the nephew put questions while suggesting safely orthodox answers, and Adelard gave more daring replies.

99 For the development of canon law, see J. A. Brundage, *Medieval Canon Law* (London, 1995). For an immensely significant revision of our understanding of the *Decretum*, see A. Winroth, *The Making of Gratian's Decretum* (Cambridge, 2000).

100 For the life of Adelard of Bath, see C. Burnett, 'Introduction', in Adelard of Bath, *Conversations with his Nephew: On the Same and the Different, Questions on Natural Science and On Birds*, ed. and trans. C. Burnett (Cambridge, 1998), pp. xi–xix; L. Cochrane, *Adelard of Bath: The First English Scientist* (London, 1994).

101 For a complete list of questions, see Adelard of Bath, *Questiones Naturales*, in *Conversations with his Nephew*, pp. 85–9.

There are passages in the *Questiones Naturales* which suggest that Adelard valued knowledge based on sense perception and rejected the use of authorities. In question 18 his nephew issued the following challenge:

work out, if you can, the way by which the positions of imagination, reason and memory were discovered by philosophers. For both Aristotle in his *Physics* and others in other works divide them in such a way that they say that imagination operates in the front part of the brain, reason in the middle, memory in the back.[102]

Adelard was happy to take up the challenge and replied:

Whoever first treated these three cells separately, I guess, learnt this very thing by experiencing it with his senses. I suppose there was a man who was well able to use his imagination to gather the forms of things, but he was injured in that front part of his head to such an extent that he lost his power of imagination, but was not deprived of reason and memory. Hence it happened that this was noted by the Philosopher. In a similar way if, by the injury of other parts, other actions of the soul were impeded, it could be stated for certain that single actions operated in single cells, seeing that the cells themselves are separated by some, albeit narrow, divisions. This then is the way that the insensible and intellectual operation of the soul has been revealed from those things which the senses note on the outside.[103]

Here knowledge would seem to begin with precise observation. Elsewhere, moreover, Adelard mocked those who followed authorities:

About animals my conversation with you is difficult. For I have learnt one thing from my Arab masters, with reason as guide, but you another: you follow a halter, being enthralled by the picture of authority. For what else can authority be called other than a halter? As brute animals are led wherever one pleases by a halter, but do not know where or why they are led, and only follow the rope by which they are held, so the authority of written words leads not a few of you into danger, since you are enthralled and bound by brutish credulity.[104]

These passages, however, are misleading since Adelard plainly did not reject authority. He apparently granted the Arab masters authoritative status, and at the start of the book he even insisted that he was putting forward their ideas rather than his: 'no one should think that when I am putting forward unknown ideas, I am doing this out of my own head, but that I am giving the views of the studies of the Arabs'.[105] It has been suggested, however, that Adelard said this to protect himself from being censured for the more radical ideas that his book contained, and

102 *Ibid.*, p. 125. 103 *Ibid.*, p. 127.
104 *Ibid.*, p. 103. 105 *Ibid.*, p. 91.

certainly no Arab sources have been identified.[106] On the other hand, he repeatedly acknowledged his debts to Plato and Aristotle, and on one occasion he even invited his nephew to accept a view which he acknowledged that he held because it was Aristotle's: 'In this accept not my own opinion, but that of Aristotle – or rather, because it is his, it's my own.'[107] Despite this particular show of deference, Adelard's point was presumably that authorities should not be followed unthinkingly, and in this respect he shared an attitude that we have already witnessed.

Similarly, Adelard's regard for sense-based knowledge must not be exaggerated. Observation formed the starting-point for many of the questions, but almost certainly he borrowed them from a list already in existence.[108] Moreover, observation rarely provided the basis for his responses, and indeed the limited value of sensory perception was frequently implied. In the first question, for example, the nephew asked why plants grew from dry and apparently seedless earth. Adelard replied that things that could be perceived by the senses were never pure earth, water, air or fire, but always a mixture of the four elements. The earth from which plants grew therefore contained water, air and fire, and it was the interaction of these elements that caused the growth of plants. The true nature of the earth was therefore beyond sense perception: 'For in such a way do these four simple elements compose this one body of the world that, although they exist as components in each composed object, they never appear to the senses as they are.'[109]

But if the senses were of limited use, Adelard did not suppose that the physical world was closed to rational exploration. This was the crux of his debate with his nephew. When the nephew asked to what the growth of plants could be attributed 'unless to the wondrous effect of the wondrous divine will', Adelard replied:

It is indeed the will of the Creator that plants should be born from the earth. But that will is not without reason.[110]

In question 4 the nephew criticized Adelard's argument and demanded that 'the execution of all things should rather be referred to God', to which Adelard responded:

I am not slighting God's role. For whatever exists is from him and through him. Nevertheless, that dependence <on God> is not <to be taken> in blanket

[106] Burnett, 'Introduction', p. xxviii; Le Goff, *Intellectuals in the Middle Ages*, pp. 54–5.
[107] Adelard of Bath, *Questiones Naturales*, in *Conversations with his Nephew*, p. 221. For his unacknowledged debt to Cicero, see Burnett, 'Introduction', pp. xxvii–xxviii.
[108] Burnett, 'Introduction', pp. xxii–xxiii.
[109] Adelard of Bath, *Questiones Naturales*, in *Conversations with his Nephew*, p. 93.
[110] *Ibid.*

fashion, without distinction. One should attend to this distinction, as far as human knowledge can go; but in the case where human knowledge completely fails, the matter should be referred to God. Thus, since we do not yet grow pale with lack of knowledge, let us return to reason.[111]

The nephew expressed the view that the workings of the natural world could only be explained as the will of God. Adelard, however, argued that God had created a world within which there was an order open to rational explanation.

Myth and poetry

In limiting the role for the senses and yet opening up the natural world as a field for rational enquiry, Adelard was typical of many of his contemporaries. This brings us to the area of twelfth-century thought that most strongly resists definition in modern terms. How were the masters to explore the natural world if not through sense perception? The answer is through myth and poetry. They composed complex stories about allegorical figures or personifications that were almost always female, such as Nature, Divine Providence, Prudence, Philosophy and Reason. Many of these stories were partly or wholly in the form of poetry. This general approach has been variously labelled. It was once thought to have been the product of a distinct group of scholars at Chartres, so references were made to the 'School of Chartres' and to 'Chartrian' scholars. These terms have persisted despite general acknowledgement that the scholars in question did not all study at Chartres and did not form a distinct group at all. The terms 'Platonism' and 'Platonist' have also been used to describe the intellectual trend because of the particular significance of Plato's work to scholars who wrote in this way. Although twelfth-century myth-makers were influenced by many classical texts, the story of creation in Plato's *Timaeus*, part of which was available in Chalcidius' third-century translation, was their single most important model.[112]

A striking example of this genre was the *Cosmographia* written by Bernard Silvestris, probably between 1143 and 1148.[113] Little is known of Bernard's life, except that he taught at Tours and dedicated his

[111] *Ibid.*, pp. 97–9.

[112] R. W. Southern, 'Humanism and the school of Chartres', in *Medieval Humanism*, pp. 61–85; B. Stock, *Myth and Science in the Twelfth Century: A Study of Bernard Silvester* (Princeton, 1972); W. Wetherbee, *Platonism and Poetry in the Twelfth Century: The Literary Influence of the School of Chartres* (Princeton, 1972).

[113] Bernard Silvestris, *The Cosmographia of Bernardus Silvestris*, trans. W. Wetherbee (New York, 1973). For the date, see Stock, *Myth and Science*, p. 11.

Cosmographia to Thierry of Chartres.[114] The *Cosmographia* consists of two books. In the first, the *Megacosmus*, Nature complains to Nous (Divine Providence) about the chaotic state of prime matter. Nous agrees to impose order and creates the universe, separating the four elements and overseeing the union of the body and soul of the universe. Bernard then describes the contents of the created universe and the way it works. The second book, the *Microcosmus*, concerns the creation of man. Nous sends Nature on a journey through the heavens to find the two goddesses, Urania (Heavenly Reason) and Physis. Nous then oversees the creation of man as microcosm, with Nature joining together the soul provided by Urania and the body provided by Physis.[115] Bernard thus found a way to discuss the creation of the universe and the way it functioned.

But almost any intellectual problem could be treated in this manner, which is why different aspects of twelfth-century thought are so hard to separate and classify. Somewhat earlier, Adelard of Bath wrote his *De eodem et diverso*, or 'On the Same and the Different'. Here Adelard explained to his nephew his reasons for travelling. He told his nephew how he visited Tours to learn from a wise man there. One evening he was just outside the city, by the River Loire, when two women appeared to him. The first, Philocosmia, tried to win him over by inviting him to choose one of her five serving-girls: Riches, Power, Honour, Fame and Pleasure. In praising these maidens, she ridiculed philosophers because they could never agree and urged him to prefer things that could be perceived by the senses to the words of philosophy. The second woman, Philosophia, then spoke up, demonstrating the compatibility of Plato and Aristotle, and rejecting the senses as deceptive, distracting and lacking the power to reflect on themselves: 'the senses cannot sense how they sense or what they themselves are'.[116] Adelard then took Philosophia's part against Philocosmia, speaking to good effect:

> When I pressed home these points on which I spoke fluently and with passion, Philocosmia, dumbstruck with a kind of shame, covered her face with her gown, withdrew backwards a little with her maidens, and left me in the middle of my speech still ready to say more.[117]

Rejoicing, Philosophia proceeded to offer Adelard the choice of her maidens: Grammar, Rhetoric, Dialectic, Arithmetic, Music, Geometry

[114] Stock, *Myth and Science*, p. 13
[115] *Ibid.*, pp. 14–17; G. R. Evans, *Alan of Lille: The Frontiers of Theology in the Later Twelfth Century* (Cambridge, 1983), pp. 134–5.
[116] Adelard of Bath, *De eodem et diverso*, in *Conversations with his Nephew*, p. 27.
[117] *Ibid.*, p. 35.

and Astronomy. She described them in detail and then departed. Adelard thus invented a story that permitted him to describe the seven liberal arts, explain the value of philosophy, and put forward a theory of knowledge.

A far more complex allegory was constructed later in the twelfth century by Alan of Lille. Born in Lille around 1116, Alan studied in Paris and possibly Chartres, before teaching in Paris and probably Montpellier. He died in 1202 or 1203.[118] The *Anticlaudianus* was composed between 1181 and 1184.[119] The story begins with Nature lamenting her failures and aspiring to create a perfect man. She therefore calls the Virtues down from heaven to assist her. Prudence (Phronesis) approves of the project but points out that while they can make the body, only God can provide the soul. Reason proposes that Prudence should go to heaven to ask God for a soul. Concord persuades Prudence to agree. Seven maidens, the liberal arts, therefore make the parts of a chariot and Concord fits them together. Reason presents five horses to pull the chariot, and they are the five senses. Prudence and Reason set off in the chariot, with Prudence investigating natural phenomena:

> The chariot is raised, leaves the ground and in its flight departs into the subtle air. As she passes through the regions of Air, Prudence carefully turns her mind to an investigation of each and every thing to which Air lays successful claim; she examines and makes a deep analysis of the elusive element. She asks herself: what is the material and origin of the clouds; in what way the earth, damp with its own moisture, sends exudations to form clouds and arranges a mantle for itself in the heavens.[120]

Ascending to the stars, the five horses refuse to go further and Reason cannot force them. Another maiden then appears: Theology. Leaving Reason behind, Theology takes Prudence further upwards. They continue to the 'realms of happiness'[121] where angels, saints and the Virgin Mary dwell. Dazzled, Prudence falls into a trance and Theology has to call on her sister, Faith, to revive her fully. Faith gives Prudence a mirror so that she can look at heaven in reflection and without being blinded by the light, and also helps her to understand the mysteries which she sees. Eventually Faith takes her into the presence of God whom she begs for the soul. God agrees and gives her a soul which she takes back

118 For the life of Alan of Lille, see J. J. Sheridan, 'Introduction', in Alan of Lille, *Anticlaudianus or The Good and Perfect Man*, trans. J. J. Sheridan (Toronto, 1973), pp. 9–11; Evans, *Alan of Lille*, pp. 1–14.

119 Sheridan, 'Introduction', in Alan of Lille, *Anticlaudianus*, p. 25; Evans, *Alan of Lille*, p. 14.

120 Alan of Lille, *Anticlaudianus*, p. 126.

121 *Ibid.*, p. 150

down to Nature. Nature then makes a body from earth, water, air and fire. Concord, aided by Arithmetic and Music, joins body and soul. The New Man is perfected by gifts from the Virtues, Reason and the liberal arts. Rumours about the New Man have spread, however, and Allecto leads the Vices against him. Nature and the Virtues assist the New Man in the ensuing battle. The New Man triumphs and rules the earth where the Virtues can now reside. This was a story which enabled Alan both to discuss the workings of the universe and to outline a theory of knowledge, including theology and faith as well as philosophy. As Alan himself put it: 'there emerge in this work the rules of grammatical syntax, the maxims of dialectical discourse, the accepted ideas of oratorical rhetoric, the wonders of mathematical lore, the melody of music, the principles of geometry, theories about writing, the excellence of the dignity of astronomy, [and] a view of the celestial theophany'.[122]

The use of myth and poetry rested upon carefully worked-out theories about allegory in which the key terms were *involucrum* and *integumentum*.[123] Originally both words referred to a physical covering, but they came to mean an allegorical covering beneath which ideas were deliberately hidden within a myth which was not straightforwardly Christian. It was believed that many classical works had been written in this way, and that concealed meanings could therefore be discovered within them. Viewed in this way, there was much to be learned from works like the *Timaeus* which offered accounts of creation that, taken literally, contradicted Christian beliefs.[124] As we have seen, scholars also set out to write works which explored truth through allegory. It is impossible to do justice to long and complex works in brief summaries, but it should be clear from the examples described above that these were texts designed to work at different levels. As Alan of Lille commented in the Prose Prologue to the *Anticlaudianus*: 'in this work the sweetness of the literal sense will soothe the ears of boys, the moral instruction will inspire the mind on the road to perfection, the sharper subtlety of the allegory will whet the advanced intellect.'[125] As a result, such works were in many respects imprecise and open to many readings. They expressed a recognition of the inadequacy of language to cope with their chosen themes and an attempt to go beyond it, to explore what was beyond words. They frequently involved reflection about language and poetry themselves; in other words, they were not only about what was beyond

[122] *Ibid.*, pp. 41–2.
[123] Stock, *Myth and Science*, pp. 11–62; Wetherbee, *Platonism and Poetry*, pp. 11–73.
[124] Stock, *Myth and Science*, p. 53; Wetherbee, *Platonism and Poetry*, pp. 38–9.
[125] Alan of Lille, *Anticlaudianus*, pp. 40–1.

words, but about the process of going beyond.[126] While they shared a common concern with language and interpretation, they were in other respects the very opposite of the dry technicality of dialectic and analysis through historical criticism and systematic textual comparison.

Diversity and conflict

The diversity within the work of the twelfth-century schools encouraged intense debate about what ought properly to have been going on, and twelfth-century schoolmen were bitter in their criticism of each other.[127] John of Salisbury's *Metalogicon*, for example, not only defended logic against its detractors, but also contained a stinging critique of those who misused it. After nearly twelve years in the schools, John returned to the Mont Sainte Geneviève, where he had first studied dialectic under Abelard. Those who had been his fellow students were still there working on dialectic and John wanted to check on their progress. He was not impressed:

I found them just as, and where, they were when I had left them. They did not seem to have progressed as much as a hand's span. Not a single tiny [new] proposition had they added toward the solution of the old problems. They themselves remained involved in and occupied with the same questions whereby they used to stir their students. They had changed in but one regard: they had unlearned moderation: they no longer knew restraint. And this to such an extent that their recovery was a matter of despair. I was accordingly convinced by experience of something which can easily be inferred [by reason]: that just as dialectic expedites other studies, so, if left alone by itself, it lies powerless and sterile. For if it is to fecundate the soul to bear the fruits of philosophy, logic must conceive from an external source.[128]

John was disgusted to find that they were debating the same old problems without finding any new solutions. Most importantly, they had failed to grasp that dialectic was useless unless applied to other branches of learning. This was a point that John developed:

Although it does not rise to other problems, dialectic resolves questions relative to itself. Thus it supplies the answers to such problems as: 'Is affirmation also enuntiation?' and 'Can two contradictory propositions be simultaneously true?' But anyone can see what [little] practical utility such information has in itself, apart from its application to particular cases. Dialectic, pure and simple, hardly ever investigates such questions as: 'Is pleasure good?' 'Should virtue

[126] See the comments of Stock, *Myth and Science*, pp. 229–30, Wetherbee, *Platonism and Poetry*, pp. 67, 72.

[127] For a detailed and brilliant account, see Ferruolo, *Origins of the University*.

[128] John of Salisbury, *Metalogicon*, p. 100.

be preferred to aught else?' 'Do good habits exist in the highest state?' and 'Should one labour when one is in need?' But upon the answer to problems such as these, depends whether or not our life will result in the attainment of happiness and salvation.[129]

John's key point was therefore that scholars preoccupied by dialectic alone failed to address ethical issues which were crucial to salvation. Pure dialecticians served no moral purpose.

John was equally critical of the masters who were obsessed with the problem of universals. They were driven by ambition and the need to establish a reputation:

Rarely, if ever, do we find a teacher who is content to follow in the footsteps of his master. Each, to make a name for himself, coins his own special error.[130]

Moreover, they baffled their students by tackling difficult issues when they were supposed to be teaching the basics:

Instruction in elementary logic does not ... constitute the proper occasion for such procedure. Simplicity, brevity, and easy subject matter are, so far as is possible, appropriate in introductory studies ... Nevertheless, at present, all are here [in introductory logical studies] declaiming on the nature of universals, and attempting to explain ... what is really a most profound question, and a matter [that should be reserved] for more advanced studies.[131]

Consequently they placed too much 'on the frail shoulders of their students' and neglected 'proper order in teaching'.[132] To cap it all, John considered that many of them were just 'wrangling over words, rather than disputing about facts', and their opinions were little different from each other 'as would be shown if it were possible to compare their meanings'.[133]

Alan of Lille conveyed the difference between good and bad scholarship in sexual terms. He wrote the *Plaint of Nature* in the 1160s.[134] At the start the poet laments, deploring the homosexual acts which have become common. A woman then appears who turns out to be Nature. Nature's crown and clothes are described in detail, for there the whole of creation is portrayed. Where man is represented, however, her tunic is

[129] *Ibid.*, pp. 100–1. [130] *Ibid.*, pp. 116–17.
[131] *Ibid.*, p. 112. [132] *Ibid.*, pp. 117–18.
[133] *Ibid.*, p. 117.
[134] For dating and summaries of this work, see N. M. Häring, 'Alan of Lille, <<De Planctu naturae>>', *Studi Medievali*, third series, 19 (1978): 797–897 at 797, 804–5; J. J. Sheridan, 'Introduction', in Alan of Lille, *The Plaint of Nature*, trans. J. J. Sheridan (Toronto, 1980), pp. 31–45; J. Ziolkowski, *Alan of Lille's Grammar of Sex: The Meaning of Grammar to a Twelfth-Century Intellectual* (Cambridge, MA, 1985), pp. 9–10.

torn. Moreover, Nature is stricken by grief. There follows a dialogue in which Nature replies to the poet's questions. She explains that she weeps because man alone disobeys her law with his sexual perversions. She tells how Venus abused the powers which Nature had delegated to her. Nature then describes a host of Vices before the Virtues appear. Finally Genius arrives and reads a sentence of excommunication directed against those who break Nature's laws. The poet then awakes.

In condemning homosexual acts, Alan made repeated use of grammatical metaphors. This was the case at the start of the work when the poet offers his lament:

Alas! Where has Nature with her fair form betaken herself? Where have the pattern of morals, the norm of chastity, the love of modesty gone? Nature weeps, moral laws get no hearing, modesty, totally dispossessed of her ancient high estate, is sent into exile. The active sex shudders in disgrace as it sees itself degenerate into the passive sex. A man turned woman blackens the fair name of his sex. The witchcraft of Venus turns him into a hermaphrodite. He is subject and predicate: one and the same term is given a double application. Man here extends too far the laws of grammar. Becoming a barbarian in grammar, he disclaims the manhood given him by Nature.[135]

In the sexual act, Alan regarded the man as active and the woman as passive. When both roles were taken by men, it was as if a word were performing two opposite grammatical functions, as subject and predicate. Putting it the other way round, adopting such a perverse grammatical practice was as if to abandon true masculinity.

Alan used similar imagery in Nature's complaint:

Man alone turns with scorn from the modulated strains of my cithern and runs deranged to the notes of mad Orpheus' lyre. For the human race, fallen from its high estate, adopts a highly irregular (grammatical) change [metaplasm] when it inverts the rules of Venus by introducing barbarisms in its arrangement of genders. Thus man, his sex changed by a ruleless Venus, in defiance of due order, by his arrangement changes what is a straightforward attribute of his. Abandoning in his deviation the true script of Venus, he is proved to be a sophistic pseudographer.[136]

A metaplasm was a change to a word in verse made necessary by the metre. A barbarism was a similar alteration to a word, but in prose and therefore without justification.[137] In this case, however, even the

135 Alan of Lille, *Plaint of Nature*, pp. 67–8; see also Ziolkowski, *Alan of Lille's Grammar of Sex*, p. 15.

136 Alan of Lille, *Plaint of Nature*, pp. 133–4; see also Ziolkowski, *Alan of Lille's Grammar of Sex*, p. 22.

137 Ziolkowski, *Alan of Lille's Grammar of Sex*, p. 22.

metaplasm was inappropriate. Man was therefore making unnecessary and improper changes to the gender of words, just as he was doing to himself. He was a false writer and a false man.

Grammatical metaphor runs throughout the *Plaint of Nature*. Indeed the work only makes sense if the metaphor is understood. Read one way, Alan was using the imagery of good and bad grammar to attack homosexual acts as perverse sexual deviancy. Read another way, however, Alan was condemning bad grammar, and perhaps bad scholarship more generally, as equivalent to sexual perversion. Good grammar and properly conducted scholarship, however, were deemed to possess the creative power of procreative sex, and the good scholar embodied pure and unadulterated masculinity. This was just one of the most striking ways in which scholars expressed their desire to condemn false learning and praise legitimate scholarship.

Towards universities

It was out of this world that universities emerged at the end of the twelfth century and the beginning of the thirteenth century. This process will be examined further in a later chapter, but it is worth pointing out key features of the twelfth-century schools which took on growing importance in the second half of the century and were to prove decisive in the emergence of stable institutions of learning.

In purely pedagogical terms, there was a growing consensus about the basic education that all students had to be given and about the ways in which they might specialize subsequently. The use of dialectic and syllogistic reasoning, for example, became increasingly commonplace and uncontroversial. Eventually all men who went to the schools and later the universities received a more or less standard training in these methods at an early stage in their intellectual formation, an experience that shaped their language and their thought processes. Furthermore, the emergence of widely accepted textbooks was crucial in defining areas for systematic teaching and research. Gratian's *Decretum* and Peter Lombard's *Sentences* were the most significant examples. Other scholars produced similar works, reflecting a general desire for order, but the *Decretum* and the *Sentences* answered common needs most effectively. These works became standard because they included a wide range of material and set it within an overall structure that seemed coherent and usable to other scholars. The *Sentences*, for example, was divided into four books: Book 1 concerned God, Book 2 examined the creation, Book 3 looked at Christ and the virtues, and Book 4 focused on the sacraments, death, judgement, hell and heaven.[138] These standard works were also popular because they were the products of teaching and could easily form the basis of an ordered curriculum. They were supported by other standard works of reference. From the early twelfth century, Anselm of Laon began to compile comments, or glosses, on the Bible from a variety of sources, chiefly patristic and Carolingian, and to insert them in the margins and between the lines of the biblical text. Anselm died in 1117 and the process was continued by his colleagues and pupils, notably his brother Ralph and Gilbert of Auxerre. Although the resulting text remained subject to variation, it nevertheless became accepted as the standard gloss on the Bible, or the *Glossa ordinaria*.[139] Around 1170, Peter Comestor produced the *Historia Scholastica*. Peter taught at the cathedral school of Notre Dame in Paris in the 1160s and became chancellor. The *Historia Scholastica* was a work of history based chiefly on the Bible.[140] Books like these established common ground for scholars working in a given field and the means with which to cover it efficiently. All students would therefore be expected to cover that ground, and masters had clear points of reference which they could use to point up the originality of their own contributions.[141] With the increasingly clear definition of both methods and fields of study, the notion of academic disciplines emerged.[142] While the meaning of terms like 'theology' remained contentious, by the end of the twelfth century debates about their meaning followed well-established lines. Although still

[138] On Peter Lombard's *Sentences*, see P. Biller, *The Measure of Multitude: Population in Medieval Thought* (Oxford, 2000), pp. 29–30, 33–7; Colish, *Peter Lombard*, vol. 1, pp. 77–90; N. Spatz, 'Approaches and attitudes to a new theology textbook: the *Sentences* of Peter Lombard', in N. van Deusen (ed.), *The Intellectual Climate of the Early University: Essays in Honor of Otto Gründler* (Kalamazoo, MI, 1997), pp. 27–52. On Gratian's *Decretum*, especially the stages in its compilation and the identity of its compiler or compilers, see J. A. Brundage, *The Medieval Origins of the Legal Profession: Canonists, Civilians, and Courts* (Chicago, 2008), pp. 96–105; Winroth, *Making of Gratian's Decretum*.

[139] B. Smalley, *The Study of the Bible in the Middle Ages* (Oxford, 1952), pp. 49–51, 56, 60–6; Smith, *Glossa Ordinaria*, pp. 2, 12–13, 17–33, 41–56, 73–6.

[140] See, for example, S. R. Daly, 'Peter Comestor: Master of Histories', *Speculum* 32 (1957): 62–73 at 67, 70–1; Ferruolo, *Origins of the University*, pp. 190–1; D. Luscombe, 'Peter Comestor', in K. Walsh and D. Wood (eds.), *The Bible in the Medieval World: Essays in Memory of Beryl Smalley* (Oxford, 1985), pp. 109–29; J. H. Morey, 'Peter Comestor, biblical paraphrase, and the medieval popular Bible', *Speculum* 68 (1993): 6–35 at 6–16; M. M. Mulchahey, *'First the Bow is Bent': Dominican Education before 1350* (Toronto, 1998), pp. 481–2; Smalley, *Study of the Bible*, pp. 178–80.

[141] See the comments of Smith, *Glossa Ordinaria*, p. 218.

[142] See G. R. Evans, *Old Arts and New Theology: The Beginnings of Theology as an Academic Discipline* (Oxford, 1980), esp. pp. 27–56.

contested, there was nevertheless a conceptual framework to which institutional structures could be related.

The status and identity of the men who worked in the schools were very significantly reinforced by the growing involvement of external political powers in their affairs. In 1155 the emperor Frederick I issued a decree in Italy known as the *Authentica Habita*. He granted his 'dutiful love to all scholars who are travelling for the sake of their studies, and especially to teachers of the divine and sacred laws: that they and their representatives may safely come to the places in which letters are studied and safely live in them'. He decreed that 'no one shall be so bold as to presume to do any injury to scholars'. Moreover, no one was 'to cause them any loss on account of a debt incurred by another man from the same district', which meant that scholars were not to be held liable for debts incurred by other scholars from the same place of origin. Having laid down penalties for infringement of these laws, Frederick went on to decree that whenever a suit was brought against scholars they could choose whether the case should be heard before their own master or before the local bishop.[143] The decree was presumably aimed at scholars in the emperor's Italian possessions, and perhaps Bologna in particular since it was issued in response to a request from masters and students from that city.[144] Whatever its effect, it offered the prospect of protection and a distinct legal identity, and a model that might be taken up elsewhere.

In the early 1170s Pope Alexander III intervened to defend scholars against the local clergy at Rheims.[145] The scholars claimed that after reproaching a local priest for unseemly behaviour they had been physically assaulted and excommunicated. In ordering an enquiry into these events, the pope accepted the scholars' claim to 'possess the liberty that no one shall dare to lay violent hands upon them or to promulgate an ecclesiastical sentence so long as they wish to remain under the jurisdiction of their own master'.[146] Again, scholars were receiving protection and recognition of a distinct legal status. Moreover, both emperor and pope put the bond between master and student at the heart of their identity.

Financial support was also an issue of fundamental concern to both masters and students. In 1179 a decree of the third Lateran Council sought to ensure that the church would provide consistent backing:

[143] Pullan, *Sources*, pp. 104–5.
[144] Brundage, *Medieval Origins of the Legal Profession*, pp. 88–9.
[145] *University Records*, no. 8, pp. 19–20.
[146] *Ibid.*, no. 8, p. 20.

Since the church of God as a kindly mother is held to provide for those needs which pertain to physical welfare and those which contribute to the progress of souls, lest the opportunity of reading and education be denied poor children who cannot be aided by the resources of their parents, let some sufficient benefice be set aside in every cathedral church for a master who shall teach the clergy of the same church and poor scholars gratis, whereby the need for a teacher shall be met and the way to knowledge opened to learners. In other churches, too, and monasteries, if in time past any provision has been made for this purpose, let it be reestablished. And for the permission to teach let no one demand any fee whatever, or ask anything from teachers under the cover of some custom, or forbid any fit person to teach if he seeks permission.[147]

Every cathedral was to employ a master, and he was not to charge for teaching the clergy and poor students. If masters were fit to teach, they were not to be forbidden to teach, not charged for permission. Almost certainly the decree was issued in response to a petition and it was probably limited in its effect: certainly it was repeated subsequently. It strongly suggests, however, that deliberate attempts were being made to put academic careers on more secure foundations.

The academic career also became more clearly defined and more secure when less frequent travelling was involved. Starting out as a student, for example, became much less of a risk once distinct traditions of learning began to develop in different places, and scholars specializing in a particular discipline started to gather in the towns that were most appropriate. Thus Bologna became known as the leading centre for legal studies, and Paris was recognized as pre-eminent in philosophy and theology. Students therefore knew where to go to find the leading masters in their chosen field. They still had to travel in pursuit of learning, but wandering was increasingly a thing of the past.

For most of the twelfth century, however, it was far from clear that any of these developments would lead to the emergence of stable academic institutions. The schools, especially in the first half of the century, were essentially chaotic. Many masters and students were swept up in their enthusiasm for dialectic and highly technical forms of argument. They also collected and compared authoritative texts, subjecting them to rigorous historical analysis. They had great confidence in the value of asking questions and challenging accepted interpretations, and they were determined to apply their methods to knowledge of God. At the same time, a belief in the value of allegorical interpretation led some scholars to deploy myth and poetry in the pursuit of truth. There was strong disagreement about the validity of different intellectual methods and procedures, and this found expression in lively criticism. This

[147] *Ibid.*, no. 9, p. 21.

intellectual diversity flourished in a highly competitive environment and within very loose institutional structures. Students were extremely mobile and their choices shaped the careers of their masters, whose reputations were therefore a crucial part of their success. If successful, however, a man could make a career out of teaching in the schools, and he might also have the opportunity to move on to another career in administration and high office. The personal stakes were very high and this doubtless contributed to the vigour with which men criticized each other. Their disorderly sense of adventure and competition gave both masters and students a strong sense of themselves as a new and distinct social group. Others could not fail to notice and to react.

2 The twelfth-century monasteries and Hugh of Saint Victor

The monasteries of the twelfth century were very different from the schools and they sometimes produced very different scholars, many of whom were ferocious critics of the masters and their students, but it is important not to misinterpret the monks' ideals and the way in which they represented themselves. They were to live apart from the world, bound by their vows not to wander from monastery to monastery. Their lives were to be shaped by specific models from the past: the apostolic life, the lives of the desert Fathers and the Rule of Saint Benedict. Compared with the mobile and competitive world of the schools, it is easy to think of the monastic world as fundamentally static, whereas in fact the twelfth century was just as much an era of innovation, change and expansion for monks as it was for students and masters in the schools. New religious orders were established and new monastic houses were founded, creating a world in which men travelled to set up or join new orders, and perhaps subsequently to establish new houses. Moreover, the lines of communication between houses were constantly alive, as monks visited other houses and exchanged letters. The different orders were often highly critical of one another, although the apparently bitter polemic sometimes disguised a willingness to tolerate different interpretations of monastic ideals and perhaps even an appreciation of diversity. Moreover, twelfth-century monks were in many respects engaged with the secular world around them. Many houses owned considerable areas of land, constituting a substantial economic force, while some monastic leaders were major political figures on the international stage. Monastic learning therefore flourished in a context that was changing just as quickly as the schools.[1]

[1] Key works on twelfth-century monastic culture include: C. Bouchard, *Holy Entrepreneurs: Cistercians, Knights, and Economic Exchange in Twelfth-Century Burgundy* (Ithaca, NY, 1991); G. Constable, 'Renewal and reform in religious life: concepts and realities', in R. L. Benson and G. Constable (eds.), *Renaissance and Renewal in the Twelfth Century* (Oxford, 1982), pp. 37–67, reprinted in *Monks, Hermits and Crusaders in Medieval Europe* (London, 1988); P. S. Gold, *The Lady and the Virgin: Image, Attitude*

Unsurprisingly, therefore, monastic learning itself was far from static, and it was not entirely divorced from the intellectual preoccupations of the schools. The first part of this chapter considers the work of Anselm of Bec and Canterbury, who was a leading figure both intellectually and politically in the late eleventh and early twelfth centuries, and who has sometimes been considered a major influence on later developments in the schools and universities.[2] In Anselm's day, however, the schools were only just beginning to take off, and it was the next generation of monastic thinkers who were compelled to respond to the likes of Peter Abelard. It was under the dynamic leadership of Bernard of Clairvaux that the Cistercian order came to prominence, and he made sure that his views were known across Europe. He was prompted in his reactions to the schools by William of Saint Thierry, who has often been considered the more subtle and complex thinker. Although she did not offer a direct response to developments in the schools, Hildegard of Bingen was equally significant if we are to understand the intellectual culture of religious houses in the twelfth century. Having examined the ways of thinking cultivated by these three key figures, the chapter will focus on actual conflict between monks and schoolmen. Finally, we will ask whether there was a way to move beyond these bitter disputes, and the last section will concern Hugh of Saint Victor whose ideas seem to offer just such a path and to point in the direction eventually taken by the University of Paris.

Anselm of Bec and Canterbury

Born in 1033, Anselm came from a minor noble family in Aosta, in northern Italy. In 1059 he went to the monastery of Bec in Normandy to study under Lanfranc. He became a monk the following year, and went on to hold the offices of prior and then abbot at Bec, before succeeding Lanfranc as archbishop of Canterbury in 1093, a position he

and Experience in Twelfth-Century France (Chicago, 1985), pp. 76–115; J. Haseldine, 'Friendship and rivalry: the role of *amicitia* in twelfth-century monastic relations', *Journal of Ecclesiastical History* 44 (1993): 390–414; P. D. Johnson, *Equal in Monastic Profession: Religious Women in Medieval France* (Chicago, 1991); C. H. Lawrence, *Medieval Monasticism: Forms of Religious Life in Western Europe in the Middle Ages*, 3rd edn (Harlow, 2001), pp. 149–205, 216–37; M. G. Newman, *The Boundaries of Charity: Cistercian Culture and Ecclesiastical Reform, 1098–1180* (Stanford, 1996); B. L. Venarde, *Women's Monasticism and Medieval Society: Nunneries in France and England, 890–1215* (Ithaca, NY, 1997).

2 For very different views on this point, see E. Gilson, *History of Christian Philosophy in the Middle Ages* (New York, 1955), p. 139; M. Haren, *Medieval Thought: The Western Intellectual Tradition from Antiquity to the Thirteenth Century*, 2nd edn (Toronto, 1992), pp. 103–4.

held until his death in 1109.[3] Anselm's intellectual interests were in some ways not far removed from those of his contemporaries in the schools. Eadmer, a monk of Canterbury who was close to Anselm, wrote a *vita*, or life, of Anselm, much of it while Anselm was still alive.[4] He noted that Anselm's *De Grammatico*, or 'On the Grammarian', 'was in the form of a disputation with a disciple, whom he introduced as the other disputant, and in it he both propounded and solved many dialectical questions'.[5] Anselm was fascinated by logic and language, and he unhesitatingly used his intellectual skills in trying to know about God.

In 1077–8 Anselm wrote the *Proslogion*, meaning an 'address', which he directed to God. In the preface he explained the aim with which he had started his work:

> I began to ask myself if it would be possible to find one single argument, needing no other proof than itself, to prove that God really exists, that he is the highest good, needing nothing, that it is he whom all things need for their being and well-being, and to prove whatever else we believe about the nature of God.[6]

As in a number of his other works, Anselm thus set himself the task of discussing God without direct use of authorities.

It is in the *Proslogion* that Anselm set out his 'ontological proof' of the existence of God. It is worth quoting in full:

> We believe that you are that thing than which nothing greater can be thought. Or is there nothing of that kind in existence, since 'the fool has said in his heart, there is no God'? But when the fool hears me use this phrase, 'something than which nothing greater can be thought', he understands what he hears; and what he understands is in his understanding, even if he does not understand that it exists. For it is one thing to have something in the understanding, but quite another to understand that it actually exists. It is like a painter who, when he thinks out beforehand what he is going to create, has it in his understanding, but he does not yet understand it as actually existing because he has not yet painted it. But when he has painted it, he both has it in his understanding and actually has it, because he has created it. So the fool has to agree that the concept of something than which nothing greater can be thought exists in his understanding, since he understood what he heard and whatever is understood is in the understanding. And certainly that than which nothing greater can

[3] For accounts of his life, see G. R. Evans, *Anselm* (London, 1989), pp. 1–26; R. W. Southern, *Saint Anselm and his Biographer: A Study of Monastic Life and Thought 1059–c. 1130* (Cambridge, 1963); R. W. Southern, *Saint Anselm: A Portrait in a Landscape* (Cambridge, 1990).

[4] Evans, *Anselm*, pp. 1–2.

[5] Eadmer, *The Life of St Anselm*, trans. R. W. Southern (London, 1962), p. 28.

[6] Anselm, *Proslogion*, preface, in *The Prayers and Meditations of Saint Anselm with the Proslogion*, trans. B. Ward (Harmondsworth, 1973), p. 238.

be thought cannot exist only in the understanding. For if it exists only in the understanding, it is possible to think of it existing also in reality, and that is greater. If that than which nothing greater can be thought exists in the understanding alone, then this thing than which nothing greater can be thought is something than which a greater can be thought. And this is clearly impossible. Therefore there can be no doubt at all that something than which nothing greater can be thought exists both in the understanding and in reality.[7]

In order to grasp Anselm's argument, it is necessary to identify his premises or assumptions. First, God is defined as 'something than which nothing greater can be thought', a definition that could be found in Cicero, Seneca, Augustine and Boethius.[8] Second, it is assumed that to exist in thought is genuinely to exist in some way. Third, Anselm takes a hierarchical approach to being, and assumes that existing outside the mind, 'in reality' as he puts it, is greater than existing only in the mind.

Thus Anselm begins with the definition of God as 'something than which nothing greater can be thought'. Then he points out that even the Fool who denies the existence of God understands when he hears the words 'something than which nothing greater can be thought'. Deploying the second assumption, Anselm argues that 'something than which nothing greater can be thought' must therefore exist in the Fool's mind, even if he does not understand it to exist in reality. It is to illustrate this point that Anselm refers to the painter who has thought what he is going to paint, but has not yet painted it: the painting exists in his mind, but he does not understand it to exist in reality. Anselm then comes to the crux of his argument. He invites the reader to suppose that 'something than which nothing greater can be thought' exists only in the mind. It would then be possible to think of it existing also in reality which, bringing in the third assumption, is greater. An absurd conclusion would then have been reached, namely that it is possible to think of something greater than 'something than which nothing greater can be thought'. According to Anselm, this absurd conclusion has been drawn because it is incorrect to suppose that 'something than which nothing greater can be thought' exists only in the mind. On the contrary, as Anselm puts it, 'Something than which nothing greater can be thought so truly exists that it is not possible to think of it as not existing.'[9] Anselm had therefore demonstrated to his own satisfaction that it was necessary to believe that God existed.

[7] *Ibid.*, 2, pp. 244–5.

[8] D. E. Luscombe, *Medieval Thought* (Oxford, 1997), p. 45; Southern, *Saint Anselm: A Portrait*, p. 129.

[9] Anselm, *Proslogion*, 3, in *The Prayers and Meditations of Saint Anselm*, p. 245.

Anselm received a reply 'on behalf of the Fool' from Gaunilo, an otherwise unknown monk from Marmoutier near Tours. Gaunilo challenged Anselm's argument in several ways, pointing out that it would seem to apply, for example, to the most wonderful island which one could imagine, even though the island did not exist:

they say that there is in the ocean somewhere an island which, because of the difficulty (or rather the impossibility) of finding that which does not exist, some have called the 'Lost Island'. And the story goes that it is blessed with all manner of priceless riches and delights in abundance, much more even than the Happy Isles, and, having no owner or inhabitant, it is superior everywhere in abundance of riches to all those other lands that men inhabit. Now, if anyone tell me that it is like this, I shall easily understand what is said, since nothing is difficult about it. But if he should then go on to say, as though it were a logical consequence of this: You cannot any more doubt that this island that is more excellent than all other lands truly exists somewhere in reality than you can doubt that it is in your mind: and since it is more excellent to exist not only in the mind alone but also in reality, therefore it must needs be that it exists. For if it did not exist, any other land existing in reality would be more excellent than it, and so this island already conceived by you to be more excellent than others, will not be more excellent. If, I say, someone wishes thus to persuade me that this island really exists beyond all doubt, I should either think that he was joking, or that I should find it hard to decide which of us I thought the bigger fool – I, if I agreed with him, or he, if he thought that he had proved the existence of this island with any certainty, unless he had first convinced me that its very excellence exists in my mind precisely as a thing existing truly and indubitably and not just as something unreal or doubtfully real.[10]

Anselm responded to all Gaunilo's objections, insisting that his argument did not apply to the most wonderful island one could imagine, but only to 'something than which nothing greater can be thought':

You claim, however, that this is as though someone asserted that it cannot be doubted that a certain island in the ocean (which is more fertile than all other lands and which, because of the difficulty or even the impossibility of discovering what does not exist, is called the 'Lost Island') truly exists in reality since anyone easily understands it when it is described in words. Now, I truly promise that if anyone should discover for me something existing either in reality or in the mind alone – except 'that-than-which-a-greater-cannot-be-thought' – to which the logic of my argument would apply, then I shall find that Lost Island and give it, never more to be lost, to that person.[11]

Anselm's point was presumably that the most wonderful island was not the greatest thing of which one could think. That was God, to whom

[10] Gaunilo, 'A reply ... on behalf of the fool', in *St Anselm's Proslogion*, trans. M. J. Charlesworth (Oxford, 1965), pp. 163–5.

[11] *Ibid.*, p. 175.

the argument applied alone. Anselm had this good-humoured exchange of views added to later copies of the *Proslogion*.

The 'ontological proof' was, however, only a small part of the *Proslogion*. Anselm very quickly turned to explore the nature of God, answering the question 'What are you, then, Lord God, you than whom nothing greater can be thought?'[12] When Eadmer described the *Proslogion*, he did not mention the proof of God's existence at all:

> it came into his mind to try to prove by one single and short argument the things which are believed and preached about God, that he is eternal, unchangeable, omnipotent, omnipresent, incomprehensible, just, righteous, merciful, true, as well as truth, goodness, justice and so on; and to show how all these qualities are united in him.[13]

For Eadmer, therefore, the *Proslogion* was entirely about the attributes of God.

Anselm's approach to the nature of God can be illustrated by his treatment of God's omnipotence. He asked how God could be omnipotent when there were things that he could not do, such as being corrupted, lying and making false what was true. Anselm explained that doing such things stemmed not from power but from powerlessness, and that it was the improper use of words that caused confusion:

> For instance we use 'to be' instead of 'not to be', and 'to do' instead of 'not to do', or 'to do nothing'. So we often say when someone denies that something exists, 'that is as you say it is', when it would be more correct for us to say, 'it is not as you say it is not'. We also say, 'he is sitting', just as we say, 'he is doing something'; or 'he is resting', just as we say 'he is doing something'. But to sit is non-doing, and to rest is to do nothing. So when we say that someone has the power to do or suffer something which is not good for him or which he ought not to do, by 'power' we really mean 'powerlessness'.[14]

In God's case Anselm was able to conclude triumphantly: 'So, Lord God, you are in fact more truly omnipotent because you cannot do anything through powerlessness, and nothing has power over you.'[15] Anselm thus generated a fuller understanding of the nature of God through close analysis of the language used to talk about him.

It is important, however, not to overestimate the importance that Anselm attached to rational arguments. He did not require a rational proof of God's existence in order to believe that God existed. He did not need a rational explanation of God's omnipotence before he could

[12] Anselm, *Proslogion*, 5, in *The Prayers and Meditations of Saint Anselm*, p. 247.
[13] Eadmer, *Life of St Anselm*, p. 29.
[14] Anselm, *Proslogion*, 7, in *The Prayers and Meditations of Saint Anselm*, p. 248.
[15] *Ibid.*

accept that God was omnipotent. In the preface he said that he had written the *Proslogion* 'from the point of view of someone trying to raise his mind to the contemplation of God, and seeking to understand what he believes'.[16] His first choice of title for the work was 'Faith in Search of Understanding'.[17] He specifically rejected the idea that belief depended upon understanding:

Lord, I am not trying to make my way to your height, for my understanding is in no way equal to that, but I do desire to understand a little of your truth which my heart already believes and loves. I do not seek to understand so that I may believe, but I believe so that I may understand; and what is more, I believe that unless I do believe I shall not understand.[18]

In Anselm's mind, the priority of faith was beyond question. Without faith, argument was meaningless.

Moreover, Anselm pointed out the limits of the understanding that could be achieved through reason. Discussing the fate of the wicked, and still addressing God, he commented: 'reason certainly cannot comprehend why through your supreme goodness you should save some, and through your supreme justice condemn others, when both are equally evil'.[19] There were, however, other ways to know God. One should turn away from the world and look inwards:

Come now, little man, turn aside for a while from your daily employment, escape for a moment from the tumult of your thoughts. Put aside your weighty cares, let your burdensome distractions wait, free yourself awhile for God and rest awhile in him. Enter the inner chamber of your soul, shut out everything except God and that which can help you in seeking him, and when you have shut the door, seek him.[20]

One should also pray, and the *Proslogion* was very much a work of prayer:

O Lord my God, teach my heart where and how to seek you, where and how to find you.[21]

Anyone wrestling with Anselm's arguments will be relieved to discover that he also prayed:

O righteous and compassionate God, whose light I seek, help me to understand what I am saying![22]

[16] *Ibid.*, preface, p. 238. [17] *Ibid.*, preface, p. 239.
[18] *Ibid.*, 1, p. 244. [19] *Ibid.*, 11, p. 253.
[20] *Ibid.*, 1, p. 239. [21] *Ibid.*, pp. 239–40.
[22] *Ibid.*, 9, p. 251.

For Anselm, knowing God was also about emotional experience, above all about longing for God and loving God:

> Let me seek you by desiring you, and desire you by seeking you; let me find you by loving you, and love you in finding you.[23]

Ultimately, however, God's role was crucial. At the end of the ontological proof, Anselm gave his thanks to God, 'for it was by your gift that I first believed, and now by your illumination I understand'.[24] Later he asked, 'How could I understand anything at all about you, except by your light and your truth?'[25] For Anselm, there were many ways to know God. Reason was not the most important, but it was a valuable tool with which to explore beliefs, and he was comfortable using it alongside prayer, introspection and love.

Bernard of Clairvaux

Some decades later, Bernard of Clairvaux took a very different view of human reason, and while drawing on the same traditions as Anselm and having much in common with him, he nevertheless set his approach to knowing God at some distance from that of the schools. Born into a noble Burgundian family in 1090, Bernard became a monk at Citeaux in 1113 and abbot of Clairvaux in 1115. He established himself as a charismatic and highly controversial leader in international politics, championing the cause of Pope Innocent II against rival claimants to the papacy for most of the 1130s, and preaching the Second Crusade at the behest of Pope Eugenius III, who had been one of his monks at Clairvaux. Right up to his death in 1153, he asserted his influence by travelling to meet people and writing letters.[26] His approach to knowing God was readily apparent in the first of his sermons on Solomon's Song of Songs. There was a long tradition of commentary on this erotic love poem, with the bride being taken to represent either the church or the individual soul joined in union with God.[27] Bernard preached eighty-six sermons on the Song of Songs, turning them into complex literary

[23] *Ibid.*, 1, p. 243. [24] *Ibid.*, 4, p. 246.

[25] *Ibid.*, 14, p. 255.

[26] For accounts of his life, see A. H. Bredero, *Bernard of Clairvaux: Between Cult and History* (Edinburgh, 1996); G. R. Evans, *Bernard of Clairvaux* (Oxford, 2000), pp. 8–21; B. S. James, *Saint Bernard of Clairvaux: An Essay in Biography* (London, 1957).

[27] J. Leclercq, *The Love of Learning and the Desire for God: A Study of Monastic Culture*, trans. C. Misrahi (London, 1978), pp. 106–9; E. A. Matter, *The Voice of My Beloved: The Song of Songs in Western Medieval Christianity* (Philadelphia, 1990), pp. 86–150.

works. He began about 1135 and laboured on them on and off until his death when he was still working on the eighty-sixth.[28]

Bernard began his first sermon on the Song of Songs by raising the question of audience:

The instructions that I address to you, my brothers, will differ from those I should deliver to people in the world, at least the manner will be different.[29]

Bernard's words were for the 'spiritually enlightened',[30] for the monastic elite. They had read the book of Ecclesiastes and the book of Proverbs to rid themselves of the 'two evils that comprise the only, or at least the main enemies of the soul: a misguided love of the world and an excessive love of self'.[31] Bernard could therefore 'proceed with this holy and contemplative discourse which ... may be delivered only to well prepared ears and minds'.[32]

Bernard put particular emphasis on the need to reject the world:

Before the flesh has been tamed and the spirit set free by zeal for truth, before the world's glamour and entanglements have been repudiated, it is a rash enterprise on any man's part to presume to study spiritual doctrines.[33]

Examining the title of the book, Bernard observed that 'Solomon' meant 'Peaceful', and invited his audience to note 'that by this kind of opening only men of peaceful minds, men who can achieve mastery over the turmoil of the passions and the distracting burden of daily chores, are invited to the study of this book'.[34] To know God, it was necessary to be virtuous. Even then, nothing could be achieved without God's help and, like Anselm, Bernard was quick to turn to prayer:

O God most kind, break your bread for this hungering flock, through my hands indeed if it should please you, but with an efficacy that is all your own.[35]

Knowing God was not therefore an intellectual exercise:

Only the touch of the Spirit can inspire a song like this, and only personal experience can unfold its meaning. Let those who are versed in the mystery revel in it; let all others burn with desire rather to attain to this experience than merely to learn about it.[36]

[28] G. R. Evans, *The Mind of St Bernard of Clairvaux* (Oxford, 1983), pp. 107–17; Matter, *Voice of My Beloved*, pp. 123–4; B. McGinn, *The Growth of Mysticism*, The Presence of God: A History of Western Christian Mysticism 2 (London, 1994), p.164.

[29] Bernard of Clairvaux, *On the Song of Songs I*, trans. K. Walsh (Kalamazoo, MI, 1971), sermon 1, p. 1.

[30] *Ibid.* [31] *Ibid.*, p. 2. [32] *Ibid.*

[33] *Ibid.* [34] *Ibid.*, p. 4. [35] *Ibid.*, p. 3.

[36] *Ibid.*, p. 6.

According to Bernard, desire led to intense personal experience of a mystery. There was no point in simply learning about this experience, and rational arguments were not the way to attain it.

Bernard's approach was not analytical and technically precise. Rather, he turned to images and metaphors to move his audience. The spiritual elite were to be ready 'to feed on bread rather than milk'. Having studied the books of Ecclesiastes and Proverbs, the monks had tasted two loaves, and now the Song of Songs was a third. Although Bernard was preaching the sermon, 'The Master of the house is present, it is the Lord you must see in the breaking of the bread.'[37] Ultimately, the Song of Songs itself provided the key metaphor:

> Only the mind disciplined by persevering study, only the man whose efforts have borne fruit under God's inspiration, the man whose years, as it were, make him ripe for marriage – years measured out not in time but in merits – only he is truly prepared for nuptial union with the divine partner.[38]

Only through long study and virtuous living was it possible to work towards 'nuptial union' with God.

Bernard discussed the acquisition of knowledge at greater length in Sermon 36 on the Song of Songs. He made it clear that some forms of ignorance were perfectly acceptable 'since there are various and countless things of which one may know nothing without detriment to salvation'.[39] It was possible to be saved, for example, without knowledge of 'the craftsman's art' or 'any of the liberal arts'.[40] Bernard did not, however, mean to suggest that the liberal arts were useless:

> Perhaps you think I have sullied too much the good name of knowledge, that I have cast aspersions on the learned and proscribed the study of letters. God forbid! I am not unmindful of the benefits its scholars conferred, and still confer, on the Church, both by refuting her opponents and instructing the simple.[41]

Scholars of the liberal arts thus served the church by opposing heretics and teaching the laity. On the other hand, there was always a danger of knowledge leading to pride and a sense of self-importance. Bernard therefore urged his monks to focus on 'the essential and primary truths' and 'the doctrines' on which their salvation was 'more intimately dependent'.[42] What mattered, however, was not just what one knew, but the manner of knowing. He therefore listed the motives with which knowledge might be acquired:

[37] *Ibid.*, p. 3. [38] *Ibid.*, p. 7.

[39] Bernard of Clairvaux, *On the Song of Songs II*, trans. K. Walsh (Kalamazoo, MI, 1976), sermon 36, p. 173.

[40] *Ibid.*, pp. 173–4. [41] *Ibid.*, p. 174. [42] *Ibid.*, p. 175.

there are some who long to know for the sole purpose of knowing, and that is shameful curiosity; others who long to know in order to become known, and that is shameful vanity ... There are others still who long for knowledge in order to sell its fruits for money or honours, and this is shameful profiteering; others again who long to know in order to be of service, and this is charity. Finally, there are those who long to know in order to benefit themselves, and this is prudence.[43]

Only those who were driven by charity or prudence avoided 'the abuse of knowledge'. The correct manner of knowing thus depended on 'the order, the application, and the sense of purpose' with which one proceeded. The correct order meant giving 'precedence to all that aids spiritual progress', true application meant pursuing 'more eagerly all that strengthens love more', while the right purpose meant pursuing it 'not through vain-glory or inquisitiveness or any base motive, but for the welfare of oneself and one's neighbour'.[44] Bernard did not think that it was possible to separate thinking and knowing from one's way of life as a whole, and from moral purpose in particular.

In practice this meant beginning with self-knowledge which would lead to humility. How could a man fail to be humbled 'on seeing the burden of sin that he carries, the oppressive weight of his mortal body, the complexities of earthly cares, the corrupting influence of sensual desires ... one to whom vice is welcome, virtue repugnant'?[45] Wracked with misery and fear, he would turn to God for consolation and mercy. Self-knowledge thus led to knowledge of God, which in turn led to love of God.[46]

Bernard summed up his whole approach at the end of the *Five Books on Consideration* that he composed between 1145 and 1152/3, and sent to his former monk, Pope Eugenius III.[47] Citing Paul's injunction 'to comprehend with all the saints what is the length, the width, the height, and the depth', he distinguished between comprehending and knowing. It was comprehension and not knowing that brought about 'fruition'.[48] Having discussed the nature of God in terms of length, width, height and depth, he wrote:

We know these things. Do we think, therefore, we have also comprehended them? It is not disputation but sanctity that comprehends them, if, however, what is comprehensible can in any way be comprehended. But unless it could, the Apostle would not have said what we should comprehend with all the

[43] *Ibid.*, p. 176. [44] *Ibid.* [45] *Ibid.*, p. 178.
[46] See also Bernard of Clairvaux, *On the Song of Songs II*, sermon 37, pp. 181–6.
[47] Evans, *Mind of St Bernard*, pp. 204–5.
[48] Bernard of Clairvaux, *Five Books on Consideration: Advice to a Pope*, trans. J. D. Anderson and E. T. Kennan (Kalamazoo, MI, 1976), p. 175, citing Ephesians 3.18.

saints. The saints, then, comprehend. Do you ask how? If you are a saint, you have comprehended and you know: if you are not, be one and you will know through your own experience. Holy affection makes a saint, and this affection is two-fold: holy fear of the Lord and holy love.[49]

Bernard valued an experience of God that went beyond knowing based on disputation, and rested instead upon fear and love of God.

One form of scholarship, however, was essential to Bernard's work, and that was knowledge and interpretation of the Bible. In his first sermon on the Song of Songs, Bernard stressed the way in which the Bible was to be interpreted. Explaining the intimacy of the first line of the Song of Songs, 'Let him kiss me with the kiss of his mouth', Bernard commented: 'How delightful a ploy of speech this, prompted into life by the kiss, with Scripture's own engaging countenance inspiring the reader and enticing him on, that he may find pleasure even in the laborious pursuit of what lies hidden, with a fascinating theme to sweeten the fatigue of research.'[50] Within the Song of Songs as a whole were expressed 'the mounting desires of the soul, its marriage song, an exultation of spirit poured forth in figurative language pregnant with delight'.[51] Scriptural texts had a beauty to be savoured, and hidden meanings to be uncovered. They did not give up their treasures easily, however. They were likely to be 'dark and impenetrable' before 'at last' becoming 'bright with meaning'.[52] Long study was necessary.

The way in which Bernard's work was shaped by his use of the Bible can be illustrated by examining a sermon that he preached on 2 Kings 5. This survives in several versions written down by those who heard him.[53] He began with a paraphrase of the opening lines and a comment on the process of interpretation:

'Naaman, captain of the army of the King of Syria, was a great and wealthy man, but also a leper. And he had in his house, as a servant, a young girl from the land of Israel.' (2 Kings 5.1–2)

That is the basic plot of the story that we are considering. History is the threshing-floor of doctrine, where good narrators separate the grain from the straw with the flail of diligence and the winnowing machine of research. Just as honey is hidden under the beeswax and the nut inside the shell, so beneath the surface of the story lies the sweetness of the moral.[54]

[49] *Ibid.*, p. 177.
[50] Bernard of Clairvaux, *On the Song of Songs I*, sermon 1, p. 3.
[51] *Ibid.*, p. 5. [52] *Ibid.*
[53] J. Leclercq, *Bernard of Clairvaux and the Cistercian Spirit* (Kalamazoo, MI, 1976), p. 129; the sermon is translated at pp. 130–5.
[54] *Ibid.*, p. 130.

Bernard thus identified different levels of interpretation. There was much to be gained from historical analysis of the literal sense, but underneath it there were moral interpretations to be discovered.

Bernard continued to paraphrase the story and to uncover those meanings:

'Following the counsel of the young girl, he went to Eliseus and knocked on the door of his house.' Eliseus means 'salvation of the Lord'. It is Jesus, the Lord of the world, who saved his people from their sins (Matthew 1.21), and of whom the prophet says: 'Your salvation, God has received me' (Psalms 68.30). And he says of himself: 'I am the salvation of the people' (Psalms 34.3).[55]

Having explained the meaning of the name Eliseus, the word 'salvation' led Bernard to recall other biblical passages containing that word. This process of linking from one passage of the Bible to another through words that occurred in each passage, or that sometimes simply sounded similar, was typical of Bernard's method. It could lead him off in any direction so that his works were often very loose in structure. Moreover, he frequently spoke through quotations to such an extent that it was impossible to distinguish his words from those of the Bible.[56]

Bernard went on to explore the meaning of Eliseus' servant:

Eliseus remained sitting in the house and sent his servant with these words: 'Go down to the Jordan and wash yourself seven times and you will be purified' (Cf 2 Kings 5.10). Our Eliseus has been lifted up bodily, he is seated at the right hand of the Father, that is in those higher places which are not yet visible to us. But he has sent his servant. This servant is the intellect or pure reason, made in the image of God (Genesis 1.27) ... Or else this servant is the Holy Spirit who makes us children: that is, naïve in the way of malice, and childlike in our simplicity. Or again, the servant is Sacred Scripture by reason of the purity of its discourses and its chaste words (Psalms 11.7).[57]

The servant could be the intellect, or the Holy Spirit, or Sacred Scripture. Bernard did not mean that a choice was necessary. On the contrary, all these interpretations were true. This was the richness of the scriptures.

But how did Bernard know that he was correct in his interpretations? He did not believe that the Bible could mean whatever anyone wanted. So what guaranteed the validity of spiritual interpretations? First, it was a matter of tradition. Bernard did not invent his interpretations out of nothing; he was steeped in earlier religious writings, and monks also

[55] *Ibid.*, pp. 130–1.
[56] See Leclercq, *Love of Learning*, pp. 87–109.
[57] Leclercq, *Bernard of Clairvaux and the Cistercian Spirit*, p. 131.

had repertories that listed the meanings of words and names.[58] Second, and much more important, God would inspire those who rejected the world, lived virtuously and prayed. Once again, scholarship and the scholar's life were inseparable. Moreover, it was the monastery that regulated the monk's way of life. Bernard cultivated ways of knowing which could only work in the monastic context.

William of Saint Thierry

A similar, but perhaps more systematic, approach was developed by William of Saint Thierry. Probably born between 1075 and 1080, and from a noble family in the region of Liège, William became a Cluniac monk between 1113 and 1115. In 1119 or 1120 he was elected abbot of Saint Thierry, near Rheims. He was a close friend of Bernard, and indeed wrote much of his *vita*. He was desperate to become a Cistercian, but only in 1135 did Bernard permit him to enter the Cistercian monastery of Signy, where he remained until his death in 1148.[59] In 1145 he wrote *The Golden Epistle*, a treatise on the monastic life that he addressed to the Carthusian monks at Mont Dieu, whom he had visited previously. He indicated that he hoped to benefit 'the younger brethren and the novices',[60] and he made it clear that they were joining the spiritual elite:

> A long journey remains for you to accomplish. For you have undertaken the loftiest of professions. It surpasses the heavens, it is on a level with the angels, it resembles angelic purity. For you have vowed not only all holiness but the perfection of all holiness and the utmost limit of all consummation. It is not for you to concern yourselves feebly with the ordinary commandments nor to give your attention only to what God lays down as of obligation; you must seek his desires, fulfill in yourselves what is God's will, the good thing, the desirable thing, the perfect thing.
>
> It is for others to serve God, it is for you to cling to him; it is for others to believe in God, know him, love him and revere him; it is for you to taste him, understand him, be acquainted with him, enjoy him.[61]

58 Leclercq, *Love of Learning*, p. 96.

59 For the life of William of Saint Thierry, see J. D. Anderson, 'Introduction', in William of Saint Thierry, *The Enigma of Faith*, trans. J. D. Anderson (Washington, DC, 1974), pp. 1–7; L. Milis, 'William of Saint Thierry, his birth, his formation and his first monastic experiences', in J. Carfantan (trans.), *William, Abbot of St Thierry: A Colloquium at the Abbey of St Thierry* (Kalamazoo, MI, 1987), pp. 9–33.

60 William of Saint Thierry, *The Golden Epistle: A Letter to the Brethren at Mont Dieu*, trans. T. Berkeley (Kalamazoo, MI, 1980), p. 3.

61 *Ibid.*, p. 14.

William went on to outline an ascent by which monks could achieve their goals. Monks went through three states. First, there were 'beginners', whose state could be called 'animal', and who were 'concerned with the body'. Second, there were those who were 'making progress', whose state could be called 'rational', and who were concerned with 'the soul'. Third, there were the 'perfect', whose state could be called 'spiritual', and who found 'rest only in God'.[62] Each of these three states consisted of three states: 'beginning', 'progress' and 'perfection'. For beginners, the beginning was 'perfect obedience', progress was 'to gain control of the body and bring it into subjection', and perfection was 'when the habitual exercise of virtue [had] become a pleasure'.[63] For those who were making progress, the beginning was 'to understand what [was] set before it by the teaching of the faith', progress was 'a life lived in accordance with that teaching', and perfection was 'when the judgment of the reason passes into a spiritual affection'.[64] There was an overlap between the state of those who were making progress and the perfect, because the stage 'when the judgment of the reason passes into a spiritual affection' was also the beginning of the perfect. Progress for the perfect was 'to look upon God's glory with face uncovered', while perfection was 'to be transformed into the same likeness, borrowing glory from that glory, enabled by the Spirit of the Lord'.[65]

Just as for Bernard, the aim was an intense kind of personal experience:

> The understanding of the one thinking becomes the contemplation of the one loving and it shapes it into certain experiences of spiritual or divine sweetness which it brings before the gaze of the spirit so that the spirit rejoices in them.[66]

But, like Bernard, William did not suppose that the experience could be achieved without God's help:

> But this way of thinking about God does not lie at the disposal of the thinker. It is a gift of grace, bestowed by the Holy Spirit who breathes where he chooses, when he chooses, how he chooses and upon whom he chooses.[67]

The monk could only do his best to prepare himself, hoping by God's grace 'to be able to will only what God wills', and thus 'to be what God is'.[68]

[62] *Ibid.*, pp. 25–6. [63] *Ibid.*, p. 27.
[64] *Ibid.* [65] *Ibid.* [66] *Ibid.*, p. 92.
[67] *Ibid.*, p. 93. [68] *Ibid.*, p. 94.

What was the role of scholarship in this process? William had clear ideas about what should be read and how.[69] Regular periods should be devoted to 'certain definite reading'.[70] The monk was to 'concentrate on certain authors' and absorb himself in them.[71] Above all, the Scriptures had to be read and meditated upon, and suitable passages had to be memorized every day.[72] Beginners should also read appropriate parts of the Fathers and the lives of the saints.[73] Reading should also generate an emotional response and lead to prayer.[74] William condemned less disciplined approaches: 'haphazard reading, constantly varied and as if lighted upon by chance does not edify but makes the mind unstable'.[75] Presumably he had the schools in mind when he attacked 'empty studies, trifling, verbose, wrangling as they are, designed to feed curiosity and ambition', holding them to 'dissipate and corrupt the spirit even when it has been brought into being or is already perfect'.[76]

At the heart of William's ascent was the relationship between intellect and love, the stage 'when the judgment of the reason passes into a spiritual affection'. The monk had to aspire to the point at which 'love itself is understanding for him' ('Amor ipse intellectus est').[77] William's precise meaning has been much debated.[78] It is clear, however, that he held the work of the Holy Spirit to be crucial:

> And when reason as it progresses mounts on high to become love, and grace comes down to meet the one who so loves and desires, it often happens that reason and love, which produce these two states, become one thing, and likewise wisdom and knowledge, which result from them.[79]

Thus human categories and definitions collapsed, and the individual could move towards greater participation in God. A process that began with obedience and the cultivation of virtue culminated in union with God. And it all took place in the monk's cell. As William put it, 'the ascent is often made from the cell into heaven'.[80] Like Bernard, William outlined a path that was particular to the religious life.

[69] See also Evans, *Mind of St Bernard*, pp. 48–9.
[70] William of Saint Thierry, *Golden Epistle*, p. 51.
[71] *Ibid.* [72] *Ibid.*, pp. 51–2. [73] *Ibid.*, p. 68. [74] *Ibid.*, p. 52.
[75] *Ibid.*, p. 51. [76] *Ibid.*, p. 84. [77] *Ibid.*, p. 68.
[78] See, for example, D. N. Bell, *The Image and Likeness: The Augustinian Spirituality of William of St Thierry*, Cistercian Studies Series 78 (Kalamazoo, MI, 1984), pp. 131–49; J.-M. Déchanet, 'Amor ipse intellectus est: la doctrine de l'amour-intellection chez Guillaume de Saint-Thierry', *Revue du Moyen Age Latin* 1 (1945): 349–74; J.-M. Déchanet, 'Introduction', in William of Saint Thierry, *Golden Epistle*, pp. xxvii–xxx; E. Gilson, *The Mystical Theology of Saint Bernard*, trans. A. H. C. Downes (London, 1940), pp. 208–10; McGinn, *Growth of Mysticism*, pp. 233–4, 242–3, 250–60; I. van't Spijker, *Fictions of the Inner Life: Religious Literature and Formation of the Self in the Eleventh and Twelfth Centuries* (Turnhout, 2004), pp. 189–95; P. Verdeyen, *La Théologie Mystique de Guillaume de Saint-Thierry* (Paris, 1990), pp. 257–69.
[79] William of Saint Thierry, *Golden Epistle*, p. 78. [80] *Ibid.*, p. 21.

Hildegard of Bingen

Hildegard of Bingen also practised a way of knowing that made sense in a religious house, but was fundamentally alien to the schools. Born the tenth child of a noble family in south-west Germany in 1098, she was offered to God as a tithe at the age of eight. She went to live in a hermitage connected with the Benedictine monastery of Disibodenberg, where she lived under the care of an anchoress, Jutta of Sponheim. Other women joined them, and a convent was set up. Jutta died in 1136, and Hildegard became abbess. In the 1140s she began to record the visions that she had experienced since childhood. Although her reputation grew, she needed reassurance and in 1146 or 1147 she wrote to Bernard of Clairvaux for advice. He accepted her visions as genuine, urging her 'to recognize this gift as grace and to respond eagerly to it with all humility and devotion'.[81] While presiding over a synod at Trier in 1147–8, Pope Eugenius III sent legates to see Hildegard and to obtain a copy of her work. The pope gave his approval, authorizing her 'in the name of Christ and St Peter to publish all that she had learned from the Holy Spirit'.[82] Many women now wished to join Hildegard, and she decided to found a new community. The monks of Disibodenberg were far from happy since Hildegard brought them fame and wealth, so the abbot refused permission. Hildegard took to her bed until the abbot was convinced that her illness was a sign of God's disapproval of the delay. Once he gave way, Hildegard was restored to health and in 1150 she moved to the new convent of Rupertsberg. She founded a second community at Eibingen in 1165. Between 1158 and 1170, she undertook four preaching tours, preaching both to religious communities and publicly to clergy and people in various parts of Germany. She died in 1179.[83]

Hildegard produced a large and astonishingly wide-ranging body of work. She wrote three visionary works: *Scivias*, an abbreviation of 'Scito vias Domini', or 'Know the Ways of the Lord',[84] between 1141 and 1151; *The Book of Life's Merits* between 1158 and 1163; and *The Book*

81 *The Letters of Hildegard of Bingen*, vol. 1, trans. J. L. Baird and R. K. Ehrman (Oxford, 1994), letter 1r, p. 31.

82 As quoted in *Hildegard of Bingen: An Anthology*, ed. F. Bowie and O. Davies (London, 1990), p. 11.

83 For accounts of Hildegard's life, see S. Flanagan, *Hildegard of Bingen: A Visionary Life* (London, 1989); F. Maddocks, *Hildegard of Bingen: The Woman of her Age* (New York, 2003); B. Newman, *Sister of Wisdom: St. Hildegard's Theology of the Feminine* (Aldershot, 1987), pp. 4–15.

84 B. J. Newman, 'Introduction', in Hildegard of Bingen, *Scivias*, trans. C. Hart and J. Bishop (New York, 1990), p. 22.

of Divine Works between 1163 and 1174. She also wrote two 'scientific' works in the 1150s. The *Natural History* described the healing powers of plants, elements, trees, animals and metals. *Causes and Cures* examined the human body, illnesses and remedies. She also wrote words and music for seventy-seven songs.

Hildegard's life was shaped by her visionary experiences. Although they were intensely personal and all-consuming, she rarely wrote about what these experiences were like for her. This is how she described them at the beginning of *Scivias*, one of the few occasions on which she offered a brief account:

> It happened that, in the eleven hundred and forty-first year of the Incarnation of the Son of God, Jesus Christ, when I was forty-two years and seven months old, Heaven was opened and a fiery light of exceeding brilliance came and permeated my whole brain, and inflamed my whole heart and my whole breast, not like a burning but like a warming flame, as the sun warms anything its rays touch. And immediately I knew the meaning of the exposition of the Scriptures, namely the Psalter, the Gospel and the other catholic volumes of both the Old and the New Testaments, though I did not have the interpretation of the words of their texts or the division of the syllables or the knowledge of cases or tenses. But I had sensed in myself wonderfully the power and mystery of secret and admirable visions from my childhood – that is, from the age of five – up to that time, as I do now. This, however, I showed to no one except a few religious persons who were living in the same manner as I; but meanwhile, until the time when God by His grace wished it to be manifested, I concealed it in quiet silence. But the visions I saw I did not perceive in dreams, or sleep, or delirium, or by the eyes of the body, or by the ears of the outer self, or in hidden places; but I received them while awake and seeing with a pure mind and the eyes and ears of the inner self, in open places, as God willed it. How this might be is hard for mortal flesh to understand.[85]

Hildegard's actual experiences are extremely difficult to analyse. It has been suggested that her visions were the product of a particular kind of migraine that involves certain types of visual experience. It has even been suggested that the paintings in the manuscript of *Scivias* that was illuminated in Hildegard's scriptorium contained the kind of visual patterns involved in this kind of migraine.[86] Such explanations

[85] Hildegard of Bingen, *Scivias*, pp. 59–60. Hildegard also discussed the nature of her visionary experiences in a letter to Guibert of Gembloux, and further information is recorded in her *vita*; see McGinn, *Growth of Mysticism*, pp. 334–6; B. Newman, 'Hildegard of Bingen: visions and validation', *Church History* 54 (1985): 163–75 at 164–7.

[86] Flanagan, *Hildegard of Bingen*, pp. 199–211; C. Singer, 'The scientific views and visions of Saint Hildegard', in *Studies in the History and Method of Science*, 2 vols. (Oxford, 1917 and 1921), vol.1, pp. 1–55, reprinted in *From Magic to Science: Essays on the Scientific Twilight* (New York, 1958), pp. 199–239.

are fascinating, but it is hard to know what to do with them since it is impossible to assess their validity.

Far more can be achieved by focusing on the textual representations of Hildegard's experiences. Indeed she herself was far more concerned with their interpretation than with the nature of her experience. Hildegard divided *Scivias*, for example, into three books, each consisting of a series of visions. She began each vision by describing what she had seen. She then presented 'a voice from heaven' which explained the vision, interpreting Hildegard's initial description line by line. In effect she created a text and then a commentary upon it. Thus the first vision in *Scivias* began:

> I saw a great mountain the colour of iron, and enthroned on it One of such great glory that it blinded my sight.[87]

Subsequently the divine voice proclaimed the meaning:

> As you see, therefore, *the great mountain the colour of iron* symbolizes the strength and stability of the eternal kingdom of God, which no fluctuation of mutability can destroy; and *the One enthroned upon it of such great glory that it blinds your sight* is the One in the kingdom of beatitude who rules the whole world with celestial divinity in the brilliance of unfading serenity, but is incomprehensible to human minds.[88]

All aspects of theology could be treated in this manner, and the visions were arranged in a careful sequence to form a coherent theological work.[89] Whatever the nature of Hildegard's inspiration, the result was an intellectually complex construction.

How is Hildegard's scholarship to be characterized? Little is known about her education except that Jutta taught her Latin. It may also be supposed that she received further instruction from monks of Disibodenberg, in particular Volmar, who was her friend and secretary until his death in 1173.[90] Clearly, however, she was deeply learned. She modelled her style on Old Testament prophets, and her visions of *Sapientia* and *Caritas* had obvious biblical roots.[91] Moreover, biblical commentary formed a significant part of her work. The divine voice that interpreted her visions also quoted passages from the Bible and interpreted them too.[92] In the *Book of Life's Merits*, for example, she took

[87] Hildegard of Bingen, *Scivias*, p. 67.
[88] *Ibid.*, pp. 67–8.
[89] Newman, 'Introduction', pp. 22–3.
[90] Flanagan, *Hildegard of Bingen*, p. 36; Newman, *Sister of Wisdom*, p. 5.
[91] Newman, *Sister of Wisdom*, pp. 25–6, 42–88.
[92] Newman, 'Introduction', p. 22; Newman, *Sister of Wisdom*, pp. 19–20.

the bridegroom and bride in the Song of Songs to stand for Solomon and *Sapientia*, and so for the Creator and the cosmos.[93] Despite all this evidence to the contrary, however, Hildegard did her utmost to present herself as unlearned. As we have seen in the passage at the start of *Scivias*, 'a fiery light' gave her immediate understanding of the scriptures, although she 'did not have the interpretation of the words of their texts or the division of the syllables or the knowledge of cases or tenses'.[94] She again played down the extent of her learning when she wrote to Bernard of Clairvaux:

> Through this vision which touches my heart and soul like a burning flame, teaching me profundities of meaning, I have an inward understanding of the Psalter, the Gospels, and other volumes. Nevertheless, I do not receive this knowledge in German. Indeed, I have no formal training at all, for I know how to read only on the most elementary level, certainly with no deep analysis. But please give me your opinion in this matter, because I am untaught and untrained in exterior material, but am only taught inwardly, in my spirit. Hence my halting, unsure speech.[95]

It was clearly true that she lacked technical training in grammar and rhetoric. Certainly she relied on her male secretaries to correct her grammar, and even then her style remained awkward and sometimes far from clear.[96] Her evaluation of her own learning should not, however, be regarded as strictly accurate, nor to indicate hostility to all learning as such. Her purpose was rather to stress the prophetic nature of her work. The less learned she was held to be, the more readily people would accept that she merely passed on things which had been given directly to her by God. Indeed, for her as much as for others, perceived lack of learning served to validate her prophetic voice. Moreover, it was her prophetic and visionary status that gave her authority as a teacher, validating and authenticating everything that she had to say about doctrine, moral behaviour and ecclesiastical reform.[97] Genuinely weak in the basics of grammar and rhetoric that were fundamental to the scholarship of the schools, she deliberately placed herself at the greatest possible distance from the ways of knowing that were prized in that context.

[93] Newman, *Sister of Wisdom*, pp. 65–6.
[94] Hildegard of Bingen, *Scivias*, p. 59.
[95] *Letters of Hildegard of Bingen*, vol. 1, letter 1, p. 28.
[96] Newman, *Sister of Wisdom*, pp. 22–5.
[97] On processes of validation and prophetic strategy, see Flanagan, *Hildegard of Bingen*, pp. 53–4; Newman, 'Hildegard of Bingen: visions and validation', pp. 163–75; Newman, *Sister of Wisdom*, pp. 34–41.

Conflict between monks and schoolmen

Despite the changes that took place in the monastic world, monastic learning had a number of distinctive and enduring features. Knowing God centred upon personal experience which was not entirely, if at all, intellectual. To attain this experience, it was necessary to reject the world and live a life of virtue, beginning with obedience and humility. Finding God also required both self-knowledge and prayer. Ultimately, however, the decisive role was played by God. It was not therefore difficult to accommodate the prophetic voice of someone like Hildegard. Usually, however, the words of God were found in the Bible, and close familiarity with the Bible was essential. More importance was attached to spiritual interpretation than to the literal sense. The words of scripture had to be memorized and so internalized that it was possible to incorporate them effortlessly into speech and writing; long study and emotional engagement were therefore required. In general, emotionally charged metaphors were used in preference to dry and technical language. It was always essential, however, to remember the audience that was being addressed. The most complex and imaginative ideas were appropriate only for the spiritual elite in religious houses. Attitudes to dialectic and disputation clearly changed, however. Anselm did not feel threatened by them and was keen to use logic and to debate with others. A generation later, Bernard of Clairvaux and William of Saint Thierry granted them little or no role in monastic learning. But even Anselm stressed the greater importance of faith when using logic.

Monastic learning was thus very different from that of the schools, and the differences became more marked. It was not that the masters failed to recognize the importance of each individual aspect of monastic learning: they did not, for example, reject self-knowledge or virtue as such. But the masters of the schools were willing to conceive of and treat these matters separately; when they brought them together, they did so in books. The monks brought them all together in the life of each individual, and it was the process of bringing them all together that mattered to them. It was impossible, for example, to think correctly if one did not live virtuously. Life and learning were inextricably linked. The context of learning was therefore all important. The monastery shaped all aspects of life, and only if all aspects of life were properly shaped could anyone hope to know or have experience of God. Their way of knowing was self-consciously particular to the monastery. From it they derived both truth and authority.

It is not therefore surprising that some monks were horrified by much of what they saw in the schools. Given their political careers and their sense of responsibility for moral and spiritual welfare beyond the cloisters, it is not surprising either that they tried to do something about it. Most notably, Bernard of Clairvaux entered into bitter conflict with two leading masters, first Peter Abelard and then Gilbert of Poitiers. William of Saint Thierry began the attack on Peter Abelard by writing to Bernard of Clairvaux and the bishop of Chartres, who had been appointed a papal legate. William criticized views which he attributed to Abelard, and called for action to be taken. Bernard made a personal approach to Abelard, but was rebuffed, and the matter ended up before the Council of Sens in 1140. Both Bernard and Abelard lobbied supporters before the Council met. The sequence of events is not entirely clear, but it seems that on the day before Abelard's case was due to be heard Bernard met with the bishops who were present at the Council. He read out extracts from Abelard's works and persuaded the bishops to condemn them there and then. When the Council met formally the next day, Abelard, perhaps aware of what had happened, appealed to the pope and left. The bishops then condemned a series of propositions attributed to Abelard, although some were partial quotations or quotations taken out of context, while others cannot be found in any of Abelard's surviving works. The condemnation was reported to Pope Innocent II, and Bernard wrote not only to the pope but to anyone who might influence him. Innocent upheld the decision and ordered that Abelard's books containing the errors should be burned. Meanwhile Peter the Venerable, abbot of Cluny, had persuaded Abelard, now an ill man, to give up his appeal. Abelard died in 1142 at a Cluniac house near Chalon.[98]

John of Salisbury described Bernard adopting similar tactics against Gilbert, bishop of Poitiers, at the Council of Rheims in 1148. Before the formal hearing, Bernard 'sent asking all the leading churchmen, those who were distinguished by their learning or sanctity or office, to meet him privately in his lodging'. He then 'delivered a short and eloquent discourse, concluding that it was their duty to remove all scandals from the church of God, and beseeching them to correct him if they thought he was mistaken in the case he had brought against master Gilbert.' Next he invited them 'to listen to the articles in which he differed from the bishop, and then to approve or reject them'. Bernard proceeded to make four statements about the nature of God,

[98] See M. T. Clanchy, *Abelard: A Medieval Life* (Oxford, 1997), pp. 288–325; J. Marenbon, *The Philosophy of Peter Abelard* (Cambridge, 1997), pp. 26–35; A. V. Murray, *Abelard and St Bernard: A Study in Twelfth Century 'Modernism'* (Manchester, 1967), pp. 51–71.

beginning with his belief that 'God is deity, and the converse'. After each statement, one of his monks wrote down what he said and read it out again, adding the question 'Do you accept this?' and getting the reply 'We do'. John noted that 'the more thoughtful men did not approve of this method: but they feared offending the abbot and his followers if they did not fall in with his wishes'. Bernard's strategy was apparently to begin with simple statements to which opposition was inconceivable and brief assent uncontroversial, and to establish a pattern out of which it would be hard to break, before presenting beliefs that were theologically more complex and ordinarily likely to stimulate more nuanced responses than his procedure permitted. Thus Bernard stated fourthly that 'Since God is simple and whatever is in God is God, the properties of the Persons are the Persons themselves, and so the Father is paternity, the Son, filiality, the Spirit, proceeding; and the converse.' At this point an archdeacon of Châlons objected that many distinguished theologians had rejected Bernard's fourth statement, and he suggested that they should delay judgement since there was about to be a Council attended by the pope, the cardinals and 'the most distinguished men in the western world'. This intervention brought the meeting to a close. According to John, the cardinals were furious when they heard about the meeting and immediately sided with Gilbert, 'saying that the abbot had attacked master Peter in exactly the same way'. Undeterred, however, Bernard went to the pope 'as a friend' and put his case 'directly'.[99]

At subsequent sessions of the Council, Gilbert defended himself vigorously. He complained that he was being held responsible for the views of other men, views that he himself condemned. He was especially exasperated to find that the writings of former students were being attributed to him; he admitted that they had heard him lecture, but he insisted that they had misunderstood him, and their writings constituted a misinterpretation of his work. He also stressed that 'he had spoken openly to the world in schools and churches, and had taught nothing in secret'. Moreover, he protested that he could never be a heretic since 'he was ready and always had been to recognize truth and respect apostolic doctrine'; if there were errors in his work, he was willing to submit.[100] When he agreed to correct his commentary on Boethius' *De Trinitate* so that it conformed to Bernard's four statements, Gilbert was finally acquitted.

[99] John of Salisbury, *The Historia Pontificalis of John of Salisbury*, trans. M. Chibnall (London, 1956), pp. 17–20.

[100] *Ibid.*, p. 22.

John notes, however, that Bernard continued to speak against Gilbert, and 'wrote many things to his discredit, both in letters and in his book *De Consideratione* to Pope Eugenius, and also in that most subtle and precious exposition of the *Song of Songs*'.[101]

The reasons for Bernard's hostility to the schools are most starkly revealed in the letters which he wrote to rally opposition to Abelard before and after the Council of Sens. His objections to the man he dubbed 'Peter the Dragon'[102] fall into three broad categories. First, he was deeply hostile to Abelard's intellectual methods. As far as Bernard was concerned, Abelard overestimated human intellectual capacity:

> mere human ingenuity is taking on itself to solve everything, and leave nothing to faith. It is trying for things above itself, prying into things too strong for it, rushing into divine things, and profaning rather than revealing what is holy.[103]

This excessive intellectual ambition reflected a lack of self-knowledge:

> He is a man who does not know his limitations, making void the virtue of the cross by the cleverness of his words. Nothing in heaven or on earth is hidden from him, except himself.[104]

In general, Abelard attached more importance to reason than to faith:

> He tries to explore with his reason what the devout mind grasps at once with a vigorous faith. Faith believes, it does not dispute. But this man, apparently holding God suspect, will not believe anything until he has first examined it with his reason.[105]

More specifically, Abelard was willing to be inventive in his use of language to refer to mysteries that Bernard considered to be beyond language:

> Master Peter has used in his books phrases that are novel and profane both in their wording and in their sense. He argues about faith against the Faith; he assails the law in the words of the law. He sees nothing 'through a glass, in a dark manner', but views everything face to face 'dwelling on high matters, on marvels beyond his reach'.[106]

[101] *Ibid.*, p. 25. For perceptive analysis of these events, see P. Godman, *The Silent Masters: Latin Literature and Its Censors in the High Middle Ages* (Princeton, 2000), pp. 123–34.

[102] *The Letters of St Bernard of Clairvaux*, trans. B. S. James (Stroud, repr. 1998), letter 242, p. 323; letter 244, p. 325.

[103] *Ibid.*, letter 238, p. 316.

[104] *Ibid.*, letter 241, p. 321.

[105] *Ibid.*, letter 249, p. 328.

[106] *Ibid.*, letter 240, p. 321. See also letter 244, p. 325.

Furthermore, Bernard was unhappy with Abelard's attitude to authorities. Bernard believed that he exalted pagan philosophers at the expense of the Fathers:

> He insults the Doctors of the Church by holding up the philosophers for exaggerated praises. He prefers their ideas and his own novelties to the doctrines and faith of the Catholic Fathers.[107]

Second, Bernard was critical of Abelard's way of life:

> Master Peter Abelard is a monk without a rule, a prelate without responsibility. He is neither in order nor of an Order. A man at variance with himself: a Herod within, a John without; a most doubtful character, having nothing of the monk about him except the name and the habit.[108]

In another letter Bernard added that he was 'an abbot without discipline, who argues with boys and consorts with women'.[109] Abelard was a monk but he had failed to reject the world and to adopt an appropriate manner of living. Quite simply, he had failed to cultivate virtue. He did not really belong to the monastic world in which it was possible to shape one's life so as to come to knowledge of God. He did not understand the essential link between life and learning.

Third, Bernard raised the subject of Abelard's audience. Bernard complained that he expected beginners to cope with advanced theology:

> Raw and inexperienced listeners hardly finished with their dialectics, and those who can hardly, so to speak, stand the first elements of the faith, are introduced by him to the mystery of the Holy Trinity, to the Holy of Holies, to the chamber of the King, and to him who is 'shrouded with darkness'.[110]

Moreover, his books were circulating widely and inverting the proper order of things:

> Although he is no longer lurking in his lair: would that his poisonous writings were still lurking in their shelves, and not being discussed at the crossroads! His books have wings: and they who hate the light because their lives are evil, have dashed into the light thinking it was darkness. Darkness is being brought into towns and castles in the place of light; and for honey poison or, I should say, poison in honey is being offered on all sides to everyone. His writings 'have passed from country to country, and from one kingdom to another'.[111]

[107] *Ibid.*, letter 239, p. 318.
[108] *Ibid.*, letter 241, p. 321.
[109] *Ibid.*, letter 244, p. 325.
[110] *Ibid.*, letter 243, p. 324.
[111] *Ibid.*, letter 239, p. 318.

Bernard was particularly horrified at the public nature of Abelard's teaching. It led to mysteries being discussed in utterly inappropriate places:

Catholic Faith, the childbearing of the Virgin, the Sacrament of the Altar, the incomprehensible mystery of the Holy Trinity, are being discussed in the streets and market places.[112]

Abelard was failing to bear in mind the proper relationship between ideas and audience. Once again he did not appreciate the need to work within the carefully controlled environment that monasteries provided. Bernard cannot have been impressed by Gilbert of Poitier's refusal to accept responsibility for students who misunderstood him, nor by the value that he attached to the openness of his teaching.[113] Monks like Bernard and masters like Abelard and Gilbert had radically different approaches to learning.

The differences between the monasteries and the schools must not, however, be overstated. There can be no doubt, for example, that conflicts were exacerbated by the personalities of men like Bernard and Abelard. It must also be remembered, as we have seen, that Bernard accorded some value to the work of the schools. John of Salisbury's account of the Council of Rheims further demonstrates that the boundaries were not clear. He notes, for example, that 'masters of the schools' like Peter Lombard and Robert of Melun were amongst those who attacked Gilbert.[114] Moreover, John himself clearly revered both Gilbert and Bernard, and he was desperate to establish the merits of both men: 'For my part I cannot believe that a man of such sanctity [Bernard] was not guided by the love of God, or that a bishop of such prudence and learning [Gilbert] should commit to writing anything whose meaning was not clear to him, however obscure it might seem to others.'[115] At Bernard's request, John even tried to arrange an informal meeting at which Bernard and Gilbert might discuss the writings of Hilary; Gilbert, however, declined on the grounds that 'they had already disputed sufficiently on the matter, and if the abbot wished to reach a full understanding of Hilary he should first seek further instruction in the liberal arts and other preliminary studies'.[116] This led John to reflect on the differences between the two men:

[112] *Ibid.*, letter 244, p. 325.
[113] On the significance of audience and context, see Godman, *Silent Masters*, pp. 3–11.
[114] John of Salisbury, *Historia Pontificalis*, p. 16.
[115] *Ibid.* [116] *Ibid.*, p. 26.

though they were both exceptionally learned and eloquent men, they excelled in different branches of learning. The abbot for his part, as his works show, was so distinguished a preacher that I can think of no-one after St Gregory comparable to him: he surpassed all in the elegance of his style and was so saturated in the Holy Scriptures that he could fully expound every subject in the words of the prophets and apostles. For he had made their speech his own, and could hardly converse or preach or write a letter except in the language of scripture ... But he had little knowledge of secular learning, in which the bishop, it is believed, had no equal in our own day. Both were keenly intelligent and gifted interpreters of scripture: but the abbot was more experienced and effective in transacting business. And though the bishop had not the text of the Bible quite so much at his fingertips, it is common knowledge that he was more thoroughly conversant with the doctors – Hilary, for example, Jerome, Augustine and others like them. His doctrine seemed obscure to beginners, but all the more compendious and profound to advanced scholars. He made use of every branch of learning as occasion demanded, knowing that all were consistent with each other, and mutually illuminating ... Both these men had many would-be imitators, but I cannot call to mind one who could touch either of them.[117]

John was evidently pained by the conflict between the two men. While acutely aware of their intellectual differences, he respected them both and valued their scholarship.

Hugh of Saint Victor

John was not alone in taking this position, and from the 1120s at least one scholar, Hugh of Saint Victor, developed a synthesis of the approaches characteristic of schools and monasteries. The house of Saint Victor was a community of canons regular that had been founded in 1108 by William of Champeaux when he retired as archdeacon and master of the cathedral school of Notre Dame. In itself this house occupied a somewhat liminal position. As canons regular, its members lived according to the Rule of Saint Augustine and aspired to live the apostolic life, but unlike monks who frequently built their houses in remote areas of the countryside, William set up his just outside the city walls of Paris on the south bank of the Seine. Moreover, he established a school that was open to students who were not members of the house, and indeed taught there until he became bishop of Châlons-sur-Marne in 1113.[118] Little

117 *Ibid.*, pp. 26–7.

118 F. T. Harkins, *Reading and the Work of Restoration: History and Scripture in the Theology of Hugh of St Victor* (Toronto, 2009), pp. 3, 5; D. Poirel, *Hugues de Saint-Victor* (Paris, 1998), pp. 25–7; P. Rorem, *Hugh of Saint Victor* (Oxford, 2009), pp. 5–9; P. Sicard, *Hugues de Saint-Victor et son Ecole* (Turnhout, 1991), pp. 7–13. For a rich analysis of the political context in which the abbey was founded and thrived during the twelfth

is known about the early life of Hugh of Saint Victor, but it is generally accepted that he came from a noble family in the diocese of Halberstadt. He entered the house of Saint Victor about 1115 and taught there from before 1125 and perhaps as early as 1120 until his death in 1141.[119] In the 1120s he wrote the *Didascalicon*, subtitled *De studio legendi*, or 'On the Study of Reading'.[120] In the preface he noted that 'there are three things particularly necessary to learn for reading: first, each man should know what he ought to read; second, in what order he ought to read, that is, what first and what afterwards; and third, in what manner he ought to read'. Hugh set out to tackle these issues, addressing first 'the reader of the arts' and then 'the reader of the Sacred Scripture'.[121] He thus offered his students an introduction to the process of studying which also depicted the ideal scholar.

In many respects Hugh was a man of the schools. He elaborated a detailed theory of human knowledge, drawing openly on classical tradition. Wisdom consisted of 'understanding' ('intelligentia') and 'knowledge' ('scientia'). 'Understanding' could be divided into the theoretical, 'which strives for the contemplation of truth', and the practical, 'which considers the regulation of morals'. 'Knowledge' could also be termed the mechanical, 'which supervises the occupations of this life'. In addition to the theoretical, practical and mechanical, Hugh identified a fourth branch of knowledge, the logical, 'which provides the knowledge necessary for correct speaking and clear argumentation'.[122] The theoretical was made up of theology, mathematics and physics,

century, see R.-H. Bautier, 'Les origines et les premiers développements de l'abbaye Saint-Victor de Paris', in J. Longère (ed.), *L'abbaye parisienne de Saint-Victor au moyen âge: communications présentées au XIIIe colloque d'humanisme médiéval de Paris (1986–1988)* (Paris, 1991), pp. 23–52. For an extremely useful overview of the history of the school of Saint Victor in the twelfth century, see D. M. Coulter, *Per Visibilia ad Invisibilia: Theological Method in Richard of St. Victor (d. 1173)* (Turnhout, 2006), pp. 233–56.

119 S. C. Ferruolo, *The Origins of the University: The Schools of Paris and their Critics, 1100–1215* (Stanford, 1985), pp. 29–31; Harkins, *Reading and the Work of Restoration*, pp. 1–3, 5; R. Moore, *Jews and Christians in the Life and Thought of Hugh of St. Victor* (Atlanta, 1998), pp. 15–21; Poirel, *Hugues de Saint-Victor*, pp. 12, 30–2; Rorem, *Hugh of Saint Victor*, pp. 9–11; Sicard, *Hugues de Saint-Victor*, pp. 13–17, 32–3; J. Taylor, 'Introduction', in Hugh of Saint Victor, *The Didascalicon: A Medieval Guide to the Arts*, trans. J. Taylor (New York, 1961), p. 38.

120 For the date at different points in the 1120s, see D. E. Luscombe, *The School of Peter Abelard: The Influence of Abelard's Thought in the Early Scholastic Period* (Cambridge, 1969), p. 188; Taylor, 'Introduction', 3. For problems in translating the title, see I. Illich, *In the Vineyard of the Text: A Commentary to Hugh's Didascalicon* (Chicago, 1993), pp. 14–15.

121 Hugh of Saint Victor, *Didascalicon*, preface, p. 44.

122 *Ibid.*, 1.11, p. 60.

and mathematics could be further divided into the quadrivium: arithmetic, music, geometry and astronomy.[123] The practical consisted of three parts, the solitary, the private and the public.[124] The mechanical contained seven sciences: fabric making, armament, commerce, agriculture, hunting, medicine and theatrics.[125] The logical could be divided into grammar and the theory of argument. The latter consisted of demonstration, probable argument and sophistic. Probable argument could be further split into dialectic and rhetoric.[126] Hugh thus identified twenty-one 'distinct sciences'[127] or arts, which he described in some detail, dividing human knowledge with clarity and technical precision.

Hugh attached great importance to these arts. In his estimation, they could 'make the student perfect'. The student should devote his first efforts to the arts 'in which are the foundation stones of all things and in which pure and simple truth is revealed'.[128] Within the twenty-one arts were the seven liberal arts which the ancients chose 'to be mastered by those who were to be educated'.[129] Upon these Hugh laid special emphasis because they contained 'the foundation of all learning'.[130] Furthermore, the study of logic was particularly valuable. Indeed it was logic 'which ought to be read first by those beginning the study of philosophy, for it teaches the nature of words and concepts, without both of which no treatise of philosophy can be explained rationally'.[131] Hugh evidently shared the preoccupations of many masters in the schools.

The same can be said of his approach to textual interpretation, although he had much to say that was distinctly original. Of the Bible, he observed that 'Sacred Scripture has three ways of conveying meaning – namely, history, allegory, and tropology'.[132] Hugh stressed that it was vital to begin with history, or the literal sense, before attempting allegorical interpretation:

> The foundation and principle of sacred learning ... is history, from which, like honey from the honeycomb, the truth of allegory is extracted.[133]

For Hugh, it was essential to grasp the full literal sense because allegory could only be based on the events and things signified by the words. He took great care to explain how things had meaning in the Bible:

[123] *Ibid.*, 2.1, p. 62; 2.6, p. 67.
[124] *Ibid.*, 2.19, p. 74. [125] *Ibid.*, 2.20, p. 74.
[126] *Ibid.*, 2.28–30, pp. 79–81.
[127] *Ibid.*, 3.21, p. 83. [128] *Ibid.*, 3.4, p. 88.
[129] *Ibid.*, 3.3, p. 86. [130] *Ibid.*, 3.4, p. 89.
[131] *Ibid.*, 1.11, p. 59. [132] *Ibid.*, 5.2, p. 120.
[133] *Ibid.*, 6.3, p. 138; see also pp. 135–6.

That the sacred utterances employ the meaning of things, moreover, we shall demonstrate by a particular short and clear example. The Scripture says: 'Watch because your adversary the Devil goeth about as a roaring lion.' Here, if we should say that the lion stands for the Devil, we should mean by 'lion' not the word but the thing. For if the two words 'devil' and 'lion' mean one and the same thing, the likeness of that same thing to itself is not adequate. It remains, therefore, that the word 'lion' signifies the animal, but that the animal in turn designates the Devil. And all other things are to be taken after this fashion, as when we say that worm, calf, stone, serpent, and other things of this sort signify Christ.[134]

Without understanding that the word 'lion' signified the animal, it would not be possible to proceed to the allegorical interpretation that the animal signified the devil. But the signification of the word 'lion' was its literal sense. From his other writings it is clear that Hugh gave the literal sense an unusually broad definition: it included the intended meaning of the human authors of scripture, even when they used figurative language and metaphor. Like many masters in the schools, while not rejecting allegorical interpretation, Hugh attached considerable weight to historical analysis.[135]

While Hugh had much in common with masters in the schools, he was also highly critical of them. For example, because he believed the seven liberal arts to be so interdependent that all of them had to be studied, he criticized those who 'select certain of them for study, and, leaving the rest untouched, think they can become perfect in these alone'.[136] He was equally appalled by those who failed to teach each art separately: 'certain persons, while they omit nothing which ought to be read, nonetheless do not know how to give each art what belongs to it, but, while treating one, lecture on them all'.[137] Such masters were not teaching, but showing off. Indeed, lack of humility was another characteristic that shocked Hugh:

134 *Ibid.*, 5.3, p. 122; quoting Peter 5.8.

135 B. T. Coolman, *The Theology of Hugh of St. Victor: An Interpretation* (Cambridge, 2010), pp. 128–9, 152–5; Coulter, *Per Visibilia ad Invisibilia*, pp. 65–92; Harkins, *Reading and the Work of Restoration*, pp. 137–96; Poirel, *Hugues de Saint-Victor*, pp. 71–7; Rorem, *Hugh of Saint Victor*, esp. pp. 28–9, 31, 32–3, 36, 48–55; B. Smalley, *The Study of the Bible in the Middle Ages* (Notre Dame, IN, 1964), pp. 93–101; D. Turner, *Eros and Allegory: Medieval Exegesis of the Song of Songs* (Kalamazoo, MI, 1995), pp. 265–74; G. A. Zinn, '*Historia fundamentum est*: the role of history in the contemplative life according to Hugh of St. Victor', in G. H. Shriver (ed.), *Contemporary Reflections on the Medieval Christian Tradition: Essays in Honor of Ray C. Petry* (Durham, NC, 1974), pp. 135–58.

136 Hugh of Saint Victor, *Didascalicon*, 3.4, p. 89.

137 *Ibid.*, 3.5, p. 89; see also p. 90, and 3.4, p. 88 for criticism of myth-makers.

> the vice of an inflated ego attacks some men because they pay too much fond attention to their own knowledge, and when they seem to themselves to have become something, they think that others whom they do not even know can neither be nor become as great. So it is that in our days certain peddlers of trifles come fuming forth; glorying in I know not what, they accuse our forefathers of simplicity and suppose that wisdom, having been born with themselves, with themselves will die. They say that the divine utterances have such a simple way of speaking that no one has to study them under masters, but can sufficiently penetrate to the hidden treasures of Truth by his own mental acumen. They wrinkle their noses and purse their lips at lecturers in divinity and do not understand that they themselves give offense to God, whose words they preach – words simple to be sure in their verbal beauty, but lacking savour when given a distorted sense. It is not my advice that you imitate men of this kind.[138]

It is hard not to read this as direct criticism of Peter Abelard's treatment of William of Champeaux and Anselm of Laon. Hugh was equally unhappy with those who studied scripture to gain wealth, honour or fame, or just to satisfy their desire 'to know about unheard-of things'.[139] Some of these criticisms could have been made by masters within the schools, but in many respects Hugh was reacting to the schools like a monk.

This is not surprising because Hugh also had a lot in common with monastic thinkers. The aim of study was to 'restore the divine likeness in man'.[140] Like William of Saint Thierry, he desired 'order and method' in reading.[141] He also valued self-knowledge: 'we are restored through instruction, so that we may recognize our nature and learn not to seek outside ourselves what we can find within'.[142] Most importantly, however, he stressed the need for the scholar to be virtuous. Restoring the divine likeness in man required not only 'contemplation of truth', but also 'the practice of virtue'.[143] The qualities necessary for 'those who study' were not only 'natural endowment' and 'practice', but also 'discipline'.[144] Discipline meant that 'by leading a praiseworthy life, they must combine moral behaviour with their knowledge'.[145] More specifically, discipline began with humility, and three lessons were particularly important for the student: 'first, that he hold no knowledge and no writing in contempt; second, that he blush to learn from no man; and third, that when he has attained learning himself, he not look down upon

[138] *Ibid.*, 3.13, pp. 96–7. [139] *Ibid.*, 5.10, p. 134.
[140] *Ibid.*, 1.8, p. 54; see also 2.1, p. 61.
[141] This was a constant refrain; see, for example, *ibid.*, 3.7, p. 91; 6.1, p. 135.
[142] *Ibid.*, 1.1, p. 47. On the relationship between order in reading, self-knowledge and restoration, and on Hugh's debt to Augustine, see Harkins, *Reading and the Work of Restoration*, esp. pp. 115–16.
[143] Hugh of Saint Victor, *Didascalicon*, 1.8, pp. 54–5.
[144] *Ibid.*, 3.6, p. 90. [145] *Ibid.*

everyone else'.[146] Another important aspect of discipline was 'quiet of life', 'whether interior, so that the mind is not distracted with illicit desires, or exterior, so that leisure and opportunity are provided for creditable and useful studies'.[147] It was equally important that students should be 'content with slender means' and not 'hanker after superfluities'.[148] Hugh summed up his view with the observation that 'All the world is a foreign soil to those who philosophize', to which he added:

> It is, therefore, a great source of virtue for the practiced mind to learn, bit by bit, first to change about in visible and transitory things, so that afterwards it may be able to leave them behind altogether. The man who finds his homeland sweet is still a tender beginner; he to whom every soil is as his native one is already strong; but he is perfect to whom the entire world is as a foreign land.[149]

This image played upon the actual experience of scholars who had left home to study, and also conveyed how important it was for all scholars, not just monks, to reject the world.

Like many monks, Hugh also set learning within a structured ascent towards an experience of God which was best expressed through metaphors such as taste and sight. The first step was 'study' which gave 'understanding' to beginners, and the *Didascalicon* was about this stage alone. The second step was 'meditation' which provided 'counsel'. At this stage one was to meditate on how to do what one had learned must be done. The third step was 'prayer', which made 'petition' since nothing good could be accomplished without divine help. The fourth step was 'performance', which Hugh described as 'seeking', when God and the supplicant worked together. The fifth and final step was 'contemplation', which involved finding, and 'in which, as by a sort of fruit of the preceding steps, one has a foretaste, even in this life, of what the future reward of good work is'.[150]

Hugh's approach was entirely compatible with monastic attitudes to learning, but his ascent also preserved the status of study and the liberal arts despite their position at the lowest stage. Crucially, the ascent did not transform the individual in such a way that the early steps became irrelevant. On the contrary, it was necessary to descend and repeat the earlier stages in order to maintain one's position or to ascend further:

> You see, then, how perfection comes to those ascending by means of these steps, so that he who has remained below cannot be perfect. Our objective,

146 *Ibid.*, 3.13, pp. 94–5. 147 *Ibid.*, 3.16, p. 99.
148 *Ibid.*, 3.18, p. 100. 149 *Ibid.*, 3.19, p. 101.
150 *Ibid.*, 5.9, p. 132.

therefore, ought to be always to keep ascending; but, because the instability of our life is such that we are not able to hold fast in one place, we are forced often to review the things we have done, and, in order not to lose the condition in which we now stand, we now and again repeat what we have been over before. For example: the man who is vigorous in his practice prays lest he grow weak; the man who is constant in his prayers meditates on what should be prayed for, lest he offend in prayer; and the man who sometimes feels less confidence in his own counsel, seeks advice in his reading. And thus it turns out that though we always have the will to ascend, nevertheless we are sometimes forced by necessity to descend – in such a way, however, that our goal lies in that will and not in this necessity. That we ascend is our goal; that we descend is for the sake of this goal. Not the latter, therefore, but the former ought to be the principal thing.[151]

Unlike William of Saint Thierry nearly twenty years later, Hugh did not envisage the permanent transformation of an individual within whom the various stages would be absorbed and fused, leading to the collapse of the categories used to structure the ascent. On the contrary, the need to repeat earlier stages meant that each stage remained distinct, to be practised on its own terms. However high an individual ascended, he could still benefit from study and the liberal arts, and the basis for sound scholarly practice remained constant.

This view informed Hugh's notion of the ideal teacher and the advice which he gave to those who aspired to fulfil this role:

The inexpensiveness of your dress and the simplicity expressed in your countenance, the innocence of your life and the holiness of your behaviour ought to teach men. You teach better by fleeing the world than by following after it. But perhaps you persist, saying, 'Well, what then? If I want to, may I not learn, at least?' I have told you above: 'Study, but do not be preoccupied with it.' Study can be a practice for you; it is not your objective. Instruction is good, but it is for beginners. You, however, have dedicated yourself to perfection, and therefore it is not enough for you if you put yourself on a level with beginners. It is fitting for you to manage more than this.[152]

Hugh's ideal master had moved on from complete preoccupation with study and the liberal arts. He had climbed the ascent so that he had other, higher priorities, but he could still study and teach. Thus Hugh shared the monastic view of the relationship between learning and life, but defined a place for the kind of work conducted in the schools.

Hugh's long-term significance is hard to assess. The abbey school was closed to non-members of the community well before the end of

[151] *Ibid.*, 5.9, p. 133. [152] *Ibid.*, 5.8, p. 131.

the twelfth century and possibly not long after Hugh's death, and it became isolated from the other Parisian schools. Nevertheless it has been argued that Hugh established an ideal and a tradition of importance to the later emergence of the University of Paris.[153] At the very least he demonstrated that it was possible to combine the very different types of learning developed in schools and monasteries, and to do so through a well-structured programme of scholarly formation.

In the interests of clarity, relations between monks and schoolmen have doubtless been oversimplified in the account above. It must be acknowledged that many schoolmen became monks, and sometimes they continued to teach; some schoolmen attacked other schoolmen on the same grounds as some of the monks; monks often criticized each other; and there was frequently mutual respect and intellectual exchange between exponents of the two approaches. Nevertheless, Bernard of Clairvaux, William of Saint Thierry and other monks offered a powerful critique of schoolmen like Abelard and Gilbert of Poitiers. Their concerns were well known at the time, and many perceived a conflict in terms of monks versus schoolmen.[154] Monks held that to know religious truth, it was necessary to reject the world and live virtuously. So, according to Bernard and others, the schools did not offer the kind of life that would make true knowing possible. They regarded the schoolmen as presumptuous in their application of reason to faith, accusing them of pursuing knowledge for the wrong reasons: for its own sake, out of desire for fame, for profit, in search of novelty. Moreover, schoolmen failed to take responsibility for the way their audience received their teaching. This was a powerful discourse that drove scholars to leave the schools and become monks, and it underpinned the attacks on individuals like Peter Abelard and Gilbert of Poitiers, men who were accused of heresy. There were many, however, like John of Salisbury, who could see merit on both sides and wished to find a way beyond conflict. It was above all Hugh of Saint Victor who fully articulated the monastic view of the proper relationship between life and learning, but also established a place for scholarship practised on its own terms. It was now possible to imagine the work of the schools continuing without being constantly threatened by the

[153] Ferruolo, *Origins of the University*, pp. 27–30, 40.

[154] See, for example, P. Delhaye, 'L'organisation scolaire au xiie siècle', *Traditio* 5 (1947): 211–68 at 225–8; M.-D. Chenu, *La théologie au douzième siècle* (Paris, 1957), pp. 343–50; Leclercq, *Love of Learning*, esp. pp. 1–9, 233–86; J. Leclercq, 'The renewal of theology', in Benson and Constable (eds.), *Renaissance and Renewal*, pp. 68–87; Ferruolo, *Origins of the University*, pp. 47–92; McGinn, *Growth of Mysticism*, pp. 367–70.

monastic critique. The school of Saint Victor could not, however, support large numbers of masters and students, and did not offer a model that could be reproduced on a large scale. There was now a discourse that effectively neutralized the monastic critique, but no large-scale institutional form for it to legitimate.

3 The University of Paris in the thirteenth century

A new kind of career, an academic career, had become possible in the twelfth-century schools. Only loosely tied to existing institutions, however, it involved a high level of risk, and the careers of specific individuals were potentially short lived. Students had a large say in who would find an audience, and those who wished to make the transition from student to master often did so by competing with their masters. At the same time, schoolmen were vulnerable to a monastic critique which insisted that religious knowledge could only be acquired by the virtuous, and that teachers must take responsibility for the effect they had on their students. Monasteries provided institutional guarantees of virtue and responsibility for reception which the schoolmen conspicuously lacked. The first part of this chapter will focus on the institutional development of a university in Paris. This involved the stabilization of the academic career, with masters asserting control over students, and the appropriation of key monastic ideals to establish a new discourse that allowed the university to negotiate a privileged position in society. The emergence of the university did not, however, bring an end to intellectual differences. Very different approaches to knowing, especially knowing about God, will be illustrated in the second and third parts of the chapter by exploring the work of Thomas Aquinas and Bonaventure, two of the most outstanding thinkers of the thirteenth century, both of whom spent significant parts of their careers in Paris. The fourth and final part of the chapter will look at moments when intellectual difference led to conflict and condemnation.

Institutionalization, cultural identity and a new discourse of learning

In the late twelfth and early thirteenth centuries, scholars in a few places began to adopt forms of collective organization that embraced or to some extent replaced the schools which had flourished independently for many years. They joined together in corporations or guilds that came to enjoy formal legal standing, and acquired rights and privileges. With hindsight it is possible to identify the emergence of the earliest universities, although no one could have offered this interpretation at the time. On the other hand, contemporaries were aware that changes were taking place, and they described the new institutions of learning as *studia generalia*. In other words, they perceived certain places as general centres of learning.[1] If the term signified more than a vague recognition of prestige, it probably referred to their ability to attract students and masters from across Europe, and their capacity to offer teaching in advanced subjects like theology, law and medicine, as well as the arts. The word 'universitas' was not applied specifically to institutions of learning; it was a very general term that could be used to describe any corporate body with legal rights, and it is a matter of chance that vernacular versions of the word have survived to refer exclusively to institutions of higher education.[2]

The process by which the first universities emerged is difficult to analyse because very little evidence survives. Historians have nevertheless tried to explain this process and to discover the origins of the medieval university, essentially offering three types of explanation. First, the emergence of universities has been explained in terms of conflict between scholars and both local ecclesiastical authorities and the town authorities. In response to these conflicts, the scholars acted collectively to protect themselves, and in the course of these conflicts they gained privileges from kings, popes and emperors.[3] The second type of explanation stresses debates amongst learned men, and especially the development of shared educational ideals to which the emerging universities gave expression.[4] The third approach treats the university as

1 G. Leff, *Paris and Oxford Universities in the Thirteenth and Fourteenth Centuries: An Institutional and Intellectual History* (New York, 1968), pp. 16–19; M. M. Mulchahey, *'First the bow is bent': Dominican Education before 1350* (Toronto, 1998), pp. 352–60; J. Verger, 'Patterns', in H. de Ridder-Symoens (ed.), *A History of the University in Europe. Vol. 1: Universities in the Middle Ages* (Cambridge, 1992), pp. 35–74 at 36–7; O. Weijers, *Terminologie des universités au xiiie siècle* (Rome, 1987), pp. 34–45.

2 For extended analysis of the term, its usages and ideological associations, see P. Michaud-Quantin, *Universitas. Expressions du mouvement communautaire dans le moyen-âge latin* (Paris, 1970). See also Weijers, *Terminologie des universités*, pp. 16–26.

3 Notable examples include H. Rashdall, *The Universities of Europe in the Middle Ages*, revised and ed. F. M. Powicke and A. B. Emden, 3 vols. (1936; repr. Oxford, 1997), esp. vol. 1, pp. 269–432; A. B. Cobban, *The Medieval Universities: Their Development and Organization* (London, 1975), esp. pp. 75–95.

4 See, for example, S. C. Ferruolo, *The Origins of the University: The Schools of Paris and their Critics, 1100–1215* (Stanford, 1985), where his argument is summarized at pp. 3, 5–8, 310–12.

a product of its urban environment. Scholars deliberately copied artisans and merchants, their classrooms were like workshops, they sold knowledge in the way that artisans and merchants sold their goods, and the university was therefore a guild like any other trade guild.[5] Recent scholarship has tended to acknowledge a measure of validity in all three approaches.[6]

The gradual emergence of *studia generalia* is generally associated with Bologna, Paris and Oxford. From early in the thirteenth century, further universities were established in two ways. Some were set up by masters and students migrating from an existing university, usually in response to conflict with local authorities. Thus, for example, Cambridge was created by scholars from Oxford (1209–14), Padua by scholars from Bologna (1222), and Orléans and Angers by Parisian scholars (1229–31). Other universities were deliberately founded by a major secular or ecclesiastical authority, often for specific political reasons. The earliest examples were Naples, set up by Emperor Frederick II in 1224, and Toulouse, created by the papacy in 1229. By 1300 there were at least eighteen universities in western Europe.[7] Amongst the earliest universities, Bologna and Paris were the most influential in terms of organization and structure, offering two very different models which later universities imitated, while developing their own manifold variations.

It is worth considering Bologna briefly in order to appreciate what was distinctive about Paris. The *studium generale* at Bologna was preeminent in the study of law, and students exercised a significant measure of control, although perhaps not as much as once thought.[8] The

[5] See J. Le Goff, *Intellectuals in the Middle Ages*, trans. T. L. Fagan (Oxford, 1993), pp. xiv–xv, 5–6, 57–8, 61–3, 93–6.

[6] See judicious comments in Ferruolo, *Origins of the University*, pp. 3, 5, 311 and J. Verger, 'A propos de la naissance de l'université de Paris: contexte social, enjeu politique, portée intellectuelle', in J. Fried (ed.), *Schulen und Studium im Sozialen Wandel des hohen und späten Mittelalters*, Vorträge und Forschungen 30 (Sigmaringen, 1986), pp. 69–96.

[7] Verger, 'Patterns', pp. 52–5. Verger suggests that the inclusion of disputed cases would raise the total to twenty-three.

[8] For traditional accounts, see M. Bellomo, *The Common Legal Past of Europe 1000–1800*, trans. L. G. Cochrane (Washington, DC, 1995), pp. 112–22; J. A. Brundage, *The Medieval Origins of the Legal Profession: Canonists, Civilians, and Courts* (Chicago, 2008), pp. 223–30, 251; A. B. Cobban, 'Medieval student power', *Past and Present* 53 (1971): 28–66 at 35–43; Cobban, *Medieval Universities*, pp. 48–74; P. Kibre, *The Nations in the Mediaeval Universities* (Cambridge, MA, 1948), pp. 3–14, 29–64; O. Pedersen, *The First Universities: Studium Generale and the Origins of University Education in Europe* (Cambridge, 1997), pp. 138–44, 160–2, 208–12; Rashdall, *Universities*, vol. 1, pp. 87–268; S. Stelling-Michaud, *L'université de Bologne et la pénétration des droits romain et canonique en Suisse aux xiiie et xive siècles* (Geneva, 1955), pp. 13–46. For significant corrections in the light of recent and ongoing research, I am extremely

crucial steps towards collective organization were taken by law students who had come from elsewhere to study in Bologna. Because they were not citizens of Bologna, they lacked the protection which citizenship gave to both person and property. Most of the students of Roman law were laymen and therefore did not enjoy the benefits of clerical status either. Moreover, many were mature adults from wealthy families, and had already acquired political and administrative experience. In order to secure a measure of protection for themselves, the law students formed loose associations which were defined approximately by the students' places of origin, and were termed 'nations'. More substantial corporations, or *universitates*, were also established, each run by a student elected as rector. In the early thirteenth century there were four such corporations, but by the middle of the century there were two: the *universitas citramontanorum* for law students from Italian towns other than Bologna, and the *universitas ultramontanorum* for law students who had come from north of the Alps. Bolognese students were denied full membership of any of these groups.

These developments were not welcomed by the commune of Bologna. In the conflict between the student corporations and the commune, the students wielded considerable power by threatening to leave the city to study elsewhere, which would deprive the masters and the city as a whole of their money. This was not an idle threat, and a group of students departed to Vicenza in 1204. The town tried to deprive the students of this power by regulating the oaths which they took. Thus the town statutes of 1211 and 1215 prohibited students from swearing that they would leave Bologna at the bidding of a particular individual. In 1217 and 1220 the commune tried to make the rectors take oaths not to leave Bologna to study elsewhere. In the face of this hostility, the students appealed to the pope. A combination of papal pressure and the fear of losing more business persuaded the commune to give in, or at least to compromise. By 1245, or even a few years earlier, foreign students were granted some of the legal rights enjoyed by citizens. The jurisdiction of the rectors was largely acknowledged in the town statutes. The statutes of the student corporations were recognized by the commune in the early 1250s. During the second half of the thirteenth

grateful to Peter Denley; see P. Denley, 'Communities within communities: student identity and student groups in late medieval Italian universities', in F. Piovan and L. S. Rea (eds.), *Studenti, università, città nella storia padovana: atti del convegno Padova 6–8 febbraio 1998* (Trieste, 2001), pp. 723–44; P. Denley, 'Communes, despots and universities: structures and trends of Italian *studi* to 1500', in J. E. Law and B. Paton (eds.), *Communes and Despots in Medieval and Renaissance Italy* (Aldershot, 2010), 295–306.

century, another student corporation was formed, a university of arts and medicine.

These developments left the masters of Bologna in a weak position. Initially they did not seek collective organization because they were mostly citizens of Bologna and therefore enjoyed legal protection. The commune imposed its authority on them at an early stage, from 1189 requiring them to swear that they would only teach in Bologna. In 1219 Pope Honorius III decreed that the licence to teach should be granted by the archdeacon of Bologna, who became known as the chancellor. The masters were financially dependent, however, on fees paid by the students and, as a result, the student corporations exercised, at least in theory, a large degree of control over the masters. To give just a few examples of the many regulations, every year the students elected the masters who were to teach, and these masters had to take an oath subjecting themselves to the rector. A master could not leave Bologna even for a matter of days without permission from both his students and the rector. Masters were fined if they did not begin and end their lectures on time, or if they failed to cover the required ground by set dates. If a master did not attract an audience of more than five students, he was fined as if he himself had been absent. Four students were elected to monitor the masters and to report infringements; to keep the masters continuously on their toes, they were not told which students had been elected to perform this role. Whether or not student corporations fully exercised the power that these rules suggest, towards the end of the thirteenth century the commune established salaried lectureships, which deprived the student corporations of their financial clout and put the city authorities in a position to control education in Bologna.

The *studium generale* at Paris, however, was run by its masters whose pre-eminence in arts and theology was internationally recognized. The early contribution of Abelard and others has been mentioned, as has the significance of papal protection. Exactly when and why the masters began to act collectively is unclear, but key steps must have been taken during the second half of the twelfth century. Unlike the masters of Bologna who were citizens of that town, most were not from Paris, and it has often been surmised that they acted to protect themselves. They were also in a stronger position to impose themselves on the students because many of them held ecclesiastical benefices and did not therefore rely entirely upon fees, while most of the students were significantly younger than their counterparts in Bologna. Whatever the precise circumstances in which the masters began to act corporately, the key surviving documents bearing witness to and formally establishing their rights and privileges were largely the product of conflict with the local town and ecclesiastical authorities. The three most significant documents were the charter granted by Philip Augustus in 1200, the statutes issued by Robert of Courson in 1215 and the bull *Parens scientiarum* of 1231.

The crisis of 1200 began when a German student sent a servant to buy wine, and the innkeeper tried to overcharge him. The student and some of his friends assaulted the innkeeper and smashed up the inn. The innkeeper went to the royal provost of Paris, who led an attack on the hostel in which a number of German students were residing. Several students were killed. The Paris masters immediately went on strike, suspending all lectures and threatening to leave unless the king punished the provost and his men. The king immediately came down on the side of the university. The provost and his men were imprisoned for life, and the king granted a charter protecting the scholars in the future. The charter included the following provisions: all citizens were obliged to report crimes they saw a layman commit against a scholar; they had to help arrest the criminal and testify in court; the royal provost and the city's magistrates were prohibited from arresting scholars or seizing their goods. The charter concluded by ordering the provost and people of Paris to take a public oath to abide by the charter, and requiring every new provost to repeat the oath before an assembly of scholars.[9] The masters and students had thus expressed their solidarity through collective action, and the king had recognized them as a distinct group, awarding them special status in relation to the people of Paris and his own officials. This status was reaffirmed by public ritual every time a new provost assumed office and performed the highly symbolic act of oath-taking.[10]

At some point before 1208–9, the masters in Paris drew up a set of statutes that does not survive. This is apparent from a bull, *Ex litteris vestre*, sent by Pope Innocent III to the masters of theology, canon law and arts at that time. The bull noted that some masters of arts had deviated from established practices by wearing inappropriate dress, failing to observe due order in lectures and disputations, and neglecting to

[9] *Chartularium*, vol. 1, no. 1, pp. 59–61. P. Kibre, *Scholarly Privileges in the Middle Ages* (London, 1961), pp. 86–7; Leff, *Paris and Oxford Universities*, p. 28; Pedersen, *The First Universities*, pp. 158–9; Rashdall, *Universities*, vol. 1, pp. 294–8; S. E. Young, '"Consilio hominum nostrorum": a comparative study of royal responses to crisis at the University of Paris, 1200–1231', *History of Universities* 22 (2007): 1–20 at 3–6.

[10] C. F. Weber, '*Ces grands privilèges*: the symbolic use of written documents in the foundation and institutionalization processes of medieval universities', *History of Universities* 19 (2004): 12–62 at 16–23.

attend funerals. The masters had responded by unanimously selecting eight colleagues to address these issues in statutes, and requiring everyone to take an oath to observe them. When a certain master G. had refused, the masters had deprived him of membership of their body. This master had now submitted, and the point of the bull was to allow his readmission.[11] Clearly the masters were capable of taking collective action on their own account, and the pope was willing to back them up.

The first surviving statutes date from 1215 and were issued by Robert of Courson as a papal legate. These statutes were partly shaped by conflict with both the town and the local ecclesiastical authorities, although there was much that reflected a consensus amongst the scholars themselves. They were certainly not imposed on the academic community by the papal legate because Robert had taught theology in Paris for many years and the opening section of the document makes it clear that he had been instructed to consult, presumably with his former colleagues: 'Let all know that, since we have had a special mandate from the pope to take effective measures to reform the state of the Parisian scholars for the better, wishing with the counsel of good men to provide for the tranquility of the scholars in the future, we have decreed and ordained in this wise.'[12] Furthermore, the following statutes, which were addressed to 'all the masters and scholars of Paris', dealt with matters that had long been of concern, including the issues known to have been the subject of the lost statutes produced by the scholars independently. In many respects they have to be interpreted as the product of cooperation as much as conflict.[13]

Modern readers are often struck by the statutes' apparent lack of organization.[14] The way in which the statutes were set out, however, reveals a great deal about the mindset of those responsible for them. The first section concerned the process of becoming a master of arts and then teaching the arts:

> No one shall lecture in the arts at Paris before he is twenty-one years of age, and he shall have heard lectures for at least six years before he begins to lecture, and he shall promise to lecture for at least two years, unless a reasonable cause prevents, which he ought to prove publicly or before examiners. He shall

[11] *Chartularium*, vol. 1, no. 8, pp. 67–8. See Rashdall, *Universities*, vol. 1, pp. 299–303; Kibre, *Scholarly Privileges*, pp. 89–90; Leff, *Paris and Oxford Universities*, pp. 24–5; Ferruolo, *Origins of the University*, p. 295.

[12] *University Records*, no. 15, pp. 27–8.

[13] Ferruolo, *Origins of the University*, pp. 282–3.

[14] See, for example, S. C. Ferruolo, 'The Paris statutes of 1215 reconsidered', *History of Universities* 5 (1985): 1–14 at 6–7; Ferruolo, *Origins of the University*, p. 305.

not be stained by any infamy, and when he is ready to lecture, he shall be examined according to the form which is contained in the writing of the lord bishop of Paris, where is contained the peace confirmed between the chancellor and scholars by judges delegated by the pope, namely, by the bishop and dean of Troyes and by P. the bishop and J. the chancellor of Paris approved and confirmed. And they shall lecture on the books of Aristotle on dialectic old and new in the schools ordinarily and not *ad cursum*. They shall also lecture on both Priscians ordinarily, or at least on one. They shall not lecture on feast days except on philosophers and rhetoric and the quadrivium and *Barbarismus* and ethics, if it please them, and the fourth book of the *Topics*. They shall not lecture on the books of Aristotle on metaphysics and natural philosophy or on summaries of them or concerning the doctrine of master David of Dinant or the heretic Amaury or Mauritius of Spain.[15]

There had long been complaints that scholars set about teaching when they were too young, when they had not studied for long enough, and when their behaviour was morally deficient. The statutes immediately set appropriate standards and indicated how magisterial candidates would be scrutinized by alluding to the resolution of a bitter conflict that had recently occurred between the scholars and the chancellor of the cathedral of Notre Dame, John of Candeilles. At issue were the way in which the chancellor exercised his right to grant the licence to teach, and the extent of his powers of jurisdiction over scholars. Previous chancellors had worked harmoniously with the scholars, but John was the first of a number of chancellors and bishops of Paris who tried to control the scholars by undermining their independence. The scholars appealed to Pope Innocent III, who backed them wholeheartedly. In 1212, after noting that he had seen nothing like this when he had studied at Paris, he ordered the bishop, dean and archdeacon of Troyes to censure the chancellor if he did not abandon the practices which offended the scholars. After a process of arbitration, it was the bishop of Paris, Peter of Nemours, who in 1213 recorded the settlement to which the statutes referred. When granting the licence to teach, the chancellor was not to exact oaths of fidelity or obedience, nor was he permitted to charge. His powers to imprison and fine scholars were also carefully circumscribed. Further rules about the granting of the licence to teach were also imposed for as long as John remained chancellor. They ensured that the licence would be given to anyone deemed fit by the masters, although John could still grant licences to candidates who did not have their backing.[16] This dispute was over well before 1215, and it

[15] *University Records*, no. 15, p. 28.

[16] See *Chartularium*, vol. 1, no. 14, pp. 73–4; nos. 16–18, pp. 75–7; Ferruolo, *Origins of the University*, pp. 296–9; Kibre, *Scholarly Privileges*, pp. 88–9; Leff, *Paris and*

was not the immediate trigger for the granting of the statutes, but the masters took care to see that the settlement in their favour was embedded within the statutes. New masters were also obliged to teach, or to be 'regent' masters, as they were called, for a minimum of two years.

This section of the statutes then dealt with the teaching that a master of arts should undertake, sorting out matters of curriculum and timetable. Set texts were specified for key subjects: the relevant works by Aristotle for dialectic; two parts of a work by Priscian and part of a work by Donatus, referred to as the *Barbarismus*, for grammar; Aristotle's *Topics* for practising the construction of certain types of argument. Dialectic and grammar were clearly established as the core subjects because they were to be taught ordinarily rather than *ad cursum*. Ordinary lectures contained in-depth analysis and were given by masters, while lectures *ad cursum* offered more general summaries, and were usually given by bachelors as part of the process by which they qualified to become masters.[17] Lectures on rhetoric, the remaining part of the trivium, and the quadrivium could be delivered on feast days, along with ethics and further practice at grammar and argument. The section concluded by prohibiting lectures on Aristotle's metaphysics and natural philosophy, along with works by recently condemned heretics, thus repeating a ban that had been issued by various bishops in 1210.[18]

The start of the second section did not specify whether it concerned students and masters of arts or all the students and masters, but particular rules within it were directed at students and masters of specific subjects.

In the *principia* and meetings of the masters and in the responsions and oppositions of the boys and youths there shall be no drinking. They may summon some friends or associates, but only a few. Donations of clothing or other things as has been customary, or more, we urge should be made, especially to the poor. None of the masters lecturing in arts shall have a cope except one round, black and reaching to the ankles, at least while it is new. Use of the pallium is permitted. No one shall wear with the round cope shoes that are ornamented or with elongated pointed toes. If any scholar in arts or theology dies, half of the masters of arts shall attend the funeral at one time, the other half the next time, and no one shall leave until the sepulture is finished, unless he has reasonable cause. If any master in arts or theology dies, all the masters shall keep vigils, each shall read or cause to be read the Psalter, each shall attend the church where is celebrated the watch until midnight or the greater part of the

Oxford Universities, pp. 25–6; Pedersen, *The First Universities*, pp. 167–70; Rashdall, *Universities*, vol. 1, pp. 304–9.

17 G. Leff, 'The *Trivium* and the three philosophies', in Ridder-Symoens (ed.), *Universities in the Middle Ages*, pp. 307–36 at 326.

18 *Chartularium*, vol. 1, no. 11, pp. 70–1; *University Records*, no. 14, pp. 26–7.

night, unless reasonable cause prevent. On the day when the master is buried, no one shall lecture or dispute.[19]

This section thus began by seeking to regulate conduct. First, the statutes tried to limit the festivities that took place at key transitional moments in a student's career. After receiving his licence to teach, a new master was admitted into the corporation of masters by means of inception, which meant acting as a master for the first time in special disputations, sometimes called 'principia'. Before becoming a master, a student had to become a bachelor. The 'responsions and oppositions' almost certainly refer to the examination process during which the candidate was obliged to respond to questions and then 'determine' a disputation. Arts students usually became bachelors at the age of about eighteen or nineteen.[20] The statutes permitted new masters and bachelors to celebrate their success, but there was to be no drinking and the scale was to remain modest.[21] Charitable giving, however, was strongly encouraged. Dress regulations for masters of arts were then set out. The last part of the section stipulated the funerary practices to be followed when students and masters in arts and theology died. This was a significant step in establishing the university's status as a corporate body. Religious ritual served to generate a sense of community in a way that was already characteristic of urban guilds and religious confraternities.[22]

The next two sections concerned all the students and masters. The first bluntly confirmed that they owned a meadow that was also claimed by the abbey of Saint Germain. The second addressed a range of issues, including some of fundamental importance to the constitution of the university.

Each master shall have jurisdiction over his scholar. No one shall occupy a classroom or house without asking the consent of the tenant, provided one has a chance to ask it. No one shall receive the licentiate from the chancellor or another for money given or promise made or other condition agreed upon.

[19] *University Records*, no. 15, p. 29.

[20] Leff, *Paris and Oxford Universities*, pp. 54–5; Pedersen, *The First Universities*, pp. 262–9; Rashdall, *Universities*, vol. 1, pp. 450–62.

[21] On drinking as a 'bonding mechanism' in universities of the fourteenth and fifteenth centuries, see R. M. Karras, *From Boys to Men: Formations of Masculinity in Late Medieval Europe* (Philadelphia, 2003), pp. 95–6.

[22] Ferruolo, 'The Paris statutes of 1215 reconsidered', p. 10; Rashdall, *Universities*, vol. 1, p. 300. On the significance of ritual in late medieval universities, and on the role of burial services in establishing the late medieval university as 'a liturgical community', see F. Rexroth, 'Ritual and the creation of social knowledge: the opening celebrations of medieval German universities', in W. J. Courtenay and J. Miethke (eds.), *Universities and Schooling in Medieval Society* (Leiden, 2000), pp. 65–80 at 79.

Also, the masters and scholars can make both between themselves and with other persons obligations and constitutions supported by faith or penalty or oath in these cases: namely the murder or mutilation of a scholar or atrocious injury done a scholar, if justice should not be forthcoming, arranging the prices of lodgings, costume, burial, lectures and disputations, so, however, that the university be not thereby dissolved or destroyed.[23]

The first sentence set down one of the key organizational principles of the university. A student joined the university by submitting to a particular master who accepted responsibility for him. At the lowest level, the university was composed of masters, each with a number of individual students clustered round him. The next sentence addressed a matter of importance in the relations between the university and the people of Paris. The university owned very little in the way of buildings, so classrooms and accommodation had to be rented. Here masters and students were reminded that they must negotiate reasonably with property owners. At this point the statutes turned abruptly to relations with the local ecclesiastical authorities, stating explicitly the key principle at stake in the conflict with the chancellor to which allusion had already been made: the chancellor had to grant the licence to teach without charging money or imposing any other kind of obligation. This was followed by the line of greatest constitutional significance in the whole document since it recognized the university as a legal corporation. The masters and students could make their own rules, require members of their body to take oaths to obey these rules, and punish those who transgressed them. Moreover, they could make legally binding agreements with other parties. This was the case with regard to a list of issues that, in addition to several matters already treated in the statutes, included the killing or injuring of scholars, and rent control. The power of the corporation was, however, limited in one important respect. The university was not to be 'dissolved or destroyed' as a consequence of their actions, which meant that they could not go on strike and leave to study elsewhere. As we shall see, this was soon to prove their strongest weapon.

After these crucial rulings for the whole body of students and masters, the statutes turned specifically to the theologians.

As to the status of the theologians, we decree that no one shall lecture at Paris before his thirty-fifth year and unless he has studied for eight years at least, and has heard the books faithfully and in classrooms, and has attended lectures in theology for five years before he gives lectures himself publicly. And none of these shall lecture before the third hour on days when masters lecture. No one

[23] *University Records*, no. 15, p. 29.

shall be admitted at Paris to formal lectures or to preachings unless he shall be of approved life and science. No one shall be a scholar at Paris who has no definite master.[24]

This section thus established a minimum age and length of study for those wishing to become masters of theology. It then settled a timetabling issue that was of fundamental importance to the smooth running of the university. Many masters of arts were also students and bachelors in the faculty of theology, so they had to be able to teach classes in arts and attend classes in theology. The statutes ruled that theology lectures had to be given after 9.00 a.m., which meant that masters of arts could teach earlier in the day before pursuing their studies in theology.[25] Two basic principles for admission to the faculty were then articulated. The first presumably applied to both masters and students: the faculty would only admit men whose virtue and learning had been found satisfactory. The second stated that every student had to be attached to a particular master, an issue that had already been touched upon with regard to the whole university. Finally, Robert of Courson declared that all who deliberately broke these rules were to be excommunicated 'unless within fifteen days of the offense they have taken care to emend their presumption before the university of masters and scholars or other persons constituted by the university'.[26]

The statutes gave papal recognition to the students and masters of Paris as a legal corporation while also expressing a complex sense of identity. By defining their privileges and regulating their activities, the statutes not only recognized the solidarity of the students and masters as a single body, but also articulated relations between various parts of the university and between the university and others, especially the chancellor and the townspeople. As already noted, however, the way in which they did this is confusing to modern readers because the overall shape of the document is unclear. Individual sections treat in quick succession issues that would seem to be unconnected. The same issues crop up in several places. Some matters are handled with considerable brevity, to the point of seeming cryptic. Hugely significant privileges and rules are treated on a par with relatively minor matters. Having set out rules for dress, funerals and lectures, the statutes declare that the students and masters can make their own rules on just these points. It has been suggested that the statutes lack order because there was

[24] *Ibid.*, pp. 29–30.

[25] Ferruolo, 'The Paris statutes of 1215 reconsidered', p. 8; Ferruolo, *Origins of the University*, p. 307.

[26] *University Records*, no. 15, p. 30.

very little time in which to consult colleagues and put the document together.[27] This explanation does not seem entirely convincing when historians have so little difficulty recasting the material under a series of thematic headings: governance, town–gown relations, conduct and so on. If Robert and his former colleagues had wanted to do this, it would not have been beyond them to recast the material as efficiently as historians do when they offer thematically structured accounts of the statutes. It may therefore be that the conceptual frameworks that seem obvious to modern academics were either not so readily apparent in 1215 or were not thought desirable.

At this point it is worth recalling two aspects of the monastic critique of the twelfth-century schools. Monks like Bernard of Clairvaux and William of Saint Thierry had insisted that life and learning were intimately connected, that a man had to live virtuously if he were to think correctly, and that meaningful scholarship could only take place within a properly regulated environment. Moreover, a master had to take responsibility for his audience, only teaching those who had undergone the necessary intellectual and moral formation. The statutes clearly sought to regulate the moral behaviour of students and masters, and to establish a formal bond between each master and his students. These regulations were not just about maintaining order, although they were certainly about that. Much more importantly, they were designed to instil the virtues necessary for good learning and to ensure the proper relationship between master and audience. Rules about conduct and behaviour were therefore interspersed with rules about, for example, curriculum precisely because life and learning were understood to be linked. Due weight must also be given to the moral significance of those rules that are not obviously about virtuous behaviour. One of the most commonly condemned manifestations of pride, for example, was the tendency to move on too quickly from one area of study to another. The statutes tackled this when setting minimum ages and periods of study for those who wished to become masters. One of the most frequently identified manifestations of the vice of curiosity was the tendency not to move on from one area of study to another, for example the inclination to carry on studying logic for its own sake rather than moving on to apply logical skills in theology. The timetabling regulations did everything possible to make it easy for arts masters to study theology. The point has been made that the statutes responded to many

[27] Ferruolo, The Paris statutes of 1215 reconsidered', p. 7; Ferruolo, *Origins of the University*, p. 305.

of the criticisms that had been directed at the schools.[28] More than that, they were built around the idea that intellectual and moral formation were inseparable, and that masters had to be responsible for their effect on their audience. In other words, the public vision of the university, the one authorized by the papacy, was fundamentally shaped by key monastic ideals.

This marked a hugely significant change in the intellectual culture of western Europe. It was not that students and masters henceforth lived and behaved like monks: they did not. At a theoretical level, however, universities were no longer vulnerable to the kind of criticism that had been leveled at the schools in the twelfth century. Actual departures from the ideals articulated in the statutes could be treated as disciplinary issues rather than matters of principle. Virtuous scholars, on the other hand, might be compared to monks. As Rutebeuf, the thirteenth-century vernacular poet, observed, 'To one who should wish to live uprightly is there any life so pleasant as is that of true scholars? ... They can not allow themselves to sit long enough at the table. Their life is as well governed as that of any monastic order.'[29] Universities were ideologically safe from the point of view of those who lived according to a religious rule, and they could now seek to be involved. The arrival of the friars will be considered shortly. In 1237 the general chapter of the Cistercian order authorized the foundation of a Cistercian house in Paris, and in 1256 Guy de l'Aumône became the first Cistercian master of theology at Paris.[30]

The university had now received privileges from the king in 1200 and the pope in 1215, but its standing was by no means secure. The bishop of Paris and his chancellor simply did not accept the corporate independence of the students and masters. At one point they excommunicated

[28] Ferruolo perceptively noted that 'despite their disorder and lack of any apparent unifying principle, the statutes of 1215 succeeded in addressing many of the principal criticisms which had been made of the schools during their previous decades of rapid growth and expansion'; 'The Paris statutes of 1215 reconsidered', p. 7 and see also pp. 7–11. See also Ferruolo, *Origins of the University*, pp. 306, 309–312.

[29] M. M. Wood, *The Spirit of Protest in Old French Literature* (New York, 1917), p. 120, n. 2.

[30] P. Dautrey, 'Croissance et adaptation chez les cisterciens au treizième siècle: les débuts du collège des Bernadins de Paris', *Analecta Cisterciensia* 32 (1976): 122–215; F. E. Kwanten, 'Le Collège Saint-Bernard à Paris: Sa fondation et ses débuts', *Revue d'histoire ecclésiastique* 43 (1948): 443–72 ; C. H. Lawrence, 'Stephen of Lexington and Cistercian university studies in the thirteenth century', *Journal of Ecclesiastical History* 11 (1960): 164–78; I. P. Wei, 'Guy de l'Aumône's "Summa de diversis questionibus theologiae"', *Traditio* 44 (1988): 275–323 at 275–6. For the dates at which other religious orders founded houses of study in Paris, see T. Sullivan, 'The *quodlibeta* of the canons regular and the monks', in C. Schabel (ed.), *Theological Quodlibeta in the Middle Ages: The Fourteenth Century* (Leiden, 2007), pp. 359–400 at 359.

the whole university on the grounds that it had contravened an earlier ordinance against conspiracies by making constitutions without the consent of the bishop, chapter or chancellor, even though this was just what the 1215 statutes had said they could do. The university had to call repeatedly for papal intervention, and a bull of 1219 insisted that the university could not be excommunicated as a whole without papal permission.[31] Matters came to a head, and the university all but disintegrated, in 1229. The crisis began in a tavern in the Rue Saint Marcel with yet another argument over a bill. This led to a series of increasingly violent clashes. Complaints were made to the bishop and the papal legate, Romano, cardinal of Saint Angelo. Romano had himself suffered from scholarly mob violence in 1225 when he had broken the university's seal and banned the university from making another one. This was one of the few issues on which the pope had backed the local ecclesiastical authorities against the university, which only received the right to have a seal in 1246. Possession of a seal was, however, of great symbolic importance for any corporate body. In reprisal for breaking their seal, a crowd of armed students and masters had attacked Romano's residence and only dispersed when royal troops came to his rescue.[32] Unsurprisingly, the papal legate was as keen as the bishop to act against violent scholars. They turned to Louis IX's regent, Blanche of Castille, for action. She sent in the provost and his men who killed several students, some of whom had apparently not been involved in the previous disorder. The masters suspended their lectures, but their complaints to the bishop and legate fell on deaf ears. They therefore announced that if they did not receive satisfaction within a month from Easter no one would be allowed to study or teach in the city or diocese of Paris for the next six years, nor would they return after that period of time unless their grievances were adequately addressed. The regent, the bishop and the papal legate remained unmoved, and so the majority of students and masters departed in what is often called the 'great dispersion', pursuing their studies in a range of other cities in western Europe.[33]

[31] *Chartularium*, vol. 1, nos. 30, 31, pp. 87–90; no. 45, pp. 102–4. Leff, *Paris and Oxford Universities*, p. 29; Rashdall, *Universities*, vol. 1, pp. 310–11. Pedersen, *The First Universities*, p. 171.

[32] Kibre, *Scholarly Privileges*, p. 91; Leff, *Paris and Oxford Universities*, p. 30; Michaud-Quantin, *Universitas*, pp. 299–303; Rashdall, *Universities*, vol. 1, p. 317; Young, '"Consilio hominum nostrorum"', pp. 6–7.

[33] *Chartularium*, vol. 1, no. 62, p. 118; no. 64, p. 119. Kibre, *Scholarly Privileges*, pp. 92–3; Leff, *Paris and Oxford Universities*, p. 31; Pedersen, *The First Universities*, p. 172; Rashdall, *Universities*, vol. 1, pp. 334–7; Young, '"Consilio hominum nostrorum"', pp. 7–8.

Mobility was one of the most powerful weapons that the students and masters could wield.[34] Once it became clear that they had not made an idle threat, the authorities started to take action. In August 1229 Louis IX confirmed the privileges granted by Philip Augustus in 1200.[35] Pope Gregory IX went into overdrive, reproaching the bishop of Paris for letting matters get out of hand, recalling his legate, ordering the bishops of Le Mans and Senlis and the archdeacon of Châlons sur Marne to act as judges in what he termed the dispute between the king and the students and masters, exhorting the king and the queen mother to recall the scholars and give them justice, reassuring the departed scholars that the matter was being investigated in full, and eventually summoning the bishop of Paris, William of Auvergne, and his chancellor, Philip, to see him in person.[36] It took two years to sort everything out, and the university resumed its teaching in 1231. In April and May of that year, Gregory IX issued a series of bulls establishing order, the most important of which was *Parens scientiarum*, 'Parent of sciences'.[37]

Unlike the statutes of 1215, *Parens scientiarum* was a carefully crafted and brilliantly assured piece of writing. The grand opening, however, has generally been ignored, perhaps because the standard edition in Denifle and Chatelain's *Chartularium Universitatis Parisiensis* fails to identify the authoritative sources embedded within it and upon which it is modelled.[38] This is unfortunate because it made a powerful claim to authority, and set out the heart of Gregory IX's message.

Parens scientiarum Parisius velut altera *Cariath Sepher, civitas litterarum*,[39] cara claret, magna quidem sed de se majora facit optari docentibus et discentibus

[34] See Leff, *Paris and Oxford Universities*, pp. 8–9; I. P. Wei, 'Scholars and travel in the twelfth and thirteenth centuries', in P. Horden (ed.), *Freedom of Movement in the Middle Ages: People, Ideas, Goods* (Donington, 2007), pp. 73–85.

[35] *Chartularium*, vol. 1, nos. 66–7, pp. 120–3. Kibre, *Scholarly Privileges*, pp. 93–4; Leff, *Paris and Oxford Universities*, p. 31; Pedersen, *The First Universities*, p. 172; Young, '"Consilio hominum nostrorum"', p. 8.

[36] *Chartularium*, vol. 1, nos. 69–71, pp. 125–9; no. 75, pp. 133–4. Kibre, *Scholarly Privileges*, p. 94; Leff, *Paris and Oxford Universities*, p. 31; Rashdall, *Universities*, vol. 1, p. 337. Given the confusion in a number of accounts, it should be noted that Philip the Chancellor and Philippe de Grève were different people; see N. Wicki, 'Introduction', in *Philippi Cancellarii Parisiensis Summa de Bono*, ed. N. Wicki (Bern, 1985), pp. 11*–13*.

[37] *Chartularium*, vol. 1, nos. 79–95, pp. 136–47. Rashdall, *Universities*, vol. 1, pp. 337–40.

[38] *Chartularium*, vol. 1, no. 79, pp. 136–9. The relevant sources are not identified in *Les Registres de Grégoire IX*, ed. L. Auvray, 4 vols. (Paris, 1896–1955), vol. 1, no. 607, cols. 385–8. Verger, however, referred to 'l'extraordinaire préambule' and noted 'les images bibliques', in 'A propos de la naissance de l'université de Paris', p. 83.

[39] Joshua 15.15. Judges 1.11. Cariath Sepher was regarded as a place where many races came together, and comparisons with Paris were therefore drawn; see B. Smalley,

gratiosa, in qua utique tamquam in officina sapientie speciali *habet argentum venarum suarum principia, et auro locus est in quo rite conflatur,*[40] ex quibus *prudentes eloquii mistici*[41] *murenulas aureas vermiculatas argento*[42] cudentes et fabricantes monilia ornata lapidibus pretiosis, immo nulli pretio comparandis sponsam Christi decorant et decorant. Ibi *ferrum de terra tollitur,*[43] quia dum terrena fragilitas fortitudine solidatur, lorica fidei, gladius spiritus et cetera inde fit christiane militie armatura, potens adversus aereas potestates. Et *lapis calore solutus in es vertitur,*[44] quia corda lapidea Sancti Spiritus afflata fervore dum ardent, incendunt et fiunt predicatione sonora preconantia laudes Christi.

This dense passage is difficult to translate, not least because the final line is open to two possible interpretations that are given as alternatives below.[45]

Paris, parent of sciences, like another *Cariath Sepher, city of letters*, and precious, shines forth. It is great indeed but concerning itself raises hopes for greater things that are pleasing to those who teach and those who learn, where, surely as if in wisdom's special workshop, *there is a mine for silver, and a place for gold which they refine*, from which those *prudent in mystical eloquence*, stamping *ornaments of gold, studded with silver*, and making necklaces elaborately, adorn and make beautiful the bride of Christ with precious stones, or rather stones beyond price. There *iron is taken out of the earth*, because when its earthly fragility is solidified by firmness, from it is made the breastplate of faith, the sword of the spirit, and other armour of Christian soldiery, potent against the aerial powers. And *copper is smelted from the ore*, because while stony hearts burn, blown on by the fervour of the Holy Spirit, they take fire ...

a. and are made to proclaim the praises of Christ with resonant preaching. [or/and]
b. and by preaching are made resonant, proclaiming the praises of Christ.[46]

'Studies on the Commentaries of Cardinal Stephen Langton (part II)', *Archives d'histoire doctrinale et littéraire du moyen âge* 5 (1930): 152–82 at 164.

40 Job 28.1.

41 Rupert of Deutz, *De Gloria et Honore Filii Hominis Super Mattheum*, ed. H. Haacke, Corpus Christianorum Continuatio Mediaevalis 29 (Turnhout, 1979), book 3, p. 72.

42 Song of Songs 1.10.

43 Job 28.2. 44 Job 28.2.

45 Modern translations differ at various points in the passage. Although I have not followed him entirely, I owe a debt to Thorndike, *University Records*, no. 19, p. 36. I am especially grateful, however, to Professor Gillian Clark and Professor David d'Avray for their learned and generous advice on the meaning of this passage.

46 In version a, 'sonora' is taken to be ablative singular with 'praedicatione'. This is how Thorndike reads the line, offering 'while stony hearts flame with the fervour of the Holy Spirit, they take fire and are made to herald praises of Christ in sounding preaching'. In version b, 'sonora' is understood to be neuter plural referring back to 'corda'.

In a way the message was plainly stated. The university was associated with wisdom, and it was credited with producing precious adornments for the spouse of Christ, in other words the church. It also manufactured the armour and weaponry that the church needed in its fight against evil. The first element of complexity came with the final line. Read one way, those who studied at the university were transformed by the Holy Spirit to become preachers. Read another way, they were transformed by preaching as well as the Holy Spirit. Both readings make grammatical sense, so it is likely that both occurred to contemporaries and were perhaps intended by those responsible for the text. There is therefore a double meaning rather than ambiguity: university scholars were transformed into preachers by preaching.

There was, however, a great deal more to this opening passage. Embedded within it was a string of quotations from the Old Testament: Joshua, Judges, Song of Songs, and above all Job. There was also a phrase from a work by Rupert of Deutz. While it is impossible to be certain that it was taken directly from there, Rupert had commented on and deployed several of the passages of the Old Testament quoted in *Parens scientiarum*, so there may be a connection awaiting further explanation.[47] More importantly, there were also verbal echoes of Gregory the Great's *Moralia in Job*, an authoritative work with which many members of the university were bound to be familiar, and upon which the opening passage of the bull clearly drew for its essential themes.[48] In a general sense, this use of authorities enhanced the dignity of the university, and indeed Gregory IX had used biblical texts to bolster the standing of the university in a number of his letters since 1229.[49] More specifically, however, two messages were driven home.

First, *Parens scientiarum* clearly gestured towards the monastic view of learning. The opening passage contained a line from the Song of Songs, the text upon which learned monks so often worked. The only

[47] Rupert had commented on Judges 1.11 and Song of Songs 1.10, and used Judges 1.11 and Job 28.1 in commentaries on other biblical texts. See *De Sancta Trinitate et Operibus Eius Libri X–XXVI*, ed. H. Haacke, Corpus Christianorum Continuatio Medievalis 22 (Turnhout, 1972), book 21, pp. 1147–8 (Judges 1.11); *Commentaria in Canticum Canticorum*, ed. H. Haacke, Corpus Christianorum Continuatio Medievalis 26 (Turnhout, 1974), book 1, pp. 28–9 (Song of Songs 1.10) and book 6, pp. 149–50 (Judges 1.12); *De Sancta Trinitate et Operibus Eius Libri I–IX*, ed. H. Haacke, Corpus Christianorum Continuatio Medievalis 21 (Turnhout, 1971), book 5, p. 332 (Job 28.1).

[48] Gregory, *Moralia in Iob Libri XI–XXII*, ed. M. Adriaen, Corpus Christianorum Series Latina 143A, (Turnhout, 1979), 18.26–8, pp. 910–15. S. Gregory the Great, *Morals on the Book of Job*, ed. C. Marriott, 3 vols. (Oxford, 1844–7), vol. 2, pp. 343–8.

[49] *Chartularium*, vol. 1, nos. 69–70, pp.125–8; no. 75, pp. 133–4.

'contemporary' writer to be quoted, Rupert of Deutz, was a monk. Much more significantly, however, three quotations were taken from Job 28.1–2, and Gregory the Great's commentary on this passage was highly pertinent. He began his discussion of Job 28.1, 'there is a mine for silver, and a place for gold which they refine', by remarking: 'In silver eloquence is customarily designated, in gold brightness of life or of wisdom.'[50] He went on to attack heretics whose pride led them to neglect the sacred books, and to repeat Paul's injunction to avoid 'profane novelties of speaking'.[51] In the context of learning, Gregory's emphasis on the importance of a good life, and his distrust of pride and novelty, had much in common with the monastic critique of the twelfth-century schools. By associating the university with an authoritative expression of this complex of ideas, *Parens scientiarum* stressed the way in which it had taken on board the monastic ideals of learning, and repeated the message conveyed by the 1215 statutes.

Second, *Parens scientiarum* introduced a theme that had been missing from the 1215 statutes: the idea of transformation. Monks like William of Saint Thierry had envisaged radical transformation in their ascents to God, and now transformation re-entered the frame. In a way this was another nod to monastic ways of thinking, except that a very different transformation was envisaged. The university was not directly responsible for transforming the individual soul in its relationship with God. Rather *Parens scientiarum* highlighted a transformation that revolved around preaching. In particular it stressed the way in which the university served the church by turning men into preachers, and Gregory the Great's commentary on Job underpinned this theme too. Commenting on the lines from Job quoted in *Parens scientiarum*, Gregory the Great stressed the importance of the unity of the church and, building on the line 'iron is taken out of the earth' (Job 28.2), deployed martial imagery to advocate the defence of the faith. Above all, he took the theme of transformation from the words of Job and applied them to the process of becoming a preacher.

Ferrum de terra tollitur. Ac si aperte dicat: Fortes uiri qui acutissimis linguarum gladiis in hac acie defendendae fidei ferrum fiunt, aliquando terra in infimis actionibus fuerunt. Peccanti quippe homini dictum est: *Terra es et in terram ibis.* Sed de terra ferrum tollitur, cum fortis propugnator Ecclesiae a terrena quam prius tenuit actione separatur. Non ergo in eo debet despici quicquid

[50] Gregory, *Moralia in Job*, 18.26, p. 910: 'In argento eloquium, in auro uitae uel sapientiae claritas designari solet.' I have preferred my own translation in this instance.

[51] I Timothy 6.20, 'O Timothee, depositum custodi, deuitans profanas uocum nouitates,' as quoted by Gregory, *Moralia in Job*, 18.26, p. 911. Gregory the Great, *Morals on the Book of Job*, vol. 2, p. 344.

fuit, qui iam coepit esse quod non fuit. An non Matthaeus in terra inuentus est, qui terrenis negotiis implicatus telonii usibus seruiebat? Sed de terra tultus, in fortitudine ferri conualuit, cuius uidelicet lingua quasi acutissimo gladio euangelii administratione Dominus infidelium corda transfixit; et qui infirmus prius despectusque fuerat per terrena negotia, fortis postmodum factus est ad caelestia praedicamenta.
Vnde adhuc subiungitur:
Et lapis solutus calore, in aes uertitur. Tunc lapis calore soluitur, cum cor durum atque a diuini amoris igne frigidum eodem diuini amoris igne tangitur, et in feruore spiritus liquatur, ut ad sequentem uitam desideriorum aestu ardeat, quam prius audiens insensibilis manebat. Ex quo ardore scilicet et emollitur ad amorem, et roboratur ad operationem; ut sicut prius durus fuerat in amore saeculi, ita se postmodum fortem exserat in amorem Dei; et quod ante audire renuebat, iam et credere et praedicare incipiat. *Lapis ergo solutus calore, in aes uertitur,* quia dura mens superni amoris igne liquefacta ad ueram fortitudinem commutatur, ut peccator qui prius insensibilis exstiterat, postmodum et per auctoritatem fortis et per praedicationem sonorus fiat.[52]

Iron is taken out of the earth.
As if he said in plain speech: 'men of strength, who by the sharpest swords of their tongues are become iron in this pitched battle of the defending of the faith, were one time but 'earth' in the lowest sphere of actions.' For to man on his sinning it was spoken; *Earth thou art, and unto earth shalt thou return.* But 'iron is taken out of the earth,' when the hardy champion of the Church is separated from an earthly course of conduct, which he before maintained. Accordingly he ought not to be contemned in any thing whatever, that he was, who has already begun to be that which he was not. Was not Matthew found in the earth, who, involved in earthly matters, served the business of the receipt of custom? But having been taken out of the earth, he was strengthened into the forcibleness of iron, in that by his tongue, as by the sharpest sword, the Lord in the enforcing of the Gospel pierced the hearts of unbelievers. And he that before was weak and contemptible by his earthly occupations, was afterwards made strong for heavenly preachings. Hence it is yet further subjoined;
And the stone being melted with heat is turned into brass.
Then is 'the stone dissolved with heat,' when the heart that is hard and cold to the fire of divine love is touched by that same fire of divine love, and melted in the glowing warmth of the Spirit, that to the life that follows it should burn with the heat of its longings, which life on hearing of before, it remained uninfluenced. By the power of which same heat, he is at once softened down to love and invigorated to practice, that as before he was hard in the love of the world, so he should afterwards give himself out strong unto the love of God, and what he declined to give ear to before, he should henceforth begin both to believe and to preach. And so, *the stone being dissolved with heat is turned into*

[52] Gregory, *Moralia in Job*, 18.27–8, p. 914.

> *brass*, because the hardened mind, being melted by the fire of love from Above, is changed to true strength. So that the sinner that was before unmoved should afterwards be made at once strong in respect of authority, and sounding in respect of preaching.[53]

The last line of this passage, 'ut peccator qui prius insensibilis exstiterat, postmodum et per auctoritatem fortis et per praedicationem sonorus fiat', could be deemed to have the same ambiguity or double meaning as *Parens scientiarum*. The translation quoted above, 'So that the sinner that was before unmoved should afterwards be made at once strong in respect of authority, and sounding in respect of preaching', has the sinner transformed into a preacher, but he could also be 'made strong by authority and resonant by preaching'. Earlier in the passage, however, there is no such possibility: 'fortis postmodum factus est ad caelestia praedicamenta' (translated above as 'he ... was afterwards made strong for heavenly preachings') and 'et quod ante audire renuebat, iam et credere et praedicare incipiat' ('and what he declined to give ear to before, he should henceforth begin both to believe and to preach') both clearly indicate a transformation that produces preachers.

The opening passage of *Parens scientiarum* was clearly modelled on Gregory's *Moralia in Job*. Relatively succinct in itself, it thus invoked a much more substantial vision of the way in which men could be changed to become preachers. While true to the statutes of 1215 in its commitment to key monastic ideals, it added a strong statement of the transformative power of the university. Perhaps this emphasis on transformation owed something to monastic culture, but it also marked the university out as very different. *Parens scientiarum* explained that the university's transformative power enabled the university to produce preachers, and thus to assist the church in its pastoral mission. In part this was a response to the particular crisis that the pope had been working to resolve: the friars' refusal to suspend teaching and to disperse from Paris had generated tensions between the friars and the secular masters, and it made sense for the pope to stress their common purpose. But it was also a huge programmatic statement. This was not an isolated expression of the university's obligation to train preachers, and preaching was soon established as an enduring feature of university life. Moreover, the Parisian masters of theology in the late twelfth and early thirteenth centuries repeatedly asserted their deep commitment to preaching, as a technique by which they would teach their students, as a key aspect of the pastoral work that they would teach their students

[53] Gregory the Great, *Morals on the Book of Job*, vol. 2, pp. 347–8.

to perform, and as the means by which they and their students would bring about reform of both clergy and laity.[54] The opening of *Parens scientiarum* was the most public expression of their ideal. It also made the point that when people dealt with the students and masters of Paris, they had to realize that they were not dealing with a disorderly mob, whatever the immediate appearances, but with a body of great religious significance.

Parens scientiarum then tackled a series of issues that had caused problems in the past, beginning with the granting of teaching licences by the chancellor. Every chancellor had to take an oath only to grant licences to teach theology and canon law to those who were worthy. To establish whether or not a candidate was worthy, he had, 'in the presence of all masters of theology in the city and other respectable and learned men by whom the truth can be learned', to 'make diligent inquiry as to the life, knowledge, facility, and also the promise and hope of success and other points which are required in such cases'. For their part, masters of theology and canon law had to swear to 'furnish faithful testimony on the aforesaid points'. The chancellor was further bound to observe the confidentiality of these references. Regarding licences in arts and medicine, the chancellor made a similar promise to 'examine the masters in good faith' and 'admit only the deserving'.[55]

Next, the bull recognized the university's status as a legal corporation. They were granted 'the function of making due constitutions or ordinances' regarding a list of issues much like that contained in the 1215 statutes, and 'of duly punishing rebels against those constitutions or ordinances by expulsion from your society'. But Gregory went a step further than the 1215 statutes.

[54] For a wonderfully vivid and detailed account of the masters' engagement with preaching, see N. Bériou, *L'avènement des maîtres de la parole. La prédication à Paris au XIIIe siècle*, 2 vols. (Paris, 1998). For expressions of their commitment, see also J. W. Baldwin, *Masters, Princes and Merchants: The Social Views of Peter the Chanter and his Circle*, 2 vols. (Princeton, 1970), vol. 1, pp. 90–1, 107–16; Ferruolo, *Origins of the University*, pp. 184–277; P. Glorieux, 'L'enseignement au moyen âge: techniques et méthodes en usage à la faculté de théologie de Paris au xiiie siècle', *Archives d'histoire doctrinale et littéraire du moyen âge* 35 (1968): 65–186 at 148–61; J. Leclercq, 'Le magistère du prédicateur au xiiie siècle', *Archives d'histoire doctrinale et littéraire du moyen âge* 15 (1946): 105–47, esp. 138–47; J. Longère, *Oeuvres oratoires de maîtres parisiens au xiie siècle: étude historique et doctrinale*, 2 vols. (Paris, 1975), vol. 1, pp. 35–44, 390–8; R. H. Rouse and M. A. Rouse, *Preachers, Florilegia and Sermons: Studies on the Manipulus florum of Thomas of Ireland* (Toronto, 1979): 48–51, 65–87. On the role of the University of Paris in thirteenth-century mendicant preaching, see D. L. d'Avray, *The Preaching of the Friars: Sermons diffused from Paris before 1300* (Oxford, 1985), esp. pp. 132–203.

[55] *University Records*, no. 19, pp. 36–7.

And if it chance that the rental of lodgings is taken from you or that – which God forbid – injury or enormous excess be inflicted on you or any of you, such as death or mutilation of a limb, unless, after due complaint has been lodged, satisfaction is given within fifteen days, it shall be permitted to you to suspend lectures until condign satisfaction is given. And if any of you shall have been unjustly imprisoned, it shall be right for you, unless the injury ceases when complaint is made, to stop lectures immediately, if it shall seem expedient.[56]

Gregory thus acknowledged their right to strike, officially granting them the power that had been specifically denied in the statutes of 1215, and that had just proved so effective.

The way in which the bishop of Paris exercised his jurisdiction had caused many problems, and the bull now turned to this thorny matter. The bishop of Paris was ordered to punish wrongdoers in a manner such that 'the honour of the scholars is preserved and crimes do not remain unpunished'. Any scholar arrested on 'probable suspicion' had to be granted bail. If a scholar had to be incarcerated, it had to be in the bishop's prison because the chancellor was forbidden to have a prison. No scholar was to be arrested for debt. There was to be no charge for lifting a ban of excommunication. Returning to the licence to teach, the chancellor was not to exact any kind of oath or payment in return for the licence.[57] The bull made it clear, however, that the university had a responsibility to maintain order amongst its members. The summer vacation was not to last for more than a month, and bachelors were permitted to continue lecturing in that time. Scholars were not to bear arms in the town, and the university was not to defend 'disturbers of the peace and of studies'. Scholarly privileges were not to be accorded to men who pretended to be scholars but did not in fact go to classes or acknowledge any master.[58] In short, the university had to do its part to prevent rowdy behaviour escalating into a crisis, and to ensure that it did not inadvertently protect young men who were not studying at all. Doubtless this part of the bull addressed some of the concerns of the bishop, king and townspeople.

The bull then turned to the curriculum. It did not attempt to set out complete programmes of study for each subject; full regulations about what was to be studied, and how long was to be spent at each stage, were drawn up and frequently revised within the various faculties during the thirteenth century.[59] Two instructions were, however, given to masters

[56] *Ibid.*, p. 37. [57] *Ibid.*, pp. 37–8. [58] *Ibid.*, p. 38.

[59] For an excellent summary of a student's career, see J. Marenbon, *Later Medieval Philosophy (1150–1350)* (London, 1987, repr. 1996), pp. 20–4.

of arts. The first concerned the set texts to be used in ordinary lectures on grammar. The second offered the prospect that the ban on teaching Aristotelian natural philosophy might soon be relaxed: the prohibited books were not to be used until they had been 'examined and purged from all suspicion of errors', a task that was never in fact accomplished by the committee that Gregory subsequently established.[60] For those studying and teaching theology, a major issue was addressed. They were to 'strive to exercise themselves praiseworthily in the faculty which they profess and not show themselves philosophers but endeavour to know God' and to 'dispute in the schools concerning those questions only which can be settled by theological works and the treatises of the holy fathers'.[61] This was an attempt to define the subject matter and methods appropriate for study in the faculty of theology, and Gregory IX had already made his point to the masters of theology in a letter of 1228.[62]

There followed a section concerning the property of scholars who died without leaving a will. The bull established procedures for notifying the heirs and giving them the opportunity to claim the property, otherwise it was to be used for the benefit of the deceased's soul.[63] Finally, the bull called on the king to respect the privileges of the masters and students, and to fine those who wronged them. In making this point, the bull returned to its opening theme. The masters and students who had been wronged and who had left the university seemed 'to have pled not so much their own case as the common cause'. The pope gave his orders to the king 'with the general need and utility of the church in view'.[64] The university's privileges had to be respected because of its value to the whole church.

Having examined Philip Augustus' charter of 1200, the statutes of 1215, and *Parens scientiarum*, and the circumstances in which these documents were produced, it is clear that the students and masters of Paris were frequently treated as a single community, and that they were capable of collective action. More than that, the masters were recognized as

60 *Chartularium*, vol. 1, no. 87, pp. 143–4. For perceptive analysis of Gregory IX's intentions on this point, and the long-term significance of his actions, see L. Bianchi, *Censure et liberté intellectuelle à l'université de Paris (XIIIe–XIVe siècles)* (Paris, 1999), pp. 103–16; L. Bianchi, 'Aristotle as a captive bride: notes on Gregory IX's attitude towards Aristotelianism', in L. Honnefelder, R. Wood, M. Dreyer and M.-A. Aris (eds.), *Albertus Magnus und die Anfänge der Aristoteles-Rezeption im lateinischen Mittelalter: Von Richardis Rufus bis zu Franciscus de Mayronis, Albertus Magnus and the Beginnings of the Medieval Reception of Aristotle in the Latin West: From Richardus Rufus to Franciscus de Mayronis* (Münster, 2005), pp. 777–94.

61 *University Records*, no. 19, p. 38.

62 *Chartularium*, vol. 1, no. 59, pp. 114–16.

63 *University Records*, no. 19, pp. 38–9.

64 *Ibid.*, p. 39.

a legal corporation and exercised their powers accordingly. Within the university as a whole, there were groups studying and teaching the arts, theology, canon law and medicine.[65] Each student was also attached to a particular master. This does not, however, constitute a full picture of the way the university was developing, and it is important to grasp its rapidly growing complexity.

Most strikingly, the documents considered thus far made no mention of the nations that were emerging in the first decades of the thirteenth century. The masters of arts divided themselves into four nations, with arts students gaining affiliation by association with their masters. Exactly when and how this took place is not known: the earliest reference to the nations dates from 1222 and there is firm evidence for a well-developed system by 1249, but their composition and structure continued to evolve in the course of the thirteenth and early fourteenth centuries. The four nations were France, Picardy, Normandy and England. Each was a very rough and somewhat arbitrary geographical grouping. Thus by the early fourteenth century the French nation consisted of masters not only from the Ile de France but also from the south of France, Spain, Italy, Greece and the East. The masters of the Picard nation came from the north of France and the Low Countries. The Norman nation was made up of masters from Normandy and Brittany. The English nation included not only English masters but masters from Germany and elsewhere in northern and eastern Europe. Each nation was a distinct and largely autonomous corporation, with its own assembly, seal, statutes, financial arrangements, records and elected officials. Each nation elected a proctor who summoned and chaired the assembly, and carried out key administrative and disciplinary functions. The system was highly democratic in that proctors were entirely subject to their assemblies and held office for no more than a month or six weeks. Together the nations constituted the faculty of arts whose rector was elected by the proctors or four other representatives chosen by the nations. The rector's period of office was also limited to a month or six weeks until it was extended to three months in 1266. The nations were responsible for organizing the teaching in the arts faculty. They maintained the schools in which the arts students were taught, mostly on the Rue du Fouarre, or 'street of straw', so named because of the straw on which the students sat. They allocated teaching space to the masters,

[65] There was no formal teaching of Roman law because its study in Paris had been prohibited in 1219 by Pope Honorius III, who wished to ensure that the theologians' pre-eminence in Paris remained unchallenged. See *Chartularium*, vol. 1, no. 32, pp. 90–3.

collected fees from the students, and organized payment of the masters. Students were not, however, obliged to attend the schools of their own nation. Many other aspects of life also revolved around the nations. Each nation employed messengers, termed *nuntii volantes* or 'flying messengers', who travelled between Paris and the lands from which the scholars came, bearing letters, property and money. Eventually they also established arrangements with bankers and merchants in Paris, called *nuntii maiores* or 'greater messengers', who provided banking services for the masters and students of the nation, arranging the transfer of funds from their families in the territories of the nation, changing money and making loans. The nations also provided the focus for the religious life of their members. The nations celebrated their own patron saints. By the fourteenth century, and probably earlier, the nations made payments to their masters for attending masses and fined them if they failed to turn up. Unsurprisingly, many masters and students felt an overwhelming sense of loyalty to their nation. Throughout the thirteenth century there were conflicts between the nations, some of them extremely violent. They were usually caused by arguments about which nation a particular master should join, disputes over the election of the rector, or the French nation's resentment that it had no more power than each of the other nations even though it had many more members. In many respects the nations shaped the everyday lives of the majority of masters and students in the university.[66]

The faculty of arts developed at the same time as the nations of which it was composed. Its status as a legal corporation with an elected rector at its head was well established by the middle of the thirteenth century. The masters teaching theology, canon law and medicine remained informal groupings until the second half of the century when they too produced written statutes, acquired seals and elected officers, including deans to preside over them. It is impossible to offer statistical analysis of the university in the thirteenth century for lack of evidence; there are, for example, no matriculation records. Nevertheless, it is clear that the faculty of arts was far larger than the others. Taking students and masters together, it has been estimated that the faculty of arts made up about two-thirds of the university. As far as masters were concerned,

[66] Cobban, *Medieval Universities*, pp. 87–90; A. Gieysztot, 'Management and resources', in Ridder-Symoens (ed.), *Universities in the Middle Ages*, pp. 108–43 at 114–16; Kibre, *Nations*, pp. 14–28, 65–115; Leff, *Paris and Oxford Universities*, pp. 51–60; Pedersen, *The First Universities*, pp. 194–5; Rashdall, *Universities*, vol. 1, pp. 311–20, 408, 414–15, 420–1; H. de Ridder-Symoens, 'Mobility', in Ridder-Symoens (ed.), *Universities in the Middle Ages*, pp. 280–304 at 282–5; R. C. Schwinges, 'Student education, student life', in Ridder-Symoens (ed.), *Universities in the Middle Ages*, pp. 195–243 at 211.

there were probably never more than ten to sixteen in any one of the higher faculties at any one time, whereas there were probably well over a hundred arts masters. Perhaps because the faculty of arts was so much larger, and perhaps also because the other faculties developed so much later, the rector, the elected head of the faculty of arts, came increasingly to act as the head of the university as a whole. By the end of the thirteenth century, all four faculties were well established as independent corporations. There was, however, a measure of interpenetration. As already mentioned, many students and bachelors in the higher faculties were also masters of arts, and until they became masters in these higher faculties they remained members of their nations in the faculty of arts, at once subject to their jurisdiction and active participants in their governmental processes. Furthermore, students in the faculty of arts had to take an oath of obedience before they could become bachelors. In the developed form of this oath, they had to swear obedience to the rector, whatever their future position might be. Many of the secular masters in the higher faculties, as well as many of the students and bachelors, were therefore bound to the rector by this oath. The federal structure of the university was most strikingly revealed at its general assembly or congregation. It was composed of all the regent masters, chaired by the rector. When a matter required discussion, each nation of the faculty of arts and each of the higher faculties considered the matter separately. Their views were reported by their proctors or deans. The four nations and the three higher faculties cast one vote each, and the decision was carried by the majority of these seven votes.[67]

Within and sometimes cutting across the structure of faculties and nations, were a growing number of colleges. The earliest were charitable foundations, developed from or modelled on hospitals, and providing little more than basic accommodation and a small financial grant for a limited number of poor scholars. The first, which became known as the Collège des Dix-Huit, was set up in 1180 by an Englishman, Jocius of London, on his way back from a pilgrimage to Jerusalem. He visited the Hospital of the blessed Mary of Paris, and saw within it a room customarily occupied by poor clerks. Acting on the advice of the dean and chancellor of Paris, he purchased the room for the accommodation of

[67] Brundage, *Medieval Origins of the Legal Profession*, pp. 246–7; Cobban, *Medieval Universities*, pp. 84–6; Gieysztor, 'Management and resources', in Ridder-Symoens (ed.), *Universities in the Middle Ages*, pp. 109–13; Leff, *Paris and Oxford Universities*, pp. 52, 60–7; Pedersen, *The First Universities*, pp. 191–4, 196–8, 200–4; Rashdall, *Universities*, vol. 1, 321–34, 408–14; N. Siraisi, 'The faculty of medicine', in Ridder-Symoens (ed.), *Universities in the Middle Ages*, pp. 360–87 at 367–8; Verger, 'Patterns', in Ridder-Symoens (ed.), *Universities in the Middle Ages*, pp. 38, 52.

eighteen scholars who would also receive a monthly payment from the alms given to the hospital. In return, the scholars were obliged only to participate in the funerary rituals of those who died in the house and to say nightly prayers. Other colleges were soon established. Some of them admitted only scholars studying a particular subject. Thus the Collège de Sorbonne, founded around 1257 by the theologian Robert of Sorbon with the active support of Louis IX, provided initially for sixteen theology students, four from each nation, and later for a total of thirty-six. Other colleges only admitted scholars from a particular region. The College of the Treasurer, for example, was founded in 1268 to house and support twelve students of theology and twelve of the arts, all to be 'chosen, when the need arises, by the two archdeacons of Grand-Caux and Petit-Caux', and all to originate 'from Grand-Caux and Petit-Caux, if in those two places they find sufficient and fit persons, or if not in the two Caux, at least from the whole diocese of Rouen'.[68] Some of these later colleges were highly complex institutions. The Sorbonne in particular regulated the lives of its members in great detail and required them all to participate in its internal management by holding various offices in turn. It also gave a great deal of support to their studies, providing an excellent library and even running special classes for extra revision and practice. The overwhelming majority of students rented houses in groups, boarded with masters, or lodged with townspeople, but for a few the colleges provided essential material support and in some cases even dominated their domestic and scholarly routines.[69]

A much more challenging degree of complexity was presented by the growing involvement of the friars and other religious orders within the university.[70] The friars included some of the university's most

[68] *University Records*, no. 36, p. 76.

[69] A. B. Cobban, 'The role of colleges in the medieval universities of northern Europe, with special reference to France and England', *Bulletin of the John Rylands University Library of Manchester* 71 (1989): 49–70 at 51–3; Gieysztor, 'Management and resources', in Ridder-Symoens (ed.), *Universities in the Middle Ages*, pp. 116–19; P. Glorieux, *Les Origines du Collège de Sorbonne* (Notre Dame, IN, 1959), pp. 17–23; Pedersen, *The First Universities*, pp. 226–9; Rashdall, *Universities*, vol. 1, pp. 497–511; Schwinges, 'Student education, student life', in Ridder-Symoens (ed.), *Universities in the Middle Ages*, p. 214. See also *Chartularium*, vol. 1, pars introductoria, no. 50, pp. 49–50; no. 448, pp. 505–14; *University Records*, no. 10, pp. 21–2; no. 42, pp. 88–98.

[70] The following account is based on: Cobban, *Medieval Universities*, pp. 91–4; Kibre, *Scholarly Privileges*, pp. 103–18; Leff, *Paris and Oxford Universities*, pp. 34–47; P. R. McKeon, 'The status of the university of Paris as *Parens Scientiarum*: an episode in the development of its autonomy', *Speculum* 39 (1964): 651–75; Mulchahey, *'First the bow is bent'*, pp. 362–4; Pedersen, *The First Universities*, pp. 173–82; Rashdall, *Universities*, vol. 1, pp. 370–97; B. Roest, *A History of Franciscan Education (c. 1210–1517)* (Leiden, 2000), pp. 1–21, 53–8; A. G. Traver, 'Rewriting history? The Parisian secular masters' *Apologia* of 1254', *History of Universities* 15 (1997–9): 9–45.

outstanding theologians, but also threatened the means by which the emerging university was asserting its autonomy. Both the Franciscan and the Dominican orders expanded dramatically in the first two decades of the thirteenth century, espousing voluntary poverty and undertaking a universal preaching mission. Right from the start, the Dominicans valued learning and set out to establish themselves in Paris and Bologna. They developed a hierarchical system of schools within the order, with the best students ending up at one of their top schools. Unlike Dominic, Francis had not himself set much store by formal learning, and the Franciscans were much slower to establish a system of education. Before long, however, they too were active as scholars in Paris. Neither order permitted its members to study or teach in the faculty of arts; they came to Paris to study theology. The rest of the university made them welcome, and friars were taught by secular masters of theology. The Dominicans received the house of Saint Jacques and associated rights partly from Jean de Barastre, a secular master of theology who had been asked to teach in their school by Pope Honorius III, and partly from the university as a whole. The Franciscans set up a new convent, the Grand Couvent des Cordeliers, with financial assistance from the king. The friars were not, however, fully tied into the emerging structure of the university. Unless a friar had been a master of arts before converting, for example, he had not taken the oath to obey the statutes of the university that masters of arts took upon inception. As the university's structure emerged, and as the university acted to assert its privileges, such anomalies began to matter. A critical point was reached when the university went on strike in 1229: the friars refused to suspend their studies, and even opened their schools to secular students who wished to continue their studies in Paris. Moreover, Roland of Cremona was granted the first Dominican chair in theology. After the masters and students returned in 1231, the Dominicans kept their chair and the mendicant schools remained open to secular students. Tension mounted thereafter not only because the friars clearly could not be relied upon to support a strike, but also because their success was damaging the careers of the secular masters. The friars were attracting growing numbers of students, thus reducing the income received by the secular masters of theology. Moreover, by converting secular masters of theology, the friars gained more chairs. In 1231 Alexander of Hales entered the Franciscan order to become the first Franciscan master of theology at Paris. Around the same time John of Saint Giles dramatically took the habit of the Dominicans in the middle of a sermon, thus creating a second Dominican chair of theology. It is not known exactly how professorial succession functioned, but it was clearly accepted that when a chair fell vacant it passed to a master from the same order. When secular masters converted, they therefore reduced the number of chairs available for secular scholars, thus damaging their career opportunities.

The resentment felt by the secular scholars was soon combined with the sense of grievance held more widely by the secular clergy whose authority and income were diminished when friars, backed by successive popes, preached, heard confession and received pious donations from the laity. Longstanding resentment turned into bitter conflict during the 1250s. Apparently the friars deemed it inappropriate to ask for magisterial status, and the chancellor in 1250 effectively excluded them by only granting a teaching licence if petition were made. Pope Innocent IV ordered the chancellor to grant the licence to any member of a religious order whom he considered to be qualified, whether or not a request had been made. In 1252 the secular masters of theology passed a statute according to which a member of a religious order could only be admitted if his order had a college in Paris, and each college could only have one chair in theology, which threatened the second Dominican chair. At Lent in 1253 disorder in the streets resulted in the provost's men killing one scholar and arresting others. The university suspended studies until justice was done, but the mendicant masters refused to join the strike, seriously undermining its effect. When the university required all masters to take an oath to act together to obtain justice, the friars again refused and were expelled from the university. In April 1253, the university passed a statute obliging all masters to take an oath to obey the statutes and to go on strike when instructed by the university. The Franciscans eventually agreed, but the Dominicans did not. The Dominican masters were therefore not only expelled but also excommunicated. The Dominicans appealed to Innocent IV, who lifted the ban of excommunication and instructed the university to readmit the Dominicans. The university did not comply, however, and in 1254 it aired its complaints in a letter addressed to all the prelates and scholars in Christendom. The general resentment of the friars seemed to be having an effect when Innocent IV issued the bull *Etsi animarum*, withdrawing the privileges of the friars with regard to preaching and hearing confession. But Innocent died in December 1254, to be succeeded by Alexander IV who backed the friars in all respects. In April 1255 he came down hard on the University of Paris with the bull *Quasi lignum vitae*. In it he ordered the reinstatement of the Dominican masters. He instructed the chancellor to grant the teaching licence to as many qualified candidates as he saw fit, thus removing the limit that had been placed on the number of masters from religious orders. Finally, he ruled that studies could only be suspended when such action had the support of two-thirds of the masters in each faculty, which, because of their numbers in the faculty of theology, ensured that the friars and the other religious orders could prevent the university going on strike. When the university refused to obey, all the masters and scholars were excommunicated. They responded by announcing the dissolution of the university and giving up all privileges that had been granted to it, so that there was now no body to which the friars could be readmitted.

The escalating conflict was accompanied by a polemical battle of increasing bitterness. Secular masters attacked the ideals of voluntary poverty that underpinned the mendicant orders. They also sought the condemnation of the *Liber introductorius in evangelium aeternum* ('Introduction to the Eternal Gospel'), a work written by a Franciscan studying in Paris called Gerard of Borgo San Donnino, in which he built on the apocalyptic theories of Joachim of Fiore to argue that the Bible had been superseded by the works of Joachim and the clergy by the friars. The most vocal secular master was William of Saint Amour, whose *De periculis novissimorum temporum* ('On the Perils of the Last Times') was condemned by the pope in 1256. During the second half of the decade, the secular masters were worn down by constant papal pressure, one after the other accepting the terms of *Quasi lignum vitae* and seeking absolution. The founding of the College of the Sorbonne was probably a constructive attempt to address the anxieties of the secular theologians in a manner that would not lead to more conflict. After Alexander IV's death in 1261, his successor, Urban IV, adopted a much more conciliatory attitude, confirming the privileges of the university. It was apparently accepted that the Dominicans should have two regent masters of theology, while the other religious orders could only have one. This was, however, a very uneasy compromise, no more stable than before the open conflicts of the 1250s. Those conflicts had brought about one very significant shift: the university had previously received almost unqualified papal backing in its struggles to be free of episcopal authority, but now the secular masters and students had been on the wrong end of papal authority, while establishing common cause with secular bishops and clergy in their opposition to the friars. The university's role in ecclesiastical politics was never again to be as straightforward as it had been in the first half of the thirteenth century. Moreover, the tensions between the secular members of the university and the friars remained, and were to flare up on many future occasions. It was impossible to escape from the problems caused by the friars and members of other religious orders who wished to be part of the university and yet to retain their identity as members of wider religious communities.

The secular students and masters were not, however, 'pure' members of the university, unconnected with the wider world. On the contrary, their need for financial support constantly reminded them of the groups to which they belonged or with which they were associated outside the university. The cost of university education was high, and probably increased from the middle of the thirteenth century. Many scholars depended on their families for money and material assistance. Most were from lesser noble families or the wealthy urban classes. Great noble families rarely sent their sons to university until much later. Few from the peasantry or the poorer urban classes could find the means to attend university, and even fewer could stay at university for long enough to become masters in the higher faculties, though there were some striking exceptions. Model letters reflect the way in which scholars found it necessary to seek assistance from their parents, siblings and clerical uncles. Another source of income was the holding of ecclesiastical benefices. A scholar might be permitted to employ another cleric to do the work while he himself was non-resident because he was at university. He paid less than the income he received, and kept the difference for himself. It is not known how many students and masters were funded in this way, but successive popes strongly encouraged the practice. In 1219, for example, Honorius III issued the bull *Super speculam*, permitting clerics to be non-resident for five years while studying theology at Paris, a privilege that was soon applied to other universities. Many popes granted benefices to individuals so that they might continue their studies, though whether or not an individual actually received his benefice depended on the local bishop's readiness to comply with papal wishes. Popes were even prepared to allow some scholars to hold more than one benefice at the same time, a financial necessity if the income from a single benefice was insufficient. From the early fourteenth century, universities regularly sent the pope ranked lists, or rolls (*rotuli*), of candidates for benefices. This funding mechanism was used to support not only theologians, but also men studying the arts and canon law. Many scholars therefore held offices in churches outside Paris and, despite their non-residence, were drawn into the local politics of the communities of which they were now members. Financial support was also provided by wealthy patrons. Royal backing could be very generous. While Henry III of England directed most of his educational patronage to Oxford, he nevertheless gave money to several Parisian students. At the end of the thirteenth century, Philip IV of France made systematic payments to scholars at Paris, as well as to two colleges, and it may be that this practice had begun earlier in the century. Other patrons included nobles, high-ranking churchmen, prominent townspeople and rich academics. Sometimes they simply funded individuals for a period of time. On occasion, however, especially in their wills, they established 'flying scholarships', or *bursae volantes*. Income from property or invested capital was used to provide grants to scholars, termed 'flying scholarships' because the holder did not have to live in a specific college. Usually, however, certain conditions had to be met: these might include coming from a particular area, attending a specific university, studying a particular subject, being studious or being poor. Financial management and responsibility for selecting holders was generally placed in the hands of the founder's family or representatives of an ecclesiastical institution. To give just one example, in her will of 1273 Margaret, countess of Flanders and Hainaut, left £300 from which the annual income was to be given to students from Flanders and Hainaut studying at Paris as chosen by either the chancellor of Paris, the Dominican prior, a representative of the Franciscans, or by two of these three. While patrons may have been primarily motivated by charity, the recipients of their generosity were bound to feel informal ties of obligation and to be drawn into the political, regional or ecclesiastical networks through which patronage operated.[71]

There was another important respect in which students and masters looked beyond the university to a wider world: very few scholars spent their entire lives at university. Most students studied for only a few years, with no intention of 'completing' the formal course. Only a tiny minority went on to teach as masters, and many masters left after a brief spell as regents, often the minimum required by the statutes. A relatively small number of secular masters of theology spent their whole

[71] J. W. Baldwin, 'Masters at Paris from 1179 to 1215: a social perspective', in R. L. Benson and G. Constable (eds.), *Renaissance and Renewal in the Twelfth Century* (Oxford, 1982), pp. 138–72 at 150–1; J. Dunbabin, 'Meeting the costs of university education in northern France, *c.* 1240–*c.* 1340', *History of Universities* 10 (1991): 1–27; C. H. Haskins, 'The life of mediaeval students as illustrated by their letters', in *Studies in Mediaeval Culture* (Oxford, 1929), pp. 1–35, as revised and expanded from *American Historical Review* 3 (1898): 203–29; Leff, *Paris and Oxford Universities*, pp. 67–8; J. Paquet, 'Coût des études, pauvreté et labeur: fonctions et métiers d'étudiants au moyen âge', *History of Universities* 2 (1982): 15–52; Pedersen, *The First Universities*, pp. 216–21; F. Pegues, 'Royal support of students in the thirteenth century', *Speculum* 31 (1956): 454–62; F. Pegues, 'Ecclesiastical provisions for the support of students in the thirteenth century', *Church History* 26 (1957): 307–18; Schwinges, 'Student education, student life', in Ridder-Symoens (ed.), *Universities in the Middle Ages*, pp. 240–1; P. Trio, 'Financing of university students in the middle ages: a new orientation', *History of Universities* 4 (1984): 1–24; J. Verger, 'Teachers', in Ridder-Symoens (ed.), *Universities in the Middle Ages*, pp. 144–68 at 151.

careers as regent masters. Otherwise, even those who enjoyed substantial teaching careers usually departed well before the end of their working lives. Some went to take up teaching posts elsewhere, but increasing numbers worked in secular and ecclesiastical government. Masters had extremely good career prospects in the church, many becoming prelates, and others taking up positions in cathedral chapters. The French and English kings also employed increasing numbers of men who could claim the title of 'master', with the English kings using them in far greater numbers for most of the thirteenth century. It is much harder to track the careers of those who did not become masters, but there is little doubt that many of them staffed the growing bureaucracies of ecclesiastical and secular government.[72] In some cases this basic career pattern has made it possible for historians to explore the role of ideas in politics by studying both the academic work of individual scholars and their subsequent actions in high office.[73] It also meant that the university had a substantial number of alumni, some of whom were very powerful men. In the fourteenth century there were occasions when the university tried to force such men to act in the university's interests by reminding them of oaths they had taken to uphold the university's privileges and statutes, and charging them with perjury when they did not take the steps required of them.[74] No such case is known in the thirteenth century, but there were frequent contacts between the university and its former members, and occasions when the latter looked to the university for support. In the 1280s bitter conflict again broke out between the secular clergy of France and the friars. The secular clergy maintained that, despite papal privileges permitting friars to preach and hear confession without authorization from the local clergy, all members of the church were still bound to confess all their sins to their own

[72] R. Avi-Yonah, 'Career trends of Parisian masters of theology, 1200–1320', *History of Universities* 6 (1986–7): 47–64; J. W. Baldwin, '*Studium et Regnum*: the penetration of university personnel into French and English administration at the turn of the twelfth and thirteenth centuries', *Revue des études islamiques* 44 (1976): 199–215; Baldwin, 'Masters at Paris', pp. 138–72; W. J. Courtenay, *Teaching Careers at the University of Paris in the Thirteenth and Fourteenth Centuries* (Notre Dame, IN, 1988); Leff, *Paris and Oxford Universities*, pp. 6–8.

[73] The pioneering work of this kind was B. Smalley, *The Becket Conflict and the Schools: A Study of Intellectuals in Politics* (Oxford, 1973). Recent outstanding examples include: J. Dunbabin, *A Hound of God: Pierre de la Palud and the Fourteenth-Century Church* (Oxford, 1991); W. C. Jordan, *Unceasing Strife, Unending Fear: Jacques de Thérines and the Freedom of the Church in the Age of the Last Capetians* (Princeton, 2005).

[74] P. Kibre, 'Academic oaths at the university of Paris in the middle ages', in J. H. Mundy, R. W. Emery and B. N. Nelson (eds.), *Essays in Medieval Life and Thought: presented in Honor of Austin Patterson Evans* (New York, 1955), pp. 123–37.

parish priests every year. Both the friars and the secular clergy wanted to be able to claim the support of the university. In 1286 the prelates of the kingdom of France met at Paris and summoned all the masters and students from all the faculties to hear their case. Four archbishops and twenty bishops were present. The archbishop of Bourges, Simon of Beaulieu, explained that they had come to complain to the masters and students about the friars' insolence 'because what we are, you will be; for I believe that there is not a prelate amongst us today who has not been taken from this university'.[75] Clearly the archbishop expected the masters and students to look into their own futures, and to identify with the interests of the secular prelates. Earlier in the century, Robert of Courson had been well aware of the extent to which this might be the case, and had made it clear that to study theology in order to achieve promotion to a prelacy was to commit mental simony.[76] Many, however, were attracted to the university precisely because of the career opportunities that they expected or hoped to be on offer as a result.[77] Even those who espoused the ideals of *Parens scientiarum* expected men transformed by the university to leave. The university was always fundamentally outward-looking.

The university that emerged in Paris in the late twelfth century and continued to develop throughout the thirteenth century was radically different from the schools that had preceded it. The university had become established as a corporation enjoying privileges granted by the king and pope. Students undertook programmes of study which, if they chose to complete them and if they did so successfully, led to the award of degrees. The degree qualified the master to teach, and he was obliged to do so for a minimum period, so the system perpetuated itself, turning the most successful students into masters through a systematic process of scholarly formation. Masters, rather than students, now had control. While there might still be competition for students, they were no longer the decisive source of funding, and they no longer made and broke magisterial careers. Students advanced their careers not by competing with their masters, but by competing with each other, in large part for the approval of their masters. They accepted the authority of their masters because they hoped to wield the same authority in their turn. The time it took to gain academic credibility was critical. The

[75] *Chartularium*, vol. 2, no. 539, pp. 8–11. See I. P. Wei, 'The masters of theology at the university of Paris in the late thirteenth and early fourteenth centuries: an authority beyond the schools', *Bulletin of the John Rylands University Library of Manchester* 75 (1993): 37–63 at 44–7, 51.

[76] Baldwin, 'Masters at Paris', p. 153, n. 67.

[77] Cobban, 'Medieval student power', pp. 29–30.

twelfth-century student felt that he was ready to assume magisterial status so quickly that he could rival his master, and the master had no means of restraining him, and limited power to offer eventual reward. The thirteenth-century student was slowed down by the structured curriculum and the need to overcome the series of obstacles that led to degrees, and the master could make him wait as he went through that sequence of stages before eventually enjoying magisterial status in the next academic generation.[78]

Every aspect of both study and life was regulated by the institution, and this institutional regulation was of huge ideological significance. Beginning with the statutes of 1215, the university's formal documents adopted key monastic values with regard to learning: the belief that only by living virtuously was it possible to think properly, and that masters had to accept responsibility for their impact on their students. In 1231 *Parens scientiarum* added the powerful vision of the university transforming the men who studied there, turning them into preachers. These formal pronouncements gave the university ideological security, freeing the scholars from the monastic critiques of the twelfth century. In so doing, it also opened the university up to monks and friars. Whatever the ideological debt to monastic culture, however, the secular masters and students were not turned into monks. The university was an extremely complex community of communities, offering masters and students a range of identities. The university as a whole was a single community. Within it, there were other communities, and communities within communities, and communities overlapping with each other: faculties, nations and colleges. There were also communities that straddled the university's conceptual boundaries: the friars and the other religious orders. All of these communities were solemnly defined, with legal privileges and rules, and capable of collective action. Formal documents drew up boundaries, created rituals of great symbolic importance, established routine practices, and claimed loyalty at times of crisis, constructing powerful identities for their members. Underpinning all these structures, each master was surrounded by the students who gained admission to the university by association with him. Individuals, moreover, were members of groups that existed with varying degrees of formality primarily outside the university: families, local churches and patronage networks. Former members of the university offered a vision of the careers that might be taken up when men

[78] Pierre Bourdieu's analysis of Parisian academia in the mid twentieth century presents the dynamic perfectly; see P. Bourdieu, *Homo Academicus*, trans. P. Collier (Cambridge, 1988), pp. 87–90.

left the university, and suggested their future interests. Being a member of the university therefore meant very different things for different men. The multiplicity of communities did not go unnoticed. Philip the Chancellor, who held office at the time of the 'great dispersion' in 1229, complained in a sermon that to make a *universitas* out of diverse nations was to create a monster. It was a monster with four heads, namely the four faculties.[79]

Unsurprisingly, in view of its structural disjunctures, the university environment was at times highly volatile. There were moments of conflict when individual masters and students had to decide where their loyalties lay: when nation fell out with nation, when secular clerics felt threatened by the friars, or when students brawled with townspeople, to give a few of the most common examples. It might seem as if the instability of the twelfth-century schools had not entirely disappeared, but that would be to underestimate the extent to which, through a process of institutionalization, the university had become a locus of power and authority, both within the institution itself and in relation to the rest of society. Individuals were tied into the corporate structure by statutes and oaths. If a man stayed in the university for any length of time, he soon acquired a stake in its continued existence. As he worked his way through the curriculum and up the career ladder, he took on responsibility for teaching, and assumed offices within the various communities of which he was a member, thus gaining status and authority. Whatever the individual's fate, however, the major conflicts had become collective rather than individual. There was, moreover, a permanence to the university as a community, and to the manifold communities that it embraced. However desperate the rhetoric of the moment, after the 'great dispersion' ended in 1231 the existence of the various corporate bodies was not seriously threatened. The university was culturally distinct, protected by a discourse that combined monastic ideals with a bold claim to transform men into agents of the church's pastoral mission, and it was not going to go away.

The intellectual excitement of the twelfth-century schools is readily detected in narrative accounts of particular lives, some of which were explored in the first chapter. The thirteenth-century university generated no such material, but the mountain of academic work that survives in written form testifies to the intellectual commitment of its scholars. Aristotle's philosophical and scientific works were still being

[79] Haskins, *Studies in Mediaeval Culture*, p. 61, n. 2; Michaud-Quantin, *Universitas*, p. 55, n. 72; J. Schneyer, *Die Sittenkritik in den Predigten Philipps des Kanzlers*, Beiträge zur Geschichte der Philosophie und Theologie des Mittelalters 39/4 (Münster, 1962), pp. 90–1.

rediscovered and translated from Greek and Arabic, and they were read and interpreted in conjunction with the work of Arab and Jewish scholars who had already grappled with these texts. There are many fine surveys of developments in philosophical and theological thought in the thirteenth century, and just as many brilliant monographs on individual thinkers. The focus here will be on two figures whose influence on others was recognized in the thirteenth century and later, and who articulated different approaches to knowing. Bonaventure was deeply influenced by Augustine and in many respects represented the theological mainstream in the thirteenth century, although there has been much disagreement about the nature of his response to Aristotle and the extent to which he incorporated Aristotelian ideas.[80] Thomas Aquinas, however, unquestionably made systematic use of Aristotle to create a powerful synthesis of different traditions.

Bonaventure

Bonaventure was born, the son of a doctor, in central Italy, in the town of Bagnoregio, between 1217 and 1221. Although Bonaventure never met Francis, he believed that he had been cured of a childhood illness when his mother called upon Francis to come to his aid. As he put it in the prologue to one of two lives of Francis that he later wrote, 'I recognize that God saved my life through him, and I realize that I have experienced his power in my very person.'[81] Bonaventure was probably educated by Franciscans in his home town before going to Paris to study the arts in the mid 1230s. He entered the Franciscan order in 1243, when he began his studies in theology. From 1253 he was in effect a regent master of theology, although as a result of the conflicts between the secular masters and the friars he did not formally receive the title until the pope insisted that it be granted in 1257. In that year he was elected minister general of the order, which plunged him into the thick of the

[80] Bonaventure has been variously interpreted as resistant to the fundamentals of Aristotelian thought, only partially informed about Aristotelian thought and therefore eclectic in his use of what he knew, and incorporating Aristotelian thought in an original fashion. For these views, see respectively: E. Gilson, *The Philosophy of Bonaventure*, trans. I. Trethowan and F. J. Sheed (London, 1938); F. Van Steenberghen, *Aristotle in the West: The Origins of Latin Aristotelianism*, trans. L. Johnston (Louvain, 1955); J. F. Quinn, *The Historical Constitution of St Bonaventure's Philosophy* (Toronto, 1973). For an incisive summary, see M. Haren, *Medieval Thought: The Western Intellectual Tradition from Antiquity to the Thirteenth Century*, 2nd edn (Toronto, 1992), pp. 165–6.

[81] Bonaventure, *The Life of St Francis (Legenda Maior)*, in Bonaventure, *The Soul's Journey into God; The Tree of Life; The Life of St Francis*, trans. E. Cousins (New York, 1978), p. 182.

controversy that was splitting the Franciscan order. As the order had developed, it had become difficult to adhere strictly and literally to the ideals of poverty that Francis had espoused. The order could not hope to carry out its preaching mission on an international scale if it did not have buildings, books and other material resources. Compromises had therefore been made, and those who accepted them were known as the Conventuals. Other members of the order, the Spiritual Franciscans, regarded these compromises as a betrayal of Francis. Some of them had also taken up the prophecies of Joachim of Fiore, identifying themselves as the new religious order that would come to the fore in the last age before the end of the world. Bonaventure's predecessor as minister general, John of Parma, was amongst them, and he was forced to resign by Pope Alexander IV. Bonaventure's formidable task was therefore to hold the order together by persuading as many as possible that the institutionalization of the order was consistent with a legitimate interpretation of the ideals of Francis, while dealing forcefully with those Spirituals who continued to dissent. As minister general, Bonaventure was based in Paris but travelled widely. He remained involved in university affairs, preaching on many occasions to university audiences. In 1273 Pope Gregory X made him a cardinal. He was heavily involved in preparations for the Council of Lyons in 1274, and played an active part in it. He died suddenly in July 1274 while the Council was still in progress.[82]

Bonaventure produced a very readable and succinct overview of his thinking in *The Soul's Journey into God*, which he wrote in 1259, having sought inspiration on Mount La Verna where Francis had received the stigmata. Francis had also experienced a vision of a seraph between whose six wings Christ had appeared on the cross, and this vision directly informed Bonaventure's writing:

> While I was there reflecting on various ways by which the soul ascends to God, there came to mind, among other things, the miracle which had occurred to blessed Francis in this very place: the vision of a winged Seraph in the form of the Crucified. While reflecting on this, I saw at once that this vision represented our father's rapture in contemplation and the road by which this rapture is reached. The six wings of the Seraph can rightly be taken to symbolize the six levels of illumination by which, as if by steps or stages, the soul can pass over to peace through ecstatic elevations of Christian wisdom.[83]

[82] For the life of Bonaventure, see E. H. Cousins, *Bonaventure and the Coincidence of Opposites* (Chicago, 1978), pp. 29–43; C. M. Cullen, *Bonaventure* (Oxford, 2006), pp. 3–14; Z. Hayes, *Bonaventure: Mystical Writings* (New York, 1999), pp. 16–18.

[83] Bonaventure, *The Soul's Journey into God*, in Bonaventure, *The Soul's Journey into God; The Tree of Life; The Life of St Francis*, Prologue, 2–3, p. 54.

The Soul's Journey into God consists of a Prologue and seven chapters. The first six chapters describe the six stages of an ascent to God, while the seventh chapter concerns the final goal. The work is relatively short, but highly complex in structure and imagery. There are several organizing principles, which vary in significance at different stages. To complicate matters further, Bonaventure's emphasis was upon synthesis and he cross-referenced from one part of the ascent to another, bringing out key themes repeatedly. He also assumed familiarity with basic ideas, and compressed his account of them accordingly.[84]

Nevertheless Bonaventure made the work accessible by repeatedly stressing one basic structure. The ascent was divided into three parts: first, looking outwards to discover vestiges of God in the material world (chapters 1 and 2); second, looking inwards to find God's image in the spirit (chapters 3 and 4); and third, looking above to contemplate God through two of his names, Being and Good (chapters 5 and 6). In so far as this programme was divided into looking outwards, inwards and above, and in so far as the first two stages concerned vestiges and image respectively, it owed much to Augustine and Hugh of Saint Victor, and it was reassuringly familiar.[85] It was briefly articulated in the titles of chapters and at various points in the text, for example in chapter 1:

> In order to contemplate the First Principle, who is most spiritual, eternal and above us, we must pass through his vestiges, which are material, temporal and outside us ... We must also enter into our soul, which is God's image, everlasting, spiritual and within us ... We must go beyond to what is eternal, most spiritual and above us, by gazing upon the First Principle.[86]

Or again a little further on in the chapter:

> our mind has three principal perceptual orientations. The first is toward exterior material objects and is the basis for its being designated as animal and sensual. The second orientation is within itself and into itself and is the basis for its being designated as spirit. The third is above itself and is the basis for its being designated as mind.[87]

Bonaventure had used and discussed more fully the distinctions between looking outwards, inwards and above in his earlier *Breviloquium*. There he had not only related the first two stages to vestige and image respectively, but had also defined the third stage in terms of similitude.

[84] D. Turner, *The Darkness of God: Negativity in Christian Mysticism* (Cambridge, 1995), p. 103, esp. n. 5.
[85] *Ibid.*, p. 108; Hayes, *Bonaventure*, pp. 54–6.
[86] Bonaventure, *The Soul's Journey*, 1.2, p. 60. See also 5.1, p. 94 and 7.1, pp. 110–11.
[87] *Ibid.*, 1.4, p. 61.

the creation of the world is a kind of book in which the Trinity shines forth, is represented and found as the fabricator of the universe in three modes of expression, namely, in the modes of vestige, image, and similitude, such that the reason for the vestige is found in all creatures, the reason for the image in intelligent creatures or rational spirits alone, and the reason for the similitude in the Godlike alone. Hence, as if by certain steplike levels, the human intellect is born to ascend by gradations to the supreme principle, which is God.[88]

That vestige, image and similitude corresponded to looking outwards, inwards and above was made clear when Bonaventure expanded on what he now called man's triple vision.

Because of this triple vision man receives a triple eye, as Hugh of St Victor says, the eye of the flesh, the eye of reason, and the eye of contemplation: the eye of the flesh by which he sees the world and those things that are in the world, the eye of reason by which he sees the soul and those things that are in the soul, the eye of contemplation by which he sees God and those things that are in God. Thus by the eye of the flesh man sees those things that are outside himself, by the eye of reason those things that are within himself, and by the eye of contemplation those things that are above himself.[89]

Did the third stage of the ascent in *The Soul's Journey into God*, chapters 5 and 6, concern similitude? This is where the work turns out to be much more difficult than it seems at first. In *The Soul's Journey into God*, Bonaventure only used the term 'similitude' with reference to the third section once, when summarizing the ascent in chapter 7.[90] This caution is understandable because the distinction that he made between image and similitude in the *Breviloquium* and earlier in his *Commentary on the Sentences* corresponded to the distinction that he made between chapters 3 and 4, within the second section on image, in *The Soul's Journey into God*.[91] On the other hand, the third section was in some sense about similitude because it concerned Being and Good, the two names of God held by Pseudo-Denys to be 'the highest "conceptual" names of God, the most "similar" of the similarities of God'.[92] Indeed, it has been convincingly argued that the three stages of *The Soul's Journey into God* correspond to Pseudo-Denys' notions of symbolic theology, representational theology and conceptual theology.[93] Bonaventure himself further reinforced his structure by relating it to 'the threefold mode of

[88] Bonaventure, *Breviloquium*, trans. E. E. Nemmers (St Louis, 1946), 2.12.1, p. 75.
[89] *Ibid.*, 2.12.5, p. 76.
[90] Bonaventure, *The Soul's Journey*, 7.1, p. 111.
[91] *Breviloquium*, 2.12, pp. 75–7. Bonaventure, *Commentaria in quatuor libros sententiarum magistri Petri Lombardi*, 2; *Opera Omnia*, 2 (Quaracchi, 1885), pp. 404–6. Turner, *Darkness of God*, pp. 110–11.
[92] Turner, *Darkness of God*, p. 114. [93] *Ibid.*, pp. 114–15.

theology: symbolic, literal and mystical, so that through the symbolic we may rightly use sensible things, through the literal we may rightly use intelligible things and through the mystical we may be lifted above to ecstasy'.[94]

The three parts of the ascent became six when each was divided into two. As far as vestige and image were concerned, this depended on a distinction between 'through' and 'in'. God was contemplated first *through* his vestiges in chapter 1, then *in* his vestiges in chapter 2. He was contemplated first *through* his image in chapter 3, then *in* his image in chapter 4. *The Soul's Journey into God* offers very little explanation of what this distinction means, observing of the three parts:

> Any one of these ways can be doubled, according to whether we consider God as *the Alpha and the Omega* (Apoc. 1.8). Or in each of these ways we can see him through a mirror or in a mirror. Or we can consider each way independently or as joined to another.[95]

Bonaventure had, however, explained this distinction in his *Commentary on the Sentences*:

> To know God *in* a creature is to know his presence and in-flowing in a creature ... But to know God *through* a creature is to be raised from knowledge of the creature to knowledge of God as if by a ladder joining them.[96]

While knowing God *through* his vestiges or his image was to be linked to God by them, it was also in a sense to be separated from God by them. It was thus to remain at a distance from God, whereas knowing God *in* his vestiges or his image was to encounter God's presence in the vestige or image, and so to get much closer.[97] When the third stage was divided to become chapters 5 and 6, the distinction between 'through' and 'in' was preserved in the chapter titles – 'On contemplating the most divine unity *through* its primary name which is Being' and 'On contemplating the most blessed Trinity *in* its name which is Good' – but nothing in the text indicates that it still held any significance for Bonaventure. There was, however, another reason for dividing the ascent into six stages: they could be related to the six powers of the soul.

> Just as there are six stages in the ascent into God, there are six stages in the powers of the soul, through which we ascend from the lowest to the highest,

94 Bonaventure, *The Soul's Journey*, 1.7, pp. 62–3.
95 *Ibid.*, 1.5, p. 61.
96 Bonaventure, *Commentaria in quatuor libros sententiarum magistri Petri Lombardi*, 1; *Opera Omnia*, 1 (Quaracchi, 1882), p. 74. My translation, but see Turner, *Darkness of God*, p. 109.
97 See Turner, *Darkness of God*, p. 109.

from the exterior to the interior, from the temporal to the eternal. These are the senses, imagination, reason, understanding, intelligence, and the summit of the mind or the spark of conscience.[98]

To grasp Bonaventure's approach more fully, however, it is necessary to examine each stage in turn.

In the Prologue and the first part of chapter 1, Bonaventure set out the conditions that had to be met before the ascent could be attempted. It was necessary to desire God:

For no one is in any way disposed for divine contemplation that leads to mystical ecstasy unless like Daniel he is a *man of desires* (Daniel 9.23).[99]

Divine assistance was required, and prayer was therefore essential:

But we cannot rise above ourselves unless a higher power lift us up. No matter how much our interior progress is ordered, nothing will come of it unless accompanied by divine aid. Divine aid is available to those who seek it from their hearts, humbly and devoutly; and this means to sigh for it in this valley of tears, through fervent prayer. Prayer, then, is the mother and source of the ascent.[100]

Unsurprisingly *The Soul's Journey into God* was at many points itself a work of prayer. In addition to prayer, Bonaventure stressed the importance of leading a virtuous life:

Whoever wishes to ascend to God must first avoid sin, which deforms our nature, then exercise his natural powers mentioned above: by praying, to receive restoring grace; by a good life, to receive purifying justice; by meditating, to receive illuminating knowledge; and by contemplating, to receive perfecting wisdom.[101]

The value of scholarly endeavour was also limited:

First, therefore, I invite the reader to the groans of prayer through Christ crucified, through whose blood we are cleansed from the filth of vice – so that he not believe that reading is sufficient without unction, speculation without devotion, investigation without wonder, observation without joy, work without piety, knowledge without love, understanding without humility, endeavour without grace, reflection as a mirror without divinely inspired wisdom.[102]

The central importance of Christ was emphasized throughout: 'All this is done through Jesus Christ.'[103] Bonaventure's approach was very much

[98] Bonaventure, *The Soul's Journey*, 1.6, p. 62. See also *Breviloquium*, 5.6.6, p. 160.
[99] Bonaventure, *The Soul's Journey*, Prologue, 3, p. 55.
[100] *Ibid.*, 1.1, pp. 59–60. [101] *Ibid.*, 1.8, p. 63.
[102] *Ibid.*, Prologue, 4, pp. 55–6. [103] *Ibid.*, 1.7, p. 62.

in line with that taken by monks like Bernard of Clairvaux and William of Saint Thierry, and by Hugh of Saint Victor in the twelfth century.

In the first two chapters, Bonaventure discussed how sense-based knowledge of the material world could lead to knowledge of God. The first chapter was entitled 'On the stages of the ascent into God and on contemplating him through his vestiges in the universe'. Bonaventure invited his reader to see 'the whole material world as a mirror through which we may pass over to God, the supreme Craftsman'.[104] His point was that God had created the universe. As a result everything in it was a vestige, literally a footprint, of God, reflecting his nature in some way. Sense-based knowledge of the created world could therefore be used by the intellect to gain some sort of understanding of the divine, and this in three ways:

> The Creator's supreme power, wisdom and benevolence shine forth in created things, as the bodily senses convey this to the interior senses in three ways. For the bodily senses assist the intellect when it investigates rationally, believes faithfully or contemplates intellectually. In contemplating, it considers the actual existence of things; in believing, the habitual course of things; and in reasoning, the potential excellence of things.[105]

First, by contemplation, things were considered 'in themselves', for example with regard to weight, number and measure. This could lead to 'knowledge of the immense power, wisdom and goodness of the Creator'.[106] Second, by faith, the world was considered with regard to its creation, sacred history and final end. This prompted thoughts of God's power, providence and justice.[107] Third, by reason, a series of hierarchies were perceived in the created world, all indicating the existence of divine perfection. For example, it could be seen 'that some things are changeable and corruptible, as are earthly bodies; others are changeable and incorruptible, as are heavenly bodies. From this [one] realises that other things are unchangeable and incorruptible, as are supercelestial realities'.[108] Sense-based knowledge was therefore valuable because, used correctly, it led to consideration of 'the power, wisdom and goodness of God as existing, living, intelligent, purely spiritual, incorruptible and unchangeable'.[109]

Chapter 2, entitled 'On contemplating God in his vestiges in the sense world', was also about sense-based knowledge, but Bonaventure now focused on the process by which sensory perception produced

[104] *Ibid.*, 1.9, p. 63. [105] *Ibid.*, 1.10, pp. 63–4.
[106] *Ibid.*, 1.11, p. 64. [107] *Ibid.*, 1.12, p. 64.
[108] *Ibid.*, 1.13, p. 64. [109] *Ibid.*, pp. 64–5.

knowledge rather than on what was perceived and known about. There were three stages in the process. The first stage was apprehension in which likenesses (or species) of sensed objects entered the soul.[110] This resulted in the second stage which was pleasure. The senses took delight in an object perceived through its likeness because of its beauty in the case of sight, its sweetness in the case of smell and hearing, or its wholesomeness in the case of taste and smell. Pleasure was based on proportion. Proportion could occur in three ways: with regard to form when there was a proper relationship between the likeness and the sensed object; with regard to power when the likeness did not overwhelm the relevant sense, for 'the senses are pained by extremes and delighted in the mean'; with regard to operation when the likeness satisfied a need on the part of the recipient.[111] The third stage was judgement, which meant understanding why pleasure was experienced. The key was 'the proportion of harmony', which Bonaventure explained in terms of abstraction from the particular and the material:

> The basis of harmony is the same in large and small objects; neither is it increased by size nor does it change or pass away as things pass away, nor is it altered by motion. It abstracts, therefore, from place, time and motion, and consequently is unchangeable, unlimited, endless and is completely spiritual.[112]

Bonaventure's point was that judgements could only be made in the light of eternal truths, and eternal truth was only to be found in God.

> judgment leads us to see eternal truths more surely. Judgment takes place through our reason abstracting from place, time and mutability, and thus from dimension, succession and change, through reason which is unchangeable, unlimited and endless. But nothing is absolutely unchangeable, unlimited and endless unless it is eternal. Everything that is eternal is either God or in God. If, therefore, everything which we judge with certainty we judge by such a reason, then it is clear that he himself is the reason of all things and the infallible rule and light of truth, in which all things shine forth infallibly, indelibly, indubitably, irrefutably, indisputably, unchangeably, boundlessly, endlessly, indivisibly and intellectually. Therefore those laws by which we judge with certainty about all sensible things that come under our consideration – since they are infallible and cannot be doubted by the intellect of the one who apprehends them, since they are as if ever present and cannot be erased from the memory of the one who recalls them, since they cannot be refuted or judged by the intellect of the one who judges because, as Augustine says, 'no one passes judgment

[110] For a full account of how Bonaventure understood this process, see Gilson, *Philosophy of Bonaventure*, pp. 341–403; Quinn, *Historical Constitution of St Bonaventure's Philosophy*, pp. 370–4.

[111] Bonaventure, *The Soul's Journey*, 2.5, p. 71.

[112] *Ibid.*, 2.6, p. 72.

on them, but by them' – these laws must be unchangeable and incorruptible since they are necessary; boundless since they are without limits; and endless since they are eternal – and for this reason they must be indivisible since they are intellectual and incorporeal, not made, but uncreated, existing eternally in the Eternal Art, by which, through which and according to which all beautiful things are formed. Therefore we cannot judge with certainty except in view of the Eternal Art which is the form that not only produces all things but also conserves and distinguishes all things, as the being which sustains the form in all things and the rule which directs all things. Through it our mind judges all things that enter it through the senses.[113]

In short, correct use of sensory perceptions depended on eternal laws that were part of the divine. To understand this was to take a step closer to God. In this light, Bonaventure attached a particular significance to numbers:

Since, therefore, all things are beautiful and in some way pleasurable, and since beauty and pleasure do not exist without proportion, and since proportion exists primarily in numbers, all things must necessarily involve numbers. Thus 'number is the foremost exemplar in the mind of the Creator', and in things, the foremost vestige leading to Wisdom.[114]

This does much to explain Bonaventure's relentless exposition of numerical patterns throughout *The Soul's Journey*, only a few of which are described here.

At the beginning of chapter 3, entitled 'On contemplating God through his image stamped upon our natural powers', Bonaventure called upon the reader to look inwards and use reason to find the image of God, and of the Trinity in particular. Sensory perception was to play no part. The key was to understand that the soul had three powers, memory, intellect and will: 'Consider, therefore, the operations and relationships of these three powers, and you will be able to see God through yourself as through an image, which is to see through a mirror in an obscure manner.'[115]

By memory, Bonaventure meant a great deal more than recollection of the past. The function of memory was threefold, to 'retain and represent … successive, simple and eternal things'.[116] With regard to successive things, the memory retained 'the past by remembrance, the present by reception and the future by foresight'.[117] It was therefore 'an image of eternity, whose indivisible presence extends to all times'.[118]

[113] *Ibid.*, 2.9, pp. 73–4.
[114] *Ibid.*, 2.10, p. 75; quoting Boethius, *De institutione arithmetica*, I.2.
[115] Bonaventure, *The Soul's Journey*, 3.1, p. 80.
[116] *Ibid.*, 3.2, p. 80. [117] *Ibid.*
[118] *Ibid.*, pp. 80–1.

By simple things, Bonaventure meant such things as 'the principles of continuous and discrete quantities like the point, the instant and the unit', which we might call basic mathematical and physical concepts.[119] Bonaventure stressed that knowledge of such principles could not be based on sense perception, and so the memory was clearly informed 'from above'.[120] By eternal things, Bonaventure meant 'the principles and axioms of the sciences, as everlasting truths held everlastingly'. These were self-evident principles that anyone would accept upon hearing them. Bonaventure cited examples from Aristotle: 'On any matter, one must either affirm or deny', and 'Every whole is greater than its part.'[121] These truths were innate, and showed that 'the memory has an unchangeable light present to itself in which it remembers immutable truths'.[122] The three activities of the memory demonstrated that 'the soul itself is an image of God and a likeness so present to itself and having God so present that the soul actually grasps him'.[123]

The intellect also had a triple function, to understand terms, propositions and inferences. Understanding terms meant understanding definitions of things. In order to convey the true nature of a thing, definitions had to use more universal terms. Understanding these terms then required the use of still more universal terms until the most universal term was reached. This meant that ultimately no particular thing could be adequately defined without an understanding of being itself. Being could be thought of in many ways short of perfection, but knowing that they were deficient was impossible without awareness of what was in no way deficient. The intellect therefore had to possess knowledge of perfect being, which was God:

> Since privations and defects can in no way be known except through something positive, our intellect does not come to the point of understanding any created being by a full analysis unless it is aided by a knowledge of the Being which is most pure, most actual, most complete and absolute, which is unqualified and Eternal Being, in which are the principles of all things in their purity. How could the intellect know that a particular being is defective and incomplete if it had no knowledge of the Being which is free from all defect?[124]

Propositions were understood when they were known with certitude to be true. That meant knowing that the truth could not be different, in other words that it was unchangeable. The human mind, however,

119 *Ibid.*, p. 80. 120 *Ibid.*, p. 81.

121 *Ibid.*, p. 80. Derived from Aristotle, *Metaphysics*, 4.15.4 (1006a 1–29) and 5.30.25 (1023b 12–36).

122 Bonaventure, *The Soul's Journey*, 3.2, p. 81.

123 *Ibid.* 124 *Ibid.*, 3.3, pp. 81–2.

was changeable, so it could only recognize the unchangeable 'by means of some light which shines in an absolutely unchangeable way'.[125] To understand an inference was to realize that 'the conclusion follows necessarily from the premises'. An inference differed from a proposition in that it might concern the contingent. Bonaventure's example was: 'If a man is running, the man is moving.' This was clearly true whether or not there was an actual man running, so the necessity of the inference did not derive from any existing thing. Nor did it derive from the existence of something in the soul alone, as that would be a fiction. The necessity of the inference could only derive from 'its exemplarity in the Eternal Art'.[126] Having examined the three functions of the intellect, Bonaventure concluded that 'it is obvious that our intellect is joined to Eternal Truth itself since it can grasp no truth with certitude if it is not taught by this Truth'.[127]

The will also had three functions, namely deliberation, judgement and desire. Deliberation involved asking 'which is better, this or that?' But it was impossible to know that one thing was better than another without knowing that it was more like the best, and this required knowledge of the best. It followed that 'the notion of the highest good is necessarily imprinted in everyone who deliberates'.[128] Judgement made with certainty had to be based on some law. Moreover, one had to be certain that the law was right and that one should not judge the law. If the law came from the mind, the mind would be entitled to judge it, so the law had be higher that the mind. The only thing higher than the human mind was its creator. It followed that 'in judging, our deliberative power touches the divine laws if it reaches a solution by a full analysis'.[129] Desire had to be understood in terms of the pursuit of happiness. True happiness was only to be found in 'the best and ultimate end'. Human desire therefore sought 'nothing except the highest good or what leads to or has some likeness to it'. Those whose desire was not ordered in this fashion were 'deceived and in error'.[130]

Bonaventure's analysis of memory, intellect and will had demonstrated the way in which the divine image was to be found within:

> See, therefore, how close the soul is to God, and how, in their operations, the memory leads to eternity, the understanding to truth and the power of choice to the highest good.[131]

[125] *Ibid.*, p. 82. [126] *Ibid.*, pp. 82–3.
[127] *Ibid.*, p. 83. [128] *Ibid.*, 3.4, p. 83.
[129] *Ibid.* [130] *Ibid.*, p. 84. [131] *Ibid.*

Moreover, Bonaventure believed that the 'order, origin and interrelatedness' of the three powers reflected the nature of the Trinity:

From memory, intelligence comes forth as its offspring, since we understand when a likeness which is in the memory leaps into the eye of the intellect in the form of a word. From memory and intelligence love is breathed forth as their mutual bond. These three – the generating mind, the word and love – are in the soul as memory, understanding and will, which are consubstantial, coequal and coeval, and interpenetrate each other. If, then, God is a perfect spirit, he has memory, understanding and will; and he has the Word generated and Love breathed forth, which are necessarily distinct since one is produced by the other – not in order of essence, nor in the order of accident, therefore in the order of persons. When, therefore, the soul considers itself, it rises through itself as through a mirror to behold the blessed Trinity of the Father, the Word and Love: three persons, coeternal, coequal and consubstantial.[132]

Bonaventure then commented on the importance of learning. He noted that the sciences were extremely helpful when the soul looked inwards in the way that he had been describing. Moreover, the sciences themselves reflected the Trinity. Philosophy as a whole was made up of natural philosophy, rational philosophy and moral philosophy. 'The first deals with the cause of being and therefore leads to the power of the Father; the second deals with the basis of understanding and therefore leads to the wisdom of the Word; the third deals with the order of living and therefore leads to the goodness of the Holy Spirit.'[133] Each of the three branches could be further subdivided into three parts: natural philosophy into metaphysics, mathematics and physics; rational philosophy into grammar, logic and rhetoric; and moral philosophy into individual, domestic and political. In each case Bonaventure found a likeness to the Trinity. Bonaventure thus deployed philosophy at a stage in the ascent when sense perception was useless, and reason was needed to explore the workings of the mind. If the process of interior scrutiny went well, there was much to be learned about God.

All these sciences have certain and infallible rules, like rays of light shining down upon our mind from the eternal law. And thus our mind, illumined and flooded by such brilliance, unless it is blind, can be led through itself to contemplate that Eternal Light. The radiation and contemplation of this Light lifts up the wise in wonder; and on the contrary it leads to confusion the fools who do not believe so that they may understand.[134]

But why were some minds blind, and why were there fools, as mentioned in the last line that so clearly echoed Anselm? Why was it so

132 *Ibid.*, 3.5, p. 84.
133 *Ibid.*, 3.6, pp. 84–5.
134 *Ibid.*, 3.7, p. 85.

difficult for most people to appreciate what Bonaventure presented as startlingly obvious? Earlier in the chapter Bonaventure had warned that sensory perceptions and the wrong kind of desire could easily obscure the image of God: 'You can see … through yourself the Truth which teaches you, if your desires and sensory images do not hinder you and interpose themselves like clouds between you and the rays of Truth.'[135] He repeated this point at the start of chapter 4, adding the distraction of worldly cares:

It seems amazing when it has been shown that God is so close to our souls that so few should be aware of the First Principle within themselves. Yet the reason is close at hand: for the human mind, distracted by cares does not enter into itself through memory; clouded by sense images, it does not turn back to itself through intelligence; allured away by concupiscence, it does not turn back to itself through desire for inner sweetness and spiritual joy. Thus lying totally in these things of sense, it cannot reenter into itself as into the image of God.[136]

This failure was unsurprising given the sinful state into which the human race had fallen. To get close to God, his help was required. While that was always in a sense the case, it was in the fourth chapter that it became the defining characteristic and essential basis of a stage in the ascent.

Chapter 4, entitled 'On contemplating God in his image reformed by the gifts of grace', considered the way in which the soul could be reformed by grace. The key was Christ:

When one has fallen down, he must lie there unless someone lend a helping hand for him to rise. So our soul could not rise completely from these things of sense to see itself and the Eternal Truth in itself unless Truth, assuming human nature in Christ, had become a ladder, restoring the first ladder that had been broken in Adam. Therefore, no matter how enlightened one may be by the light of natural and acquired knowledge, he cannot enter into himself to delight within himself in the Lord unless Christ be his mediator.[137]

When the soul, as image of God, was reformed, it was 'purified, illumined and perfected' by the three theological virtues, faith, hope and love. By their means, the soul recovered its spiritual senses so that it could see, hear, smell, taste and embrace its spouse, and sing the Song of Songs 'which was composed for the exercise of contemplation in this fourth stage'. All this was 'more a matter of affective experience than rational consideration'.[138] The soul was 'prepared for spiritual ecstasy through devotion, admiration and exultation', each of which

[135] *Ibid.*, 3.3, p. 83. [136] *Ibid.*, 4.1, p. 87.
[137] *Ibid.*, 4.2, pp. 87–8. [138] *Ibid.*, 4.3, p. 89.

was expressed in a passage from the Song of Songs.[139] As a result of the effect of grace, the soul itself was ordered hierarchically: 'When this is achieved, our spirit is made hierarchical in order to mount upward, according to its conformity to the heavenly Jerusalem which no man enters unless it first descend into his heart through grace.'[140] It was then possible to contemplate God within: 'From all this, God is seen as all in all when we contemplate him in our minds, where he dwells through the gifts of the most abundant charity'.[141] A different kind of scholarship was now appropriate: 'For this stage of contemplation the study of the divinely imparted Scripture is especially helpful just as philosophy is for the preceding stage.'[142] The transition from the third to the fourth stage in the ascent was crucial. It marked the shift from nature to grace, from the rational to the affective, and from the study of philosophy to the study of the Bible. It divided the six-stage ascent into two halves, creating a binary structure in addition to the tripartite one which Bonaventure preferred to stress.

At the opening of the fifth chapter, however, the tripartite structure returned to the fore:

> We can contemplate God not only outside us and within us, but also above us: outside through his vestiges, within through his image and above through the light which shines upon our minds, which is the light of Eternal Truth.[143]

Chapters 1 and 2 had looked outwards, chapters 3 and 4 had looked within, and now chapters 5 and 6 would look above. They did so by examining two names for God, each of which had been called God's primary name by a different authority. Chapter 5 contemplated God as Being, with the emphasis on the Old Testament and God's unity, while chapter 6 considered God as Good, with its main focus on the New Testament and the Trinity.

Chapter 5 was entitled 'On contemplating the divine unity through its primary name which is Being'. Having outlined his programme for chapters 5 and 6, Bonaventure proceeded to explain that 'being itself is so certain in itself that it cannot be thought not to be'. He based his thinking on a comparison between being and non-being. His key point was that non-being was 'the privation of being', so it could only be understood in terms of being. Being, on the other hand, was not understood in terms of something else because everything that was understood was understood as non-being or a form of being. Moreover, every

[139] *Ibid.* [140] *Ibid.*, 4.4, p. 90.
[141] *Ibid.*, pp. 90–1. [142] *Ibid.*, 4.5, p. 91.
[143] *Ibid.*, 5.1, p. 94.

limited form of being, a particular being for example, was understood in terms of pure being. Since non-being could only be understood in terms of being, and every type of being in terms of pure being, it followed that pure, divine being was 'what first comes into the intellect'.[144] As the first thing to enter the intellect, being was therefore the means by which all other knowing was possible, and yet the intellect struggled to grasp this:

Strange, then, is the blindness of the intellect, which does not consider that which it sees first and without which it can know nothing.[145]

Bonaventure made a comparison with light: the eye saw things by means of light, but either did not see light itself or did not notice it.

Thus our mind, accustomed to the darkness of beings and the images of the things of sense, when it glimpses the light of the supreme Being, seems to itself to see nothing. It does not realize that this very darkness is the supreme illumination of our mind, just as when the eye sees pure light, it seems to itself to see nothing.[146]

Bonaventure then considered the nature of pure being, stressing that it was 'eternal, utterly simple, most actual, most perfect and supremely one'.[147] Calling on the reader to wonder, he described being itself in a series of paradoxes, using pairs of adjectives, some of which were apparently contradictory:

But you have something here to lift you up in wonder, for Being itself is first and last; it is eternal and most present; it is utterly simple and the greatest; it is most actual and most unchangeable; it is most perfect and most immense; it is supremely one and yet all-inclusive.[148]

Moreover, within each pair, being was one thing because it was the other. At this stage, this was something that was open to explanation. Thus, to take the first two pairs mentioned above:

If you wonder at this with a pure mind, you will be flooded with a greater light when you see further that it is last because it is first. For because it is first, it does all things for itself; and therefore it must necessarily be the ultimate end, the beginning and the consummation, the Alpha and the Omega. It is most present precisely because it is eternal. For because it is eternal, it does not flow from another, nor of itself cease to be, nor pass from one state to another; therefore it has neither past nor future, but only present being.[149]

144 *Ibid.*, 5.3, p. 96. 145 *Ibid.*, 5.4, p. 96.
146 *Ibid.*, pp. 96–7. 147 *Ibid.*, 5.5, p. 97.
148 *Ibid.*, 5.7, p. 98. 149 *Ibid.*, pp. 98–9.

Gradually, however, Bonaventure moved from paradoxes that could be explained to contradictions that could not:

> Because it is eternal and most present, it therefore encompasses and enters all duration as if it were at one and the same time its centre and its circumference. Because it is utterly simple and the greatest, it is, therefore, totally within all things and totally outside them.[150]

Bonaventure was adopting an apophatic strategy that highlighted the inadequacy of human language in describing God, and the need to break language down to advance beyond its limitations.

The sixth chapter was entitled 'On contemplating the most blessed Trinity in its name which is Good'. Echoing Anselm's *Proslogion*, Bonaventure asserted that 'the highest good is without qualification that than which no greater can be thought', and that 'it cannot rightly be thought not to be, since to be is in all ways better than not to be'. Turning then to the Trinity, he further claimed that the highest good 'cannot rightly be thought of unless it be thought of as three in one'.[151] He based this claim on the Dionysian view of good as self-diffusive: 'For good is said to be self-diffusive; therefore the highest good must be most self-diffusive.' His argument further depended on the notion that there was a hierarchy of types of love. First, love of another was superior to love of self, so a second person was required in God. But then it was better for two people to share their love with yet another, so there had to be a third person in God. God had to have, as Bonaventure put it, a 'beloved and a cobeloved'. These second and third persons could not, however, be part of God's creation because 'the diffusion in time in creation is no more than a centre or point in relation to the immensity of the divine goodness'. If one thought of diffusion from God to the created world, one could think of another diffusion greater than this, 'namely, one in which the one diffusing communicates to the other his entire substance and nature'. And, since being was superior to not being, such diffusion had actually to exist. In other words, there had genuinely to be second and third persons in God, if God was to be the highest good and supremely self-diffusive.[152]

Immediately, however, Bonaventure recognized that he was not simply presenting an argument to be followed.

> But when you contemplate these things, do not think that you comprehend the incomprehensible.[153]

[150] *Ibid.*, 5.8, p. 100. [151] *Ibid.*, 6.2, pp. 102–3.
[152] *Ibid.*, pp. 103–4. See Hayes, *Bonaventure*, pp. 108–11.
[153] Bonaventure, *The Soul's Journey*, 6.3, pp. 104–5.

He called upon the reader to wonder at the nature of the Trinity, once again adopting an apophatic strategy and offering a series of paradoxes.

For here is supreme communicability with individuality of persons, supreme consubstantiality with plurality of hypostases, supreme configurability with distinct personality, supreme coequality with degree, supreme coeternity with emanation, supreme mutual intimacy with mission. Who would not be lifted up in admiration at the sight of such marvels?[154]

Bonaventure then switched his focus to Christ, inviting the reader to wonder at 'the superwonderful union of God and man in the unity of the Person of Christ'.[155] Contemplation of God as Being had already led to a series of wonder-inducing paradoxes, and now it was necessary to consider that in the divine Being 'is joined the First Principle with the last, God with man, who was formed on the sixth day; the eternal is joined with temporal man, born of the Virgin in the fullness of time, the most simple with the most composite, the most actual with the one who suffered supremely and died, the most perfect and immense with the lowly, the supreme and all-inclusive one with a composite individual distinct from the others, that is, the man Jesus Christ.'[156] Similarly, it was necessary to add to the paradoxes that resulted from contemplating God as Good, wondering that 'in Christ personal union exists with a trinity of substances and a duality of natures; that complete agreement exists with a plurality of wills; that mutual predication of God and man exists with a plurality of properties; that coadoration exists with a plurality of excellence; that coexaltation above all things exists with a plurality of dignity; that codomination exists with a plurality of powers'.[157] Now, at the sixth stage, 'the perfection of the mind's illumination' had been reached.[158]

That left only the goal of the journey, described in the seventh chapter, entitled 'On spiritual and mystical ecstasy in which rest is given to our intellect when through ecstasy our affection passes over entirely into God'. Having found God outside itself, within itself, and above itself, the mind had now to look beyond itself, 'to transcend and pass over not only this sense world but even itself'.[159] Christ was the means by which this might be accomplished, as had been shown to Francis on Mount La Verna. At this critical juncture the intellect had to be abandoned, and it was love alone that took the final step:

[154] *Ibid.*, p. 105. [155] *Ibid.*, 6.4, p. 106.
[156] *Ibid.*, 6.5, p. 107. [157] *Ibid.*, 6.6, p. 108.
[158] *Ibid.*, 6.7, p. 108. [159] *Ibid.*, 7.1, p. 111.

In this passing over, if it is to be perfect, all intellectual activities must be left behind and the height of our affection must be totally transferred and transformed into God.[160]

Human endeavour did not count for much; there was little point in asking questions, talking or writing. God's giving was what mattered.

Since, therefore, in this regard nature can do nothing and effort can do but little, little importance should be given to inquiry, but much to unction; little importance should be given to the tongue, but much to inner joy; little importance should be given to words and to writing, but all to the gift of God, that is, the Holy Spirit.[161]

To emphasize the uselessness of words in the face of the ineffable, Bonaventure returned to the use of paradox, quoting directly from Pseudo-Denys' *Mystical Theology*. Pseudo-Denys had prayed to be directed into the 'summit of mystical communication':

There new, absolute and unchangeable mysteries of theology are hidden in the superluminous darkness of a silence teaching secretly in the utmost obscurity which is supermanifest – a darkness which is super-resplendent and in which everything shines forth and which fills to overflowing invisible intellects with the splendours of invisible goods that surpass all good.[162]

Bonaventure also quoted Pseudo-Denys when he described this as a 'state of unknowing'.[163] In the *Breviloquium* he described how the spirit was 'carried beyond its own self into darkness and delight' by 'a certain learned ignorance'.[164]

There has been considerable disagreement about the nature of the ascent outlined in *The Soul's Journey into God*, especially regarding its intended audience and its relationship with lived experience. It has been argued that the three basic parts offer three distinct ways of approaching God that could be pursued entirely independently of each other.[165] On similar lines, it has even been suggested that the six stages can be seen as 'representations of different spiritualities that speak to different types of religious persons'.[166] While the text is open to such readings, they ignore the unity of the ascent as a whole and the tremendous care with which Bonaventure constructed the relationships between the various stages. Recognizing this, it has been argued that the ascent should not be seen as 'a series of successive steps' in which moving to a higher level entails abandonment of the one below it. Rather, Bonaventure's

[160] *Ibid.*, 7.4, p. 113. [161] *Ibid.*, 7.5, p. 113.
[162] *Ibid.*, p. 114. [163] *Ibid.*, pp. 114–15.
[164] *Breviloquium*, 5.6.7, p. 160.
[165] E. Cousins, 'Introduction', in Bonaventure, *The Soul's Journey*, p. 23.
[166] Hayes, *Bonaventure*, p. 32.

conception of hierarchy was such that 'every step contains within it all that is contained in the lower', so that 'at each step the progress of the soul is understood to be inclusive, as containing all that precedes that step'.[167] This fits entirely with the view of human knowledge that Bonaventure expressed in *Retracing the Arts to Theology* (*De reductione artium ad theologiam*) where he identified six illuminations: sacred scripture, sense perception, mechanical knowledge, rational philosophy, natural philosophy and moral philosophy. He maintained that 'all these branches of knowledge' were 'ordained for the knowledge of Sacred Scripture; they are contained in it; they are perfected by it; and by means of it they are ordained for eternal illumination'.[168]

Taken as a whole, however, the ascent in *The Soul's Journey into God* was clearly not a realistic possibility for everyone. It supposed a very high degree of learning, including the arts and theology, and can only have been meaningful in its entirety for an intellectual elite. It has been described as 'a university guidebook', as 'a general portrait of how the immediate learning experiences of university students should be understood at their more lasting, deeper, and more tested levels'.[169] To some extent, however, it seems likely that Bonaventure had a specifically Franciscan audience in mind. One of the tensions threatening the unity of the order arose from the growing dominance of university-educated men whose attitude to learning was very different from that which Francis himself had espoused. *The Soul's Journey* sought to reconcile university learning with the spiritual traditions established by Francis. Bonaventure wanted to show that the unlearned Francis was a meaningful model for learned men, and that learning did not make it impossible to follow his ideals of poverty.

The Soul's Journey was not, however, a programme of study to be followed step by step. In other works Bonaventure structured human knowledge differently. For example, in *Retracing the Arts to Theology* he offered two schemes. He began by discussing four lights: the external light of mechanical skill, the lower light of sense perception, the inner light of philosophical knowledge, and finally the higher light of grace and sacred scripture. He then presented a modified classification

167 Turner, *Darkness of God*, pp. 112–13.

168 Bonaventure, *De Reductione Artium ad Theologiam*, trans. Sister Emma Thérèse Healy (New York, 1955) reprinted in A. Hyman and J. J. Walsh (eds.), *Philosophy in the Middle Ages: The Christian, Islamic, and Jewish Traditions* (Indianapolis, 1973, repr. 1978), p. 425.

169 S. F. Brown, 'Introduction', in Bonaventure, *The Journey of the Mind to God*, trans. P. Boehner, ed. with introduction and notes by S. F. Brown (Indianapolis, 1993), p. xi; see also pp. 69–71.

consisting of the six illuminations mentioned above. Bonaventure regarded these as complementary ways of thinking about how God should be approached, entirely consistent with each other, and allowing him to make different points about religious and intellectual formation.

For Bonaventure, there was much to be learned about God on the basis of sense perception. A large part of rational thought, however, was not sense-based: by looking inward, it was possible to discover innate ideas that brought much greater illumination. Ultimately, however, the intellect failed in pursuit of God, language collapsed into paradox and contradiction, and it was love that had the potential for union with God. Indeed, from the outset knowledge of God was only possible for those who lived virtuously, desiring God and receiving his help. Bonaventure's approach was entirely consistent with that of twelfth-century monks like Bernard of Clairvaux and William of Saint Thierry. Like Hugh of Saint Victor, however, he granted a role for learning. Indeed, he gave learning an even greater role than Hugh because different forms of scholarship came into play at different stages in the ascent. The practices of the university therefore generated many different forms of valuable knowledge.

Aquinas

Thomas Aquinas was born in southern Italy in 1224 or 1225, probably at the family castle of Roccasecca. As a child he was sent as an oblate to the abbey of Monte Cassino. From 1239 to 1244, he studied the arts at the university of Naples. In view of his subsequent scholarship, it is perhaps not insignificant that at Naples students were taught works by Aristotle that were formally banned in Paris. He joined the Dominican order in 1244, but was seized and held by his family for over a year because they wished him to enter a traditional monastic order. Once he was released, he was sent by the Dominican order to Paris where, from 1245 to 1248, he was taught in the convent of Saint Jacques by Albert the Great. He moved to Cologne in 1248, where he continued his studies under Albert and was ordained as a priest. In 1252 he returned to Paris, where he studied theology until 1256. From 1256 to 1259 he was a master of theology in Paris. It was probably during this spell in Paris that he began his *Summa Contra Gentiles*, which, according to a fourteenth-century chronicle, he wrote at the request of Raymund of Pennaforte, a former master general of the Dominican order, to assist Dominicans who were preaching in Spain in opposition to Moslems, Jews and heretics. He spent the years between 1259 and 1269 in Italy, at Naples, at Orvieto, where he completed the *Summa Contra Gentiles* in 1264, and in Rome, where he set up a studium at the convent of Santa Sabina. It was there that he began the *Summa Theologiae* in 1266, a summary of theology for beginners, although there has been some debate about the level at which he intended to pitch the work. From 1269 to 1272 he was once again a master of theology in Paris. He left in 1272 to establish a provincial studium at the priory of San Domenico in Naples, where his lectures were also open to members of the university. He stopped writing in 1273, saying that he could not go on 'because all that I have written seems like straw to me'. Historians have speculated that he suffered a stroke or some sort of breakdown. Whatever the cause, he left the third and final part of the *Summa Theologiae* unfinished, and his followers added a *Supplement* made up of extracts taken from his *Commentary on the Sentences*. In 1274 he set off to attend the Council of Lyons, but hit his head on a tree branch, perhaps while travelling on a donkey. He died south of Rome, at the Cistercian abbey of Fossanova, on 7 March 1274.[170]

Aquinas produced a vast body of work. Seeking to explain his prodigious output, contemporaries noted his extraordinary powers of memory and concentration, prompting numerous anecdotal recollections and stories. It was said that he would dictate to three or even four secretaries at the same time, to each on a different subject.[171] While dining with King Louis IX, he supposedly became absorbed in thinking about Manichean heresy, suddenly thumped the table in triumph, and then called for a secretary to whom he could dictate his refutation of the heresy, before having to explain that he had thought that he was at his desk.[172] It is extremely difficult to give an account of his work, certainly not because it lacks clarity, but because his all-embracing overviews were vast and detailed, unlike Bonaventure's compressed summaries, and above all because each component of his thought relates to every other component, and he made readers very aware of this. Understanding any one point seems to depend upon understanding the whole web of interconnected ideas. It is impossible not to wonder at his apparent ability to keep all aspects of his thought in mind simultaneously and to sustain them all consistently. Rather than attempting to summarize 'everything', the following account plots a

[170] The finest account of Aquinas' life is J. A. Weisheipl, *Friar Thomas d'Aquino: His Life, Thought and Works* (New York, 1974). Almost all histories of medieval thought contain a brief biographical summary.

[171] Weisheipl, *Friar Thomas*, p. 137.

[172] B. Davies, *The Thought of Thomas Aquinas* (Oxford, 1992), p. 8.

particular path through his work, designed to allow comparison with Bonaventure on key issues.[173]

Aquinas held that there were two ways of knowing, by natural reason and by grace. He stated this most clearly when discussing knowledge of God. In the *Summa Theologiae*, for example, he observed: 'By grace we have a more perfect knowledge of God than we have by natural reason.'[174] In the *Summa Contra Gentiles*, he wrote:

> There are two ways of knowing what we hold to be true about God. There are some truths about God that exceed the capacity of human reason – for example the fact that God is three and one. There are also some truths that natural reason can attain, such as that God exists, that he is one, and other truths of this kind. These are truths about God that have been conclusively proved by philosophers making use of their natural reason.[175]

Clearly knowledge obtained through grace was superior to natural knowledge achieved through the use of reason. As we shall see, however, Aquinas valued natural knowing very highly, and tried to explain how it worked in great detail.

Before attempting to give an account of how Aquinas thought natural knowing worked, two general points are worth making. First, for Aquinas, all natural knowledge was sense-based: 'in this life all knowledge that is in our intellects originates in the senses'.[176] He did not mean that it was only possible to know what was actually perceived through the senses, but that the process of knowing always began with and proceeded with reference back to what had been sensed: 'things that are not perceived by the senses cannot be grasped by the human intellect except in so far as knowledge of them is gathered from the senses'.[177] Second, however, data provided by the senses did not itself constitute intellectual knowledge. For intellectual knowledge to be achieved, the intellect itself had to act upon and receive what was provided by the senses. He explained this process by distinguishing between two powers. One was the *intellectus agens*, which is generally translated as the

[173] Every history of medieval thought has a summary seeking to cover the main characteristics of Aquinas' work, and I have chosen to address those aspects which as a student I could not follow, and with which my own students have most difficulty.

[174] ST, 1a.12.13 (vol. 3, p. 43).

[175] *Summa Contra Gentiles*, 1.3, in P. E. Sigmund (trans. and ed.), *St. Thomas Aquinas on Politics and Ethics* (New York, 1988), p. 3; see also Thomas Aquinas, *On the Truth of the Catholic Faith. Summa Contra Gentiles*, trans. A. C. Pegis, 5 vols. (New York, 1955–7), vol. 1, p. 63. Henceforth SCG.

[176] SCG 1.3, in Sigmund, *St. Thomas Aquinas on Politics and Ethics*, p. 3; see also Thomas Aquinas, *On the Truth of the Catholic Faith. Summa Contra Gentiles*, trans. Pegis, vol. 1, p. 64.

[177] *Ibid.*

'agent intellect' or the 'active intellect'. The other was the *intellectus possibilis*, which historians variously call the 'potential intellect', 'possible intellect', 'receptive intellect' or occasionally 'passive intellect'. The two terms were taken from the work of Aristotle, but it was not entirely clear what he meant by them. Consequently later scholars, not least in the University of Paris, interpreted him very differently. Was there just one active intellect shared by everyone, which could perhaps be identified with God? Or was there a single potential intellect shared by all? These matters were a cause of great controversy in thirteenth-century Paris, but according to Aquinas, and he thought he was agreeing with Aristotle, each individual soul had an agent intellect and a potential intellect.

As Aquinas explained it, when a thing was perceived by the senses an image which he called a 'phantasm' was produced and stored in the imagination. From the phantasm, the agent intellect abstracted an idea of the perceived object's defining characteristics, of what made it what it was, of its 'whatness' or 'quiddity'. Aquinas also called it a 'form' and an 'intelligible species'. Having been abstracted from phantasms by the agent intellect, these intelligible species were retained in the potential intellect. Thus, considering whether intellectual knowledge was taken from sensible things, he explained:

> That higher, superior agent which Aristotle calls the agent intellect ... by a process of abstraction makes images [phantasms] received from the senses actually intelligible. According to this, then, intellectual activity is caused by the senses by way of these images [phantasms]. However, since these images [phantasms] are not capable of effecting a change in the possible intellect but must be made actually intelligible by the agent intellect, it is not right to say that sensible knowledge is the total and complete cause of intellectual knowledge – better to say that it is somehow the material of the cause.[178]

When asking whether the intellect could understand through intelligible species without turning to phantasms, he explained that the intellect could only deal with quiddities, and since these existed in particular material things which were apprehended through the senses, the intellect had to turn to phantasms in order to obtain the intelligible species which would permit understanding:

> The proper object of the human intellect ... since it is joined to a body, is a nature or 'whatness' [quidditas] found in corporeal matter ... But by definition a nature of this kind exists in an individual which has corporeal matter, for instance it is of the nature of stone that it should exist in this or that particular stone, or of the nature of horse that it should exist in this or that

178 ST 1a.84.6 (vol. 12, p. 37).

particular horse, etc. Thus the nature of stone or any other material reality cannot be known truly and completely except in so far as it exists in a particular thing. Now we apprehend the particular through the senses and imagination. Therefore if it is actually to understand its proper object, then the intellect must needs turn to sense images [phantasms] in order to look at universal natures existing in particular things.[179]

Looking more closely at the process of abstraction from phantasms, he explained that it meant isolating the universal 'definition of the species' from the 'individuating conditions' which made, for example, one stone distinct from any other stone:

I claim likewise that whatever pertains to the definition of any species of material reality, for instance stone or man or horse, can be considered without individuating conditions which are no part of the definition of the species. And this is what I mean by abstracting the universal from the particular, the idea [intelligible species] from sense images [phantasms], to consider the nature of a species without considering individuating conditions represented by sense images [phantasms].[180]

Once the intelligible species had been abstracted from the phantasms, they could be used by the intellect in thought; they were 'that by which the intellect understands'.[181] First, the potential intellect could form a 'mental word, which is nothing other than a concept of mind expressing what he is thinking about'.[182] Aquinas also referred to this concept as a 'definition' and, in a technical sense unrelated to moral purpose, an 'intention'.[183] Second, it could compose or divide, by which he meant constructing propositions or statements that either affirmed or denied something about something else. It was the definition or these propositions, rather than the intelligible species, that were signified by words:

first, there is an effect produced in the possible intellect in so far as it is informed by an intelligible species; and then, secondly, when it is thus informed, it formulates either a definition or else division or composition, which is then signified by words. Thus the meaning which a name signifies is a definition, and a proposition signifies the intellect's composing or dividing. Therefore words do not signify the intelligible species, but those things which the intellect formulates for itself in order to understand things outside.[184]

179 ST 1a.84.7 (vol. 12, pp. 41–3).
180 ST 1a.85.1.ad1 (vol. 12, p. 53).
181 ST 1a.85.2 (vol. 12, p. 61).
182 ST 1a2ae.93.1.ad2 (vol. 28, p.55).
183 For a brief but invaluable summary of the different meanings attached to the term 'intention', see Marenbon, *Later Medieval Philosophy*, pp. 139–40.
184 ST 1a.85.2 (vol. 12, p. 63); I have adapted the translation.

It was when the intellect constructed propositions pertaining to things outside itself that it could know the truth by judging that there was a correspondence between a thing outside itself and its concept of that thing:

truth is defined as conformity between intellect and thing. Hence to know that conformity is to know truth. Sense however does not know that conformity in any way; for although sight possesses the likeness of the visible thing, it does not know the correspondence between the thing and what it apprehends about it. Intellect can know its own conformity to the thing known; yet it does not grasp that conformity in the mere act of knowing the quiddity of a thing. But when the intellect judges that the thing corresponds to the form of the thing which it apprehends, then for the first time it knows and affirms the truth. This it does in the act of composing and dividing; for in every proposition some form signified by the predicate is either joined to some thing signified by the subject or separated from it.[185]

It was also when propositions were formulated that mistakes could be made:

in affirming and denying one thing of another, intellect can be deceived in affirming of a thing whose quiddity it understands, something which does not follow from the quiddity or is incompatible with it.[186]

Although Aquinas maintained that fundamentally the intellect could not go wrong when abstracting quiddities ('with respect to the quiddity of a thing, speaking essentially, the intellect makes no mistakes'[187]), he recognized that there could be mistakes 'accidentally' when the quiddity itself implied a false proposition:

Since falsity is in the intellect only in its function of combining concepts in the judgment, there can be falsity in the operation of knowing quiddities accidentally, in so far as some element of judgment enters in. This can happen in two ways: in one way when the intellect attributes the definition of one thing to another, e.g. by saying the definition of circle applies to man; so that the definition of the one is false of another; in another way when the intellect puts together in one definition elements which are incompatible: so that the definition is not only false as applied to some thing, but false in itself. Thus the reason why the intellect is false in forming the definition, 'four-footed rational animal', is that it is false in making the judgment, 'some rational animal is four-footed'.[188]

[185] ST 1a.16.3 (vol. 4, p. 81); I have adapted the translation.
[186] ST 1a.17.3 (vol. 4, p. 109); I have adapted the translation.
[187] ST 1a.85.6 (vol. 12, p. 81); I have adapted the translation.
[188] ST 1a.17.3 (vol. 4, p. 109); I have adapted the translation. See also 1a.85.6 (vol. 12, p. 81).

Having reached the stage of forming propositions, however, it was possible to proceed to reasoning by syllogisms.

It is worth emphasizing again that for Aquinas all thought involved recourse to phantasms in some way. As he put it, 'It is impossible for our intellect, in its present state of being joined to a body capable of receiving impressions, actually to understand anything without turning to phantasms.' He considered this to be evident because the intellect used no corporeal organ and, if it did not depend on faculties like the senses and the imagination which did use corporeal organs, should have been able to function even when there was physical damage to the corporeal organs on which the senses and imagination relied. It could be observed, however, that 'if acts of the imagination are impeded by an injury to its organ – for instance, in a seizure – or, similarly, if acts of sense memory are impeded – for instance, in a coma – a man is impeded from actually understanding even things which he had known before', so obviously intellect was dependent on the senses and the imagination, which provided it with phantasms. Moreover, Aquinas also cited the routine experience of understanding: 'As anyone can experience for himself, if he attempts to understand anything, he will form phantasms for himself which serve as examples in which he can, as it were, look at what he is attempting to understand.' Phantasms were therefore always involved in knowing.[189]

Exactly how phantasms were involved, however, depended on what was being known. How the intellect knew individual things required some explanation because, as we have seen, it depended on quiddities, or intelligible species, which were universals bearing no trace of particular things.

> Directly and immediately our intellect cannot know the singular in material realities. The reason is that the principle of singularity in material things is individual matter, and our intellect ... understands by abstracting intelligible species from this sort of matter. But what is abstracted from individual matter is universal. Therefore our intellect has direct knowledge only of universals.[190]

While the intellect could not have direct knowledge of individual things, by reflecting on the process by which intelligible species were abstracted it could work its way back to phantasms and thus know particular things 'indirectly and by a quasi-reflection'.[191]

Even things that Aquinas did not think could be sensed at all could only be known in the intellect through processes involving phantasms

[189] ST 1a.84.7 (vol. 12, p. 41); I have adapted the translation.
[190] ST 1a.86.1 (vol. 12, p. 91); I have adapted the translation.
[191] *Ibid.*

which were sense-based. Thus knowledge of the self required reflection on the process of knowing through sense perception: 'Since it is connatural for our intellect in the present life to look to material, sensible things … it follows that our intellect understands itself according as it is made actual by species abstracted from sensible realities by the light of the agent intellect.'[192] Or again: 'While the soul is joined to the body, it understands by turning to sense images; it cannot even understand itself except in that it comes to be actually understanding through a species abstracted from sense images.'[193] So self-awareness was also achieved indirectly, through awareness of the sense-based process of knowing other things. Thinking about things that did not actually exist involved phantasms too. Phantasms were retained in the imagination or phantasy, which was 'a treasure-store of forms received through the senses'.[194] In the imagination, it was possible to combine phantasms to form new ones: 'in the imagination we can form the image of a golden mountain from those of gold and a mountain'.[195] Thus, again through phantasms, it was possible to think about things that did not exist and had therefore not actually been sensed.

What about God? Although God could not be known directly through the senses, Aquinas was clear that some knowledge about God, above all knowledge that he existed, was obtainable on the basis of what could be sensed: 'our intellect is led from the objects of the senses to the knowledge of the existence of God'.[196] This knowledge was not easily achieved, but it was very much the point of philosophy: 'To know what reason can investigate concerning God requires that one already have a knowledge of many things, since almost all of philosophy is directed towards the knowledge of God.'[197] His approach to proving the existence of God was quite different from Anselm's, and indeed, while not naming Anselm, he explicitly rejected the ontological proof. He pointed out that 'someone hearing the word "God" may very well not understand it to mean "that than which nothing greater can be thought"'. Even if that meaning were accepted, the argument simply did not work:

192 ST 1a.87.1 as cited in Davies, *Thought of Thomas Aquinas*, p. 214.

193 ST 1a.89.2 as cited in Davies, *Thought of Thomas Aquinas*, p. 214.

194 ST 1a.78.4 (vol. 11, p. 139).

195 ST 1a.12.9 (vol. 3, p. 33).

196 SCG 1.3, in Sigmund, *St. Thomas Aquinas on Politics and Ethics*, p. 3; see also Thomas Aquinas, *On the Truth of the Catholic Faith. Summa Contra Gentiles*, trans. Pegis, vol. 1, p. 64.

197 SCG 1.4, in Sigmund, *St. Thomas Aquinas on Politics and Ethics*, p. 4; see also Thomas Aquinas, *On the Truth of the Catholic Faith. Summa Contra Gentiles*, trans. Pegis, vol. 1, p. 67.

> And even if the meaning of the word 'God' were generally recognized to be 'that than which nothing greater can be thought', nothing thus defined would thereby be granted existence in the world of fact, but merely as thought about. Unless one is given that something in fact exists than which nothing greater can be thought – and this nobody denying the existence of God would grant – the conclusion that God in fact exists does not follow.[198]

Aquinas' approach was to argue from effect to cause, the effects being open to sense perception: 'From effects evident to us ... we can demonstrate what in itself is not evident to us, namely, that God exists.'[199]

Aquinas offered five ways in which it was possible to prove the existence of God. The first was based on our observation of 'motion', by which he meant what we would call 'change':

> Some things in the world are certainly in process of change: this we plainly see. Now anything in process of change is being changed by something else. This is so because it is characteristic of things in process of change that they do not yet have the perfection towards which they move, though able to have it; whereas it is characteristic of something causing change to have that perfection already. For to cause change is to bring into being what was previously only able to be, and this can only be done by something that already is ... Now the same thing cannot at the same time be both actually x and potentially x, though it can be actually x and potentially y ... Consequently, a thing in process of change cannot itself cause that same change; it cannot change itself. Of necessity therefore anything in process of change is being changed by something else. Moreover, this something else, if in process of change, is being changed by yet another thing; and this last by another. Now we must stop somewhere, otherwise there will be no first cause of the change, and, as a result, no subsequent causes. For it is only when acted upon by the first cause that the intermediate causes will produce the change ... Hence one is bound to arrive at some first cause of change not itself being changed by anything, and this is what everybody understands as God.[200]

Aquinas' argument was that we can see that things change. Nothing can change itself; anything that is changing has to be changed by something else. If that something else is changing, it too has to be changed by something else. This chain of things being changed by something else cannot go on for ever or there would be no first mover, or first cause of change. Crucially, however, if there were no first mover, something changing other things but not being changed itself, something therefore different in nature from any other thing, there would be nothing to set off the chain of things changing other things, and thus no movement

[198] ST 1a.2.1 (vol. 2, pp. 7–9).
[199] ST 1a.2.2 (vol. 2, p.11).
[200] ST 1a.2.3 (vol. 2, pp. 13–15).

at all. But we can see that that there is change, so something must have set it off: 'one is bound to arrive at some first cause of change not itself being changed by anything, and this is what everybody understands by God'.

The second and third proofs depended on similar objections to an infinite series. The second concerned causation, and began with the statement: 'In the observable world causes are found to be in ordered series; we never observe, nor ever could, something causing itself, for this would mean it preceded itself, and this is not possible.' Aquinas then argued that this series of causes could not be infinite because 'if you eliminate a cause you also eliminate its effects, so that you cannot have a last cause, nor an intermediate one unless you have a first'. If there were no first cause, 'there would be no intermediate causes either, and no last effect, and this would be an open mistake'. It was therefore necessary 'to suppose some first cause, to which everyone gives the name "God"'.[201]

The third proof applied the same idea about infinite series to sequences of things bringing other things into existence. It was complicated by the distinction that Aquinas felt obliged to make between things that had to exist and things that did not. He began by establishing that there had to be some things that must exist because 'if everything need not be, once upon a time there was nothing', and 'if that were true there would be nothing even now, because something that does not exist can only be brought into being by something already existing'. Since things clearly did exist, 'there has got to be something that must be'. Turning specifically to things that must exist, Aquinas argued that such a thing 'may or may not owe this necessity to something else'. Things that owed the necessity of their existence to something else would form a 'series of things which must be and owe this to other things'. This series could not be infinite, and one had 'to suppose something which must be, and owes this to no other thing than itself; indeed it itself is the cause that other things must be'.[202] The point was that if one did not make such a supposition, Aquinas held that nothing would exist, and our senses told us that things did exist.

The fourth proof was 'based on the gradation observed in things', and the key point was that judgements about relative values could only be made if there were an absolute:

> Some things are found to be more good, more true, more noble, and so on, and other things less. But such comparative terms describe varying degrees of

[201] ST 1a.2.3 (vol. 2, p. 15).
[202] *Ibid.*

approximation to a superlative; for example, things are hotter and hotter the nearer they approach what is hottest. Something therefore is the truest and best and most noble of things, and hence the most fully in being; for Aristotle says that the truest things are the things most fully in being.[203]

So our perception that some things are better than others meant we had to suppose the existence of something that was the best. Aquinas then took from Aristotle the notion that goodness and being were identical, so that the best was the most fully in being. He further cited Aristotle to the effect that the thing possessing some property most fully is the cause of that property in other things. He concluded: 'There is something therefore which causes in all other things their being, their goodness, and whatever other perfection they have. And this we call "God".'[204]

The fifth proof rested on our perception of 'the guidedness of nature':

An orderedness of actions to an end is observed in all bodies obeying natural laws, even when they lack awareness. For their behaviour hardly ever varies, and will practically always turn out well; which shows that they truly tend to a goal, and do not merely hit it by accident. Nothing however that lacks awareness tends to a goal, except under the direction of someone with awareness and with understanding; the arrow, for example, requires an archer. Everything in nature, therefore, is directed to its goal by someone with understanding, and this we call 'God'.[205]

According to Aquinas, it could be seen that things that lacked consciousness nevertheless fulfilled a purpose within the natural order. Since they could not direct themselves to fulfil this purpose, because they lacked consciousness, it followed that there must be an intelligent being directing them to fill their role in the natural order, 'and this we call "God"'.

Aquinas thus argued that knowledge of the material world based on sense perception made it possible also to know by natural reason that God existed. While not everyone could do this, for those who could there was certain knowledge that God existed. He did not suppose for a moment, however, that this constituted a complete knowledge or understanding of God. It involved arguing from effect to cause, and the effects were so unequal to the cause that only limited knowledge of the cause was possible:

The knowledge that is natural to us has its source in the senses and extends just so far as it can be led by sensible things; from these, however, our understanding

203 ST 1a.2.3 (vol. 2, pp. 15–17).
204 ST 1a.2.3 (vol. 2, p. 17). 205 *Ibid.*

cannot reach to the divine essence. Sensible creatures are effects of God which are less than typical of the power of their cause, so knowing them does not lead us to understand the whole power of God and thus we do not see his essence.[206]

Aquinas was equally aware of the inadequacy of language when referring to God:

Aristotle says that words are signs for thoughts and thoughts are likenesses of things, so words refer to things indirectly through thoughts. How we refer to a thing depends on how we understand it. We have seen already that in this life we do not see the essence of God, we only know him from creatures; we think of him as their source, and then as surpassing them all and as lacking anything that is merely creaturely. It is the knowledge we have of creatures that enables us to use words to refer to God, and so these words do not express the divine essence as it is in itself.[207]

Language was rooted in the created world, and only knowledge of that world made it possible to use words of God. Words were therefore unequal to the task of referring to God's true nature. It followed that 'God is said to have no name, or to be beyond naming because his essence is beyond what we understand of him and the meaning of the names we use'.[208] There was less difficulty when negative terms were used to say 'what he is not', but positive terms like 'good' or 'wise' were bound to 'fail to represent adequately what he is'.[209]

There was, however, the second way of knowing: 'By grace we have a more perfect knowledge of God than we have by natural reason.'[210] Aquinas defined grace as 'a certain participation in the divine nature, which surpasses every nature'.[211] It could have a powerful effect on knowing:

[Natural reason] depends on two things: images [phantasms] derived from the sensible world and the natural intellectual light by which we abstract intelligible concepts from these images. In both these respects human knowledge is helped by the revelation of grace. The light of grace strengthens the intellectual light and at the same time prophetic visions provide us with God-given images which are better suited to express divine things than those we receive naturally from the sensible world. Moreover, God has given us sensible signs and spoken words to show us something of the divine.[212]

206 ST 1a.12.12 (vol. 3, p. 41).
207 ST 1a.13.1 (vol. 3, p. 49).
208 ST 1a.13.1.ad1 (vol. 3, p. 49).
209 ST 1a.13.2 (vol. 3, pp. 53–5).
210 ST 1a.12.13 (vol. 3, p. 43).
211 ST 1a2e.112.1 (vol. 30, p. 145).
212 ST 1a.12.13 (vol. 3, pp. 43–5).

Thus grace both strengthened the capacity to know by natural reason and offered entirely different sources of knowledge about God.

Revealed knowledge came in many forms. Aquinas defined prophecy, for example, as knowledge revealed by God and beyond natural human capacity. As he explained, 'Those truths which surpass all human knowledge and which are revealed from God cannot find confirmation in that human reasoning which they transcend, but only in the working of divine power.'[213] Prophetic knowledge could concern anything:

> prophetic knowledge is brought about by a divine light which makes possible the knowledge of all realities, whether they be human or divine, spiritual or corporeal. And so prophetic revelation extends to all such realities.[214]

On the other hand, types of prophetic knowledge were ordered in a hierarchy:

> Yet we should consider that because prophecy relates to what is far from our range of knowledge, then the more a reality is distant from human knowledge, the more properly will that reality belong to prophecy.
>
> There are three degrees of remoteness from human knowing. The first covers what is hidden from this or that individual, whether in sense or intellect, yet is not hidden from men in general; just as a man knows by his senses what is adjacent to him in place while another person, with the same senses, fails to know because he is not adjacent. Thus ... the thoughts of one person's heart can be manifested prophetically to another. In this way too the knowledge which one has by demonstration can be revealed to us in prophecy.
>
> The second degree comprises those truths which universally surpass the knowledge of all men, not because they are intrinsically unknowable, but because of a defect in human knowledge. An example of this is the mystery of the Trinity ...
>
> Third, and most remote of all, is that which surpasses the knowledge of all men, because the truths concerned are not knowable; such are future contingents whose truth is not determined.
>
> Now because what is universal and self-caused surpasses what is particular and caused by another, so the revelation of future events most properly belongs to prophecy.[215]

Thus prophecy was especially about the future. There were, however, no rules about who might receive prophetic knowledge; God could give it to anyone, without regard for 'natural dispositions'.[216] Intellectual ability and education were also irrelevant, and masters of theology did

[213] ST 2a2ae.171.1 (vol. 45, p. 7).
[214] ST 2a2ae.171.3 (vol. 45, p. 15)
[215] ST 2a2ae.171.4 (vol. 45, pp. 15–17).
[216] ST 2a2ae.172.3 (vol. 45, pp. 34–9).

not always respond positively to those who claimed to have received prophetic knowledge.[217]

It was even possible that someone in this life might see God in his essence, but it would require God to remove that person entirely from the normal processes of knowing. This was the experience of 'rapture', which was related in some way to prophecy.[218] Paul had said of himself, 'I know a man in Christ who was caught up to the third heaven.'[219] Aquinas explained that this was when someone 'by the spirit of God is uplifted to a supernatural level, with abstraction from the senses'.[220] Beginning with a brief account of natural, sense-based knowing of individual things, he went on to explain in detail why rapture required complete removal from the senses:

> The divine essence cannot be seen by any knowing faculty of man other than the intellect. But the human intellect only turns to sense-objects through the medium of phantasms, which it receives from the senses by means of intelligible species, and through considering which it judges and disposes of sense-objects. And so in every operation by which our intellect is abstracted from phantasms, it must also be abstracted from the senses.
>
> But the intellect of man in this life must be abstracted from phantasms, if it is to see the essence of God. For the essence of God cannot be seen through any phantasm, nor even through any created intelligible species, because the essence of God infinitely exceeds not only all bodies, which are represented by phantasms, but also all created intelligibles.
>
> When the intellect of man is raised to the highest vision of God's essence, it must be that the mind's whole attention is called there, so that it understands nothing else from phantasms, but is totally carried to God. Hence it is impossible that a man in this life should see God in his essence without abstraction from the senses.[221]

Aquinas recalled that the intellect knew individual things by working back through intelligible species and phantasms. He then made the point that the intellect could not know God's essence through the medium of anything created. It could not therefore know God's essence

[217] See J. M. Cocking, *Imagination: A Study in the History of Ideas* (London, 1991), p. 155; I. P. Wei, 'Predicting the future to judge the present: Paris theologians and attitudes to the future', in J. A. Burrow and I. P. Wei (eds.), *Medieval Futures: Attitudes to the Future in the Middle Ages* (Woodbridge, 2000), pp. 19–36 at 33–5.

[218] On the relationship between prophecy and rapture, see ST 2a2ae.175.3 (vol. 45, p. 105).

[219] 2 Corinthians 12.2.

[220] ST 2a2ae.175.1 (vol. 45, p. 97).

[221] ST 2a2ae.175.4 (vol. 45, p. 109). I have substantially altered the translation, in part aided by *The 'Summa Theologica' of St. Thomas Aquinas: Second Part of the Second Part QQ. CLXXI–CLXXXIX*, trans. Fathers of the English Dominican Province (London, 1934), pp. 71–2.

through intelligible species and phantasms because they were created. Moreover, it could not simultaneously know God's essence directly and other things using phantasms. Since both intelligible species and phantasms originated in the senses, being removed from them meant also being removed or abstracted from the senses. It went without saying that, like prophecy, rapture could never be taught.

Teaching, however, was fundamental to the purpose of the university, and Aquinas analysed the process of teaching in the light of his ideas about knowing when he considered whether one man could teach another. He began his analysis by recalling Aristotle's view that 'the passive intellect of the human soul is in a state of pure potentiality with regard to intelligible impressions', from which it followed that the teacher caused knowledge in the student by 'reducing' his passive intellect 'from a state of potentiality to a state of actuality'. Aquinas further noted that effects coming from an external source could come either from that external source alone or sometimes from an external source and sometimes from an internal source. Teaching fell into this latter category, so he elaborated on what it meant, using the example of health and medicine. Good health in a sick person was sometimes caused by an external source, the art of medicine, and sometimes by an internal source, the power of nature. He made two further points about instances when effects came from both external and internal sources, continuing to use the medical example. First, 'art imitates nature in its workings'; thus 'just as nature cures a sick man by altering and digesting and expelling the matter causing his sickness, so does the art of medicine'. Second, the external cause, the art, 'does not operate as principal agency, but rather as an aid to the principal agency (namely, the internal cause), by supporting it and providing it with the means it uses to produce the effect'; thus the physician provided food and medicine that nature could use to bring about a cure.[222]

Aquinas then considered knowledge within this framework. It could be acquired from an internal source, 'as is clear in the case of one who acquires knowledge through his own research'. Here the cause of knowledge was the light of the agent intellect 'through which certain universal principles of all the branches of knowledge are known naturally and immediately'. When a man applied these principles to specific cases, known through sense perception, he acquired 'knowledge by his own research of things of which he was ignorant, thus proceeding from the known to the unknown'. Knowledge could also be acquired from an external source, through being taught, and there were two ways in

[222] ST 1a.117.2 (vol. 15, pp. 131–3).

which the master could lead his disciple 'from the already known to the unknown'. First, he could present the disciple with intellectual tools which his intellect could use to acquire knowledge, 'as when he puts before him certain less universal propositions on which the learner can form a judgment from previous knowledge, or as when he puts to him concrete examples ... from which the learner's mind is led on to knowledge of the truth of what was previously unknown'. Second, the master could set out 'the relationship of principles to conclusions' when his disciple perhaps lacked the ability to work it out for himself.[223] The disciple learned chiefly because of what happened within himself, while the master provided 'only external help, in the same way as the physician who heals'.[224]

Aquinas acknowledged, however, that some people would have to be taught simply to accept truths that others could prove through reason. What others genuinely understood, they would have to believe as matters of faith. This was partly so that people could obtain knowledge of divine truth more quickly. Proving God's existence and other things about him was an aspect of metaphysics, which was the last science to be studied because it presupposed many others. People could not be allowed to come to knowledge of God only after much of their life was over. It was also necessary to ensure that knowledge of God was more widespread. Many people could not get anywhere with study, either because they lacked the intelligence, or they had to work to support themselves, or they were lazy, and they would never have knowledge of God unless it were presented to them as a matter of faith. Finally, it was important that people should have certainty. Human reason was thoroughly deficient with regard to divine matters, and philosophers made mistakes and disagreed with each other even over human issues. Divine truths had to be taught through faith to provide certain knowledge about God.[225] Aquinas was intensely aware that teaching had to be conducted at different levels for different audiences.

The serious scholar, however, had to think hard about how he approached his study. Aquinas defined *studiositas* as a virtue which moderated the natural desire to know, and was linked in a subordinate capacity to temperance.[226] Opposed to *studiositas* was the vice of *curiositas* which was concerned not directly with knowing, but with 'the appetite and eagerness to acquire knowledge'.[227] Aquinas explained

223 ST 1a.117.2 (vol. 15, pp. 133–5).
224 ST 1a.117.2.ad1 (vol 15, p. 135).
225 ST 2a2ae.2.4 (vol. 31, pp. 77–9).
226 ST 2a2ae.166.2 (vol. 44, pp. 197).
227 ST 2a2ae.160.2 (vol. 44, p. 87); ST 2a2ae.167.1 (vol. 44, pp. 202–3); my translation.

that knowing the truth was good in itself, but could be bad accidentally. It could be bad because of some consequence, 'as when somebody swells with pride' or 'when somebody uses knowledge of the truth in order to sin'. There could also be vice, the vice of *curiositas*, because of 'inordinateness of the appetite and eagerness to learn the truth'. This inordinateness could arise in four ways: first, 'when attention to the less useful distracts people from the studies incumbent on their office'; second, 'when a person studies from an illicit source'; third, 'when a person strives to know the truth about creatures without heeding its rightful end, namely knowing about God'; and fourth, 'when a person applies himself to grasp truths beyond his capacity', because people easily fell into error by doing this.[228] It was important that the scholar maintained a correct sense of purpose and did not get carried away in pursuit of knowledge.

Aquinas also discussed the context in which study and teaching took place, showing his sensitivity to the criticisms that the friars received from the secular clergy. Was it licit for religious to teach, preach and perform other tasks of this kind? He maintained that it was entirely permissible because they were 'not obliged by any vow or any precept of their rule to refrain from such things', nor were they 'less suited for doing them because of any sin committed'. It was also proper for them to receive holy orders or whatever jurisdiction was necessary. Moreover, they were especially suited to this kind of work because they had embraced 'the practice of holiness'.[229] Aquinas thus invoked the idea that a life ordered to virtue was fundamental to scholarship and teaching. He offered an interesting variation on this theme when considering whether a religious order should be founded for study, an issue especially pertinent to the Dominicans. He argued that study was indeed fitting for a religious order for three reasons. First, he maintained that study promoted the contemplative life in two ways: 'directly, by disposing for contemplation through illumination of the intellect', and 'indirectly, by removing the dangers of contemplation of divine things by those who are ignorant of Scripture'. Second, he argued that 'the study of letters is necessary for a religious order founded for preaching and similar works', so the pastoral value of learning was emphasized. Third, he explained that 'study befits a religious order as regards that which is common to all religious orders' in that 'it helps to avoid concupiscence of the flesh', 'it eliminates the desire for wealth' and 'it teaches obedience'.[230] Aquinas therefore held

[228] ST 2a2ae.167.1 (vol. 44, pp. 203–5); I have adapted the translation.
[229] ST 2a2ae.187.1 (vol. 47, pp. 147–9).
[230] ST 2a2ae.188.5 (vol. 47, pp. 199–201); I have adapted the translation.

that study aided both contemplation and pastoral work. Moreover, he reversed the usual relationship between learning and virtue, arguing that learning bred virtue.

There remained the further question of what should be presented to a wider audience that included the uneducated. Should there be public disputations with infidels? With regard to the disputant, intention was the key issue. If he disputed 'as though he had doubts about the faith and did not hold its truth for certain but proposed to test it with arguments', he certainly sinned as someone who doubted the faith and was himself an infidel. His actions were praiseworthy, however, if he disputed to refute errors or even to develop his skills. Matters were more complicated when it came to the audience, and it was necessary to consider whether they were instructed and firm in faith, or simple and hesitant. There was no danger in disputing about the faith before those who were wise and secure in faith, but an audience of simple people required more careful assessment. If they were troubled by infidels, for example by Jews, heretics or pagans, who were trying to corrupt their faith, it was necessary to dispute publicly about the faith as long as suitable men could be found who were capable of refuting errors. In this instance, the simple would be strengthened in their faith, and infidels would no longer have the power to deceive. Moreover, error would be confirmed if there were silence from those who were supposed to resist perversion of the faith. If, however, simple people were not at all troubled in this regard, as in lands where there were no infidels, it was dangerous to dispute publicly about the faith before them. Their faith was firmer because they had heard nothing contrary to what they believed, and it would do them no good to hear how infidels attacked the faith. Aquinas thus maintained that unless an audience was well informed or already shaken in its beliefs, public disputation about the faith was best avoided.[231] Once again he displayed great sensitivity to the potential needs of different types of audience, and he defined the master's responsibilities accordingly.

Aquinas presented a theory of knowing in which he was hugely influenced by Aristotle, and in which all natural knowledge was based more or less directly on sense perception. Through grace, however, God could strengthen the natural process by which the agent intellect abstracted quiddities and intelligible species from phantasms. Moreover, God could also act outside the natural process to reveal knowledge directly, for example though prophecy. He could even lift an individual entirely out of sense-based knowing and into rapture, so that the intellect saw God

[231] ST 2a2ae.10.7 (vol. 32, pp. 57–9).

in his essence. Aquinas did not doubt the value of knowledge generated in the university, and he explained the processes of study and teaching in terms of natural knowing. When the master taught his student, he supported the natural processes operating within his pupil, and in this he was like a physician healing his patient. There were, however, moral issues to consider. The scholar had to pursue useful knowledge, shun inappropriate sources of knowledge, remember that the point of studying the created world was to know about God, and be aware of his own limitations. In short, he must resist *curiositas* and moderate his desire to know by practising the virtue of *studiositas*. In general, living virtuously was necessary for sound scholarship, but study also fostered virtue. It was necessary to remember, however, that many people needed to be taught to believe the truth rather than to understand it fully, and it was potentially dangerous to hold disputations about the faith in public. The master always had a responsibility to assess his audience and to teach accordingly.

Conflict and condemnation

Aquinas and Bonaventure both insisted on the importance of virtue if true knowledge was to be obtained, and Aquinas was especially keen to stress the master's responsibility for the reception of his teaching by different types of audience; they both therefore adhered to the values that the university had adopted from twelfth-century monks. Moreover, they both stressed the importance of scholarship and learning, attaching high value to the work of the university. It will be apparent, however, that Bonaventure and Aquinas were very different in their ideas about knowing. Both believed that sense-based knowledge of the created world made it possible to know something about God, but while for Aquinas this was the basis for all natural knowledge of God, Bonaventure held that much rational thought required introspection that was not sense-based. Looking within, Bonaventure found innate ideas that were much more valuable, whereas Aquinas did not think that innate ideas existed. Aquinas drew systematically upon Aristotle's thinking, so that his interpretation of Aristotle was significant at every level of his work, while Bonaventure was much more selective in the way he deployed Aristotelian principles, continuing to rely much more heavily on Augustine for his basic framework. Aquinas and Bonaventure developed these fundamentally different approaches while the reception of newly translated Aristotelian texts caused bitter conflicts within the

University of Paris. In 1255 the arts faculty issued a statute requiring that all Aristotle's known works be studied, almost certainly reflecting what had been the practice for some time.[232] By now many of the works of the twelfth-century Muslim scholar, Averroes, had also been translated and were available in Paris, and his interpretations of Aristotle were also being used. A number of masters of arts specialized in the analysis of Aristotle's work, and they did not consider it their brief to find a way of bringing Aristotle's ideas into line with Christian belief, still less to create some kind of synthesis. The extent to which they intended to challenge Christian orthodoxy was and is far from clear. Historians disagree also about whether there was a 'school' or 'movement', but they have referred to elements within the arts faculty as 'radical Aristotelians', 'heterodox Aristotelians' and 'Latin Averroists'. There is no doubt, however, that some arts masters, notably Siger of Brabant and Boethius of Dacia, were articulating ideas that were incompatible with Christian belief, and that they did not devote much time to criticizing them from a Christian perspective. Many others, especially in the faculty of theology, were horrified, and considered it their duty to take action.

One of the most controversial issues concerned what is usually termed the unity (or sometimes the 'unicity') of the intellect. According to Siger of Brabant, Aristotle argued that there was just one potential intellect shared by everyone. Albert the Great and Bonaventure had already taken Averroes to advocate this view in his commentary on Aristotle, and they had argued against it. Siger, however, did not explicitly reject it. In 1270, without naming Siger, Aquinas attacked his work in a treatise entitled *On the Unity of the Intellect against the Averroists*. He explained the context at the start of the treatise:

> For a long time now there has been spreading among many people an error concerning the intellect, arising from the words of Averroes. He tries to assert that the intellect that Aristotle calls the possible intellect, but that he himself calls by the unsuitable name 'material', is a substance separate in its being from the body and not united to it in some way as its form, and furthermore that this possible intellect is one for all men. Against these views we have already written many things in the past. But because the boldness of those who err has not ceased to strive against the truth, we will try again to write something against this same error to refute it clearly.[233]

232 *Chartularium*, vol. 1, no. 246, pp. 277–9; *University Records*, no. 28, pp. 64–6.

233 Thomas Aquinas, *On the Unity of the Intellect against the Averroists (De Unitate Intellectus Contra Averroistas)*, trans. B. H. Zedler (Milwaukee, 1968), pp. 21–2.

In his treatise Aquinas aimed 'to show that the above-mentioned position is no less against the principles of philosophy than against the teachings of faith'.[234] The issue was contentious, however, because the notion of a single potential intellect undermined key Christian beliefs. As Aquinas explained: 'if we deny to men a diversity of the intellect, which alone among the parts of the soul seems to be incorruptible and immortal, it follows that after death nothing of the souls of men would remain except that single substance of intellect; and so the recompense of rewards and punishments and also their diversity would be destroyed'.[235] If there were only one intellect for everyone, individuals would not survive as individuals after death, and they could not therefore receive the specific punishments or rewards that were their due in the next life. This was not a matter on which theologians could permit any vagueness whatsoever.

A second cause of controversy was Aristotle's view about the eternity of the world. He argued that the world was eternal in its origins, that it had no beginning, an idea rehearsed by both Siger of Brabant and Boethius of Dacia. This plainly contradicted the account of creation in Genesis. Bonaventure dismissed the view of anyone who supported Aristotle as contradictory:

> It is impossible for that which has being after non-being to have eternal being, because this implies a contradiction. But the world has being after non-being. Therefore it is impossible that it be eternal.[236]

Aquinas, however, maintained that while arguments in favour of the eternity of the world were flawed, so were those that could be advanced in an attempt to prove that it had a beginning. The truth on this matter had to be accepted as a matter of faith: 'we hold by faith alone that the world has not existed forever; this truth cannot be proved demonstratively'.[237] One of his key points was that the efficient cause in this matter was the will of God, and this was not open to rational investigation:

> God's will cannot be investigated by reason, except as regards those matters which God must will with absolute necessity; such however, are not those things which he wills with reference to creatures, as we said above. But the divine will can be made known to man by revelation, on which faith is based.

[234] *Ibid.*, p. 22.
[235] *Ibid.*
[236] Bonaventure, *Commentary on the Sentences*, 2.1.1.1.2, in St Thomas Aquinas, Siger of Brabant, St Bonaventure, *On the Eternity of the World (De Aeternitate Mundi)*, trans. C. Vollert, L. H. Kendzierski, P. M. Byrne (Milwaukee, 1964), p. 109.
[237] ST 1a.46.2, in Thomas Aquinas, Siger of Brabant, Bonaventure, *On the Eternity of the World*, p. 65.

That the world had a beginning, therefore, is an object of faith, but not of demonstration or science.[238]

Furthermore, Aquinas considered it dangerous to put forward unconvincing arguments on the matter since 'this would furnish infidels with an occasion for scoffing, as they would think that we assent to truths of faith on such grounds'.[239] Theologians who felt obliged to counter ideas emerging from the arts faculty were far from in harmony with each other.

Indeed Bonaventure and Aquinas responded very differently to the crisis over some of the teaching in the arts faculty, and in ways that reveal much about their fundamental approaches to scholarship and teaching. Although Aquinas was clear that natural reason had its limits, hence for example his view that it was impossible to prove by reason that the world had a beginning, he had supreme confidence that the results of correct reasoning would never conflict with faith:

Although the truth of the Christian faith exceeds the capacity of human reason, truths that reason is fitted by nature to know cannot be contrary to the truth of faith. The things that reason is fitted by nature to know are clearly most true, and it would be impossible to think of them as false. It is also wrong to think that something that is held by faith could be false since it is clearly confirmed by God. Since we know by definition that what is false is contrary to the truth, it is impossible for the principles that reason knows by nature to be contrary to the truth of faith ... We conclude therefore that any arguments made against the doctrines of faith are incorrectly derived from the self-evident first principles of nature. Such conclusions do not have the force of proofs, but are either doubtful opinions or sophistries, and so it is possible to answer them.[240]

If an argument based on reason conflicted with faith, Aquinas was sure that the argument was flawed. Once the argument had been corrected, there would be no problem. So when masters of arts like Siger seemed to offer rational support for heterodox views, he set about proving that their arguments were wrong.

Bonaventure's response, however, was to play down the significance of reason, and demand that others do the same. For most of his career, he had probably regarded the Paris curriculum as a perfectly acceptable programme of study. In response to turbulence within his order, *The Soul's Journey into God* offered a serene and all-embracing vision: everything had a part to play in seeking knowledge of God, including

238 *Ibid.*, p. 66. 239 *Ibid.*
240 SCG 1.7, in Sigmund, *St. Thomas Aquinas on Politics and Ethics*, pp. 4–5; see also Thomas Aquinas, *On the Truth of the Catholic Faith. Summa Contra Gentiles*, trans. Pegis, vol. 1, pp. 74–5.

the sciences and pagan learning. The ascent indicated their relative importance, and how they fitted together. When, however, there was controversy and crisis at the University of Paris, this was not enough and Bonaventure expressed his priorities very forcefully. In 1273 he produced his *Conferences on the Hexaemeron*. He condemned 'the darkness of curiosity' and declared that it was 'patently obvious ... that there is no sure passage to wisdom through science'.[241] He attacked those who preferred the study of science to wisdom:

> Some wish to be all-wise and all-knowing, but it happens to them just as to the woman: 'And the woman saw that the tree was good to eat, and fair to the eyes' (Genesis 3.6). They see the beauty of transitory science and being delighted, they linger, they savour, and they are [deceived]. We do not belong to the party of their companions, the disciples of Solomon, but to that of David his father, who preferred the study of sanctity and wisdom to that of science.[242]

Science was dangerously tempting: 'unless it is watched very carefully, there is easy ruin in science'. A sense of religious purpose had always to be maintained: 'We should desire to know nothing unless we become more holy and go forward in the wisdom which takes us toward God.'[243]

Bonaventure did not suggest that study should be abandoned, but it had to be conducted in the proper manner. Above all, order had to be observed. He noted that there were four types of text to be studied: 'the books of the Holy Scriptures'; 'the books of the originals, namely the saints', by which he meant the writings of the Fathers; 'the summas of the masters'; and 'the writings of worldly learning', by which he meant pagan philosophy.[244] Bonaventure gave absolute priority to the Bible:

> Thus, let him who wishes to learn, seek science at its source, namely, in Holy Scripture, since 'the knowledge of salvation given for the remission of our sins' (Luke 1.77) is not found among the philosophers, nor among the summas of the masters, since they draw from the originals of the saints. But certain science cannot be taken from the originals beyond what the saints draw from Holy Scripture, since the saints could be deceived.[245]

It followed that 'the disciple of Christ ought first to study Holy Scripture, in which there is no error'. Moreover, familiarity with the whole of the Bible was required.[246]

That did not mean, however, that it was pointless to study the other kinds of text. The writings of the Fathers had to be studied because

241 Bonaventure, *Conferences on the Hexameron*, vision 3, discussion 7, in Hyman and Walsh (eds.), *Philosophy in the Middle Ages*, pp. 417–18.
242 *Ibid.*, p. 418. 243 *Ibid.*
244 *Ibid.*, p. 419. 245 *Ibid.* 246 *Ibid.*

it was impossible to understand the Bible without them. But they too were extremely difficult, with the result that 'some studying them have fallen into many errors and heresies'.[247] It was therefore necessary to turn to the summas of the masters for explanation. The summas of the masters, however, cited many philosophers, so they also had to be studied. This movement away from the Bible was fraught with increasing danger.

> Thus there is danger in descending to the originals; there is more danger in descending to the summas of the masters; but the greatest danger lies in descending to philosophy.[248]

The writings of the Fathers might be wrongly preferred to the Bible because they contained 'pretty words'. The summas of the masters could be deeply misleading because the masters sometimes misunderstood the Fathers. Philosophy, however, was most dangerous of all because it led some to neglect of the Bible. The answer was to 'drink moderately from philosophy'. Bonaventure condemned those who gave themselves 'entirely to philosophy'; they were 'bent over in submission to infinite errors, (treating) the sayings of certain philosophers as though they were the life-giving ferment of Scripture'. Francis had set the right example: when the sultan treated faith as a matter for debate, Francis told him that 'faith is above reason and is proved only by the authority of Scripture and the divine power, which is manifested in miracles'. Bonaventure concluded that 'the water of philosophical science is not to be mingled with the wine of Holy Scripture merely so that the wine is transmitted into water'.[249] The order was thus perfectly clear, but unfortunately contemporary practice was seriously at fault.

> The order thus is that first of all the letter and the spirit of Holy Scripture is studied, and then the originals are read, and they are subordinated to Scripture. Likewise in passing over to the study of the writings of the philosophers; but the contrary is always done, since the professors, even if not openly, secretly read, copy, and conceal the quartos of the philosophers as though they were idols.[250]

Bonaventure had strong views about how learning should be pursued within both the Franciscan order and the university. Complete preoccupation with the study of pagan philosophy was dangerous, and a proper sense of order should be re-established.

Bonaventure was not the only one to take this view, and some believed that authoritative intervention was required. In 1270, on 10 December,

[247] *Ibid.* [248] *Ibid.*
[249] *Ibid.*, pp. 419–20. [250] *Ibid.*, p. 420.

the bishop of Paris, Stephen Tempier, condemned thirteen propositions including the view that there was only one intellect for everyone, and the claim that the world was eternal.[251] In 1277 Pope John XXI called for further action, asking the bishop to conduct an investigation into errors being propagated in the university. A commission of theologians rapidly produced a report, and on 7 March the bishop issued a condemnation of 219 propositions.[252] The list was a bizarre and puzzling mishmash. While it seems to have been aimed at arts masters like Siger of Brabant and Boethius of Dacia, it failed to represent their views accurately. It also included propositions that no Parisian scholar is known to have put forward anywhere in the university. Moreover, it even condemned some views that had formed part of the teaching of Thomas Aquinas, who had died in 1274, prompting bitter exchanges in Paris between Dominican defenders of Aquinas and Franciscan critics over the next few years.[253]

The long-term significance of these condemnations, especially those of 1277, has been much disputed. For some historians the condemnations of 1277 were a watershed in the intellectual history of western Europe, changing the direction of medieval thought, whereas for others they did not seriously interrupt or redirect ongoing processes of intellectual inquiry.[254] Much depends on whether historians choose to emphasize conflict or cooperation in their accounts of thirteenth-century intellectual culture. For those who construct narratives of conflict, the reception of Aristotle and his Arab commentators created bitter divisions between 'radical' Aristotelians in the arts faculty and 'traditional' theologians who remained wedded to Augustine. Aquinas is located in the middle as the man who tried to 'synthesize' Aristotelian philosophy and Christian faith. The condemnations of 1277 are held to have marked the defeat of the extremists in the arts faculty, to have

[251] *Chartularium*, vol. 1, no. 432, pp. 486–7; *University Records*, no. 38, pp. 80–1.

[252] *Chartularium*, vol. 1, no. 473, pp. 543–58. Partially translated in Hyman and Walsh (eds.), *Philosophy in the Middle Ages*, pp. 542–9.

[253] For detailed analysis of the 1277 condemnation, see Bianchi, *Censure et liberté intellectuelle*, pp. 165–230; R. Hissette, *Enquête sur les 219 articles condamnés à Paris le 7 mars 1277* (Louvain, 1977); M. M. McLaughlin, *Intellectual Freedom and its Limitations in the University of Paris in the Thirteenth and Fourteenth Centuries* (New York, 1977), pp. 74–95; J. M. M. H. Thijssen, *Censure and Heresy at the University of Paris 1200–1400* (Philadelphia, 1998), pp. 40–56; L. E. Wilshire, 'The condemnations of 1277 and the intellectual climate of the medieval university', in N. Van Deusen (ed.), *The Intellectual Climate of the Early University: Essays in Honor of Otto Gründler* (Kalamazoo, MI, 1997), pp. 151–93.

[254] Contrast, for example, D. E. Luscombe, *Medieval Thought* (Oxford, 1997), esp. pp. 114–21, and Marenbon, *Later Medieval Philosophy*, esp. pp. 73–4. For a summary of different interpretations, see Bianchi, *Censure et liberté intellectuelle*, pp. 203–7.

set back the approach pioneered by Aquinas, and even to have closed a period of freedom of thought.[255] Other historians, however, question whether the work of Siger of Brabant and a few others added up to a significant movement, and point out that the overwhelming majority of arts masters deferred to theology as the superior discipline, and prepared their students for potential study of theology in the future, making cooperation between faculties the dominant feature of intellectual life in the university.[256]

Without doubt Parisian masters developed very different theories about knowing, as we have seen by examining the work of Bonaventure and Aquinas. Because this bore upon matters of faith, so that differences were deemed important, there were frequent controversies, and leading figures were therefore involved in well-publicized conflicts. It should be noted, however, that these conflicts were played out within the university, albeit with occasional intervention from external ecclesiastical authority. While formal censure of academic work rested on the authority of the bishop and chancellor, cases were effectively decided by the regent masters of theology as a body. Even when religious orders took action against their own members in the second half of the thirteenth century, and cases began to go directly to the papal courts in the early fourteenth, special commissions of theologians from Paris played a decisive role in evaluating suspect views.[257] Whereas in the twelfth century conflicts had taken place between men in different contexts of learning, between schoolmen and monks, now battles were fought between men whose identity had been substantially formed by the university. As a result, however extreme the language in which they criticized each other, they had a good deal in common. Moreover, whatever their disagreements about how knowledge was acquired and whatever conclusions they drew using their chosen methods, they all agreed that it was possible to know truths. The notion that knowing the truth required virtuous behaviour was built into university statutes and

255 For very different, but equally brilliant, narratives of conflict, see E. Gilson, *History of Christian Philosophy in the Middle Ages* (London, 1955); Van Steenberghen, *Aristotle in the West.*

256 See, for example, Marenbon, *Later Medieval Thought*, esp. pp. 67, 73–4. Marenbon also summarizes narratives of conflict very effectively.

257 W. J. Courtenay, 'Inquiry and inquisition: academic freedom in medieval universities', *Church History* 58 (1989): 168–81 at pp. 173–7; W. J. Courtenay, 'Dominicans and suspect opinion in the thirteenth century: the cases of Stephen of Venizy, Peter of Tarentaise, and the articles of 1270 and 1271', *Vivarium* 32 (1994): 186–95. For detailed analysis of procedures and different forms of censure, and for differing assessments of the impact of censure on academic freedom, see also Bianchi, *Censure et liberté intellectuelle*, pp. 21–67; Thijssen, *Censure and Heresy*, esp. pp. 1–39.

articulated by masters of theology. In justifying the university's existence, key documents also explained that it turned men into preachers, asserting the overriding importance of its pastoral role. The university's standing as a locus of intellectual and moral authority was not disputed. Masters of theology devoted much time and effort to consideration of how the university's pastoral role was to be fulfilled, and working out what people outside the university needed to know in order to be saved in the next life. Whether the intellectual culture of the thirteenth-century university should be characterized in terms of conflict or cooperation must depend at least in part on the balance between disagreement and consensus in their consideration of their pastoral role and in the substance of their pastoral teaching.

4 Communication and control

In the second half of the twelfth century, the Parisian theologians placed greatest emphasis on moral theology and pastoral mission. All too often this has been presented as a period of intellectual decline; the scholars of this period supposedly had second-rate minds, and we have to wait until the thirteenth century for things to become interesting again. This, however, is to judge their work from a perspective that was not shared by Parisian scholars themselves, not even those of the first half of the twelfth century. Repeatedly ethics and moral theology were presented as the ultimate goals of academic study. Thus, in Peter Abelard's *Dialogue between a Philosopher, a Jew and a Christian*, the Philosopher declares at the very start that the whole point of his long study of the various other disciplines was finally to study moral philosophy:

> So having devoted myself to our schools for a long time, and having been educated in both their reasons and their authorities, at last I brought myself to moral philosophy, which is the aim of all the disciplines and for the sake of which I judged all the rest should be mere preliminaries.[1]

Later, in the exchange between the Philosopher and the Christian, the latter refers to ethics as 'the goal and summation of all disciplines', renaming it 'divinity' in the context of Christian study in order to stress the goal of understanding God rather than the means of getting there:

> we're really proceeding now toward the goal and summation of all disciplines. Surely the discipline you have usually called 'ethics' – that is, morals – we have usually called 'divinity'. That is, whereas we call it such from what it is directed at comprehending, namely God, you do so from the means by which it arrives there, namely the moral goods you call 'virtues'.[2]

[1] Peter Abelard, *Dialogue between a Philosopher, a Jew and a Christian*, in *Ethical Writings*, trans. P. V. Spade (Indianapolis, 1995), preface, p. 59.

[2] *Ibid.*, 2.148, p. 93.

The Philosopher then declares that compared with ethics 'all the other arts' teachings become vile'. They only have value in so far as they perform an ancillary role, assisting the scholar to reach the ultimate form of study.

Nothing fruitful is apparent in them, except to the extent that they serve this ultimate philosophy like busy maidservants around their mistress. For what is there to the study of grammar, dialectic or the other arts that has to do with seeking out true human blessedness? They all lie far below this pinnacle and aren't strong enough to raise themselves up to such a peak. But they do deal with certain kinds of speech or busy themselves with some of the natures of things, as if providing certain steps up to this loftiness. For we must speak about it and make it known by using some of the natures of things as an example or analogy. Thus through them we reach it, as though reaching the mistress through a kind of escort by the maidservants.[3]

John of Salisbury exhibited exactly the same priorities in his *Metalogicon*: 'Of all branches of learning, that which confers the greatest beauty is Ethics, the most excellent part of philosophy, without which the latter would not even deserve its name.'[4] This attitude was much in evidence when he criticized his contemporaries for being obsessed with dialectic on its own rather than deploying it to address moral issues:

Dialectic, pure and simple, hardly ever investigates such questions as: 'Is pleasure good?' 'Should virtue be preferred to aught else?' 'Do good habits exist in the highest state?' and 'Should one labour when one is in need?' But upon the answer to problems such as these, depends whether or not our life will result in the attainment of happiness and salvation.[5]

In the thirteenth century theologians used Aristotelian concepts to discuss the nature and purpose of theology. Was theology a science? Increasingly they decided that it was, in which case they had to consider whether it was a practical science or a theoretical science.[6] Characteristically, Thomas Aquinas gave a distinctive twist to the debate. In Aristotelian terms, a science had to be based on self-evident first principles. Drawing on Aristotle, Aquinas argued that this criterion might be met in different ways, so that some sciences rested on

[3] *Ibid.*, 2.152, pp. 93–4.
[4] John of Salisbury, *The Metalogicon of John of Salisbury: A Twelfth-Century Defense of the Verbal and Logical Arts of the Trivium*, trans. D. D. McGarry (Berkeley, 1955), 1.24, p. 67.
[5] *Ibid.*, 2.11, pp. 100–1.
[6] For accounts of thirteenth-century discussions of theology as a science, see M.-D. Chenu, *La théologie comme science au xiiie siècle* (Paris, 1957); G. Turner, 'St Thomas Aquinas on the "scientific" nature of theology', *New Blackfriars* 78 (1997): 464–76.

first principles that were known by natural understanding, while others derived their first principles from other higher sciences:

sciences are of two kinds: some work from premises recognized in the innate light of intelligence, for instance arithmetic, geometry, and sciences of the same sort; while others work from premises recognized in the light of a higher science, for instance optics starts out from principles marked out by geometry, and harmony from principles indicated by arithmetic.[7]

Theology, according to Aquinas, was a science of the second type, a 'subalternated' science, because it was based on principles derived from a superior source, specifically those that God chose to reveal:

In this second manner is Christian theology a science, for it flows from founts recognized in the light of a higher science, namely God's very own which he shares with the blessed. Hence as harmony credits its principles which are taken from arithmetic, so Christian theology takes on faith its principles revealed by God.[8]

Aquinas further maintained that theology was 'a single science':

Now since holy Scripture looks at things in that they are divinely revealed ... all things whatsoever that can be divinely revealed share in the same formal objective meaning. On that account they are included under theology as under a single science.[9]

This was important to bear in mind when considering whether theology was a practical or a theoretical science. It could be argued that theology was a practical science because 'Aristotle says that "a practical science is that which ends in action"', and 'Christian theology is for action, according to St James, "Be ye doers of the word and not hearers only".'[10] Against this, it could be argued that theology was 'more contemplative than practical' because 'every practical science is concerned with what men can do and make, thus ethics is about human acts and architecture about building. Christian theology, however, is about God, who makes men and is not made by them'.[11] Bearing in mind that theology was a single science, Aquinas held that it was both theoretical and practical:

[7] ST 1a.1.2 (vol. 1, p. 11). For the Aristotelian origins of the notion of a subalternated science, see Chenu, *La théologie comme science*, p. 72, n. 1; Turner, 'St Thomas Aquinas on the "scientific" nature of theology', p. 468.

[8] ST 1a.1.2 (vol. 1, p. 11).

[9] ST 1a.1.3 (vol. 1, pp. 13–15). I have adjusted the translation to maintain consist use of key terms.

[10] ST 1a.1.4.ad1 (vol. 1, p. 15), citing Aristotle, *Metaphysics*, 2.1 993b21, and James 1.22.

[11] ST 1a.1.4.sed contra (vol. 1, p. 17).

> Whereas some among the philosophical sciences are theoretical and others are practical, theology takes over both functions, in this being like the single knowledge whereby God knows himself and the things he makes.[12]

It was, however, 'more theoretical than practical' because 'it is mainly concerned with the divine things which are, rather than with things men do; it deals with human acts only in so far as they prepare men for that achieved knowledge of God on which their eternal bliss reposes'.[13] Aquinas thus contrived to set the contemplative above the practical, while including moral theology and the saving of souls as part of theology's fundamental purpose. For many of his colleagues, however, the practical outweighed the theoretical. Bonaventure, for example, said that the point of theology was both to further contemplation and to make us good, but chiefly the latter.[14] However they viewed the relative status of the practical and the theoretical within theology, thirteenth-century theologians used Aristotelian epistemology to demonstrate that the practical was always an essential goal. So when Parisian masters addressed moral questions, they were not failing to have anything to say about the really exciting issues; rather they were following the idea that this should be the culmination of all study, an idea that was deeply embedded in their sense of their own calling.

Moreover, while moral philosophy and theology were presented as the culmination of study, we should not be misled into thinking that they turned to these matters only in the later stages of their academic careers. On the contrary, they had been studying ethics from their earliest days in the schools because it was taught as part of grammar and rhetoric. These subjects were taught by commentary on classical texts, and masters were expected to explain passages that raised questions of morality, a practice entirely in line with ancient Roman pedagogy. The result was that works of moral theology contained citations, extracts, precepts and examples drawn from the pagan texts that were deemed to possess authority in grammar and rhetoric.[15] Once Aristotle's *Politics* and *Ethics* became available for study, these too formed key elements

[12] ST 1a.1.4 (vol. 1, p. 17). I have adjusted the translation to maintain consist use of key terms.

[13] *Ibid.*

[14] Bonaventure, *Commentaria in quatuor libros sententiarum Magistri Petri Lombardi*, 1; *Opera Omnia* 1 (Quaracchi, 1882), Prooemium, quaestio 3, pp. 12–13.

[15] P. Delhaye, 'L'enseignement de la philosophie morale au XIIe siècle', *Mediaeval Studies* 11 (1949): 77–99, reprinted in *Enseignement et Morale au XIIe Siècle* (Fribourg, 1988), pp. 59–81; P. Delhaye, '<<Grammatica>> et <<Ethica>> au xiie siècle', *Recherches de théologie ancienne et médiévale* 25 (1958): 59–110, reprinted in *Enseignement et Morale*, pp. 83–134. For a longer-term perspective, see C. S. Jaeger, *The Envy of Angels: Cathedral Schools and Social Ideals in Medieval Europe, 950–1200* (Philadelphia, 1994), pp. 118–79.

of an education in the faculty of arts, and were hugely important for many theologians.[16] Moral concerns thus permeated scholarly endeavour from start to finish.

In order to understand the significance of their ethical and moral teaching, the first part of this chapter will explore the ways in which thirteenth-century masters of theology saw themselves and their role in relation to the rest of society. The second part will show how they developed a number of fundamental ideas that made it seem possible to save people from eternal damnation provided that they paid heed to the masters' expert advice on all aspects of human life. Thus the masters' thinking about the afterlife, especially purgatory, the ethical significance of intention and the role of the devil, all served to construct the notion of individual Christians whose personal responsibility for their own salvation would prompt them to seek or accept authoritative rulings on what was licit and illicit in all their actions. The third part of the chapter will set out the chief means by which the masters expected that their authoritative teaching would be communicated beyond the university. The masters of Paris played a key role in what has been called 'a pastoral revolution', and the prospect of saving souls throughout Christendom by their intellectual and pedagogical efforts must have generated a sense of excitement quite as intoxicating as that gained from the study of newly translated texts from the past.

Self-image

The masters regarded their analysis of moral issues and the communication of their views as fundamental aspects of their work that gave them a distinctive and authoritative role in society. This is clear from quodlibetal disputations held in the second half of the thirteenth century, during which they were often asked about themselves and the problems that they faced.[17] They were in effect invited to justify themselves, and as a result quodlibetal questions reveal much about the way in which the masters of theology perceived themselves and the value that they attached to their work.

[16] On the reception of Aristotle's *Politics* and *Ethics*, see P. Biller, *The Measure of Multitude: Population in Medieval Thought* (Oxford, 2000), pp. 50–2, 296–311; J. Dunbabin, 'The reception and interpretation of Aristotle's *Politics*', in N. Kretzmann, A. Kenny and J. Pinborg (eds.), *The Cambridge History of Later Medieval Philosophy* (Cambridge, 1982), pp. 723–37; G. Wieland, 'The reception and interpretation of Aristotle's *Ethics*', in Kretzmann, Kenny and Pinborg (eds.), *The Cambridge History of Later Medieval Philosophy*, pp. 657–72.

[17] See n. 181 below for the nature of quodlibetal disputations.

In 1269, for example, Aquinas tackled an issue that was put to many masters in one form or another. How could they justify remaining in the schools rather than working directly to save souls? Aquinas was asked whether someone was bound to give up studying theology to pursue the salvation of souls, even if he were fit to teach others.[18] Using an image derived from Aristotle, he responded by comparing the master of theology with an architect.[19] By contrast, the ordinary priests who had direct responsibility for the cure of souls were like manual labourers. In any construction, Aquinas explained, the architect who arranged the construction was more important than a manual worker who followed instructions. Thus in the construction of buildings the architect was more highly paid than the manual workers who hewed planks and cut stone. In the work of spiritual construction, those who were directly concerned with the cure of souls, for example by administering the sacraments, were like manual workers. However, both bishops, who arranged how these priests should carry out their duty, and the doctors of theology, who investigated the means of salvation and taught them to others, were like architects. It was therefore better to teach sacred doctrine, and more meritorious if done with good intention, than to be concerned with the salvation of individuals. It was also better to instruct in matters pertaining to salvation those who could benefit both themselves and others rather than simple folk who could only benefit themselves. Aquinas added just one qualification: in certain cases of necessity both bishops and doctors would have to lay aside their office and attend directly to the salvation of souls. This was not, however, the ordinary state of affairs. Normally the masters, too exalted to attend directly to the cure of souls, were responsible for those who did. Like bishops, they had a definite status within a hierarchy. But whereas bishops ruled, the masters carried out a process of inquiry which resulted in teaching. Operating at a higher level of understanding, they passed on the fruits of their learning and thus played a crucial role in ensuring right order within the church.

[18] Quodlibet I.14. Thomas Aquinas, *Quaestiones de quolibet*, Sancti Thomae de Aquino Opera Omnia 25, 2 vols. (Rome, 1996), vol. 2, pp. 194–7. See E. Marmursztejn, 'A normative power in the making: theological *quodlibeta* and the authority of the masters at Paris at the end of the thirteenth century', in C. Schabel (ed.), *Theological Quodlibeta in the Middle Ages: The Thirteenth Century* (Leiden, 2006), pp. 345–402 at 358–9; E. Marmursztejn, *L'autorité des maîtres: scolastique, normes et société au xiiie siècle* (Paris, 2007), pp. 49–54; I. P. Wei, 'The self-image of the masters of theology at the university of Paris in the late thirteenth and early fourteenth centuries', *Journal of Ecclesiastical History* 46 (1995): 398–431 at 409–10.

[19] On the Aristotelian origins of the metaphor of the architect, see Marmursztejn, 'A normative power in the making', p. 358, n. 37.

Henry of Ghent was another master who faced numerous questions about the magisterial life, and he too had to justify his continuing presence in the schools. In 1276, for example, he was asked whether a man with sufficient instruction should remain in the schools in the hope of further profit, rather than leaving to work for the salvation of souls.[20] Henry's response was a painstaking yet passionate justification of the magisterial career in which he examined the circumstances in which it should be assumed and the reasons for its importance. Should an individual remain in the schools or depart to assume direct responsibility for the cure of souls? First, Henry supposed that the individual was suited both to making further progress in his studies if he remained and to saving souls if he moved on. Someone suited to the cure of souls but not to making progress in study acted foolishly in committing himself to study. On the other hand, someone suited to study but not to the cure of souls should transfer to study so that he might learn how to promote the salvation of souls. For any problem to exist, therefore, it had to be supposed that the individual was sufficiently capable to take either course of action. This being the case, Henry made a distinction between considering the matter with regard to the individual who had to choose and considering it with regard to what might be chosen.

First, he considered the matter with regard to the individual. Either he was equally capable of benefiting himself and the church in either activity, or he was more capable of achieving this benefit in one activity than the other. In the latter case there was no problem. The individual should do what he was best at for the greater benefit of himself and others. But if he was equally suited to both activities, and if equal opportunity to do both presented itself, the question became much more tricky. Then the matter would have to be considered with regard to what might be chosen. From this point of view, either there was an equal need for him to study and to undertake the cure of souls, or there was a greater need for him to perform one of these activities. In the latter case it would obviously be better for him to undertake the task where he was most needed. If, however, there was equality in this respect also, a further distinction had to be made: either it was the case that by lecturing and disputing in the schools he would benefit not only himself, but also others; or this was not the case and he would have to spend a lot of time studying before he could benefit others in

[20] Quodlibet I.35. *Henrici de Gandavo Quodlibet I*, ed. R. Macken (Louvain, 1979), pp. 195–202. See Marmursztejn, 'A normative power in the making', pp. 358–9; Marmursztejn, *L'autorité des maîtres*, pp. 49–54, 142; Wei, 'The self-image of the masters of theology', pp. 413–16.

this way. In the first case, Henry was convinced that the calling of a master of theology was superior because in teaching others to be of use all over the world, in elucidating the truth with regard to the faith and the scriptures, and in defending the truth against the impious and heretics, he could benefit the whole church rather than just one particular church.

Henry emphasized his point by adding another qualification that permitted him to wax lyrical on the fundamental purpose of a master of theology. If a school were sufficiently provided for by other doctors so that he was hardly needed, and a church to which he could transfer himself needed him badly, then it would be better if he left the schools. For the whole point of a master's existence was to serve others and not himself. So when a master found that others taught more effectively than himself, he should move on to where his teaching was actually needed. The work of a master must be taken up because of others, as a necessary task and in response to need. It could only be compared with the office of a prelate. Henry therefore had no doubts about masters who attracted students. It did not matter if they were perhaps not as good as their predecessors. It was much better and more fruitful both for themselves and for others if they taught publicly in the schools so that they could make masters and doctors of others rather than leaving to become merely the instructors of children. The point was that a university theologian could do so much more good than an ordinary clergyman. To illustrate this and to give it emotional impact, Henry took up the image used earlier by Aquinas and compared the master of theology with an architect and the ordinary clergyman with a manual labourer. The work of the master was as far from the work of the ordinary clergyman as the work of an architect was from the work of manual labourers. For the architect taught the principles of building while the labourer applied the rules given to him, rules which he was frequently unable to explain. Similarly the 'rural doctors and preachers' were frequently ignorant of the reasons behind those things which they taught and preached, but they taught them with confidence because they knew that what they taught had been accepted by the university masters. Just as a good architect, vital for the direction of some great building project, would be worthy of reproach if he refused to do the work of an architect but applied himself to stonemasonry, so would the great master, vital in the work of the schools, be worthy of reproach if he devoted himself to hewing the spiritual stones of simple souls when it would be much better if he taught simple men the principles of this task. In what by his own admission was fast becoming a sermon as much as a quaestio, Henry was even able to explain the qualification which he had made earlier in terms of this image. If an architect found that there were many better architects around and that he was in the way, it would be better for himself and the building under construction if he turned to manual labour. It was just like the master who ought to leave the schools when others could do the job more effectively.

At this point Henry returned to the structure of his quaestio. He had just been discussing the case of a master who by lecturing and disputing in the schools would benefit not only himself but also others. Now, referring back to his earlier distinction, he turned to the case of someone who was not yet able to offer immediate benefit to others in this way, but who needed to spend a long time before he could achieve this. Again Henry made a distinction. Either there were great hopes that such a man could attain the high and lofty status of a leading master, or there were genuine fears that he would never be fit for promotion. In the first case, Henry said that it would be much better if he stayed in the schools to become a great architect and a leading light in the church, rather than leaving at once to remain like a stonemason and a lesser light. But in the second case, Henry thought it would be much better and more useful for himself and the church if he left. When he was sufficiently trained to be able to help others he should go and use well what he had acquired, taking up an office for which he was prepared and suited. This was far better than struggling to attain a status which he might never achieve. Even if he did achieve it, it would only be with great trouble, he would hardly benefit anyone, and people would question his right to the position. So in this case, the proper course of action was not in doubt. However, perhaps noticing some members of his audience looking rather uncomfortable, Henry softened his line slightly with one final qualification. Someone who had studied for a long time and whose promotion was near could await promotion even though there was no question of him becoming a great doctor. As a result of his status he would command greater credibility and greater confidence would be vested in him, and so he could be of greater benefit to himself and to others. But when he had been promoted, he should leave the schools as quickly as was convenient and proper.

It is striking how the crucial issue in Henry's discussion is at every stage the contribution that would be made to society outside the schools. The master only existed to serve others and so it was not always better to remain in the schools. But if he had the ability and there was no greater need for him elsewhere, he should certainly remain. In this way he could make his greatest possible contribution to society. The whole church would benefit if he taught others, if he elucidated the true faith and the scriptures, and if he defended the truth against heretics. His role was to direct ordinary priests and preachers, and he would be wrong to abandon this task. He was the great architect. His office was necessary to the church like that of the prelate. In this way Henry defined and justified the work of the master entirely in terms of functions that took on meaning outside the schools.

The masters were asked many such questions about their work, and an entirely consistent view emerges from them. They saw themselves as a distinct and self-aware group whose work was vital to the common good. Their contributions to society were numerous: they removed doubt and error, elucidated the truth, defended the faith, and taught others how to preach, teach and see to the cure of souls throughout the church. They were at the top of a hierarchy of knowledge, dealing with problems which others could not begin to comprehend. Lesser men, however, accepted their views as authoritative so that the masters had ever to be mindful of their impact on both their immediate audience and a wider audience beyond the schools. Indeed, great masters benefited the entire church by playing this directing role. Hence their high status as men who merited comparison with bishops and prelates in this world, and who would rank alongside martyrs and virgins in heaven.[21]

The explicit claim to enjoy a status comparable to that of prelates had the potential to cause problems in practice, but this issue was addressed only occasionally. In 1290, however, Godfrey of Fontaines considered what a master should do if he found himself in conflict with a bishop. What should a master do if he were faced with a question and he firmly held one side of the argument to be true but a bishop condemned this view as false so that anyone who asserted or taught it would incur excommunication? Which side of the argument should the master expound?[22] It could be argued that the master should expound the side of the argument which he held to be false because no one should do anything leading to his excommunication. On the other hand, it could be argued that no one ought to lie, especially not a master of theology.

Godfrey began his response by repeating the principle that teaching the truth came into the category of affirmative precepts which oblige for all time, but not at every moment, while not teaching falsehood fell into the category of negative precepts which apply for all time and at every

21 For their claim to rank with martyrs and virgins, see Marmursztejn, *L'autorité des maîtres*, p. 30; Wei, 'The self-image of the masters of theology', pp. 402–3.

22 Quodlibet VII.18. *Les quodlibet cinq, six et sept de Godefroid de Fontaines*, ed. M. de Wulf and J. Hoffmans (Louvain, 1914), pp. 402–5. See Marmursztejn, 'A normative power in the making', p. 363; Marmursztejn, *L'autorité des maîtres*, pp. 69–71; Wei, 'The self-image of the masters of theology', 426–8.

moment. So while the master could never teach falsehoods, the truth did not always have to be expounded: that depended on circumstances of time and place. Godfrey then made a basic distinction with regard to the specific case in hand. Either the truth which the master thought he knew concerned matters necessary to salvation or it concerned less important issues such that neither side of the argument ran counter to the true faith or good morals. In the latter case, Godfrey argued that the master should put forward neither side of the argument. Obviously he could not teach the view he held to be false; that was prohibited by a negative precept which applied at all times. On the other hand, teaching the view he held to be true was enjoined by an affirmative precept which applied in the right circumstances of time and place. However, these were not the right circumstances because he was prohibited by a precept from a superior. Since it was not actually wrong to omit the prohibited action, he had to obey. As long as he was in the place where the prelate had jurisdiction and the precept was in force, it was neither the time nor the place to tell this particular truth. Godfrey also stressed the importance of obedience. If the view condemned by the bishop appeared to be certainly true, probably true or even debatable, the condemnation and excommunication might seem misguided because it impeded enquiry and knowledge of the truth. However, the individual should not set himself up in opposition by contradicting the prelate or urging disobedience. For when no crisis required this truth to be taught, if any individual were permitted to oppose the prelate, the chain of obedience would be broken. On the other hand, the prelate should be pressed to revoke the condemnation and excommunication. For although the resulting harm did not concern salvation, it nevertheless worked against the perfect understanding necessary in at least some measure for men to deal freely with truth. However, there was yet another reason why the master could not openly oppose the bishop: scandal had to be avoided just as much as disobedience. Infidels and many of the faithful would be scandalized by the ignorance and simpleness of prelates who deemed something erroneous and contrary to the faith which in fact ran counter to neither faith nor good morals. Even the faithful who did not really understand the issues would hold the faith in less esteem.

So if the issues at stake did not pertain to salvation, the master could not openly challenge the bishop. But what if they did pertain to salvation? If the truth to which the master held was absolutely certain, based on the authority of scripture and true reasoning, the bishop's prohibition was entirely mistaken and did not bind anyone. For a sentence of excommunication containing manifest error was not binding;

the excommunication of anyone teaching that God created heaven and earth was the example cited by Godfrey. So in this case the master must speak his mind, even though he would appear disobedient and some might be scandalized.

But what if the view condemned as false were indeed false and yet the master, using scripture or reason, genuinely believed it to be true and necessary for salvation? He would either have to set aside his conscience or condemn a prohibition and excommunication which were in fact quite proper. Godfrey concluded that the master must say what he believed to be true, for acting against one's conscience, although mistaken, was a greater sin than following it into error. In this case the master sinned more grievously if he failed to expound what his conscience mistakenly judged to be true doctrine because he feared punishment and wished to obey his superior lest he incur excommunication. It was worse to sin directly against God than against a man. Godfrey concluded his analysis by remarking generally that although manifest error on the part of a prelate was not to be supposed lightly, if the faithful doctor found something had been condemned as false which he believed to be true, he ought to try to expose this in a proper way. Godfrey had thus affirmed the master's duty to expound the truth, a duty which might lead him to defy a bishop.

Henry of Ghent faced similar issues in 1291 when he was asked whether it was licit to dispute about the power of prelates.[23] Henry approached the matter in terms of the intention that lay behind the disputation. The intention might be to diminish the power of prelates and obedience to them, to extend their power and obedience to them, or to clarify the nature and extent of their power, thus establishing who should obey them. To dispute about the power of prelates in the first case was entirely illicit. It was to oppose divine order and the public good since prelates derived their power from God for the public utility of the church. Those guilty were eternally damned and since they were often rebellious enemies of the prelates, the prelates usually disliked this kind of disputation and rightly banned them. To dispute about the power of prelates with the intention of extending that power was also illicit. Again it was to work against the order established by God. It was less serious than the first case since it was in a way to favour the church and the prelates. But prelates ought to disapprove of it because

[23] Quodlibet XV.15. *Henrici de Gandavo Quodlibet XV*, ed. G. Etzkorn and G. A. Wilson (Leuven, 2007), pp. 147–54. See Marmursztejn, 'A normative power in the making', pp. 363–4; Marmursztejn, *L'autorité des maîtres*, pp. 69, 71–3; Wei, 'The self-image of the masters of theology', pp. 428–30.

many participants hoped to gain by flattery. Furthermore, good men did not wish to be esteemed above their true worth, often preferring to be esteemed below it. Moreover, those who extended the power of prelates in the hope that it would work to their advantage would diminish that power when they feared that it would work against them.

To dispute about the power of prelates with the intention of establishing its true nature was, however, entirely licit and highly beneficial. Indeed it was necessary and should be welcomed by prelates. From such disputations many prelates often learned how to use their power legitimately and how to avoid abuses. Their subjects on the other hand learned when they must obey their prelates, how to avoid rebellion, and how to resist their prelates when obedience was illicit. Without the disputation both parties might remain in ignorance. Henry made it clear that he did not mean subjects to judge the commands of their superiors when they contained nothing contrary to divine precepts. But when this was feared, the power of the prelates must be scrutinized and assessed by disputation. The good would be distilled by the disputation and obediently implemented. Henry therefore argued that prelates should seek this kind of disputation. They certainly should not avoid it as this would render their precepts suspect. Henry added two final qualifications. He conceded that no doubt would be cast upon a prelate's precepts if he prohibited a disputation when those involved were jealous and suspect. Furthermore, he accepted that it was best not to dispute about prelates' powers when there was no fear of divine precepts being contravened. Nevertheless, Henry was in effect claiming the power to scrutinize the work of the prelates and to regulate it through disputation. Thus on the rare occasions when masters considered how they should relate to prelates and bishops, they showed an unwavering commitment to the fulfilment of their functions. It was a commitment which in a sense gave them authority over bishops and other prelates.

Some quodlibetal questions also point to an abiding tension between theologians and lawyers. During the second half of the twelfth century, canon law became an independent discipline, clearly distinct from theology, and those who studied and practised canon law and Roman law developed a strong sense of their own identity.[24] While, as we shall see in Chapters 5 and 6, Parisian theologians were familiar with developments in canon and Roman law, and did not hesitate to cite legal authorities and draw upon legal analysis, theologians and lawyers held

[24] See M. Bellomo, *The Common Legal Past of Europe 1000–1800* (Washington, DC, 1995); J. A. Brundage, *The Medieval Origins of the Legal Profession: Canonists, Civilians, and Courts* (Chicago, 2008).

conflicting views on how future prelates might best be trained. In 1293, for example, Godfrey of Fontaines was asked whether the church could be governed better by a good lawyer than by a theologian.[25] This gave Godfrey the opportunity to insist that the fundamental purpose of the prelate could only be fulfilled with the help of theology. He began his analysis by offering three possible interpretations of the word 'church'. First, it could mean the physical building in which God was worshipped. Second, it could refer to the faithful who worshipped God and used the building. Third, it could mean the temporal goods, such as dues and possessions, which physically sustained the ministers of the church.

Taking the first definition, Godfrey pointed out that the immediate care of church buildings was best left neither to a theologian nor to a lawyer, but to a good craftsman. Although the prelate was responsible for maintaining the church in this sense, he did not have to acquire manual skills because this was not the real point of his office. Rather he had to have the diligence and prudence to see that when necessary the work was given to men with the appropriate skills. Similarly with the temporal goods of the church, the third definition, the prelate needed only the prudence to put the right men in charge. On the other hand, when the goods of the church had to be defended against attack, the situation at first seemed slightly different. If a secular power used violence against the church, neither theology nor law were much help; the prelate had to do his best to find a remedy. If, however, secular learning were cunningly used against the church, Godfrey acknowledged that a lawyer was more useful than a theologian. The lawyer knew how to defend the goods and liberties of the church against such assailants, and even how to recover them. The lawyer was also more useful in settling legal disputes between the prelate's subjects. However, none of this constituted the real point of the prelate's office and so, as before, the prelate required only the diligence to provide himself with men who could do all this. He needed a good official and a good advocate, but he did not have to be one himself, just as he did not need to be a good craftsman.

Godfrey then turned to the second definition of the church: the faithful. The government of the church in this sense was the real point of the prelate's office. Here the theologian was incomparably more valuable than the lawyer. A man perfect in both fields would be more valuable still, but he would derive more worth from his theology than from his

[25] Quodlibet X.18. *Le dixième quodlibet de Godefroid de Fontaines*, ed. J. Hoffmans (Louvain, 1931), pp. 395–8. See Marmursztejn, 'A normative power in the making', pp. 354–5; Wei, 'The self-image of the masters of theology', pp. 404–5.

law. This was obvious if one considered what pertained to the good of the church in this second sense. What mattered was instruction in the faith through the preaching of the truth and instruction in morals through exhortation. These were matters of theology, not law, as was the administration of the sacraments. Godfrey concluded with some stern criticism of his contemporaries. The prelates of his day did not see the real point of their office in relation to the church in the sense of the faithful, nor even in the lesser sense of church buildings. Rather they seemed to define the church in terms of temporal goods and exercise their office accordingly. The result was great perversity and abuse. Godfrey was thus in no doubt that theological training was more important for prelates than legal training. Law might be useful for the fulfilment of his secondary functions, but the prelate could always find others to perform them for him. When these secondary functions were elevated to primary status, the result was corruption. Theological learning was therefore essential for the good prelate to carry out his true task, the government of the faithful. This implied an important role for the masters of theology whose distinctive responsibility for this kind of training they frequently stressed.

As well as training others, many masters went on to become major prelates themselves. Most significantly, however, they claimed an immediate authority as academic theologians at the University of Paris, an authority that did not always fit with the ordinary jurisdictional structure of the church through which lawyers expected to exercise power. Moreover, they did so with great self-confidence and optimism, readily likening themselves to major prelates and showing little theoretical interest in limitations on their power or concern about friction with other members of the church. They claimed a place at the summit of a hierarchy of learning with an obligation to respond to the needs of the whole Christian community. Moreover, they assumed that their authority would be widely acknowledged and would have an impact. This does much to explain their relentless and detailed scrutiny of all aspects of life.

Generating a need for masters of theology and their judgements in Christian society

One of the most convincing and enduring theses about the role and status of learned men in the middle ages was put forward by R. I. Moore in his work on the persecution of minorities. By establishing a discourse of 'the other' that justified the persecution of several otherwise unrelated groups by the various ecclesiastical and secular bureaucracies in which they were employed, the 'literati', as Moore termed them, empowered themselves.[26] It is important to grasp, however, that learned men produced a discourse about Christians which they directed at Christians, and it too had the potential to empower the scholarly authors of the discourse because it implied a need for all members of Christendom to know what the Paris theologians had to say on every conceivable issue. Paradoxically, this discourse stressed each individual's responsibility for her or his own salvation, giving grounds for both hope and fear. So much was at stake, however, and sin so hard to avoid, that no ordinary Christian could cope alone. Who then could resist the authoritative guidance that the Paris theologians had to offer?

Purgatory

In the early twelfth century there was much uncertainty about the afterlife, and no consistent view was expressed. By the second half of the thirteenth century, however, Parisian theologians were in broad agreement about what happened to souls when they became separated from their bodies after death: some went to heaven, others went to hell and a third group went to purgatory. The souls in purgatory were punished because, having confessed their sins, they had not completed penance in this life, or because they were guilty of venial sins. Eventually, however, they were purged and went to heaven. The fire that purged them was corporeal fire, and the suffering it caused was greater than that of any penance that might be undertaken in this life.[27] The length of time that they spent in purgatory could be reduced by the living if they held masses, prayed, gave alms, fasted or performed other good works on behalf of the souls in purgatory; these were known as suffrages. There was no direct scriptural authority for the existence of purgatory, although many biblical passages could be granted a supporting role.[28] Without doubt the masters drew upon patristic authorities, notably Augustine and Gregory.[29] Historians have disagreed, however, about how radically ideas about purgatory actually changed, about the

[26] R. I. Moore, *The Formation of a Persecuting Society: Power and Deviance in Western Europe, 950–1250* (Oxford, 1987).

[27] For a rich account of how thirteenth-century masters explained the suffering of the separated soul, see D. Mowbray, *Pain and Suffering in Medieval Theology: Academic Debates at the University of Paris in the Thirteenth Century* (Woodbridge, 2009), pp. 104–30.

[28] J. Le Goff, *The Birth of Purgatory*, trans. A. Goldhammer (London, 1984), pp. 41–4.

[29] Le Goff, *Birth of Purgatory*, pp. 61–85, 88–95. But for important corrections, see G. R. Roberts, 'Purgatory: "birth" or evolution?', *Journal of Ecclesiastical History* 36 (1985): 634–46.

relationship between the ideas of Parisian masters and the beliefs of the laity, and about the extent to which the masters' ideas reflected or even helped to bring about broader social transformations.

The most famous work in this field is Jacques Le Goff's *The Birth of Purgatory*. He convincingly established that the noun 'purgatorium', or 'purgatory', did not exist until it was used in the Paris schools in the late twelfth century. He also argued that at the same time the Parisian masters gave purgatory a distinct spatial location. While acknowledging a long intellectual history and a formative role for popular beliefs and folklore, he regarded the changes brought about by Parisian masters in the 1170s as so significant as to justify the view that it was only then that purgatory was born. This was largely because he linked their work on purgatory to profound changes affecting the whole of western Europe. First, he explained the importance of their thinking in relation to the emergence of new socio-economic structures. The new ideas about purgatory took on meaning in a more complex society in which they reflected new judicial practices and the growth of towns where they gave hope to and increased the status of urban groups hitherto regarded with contempt. Second, Le Goff related their work to profound mental shifts. The introduction of purgatory as an intermediary between heaven and hell reflected a wider shift from binary to ternary patterns in ways of thinking. It also expressed new conceptions of space, time and number, and a new value attached to earthly life. At the same time, Le Goff argued, these ideas were developed in conscious opposition to heresy and the Greek church. In general, moreover, they served to empower the church.

A very different analysis was offered by Aaron Gurevich, who argued that the idea of purgatory existed in popular culture long before the twelfth century. While views of the afterlife were unstructured, purgatory was not understood to be a clearly distinct place, and the noun 'purgatorium' did not exist, souls were purged and then went to heaven, so the basic function of purgatory was well established in popular belief. Gurevich rested his case on vision literature. Although the visions were recorded by educated churchmen and were in part shaped by literary tradition, Gurevich took them to be based on the experiences of real people in the terms in which they understood them, and he stressed popular and folkloric elements contained within the visions. Crucially, he regarded popular culture and the folkloric as distinct from elite scholarly culture, and indeed set them in opposition to each other. His view was that Parisian masters developed their ideas about purgatory because of pressure from below. Preachers, parish priests and those who wrote works that were to be expounded to the illiterate, in other words those clergy who had direct contact with ordinary people, had to cope with their anxieties and concerns, and they took up their beliefs. The Parisian masters were thus driven to recognize what was already a widespread belief in purgatory.[30]

Without doubt, the visions show that many aspects of the idea of purgatory existed before the twelfth century. One from many possible examples will suffice to make the point. The vision of Drythelm was recorded by Bede in his *Ecclesiastical History* in the eighth century.[31] Drythelm was a pious head of a household who lived in the north of England. He became ill, died at nightfall, but revived in the morning. Having disposed of his property, he entered the monastery of Melrose and withdrew to a hermitage where he recounted what he had seen. A guide with 'a shining countenance and a bright garment' had led him to a vast valley. On one side of the valley there were flames while on the other there was ice and snow, and souls leaped back and forth as each side proved unbearable. Drythelm thought that this might be hell, but his guide said that this was not the case. The guide led him through the valley to a place of darkness until they reached a huge pit from which balls of flames rose and fell. Left alone, Drythelm observed that the flames were full of souls while a terrible stench filled the place. He also saw laughing devils dragging lamenting souls into the pit; these souls included a clergyman, a layman and a woman. The guide returned to chase off devils who were menacing Drythelm himself and to lead him into lightness, where they faced a vast wall through which there was apparently no means to go. By some means which Drythelm could not comprehend, they passed beyond the wall into 'a vast and delightful field' full of sweet-smelling flowers and brilliant light, occupied by 'innumerable assemblies of men and women in white and many groups seated together rejoicing'. Drythelm thought that this might be heaven, but his guide told him that it was not. Further on, Drythelm encountered a more beautiful light, heard sweet singing, and smelled a more wonderful fragrance. Though he hoped to enter this place, his guide led

30 A. Gurevich, *Medieval Popular Culture: Problems of Belief and Perception*, trans. J. M. Bak and P. A. Hollingsworth (Cambridge, 1988), pp. 109–49; A. J. Gurevich, 'Popular and scholarly medieval cultural traditions: notes in the margin of Jacques Le Goff's book', *Journal of Medieval History* 9 (1983): 71–90.

31 E. Gardiner (ed.), *Visions of Heaven and Hell before Dante* (New York, 1989), pp. 57–63. For discussion of the genre and other examples, see A. E. Bernstein, 'Heaven, hell and purgatory: 1100–1500', in M. Rubin and W. Simons (eds.), *The Cambridge History of Christianity. Vol. 4: Christianity in Western Europe c. 1100–c. 1500* (Cambridge, 2009), pp. 200–16 at 204–6; Gurevich, *Medieval Popular Culture*, pp. 104–52; Le Goff, *Birth of Purgatory*, pp. 107–22, 177–205.

him back to the field from which they had just come. There the guide explained what Drythelm had seen:

That valley you saw so dreadful because of the consuming flames and cutting cold is the place to try and punish the souls of those who delay to confess and amend their sins, but eventually have recourse to repentance at the point of death, and so depart from this life. Nevertheless, because they finally confessed and repented at death, they will all be received into the kingdom of heaven at the Day of Judgment. Many, however, are aided before the Day of Judgment by the prayers, alms and fasting of the living, and more especially by Masses. That fiery and stinking pit that you saw is the mouth of hell, and whoever falls into it shall never be delivered for all eternity. This flowery place, in which you see these most beautiful people, so bright and merry, is the reception place for the souls of those who depart from the body after doing good works, but who are not so perfect as to deserve to be admitted immediately into the kingdom of heaven. Yet at the Day of Judgment they shall all see Christ and partake of the joys of his kingdom; for they who are perfect in thought, word and deed immediately enter the kingdom of heaven as soon as they depart from their bodies. That is in the place with the odor and bright light where you heard the sound of sweet singing.[32]

After his guide had promised that he would go to heaven after death provided that he spoke and behaved ‘in righteousness and simplicity’, Drythelm returned reluctantly to life. Subsequently Drythelm would only recount what he had seen to those who lived piously, and he subjected himself to extreme penance by praying while standing in a river, even in winter. When others remarked on his ability to endure the cold, he replied that he had seen worse. Thus ‘he helped the salvation of many by his words and example’.[33]

Drythelm’s vision presented an afterlife consisting of four places: heaven, hell, a valley full of fire and ice for those who repented and confessed only at the point of death, and a beautiful field for those who lived virtuously but were insufficiently perfect to go straight to heaven. Those who found themselves in either of the last two places eventually went to heaven. Clearly this differed from the later division of the afterlife into heaven, hell and purgatory, but the valley of fire and ice fulfilled much the same role as purgatory was later to do. Although it was not called purgatory and there was no reference to purgation, it punished sinners who had confessed so that they could get to heaven in the end, and suffrages could speed them on their way. Furthermore, the horrific nature of punishment in the valley was emphasized by Drythelm’s

[32] Gardiner (ed.), *Visions of Heaven and Hell*, p. 61.
[33] *Ibid.*, p. 63.

comparison between his extreme penitential acts and what he had seen there.

Visions of this kind cannot be used to choose between the views of Le Goff and Gurevich because it is impossible to separate and quantify the 'learned' and the 'popular' within them. Moreover, any attempt to perform this impossible task is deeply anachronistic since the Parisian masters themselves regarded these visions as straightforwardly genuine and used them as evidence in their attempts to understand the afterlife. The idea that these visions could be seen as in opposition to learning would have made no sense to them whatsoever. To give just one example, Hugh of Saint Victor gave careful attention to the nature and value of visions of the afterlife. Having asserted on the basis of 'many examples' that good and evil angels were present when the soul left the body at the moment of death, he proceeded to discuss in detail the sources of knowledge about the fate of souls after death:

> we also know that the souls themselves, when still placed in the body before departure, have sometimes foreknowledge of many things which are to be upon them, whether from the response of their interior consciousness or through revelations made externally. We know also that the souls which have sometimes been snatched away and again returned to the bodies have narrated certain visions and revelations made to them either about the torments of the impious or about the joys of the just.[34]

Because he was in the middle of discussing whether or not separated souls were located in place and space, Hugh was primarily struck by the apparently corporeal nature of the experiences that were related in visions when souls returned to their bodies:

> in all these [visions] they have recited nothing except either the corporeal or something similar to the corporeal, namely, rivers, flames, bridges, ships, houses, groves, fields, flowers, black men, white men, etc., such as are customarily seen and had in this world, either to be loved unto joy or to be feared unto torment, also that they, when loosed from bodies, are taken by the hands, guided by the feet, suspended by the neck, shipped, cast headlong, and other things of this kind which can by no means happen except to corporeal nature.[35]

Hugh did not question the authenticity of these visions. His point was that if the corporeal nature of these experiences was accepted, it followed that separated souls possessed some sort of bodily likeness:

[34] Hugh of Saint Victor, *On the Sacraments of the Christian Faith (De Sacramentis)*, trans. R. J. Deferrari (Cambridge, MA, 1951), 2.16.2, p. 436.

[35] *Ibid.*

If we believe that all these things exist there thus visibly and corporeally, beside other incongruous things that arise, we confess truly that the souls themselves even separated from bodies are bodies composed of members in the likeness of bodies and yet distinct.[36]

Hugh was thus using visions as a source of information about the nature of separated souls. It led him to recount a story about a pilgrim that he himself had heard. He was careful to set out the chain of communication by which he came to know the story, stressing the impeccable credentials of the key narrators. Hugh had been told the story by 'a certain brother of approved testimony' who had received it from his abbot. The abbot had picked up the story when travelling to visit some other brothers. Breaking his journey in a village overnight, he 'learned that a famous event had taken place a few days before among the inhabitants of that place', presumably from the inhabitants themselves. Although Hugh did not dwell on this last link in the chain, there was no suggestion that he regarded it as weak.[37] The story concerned a pilgrim who left the village before dawn and was separated from his companions in a nearby forest. He encountered a devil masquerading as Saint James who praised him for his devotion, assured him that he would soon receive great reward, and set out the miseries of this life, inducing 'contempt of life' and removing 'fear of death'. Thus deceived, the pilgrim cut his own throat. When his companions found his body, they took it back to the village and falsely accused his host of his murder. The host begged for divine aid, and the pilgrim came back to life, explaining that the host was innocent. He further 'reported that he had been led to torments by the same evil angel by whom he had been persuaded to kill himself', until the real Saint James 'snatched him off to heaven' where, after many prayers on his behalf, he was given permission to return to life. While in heaven 'he saw many thousands of angels', but they were so unlike anything in this world that he could say little about them.[38]

Although this vision did not reveal much about the afterlife, it allowed Hugh to develop his thinking about separated souls:

Indeed we wished to recall this lest it seem a marvel if, when souls have departed from bodies, certain signs similar to the corporeal are presented for the demonstration of the spiritual, which, unless they were seen in and through such a corporeal likeness would by no means be mentioned by these same souls when returned to bodies, living in bodies, and knowing only corporeal things. For although being stripped of bodies there, they were able in one way to see those things; yet they would not be able to tell us in another way.[39]

[36] *Ibid.* [37] *Ibid.*
[38] *Ibid.*, pp. 436–7. [39] *Ibid.*, p. 437.

Hugh's point was that if souls were to leave their bodies and report back on the afterlife, they would have to experience the spiritual in a quasi corporeal way or they would be unable to understand and communicate that experience once they were back in their bodies. While he conceded that separated souls that were not going to return to their bodies probably did not perceive in this way, it allowed him to suggest that some kind of quasi corporeal experience was not entirely alien to separated souls, which was important because he was just about to insist that they were punished by corporeal and material fire. For Hugh, visions had genuine value and authority as sources that informed theological analysis. This was confirmed when he used visions as evidence for the view that purgatorial punishment probably took place in this world; its location had 'by no means been determined, except that by the many examples and revelations of the souls which have been placed in punishment of this kind it has been shown very often that that punishment is exercised in this world'.[40]

Visions were therefore understood by masters to give them access to experience outside the schools, and were deployed by them, in combination with scriptural and patristic authorities, as part of their scholarly output. They themselves thought that they were responding to the experiences of the unlearned, appropriating them and incorporating them into their discourse, a discourse that they sought to present back to the rest of society. What then were the essential features of the discourse that they constructed and wished to project back? Following the work of other historians, it is important to trace the emergence of a simplified division of the dead into three groups according to which separated souls rose directly to heaven, plunged straight to hell or spent time in purgatory. It is also important to identify the moment at which the noun 'purgatorium' came into being and purgatory received a name, and to consider the extent to which this was linked with a clear spatial location. But these were not the features that mattered most for the authority of the masters. In this regard, it is necessary to understand how their idea of purgatory underpinned their pastoral strategies and generated the need for further judgements to be made by them. Before these features can be identified, however, it is necessary to explore the work of individual masters in some detail because misleading accounts have been given.

Hugh of Saint Victor Continuing to explore the work of Hugh of Saint Victor, the second book of his *De sacramentis* included a

[40] *Ibid.*, 2.16.4, p. 440.

section 'on the end of man and on those who seek that end'. He began with the emphasis on hope: it was not necessary to be perfect to be saved.

Scripture says: 'Blessed are the dead, who die in the Lord' (Cf. Apoc. 14.13). They die in the Lord who dying in the flesh indeed are yet found living in the Lord. What is 'in the Lord'? In faith and hope and charity ... Let no one, therefore, say to me: Those who have little faith and little hope and little charity are not saved. I do not measure. Let them grow as much as they wish; the greater, the better. Yet I do not dare condemn them, however little they are. From the moment they are born from God, they are sons of God. Do you think that God will save His great sons and will condemn His small ones? Scripture says to me: 'Your eyes have seen my imperfection, and in your book all will be inscribed' (Cf. Psalm 138. 16). If all, then both small and large.[41]

He continued in this vein, stressing that 'the imperfect also will be saved'.[42] When, however, he turned to the questions that were often asked about death, uncertainty and fear came to the fore:

Men ask about the departure of souls from bodies, how they depart, and whither they proceed on departing, or whither they proceed when they have arrived, what they find or what they perceive or endure. But all these things ought to be feared rather than asked. Therefore, since they are hidden, let them not be asked or be found but let them be feared. For who can be secure proceeding into uncertainty?[43]

By linking fear and uncertainty, Hugh found a purpose for the gaps in the authorities. There was, however, one certainty, and that was the need to live well to avoid an evil death.[44]

Hugh then turned to the questions that many asked. The first question concerned the nature of the soul's existence after death, and especially whether or not it was located in space. One view was that when souls departed from bodies they 'go forth that they may begin to exist outside, as if cut off'. Another view took the notion of departure less literally, maintaining that 'they withdraw themselves from the animation of bodies, and gathering, as it were, to themselves, they cease from the quickening of bodies so that they subsist on themselves'. In the first case, the soul would be like corporeal breath: when exhaled 'it goes out of the body and begins essentially and locally outside the body, while before it was essentially and locally contained within the body'. In the second case, the soul could be likened to moisture in the bark of a tree: 'When indeed the bark begins to dry on a tree, the moisture goes out

41 *Ibid.*, 2.16.1, p. 433. 42 *Ibid.*
43 *Ibid.*, 2.16.2, pp. 433–4. 44 *Ibid.*, p. 434.

from it and is contracted toward the inner portions, and it does not go out so that it is outside but remains more within.'[45] Hugh seemed to favour the second approach:

> it seems that in a measure [the separated soul] is outside all body, because subsisting alone in itself it is not poured forth for the quickening of the body. When indeed it is not in a body, it is not in a place, because place exists only in a body. Now when it is outside a body, it is also outside a place, because between itself and a body there is no place, and it is equally distant from all body since between itself and all body there is no body.[46]

Thus when the soul left the body, it could not be located in a place or in space. Putting it the other way round, Hugh observed: 'If there were space, there would be place; if there were place, there would be body.'[47] The impossibility of locating the soul in place and space was evident from the way the soul existed when in a body. Even though the soul moved the body physically, it did not itself move in space. In this respect it was like wisdom which was said to be in the heart but was not said to move around physically.[48] While Hugh thus rehearsed arguments in support of one particular answer to the question, he was careful to distance himself from the conclusion. Many asked these questions and 'they' advanced these views. Hugh stressed that 'in hidden things we should not be too curious, lest perhaps we presume more than we can', refusing to commit himself further.[49]

Hugh was sure, however, that 'on the departure of souls there is at hand the presence of evil or good angels who according to merits either carry them to torments or lead them to rest'.[50] This brought Hugh to the second major question that concerned the way in which separated souls suffered punishment. He noted that 'Certain men think that souls can be tortured by corporeal punishments only through bodies and while remaining in bodies', concluding therefore that separated souls 'sustain only those punishments which conscience, the accuser within, inflicts'. Hugh stated categorically, however, 'on the authority of the Sacred Scripture and Catholic faith', that separated souls were 'tortured by corporeal and material fire'.[51] He could provide no rational explanation, but insisted that it should not be a source of wonder. If, for example, souls felt material fire through bodies, they might well

[45] *Ibid.* [46] *Ibid.* [47] *Ibid.*, p. 435.

[48] *Ibid.*: 'Even when, being placed in a body, the soul moves the body locally, yet it itself does not move locally. For if it is thought to move locally because it is in a body which moves locally, why similarly should not wisdom be said to move locally, since it is in the heart which moves locally.'

[49] *Ibid.* [50] *Ibid.*, p. 436.

[51] *Ibid.*, 2.16.3, p. 438. See also Mowbray, *Pain and Suffering*, p. 112.

be expected to feel it to a much greater extent when soul and fire were directly engaged with no body between them.[52] A little earlier in the discussion, Hugh had speculated that souls which had taken pleasure in corporeal images while still in the body might not entirely lose the 'corporeal capacity to suffer' when they left the body because 'the images of corporeal things' had been 'impressed by the experience of wicked delight'.[53] Ultimately, however, the important thing for Hugh was to be clear that 'sinful souls which have not corrected blame in this life have punishment after this life'.[54]

This left Hugh free to consider the 'corporeal places' where corporeal punishments were inflicted. There was much about which he was uncertain, but he was entirely clear that the souls could be divided into four groups: the perfectly good, the very evil, the imperfectly good and the imperfect or less evil.[55] The perfectly good, which included those who were purged of sin before death, went directly up to heaven.[56] This was the only group about which there was complete certainty. The very evil went straight to hell, but where was hell? Perhaps it was 'within a hollow of the land or outside in some region of its circumference', but more probably it was 'placed within the earth as a kind of prison or workhouse for the shades'.[57] The imperfectly good were to suffer purgatorial punishment after death before eventually going to heaven once fully purged:

> In this those who have departed from this life with certain faults but are just and predestined for life are tormented temporarily so as to be purged.[58]

The location of this purgatorial punishment was undetermined, but it was probably in this world, each soul being punished where it had committed its sin.[59] The ultimate fate of the imperfect or less evil was clear: they were damned and would end up in hell. But where were they now?

> not unfittingly can it be asked whether the souls of those to be damned, that is, of those who among the impious and the most wretched were by a certain measure of living lower in malice, are straightway on departing from the bodies

[52] Hugh of Saint Victor, *On the Sacraments*, 2.16.3, p. 438: 'If they can be affected when between themselves and that by which they are affected there is that medium through which they are affected, is it not entirely probable that they would be much more affected when they are joined immediately with that by which they are affected?'

[53] *Ibid.*, 2.16.2, p. 438. [54] *Ibid.*, 2.16.3, p. 439.

[55] *Ibid.*, 2.16.4, p. 441. [56] *Ibid.*, pp. 440, 441.

[57] *Ibid.*, p. 440. See also p. 441, where Gregory is cited.

[58] *Ibid.*, p. 440. [59] *Ibid.*

snatched to the places of hell or indeed are meanwhile separated from those severer torments of hell in certain other penal places.[60]

So it was possible that the less evil did not go straight to hell until 'certain lighter punishments have been disposed of according to the mode or measure of their faults'.[61] Quite what the point of this delay might be, since purgation could not take place, Hugh could not say, if indeed there was such a delay at all.

Hugh went on to consider the nature of the torments in hell, a discussion that became a series of lengthy quotations from Augustine and Gregory.[62] Still presenting quotations without further comment, Hugh placed great emphasis on suffrages. Through Augustine in particular, he made it clear that masses, alms and prayers were of great benefit to souls undergoing purgatorial punishments. For the very good, they were 'acts of grace'; for the not very bad, they were 'propitiations'; for the very bad, they were of no help but still provided 'consolations of some sort to the living'. For those undergoing purgatorial punishment, however, they brought great benefit, either bringing their punishment to an end or making it more bearable.[63]

Hugh's view of the afterlife was riddled with uncertainty and there was much that he simply did not know or could not explain. He divided the souls of the dead into four groups, though somewhat tentatively with regard to the 'imperfect or less evil'. The 'imperfectly good' were, however, purged before going to heaven, and suffrages would reduce their suffering or the time spent being purged. He was concerned about spatial location, rehearsing the idea that separated souls could not have spatial location at all before suggesting the likelihood that souls undergoing purgatorial punishment were to be found in this world where they had committed their sins. He was clear, however, that the existence of this process offered hope of salvation while uncertainty about the afterlife should engender fear.

Peter Lombard Peter Lombard's treatment of relevant issues in his *Sentences* was relatively brief. Distinction 21 of book 4 concerned 'sins which are remitted after this life'. First, Peter considered whether some sins were remitted after this life, and cited authorities to show that this was indeed the case.[64] To refine his answer, he focused

[60] *Ibid.*, p. 441. [61] *Ibid.*
[62] *Ibid.*, 2.16.5, pp. 441–8.
[63] *Ibid.*, 2.16.6–7, pp. 448–50.
[64] Peter Lombard, *Sententiae*, 4.21.1 (vol. 2, p. 379).

on 1 Corinthians 3.11–15, one of the most frequently cited biblical passages in these discussions:

> For no other foundation can any one lay than that which is laid, which is Jesus Christ. Now if any one builds on the foundation with gold, silver, precious stones, wood, hay, stubble – each man's work will become manifest; for the Day will disclose it, because it will be revealed with fire, and the fire will test what sort of work each one has done. If the work which any man has built on the foundation survives, he will receive a reward. If any man's work is burned up, he will suffer loss, though he himself will be saved, but only as through fire.

Peter offered the following interpretation: 'this clearly shows that those who build with wood, hay and straw carry with them combustible buildings, that is venial sins, which are burned in purgatorial fire; thus it is certain that venial sins are destroyed after this life'.[65] Next Peter advanced the view that some were purged in fire more quickly and others more slowly, depending on the extent to which they had loved the transitory things of this world; wood, hay and straw corresponded to different degrees of sin in this regard, with wood burning for longest, hay for a shorter time, and straw for the shortest time.[66]

Peter then considered whether everyone who went to heaven had to undergo purgatorial fire first. He noted Augustine's view that those who built with gold, silver and precious stones were safe from both the eternal fire of hell and purgatorial fire. It could be objected that no one was so perfect as to avoid venial sin, and so those who built with gold, silver and precious stones also built with wood, hay and straw, and therefore had to undergo purgatorial fire. In other words, no one was saved without suffering purgatorial fire. Peter dismissed this objection: not everyone who sinned venially built with wood, hay and straw, just as not every one who contemplated God, loved his neighbour and did good works built with gold, silver and precious stones. Most importantly, the same person could not build in both ways. Even if someone who built with gold, silver and precious stones also sinned venially, his sin would be annihilated by the fervour of his charity like a drop of water in a furnace, and so he would carry nothing combustible with him.[67]

Peter then considered the fate of those whose sins were not thus disposed of. First, he noted that the same sin would be punished much more severely in purgatorial fire than in this life.[68] He then tackled the view that only the penalty for sin might be remitted in future, not the

[65] *Ibid.*, 4.21.2 (vol. 2, p. 380).
[66] *Ibid.*, 4.21.3–4, (vol. 2, pp. 380–1).
[67] *Ibid.*, 4.21.4–5 (vol. 2, pp. 381–2).
[68] *Ibid.*, 4.21.5 (vol. 2, pp. 382–3).

sin itself. Some argued that if someone was truly repentant, all his sins were remitted and only the penalty might remain. Thus when a true penitent died, he passed on without sin, whereas someone who was not a true penitent at death bore a stain that could never be removed. Someone who built with wood, hay and straw repented truly and therefore passed on without sin. This constituted a much tougher line on who could hope to get to heaven, and Peter had no truck with this view: it was possible to be truly penitent but to have failed to repent one or more venial sins that would be purged after death.[69]

Distinction 45 of book 4 concerned the various receptacles in which the souls of the dead resided and suffrages for the dead. Peter divided the souls of the dead into four groups before the Last Judgement. At the two extremes, there were the very good for whom suffrages were actions of grace, and the very bad for whom suffrages were useless, although they might console the living. Peter cast the two intermediate groups as the 'moderately bad' for whom suffrages might reduce the severity of their punishment in this interim period, and the 'moderately good' for whom suffrages might win full absolution. Peter did not discuss the precise locations in which these souls were to be found.[70] Peter then inquired as to the fate of two people, one rich and one poor, who were equally good within the category of 'moderately good', so that they both needed suffrages, and were equally deserving of help after death. For the rich person, special as well as common prayers were said, and vast alms were given, while only the common prayers were said for the pauper. Would the pauper be helped as much by relatively limited suffrages as the rich person by more substantial suffrages? If the pauper did not derive just as much benefit from more limited suffrages, he would not be treated according to his merits. But if he did, what was the point of rich people spending on suffrages? According to Peter, it could well be argued that the very different suffrages offered on their behalves were of equal value to them because the same benefit could be gained in different ways. Peter did not expand on the implications of this view; perhaps it was simply fitting for rich families to spend more lavishly on funerals, or perhaps the rich needed more help. Either way, there was another point of view because it could also be argued that greater help brought quicker, though not more complete, absolution for the rich. Peter did not come down on one side or the other.[71]

[69] *Ibid.*, 4.21.5–6 (vol. 2, p. 383).
[70] *Ibid.*, 4.45.1–2 (vol. 2, pp. 523–5).
[71] *Ibid.*, 4.45.4 (vol. 2, p. 526). See P. W. Rosemann, *Peter Lombard* (Oxford, 2004), p. 183, for the suggestion that Peter meant that 'the elaborate prayers offered for the wealthy person produce the same effect in the eyes of God as the simple prayers made

Like Hugh, Peter Lombard held that separated souls were in four groups, and indeed he did so with greater confidence. He was equally clear about the value of suffrages, extending their benefit to two of the four groups. His view that venial sins could be purged after death suggested hope, but his explicit statement that any given sin would be more severely punished by purgatorial fire than in this life offered grounds for fear. He showed no interest in questions of spatial location.

Peter Comestor As explained above, it has been claimed that the Parisian masters of the late twelfth century wrought significant changes. Peter Comestor discussed the afterlife in his *De sacramentis*, written between 1165 and 1170.[72] Throughout he referred to purgatorial fire rather than purgatory. Citing Augustine, he said that the purgation 'in purgatorial fire' of those who were to be saved took place more or less quickly depending on differences in sin and penance.[73] He then explained that this was the means by which those who had not been able to complete penance in this life could complete it in the next and be saved:

> There are those who cannot complete the penance enjoined in this life because prevented by death. Concerning them it is said that they are to pass through fire so that there they may complete what they could not do in this life, and thus be saved.[74]

Perhaps concerned that some might be tempted to postpone completion of penance, he stressed that punishment in the next life was much more severe than punishment in this life.[75] The key point was that God was both merciful and just. Out of mercy he forgave penitents, sparing them eternal punishment. Out of justice, however, he did not let sins go unpunished. Echoing Gregory, he noted that either man or God must administer punishment.[76] Man should therefore take care to correct his faults in this life lest he had to suffer pain in the next.[77] Peter acknowledged, however, that contrition of the heart might be so great that the penitent was immune from purgatorial fire even though penance had not been completed.[78] Those who died without repenting suffered eternal punishment.[79]

for the poor man, but that it is nonetheless appropriate for the affluent man's family to go to greater expense in the funeral of their relative'.

72 Le Goff, *Birth of Purgatory*, pp. 156–7.

73 Pierre le Mangeur, *De Sacramentis*, ed. R. M. Martin, *Spicilegium Sacrum Lovaniense* 17 (Louvain, 1937), p. 81.

74 *Ibid.* 75 *Ibid.*

76 Gregory the Great, *Moralia in Iob Libri I–X*, ed. M. Adriaen, Corpus Christianorum Series Latina 143 (Turnhout, 1979), 9.34.54, p. 495.

77 Pierre le Mangeur, *De Sacramentis*, p. 81.

78 *Ibid.*, pp. 81–2. 79 *Ibid.*, p. 82.

Peter then worried about those who completed the penance enjoined upon them perfectly, but who had not received a penance of sufficient severity because of the priest's negligence or ignorance. Would they be freed from all further punishment when they died? Peter considered that their contrition might be so great that they were indeed freed, or that God might add a further punishment to be suffered in purgatorial fire, but only God could know the extent of contrition.[80]

Turning to the nature of purgatorial fire, Peter noted differences of opinion. Some said that it was a material fire. This did not mean that it was the ordinary fire of everyday experience: it was not 'elementary' fire that could be fed by wood. But it was a fire that existed in the sub-lunary realm and would perish after the day of judgement with other transitory things. Others said that it was simply pain that was called fire because it was severe and burned like fire. Moreover, to distinguish it from annihilating and eternal pain, it was called purgatorial fire because it was not annihilating but purged through temporary pain so that the sufferer would not be punished eternally.[81] Peter did not come down on one side or the other, but returned to the question of who passed through purgatorial fire. Whatever the nature of the fire, it was to be believed that those faithful passed through it who had not completed penance in this life. Elaborating on his earlier analysis, he noted that some felt it more than others, that some were liberated more quickly than others, indeed that some were punished right up to the day of judgement while others were released sooner. It all depended on the quantity of sin and penance, and the intensity of punishment.[82] The perfectly good, however, were believed to be immune from purgatorial fire because, although it was impossible to be without some venial sins, theirs were consumed by the fervour of charity like a drop of water in a fiery furnace, so that they carried nothing flammable with them.[83]

Greater significance has been attached, however, to a sermon that Peter wrote later for the dedication of a church and which opened with a line from Psalm 122: 'Jerusalem is builded as a city that is compact together.'[84] Among other things, Peter noted, Jerusalem could be taken to stand for the Church Triumphant which consisted of angels and the spirits of the blessed. Elaborating the theme of construction, he observed:

[80] *Ibid.* [81] *Ibid.*
[82] *Ibid.*, pp. 82–3. [83] *Ibid.*, p. 83.
[84] This sermon was attributed to Hildebert of Lavardin. On its reattribution to Peter Comestor, see Le Goff, *Birth of Purgatory*, pp. 154–5

In the building of a city three things come together: first, stones are violently extracted from the quarry with hammers and iron crow-bars, with a great deal of human labour and sweat; second, they are polished, smoothed and squared off with the chisel, the axe and the ruler; third, they are put in their places by the artisan's hand. Likewise in the building of the heavenly Jerusalem, three things are to be considered: separation, polishing and positioning. Separation is violent; polishing is purgatorial; positioning is eternal. In the first, man is in distress and affliction; in the second, in suffering and expectation; in the third, in glory and exultation. Through the first, man is sifted like wheat; in the second, man is tested like silver; in the third, he is restored to the treasury.[85]

Thus Peter likened the separation of the soul from the body at death to the hewing of a stone from a quarry, the process of purgation after death to the polishing of individual stones, and the positioning of stones in a building to the elevation of purged souls to heaven.

Peter continued this image, explaining that prior to the separation of their bodies and souls the living were like stones still in the quarry, the mass of their bodies pressing them together. Getting to heaven involved many tribulations. After the woes of separation, it was rare for someone to be found fit to go straight to heaven. Most passed on with wood, hay and straw, and 'were polished in purgatory', and here Peter used the noun 'purgatory', after which they were raised up to heaven. Peter went on to explain how the church represented these three stages in the liturgical calendar. The vigil of All Saints, a fast day and therefore a day of affliction, stood for separation. All Saints' Day itself, which signified the superabundance of joy in which the saints feasted with God, corresponded to positioning. The Commemoration of the Dead was bound up with polishing because it worked so that 'those who are being polished in purgatory obtain full absolution or mitigation of their pain', and again Peter used the noun 'purgatory'.[86]

Whereas in his *De sacramentis* Peter had referred only to purgatorial fire, now he twice used the noun 'purgatory'. While admitting the possibility that there may have been a later emendation of the sermon, Le Goff considers that 'it is more likely that Peter did indeed employ the noun *purgatorium* and that he was therefore if not the inventor, then at least one of the earliest users, of a neologism related to … a revolutionary change in ideas concerning the geography of the other world'. Le Goff thus argues that before 1170 Peter only referred to purgatorial fire, but that his thinking developed so that he began to use the noun between 1170 and his death in 1178 or 1179.[87]

85 PL vol. 171, col. 740.
86 *Ibid.*, cols. 740–1.
87 Le Goff, *Birth of Purgatory*, p. 157.

It is not entirely clear whether Peter Comestor divided separated souls into three groups or four. He only discussed those who went to heaven, either directly or after purgation, so there is no clue as to whether he thought there were one or two other categories, the not entirely wicked as well as the wicked. Like his predecessors, he struck a careful balance between hope and fear. Purgatory allowed those who had repented to complete penance that they had not had time to finish in this life, and the most contrite might even be spared this obligation. For most in this position, however, the harsher punishment of purgatory was to be dreaded. In his later work he probably used the noun 'purgatorium', but it was not accompanied by any apparent interest in the spatial location of purgatory. It is far from obvious that his work represented a radical break with the past.

Peter the Chanter The other late twelfth-century Parisian master who has been credited with mould-breaking work is Peter the Chanter. He offered his clearest overview of the afterlife in his *Summa de Sacramentis et animae consiliis* while discussing punishments of sins, and he made frequent use of the noun 'purgatorium'. He was much exercised by the punishments that God inflicted for venial sins, and especially whether someone might receive eternal punishment for a venial sin.[88] This was not a straightforward matter because of those who died having committed both mortal and venial sin. They went to hell because of their mortal sin. How then were they punished, if at all, for their venial sin? It seemed absurd to suppose that someone might receive a temporary and purgatorial punishment in hell, but it also seemed unjust that someone should receive an eternal punishment in hell for a venial sin.[89]

In the course of a long and intricate discussion in which he assessed a multitude of different opinions and interpretations, Peter considered a view according to which punishment for the venial sin was absorbed into the punishment for the mortal sin. This could be understood by analogy with a man who committed a crime for which he deserved punishment but who, before receiving a specific punishment for this crime, committed a much worse crime for which he deserved and received the death penalty. This punishment seemed to absorb the punishment due for the first and less serious crime in that there was no punishment at all for the first crime unless it was understood to be part of the punishment

88 Pierre le Chantre, *Summa de sacramentis et animae consiliis*, deuxième partie, ed. J.-A. Dugauquier, Analecta Mediaevalia Namuracensia 7 (Louvain, 1957), 90–4, pp. 91–107.

89 *Ibid.*, 90, pp. 92–3.

for the second and greater crime.[90] Peter, however, found the analogy to be wanting because a human judge could not inflict further punishment after the death penalty, whereas God could always make a punishment worse, however grave it had been in the first place. It followed that God could always add punishment for venial sin to punishment for mortal sin.[91]

Pursuing this thought, Peter noted that venial sin received specific punishment in the form of penance in this life, and similarly it received specific punishment in purgatory, so why not also in hell?[92] Peter was using the noun 'purgatorium', and further discussion led him to take an important stance on the grouping of separated souls between death and the Last Judgement. There were those who said that God remitted the venial sin of those who were going to hell with regard to punishment because it sufficed to punish them for their mortal sins, which meant that their venial sin went unpunished. God did not, however, remit their venial sin with regard to guilt because they always remained guilty of that venial sin.[93] Others claimed that the venial sins of the reprobate were punished in purgatory just like the venial sins of the predestined. According to this view, the reprobate passed through purgatory before going to hell. They were purged in purgatory, and their venial sins were remitted with regard both to punishment, which meant that they did not have to be punished for them elsewhere, and to guilt. This view struck Peter as absurd because the predestined would be in no better state than the reprobate.[94] It led him to offer an important clarification:

> Distinctions are usually made with regard to the places where the good and the wicked go after this life. The good go either straight to heaven if they carry nothing flammable with them, or first to purgatory and then to heaven if they carry venial sins with them. Diverse receptacles are not to be distinguished for the wicked who are said to pass straight to hell.[95]

This was not the main point of Peter's discussion but he chose to state it emphatically, going on to reinforce it with further arguments. The predestined deserved to be purged of their venial sins in purgatory because they had previously acted well and with charity, whereas the wicked deserved no such thing because they were entirely without charity.[96] There were also those who said that the wicked passed through purgatory, not that they might be purged, but with purgatory serving as a kind of vehicle by which they were transmitted to eternal fire. To Peter, however, it was not

[90] *Ibid.*, 92, p. 102. [91] *Ibid.*, p. 103.
[92] *Ibid.* [93] *Ibid.*, 93, p. 104.
[94] *Ibid.* [95] *Ibid.* [96] *Ibid.*, pp. 104–5.

clear on what authority they based this view.[97] Moreover, it did not help address the problem of understanding how venial sin was punished when someone died and went to hell because of mortal sin, and it was to this problem that Peter reverted. He had used the noun 'purgatorium' and he had made it very clear that there were only three paths after death. While he was emphatic in his pronouncement, it was not the point of his argument, and it arose merely as an aside. It is difficult to understand how this departure from the work of other recent masters passed into the literary output of the schools with so little fanfare.

But was the use of the noun 'purgatorium' linked to a strong sense of spatial location, as has been suggested? Peter the Chanter used the term 'purgatory' again when discussing alms as remedies against venial sin.[98] Alms given on behalf of the dead reduced their purgatorial punishment. If therefore someone gave alms for a living friend, was the friend's penitential punishment reduced? Peter said that it was, offering the following explanation:

> For there are two purgatories. One purgatory is in the future after death and it can be reduced principally by the celebration of masses, and secondarily by other good works. The other purgatory is penance that has been enjoined, and it can be mitigated by the same things.[99]

Thus, for Peter, purgatory was not a single entity, and unsurprisingly he did not consider where it might be located. Le Goff commented that for Peter purgatory was 'a state rather than a place'.[100]

If Peter's view of purgatory turned out to be rather less clear than at first appeared, he was vehement about the severity of the punishment that was to be endured there. When discussing punishments due for venial sins, he asked whether someone who deserved purgatorial punishment for venial sin because he died without contrition for that sin deserved greater punishment than someone did for mortal sin for which he had been contrite and completed penance enjoined by a confessor. His answer was yes, and it led him to repeat an important point: any punishment enjoined in this life was lighter than purgatorial punishment.[101] He returned to this theme in his *Verbum Adbreviatum*, when discussing the quantity and harshness of penance. His purpose was to

[97] *Ibid.*, p. 105.

[98] Pierre le Chantre, *Summa de sacramentis et animae consiliis*, troisième partie (III, 2a), *Liber casuum conscientiae*, ed. J.-A. Dugauquier, Analecta Mediaevalia Namurcensia 16 (Louvain, 1963), 257, pp. 263–4.

[99] *Ibid.*, p. 264.

[100] Le Goff, *Birth of Purgatory*, p. 166.

[101] Pierre le Chantre, *Summa de sacramentis et animae consiliis*, deuxième partie, 98, pp. 121–2.

prove that penance should be severe and involve great suffering. He did this by explaining that as far as humanly possible penance must be equal to purgatory, and by stressing the extreme nature of punishment in purgatory. He therefore quoted Bede to the effect that in purgatorial fire 'the lightest punishment is more serious and harsh than the most exquisite torments of all the martyrs', exhorted his readers to think about the 'incomparable punishment of purgatory' and cited Hebrews 10.31, 'It is a fearful thing to fall into the hands of the living God.'[102]

Peter the Chanter seems to offer a more radical break in his work on purgatory than Peter Comestor. Incontestably he used the noun 'purgatorium', and he did so with frequency. Moreover, he was absolutely clear that separated souls were faced with three possible destinations after death: heaven, hell, or purgatory. On the other hand, he showed no explicit interest in purgatory as a place, and on occasion it did not even seem to be an entirely coherent entity. He was clear, however, about the value of suffrages and very clear that punishment in purgatory was much more painful than anything that could be suffered in this life.

William of Auvergne William of Auvergne, who was a master of theology in the 1220s and then bishop of Paris, wrote about purgatory in his *De universo* which he composed in the 1230s.[103] When he did so, his first concern was to establish that it existed and where. He then considered particular problems relating to the nature of fire in both hell and purgatory. He wanted to explain how hell fire did not consume the bodies that it burned. The problem with purgatorial fire was to explain how it burned souls that were separated from their bodies, and here he had to contend with an unnamed authority which denied the corporeal nature of purgatorial fire. He also wished to account for the variety of tortures that were inflicted in purgatory and hell, many not involving fire at all. It is worth exploring his arguments in detail because they have been the subject of some controversy. Alan Bernstein has argued that William held purgatorial fire to be incorporeal but considered this to be a truth that should be taught only to the theological elite; teaching beyond the schools should stress the material nature of purgatorial fire lest the prospect of punishment after death seem insufficiently

102 *Petri Cantoris Parisiensis Verbum Adbreviatum*, Textus Conflatus, ed. M. Boutry, Corpus Christianorum Continuatio Medievalis 196 (Turnhout, 2004), 2.55, p. 817.

103 See A. E. Bernstein, 'Theology between heresy and folklore: William of Auvergne on punishment after death', *Studies in Medieval and Renaissance History* 5 (1982): 5–44 at 6–8, 14–19; Le Goff, *Birth of Purgatory*, p. 242.

threatening.[104] According to Jacques Le Goff and Jérôme Baschet, on the other hand, William consistently upheld the corporeal nature of purgatorial fire.[105]

William began by asking whether the place for the purgation of souls that they called purgatory was separate from both hell and where people live. He stated that it was, and proceeded to offer a series of interconnected arguments to show that this was the case. First, it was obvious that much remained to be purged in some souls because their bodies had died before they were able to complete penance in this life, an eventuality that was made especially likely by sudden or unforeseen death. It was necessary that there should be a place in which they could complete their penance, and this was what they called purgatory. It might be objected that souls went directly either to heaven or hell, depending on whether or not they had mortal sin, but William said that intelligent men had no doubt that some sins were less serious, and that infernal punishment was not due for these sins. It was, however, impossible that anyone should go to heaven with such sins, hence the need for purgation and for some place in which it could occur. William went on to elaborate these arguments, stressing the differences between types of sin, and ridiculing the arguments that would follow if one did not accept his point. Lest anyone should doubt God's mercy and justice, he concluded that purgatory was useful in terms of souls achieving salvation, but that fear of future purgation made men begin penitential purgation more willingly and quickly in this life, and try harder to complete it before death.[106] Thus, right from the start of his analysis, William divided the immediate fate of separated souls into three, used the noun 'purgatorium', put a strong emphasis on place, and balanced hope of salvation against fear of punishment in purgatory.

Having presented all these arguments, William explained that indubitable faith in purgatory stemmed from visions and apparitions of souls who were undergoing purgation after death. Many often appeared to their friends to obtain their help in the form of suffrages, and to warn

[104] A. E. Bernstein, 'Esoteric theology: William of Auvergne on the fires of hell and purgatory', *Speculum* 57 (1982): 509–31; for a summary of the argument, see A. E. Bernstein, 'The invocation of hell in thirteenth-century Paris', in J. Hankins, J. Monfasani and F. Purnell (eds.), *Supplementum Festivum: Studies in Honor of Paul Oskar Kristeller*, Medieval and Renaissance Texts and Studies 49 (Binghamton, New York, 1987), pp. 13–54 at 23–4.

[105] J. Baschet, *Les justices de l'au-delà: les représentations de l'enfer en France et en Italie (XIIe-XVe siècle)* (Rome, 1993), pp. 43–6 ; Le Goff, *Birth of Purgatory*, pp. 244–5.

[106] *Guilielmi Alverni … Opera Omnia*, 2 vols. (Paris, 1674; repr. Frankfurt am Main, 1963), vol. 1, *De universo*, LX, pp. 676–8. See Bernstein, 'Theology between heresy and folklore', pp. 31–2.

them so that they could avoid future punishments. Many also appeared to holy men, seeking suffrages from them or wanting them to get their friends to arrange suffrages. Returning to life, they recounted and bore witness to the state of souls undergoing purgation, both their own souls and the souls of others. Accounts of these apparitions were not only entertaining to hear but also useful and salutary because they led men to correct their vices and sins, and encouraged them to love sanctity and desire eternal happiness. As further proof, William then asserted that all three great religions agreed that souls were purged after death, and that even peoples who had no faith invariably offered suffrages to free the souls of the dead so that they might reach the heavens or become like their gods. William then clarified what was distinctive about Christian belief. The Christian people believed that the souls of the dead could be helped by prayers, alms, masses and every kind of pious work. There were, however, two qualifications. First, this only applied up to the day of universal judgement. Second, not everyone could be perfectly purged for Christians did not believe that those who were already in hell or the souls of children who died before baptism could be purged. Only those who repented in this life could be purged, and only they could benefit from the suffrages that he had just listed.[107] Once again William went on to explore the logical consequences of refusal to accept his position, and to denigrate the possible conclusions that would have to be drawn. Only one other line of argument contained some truth: those who denied the existence of purgatory might argue that interior penance sufficed, removing the need for purgatorial punishment after death. The main drawback to this was that suffrages would be rendered pointless. Nevertheless, provided that the pain of interior penance varied according to the seriousness of the sin, William conceded that this might be enough to satisfy divine justice and to remove the need for further punishment. In most cases, however, he contended that divine justice was not completely satisfied by interior penance which had therefore to be supplemented.[108]

William further based his case for the existence of purgatory on the very nature of penance. Interior penance was a spiritual judgement in which the soul judged itself to deserve infernal punishments for its sins. It therefore subjected itself not only to spiritual torments but also to corporeal afflictions such as fasts, works and whippings. When the soul

[107] *De universo*, LXI, p. 678. See Bernstein, 'Theology between heresy and folklore', pp. 36–8.

[108] *De universo*, LXI, pp. 678–9. See Bernstein, 'Theology between heresy and folklore', pp. 33–4.

saw that this was not enough fully to satisfy the justice of the Creator, it prayed for his mercy, imploring him to set aside the punishments that were deserved. Thus William argued that the penitent soul knew itself that interior penance and corporeal punishments in this life were not enough. He therefore remarked that those who denied the existence of purgatory simply did not understand the nature of penance. Indeed, William insisted, the afflictions of purgatory were 'incomparably greater' than anything penitents could inflict on themselves in this life. William illustrated that this was just by offering two scenarios taken from this life. If a servant fled, it was not enough for him simply to return to his master; he was justly required to perform other works to compensate his master for the time during which he had been defrauded of his labour. Similarly, a knight who abandoned his king when war threatened could not just go back to the king; he had to give him satisfaction for broken faith and losses he had caused. In the same way, it was not enough for sinners simply to return to God: they had to pay for the affront and injury they had caused by withdrawing their servitude. William conceded, however, that there might be cases where the humility, devotion and interior affliction were so great that God was satisfied without further punishment. These exceptional cases apart, souls had to undergo purgation after death.[109]

But where did this purgation take place? This was a tricky question because whether purgatory was a distinct and separate place 'no law or other writing determines'. Visions, however, indicated that purgation and supplementary penances occurred in many places on this earth, and reason supported this view. Since these purgations supplemented penances, it would be wrong for them to be in any place other than that of the penitents. William declared a general principle to the effect that the whole and its parts should always be in the same place; thus where a man was, his feet and hands should also be. These purgations were parts of penances, so it followed that they must occur in the same place as the original penances begun in this life.[110]

William then turned to the nature of fire in purgatory and hell. Having regard for those who only believed what they saw with their own eyes or learned from innumerable and unimpeachable testimony, he pointed out the many different and extraordinary types of fire that existed in this world. To cite just his first example, Greek fire burned water, and Aristotle explained how to make nine different types. William's next

[109] *De universo*, LXII, p. 679. See Bernstein, 'Theology between heresy and folklore', pp. 34–6.

[110] *De universo*, LXII, p. 679.

key point was again an appeal to experience. Anyone could see that the corporeal frequently had a huge effect on souls, delighting and troubling them, and either way causing them to suffer greatly; women and riches were the specific stimulants cited. So it was hardly shocking or surprising if there was a kind of corporeal fire that could torture human souls both when in bodies and when separated from bodies. William then stressed the justice of this arrangement, chiefly by citing examples from the Old Testament. Since God spoke from a burning bush that was not consumed by fire, he could surely create a fire that would not consume what it burned in order to exercise his justice by torturing the souls of the impious and avenging injuries done to him. If the most just creator created a rain of fire and brimstone to punish the people of Sodom for a particular injury and abuse, how much more appropriate for him to create a fire to punish all injuries and abuses against God. If he parted the Red Sea, against the nature of water, how much better for his honour and glory, and for the beauty and goodness of his justice, to create a fire against the nature of fire to torture the souls of those he considered his enemies.[111]

William proceeded to focus on hell and the way in which the bodies of the damned were not consumed or destroyed by fire. Once again he appealed to nature to show that such a fire was not out of the ordinary, citing first the salamander which lived in fire without harm. Then, adopting a by now familiar pattern, he pointed to the requirements of justice. If the bodies of the damned were destroyed by fire, their punishment would not be everlasting, yet the beauty of divine justice required that it should be eternal.[112]

Next, William turned to the nature of purgatorial fire. He noted that a wise and learned Christian said that human souls suffered only by the imagination of fire, in other words that purgatorial fire was not corporeal. Bernstein argues convincingly that William had Augustine in mind.[113] William then set out to explore the arguments that might support this view, making it very clear that this is what he was doing, and carefully distancing himself from the view in question.[114] He began by discussing the way in which the soul suffered in this life when its body was burned by fire. Because the soul was a spiritual substance, it was

[111] *Ibid.*, LXIII, p. 680. [112] *Ibid.*, LXIV, p. 681.

[113] Bernstein, 'Esoteric theology', pp. 517–18, citing Augustine, *De Genesi ad litteram*, 12.32–3 (PL vol. 34, cols. 480–1). Le Goff, *Birth of Purgatory*, p. 244, seems to indicate that the ideas in question were close to those of Origen; Baschet does not offer an identification. I am very grateful to Professor Bernstein for his advice on this point.

[114] Baschet, *Les justices de l'au-delà*, p. 44, n. 101, makes a similar point.

impossible for there to be any corporeal form within it, which meant that the torment had to be a spiritual form. Indeed when all corporeal and sensible things were apprehended, they made spiritual impressions like this. The impression itself was not heat, yet the soul said to itself that it was burning and suffered in this way. The soul could not be hot or cold because these were corporeal qualities and could only exist in bodies. The soul therefore considered that it burned despite there being no heat in it. Impressed through the body from the fire, the spiritual form, which was not itself fire or heat, nevertheless scorched the soul and made it burn, as the soul itself confessed. It was not therefore surprising if the soul judged that it was being burned only by the imagination of fire since the imagination was entirely spiritual and therefore closer to the soul by its nature. In disposing of objections to this analysis of the way in which sense-based experience produced genuine passions in the soul which were not themselves corporeal in nature, William referred to the process by which 'species' or 'phantasms' were abstracted from sense-based perceptions to impress passions on the soul. This led William to discuss the nature of the imagination, stressing that by conjuring up species or phantasms it could make just as strong an impression on the soul as the senses. This was clear in men of strong imagination who took as much pleasure in imagining the sight of delightful things as in actually seeing them. Various examples followed, including someone upon whom the mere sight of medicine had the desired effect, which must have been caused by the species or 'similitude impressed on his soul' because he had no contact with the actual substance of the medicine, neither the taste nor the smell. It therefore made sense to think that a strong species, one which was strong in making a sad or happy apprehension, sufficed on its own to bring about sadness or happiness in souls, and that the extent of these passions depended on the degree of strength of these species and the things of which they were species. Dreams were a particular case of the imagination at work. Sometimes people dreamed that they were burning in fire and suffering terribly, as if it were actually happening, when in fact fire was not present in substance and it was the species of fire in their imagination which caused them to suffer. Similarly people dreamed that they possessed and then lost great riches, which caused them pleasure and then sadness although actual riches were never present, only species or phantasms in their souls.[115]

William was now able to offer an overall assessment of the view of the wise man to whom he had referred earlier. Given the way in which

[115] *De universo*, LXV, pp. 681–2.

physical suffering effected the soul in this life and the way in which the imagination worked, it was entirely understandable that he should think that souls separated from their bodies could be tortured by the apprehension of fire alone, without the presence of actual fire. Moreover, this would neatly explain the range of torments supposed to take place in purgatory because God could torture souls in all sorts of ways through the imagination 'since it was possible for him, through his omnipotence, to represent or describe all horrors and the strongest species of all kinds of torments in the imagination'. If, however, God could inflict punishment in this way, why had he created the kind of fire that William had described previously, a fire that was corporeal and yet could torture separated souls? What if someone said that it had been created superfluously? William replied in his own voice, clearly asserting what he regarded as the truth. The creation of this special kind of fire was not superfluous for a number of reasons. First, 'it has many uses of which one is that it corporeally and truly tortures the bodies of souls and also the souls themselves'. This compressed statement presumably refers to the fire's capacity to torture bodies in hell and separated souls in purgatory. Second, 'since God is the God of truth, and he is truth, it does not befit the magnificence of his glory to use the lies of dreams'. Third, 'just dreaming of fires would not sufficiently deter men from vices and sins because very few could understand that souls can be tortured by either dreams or the imaginings of punishments'. Showing due caution, William added that the omnipotent creator could take vengeance on his enemies in many ways that were unknown to all, including himself and other men.[116]

It is this last passage that has sown confusion amongst later historians. The opening line is far from clear: 'What if someone said that fire of this kind had been created superfluously?' Bernstein takes it to refer to the incorporeal species of fire that had just been discussed, and is surprised when William goes on to insist that it burns corporeally, and that it is unlike fire in dreams. According to Bernstein, 'The resolution of this apparent contradiction lies in the distinction between esoteric and exoteric knowledge, between what may be taught to theology students and what may be preached publicly. William employed this distinction to preserve the threat of punishment after death.'[117] Seizing on William's point about dreams lacking deterrent effect, Bernstein has William teaching his students that purgatorial fire was incorporeal, which was the truth, but wanting

[116] *Ibid.*, p. 682.
[117] Bernstein, 'Esoteric theology', p. 515.

everyone else to be told that it was corporeal so that they would be sufficiently frightened to abandon sin. If, however, 'fire of this kind' is taken to refer to the special kind of corporeal fire that can nevertheless burn separated souls in purgatory and hell which William had previously discussed, there is no contradiction to explain. When he established the nature of this fire, he argued directly, drawing his own conclusions. When he discussed the view that souls in purgatory were tortured through the imagination by the species of fire rather than actual fire, he indicated expressly that he was assessing a view put forward by someone else, concluding that the view was reasonable and that it was possible for God to work in this way. But God had chosen another means of punishment, the special kind of corporeal fire, and it was this decision on God's part that William then tried to explain. God had already chosen to work in a way that would deter people from sin, so there was no reason for theologians to decide to preach something they knew to be untrue.

As noted above, one of the attractions of the idea that God punished souls through the imagination was that it made it easy to explain the range of torments supposedly suffered in purgatory and hell. William therefore considered whether there was nothing but fire in hell or whether there were other corporeal features. Noting that 'poets' referred to rivers and stakes, he suggested that they were perhaps speaking metaphorically. According to Christian doctrine, however, hell also contained extremely cold waters. But, in line with his preceding analysis, William stressed the key point that neither these waters nor hell fire were exactly like fire and water in this life since the fire was inextinguishable and the waters could not be consumed and perhaps not heated either.[118] William did not refer again to the range of punishments in purgatory, but the same points presumably applied.

William was therefore clear that after death the separated soul faced three possible destinations: heaven, hell or purgatory. By now the use of the noun 'purgatorium' was apparently routine. He showed a strong interest in the location of purgatory, but did not discover a single place in which it could be found. Rather purgatory consisted of the many places on this earth where souls had begun penances in this life and must now complete them after death, which threw the emphasis back on to the process of purgation. While being very clear that souls in purgatory would eventually get to heaven, and that suffrages could speed their release, William repeatedly stressed that punishment in purgatory

[118] *De universo*, LXV, p. 682.

was to be feared, and in doing so he stuck to the traditional line that purgatorial fire was corporeal and to be feared as a punishment far more painful than any penance in this life.

Aquinas A summary of Aquinas' views on purgatory can be found in the supplement which his followers added to his unfinished *Summa Theologiae* after his death in 1274, drawing upon his other works, especially his *Commentary on the Sentences*, usually quoting sections word for word.[119] Without direct reference to purgatory, Aquinas considered the general relationship between the separated soul and place when he considered 'whether places are appointed to receive souls after death'. He explained that separated souls were indeed received in places, but that the way in which they existed in places was far from straightforward and in many respects beyond human understanding. His key point was that there could be 'fittingness' or 'congruity' in the relationship between spiritual and corporeal substances. Thus, although separated souls had no bodies, 'nevertheless certain corporeal places are appointed to them by way of congruity in reference to their degree of nobility (wherein they are as though in a place, after the manner in which incorporeal things can be in a place), according as they more or less approach to the first substance (to which the highest place is fittingly assigned), namely God'. It followed that 'those souls that have a perfect share of the Godhead are in heaven, and that those souls that are deprived of that share are assigned to a contrary place'. Aquinas acknowledged, however, that this left a great deal unexplained: 'Incorporeal things are not in place after a manner known and familiar to us, in which way we say that bodies are properly in place; but they are in place after a manner befitting spiritual substances, a manner that cannot be fully manifest to us.' Despite this uncertainty, Aquinas was sure that place contributed to the punishment or reward of separated souls because knowing where they had been sent brought them joy or sorrow.[120]

Still without explicit reference to purgatory, Aquinas outlined its role when considering 'whether souls are conveyed to heaven or hell immediately after death'. He explained what happened to separated souls by analogy with bodies which rose or fell according to their 'gravity or levity' unless some obstacle held them back. Similarly, the soul received its due reward or punishment according to its 'merit or demerit' unless

119 Le Goff, *Birth of Purgatory*, p. 267.

120 ST, Supplement, 69.1, *Summa Theologica. First Complete American Edition*, trans. Fathers of the English Dominican Province, 3 vols. (New York, 1947–8), vol. 3, pp. 2829–30.

some obstacle intervened. The potential obstacle was venial sin, which could delay reward. Thus separated souls went straight to heaven or hell after death unless they were held back from heaven by venial sin which had to be cleansed from them before they could go to heaven.[121]

When considering 'whether there is a purgatory after this life', Aquinas explained that cleansing the soul of venial sin was not the only reason for purgatory's existence:

> For if the debt of punishment is not paid in full after the stain of sin has been washed away by contrition, nor again are venial sins always removed when mortal sins are remitted, and if justice demands that sin be set in order by due punishment, it follows that one who after contrition for his fault and after being absolved, dies before making due satisfaction, is punished after this life. Wherefore those who deny purgatory speak against the justice of God: for which reason such a statement is erroneous and contrary to faith.[122]

Purgatory thus existed also to allow the soul to complete penance that had been left unfinished at the moment of death.

If the existence of purgatory was therefore certain, its location remained far from clear. Addressing the question 'whether it is the same place where souls are cleansed, and the damned punished', Aquinas noted that 'nothing is clearly stated in Scripture about the situation of purgatory, nor is it possible to offer convincing arguments on this question'. He considered it probable, however, and 'more in keeping with the statements of holy men and the revelations made to many', that purgatory's location was 'twofold'. First, 'according to the common law', it was below and close to hell, which meant that the same fire burned in purgatory and hell. Second, 'according to dispensation', purgatorial punishment occurred 'in various places', either so that the living might learn or to help the dead whose punishments would be lessened by the prayers of the church once the living knew of their suffering. Aquinas dismissed two other views. Some said that purgatory was experienced in the place where sin was committed, but this was unlikely because 'a man may be punished at the same time for sins committed in various places'. Others thought that purgatory was above this world because the souls undergoing purgation were in a state between this world and God, but this made no sense since they were being punished for 'that which is lowest in them, namely sin'.[123] The location of purgatory was thus difficult to pin down in Aquinas' analysis. It could be understood as existing below this world, near to hell, or as being at various places

[121] ST, Supplement, 69.2, *Summa Theologica*, vol. 3, pp. 2830–1.
[122] ST, Supplement, *Summa Theologica*, vol. 3, appendix 2.1, p. 3022.
[123] ST, Supplement, *Summa Theologica*, vol. 3, appendix 2.2, p. 3023.

in this world where it would be noticed by the living. In so far as both were true, it is hard to identify a clear sense of place at all, a view that was consistent with his claims about spiritual substances being in place in a way beyond our comprehension.

About one matter Aquinas was entirely clear, however: pain suffered in purgatory was invariably greater than that suffered in this life. Asked 'whether the pains of purgatory surpass all the temporal pains of this life', he explained that there was 'a twofold pain' in purgatory. One was 'the pain of loss, namely the delay of the divine vision', while the other was 'the pain of sense, namely punishment by corporeal fire', and 'with regard to both the least pain of purgatory surpasses the greatest pain of this life'. This was so because in general the more strongly something was desired, the more painful its absence, and the soul's desire for God was greater after death because it was no longer held back by a body, and because of its awareness that it would have been in heaven already but for the need to be cleansed. Moreover, the soul felt greater pain when it was inflicted directly on the soul and not through the body.[124] Aquinas thus confirmed that purgatory was very much to be feared.

That purgatorial pain derived from material fire was made very clear when he discussed 'whether the separated soul can suffer from a bodily fire'. He discussed a number of existing explanations. Some said that simply seeing the fire caused the soul to suffer. Others argued that it was because the soul apprehended the fire as hurtful to itself that it experienced fear and sorrow. Another view was that while the fire could not act on the soul as a corporeal thing, it could do so as 'the instrument of the vengeance of divine justice'. Aquinas found each view wanting on its own, but combined them to establish a satisfactory solution. First, he explained that the separated soul could, in spite of its incorporeal nature, be united with corporeal fire in the same way that it could be in a physical place. Second, however, whereas no place could by its nature detain a soul, corporeal fire was 'enabled as the instrument of the vengeance of divine justice … to detain a spirit' so that it had 'a penal effect on it, by hindering it from fulfilling its own will'. Third, this meant that the soul saw the fire as hurtful, which added to its torment.[125]

Aquinas also discussed 'whether this punishment is voluntary'. He drew a distinction between absolute and conditional voluntariness, and punishment could not be placed in the first category because 'the very

124 ST, Supplement, *Summa Theologica*, vol. 3, appendix 1.2.1, p. 3018.

125 ST, Supplement, 70.3, *Summa Theologica*, vol. 3, pp. 2840–3. For a more detailed account of Aquinas' explanation of how the separated soul suffered from corporeal fire, see Mowbray, *Pain and Suffering*, pp. 115–17.

notion of punishment is that it be contrary to the will'. It was possible, however, to view punishment as conditionally voluntary, and in this case he made a further distinction. First, it might be that 'by being punished we obtain some good', so that the will itself undertook punishment or accepted it gladly, and martyrdom was the example he gave. Second, it might be that 'although we gain no good by the punishment, we cannot obtain a good without being punished', and then the will did not undertake the punishment but submitted to it. It was in this last sense that punishment in purgatory could be regarded as voluntary.[126]

Considering the nature of punishment in purgatory further, he discussed 'whether the souls in purgatory are punished by the demons'. He was sure that souls in purgatory were cleansed 'by the divine justice alone' and not by demons or, for that matter, angels. It was possible, however, that they took them there, and perhaps even that the demons stayed to watch.[127] Aquinas also addressed the contentious issue of 'whether venial sin is expiated by the pains of purgatory as regards the guilt', and answered in the affirmative, concluding unequivocally that 'venial sin in one who dies in a state of grace, is remitted after this life by the fire of purgatory'.[128] His response to the question 'whether the fire of purgatory delivers from the debt of punishment' was also straightforwardly affirmative.[129] He was equally clear that, quite apart from the question of unequal penances remaining to be completed, the need to get rid of venial sin meant that some would spend longer than others in purgatory:

> Some venial sins cling more persistently than others, according as the affections are more inclined to them, and more firmly fixed in them. And since that which clings more persistently is more slowly cleansed, it follows that some are tormented in purgatory longer than others, for as much as their affections were steeped in venial sins.[130]

The issue of the varying lengths of time that might be spent in purgatory was more challenging when it came to the effects of suffrages. Considering 'whether suffrages offered for one deceased person profit the person for whom they are offered more than others', Aquinas noted two opinions. According to some, the most worthy derived the main benefit from such suffrages rather than those for whom they were

[126] ST, Supplement, *Summa Theologica*, vol. 3, appendix 1.2.2, p. 3018–19.
[127] ST, Supplement, *Summa Theologica*, vol. 3, appendix 1.2.3, p. 3019.
[128] ST, Supplement, *Summa Theologica*, vol. 3, appendix 1.2.4, p. 3019–21. See *De malo*, 7.11 for more nuanced analysis.
[129] ST, Supplement, *Summa Theologica*, vol. 3, appendix 1.2.5, p. 3021.
[130] ST, Supplement, *Summa Theologica*, vol. 3, appendix 1.2.6, p. 3021.

offered. To illustrate this, they pointed out that when a candle was lit for a rich man others present would benefit just as much, or even more if they had sharper eyesight. Similarly, when a lesson was taught to an individual, others who heard would gain just as much, or even more if they had greater intelligence. They explained that the church encouraged prayers on behalf of particular individuals in order 'to excite the devotion of the faithful, who are more inclined to offer special than common suffrages, and pray more fervently for their kinsfolk than for strangers'. Others, however, maintained that suffrages were of greater benefit to those for whom they were offered. Aquinas held that there was truth on both sides, depending on where the value of suffrages was thought to come from. First, in so far as their value came from charity, 'which makes all goods common', they mainly benefited 'the person who is more full of charity', even though they were not offered for him; this individual derived 'a certain inward consolation' from rejoicing at another's reduced punishment. Second, however, in so far as the value of suffrages derived from one person's intention to make satisfaction for another, and because satisfaction led to the remission of punishment, they entirely benefited the person for whom they were offered. Aquinas concluded that with regard to the remission of punishment suffrages chiefly benefited the person for whom they were offered, and so there was 'more truth in the second opinion than in the first'.[131] In short, those for whom suffrages were offered spent less time in purgatory than others. The injustice that this might be thought to create was highlighted when Aquinas was asked in a quodlibetal disputation 'whether one of two persons who are worthy of the same punishment lingers longer in purgatory than the other'. Focusing on the power of prayers, Aquinas' argument was essentially the same. While he conceded that there was a sense in which prayers were of most benefit to those who had greater charity, he attached far greater weight to the intention of those who prayed so that others might be released from the debt of punishment: 'And so we must say that prayers made in this latter manner avail only for those for whom they are made and, if many prayers are made for someone he is more quickly freed from the punishment of purgatory than others for whom they are not made, even if they brought equal sins with them.'[132]

The pattern of heaven, hell and purgatory as the three possible destinations of separated souls after death was now well established, as was

[131] ST, Supplement, 71.12, *Summa Theologica*, vol. 3, pp. 2855–6.

[132] Quodlibet II.14, *Quodlibetal Questions 1 and 2*, trans. S. Edwards (Toronto, 1983), pp. 106–9; Thomas Aquinas, *Quaestiones de quolibet*, vol. 2, pp. 233–4.

use of the noun 'purgatory'. But spatial location remained vague since the manner in which a separated soul could be in a place at all was beyond human understanding, and purgatory itself could be located both below this world, near hell, and in various places in this world. Aquinas affirmed, however, that suffrages helped souls in purgatory, and that pain experienced in purgatory was far worse than any pain in this life.

Bonaventure In his *Breviloquium*, Bonaventure summed up the key points about purgatory:

> with regard to the punishment of purgatory, the following points must be held: that the fire of purgatory is a physical fire which torments the spirits of the just who in this life did not fulfill the penance and due satisfaction [for their sins]. These are punished to a greater or lesser degree according as they took with them from this life more or less of what must be burned away. They are afflicted less severely than in hell, but more so than in this present world. This penalty is not so severe as to deprive them of hope and of the knowledge that they are not in hell, although because of the greatness of their punishments they might not always avert to this. By means of this suffering, inflicted by a physical fire, their spirits are purged of the guilt and dregs of sin, as well as its after-effects. When they are wholly cleansed, they take flight immediately and are brought into the glory of paradise.[133]

He explained that because some just people died without completing penance in this life, and because sin could not go unpunished lest 'the beauty of eternal order' be disturbed, these people had to be 'temporarily punished according to their deserts and the guilt of their sin' and eventually get to heaven, hence the need for purgatory. The fire by which the soul was punished in purgatory was material in its nature because by sinning the soul had shown contempt for the highest good and thrown itself down to the depths, and justice therefore required that it be punished by being united to something at a lower level of being. The punishment varied in severity and length of time because it had to correspond to the seriousness of the sin committed and the amount of penance completed before death. The punishment was more severe than in this life because doing penance in this life was voluntary while punishment in purgatory was not, and the severity of the punishment made up for the lack of willing acceptance of the punishment. Hope existed, however, because souls in purgatory possessed grace and so could not despair. Once purified, souls went to heaven because it

[133] Bonaventure, *Breviloquium*, trans. D. V. Monti (New York, 2005), 7.2.2, pp. 269–70.

would not 'befit the divine mercy or justice further to delay glory once God finds the vessel to be suitable'.[134] Bonaventure also confirmed that suffrages benefited souls in purgatory, but not those in hell or heaven. Furthermore, suffrages directed to particular individuals were of greater benefit to those individuals 'if the intention of the petitioner is righteous and God-conformed, and since something the Church has instituted assuredly cannot be without effect'.[135]

Conclusion Reviewing the work of the masters over the twelfth and thirteenth centuries, it is possible to identify a number of developments. Whereas masters in the early twelfth century tended to divide separated souls into four groups immediately after death, it became accepted that there were only three groups corresponding to three possible destinations: heaven, hell and purgatory. From the late twelfth century, while references to purgatorial fire and punishment still abounded, the noun 'purgatorium' entered the vocabulary of the schools and was used as a matter of routine. The extent to which purgatory was given spatial location is less clear, however. Certainly the question of space was treated by the masters with greater frequency, but they did not agree on where it was to be found. It might be near hell or on this earth, and in the latter case it might be where penance was being performed before death intervened or where the living would take notice. Whatever the case, separated souls were not in place in any sense that the living could comprehend. The spatialization of purgatory therefore remained problematic.

Of greater significance for the authority of the masters were a series of binary patterns that underpinned their pastoral strategies by generating a need for their further judgements. Their thinking about purgatory consistently stressed distinctive relationships between the individual and the community, between this life and the next, and between fear and hope. In each case the effect was to construct a notion of the individual Christian who was obliged to accept personal responsibility for his or her behaviour and future fate, but who could and indeed should seek assistance from those who could give expert moral guidance.

As has been noted by several historians, the idea of purgatory meant that everyone was judged individually at the point of death before eventually facing the Last Judgement with everyone else at the end of time.[136] The personal life story of the individual was brought to the

134 *Ibid.*, 7.2.3–6, pp. 270–2.

135 *Ibid.*, 7.3.5, p. 276.

136 Bernstein, 'Heaven, hell and purgatory: 1100–1500', p. 208; Gurevich, *Medieval Popular Culture*, pp. 120–1; Le Goff, *Birth of Purgatory*, pp. 210–11, 230–4, 292–3.

fore by this immediate reckoning. On the other hand, the individual was not left isolated. As long as the individual repented of his mortal sins and confessed before death, entry to heaven via purgatory was assured, a process that brought the individual into relationship with the church. After death suffrages would help the individual in purgatory, which meant benefiting from membership of community networks of many kinds, most obviously family and friends as well as the church. Practices linked to belief in purgatory thus bound communities together and empowered the church.[137]

Ideas about purgatory also brought the next life into a particular kind of relationship with this life. However alien and incomprehensible the manner in which separated souls might exist in a place, notions of measurement prevalent in this world continued to play out in purgatory. This was most obviously true of time.[138] The experience of purgatory took place in finite time, and the length of time that the soul spent in purgatory was set in the first place by the number and seriousness of sins committed, and by the penance undertaken and the amount completed, and then it might be reduced by suffrages. That which was measurable was open to human understanding and to some extent human control. It was a field in which expert knowledge could make a difference.

In some respects the prospect of going to purgatory offered hope because it enabled those who had not completed penance or who were guilty of venial sins to find a route to heaven. As Hugh of Saint Victor had put it, it was not necessary to be perfect to achieve salvation. But the masters recognized the danger that many might therefore feel free to do as they pleased in this life, intending to repent at the end, thus postponing due punishment until the next life. Fear of hell, which continued to be a major theme in sermons and *exempla*, was not considered enough to prevent this possibility.[139] The masters were therefore consistent in seeking to conjure up fear of purgatory.[140] The pain of punishment in purgatory was always presented as far worse than the worst punishment

137 Bernstein, 'Heaven, hell and purgatory: 1100–1500', p. 208; Bernstein, 'Theology between heresy and folklore', pp. 42–3; Le Goff, *Birth of Purgatory*, pp. 12, 248–9, 254, 320.

138 See Bernstein, 'Heaven, hell and purgatory: 1100–1500', pp. 209, 211–13; Le Goff, *Birth of Purgatory*, pp. 227–30, 233, 290–5.

139 On the Paris theologians' discussions of hell, and on representations of hell in sermons and *exempla*, see Baschet, *Les justices de l'au-delà*, esp. pp. 33–83; Bernstein, 'Theology between heresy and folklore', pp. 5–44; Bernstein, 'The invocation of hell in thirteenth-century Paris', pp. 13–54; Bernstein, 'Esoteric theology', pp. 509–31.

140 On hope and fear, see Bernstein, 'Heaven, hell and purgatory: 1100–1500', p. 208; Le Goff, *Birth of Purgatory*, pp. 259, 301, 305–6, 310–15, 319, 328, 349, 358.

in this life. William of Auvergne put his finger on the intended effect when he said that fear of purgatory made people more willing to undertake penance in this life and more concerned to finish it. It followed that they would be more ready to listen to those who understood how penance worked.

Essentially, these binary patterns were built around and helped to construct the figure of an individual Christian who expected to face a personal judgement immediately after death, who hoped ultimately to be saved but feared the pain of purgatory, and who understood the prospect in terms of the measurable. It created intense pressure on that individual to accept responsibility for what would happen and thereby generated a need for that individual to know about the crucial factors. Exactly which forms of behaviour were sinful and which were licit? What was a mortal sin and what was venial? In a complex society, when choices were not straightforward, what was the least sinful option? What exactly should be confessed? These were not, however, questions that most people could answer on their own. Fortunately, they were not on their own. In addition to family, friends and the church in general, there were the masters of Paris who were experts in just the kind of knowledge that was required, who could scrutinize any activity and assess its degree of sinfulness, who could advise when standard behaviour seemed to fall foul of religious beliefs, who could work out the best strategy when several rules seemed to create an impossible situation, and who reckoned to disseminate their expertise through educational and ecclesiastical structures. Every individual was subject to these pressures, so the field for the masters' expertise was universal.

Ethic of intention

The pressure on individuals both to take responsibility for their own salvation and to seek help was similarly increased by the masters' work on the moral significance of intention. The key steps were taken by Peter Abelard. He argued that sin lay in consent to anything that was inappropriate because it showed 'scorn for God'.[141] Scorn for God meant 'not to do for his sake what we believe we ought to do for his sake, or not to renounce for his sake what we believe ought to be renounced'.[142] He clarified what he meant by consent by explaining at length what was not a sin. First, sin was not simply a matter of the will, so that it

[141] Peter Abelard, *Ethics*, 1.7, in *Ethical Writings*, trans. P. V. Spade (Indianapolis, 1995), p. 2.
[142] *Ibid.*, 1.8, p. 3.

was not a sin to will a bad act. He demonstrated his point by showing that it was possible to 'sin without any bad will'.[143] This was clear if one imagined an innocent person whose cruel master wished to kill him and who fled, doing everything he could to escape his master. In the end, however, he was found by his master, and 'under duress and against his will, he kills his master in order not to be killed by him'.[144] His will was not bad because he only willed to avoid death, and 'yet he did wrong in consenting (even though he was under duress from the fear of death) to an unjust slaying he should have borne rather than inflicted'.[145] He therefore sinned entirely because he consented to the killing, and not at all because of his will which was not bad. As Abelard put it, 'it is plain that sin is sometimes committed without any bad will at all, so that it is clear from this that willing isn't said to be what sin is'.[146]

Abelard reinforced his point that sin arose from consent and not the will by showing that a bad will did not invariably lead to sin. He imagined his reader insisting that when duress was not involved a bad will was itself sinful.

Of course, you will say, this [Abelard's previous point] holds where we sin under duress, but it doesn't hold where we sin willingly. For example, if we want to commit some deed we know shouldn't be committed by us. In that case, surely, the bad willing and the sin appear to be the same. For example, someone sees a woman and falls into lust. His mind is stirred by the pleasure of the flesh, with the result that he is set on fire for the shamefulness of sex. So, you say, what else is this willing and shameful desire but sin?[147]

To this Abelard replied:

What if this willing is curbed by the virtue of moderation but not extinguished, stays for the fight, holds out for the struggle, and doesn't give up even when defeated? For where is the fight if the material for the fight is absent? Where does the great reward come from if there is nothing serious we put up with? When the struggle has passed, there is no fighting left but only the receiving of the reward. We struggle by fighting here in order that, triumphant in the struggle, we might receive a crown elsewhere. But to have a fight it's proper to have an enemy who resists, not one who gives up altogether. Now this enemy is our bad will, the one we triumph over when we subject it to the divine will. But we don't entirely extinguish it, so that we always have a will we might strive against.[148]

Essentially Abelard's argument was that resisting a bad will was a fine achievement that merited reward. There was only sin if the bad will was

[143] *Ibid.*, 1.10, p. 3.
[144] *Ibid.*, 1.11, p. 3.
[145] *Ibid.*, 1.15, p. 4.
[146] *Ibid.*, 1.20, p. 5.
[147] *Ibid.*, 1.21, p. 5.
[148] *Ibid.*, 1.22, pp. 5–6.

not resisted and consent was given. So, in the example that had been raised, 'it isn't the lusting after a woman but the consenting to the lust that is the sin. It isn't the will to have sex with her that is damnable but the will's consent.'[149]

Abelard then moved on to explain that once consent had been given to evil the sin had been committed in full; carrying out the sinful act to which consent had been given did not make the sin any greater.

> Now we consent to what isn't allowed when we don't draw back from committing it and are wholly ready to carry it out should the opportunity arise. So whoever is found in this condition has incurred full guilt. Adding on the performance of the deed doesn't add anything to increase the sin. Instead, for God, someone who tries as hard as he can to go through with it is just as guilty as one who does go through with it insofar as he is able.[150]

To show that actions were not part of the sin, he argued that things that ought not to be done could be done without sin.

> Now as for things that ought not to be done, I don't think it escapes anyone how often they are done without sin, for example when they are committed through force or ignorance. For instance, if a woman subjected to force has sex with someone else's husband, or if a man somehow deceived sleeps with a woman he thought was his wife, or if by mistake he kills someone he believed should be killed by him in his role as judge. So it isn't a sin to lust after someone else's wife, or to have sex with her; the sin is rather to consent to this lust or to this action.[151]

That sin did not depend on action could also be shown by the fact that the same act could be sinful or sinless, depending on the intention of the person who performed the act.

> For God doesn't think about the things that are done but rather in what mind they are done. The merit or praiseworthiness of the doer doesn't consist in the deed but in the intention. Often in fact the same thing is done by different people, through the justice of one and the viciousness of the other. For example, if two people hang a criminal, one out of a zeal for justice and the other out of hatred springing from an old feud, then although the hanging is the same action, and although they certainly do what is good to be done and what justice demands, nevertheless through the difference in their intention the same thing is done by different people, one badly and the other well.[152]

Abelard was evidently aware that his argument might seem subversive since it was normal to punish people for what they actually did.

[149] *Ibid.*, 1.27, p. 6. [150] *Ibid.*, 1.29–30, p. 7.
[151] *Ibid.*, 1.49, pp. 10–11. [152] *Ibid.*, 1.57–8, pp. 12–13.

There are people too who get more than a little upset when they hear us say the doing of a sin isn't properly said to be the sin, or doesn't add anything to enlarge the sin. Why, they ask, is a harder atonement exacted of penitents for performing the deed than for being guilty of the fault?[153]

Abelard was entirely happy with this state of affairs. This was partly because it was impossible for humans to judge intentions; they could only judge what they could see, which meant actions rather than intentions. Only God could apprehend and therefore judge intentions.[154] It was also because of a pragmatic and entirely proper concern for the consequences of actions in terms of social order. Actions that harmed others, damaged the community or caused scandal were rightly punished with severity.

For everything that can contribute to common ruin or to public disadvantage is to be punished with the greater rebuke. What causes greater offense deserves a heavier penalty among us, and the greater scandal for people incurs the greater punishment among people – even if a slighter fault preceded it.[155]

Similarly actions were rewarded or punished in order to shape future behaviour by providing examples for people to follow or reject.

we aren't denying that in this life something is awarded for these good or bad deeds, in order that we may be further encouraged to good deeds or kept from bad ones by present repayment as profit or penalty, and in order that some people should take their examples from others in doing things that are proper or shunning those that are improper.[156]

God, however, judged the individual truly in terms of intention rather than the results of actions.

God pays attention only to the mind in rewarding good or evil, not to the results of the deeds. He doesn't think about what arises from our fault or from our good will, but judges the mind itself in its intention's purpose, not in the result of the outward deed.[157]

Abelard was also careful not to suggest that moral judgement was entirely subjective. Belief that one was acting well and in a manner pleasing to God did not always make an intention good. The intention was only good if one was correct in this assessment.

an intention isn't to be called good because it appears good, but more than that, because it is such as it is considered to be – that is, when if one believes that what he is aiming at is pleasing to God, he is in addition not deceived in his evaluation.[158]

153 *Ibid.*, 1.77, p. 17. 154 *Ibid.*, 1.82–3, p. 18. 155 *Ibid.*, 1.86, p. 19.
156 *Ibid.*, 1.100, p. 21. 157 *Ibid.*, 1.90, p. 20. 158 *Ibid.*, 1.109, p. 24.

Nevertheless, whether or not a person committed a sin did indeed depend on what they believed to be right, and they were obliged to follow their conscience. As an example, Abelard cited those who crucified Christ. Sometimes the term 'sin' was used loosely of wrong actions, and in this sense they could be said to have sinned. But in the truer sense of failing to do what one believed to be good and pleasing to God, they could not be said to have sinned.

> Thus those who persecuted Christ or his followers, and believed they should be persecuted, we say sinned through action. Nevertheless, they would have sinned more seriously through fault if they had spared them contrary to conscience.[159]

While the church continued to condemn specific acts and to rail against sinful desires, theologians like Abelard turned identifying sin into a complex business which did not simply depend on actions or even desires. Figuring out whether or not an individual had sinned, and how seriously, required careful investigation and sophisticated analysis. In one sense only the individual could look inwards to discover intention, but the masters, and those they had taught, were manifestly equipped to help individuals assess and respond to the fruits of their introspection.

Devil

Against this relentless emphasis on personal responsibility, it might be objected that the devil led people astray and was therefore at least partly to blame. The role of the devil, however, became less and less important in the intellectual view of the world, a trend that can be traced back to Anselm's *Cur Deus Homo*, or 'Why God Became Man'. According to the traditional account, known as the ransom theory, man had submitted to the devil of his own free will so that the devil gained lawful possession of him. If God simply released man from the devil, he would be failing to respect the devil's lawful rights, thus perpetrating an injustice. But when the devil killed Christ who did not deserve to die, the devil lost his just claims over man. By giving the life of Christ, God paid a ransom that obtained the just release of man. This is Anselm's succinct outline of this argument:

> But, to proceed, take that other thing which we are in the habit of saying: that God, in order to set mankind free, was obliged to act against the devil by justice rather than mighty power. We reason that thus the devil, having killed him in whom there was no guilt deserving death and who was God, would justly

[159] *Ibid.*, 1.131, p. 29.

lose the power which he used to have over sinners. Otherwise, so we argue, God would have been doing unjust violence against the devil, since the latter was the lawful possessor of man; for the devil had not gained his hold over man with violence: rather it was man who had gone over to the devil of his own free will.[160]

Anselm rejected this view on a number of grounds. First, both the devil and man belonged to God and were entirely subject to him. God could therefore do whatever he wanted with perfect justice.

given that neither the devil nor man belongs to anyone but God, and that neither stands outside God's power: what action did God need to take with, concerning, or in the case of, someone who was his own, apart from punishing this bond-slave of his who had persuaded his fellow bond-slave to desert his master and come over to join him, and had treacherously taken in the fugitive and, a thief himself, had received a thief along with the stolen property of his master? For they were both thieves, since one was stealing his own person from his master at the instigation of the other. Supposing God were to act in this way, could any action be juster?[161]

Anselm's second objection was that 'although man was being justly tormented when he was tormented by the devil, the devil himself was not acting justly in tormenting him'.[162] On the contrary, the devil was acting out of malice, but God allowed him to do it. Anselm's basic point was that the same action could be just and unjust from different points of view. Suppose someone struck an innocent person, and this person hit back, despite being under an obligation not to avenge himself. It was just that the original assailant should be struck, but not that his victim should do the striking.[163] Third, Anselm examined a passage from Paul's letter to the Colossians that could be taken to support the ransom theory. The passage referred to the 'bond of the decree' which was against us and was annulled by Christ's death. It could be argued that 'the meaning of this is that the devil, prior to the passion of Christ, used to demand sin from mankind justly, as if under the terms of a bond forming part of some agreement, as a sort of interest levied on the first sin which he persuaded man to commit, and that thus he appears to prove his jurisdiction over mankind'. Anselm maintained, however, that the decree came from God not the devil, 'For it was decreed by the just judgment of God and, as it were, confirmed by a bond, in order that man, having sinned of his own free will, would not be able, through

[160] Anselm, *Why God Became Man*, 1.7, in Anselm of Canterbury, *The Major Works*, ed. B. Davies and G. R. Evans (Oxford, 1998), p. 272.
[161] *Ibid.* [162] *Ibid.*
[163] *Ibid.*, pp. 272–3.

his own efforts, to avoid either sin or the punishment for sin.' Thus the bond and its annulment reflected a relationship between God and man in which the devil enjoyed no rights.[164] Finally, Anselm argued that 'just as there is no injustice whatsoever in a good angel, similarly there is absolutely no justice in a bad one', concluding that 'there was nothing in the devil, therefore, which made God obliged not to use his mighty power against him for the purpose of liberating mankind'.[165]

Anselm's explanation of why God became man is generally known as his 'satisfaction theory'. It was essential to remember that 'it was God's plan to make up for the number of angels who had fallen, by drawing upon the human race, which he created sinless'.[166] But man had sinned and fallen, so the question was how he could be restored so that he could play his part in God's plan. Man owed obedience to God, and when he sinned through disobedience it was not enough simply to return what he had taken away; 'rather, he ought to pay back more than he took, in proportion to the insult which he has inflicted'.[167] In general it was 'not fitting for God to forgive a sin without punishment'.[168] More specifically, humans who had sinned and had not paid recompense to God, having been let off unpunished, would not be fitting companions for the good angels in heaven.[169] Paying recompense was impossible, however, because it 'ought to be proportional to the magnitude of the sin', and yet in fact man owed everything to God already, including everything that Boso, with whom Anselm was in dialogue, said he would give God in recompense for sin: 'penitence, a contrite and humbled heart, fasting and many kinds of bodily labour, the showing of pity through giving and forgiveness, and obedience'.[170] Even if man did not owe everything to God already, recompense for 'even so small a sin as one glance contrary to the will of God' would have to be greater than the whole of creation.[171] Recompense could not therefore be made 'unless there should be someone who would make a payment to God greater than everything that exists apart from God'. Someone who could do this 'from his own property' would have himself to be 'superior to everything that exists apart from God'. But 'there is nothing superior to all that exists which is not God – except God'. This brought Anselm to the crux of his argument because he could say that only God could pay the necessary recompense, but that only man ought to pay it. It followed that only a God/man would be able to pay and do so in such a way that man would

[164] *Ibid.*, pp. 273–4. [165] *Ibid.*, p. 274.
[166] *Ibid.*, 1.16, pp. 289–90. [167] *Ibid.*, 1.11, p. 283.
[168] *Ibid.*, 1.12, p. 284. [169] *Ibid.*, 1.19, p. 301.
[170] *Ibid.*, 1.20, p. 303. [171] *Ibid.*, 1.21, p. 305.

have paid his debt to God. As Anselm summed up: 'If, therefore, as is agreed, it is necessary that the heavenly city should have its full complement made up by members of the human race, and this cannot be the case if the recompense of which we have spoken is not paid, which no one can pay except God, and no one ought to pay except man: it is necessary that a God-Man should pay it.'[172] Anselm effectively sidelined the devil in this explanation of why God became man. The satisfaction theory did not immediately and entirely replace the ransom theory.[173] Nevertheless, the devil's role was increasingly reduced in the world view constructed by Paris theologians.

Thomas Aquinas' work in the thirteenth century showed the limits now placed on the devil's powers and the way in which sin, for example, could be explained without reference to him. Certainly the devil and his fellow demons were able to incite men to sin, when permitted to do so by God.[174] This was possible because the devil could 'persuade or provide what is desirable'.[175] He could also have an interior effect on the imagination and the sense appetite, causing 'images to appear within and passions to be felt'.[176] But this did not mean that all sins were caused by the devil, or that the devil could ever force someone to sin. Indirectly, it was true that 'the devil is the cause of all our sins because he instigated the first man to sin and it was from this sin that there resulted a proneness to sin in the whole human race'. Directly, however, 'the devil is not the cause of every sin for not all sins are committed at the devil's instigation, some being committed from free choice and weakness of the flesh'. Even if the devil did not exist, men would still have desires which would cause sin unless they were controlled by reason. Whether or not these desires were controlled by reason depended on free will, not the devil.[177] Even when the devil played a part, he was not the direct cause of sin; that was always the will of the person who sinned.[178] Moreover, when the devil forced a man to commit a sinful act by so affecting the imagination and sense appetite that his reason was totally impeded, it could not be considered a sin precisely because he could not use his reason. As long as his reason was not totally overwhelmed, however, he had the power to resist sin, and so the devil did not have

[172] *Ibid.*, 2.6, pp. 319–20.
[173] J. B. Russell, *Lucifer: The Devil in the Middle Ages* (Ithaca, NY, 1984), pp. 171–2, 177–8.
[174] ST 1a.114.1 (vol. 15, pp. 74–5).
[175] ST 1a2ae.80.1 (vol. 25, pp. 220–1).
[176] ST 1a2ae.80.2 (vol. 25, pp. 222–3).
[177] ST 1a.114.3 (vol. 15, pp. 78–81); 1a2ae.80.4 (vol. 25, pp. 228–9).
[178] ST 1a2ae.80.1 (vol. 25, pp. 218–21).

complete power to force a man to sin.[179] Theologians did not doubt the existence of the devil, and he remained a stalwart figure in sermons and *exempla*, perhaps reflecting the desire of preachers to respond to popular belief.[180] Once again, however, the trend was to throw responsibility decisively onto the individual Christian, a responsibility that could only be properly fulfilled with adequate knowledge that the masters believed it was their responsibility to provide.

Means of communication

If ideas about purgatory, intention and the devil were to generate a general need for the masters' judgements on all aspects of human life, and if these further judgements were to have any effect, the masters had to be able to communicate their rulings to a wide audience. Moreover, they had to do so in ways that conveyed and reinforced their authority. They were not simply passing on neutral information that people could take or leave as they saw fit. On the contrary, the message had to be presented in a form that would command respect. The masters therefore refined and theorized their techniques of communication, and spent a great deal of time and effort putting them into practice.

Quodlibetal disputations

Most obviously Parisian masters communicated their views to their students through lectures and disputations, and doubtless through informal supervision and discussion. Students also had the opportunity to share their ideas with each other both formally during disputations and informally. Since, as we have seen, most masters and students left Paris to take up jobs elsewhere, this alone meant that ideas would eventually pass beyond the schools. One form of disputation, however, constituted a more immediate form of public engagement in itself. Quodlibetal disputations, or quodlibets, were public disputations at which questions were asked by anyone (*a quolibet*) about anything (*de quolibet*), hence the name. They could only be held by regent masters at Advent or Lent. Masters were not, however, obliged to hold quodlibets, and very few ever held them twice a year. Each quodlibet consisted of two sessions. The first was the *disputatio*. The audience was extremely varied and

179 ST 1a2ae.80.3 (vol. 25, pp. 224–7).

180 See A. E. Bernstein, 'Teaching and preaching confession in thirteenth-century Paris', in A. Ferreiro (ed.), *The Devil, Heresy and Witchcraft in the Middle Ages: Essays in Honor of Jeffrey B. Russell* (Leiden, 1998), pp. 111–30.

could include men who were not members of the university: it was a solemn and public occasion. The audience had a crucial role to play because it dictated the subject matter of the disputation; the master did not set the questions. At the first session these questions would be discussed, and the presiding master might or might not say very much. But at the second session, the *determinatio*, which was held within a few days, only the master spoke. He reordered the questions that had been raised haphazardly at the first session within a meaningful framework, and gave a definitive *solutio* or *determinatio* to each one in turn. These questions reflected the interests and preoccupations of the audience, and they ranged from abstract questions of philosophy and theology to questions which looked beyond the schools, referring to contemporary events and dealing with political and social issues at all levels of society. Surviving manuscripts and library lists indicate that these determinations passed to other schools and universities. Furthermore, quodlibetal questions were collected in manuscripts intended for use outside the university. There are also references to masters putting their determinations in writing and under seal, although no quodlibetal question is known to survive in this form. Quodlibetal questions were also included in summas and manuals designed to assist confessors. Quodlibets therefore reflected both a magisterial response to the needs of a wider clerical audience and the first step in a process of transmission beyond the university.[181]

Preaching

Preaching was another integral part of the life of the schools and the university as it emerged from the late twelfth century. We have already

[181] On quodlibetal disputations, see L. E. Boyle, 'The quodlibets of St. Thomas and pastoral care', *The Thomist* 38 (1974): 232–56; P. Glorieux, *La littérature quodlibétique de 1260 à 1320*, 2 vols. (Paris, 1925 and 1935); P. Glorieux, 'L'enseignement au moyen âge: techniques et méthodes en usage à la faculté de théologie de Paris au xiiie siècle', *Archives d'histoire doctrinale et littéraire du moyen âge* 35 (1968): 65–186 at 128–34; J. Hamesse, 'Theological quaestiones quodlibetales', in Schabel (ed.), *Theological Quodlibeta in the Middle Ages: The Thirteenth Century*, pp. 17–48; I. P. Wei, 'The masters of theology at the University of Paris in the late thirteenth and early fourteenth centuries: an authority beyond the schools', *Bulletin of the John Rylands University Library of Manchester* 75 (1993): 37–63 at 39–44; J. F. Wippel, 'The quodlibetal question as a distinctive literary genre', in *Les genres littéraires dans les sources théologiques et philosophiques médiévales: definition, critique et exploitation. Actes du colloque international de Louvain-la-Neuve 25–27 mai 1981* (Louvain-la-Neuve, 1982), pp. 67–84; J. F. Wippel, 'Quodlibetal questions, chiefly in theology faculties', in *Les questions disputées et les questions quodlibétiques dans les facultés de théologie, de droit et de médecine*, Typologie des sources du moyen âge occidental 44–45 (Turnhout, 1985), pp. 151–222.

seen how Gregory IX's bull of 1231, *Parens scientiarum*, asserted the university's power to transform men into preachers. Students and masters were expected both to hear and to give sermons, and this expectation was embedded in the regulations and routines of the university as an institution. There were no classes in preaching as such, but a close relationship between study and preaching was taken for granted. While the liberal arts clearly contributed to oratorical technique, it was the role of theology that was stressed. From the late twelfth century, masters of theology at Paris were clearly aware that most of those they taught would spend some part of their lives preaching, and they indicated that part of their task was to train preachers.[182] Stephen Langton declared that 'it is the master's duty ... to incite his promising pupils to preach'.[183] It was, moreover, especially the study of the Bible that was seen as essential in the production of preachers. In his preface to *The Art of Preaching*, Alan of Lille took Jacob's ladder to represent an ascent to perfection that culminated in preaching after three stages that involved studying, being taught and teaching the Bible:

> Jacob beheld a ladder reaching from earth to heaven, on which angels were ascending and descending. The ladder represents the progress of the catholic man in his ascent from the beginning of faith to the full development of the perfect man. The first rung of this ladder is confession; the second, prayer; the third, thanksgiving; the fourth, the careful study of the Scriptures; the fifth, to inquire of someone more experienced if one comes upon any point in Scripture which is not clear; the sixth, the expounding of Scripture; the seventh, preaching.[184]

Peter the Chanter regarded preaching as one of the master's three main duties, and in a sense the most important of all. He likened biblical study to a building in which *lectio* was the foundation, *disputatio* the walls and preaching the roof:

> The practice of bible study consists in three things: reading, disputation, preaching ... Reading is, as it were, the foundation and basement for what follows, for through it the rest is achieved. Disputation is the wall in the building of study, for nothing is fully understood or faithfully preached, if it is not first chewed by the tooth of disputation. Preaching, which is supported by the former, is the roof, sheltering the faithful from the heat and wind of temptation. We should

[182] N. Bériou, *L'avènement des maîtres de la parole. La prédication à Paris au XIIIe siècle*, 2 vols. (Paris, 1998), vol. 1, p. 44 ; R. H. and M. H. Rouse, *Preachers, Florilegia and Sermons: Studies on the Manipulus Florum of Thomas of Ireland* (Toronto, 1979), p. 48.

[183] As quoted *ibid.*, p. 50.

[184] Alan of Lille, *The Art of Preaching*, trans. G. R. Evans (Kalamazoo, MI, 1981), preface, p. 15.

preach after, not before, the reading of Holy Scripture and the investigation of doubtful matters by disputation.[185]

The idea that preaching was shaped by disputation persisted in the thirteenth century. In the 1280s, Servais of Mont Saint Eloi, sometimes referred to as Gervais or Gervase, reflecting the various versions of his name that occur in manuscripts, preferred to rank disputation ahead of preaching in terms of merit, but based this judgement on the same view of preaching as dependent on the fruits of disputation. In a quodlibetal disputation he was asked whether the act of disputation or teaching was better and more meritorious than the act of preaching.[186] On the one hand, it could be argued that preaching was more meritorious because it did most for the edification of the people. On the other, it could be maintained that disputation was more meritorious because it did most for the defence of the faith, which was of the greatest necessity. Servais solved the problem by establishing four criteria by which to judge the merit of an act: charity, effort of will, the difficulty of the task, and the excellence of the ends. As far as charity and effort of will were concerned, the two activities were equal; they could arise out of equal charity and they could be exercised with equal effort of will. With regard to

[185] Peter the Chanter, *Verbum abbreviatum*, PL vol. 205, col. 25, trans. B. Smalley, *The Study of the Bible in the Middle Ages* (Oxford, 1952), p. 208, as quoted by P. B. Roberts, 'Sermons and preaching in/and the medieval university', in R. B. Begley and J. W. Koterski (eds.), *Medieval Education* (New York, 2005), pp. 83–98 at 83–4. See also J. W. Baldwin, *Masters, Princes and Merchants: The Social Views of Peter the Chanter and his Circle*, 2 vols. (Princeton, 1970), vol. 1, pp. 90–1 for translation of a longer version. Thomas of Chobham also held the academic duties of the theologian to consist of reading, disputing and preaching; see J. J. Murphy, *Rhetoric in the Middle Ages: A History of Rhetorical Theory from St Augustine to the Renaissance* (Berkeley, 1974), p. 320. On the relevance of biblical study to preaching, see Bériou, *L'avènement des maîtres*, vol. 1, pp. 44–5, 169–71; Roberts, 'Sermons and preaching', pp. 94–5; D. d'Avray, *The Preaching of the Friars: Sermons diffused from Paris before 1300* (Oxford, 1985), pp. 185–91; B. Smalley, *English Friars and Antiquity in the Early Fourteenth Century* (Oxford, 1960), pp. 28–44.

[186] Quodlibetal question 40. B. N. lat. 15350, f. 277va–vb; J. Leclercq, 'L'idéal du théologien au moyen âge: textes inédites', *Revue des sciences religieuses* 21 (1947): 121–48 at 129–30. Servais' quodlibets survive as a series of 85 questions in this manuscript and the numbering of his questions refers to their place in this series. For the date, see P. Glorieux, 'Les quodlibets de Gervais de Mont-Saint-Eloi', *Recherches de théologie ancienne et médiévale* 20 (1953): 129–34 ; T. Sullivan, 'The *quodlibeta* of the canons regular and the monks', in C. Schabel (ed.), *Theological Quodlibeta in the Middle Ages: The Fourteenth Century* (Leiden, 2007), pp. 359–400 at 363–5. On this question, see also A. L. Gabriel, 'The ideal master of the medieval university', *Catholic Historical Review* 60 (1974): 1–40 at 29; Wei, 'The self-image of the masters of theology', pp. 418–19. For an explanation of why Servais is to be preferred to Gervais or Gervase, see R. Hissette, 'Une question quodlibétique de Servais du Mont-Saint-Eloi sur le pouvoir doctrinal de l'évêque', *Recherches de théologie ancienne et médiévale* 49 (1982): 234–42 at 234–5, n. 1.

the difficulty of the task, however, disputation clearly excelled because it was more difficult to explain something than simply to teach that it was so, and explanations were worked out in disputations which were then deployed in preaching. With regard to the excellence of its ends, disputation was again superior because its purpose was the defence of the faith against the cunning of heretics and the provision of principles to inform preaching; the art of disputation was therefore architectonic whereas preaching was merely operative and hence inferior. Greater merit was therefore attached to disputation in large part because of the way it underpinned preaching.

When discussion focused on the nature of preaching and the qualities required of a preacher, learning again came to the fore, in conjunction with virtue.[187] In defining preaching, Alan of Lille stressed the need for the preacher to be able to use reason and to cite authority.

> Preaching is an open and public instruction in faith and behaviour, whose purpose is the forming of men; it derives from the path of reason and from the fountainhead of the 'authorities'.[188]

There were, however, other considerations relating to performance and the preacher's relationship with his audience. He had to avoid providing superficial entertainment:

> Preaching should not contain jesting words, or childish remarks, or that melodiousness and harmony which result from the use of rhythm or metrical lines; these are better fitted to delight the ear than edify the soul. Such preaching is theatrical and full of buffoonery, and in every way is to be condemned.[189]

Nevertheless, it was important to make an impact on the audience:

> There should be some weight in the thought of a good sermon, so that it may move the spirits of its hearers, stir up the mind, and encourage repentance. Let the sermon rain down doctrines, thunder forth admonitions, soothe with praises, and so in every way work for the good of our neighbours.[190]

Alan's outline of the structure of a sermon shows how learning was to be combined with performative strategies. The sermon should begin with an authoritative text:

> This should be the form of preaching: it should develop from, as it were, its own proper foundation, from a theological authority – especially a text from

[187] J. Leclercq, 'Le magistère du prédicateur au xiiie siècle', *Archives d'histoire doctrinaire et littéraire du moyen âge* 15 (1946): 105–47 at 108, 138.
[188] Alan of Lille, *Art of Preaching*, 1, pp. 16–17.
[189] *Ibid.*, p. 18. [190] *Ibid.*, pp. 19–20.

the Gospels, the Psalms, the Epistles of Paul, or the Books of Solomon, for in these, in particular, edifying instruction resounds.[191]

The preacher had then to 'win the good will of his audience'. This meant being clear about his own motives, stressing that he was acting for their spiritual instruction and not for his own material gain or popularity. It was essential that he present himself with humility with regard to his own virtue and learning:

> He should assure his listeners that … he does not speak as one greater in knowledge or in wisdom, or as one who lives a better life, but because things are sometimes revealed to the little ones which are not shown to the great; and at such a time, the great ought to be silent. And because if sometimes the great do not wish to preach, it is not surprising if lesser men then prattle. For if the learned are silent, the very stones will speak and cry out.[192]

The preacher should then expound the meaning of the text that he had already presented. It was important that the text not be 'too obscure or too difficult, in case his listeners are put off by it and so listen less attentively'. But his learning was essential because other authorities had to be brought in to back up the first, and these could include 'sayings of the pagan writers'. It was also important to stimulate an emotional response with 'moving words which soften hearts and encourage tears', and then to control it:

> When the preacher sees that his hearers' minds are moved, and that they weep freely, and that their expressions are downcast, he should hold back a little, but not too much.[193]

To avoid boredom, the sermon should not be too long, and *exempla* should also be used to prove his points.[194] Later in *The Art of Preaching*, when explaining that sermons should be preached by prelates, Alan again stressed that, in addition to leading an exemplary life and following his own exhortations, the preacher must have knowledge:

> Preachers need knowledge, that they may be thoroughly conversant with both Testaments, and experienced in the weighing of texts, fluent in words, circumspect in all their deeds, despisers of the world, conscientious in doing their duty.[195]

By the thirteenth century there was considerable pressure on masters of theology to deploy their learning to good effect. Servais of Mont Saint Eloi was asked whether a master or bachelor sinned mortally if he hid

191 *Ibid.*, p. 20. 192 *Ibid.*, p. 21.
193 *Ibid.*, pp. 21–2. 194 *Ibid.*, p. 22.
195 *Ibid.*, 38, p. 144.

a sermon that he had written or refused to give it to a colleague who requested it and whom he knew would probably return it undamaged.[196] Servais argued that in a case of necessity one was bound to help, so it was a mortal sin to hide a sermon out of avarice when someone needed it. A sermon could be withheld out of human providence without any sin at all, however. Taking himself as an example, Servais felt that there was nothing wrong in having sermons in reserve. If he preached a sermon in a Carthusian house or elsewhere where the audience was small and he thought to repeat it another year (perhaps because he would not have time to compose another), he could refuse to let anyone else have it. This was because he could not use a sermon which he had communicated to other preachers for he would fear reproach from someone who could show him the whole sermon which he had just preached already in his notebook. The crucial point was that preaching sermons that were in notebooks was contrary to the proper status of masters; after all, people had quite enough of that in ordinary sermons. It was therefore licit to hide a sermon lest the master did something which defiled his status. Clearly, when people heard a master of theology preach, they were entitled to expect something out of the ordinary. A master's sermon had to be of a certain quality and, according to Servais, it would seem that this quality was originality.

Given the frequency with which masters and students were obliged to preach to each other in the thirteenth century, it is easy to imagine desperate attempts to 'borrow' sermons, as well as an audience which would be quick to spot a 'repeat'. University sermons were preached on days when the faculty of theology was not engaged in any other form of teaching. In other words, they took place on all Sundays, on festivals that occurred during the week and were celebrated by all the faculties in the university, and also on festivals that were celebrated by the faculty of theology alone. When the theologians worked and the other faculties stopped, however, there were no sermons. On those festivals when the theologians stopped, two sermons had to be preached, one in the morning and the *collatio* in the evening, the latter generally having to take up the theme of the former. The faculty of theology also stopped work on the eve of some festivals. Attendance at these sermons was obligatory for all members of all the faculties of the university. On Sundays they usually took place at the house of the Dominicans and during the week they normally occurred at the house of the Franciscans, although this did not imply that only friars did the preaching. The preaching of

196 Quodlibetal question 43. B. N. lat. 15350, f. 278rb–va; Leclercq, 'Le magistère du prédicateur', p. 124; Wei, 'The self-image of the masters', pp. 419–20.

these sermons was equally obligatory for both masters and bachelors in the faculty of theology. Preaching by the masters was organized by four regent masters deputed by the faculty who assigned particular sermons to specific masters who were then bound to preach or to find a replacement. The Paris statutes give no details about how the preaching of the bachelors was arranged, but in Oxford sermons were assigned, with at least forty days' warning, by two bachelors who were deputed to work with the chancellor on this, and since Oxford frequently followed Parisian practice, a similar arrangement may well have operated in Paris. In any case, there can be no doubt that the assignment of sermons was organized through the faculty and that details of who was to preach and when were made known at meetings of the faculty when all the bachelors were present.[197]

These sermons were an essential part of the process of learning and teaching in the faculty of theology. A collection of notes taken during courses by a student at Paris in the mid thirteenth century contains material relating to all disciplines taught in the faculties of arts and theology, and it includes questions about preaching along with themes and plans of sermons, showing that students learned preaching as they studied other disciplines.[198] Fourteenth-century statutes also reveal how preaching was built into the processes of teaching and examination; knowing how to preach was a condition for advancing through the stages of one's career as a bachelor and eventually for receiving the licence. Even in his first years in the faculty, a bachelor had to preach two collations or a sermon and a collation 'in his own person, to prove himself in eloquence and the art of preaching'.[199] Until he had done so, he could not progress to the next stage of his education. When he did become a *bacalarius cursor*, he was again bound to preach at least one collation every year. While he was expounding the Sentences, there does not appear to have been any obligation to preach, but once he became a *bacalarius formatus* he had to preach one sermon and its collation every year, and also one collation after a sermon given by a master,

[197] To reconstruct the way the faculty of theology worked in the thirteenth century, historians have frequently used the two earliest collections of statutes that date from the fourteenth century. It is, however, generally accepted that these statutes were compiled from rules already in force. See *Chartularium*, vol. 2, no. 1188, pp. 691–7 and no. 1189, pp. 697–704. See also M. M. Davy, *Les sermons universitaires parisiens de 1230–1231* (Paris, 1931), pp. 25–8; Glorieux 'L'enseignement', pp. 95, 98, 148–64. For the most nuanced account, however, see Bériou, *L'avènement des maîtres*, vol. 1, pp. 109–17.

[198] Leclercq, 'Le magistère du prédicateur', p. 116. On the taking of notes, see Bériou, *L'avènement des maîtres*, vol. 1, pp. 73–103.

[199] *Chartularium*, vol. 2, no. 1189, p. 699, item 27.

provided that he was warned two months in advance. If he failed to fulfil these obligations, his licence would be held back for two years. It was possible in certain circumstances for some other bachelor to preach in his place, but this practice was strictly limited as each bachelor could only preach in another's place once a year. In some cases, a sermon might also be preached instead of participation in a quodlibetal disputation.[200] When the bachelor became a master, the process of inception included the preaching of a sermon.[201] Thereafter, as already explained, the obligation to preach remained.

Preaching was therefore a key part of the intellectual and moral formation of the men who attended university, and it bound them together in community. Crucially, however, it also provided a point of direct contact between intellectuals and the rest of society. Masters regularly preached not only to students and each other, but also to a much wider audience, especially in Paris. Many of their sermons were preached *ad populum*, or 'to the people', in the numerous churches of Paris.[202] These sermons for lay audiences were delivered in French but written down and preserved in Latin, from which they could be translated subsequently into any vernacular language anywhere in Europe. Some manuscripts include elements of vernacular within the Latin text, which doubtless aided those preparing to preach in the vernacular and perhaps indicates that some sermons were delivered partly in Latin and partly in the vernacular: there is much that remains uncertain about the actual performance of preaching.[203] Numerous surviving collections of sermons bear witness, however, to the pastoral function that the masters exercised in Paris.[204] Lists of works offered by the *stationarii* of Paris in 1286 and 1304 include many volumes of sermons that could be used for non-university preaching.[205] Preaching was therefore a means by

200 *Ibid.*, pp. 697–704.

201 Baldwin, *Masters, Princes and Merchants*, vol. 1, pp. 111–16; J. Hamesse, 'Introduction: the university', in J. Hamesse, B. M. Kienzle, D. L. Stoudt, A. T. Thayer (eds.), *Medieval Sermons and Society: Cloister, City, University* (Louvain-la-Neuve, 1998), pp. 312–13; N. K. Spatz, 'Imagery in university inception sermons', in *Medieval Sermons and Society*, pp. 329–42.

202 Roberts, 'Sermons and preaching in/and the medieval university', pp. 87–90.

203 Bériou, *L'avènement des maîtres*, vol. 1, pp. 231–8; d'Avray, *Preaching of the Friars*, pp. 90–5; Rouse and Rouse, *Preachers*, pp. 79–80.

204 See, for example, N. Bériou, 'La prédication au béguinage de Paris pendant l'année liturgique 1272–1273', *Recherches Augustiniennes* 13 (1978): 105–229; N. Beriou, *La prédication de Ranulphe de la Houblonnière: sermons aux clercs et aux simples gens à Paris au xiiie siècle*, 2 vols. (Paris, 1987); Bériou, *L'avènement des maîtres*, vol. 1, pp. 125–9, 215–91.

205 Glorieux, 'L'enseignement', pp. 159–60. See also d'Avray, *Preaching of the Friars*, pp. 273–81.

which Parisian intellectuals communicated directly with and asserted authority over the rest of society.

As well as communicating directly by preaching themselves, Parisian scholars had a profound influence on preaching across western Europe. In part this was a matter of former students and indeed masters themselves leaving Paris and preaching as part of whatever role they went on to play in the church. But even for those who never went to Paris at all, a whole host of preaching aids was produced in Paris. Books and manuals on the art of preaching taught the theory of preaching. Alan of Lille's *Art of Preaching*, discussed above, was an early example of a genre that grew rapidly in technical sophistication after about 1200.[206] Collections of model sermons provided basic plans, while *florilegia* and collections of *exempla* gave quick access to the raw material that could be used within them, often setting out material according to the social group which it would best serve. Books of distinctions listed words used in the Bible and explained the different meanings that they could have, often illustrating each meaning with a biblical passage. Biblical concordances were produced by the end of the thirteenth century. Alphabetical organization of key terms, the use of Arabic numerals to number the pages and divisions of a work, and the design of clear layouts became standard features of reference works that were quick and easy to use.[207]

From the late twelfth century, sermons were much more carefully organized, and their structures became increasingly complex during the thirteenth century. Although the extent to which this process was influenced by the intellectual methods and practices developed in universities has been much debated, the new form is often referred to as 'the university style' and it is generally described as 'thematic' because sermons were characterized chiefly by the way in which an opening theme, usually a biblical text, was then divided into parts. This meant expounding the meaning and significance of the text in a series of parts or sections, some of which might be further subdivided or broken down into subsections. There was a range of conceptual bases for this process of division, explained in terms of rhetorical theory by preaching

[206] Murphy, *Rhetoric in the Middle Ages*, pp. 303–11.

[207] On the development of preaching aids, see Bériou, *L'avènement des maîtres*, vol. 1, pp. 177–96; d'Avray, *Preaching of the Friars*, pp. 64–90; M. M. Mulchahey, *'First the Bow is Bent': Dominican Education before 1350* (Toronto, 1998), pp. 400–79; Murphy, *Rhetoric in the Middle Ages*, pp. 342–3; Roberts, 'Sermons and preaching in/and the medieval university', pp. 92–4; R. H. Rouse and M. A. Rouse, '*Statim invenire*: schools, preachers, and new attitudes to the page', in R. L. Benson and G. Constable (eds.), *Renaissance and Renewal in the Twelfth Century* (Cambridge, MA, 1982), pp. 201–25.

manuals, and the framework that was to be deployed was justified at some length, often using both reason and authority, which meant further scriptural quotations.[208]

The production of preaching aids and the development of preaching techniques were by no means exclusive to Paris, but it was without doubt a key centre for the education of preachers and for the production and diffusion of preaching aids, a role that only increased with the arrival of the friars.[209] Paris' early success was most strikingly recounted by Jacques de Vitry in his *Historia occidentalis*, with Foulques de Neuilly as the figure emblematic of its outreach. According to Jacques, Foulques was a poorly educated rural priest whose morals left much to be desired. When he changed his ways, he became aware of his own ignorance and therefore went to Paris where he attended the lectures of Peter the Chanter during the week, taking notes on wax tablets, so that he could pass on what he learned to his parishioners in his Sunday sermon. Priests in the area around Neuilly, which was to the east of Paris, began to ask him to preach in their parishes as well. Eventually Peter the Chanter made him preach to a learned audience at the church of Saint Severin in Paris. He went on to travel widely, preaching with dramatic success across a large part of western Europe. Still following Jacques' account, others were moved by his example to become notable preachers, including men with serious academic credentials like Stephen Langton and Robert of Courson.[210] From the late twelfth century, Paris was thus understood to be a source from which moral teaching flowed through sermons to Christendom as a whole. Preachers themselves glorified Paris in these terms, one unnamed friar in the 1270s concluding his sermon by inviting his audience to pray for the University of Paris so that God would protect in peace 'this fountain/spring from which streams flow through the whole church of God'.[211]

[208] On the structure of sermons, see Evans, 'Introduction', in Alan of Lille, *The Art of Preaching*, pp. 5–6; Bériou, *L'avènement des maîtres*, vol. 1, pp. 134–69; d'Avray, *Preaching of the Friars*, pp. 7–8, 10, 163–80; Murphy, *Rhetoric in the Middle Ages*, pp. 275–6, 310–33; Roberts, 'Sermons and preaching in/and the medieval university', pp. 90–2; Rouse and Rouse, '*Statim invenire*', pp. 216–18; Rouse and Rouse, *Preachers*, pp. 65–90.

[209] d'Avray, *Preaching of the Friars* pp. 6–8, 22, 132–63.

[210] Jacques de Vitry, *Historia occidentalis*, ed. J. F. Hinnebusch, Spicilegium Friburgense 17 (Fribourg, 1972), pp. 89–103. See also Baldwin, *Masters, Princes and Merchants*, vol. 1, pp. 36–9; Bériou, *L'avènement des maîtres*, vol. 1, pp. 46–7; d'Avray, *Preaching of the Friars*, pp. 22–4.

[211] Bériou, 'La prédication au béguinage de Paris', p. 137.

Confession

Another mode of communication, and arguably also control, was confession. Preaching and confession were closely linked because confessions were often heard after a sermon had been preached.[212] The requirement to make annual confession was established in 1215 by the fourth Lateran Council in the canon *Omnis utriusque sexus* when it was decreed that all adults should make individual confessions to their own parish priest at least once a year. They were to confess all their sins, and to do their best to carry out the penances imposed on them. They were further enjoined to receive the eucharist at least at Easter unless their priest advised that there was good reason not to, and the penalties for failure were a lifelong ban on entering a church and denial of Christian burial. Since it was usually necessary to confess before taking the eucharist, this in effect tied annual confession to the celebration of Easter. The decree was to be frequently published in churches so that no one could claim to be unaware of it. Anyone who wanted to confess to a priest other than their own had to get their own priest's permission. The priest who heard confession was to be 'discerning and prudent', and to make careful inquiry into the circumstances in which sin had been committed. Here the traditional image of the medical doctor curing the sick was deployed. Finally, the priest was required to keep confessions secret or face not only deposition from priestly office but also confinement 'to a strict monastery to do perpetual penance'.[213] This attempt to prescribe annual confession reflected existing practices in some areas, statutes recently enacted by bishops such as Eudes de Sully in Paris and Stephen Langton in Canterbury, and the thinking of Parisian theologians.[214]

Ideas about penance and confession had developed rapidly during the twelfth century. One vital issue was the relative significance of inner contrition and confession to a priest in gaining remission of sins. Following Augustine, it was generally agreed that penance involved contrition of heart, profession of the mouth, and satisfaction in deed.[215]

[212] d'Avray, *Preaching of the Friars*, p. 184; J. H. Arnold, *Belief and Unbelief in Medieval Europe* (London, 2005), p. 173.

[213] *Decrees of the Ecumenical Councils*, ed. N. P. Tanner, 2 vols. (London, 1990), vol. 1, p. 245.

[214] P. Biller, 'Confession in the middle ages: introduction', in P. Biller and A. J. Minnis (eds.), *Handling Sin: Confession in the Middle Ages* (York, 1998), p. 8.

[215] See P. J. Payer, *Sex and the New Medieval Literature of Confession, 1150–1300* (Toronto, 2009), p. 51; L. Smith, 'William of Auvergne and confession', in Biller and Minnis (eds.), *Handling Sin*, pp. 95–107 at 99. See also Alan of Lille, *Art of Preaching*, 31, p. 126.

Although consensus was slow to emerge, Abelard, Hugh of Saint Victor, Peter Lombard and Alan of Lille treated inner contrition as the essential component that brought about remission of sin.[216] They were quick, however, to maintain the importance of confession and to stress the significance of the role of the priest. Hugh of Saint Victor, for example, made his point as a criticism of those who overstated the role of contrition:

Certain men try to ascribe the power of forgiving sins to God alone, and they by no means admit that man can be made a participant in it ... In similar manner now in the Church of today they say that the ministries of the priests have no more power than as a kind of sign only, that he indeed who is first absolved by the Lord through contrition of heart within, afterwards is shown to have been absolved by them through the confession of the mouth. Now they wish to prove that sins are forgiven only in the contrition of the heart before the confession of the mouth ... However, after contrition of the heart confession of mouth is also necessary, because, if anyone, even after obtaining pardon for sins, shall neglect to confess these same sins of his, as if a contemner of a divine institution, although he may not be held as a defendant for the sins which are already forgiven, he will nevertheless be a defendant for contempt, or perhaps because the sins themselves presently return to the stubborn, which before were forgiven him who was humbled by the sting of conscience.[217]

Thus, while Hugh accepted that contrition of the heart brought remission of sin, he insisted that confession to a priest was more than a sign that this had taken place; failure to confess showed contempt for a divine institution, and indicated that the same sins were likely to be repeated soon. More than this, it was at the point of confession that God, acting through the priest, freed sinners from eternal suffering: 'as they confess through the ministry of the priests [God] absolves them from the exterior bond, that is, from the debt of damnation'.[218] Confession to a priest was also appropriate because it involved humility and obedience which served to remedy the pride involved in the sin:

Since then every sin is committed through pride, it is necessary for all repentance to be tempered through humility, in order that obedience may crush

[216] P. Anciaux, *La théologie du sacrement de pénitence au xiie siècle* (Louvain, 1949), pp. 164–231, 273–4, 351–3, 475; M. L. Colish, *Peter Lombard*, 2 vols. (Leiden, 1994), vol. 2, pp. 588–609; Payer, *Sex and the New Medieval Literature of Confession*, pp. 16–18; T. N. Tentler, *Sin and Confession on the Eve of the Reformation* (Princeton, 1977), pp. 18–19, 22–4; Baldwin, *Masters, Princes and Merchants*, vol. 1, p. 50. For different interpretations of the emphasis that Peter Lombard put on contrition, see Colish, *Peter Lombard*, pp. 602–9; Rosemann, *Peter Lombard*, pp. 163–8.

[217] Hugh of Saint Victor, *On the Sacraments*, 2.14.8, pp. 416–17.

[218] *Ibid.*, p. 418.

disobedience and the devotion of humility suppress the swelling of elation. Therefore, it is very fitting that we who have been insolent to God by sinning be suppliants also to the servants of God by repenting to men.[219]

Finally, Hugh considered that the effort involved in making confession would make people more careful to avoid sin in the future:

For this too is most salutary for the sinner, that he learn how far he has receded from God by sinning when he returns to God with such difficulty by repenting, because he is also made more cautious in the future when the way to remission is not opened without the grave labour of repenting.[220]

The general tendency to stress the importance of contrition, while finding plenty of reasons to maintain the authority of the priest, lasted until Thomas Aquinas struck a new balance between the two. He maintained that contrition was not sufficient to gain forgiveness without the priest's actions in performing the sacrament because it was the performance of the sacrament that produced grace. The penitent had to be appropriately disposed, but the power of the sacrament could not be relegated to a secondary position.[221] This was the prevalent position until the early fourteenth century when Duns Scotus shifted the balance still further towards the role of the priest. In exceptional cases perfect contrition on the part of the penitent was enough to obtain God's forgiveness before confession. Usually, however, imperfect sorrow, attrition rather than contrition, was adequate because the power of the sacrament made up for deficiencies in the penitent's disposition, which made it theoretically easier to obtain remission of sin.[222]

Another fundamental debate concerning the role of the priest focused on his knowledge and ability to make informed judgements. This was discussed in terms of the 'keys' which Christ had given to Peter and which had now passed to all priests. According to Matthew, Christ had said to Peter: 'I will give you the keys of the kingdom of heaven, and whatever you bind on earth shall be bound in heaven, and whatever you loose on earth shall be loosed in heaven.'[223] No one doubted that the authority to bind and loose was one of the keys, although there was disagreement about what this involved, as we have just seen. But was the knowledge necessary to exercise this authority a second key? According to some, knowledge was a key, whatever the shortcomings of many priests. Peter Lombard, for example, said that 'the use of these keys, however, is multiple, namely, to discern those who are to be bound and

[219] *Ibid.*, p. 421. [220] *Ibid.*
[221] Tentler, *Sin and Confession*, pp. 24–6.
[222] *Ibid.*, pp. 26–7. [223] Matthew 16.19.

loosed, and then to bind and loose'.[224] With sadness, however, he had to acknowledge that:

It can soundly be said that not all priests have the second of these keys, that is to say, the knowledge to discern: which is to be deplored and lamented. For many, although lacking discernment and devoid of the knowledge by which the priest must distinguish himself, presume to accede to the grade of the priesthood, being unworthy of it in knowledge and life, [people] who neither before nor after [being received into] the priesthood have the knowledge to discern who is to be bound or loosed.[225]

It was therefore necessary to remember that God's judgement never failed, even though the church's judgement sometimes did. It also followed that the penitent should 'seek out a priest of wisdom and discernment', and confess to a lay companion if no such priest was to be found.[226] Others who regarded knowledge as a key did not throw this responsibility on the penitent, preferring to insist that priests always had some basic knowledge. Against this, others, like Peter Abelard, said that there was only one key, the power to bind and loose, but that knowledge helped in its use. Peter the Chanter and Robert of Courson fell into this camp, arguing that the priest gained no knowledge through ordination, but was obliged to acquire it. This was a view that created a need for theologians to generate and communicate the knowledge that confessors required.[227]

It is difficult to assess exactly how much scholarly work was produced with confession in mind. Some works of moral theology, for example by Peter the Chanter and Robert of Courcon, focused on very specific moral problems explicitly for the benefit of confessors.[228] Many quodlibetal questions in the thirteenth century, while making no reference to confession, may also have been asked by those who had encountered particular problems when hearing confession, and they may have been answered with this context in mind. The relentless consideration of small circumstantial variations pertaining to a specific sin really only makes sense in this setting. In general the study of moral theology and especially the experience of problem-solving in disputations would

224 Peter Lombard, *Sententiae*, 4.18.3 (vol. 2, p. 356); as translated by Rosemann, *Peter Lombard*, p. 166.

225 Peter Lombard, *Sententiae*, 4.19.1.3 (vol. 2, p. 365); as translated by Rosemann, *Peter Lombard*, pp. 166–7.

226 Peter Lombard, *Sententiae*, 4.17.4.6 (vol. 2, p. 352); as translated by Rosemann, *Peter Lombard*, p. 167.

227 Baldwin, *Masters, Princes and Merchants*, vol. 1, pp. 52–3. See also Payer, *Sex and the New Medieval Literature of Confession*, pp. 31–5.

228 Baldwin, *Masters, Princes and Merchants*, vol. 1, p. 53.

have prepared men to respond intelligently when hearing confession.[229] Students and masters were therefore very likely to leave Paris with the knowledge and skills necessary to be effective confessors. The work of Parisian masters was communicated to a significantly wider audience, however, extending beyond those who had actually been to Paris, through summas, guides and manuals for confessors. Many were written by men who had studied and taught at Paris, incorporating the work of their teachers and colleagues as well as their own. Examples from the late twelfth and early thirteenth centuries include Alan of Lille's *Liber poenitentialis* around 1200, Robert of Flamborough's *Liber poenitentialis* between 1208 and 1213, Peter of Poitiers' *Summa de confessione* after the fourth Lateran Council of 1215 and Thomas of Chobham's *Summa confessorum* at around the same time.[230] During the thirteenth century many more examples of the genre were produced by friars, especially Dominicans.[231] The *Summa confessorum*, written by the German Dominican John of Freiburg, incorporated much material produced by Thomas Aquinas, especially extracts from his quodlibets and from the second part of the second part of his *Summa Theologiae* (the *Secunda secundae*), which also circulated separately from and more widely than the rest of the *Summa Theologiae* because it could be read as an independent treatise on the virtues and vices, thus fulfilling a role in pastoral training.[232] Several of these works, notably those by Thomas of Chobham and John of Freiburg, were widely diffused, both in their own right and when copied by other writers of confessors' manuals,

229 See d'Avray, *Preaching of the Friars*, p. 184.

230 Baldwin, *Masters, Princes and Merchants*, vol. 1, pp. 32–6; Biller, 'Confession in the middle ages', pp. 9, 12; P. Biller, *The Measure of Multitude: Population in Medieval Thought* (Oxford, 2000), pp. 185–6 ; P. Michaud-Quantin, *Sommes de casuistique et manuels de confession au moyen âge (XII–XVI siècles)* (Louvain, 1962), pp. 16–19, 21–4. For analysis of the genre and its development, see L. E. Boyle, '*Summae confessorum*', in *Les genres littéraires dans les sources théologiques et philosophiques médiévales*, pp. 227–37; P. J. Payer, 'Confession and the study of sex in the middle ages', in V. L. Bullough and J. A. Brundage (eds.), *Handbook of Medieval Sexuality* (New York, 1996), pp. 3–31 at 8–11; Payer, *Sex and the New Medieval Literature of Confession*, pp. 2–6, 8–9, 12–44.

231 Biller, 'Confession in the middle ages', pp. 9–10; Biller, *Measure of Multitude*, p. 186; Payer, *Sex and the New Medieval Literature of Confession*, p. 5.

232 L. E. Boyle, 'The *Summa confessorum* of John of Freiburg and the popularization of the moral teaching of St. Thomas and of some of his contemporaries', in A. A. Maurer *et al.* (eds.), *St. Thomas Aquinas, 1274–1974: Commemorative Studies* (Toronto, 1974), vol. 2, pp. 245–68 at 254–8, reprinted in L. E. Boyle, *Pastoral Care, Clerical Education and Canon Law, 1200–1400* (London, 1981), third item, same pagination; L. E. Boyle, 'The quodlibets of St. Thomas and pastoral care', *The Thomist* 38 (1974): 232–56 at 242–51, reprinted in Boyle, *Pastoral Care*, second item, same pagination; L. E. Boyle, *The Setting of the Summa Theologiae of Saint Thomas*, The Etienne Gilson Series 5 (Toronto, 1982), pp. 20–9.

and there can be no doubt that they communicated the ideas of Parisian scholars to a large clerical audience.[233] It may even be that some works were read by and perhaps even intended for educated and pious laypeople, although this cannot have been common.[234] Frustratingly, the very nature of confession ensured that there are no records of what was said in the course of actual confessions; only occasionally do we come across tantalizing glimpses of what went on.[235] The guides and manuals give us every reason to think, however, that during these 'interactive' exchanges the ideas of the Parisian masters reached a wide audience.

Target audiences

One further aspect of the process of communication needs to be emphasized. Scholarly discussion of preaching and confession frequently envisaged a highly differentiated audience, with strategies and moral messages adapted to the perceived characteristics and needs of different social groups. In part this reflected a long tradition of imitating Paul, who told the Corinthians that he had become 'all things to all men, that I might by all means save some', with the result that depictions of saints had long stressed their ability to speak and behave in different ways to different types of people.[236] From the twelfth century, this ability to adapt appropriately to different audiences was increasingly expected of preachers and confessors, and to this end works designed to assist them took account of the various social groups that might be encountered. The groups into which society was divided were of many different kinds, but increasingly groups defined by occupation or profession were included along with groups marked out by religious status, social class and sexual or marital condition. Thus, in the chapter in *The Art of Preaching* entitled 'To whom preaching should be delivered',

[233] Biller, 'Confession in the middle ages', p. 12; Boyle, 'The *Summa confessorum* of John of Freiburg', pp. 258–68.

[234] See Smith, 'William of Auvergne and confession', in Biller and Minnis (eds.), *Handling Sin*, pp. 106–7, for the suggestion that William's work on penance was produced for a lay readership and that there may have been 'an educated, interested, devout reading public'. For the view that it must have been rare for laypeople to read such works and that they were not written for this kind of readership, see T. N. Tentler, 'The summa for confessors as an instrument of social control', in C. Trinkaus and H. A. Oberman (eds.), *The Pursuit of Holiness in Late Medieval and Renaissance Religion* (Leiden, 1974), pp. 103–37 at 114.

[235] For an excellent account of how the process was envisaged in summas, guides and manuals for confessors, see Payer, *Sex and the New Medieval Literature of Confession*, pp. 45–74.

[236] 1 Corinthians 9.22. See A. Murray, *Reason and Society in the Middle Ages* (Oxford, 1978), pp. 386–8.

Alan of Lille listed the faithful, the unworthy and obstinate, the young, adults, the dissipated, the poor, the rich, soldiers, public speakers, the learned, prelates, princes, monks, married people, widows and virgins.[237] An early thirteenth-century preaching manual, after an even longer list of groups, advised: 'Not only the sermons but also the sentences and the complete manner of speaking and style of writing should vary according to the variety of persons.'[238] Many confessors' manuals also gave instructions on how to interrogate different groups, indicating the sins that were either an inevitable part of a particular job or for which it gave frequent opportunity. The processes by which scholars' ideas were communicated thus involved a sharp sense that society was made up of different social groups, each of which needed to be targeted specifically.[239]

Conclusion

From an early stage in their education, when learning basic grammar and rhetoric, Parisian theologians had studied ethics. They also regarded moral philosophy and moral theology as fundamental goals of the philosopher and theologian. Furthermore, they believed that they were at the top of a hierarchy of learning, with an obligation to disseminate their ideas to the rest of Christian society. It was this role that,

[237] Alan of Lille, *The Art of Preaching*, 39, pp. 146–9. See G. Constable, *Three Studies in Medieval Religious and Social Thought: The Interpretation of Mary and Martha; The Ideal of the Imitation of Christ; The Orders of Society* (Cambridge, 1995), p. 329. On preoccupation with groups and types in the twelfth century, see C. W. Bynum, 'Did the twelfth century discover the individual?', in *Jesus as Mother: Studies in the Spirituality of the High Middle Ages* (Berkeley, 1982), pp. 82–109; see also an earlier version in *Journal of Ecclesiastical History* 31 (1980): 1–17.

[238] As quoted by Constable, *Three Studies in Medieval Religious and Social Thought*, p. 329.

[239] On different social types with regard to preaching and confession, see: Bériou, *L'avènement des maîtres*, vol. 1, pp. 293–383; Biller, 'Confession in the middle ages', pp. 16–18; Constable, *Three Studies in Medieval Religious and Social Thought*, pp. 329–31; D. L. d'Avray and M. Tausche, 'Marriage sermons in *ad status* collections of the central middle ages', *Archives d'histoire doctrinale et littéraire du moyen âge* 47 (1980): 71–119 at 71–5; J. Le Goff, 'Trades and professions as represented in medieval confessors' manuals', in *Time, Work and Culture in the Middle Ages* (Chicago, 1980), pp. 107–21; P. Michaud-Quantin, 'Le vocabulaire des catégories sociales chez les canonistes et les moralistes du xiiie siècle', in D. Roche and C. E. Labrousse (eds.), *Ordres et Classes. Colloque d'Histoire Sociale. Saint-Cloud 24–25 mai 1967* (Paris, 1973), pp. 73–86 at 82–5; P. Michaud-Quantin, 'Les catégories sociales dans le vocabulaire des canonistes et moralistes au xiiie siècle', in *Etudes sur le vocabulaire philosophique du moyen âge* (Rome, 1970), pp. 163–86; C. Muessig, 'Audience and preacher: *ad status* sermons and social classification', in C. Muessig (ed.), *Preacher, Sermon and Audience in the Middle Ages* (Leiden, 2002), pp. 255–76.

in their view, gave them status and authority. They did not, however, dispense neutral information; their ideas and the means by which they communicated them were meant to shape behaviour, and one historian has described it as a system of 'social control'.[240] Basic ideas about the afterlife, intention and the devil demanded that individuals assess their current behaviour and ponder their ultimate fate while burdened with both fear and hope. Crucially, however, they could not negotiate the moral issues that they faced without the advice that theologians had to offer. The masters of theology thus conjured up the image of the individual Christian, badly in need of their authoritative teachings. Disputations, sermons and confession were the techniques by which theologians sought to address this need. They were occasions on which the masters, or those they had taught, performed with authority, ministering to a complex audience that they analysed with care. It remains to consider what kind of behaviour the masters of theology wished to produce.

[240] Tentler, 'The summa for confessors as an instrument of social control', pp. 103–37.

5 Sex and marriage

Parisian scholars had a great deal to say about sex, marriage and, consequently, what we would term 'gender'. This chapter will seek to identify key aspects of their thought on this fundamental aspect of human experience. In doing so, it will consider the extent to which they agreed with each other, thus establishing a consistent and coherent set of ideas.[1] While the most obvious subjective reactions to medieval values rarely serve any worthwhile analytical purpose, it is particularly difficult in the twenty-first century not to be taken aback at some of the ideas expressed about women, at least at the first encounter. Since numerous accounts of medieval ideas about sexuality and gender have cast medieval scholars as rabid misogynists, the validity of this label also needs to be considered.[2] The first three sections will set out key ideas on the nature of men and women, marriage and marital sex. The last part of the chapter will take as a case study a number of quodlibetal questions relating to marriage. This will allow us to examine the way in which scholars applied their basic ideas to practical problems and the impact that they expected their ideas to have on sexually active couples. A close reading of some of these questions will also allow us to explore the language that they used when discussing what we could call 'gender', and what this reveals about their attitudes. Finally, we will also be in a position to reflect on why scholars had so much to say about sex. Before going further, it should also be noted that in this field the overlap between theology and canon law was especially strong because the

[1] For the view that the period witnessed 'an emerging consensus about what was thought to be the correct theological and moral account of sex', see P. J. Payer, *The Bridling of Desire: Views of Sex in the Later Middle Ages* (Toronto, 1993), esp. pp. 9–12, 179–83. See also J. A. Brundage, *Law, Sex, and Christian Society in Medieval Europe* (Chicago, 1987), p. 485: 'By the mid-thirteenth-century Western churchmen had arrived at a fairly clear consensus about the goals of the Church's sexual policy.'

[2] For extreme examples of the tendency to characterize medieval scholars as misogynists, see Payer, *Bridling of Desire*, pp. 6–7.

same issues were treated in both disciplines, and theologians frequently cited canon law texts in their work.[3]

The nature of men and women

When the Parisian masters discussed the nature of men and women, their basic understanding of gender difference came immediately to the fore. Almost invariably they began with the idea that woman had been created to help man in procreation. Thus Hugh of Saint Victor noted that God 'made woman as an assistance to man in the propagation of the race'.[4] This idea was based on Genesis 2.18, 'It is not good for man to be alone; let us make him a help that is like himself', and it was often elaborated to set up a series of binary oppositions between male and female, all of which made the male superior to the female. When Thomas Aquinas considered whether woman should have been made in the original creation of things, for example, he began his response by invoking the notion of woman as procreative assistant to man:

> It was absolutely necessary to make woman, for the reason Scripture mentions, as a help to man; not indeed to help him in any other work … because where any other work is concerned man can get help more conveniently from another man, but to help him in the work of procreation.[5]

The idea that in everything except procreation a man would receive more valuable assistance from another man was taken from Augustine and repeated by many thirteenth-century theologians including Albert the Great and Bonaventure.[6] Aquinas developed his analysis by presenting a hierarchy of living beings considered in terms of the way they procreated. His argument depended on three assumptions: first, that procreation should be understood in terms of active and passive powers; second, that some functions in life were nobler than others; and third, combining the first two assumptions, that the active power was nobler than the passive. At the bottom of the hierarchy, in a category that we might struggle to recognize today, were living beings 'which have no active procreative power themselves, but are procreated by an agent of a different species; like those plants and animals which are

[3] See P. Biller, *The Measure of Multitude: Population in Medieval Thought* (Oxford, 2000), p. 38.

[4] Hugh of Saint Victor, *On the Sacraments of the Christian Faith (De Sacramentis)*, trans. R. J. Deferrari (Cambridge, MA, 1951), 2.11.2, p. 325.

[5] ST 1a.92.1 (vol. 13, pp. 35–7). I have adjusted the translation.

[6] Payer, *Bridling of Desire*, p. 28.

generated without seed by the active force of heavenly bodies out of suitable matter'. Above them came beings 'which have their active and passive procreative powers joined together, as, for example, those plants which are generated from seed'. Because plants had 'no nobler function than procreation', it was 'proper that they should be procreating all the time, and have the active power of procreation joined to the passive'. In the next category, going up the hierarchical scale, were the 'perfect animals, which have the active power of procreation in the male sex and the passive in the female':

> And because animals are capable of a vital function which is nobler than that of procreation, a function which their life is chiefly directed to, the consequence is that in perfect animals the male and the female sex are not continually joined together, but only at times of mating. So we may fancy, if we like, that in mating male and female constitute a whole or unity, rather like that of a plant in which the male and the female principles are permanently joined together.

The point was that when living beings had a function nobler than procreation, the male and the female were separated from each other so that the male could exercise the nobler function on his own, but they could combine on occasion for purposes of procreation with the male having the nobler active power and the female the less noble passive power. At the top of the hierarchy, however, was the human being ('homo' in Latin) 'whose life is directed to a nobler function still, that of understanding things'. Given this higher purpose, 'there was more reason than ever … for emphasizing the distinction between the sexes, which was done by producing the woman separately from the man, while at the same time joining them together in a union of the flesh for the work of creation'. In other words, it was even more important to separate male and female humans so that the male could pursue understanding without the distractions of procreation, while the female stood ready to unite with him for procreation. One of the opening arguments in the *quaestio* had presented woman as a defective male. Aquinas agreed that 'as regards nature in the individual' the female was indeed defective. Presumably this was because she did not pursue understanding, but he offered an essentially physiological explanation for women being conceived: 'the active power in the seed of the male tends to produce something like itself, perfect in masculinity; but the procreation of the female is the result either of the debility of the active power, of some unsuitability of the material, or of some change effected by external influences, like the south wind, for example, which is damp'. With regard to 'nature in the species as a whole', however, the female was not defective, but 'directed to the work of procreation', as God intended.[7] Man and woman were thus constructed in terms of a series of binary oppositions: active – passive; understanding – procreation (as primary functions); noble – less noble; perfect – defective (at least regarding the individual). These patterns were not invented by or in any way particular to Aquinas. Rather, as we will see, they ran through and frequently structured the views of Parisian intellectuals on all matters to do with what we would call sexuality.

Given their understanding of woman as naturally inferior to man, it is not surprising that scholars considered that women should be subject to men. In the *Summa Theologiae*, Aquinas explained the existence of a particular kind of female subjection even before the first sin had been committed and the Fall had taken place:

> Subjection is of two kinds; one is that of slavery, in which the ruler manages the subject for his own advantage, and this sort of subjection came in after sin. But the other kind of subjection is domestic or civil, in which the ruler manages his subjects for their advantage and benefit. And this sort of subjection would have obtained even before sin. For the human group would have lacked the benefit of order had some of its members not been governed by others who were wiser. Such is the subjection in which woman is by nature subordinate to man, because the power of rational discernment is by nature stronger in man.[8]

So woman was not a slave, but man's greater ability to think rationally meant that he should rule her in her own best interests. Or, as Aquinas put it in his *Summa Contra Gentiles*, 'the female requires the male, not only for procreation, as in other animals, but also for governance: because the male excels both in intelligence and in strength'.[9] Thus far the masters were all in general agreement, and it is hardly surprising that they should be regarded as misogynistic in the twenty-first century.

Marriage

Purpose

What about when the masters left the nature of men and women in general and focused on the institution of marriage in particular? Much of their work in this field concerned the purpose of marriage. There was

[7] ST 1a.92.1 and 1a.92.1.ad1 (vol. 13, p. 37). For Aquinas' debt to Aristotle regarding the nature of men and women, see P. Allen, *The Concept of Woman: The Aristotelian Revolution, 750 B.C.–A.D. 1250*, 2nd edn (Grand Rapids, MI, 1997), pp. 385–407.

[8] ST 1a.92.1.ad2 (vol. 13, pp. 37–9).

[9] Thomas Aquinas, *The Summa Contra Gentiles of Saint Thomas Aquinas: The Third Book (Part II – Chapters LXXXIV–CLXIII)*, trans. The English Dominican Fathers (London, 1928), 3.123, p. 115. Henceforth SCG.

general agreement that marriage served two purposes, each having been established or instituted on a different occasion. The first purpose of marriage was procreation, and to this end it had been instituted before the Fall when God commanded the first man and woman to 'Be fruitful and multiply, and fill the earth' (Genesis 1.28). This purpose continued to be valid after the Fall and was termed marriage *ad officium*. The second purpose of marriage was to serve as a concession to the weakness of the flesh, and in this respect it had been instituted after the Fall. The ideal way of life was virginity or celibacy, but those who were too weak to resist temptation should marry rather than commit fornication or adultery. Here Paul was cited: 'But if they cannot contain, let them marry: for it is better to marry than to burn' (1 Corinthians 7.9). Marriage was in this sense an inferior way of life, but it was permissable as a remedy for sin, and it was termed marriage *ad remedium*. Hugh of Saint Victor summed up the twofold institution and its double purpose as follows:

> The institution of marriage is twofold: one before sin for office, the other after sin for remedy; the first, that nature might be multiplied; the second, that nature might be supported and vice checked.

Hugh explained further:

> Now the office of marriage is this, that the mingling of flesh was established before sin not for the remedy of weakness but for the multiplication of progeny; after sin, blessed Augustine testifies that the very same was conceded as a remedy for weakness, saying: The weakness of both sexes inclining toward the ruin of shamefulness is rightly supported by the honour of marriage, so that what was office for the sound is remedy for the sick.[10]

Gratian's *Decretum* had as much influence on theologians as canon lawyers in this area:

> The first institution of marriage was effected in Paradise such that there would have been 'an unstained bed and honourable marriage' [Hebrews 13.4] resulting in conception without ardour and birth without pain. The second, to eliminate unlawful movement, was effected outside Paradise such that the infirmity that is prone to foul ruin might be rescued by the uprightness of marriage.[11]

All these basic points were rehearsed by Peter Lombard in his *Sentences*.[12]

[10] Hugh of Saint Victor, *On the Sacraments*, 2.11.3, p. 325.

[11] Payer, *Bridling of Desire*, Appendix 1, p. 185. For the adoption of this view by other canonists, see Brundage, *Law, Sex, and Christian Society*, pp. 271–2.

[12] Peter Lombard, *Sententiae*, 4.26.1–2 (vol. 2, pp. 416–17), 4.30.3.2 (vol. 2, p. 441). For a useful guide to the treatment of marriage and sex in Peter Lombard's *Sentences*, see Biller, *Measure of Multitude*, pp. 57–9.

Different scholars attached different weight to these two purposes, but they were never seen as contradictory. Rather they worked together: marital sex was preferable to non-marital sex, provided always that procreation was the aim. So there were no major disputes here, although in the thirteenth century much greater emphasis was put on the naturalness of marriage.[13] Thomas Aquinas, for example, considered 'whether matrimony is of natural law'. He argued that it was not natural 'as resulting of necessity from the principles of nature', in the way that 'upward movement is natural to fire'. It was, however, natural as something 'to which nature inclines, although it comes to pass through the intervention of the free-will'. Drawing heavily on Aristotle, he explained that natural reason inclined to marriage in two ways:

First, in relation to the principal end of matrimony, namely the good of the offspring. For nature intends not only the begetting of offspring, but also its education and development until it reach the perfect state of man as man, and that is the state of virtue ... Now a child cannot be brought up and instructed unless it have certain and definite parents, and this would not be the case unless there were a tie between the man and a definite woman, and it is in this that matrimony consists. Secondly, in relation to the secondary end of matrimony, which is the mutual services which married persons render one another in household matters. For just as natural reason dictates that men should live together, since one is not self-sufficient in all things concerning life, for which reason man is described as being naturally inclined to political society, so too among those works that are necessary for human life some are becoming to men, others to women. Wherefore nature inculcates that society of man and woman which consists in matrimony. These two reasons are given by the Philosopher.[14]

For Aquinas, therefore, the chief purpose of marriage was the production of children, and crucially he took this to mean not just procreation but also their proper upbringing. He therefore used the same argument when condemning fornication, explaining further why both parents had to be involved in raising children properly and why this required that they be married. With some animals, and Aquinas cited dogs as an example, the female was able to bring up the offspring on her own, and so the male and female did not stay together. In every case in which the female could not raise the offspring on her own, the male and female remained together until the offspring had been successfully reared. Because the young of some birds, for example, had to be brought food

[13] See Payer, *Bridling of Desire*, pp. 66–8.

[14] Thomas Aquinas, *The 'Summa Theologica' of St. Thomas Aquinas: Third Part (Supplement) QQ. XXXIV–LXVIII*, trans. Fathers of the English Dominican Province (London, 1922), 41.1, pp. 77–8. Henceforth *Supplement*. On the growing importance of natural law and Aristotle in theological discussions of marriage in the thirteenth century, see Biller, *Measure of Multitude*, pp. 45–52.

while also needing to be incubated, the female could not possibly raise them on her own and so the male stayed to help. Where did humans fit into this picture?

Now it is clear that in the human species the female is far from sufficing alone for the rearing of the children, since the needs of human life require many things that one person alone cannot provide. It is therefore in keeping with human nature that the man remain with the woman after coition, and not leave her at once, indulging in promiscuous intercourse, as those do who have the habit of fornication.

With humans, however, it was not just that there was too much work for one parent. A child needed not only food for its body but also 'instruction for its soul'. Moreover, whereas other animals could provide for themselves by 'natural forethought', 'man lives by reason, which can attain to forethought only after long experience: so that children need to be instructed by their parents who are experienced'. This instruction could not begin at once and took a long time, and had to be backed up with punishment. According to Aquinas, this was beyond a woman's capabilities because she lacked a man's rational powers and physical strength: 'Now a woman is insufficient for these things, in fact there is more need for a man for such things, for his reason is more perfect for instruction, and his arm is stronger for punishment.' It followed that it was natural for the man to remain with the woman not just for a short time but in a 'lasting fellowship' which was called matrimony.[15]

While Aquinas and other thirteenth-century masters added arguments from nature, marriage was always granted a spiritual aspect. Hugh of Saint Victor, for example, stressed its divine origins:

The author of marriage is God. For He himself decreed that there be marriage, when He made woman as an assistance to man in the propagation of the race. Adam also knowing in spirit for what use woman had been made, when she had been brought to him, said, 'This now is bone of my bones, and flesh of my flesh. Wherefore a man shall leave father and mother, and shall cleave to his wife: and they shall be two in one flesh' (Cf. Gen. 2.23 and 24). And Christ also in Cana of Galilee (Cf. John 2), not only by corporeal presence but also by the exhibition of a miracle consecrated nuptials. All this shows that marriage is from God and is good.[16]

Drawing on Augustine, masters frequently said that marriage, and especially sexual intercourse between husband and wife, were excused by the three 'goods' of marriage: offspring (*proles*), fidelity (*fides*) and

[15] SCG 3.122, pp. 112–13. See also ST 2a2ae.154.2 (vol. 43, pp. 135–6).
[16] Hugh of Saint Victor, *On the Sacraments*, 2.11.2, p. 325.

sacrament (*sacramentum*). By the latter, they meant not that marriage was one of the seven sacraments, but that marriage could not be dissolved because it symbolized the union between Christ and the church.[17] When Aquinas explained how marriage acted as remedy for concupiscence, he included the idea that 'marriage affords a remedy by the grace given therein' when concupiscence was repressed 'in its root', as well as by marital sex.[18] While naturalistic arguments became more common in the thirteenth century, they did not alter the fundamental views of the purposes of marriage.

Making a marriage: consent and consummation

While there were no major disputes about the purposes of marriage, there were significant disagreements when it came to defining what constituted a marriage. Scholars disagreed over the point at which a marriage became fully and irrevocably established. Was it when the couple consented to marry, without regard to consummation that might or might not take place subsequently? Or was it when the couple had sex for the first time? This mattered in theory because of the marriage between Mary and Joseph. Since Mary was a virgin when Christ was born, she and Joseph had not been properly married if consummation was necessary to make a marriage, a view which could not be comfortably held.[19] It mattered in practice because actual marriage disputes had to be settled in ecclesiastical courts, and it was necessary to be clear about whether couples could separate if their marriages had not yet been consummated.

The view that consent established a fully valid marriage prevailed, with Hugh of Saint Victor as a strong advocate:

> This association then is marriage, which is consecrated by a compact of mutual agreement, when each by voluntary promise makes himself debtor to the other, so that thereafter he neither passes over to association with another, while the other is living, nor disjoins himself from that association which is established reciprocally ... Now if anyone asks when marriage begins to be, we say that from the moment when such a consent as we have defined above has been made between male and female, immediately from that moment marriage is and even

[17] Payer, *Bridling of Desire*, pp. 69–71; P. J. Payer, *Sex and the New Medieval Literature of Confession, 1150–1300* (Toronto, 2009), pp. 175–6. See, for example, Peter Lombard, *Sententiae*, 4.26.6.1 (vol. 2, pp. 419–20).

[18] *Supplement*, 42.3.ad4, pp. 92–3.

[19] See P. S. Gold, 'The marriage of Mary and Joseph in the twelfth-century ideology of marriage', in V. L. Bullough and J. A. Brundage (eds.), *Sexual Practices and the Medieval Church* (Buffalo, 1982), pp. 102–17.

if the joining of flesh follows afterwards nothing more is contributed to the marriage with reference to the virtue of the sacrament.[20]

Most influentially, Peter Lombard was equally clear that it was an error to maintain that marriage could not be contracted without sexual intercourse. Moreover, to suppose that the marriage of Mary and Joseph did not exist or was less than perfect was wicked; rather absence of carnal relations made their marriage more holy and more perfect.[21]

The significance attached to consent was further evident in scholars' treatment of another issue related to the making of a marriage, the precise words used by the parties involved. A distinction was drawn between present consent, using words in the present tense, and future consent, promising to marry in the future with words in the future tense. Peter Lombard, for example, stated very clearly that marriage was established by present and not future consent.[22] It was generally agreed, moreover, that if a couple promised to marry in the future, and then one of them married someone else with present consent, the second relationship stood as the true marriage. As Hugh put it:

But you say to me: Someone promised or by chance swore to someone that he at an agreeable time would marry her and she similarly promised or swore that she would wed him. Meanwhile, by mutual agreement, one or both passed to association with another; he took another wife and she wed another husband. What must be done then? On account of the former promise must the compact of the second agreement be severed? But consider that it is one thing to do and quite a different thing to promise. He who promises does not yet do; but he who does, already does what he does. In him who promises, if he does not do what he promises, there is falsehood. But in him who does, even if he repents after the deed, nevertheless what has been done has been completely done. He then who has promised that he would take a wife, nevertheless has not yet taken a wife, and she who promised that she would wed, has not yet wed; there was still no marriage but there should have been. But afterwards he took a wife and she wed a husband, there was already marriage on both sides, and what has been done cannot be dissolved, even if what was promised was not fulfilled. Therefore, the preceding lie must be corrected by penitence, but the following marriage must not be dissolved.[23]

The power of consent using words in the present tense was further emphasized when scholars considered the status of a marriage that was made with present consent but left unconsummated. This marriage

[20] Hugh of Saint Victor, *On the Sacraments*, 2.11.4–5, pp. 329–30.

[21] Peter Lombard, *Sententiae*, 4.26.6.3 (vol. 2, p. 421); see also 4.27.3.2 (vol. 2, p. 423). For canonists making similar points, see Brundage, *Law, Sex, and Christian Society*, p. 274.

[22] Peter Lombard, *Sententiae*, 4.27.3.1 (vol. 2, pp. 422–3).

[23] Hugh of Saint Victor, *On the Sacraments*, 2.11.5, p. 330.

stood even if one of the partners subsequently entered a marriage with a different partner and consummated it; this second relationship was adultery. Hugh noted that 'certain men' thought that the second relationship should be accepted as the true marriage 'because in this case more seems to have taken place, where after consent even the mingling of flesh has followed', but he dismissed this view since on this basis a third relationship might later be accepted as the valid marriage on the grounds that 'carnal copulation has taken place more often than in the second'.[24]

The most important advocate of a different approach was Gratian who argued that there were two stages in the making of a marriage: first consent, and then consummation. According to this view, both consent and consummation were necessary to establish a marriage, but it was consummation that made the marriage complete and indissoluble. This became known as the 'Italian solution' whereas the view that present consent was sufficient on its own to establish a marriage was called the 'French solution'. In the middle decades of the twelfth century, canonists associated with Bologna backed Gratian, while only Parisian canonists supported the consent theory. Eventually, however, the consent theory became dominant in canon law just as in theology. The key figure in this development was probably Huguccio, and from the late 1180s the consent theory was accepted by virtually all canonists, and was increasingly evident in papal decisions.[25]

Sex did not become entirely irrelevant to the making of a marriage, however. In the second half of the twelfth century, Pope Alexander III ruled that present consent established a marriage, but that it could be dissolved for a variety of reasons up to the point of consummation. He also maintained that when consent had been given subject to the fulfilment of certain conditions, the marriage became fully established if sexual intercourse took place, even though the conditions had not been met. Moreover, future consent followed by sexual intercourse also set up a valid marriage, a position that Peter Lombard had already taken.[26] In the thirteenth century Aquinas expressed the same view, explaining that sexual intercourse after future consent was taken to establish a marriage based on present consent. This was not so according to the tribunal of conscience which demanded 'inward consent' without which even words expressing present consent did not make a marriage.

[24] *Ibid.*, p. 331.
[25] Brundage, *Law, Sex, and Christian Society*, pp. 235–8, 262–9; Gold, 'The marriage of Mary and Joseph', pp. 103–7.
[26] Brundage, *Law, Sex, and Christian Society*, pp. 264, 333–5.

The church, however, had to judge on the basis of external evidence, and 'since nothing is more expressly significant of consent than carnal intercourse, it follows that in the judgment of the Church carnal intercourse following on betrothal is declared to make a marriage, unless there appear clear signs of deceit or fraud'.[27] There was therefore an element of compromise in the settlement of the dispute about what made a marriage.

The emphasis on free and mutual consent had striking implications in another regard entirely because it granted individuals independence from their families in choice of marriage partner, and it treated men and women equally in this respect. This was clear in Hugh's description of marriage as 'a compact of mutual agreement, when each by voluntary promise makes himself debtor to the other', and it was a point on which all scholars agreed. Peter Lombard stated succinctly that present consent was enough to establish a marriage while the giving of the marriage partners by their parents pertained only to the fittingness and solemnity of the marriage, as did the priest's blessing.[28] Aquinas discussed the daughter's independence of her father in choice of husband when considering 'whether consent given secretly in words of the present makes a marriage'. He answered the main question in the affirmative because while 'consent expressed in words of the present between persons lawfully qualified to contract' was essential to the sacrament, everything else belonged to 'the solemnization of the sacrament, as being done in order that marriage may be more fittingly performed'. The omission of whatever solemnized the marriage was a sin, but the marriage was valid. One of the opening objections, however, had suggested that secret marriages could not be valid because the woman was in her father's power which meant that his consent was necessary if she was to be transferred to her husband's power, and it could not be given if the marriage was secret. Aquinas dismissed this argument because it rested on a misunderstanding of the father's authority:

> The maid is in her father's power, not as a female slave without power over her own body, but as a daughter, for the purpose of education. Hence, in so far as she is free, she can give herself into another's power without her father's consent, even as a son or daughter, since they are free, may enter religion without their parents' consent.[29]

If implemented in practice, the need for free consent had the potential to bring the church into conflict with aristocratic families which

[27] *Supplement*, 46.2, p. 126.
[28] Peter Lombard, *Sententiae*, 4.28.2.1 (vol. 2, p. 433).
[29] *Supplement*, 45.5.ad1, p. 121.

reckoned to make politically and economically advantageous matches for their offspring; the consent of the individual, female or male, did not come into it.[30] We must not exaggerate the challenge to the social order, however. The woman began subject to her father's authority and ended up subject to her husband's, so it was only in the process of passing from one to other that in theory her consent was needed. Aquinas, moreover, did not envisage even sons ignoring their fathers. A father could not force his son to marry, 'but he may induce him for a reasonable cause; and thus the son will be affected by his father's command in the same way as he is affected by that cause, so that if the cause be compelling as indicating either obligation or fitness, his father's command will compel him in the same measure'.[31] Nonetheless, the individual marriage partner was not supposed to be entirely subject to family pressure, and the woman was theoretically in the same position as the man.[32]

Marital affection

The theme of equality between wife and husband was also apparent when scholars discussed companionship and love in marriage, or marital affection as it was termed. Hugh of Saint Victor, for example, pointed out that marriage must involve consent to more than sex since fornicators and adulterers agreed to that. To understand what was consented to in marriage, Hugh looked to the relationship that God established between the first man and the first woman after creating the woman from the man's side:

since she was given as a companion, not a servant or a mistress, she was to be produced not from the highest or from the lowest part but from the middle. For if she had been made from the head, she would have been made from the highest and she would seem to have been created for domination. But if she had been made from the feet, she would have been made from the lowest and she would seem to have been subjected to slavery. She was made from the middle, that she might be proved to have been made for equality of association. Yet in a certain way she was inferior to him, in that she was made from him, so that she might always look to him as to her beginning and cleaving to him

30 On tensions between lay and ecclesiastical attitudes to marriage, see G. Duby, *Medieval Marriage: Two Models from Twelfth-Century France*, trans. E. Forster (Baltimore, 1978); G. Duby, *The Knight, the Lady, and the Priest: The Making of Modern Marriage in Medieval France*, trans. B. Bray (New York, 1983). For an account emphasizing eventual lay acceptance of the church's view of marriage, see C. N. L. Brooke, *The Medieval Idea of Marriage* (Oxford, 1989), pp. 119–43.

31 *Supplement*, 47.6, p. 137.

32 The basic point was made repeatedly by canonists; see Brundage, *Law, Sex, and Christian Society*, pp. 275, 332–3, 335–6, 364, 414, 437–9.

indivisibly might not separate herself from that association which ought to have been established reciprocally.[33]

The creation from the man's side rather than his head or feet thus indicated a measure of equality in the relationship, but that she was created from him at all brought hierarchy back into play. Peter Lombard used the same image to emphasize that the woman was created neither to be a slave nor a mistress, but for marital companionship:

Why woman was formed from the man's side and not from some other part of his body ... she was formed not from just any part of his body, but from his side, so that it should be shown that she was created for the partnership of love, lest, if perhaps she had been made from his head, she should be perceived as set over man in domination; or if from his feet, as if subject to him in servitude. Therefore, since she was made neither to dominate, nor to serve the man, but as his partner, she had to be produced neither from his head, nor from his feet, but from his side, so that he would know that she was to be placed beside himself whom he had learned had been taken from his side.[34]

Robert of Sorbon, a master of theology at Paris between 1250 and 1274, used the image again to stress equality. He began by quoting Genesis 2.18, 'It is not good for man to be alone; let us make him a help like unto himself', and commented:

'like unto himself' – this corresponds to equivalence. By this is indicated that the woman must be the equal of the man, or his companion, not under him and not above him. Also, woman was made from man's rib, not from the upper part or from the lower, but from the middle, that by it might be designated that woman must be man's equal.[35]

Aquinas was another to deploy this image when considering whether woman should have been made from man's rib:

It was right and proper for the woman to be formed from the man's rib. First, in order to signify the companionship there should be between man and woman; the woman should neither *have authority over the man* (Timothy 2.12) – and therefore she was not formed from his head; nor should she be despised by the man, as though she were merely his slave – and so she was not formed from his feet.[36]

[33] Hugh of Saint Victor, *On the Sacraments*, 2.11.4, p. 329.

[34] Peter Lombard, *Sententiae*, 2.18.2 (vol. 1, pp. 416–17), as translated in Peter Lombard, *The Sentences. Book 2: On Creation*, trans. G. Silano (Toronto, 2008), p. 77; see also 4.28.4.1 (vol. 2, p. 435).

[35] Quoted by E. Kooper, 'Loving the unequal equal: medieval theologians and marital affection', in R. R. Edwards and S. Spector (eds.), *The Olde Daunce: Love, Friendship, Sex and Marriage in the Medieval World* (New York, 1991), pp. 44–56 at 45.

[36] ST 1a.92.3 (vol. 13, p. 43).

Denying that the wife was like a slave to her husband was not meant to indicate complete equality, but the emphasis on companionship was nevertheless striking. Elsewhere, when explaining the indissolubility of marriage, Aquinas characterized the relationship between husband and wife as 'the greatest friendship', 'for they are made one not only in the act of carnal intercourse, which even among dumb animals causes an agreeable fellowship, but also as partners in the whole intercourse of daily life'.[37] When proving that marriage should be the union of one man with one woman, he observed that 'equality is a condition of friendship'. The woman could not have more than one husband because the paternity of her children would be uncertain. The man, however, should not have more than one wife because experience showed that women in polygamous marriages were treated like servants, and, moreover, the friendship between them would not be equal since the wife's friendship would be servile rather than freely bestowed.[38]

While scholars like Hugh and Aquinas either referred to or left open the possibility of male dominance, their references to equality, companionship and friendship were very different from their other statements about men and women, some of which were quoted earlier. Other theologians used very similar language. The point is that when Parisian masters talked about marital affection they adopted a very different tone from when they discussed the nature of men and women, and came up with much more positive views of women. They were not entirely consistent, and it is all too easy to present a simplistic and misleading view of them as unqualified misogynists.

Marital sex

Conjugal debt

The marital affection about which scholars spoke so warmly had little to do with sex, but marital sex was a major concern for theologians. As already explained, one of the points of marriage was to prevent sex outside marriage, and this tied in with the theory of conjugal debt upon which all scholars were in agreement. According to this theory, each partner in a marriage had a moral obligation to have sex when the other partner wanted it, lest he or she be tempted elsewhere. As expressed in terms of the debt, when one partner demanded or asked that the debt

[37] SCG 3.123, pp. 115–16. [38] SCG 3.124, pp. 118–19.

be paid, the other was bound to pay or render it.[39] The key authority underpinning the theory was Paul's first letter to the Corinthians: 'Let the husband pay the debt to his wife, and the wife also in like manner to the husband. The wife does not have power over her own body, but the husband; likewise, the husband does not have power over his own body, but the wife.'[40] This debt was enforceable in ecclesiastical law courts and both husband and wife had to remain free to pay it.[41] Neither could take a vow of continence or enter religion without the other's agreement to forgo the debt, a point Peter Lombard made repeatedly.[42] As Aquinas explained:

> No one can make an offering to God of what belongs to another. Wherefore since by a consummated marriage the husband's body already belongs to his wife, he cannot by a vow of continence offer it to God without her consent.[43]

Or again:

> A vow is a voluntary act, as its very name implies: and consequently a vow can only be about those goods which are subject to our will, and those in which one person is bound to another do not come under this head. Therefore in matters of this kind one person cannot take a vow without the consent of the one to whom he is bound. Consequently, since husband and wife are mutually bound as regards the payment of the debt which is an obstacle to continence, the one cannot vow continence without the other's consent; and if he take the vow he sins, and must not keep the vow, but must do penance for an ill-taken vow.[44]

There was, however, an important difference between asking for the debt and paying it. It was agreed that while payment of the debt was obligatory, demanding it was not, and so a vow not to demand payment was permissible.[45] There was also a two-month period after consent had established the marriage during which either party was entitled to refuse to consummate the marriage to leave open the possibility of entering religion:

> Before consummation the body of one consort is not absolutely delivered into the power of the other, but conditionally, provided neither consort meanwhile

[39] For discussion of the terminology and appropriate translation, see Payer, *Bridling of Desire*, pp. 89–90.

[40] 1 Corinthians 7.3–4.

[41] For the canonists' adherence to the theory of conjugal debt, see Brundage, *Law, Sex, and Christian Society*, pp. 198, 241–2, 282–4, 358–60, 447.

[42] Peter Lombard, *Sententiae*, 4.27.2 (vol. 2, p. 422), 4.27.5.2 (vol. 2, p. 424), 4.27.7–8.1–6 (vol. 2, pp. 425–7), 4.32.2.1–4 (vol. 2, pp. 452–4).

[43] *Supplement*, 61.1, p. 288.

[44] *Supplement*, 64.6, p. 321.

[45] Payer, *Bridling of Desire*, p. 94; Payer, *Sex and the New Medieval Literature of Confession*, p. 178.

seek the fruit of a better life [i.e. enter religion]. But by marital intercourse the aforesaid delivery is completed, because then each of them enters into bodily possession of the power transferred to him. Wherefore also before consummation they are not bound to pay the marriage debt forthwith after contracting marriage by words of the present, but a space of two months is allowed them for three reasons. First that they may deliberate meanwhile about entering religion; secondly, to prepare what is necessary for the solemnization of the wedding; thirdly, lest the husband think little of a gift he has not longed to possess.[46]

The wife of a man found to be impotent when they tried to consummate the marriage could also get their marriage annulled because her husband was incapable of paying the debt. Aquinas explained: 'In marriage there is a contract whereby one is bound to pay the other the marital debt: wherefore just as in other contracts, the bond is unfitting if a person bind himself to what he cannot give or do, so the marriage contract is unfitting, if it be made by one who cannot pay the marital debt.' If the cause were natural and temporary, and could be cured by medicine or in time, the marriage stood. But if the cause were natural and permanent, the marriage was void, the impotent man could never marry, and the woman was free to marry. Aquinas said that the church expected the couple to try to consummate their marriage for three years after which time it would regard the impotence as permanent and dissolve the marriage. If, however, the man subsequently proved not to be impotent, the marriage was to be reinstated.[47] There was also the possibility of impotence being caused by a curse. If the effect was temporary, the marriage was valid. If, however, it was permanent, the marriage was void, and once again it took three years to establish that this was the case. If the curse had rendered the man impotent with regard to all women, he could not marry again, but if it had left him 'impotent in relation to one woman and not to another', he was free to marry another woman.[48]

The theory of conjugal debt granted equal rights and obligations to husband and wife. Peter Lombard, for example, stated explicitly that while in all other matters the man was set over the woman, 'in paying the carnal debt they are equals'.[49] When theologians imagined it working in practice, however, it turned out that demanding the debt might mean different things to husband and wife. While both could simply

[46] *Supplement*, 61.2.ad2, p. 290. See also Payer, *Bridling of Desire*, pp. 90–2.

[47] *Supplement*, 58.1, pp. 254–5. On impotence, see Brundage, *Law, Sex, and Christian Society*, pp. 290–2, 339, 376–8, 457–8; Payer, *Bridling of* Desire, pp. 73–5.

[48] *Supplement*, 58.2, pp. 258–9.

[49] Peter Lombard, *Sententiae*, 4.32.1.1 (vol. 2, p. 451).

ask in words, the wife might be too ashamed to speak and so give signs to which her husband was bound to respond. As Aquinas had it:

> The debt may be demanded in two ways. First, explicitly, as when they ask one another by words; secondly, implicitly, when namely the husband knows by certain signs that the wife would wish him to pay the debt, but is silent through shame. And so even though she does not ask for the debt explicitly in words, the husband is bound to pay it, whenever his wife shows signs of wishing him to do so.[50]

When the wife asked implicitly by signs, it could also be called asking 'interpretively, as when she is ashamed and her husband feels that she desires him to pay the debt'.[51] The husband did not experience the same reticence because he had 'the more noble part in the marriage act', and so it was 'natural that he should be less ashamed than the wife to ask for the debt'.[52] In other words, the woman's shame stemmed from her passive role in sexual intercourse, and so the opposition between active and passive patterned even an area of equality.[53]

Sexual positions

While the conjugal debt established an obligation for each partner to satisfy the other's demands, this certainly did not mean that any demand was acceptable and free of sin, or that couples could do whatever they wanted. Moderation was required in demanding payment, and this was invariably treated as a point that applied to women in particular. A wife could not repeatedly demand payment to the point at which her husband could no longer comply: 'If the husband be rendered incapable of paying the debt through a cause consequent upon marriage, for instance through having already paid the debt and being unable to pay it, the wife has no right to ask again, and in doing so she behaves as a harlot rather than as a wife.'[54] Nor should the husband accede to his wife's demands if it would endanger his health: 'the husband is bound to pay the debt to his wife, in matters pertaining to the begetting of children, with due regard however to his own welfare'.[55]

50 *Supplement*, 64.2, p. 315.
51 *Supplement*, 53.1.ad4, p. 186.
52 *Supplement*, 64.5.ad2, p. 320.
53 For a brilliant critique of the notion that the theory of conjugal debt entailed equality between wife and husband, see D. Elliott, *Spiritual Marriage: Sexual Abstinence in Medieval Wedlock* (Princeton, 1993), pp. 148–55.
54 *Supplement* 64.1.ad3, p. 313.
55 *Supplement* 64.1, p. 313. See also Payer, *Bridling of Desire*, p. 95.

There were also major concerns about how married couples had sex. Intercourse had to be vaginal and then the couple had to adopt an acceptable position.

Use of a spouse is against nature when it bypasses the proper vessel, or the proper manner instituted by nature in terms of the position. The first case is always a mortal sin because offspring cannot result and so the intention of nature is totally frustrated. In the second case it is not always a mortal sin, as some say, but can be a sign of deadly concupiscence. Sometimes it can even be without sin when the disposition of the body does not allow the other way. Otherwise the gravity is in proportion to the distance from the natural manner.[56]

Anything other than vaginal sex could not lead to procreation, the proper aim of marital sex, and was therefore unnatural and a mortal sin. In most cases only what we now call the missionary position was regarded as natural and acceptable. Other positions might be allowed because of obesity or pregnancy. In general, however, sex with the man entering the woman from behind was unacceptable because that was how animals did it. Sex with the woman on top was also unacceptable because it represented an inversion of the natural order which required male dominance, and therefore the man on top. These 'unnatural' positions were also thought to make conception less likely or impossible, which made them even more sinful.[57]

Times

There were also times at which couples were not supposed to have sex. According to a long tradition to be found in the Church Fathers and in penitential literature going back to the sixth century, sex was forbidden on feast days and fast days, and when the wife was menstruating, pregnant, or after she had given birth. In general the scholars of the twelfth and thirteenth centuries continued to advocate these rules, but treated offences against them as much less serious than had the older penitentials. It was thus a venial sin to ask for payment of the debt on a holy day, but no sin at all to render it, as the conjugal debt required. Views were more varied when the condition of the wife was the determining factor, but it could, for example, be a mortal sin knowingly to

[56] Aquinas *In 4 Sent 31*, expositio textus, as quoted by Payer, *Bridling of Desire*, p. 79.

[57] Brundage, *Law, Sex, and Christian Society*, pp. 199, 225, 286, 367, 452–3; Payer, *Bridling of Desire*, pp. 76–9. For theologians' views on contraception, see Biller, *Measure of Multitude*, pp. 166–77; J. T. Noonan, *Contraception: A History of its Treatment by the Catholic Theologians and Canonists*, enlarged edn (Cambridge, MA, 1986).

seek payment of the debt when the wife was menstruating unless it was to avoid a greater sin.[58]

Sexual pleasure

Thus far there would seem to have been general agreement on most matters pertaining to marital sex, but there was much less certainty once intention came into play, especially in relation to sexual pleasure. A standard view identified four possible intentions: first, to have children; second, to pay the debt; third, to overcome incontinence or to avoid fornication; and, fourth, to satisfy lust or pursue sexual pleasure for its own sake.[59] The latter was the least problematic as it was always regarded as a sin. Whether it was mortal or venial sin, however, was a matter of debate. The problem with sexual pleasure, according to Aquinas, was that it completely undermined the use of reason: 'Now there is a loss of reason incidental to the union of man and woman, both because the reason is carried away entirely on account of the vehemence of the pleasure, so that it is unable to understand anything at the same time, as the Philosopher says [Ethics 7.11]; and again because of the tribulation of the flesh which such persons have to suffer from solicitude for temporal things [1 Corinthians 7.28].' That was why the goods of marriage were necessary as a form of compensation.[60] Furthermore, impairment of reason had moral consequences: 'That men be too much given to the pleasure of copulation is corruptive of good morals: because, since, more than any other, this pleasure absorbs the mind, the reason would be hindered in things pertaining to rectitude.'[61]

Peter Lombard established that the pursuit of sexual pleasure for its own sake involved sin. Referring to the goods of marriage, he said: 'However, when these goods are absent, namely fidelity and offspring, it does not seem that intercourse is defended from being a crime. Whence in the *Sentences* of Sextus the Pythagorean we read, "Every too ardent lover of his own wife is an adulterer".'[62] He went on to cite part of

[58] Brundage, *Law, Sex, and Christian Society*, pp. 198–9, 225, 242, 285, 367–8, 451–2; Payer, *Bridling of Desire*, pp. 97–110; Payer, *Sex and the New Medieval Literature of Confession*, pp. 182–5.

[59] Payer, *Bridling of Desire*, pp. 85–6; Payer, *Sex and the New Medieval Literature of Confession*, p. 176.

[60] *Supplement* 49.1, pp. 144–5. For Peter the Chanter's similar view, see J. W. Baldwin, *The Language of Sex: Five Voices from Northern France around 1200* (Chicago, 1994), p. 126.

[61] SCG 3.125, p. 120.

[62] Peter Lombard, *Sententiae*, 4.31.5.2 (vol. 2, p. 447). As translated by Payer, *Bridling of Desire*, p. 118. See Payer, *Bridling of Desire*, pp. 120–4 for discussion of the Sextus text and its authorship.

Gregory's response to a question about whether a man could enter a church after intercourse: 'but because the licit commingling of a spouse is not possible without carnal pleasure he must refrain from entering the sacred place because the pleasure itself is in no way possible without fault'.[63] Peter took this to refer to sex when the good of offspring was lacking, in which case pleasure could not be without sin.[64] To these arguments from authority, Aquinas added one from nature: 'to make use of sexual intercourse on account of its inherent pleasure, without reference to the end for which nature intended it, is to act against nature'.[65] Aquinas also expressed the general view amongst theologians when he argued that whether the sin involved was venial or mortal depended on whether the husband would only have sought pleasure with his wife, in which case it was a venial sin, or would have been perfectly happy to experience it with any woman, in which case it was a mortal sin:

> But if the motive be lust, yet not excluding the marriage blessings, namely that he would by no means be willing to go to another woman, it is a venial sin; while if he exclude the marriage blessings, so as to be disposed to act in like manner with any woman, it is a mortal sin.[66]

Or again:

> if pleasure be sought in such a way as to exclude the honesty of marriage, so that, to wit, it is not as a wife but as a woman that a man treats his wife, and that he is ready to use her in the same way if she were not his wife, it is a mortal sin; wherefore such a man is said to be too ardent a lover of his wife, because his ardour carries him away from the goods of marriage. If, however, he seek pleasure within the bounds of marriage, so that it would not be sought in another than his wife, it is a venial sin.[67]

Only Durand of Saint Pourçain, a Dominican master of theology in the early fourteenth century, argued that the sin was always venial rather than mortal.[68] Canon lawyers were more divided, with Huguccio saying that it was a mortal sin and the Ordinary Gloss on the *Decretum* taking the view that it was venial unless some other factor came into play.[69]

Sex when the intention was to overcome incontinence or to avoid fornication was a trickier matter. This was sometimes taken to include the actions of someone who initiated sex with a partner who was aroused

63 Peter Lombard, *Sententiae*, 4.31.8.2 (vol. 2, p. 450). As translated by Payer, *Bridling of Desire*, p. 125 from Gratian.
64 Peter Lombard, *Sententiae*, 4.31.8.3 (vol. 2, p. 451).
65 *Supplement*, 65.3, p. 339. 66 *Supplement*, 41.4, p. 85.
67 *Supplement*, 49.6, p. 158.
68 Payer, *Bridling of Desire*, pp. 127–8.
69 *Ibid.*, pp. 125–6.

and might seek sex outside the marriage, or who simply paid the debt when asked by such a partner, and these actions were generally seen as meritorious.[70] The real issue, however, was how to assess the actions of the person who demanded payment of the debt to avoid himself or herself seeking sex outside the marriage. Peter Lombard analysed the significance of Paul's first letter to the Corinthians which said that marriage was granted as an indulgence. According to Peter, indulgence could take the form of either concession or permission. Marital union solely to have children was *conceded*, while marital union which was not necessary for procreation and which took place because of incontinence was *permitted*. This second form of indulgence was more limited in its effect which meant that there was still some fault, although it was light, and therefore venial sin.[71] Most theologians shared the view that to initiate marital sex to avoid other illicit sexual activity on one's own part was to commit venial sin. Further reasons were discovered, however. Aquinas' view was that 'there are only two ways in which married persons can come together without any sin at all, namely in order to have offspring, and in order to pay the debt; otherwise it is always at least a venial sin'.[72] Invoking the distinction between having sex to stop one's partner going outside the marriage and having sex to stop oneself doing the same thing, he explained:

> If a man intends by the marriage act to prevent fornication in his wife, it is not sin, because this is a kind of payment of the debt that comes under the good of faith. But if he intends to avoid fornication in himself, then there is a certain superfluity, and accordingly there is a venial sin.[73]

Only Durand of Saint Pourçain, once again going against the mainstream, thought it probable that there was no sin at all since it was entirely rational to have sex with one's spouse to avoid fornication.[74] For the overwhelming majority of scholars, however, marriage was not entirely effective as a remedy for sin in this case.

It might be supposed that there were no further problems regarding intention and sexual pleasure in marital sex: you committed no sin as long as you had sex in order to have children or to satisfy your partner's demand for payment of the debt, and provided that it was in a proper way and at the right time. Many scholars, indeed a growing majority,

[70] *Ibid.*, p. 112.
[71] Peter Lombard, *Sententiae*, 4.31.6.1–2 (vol. 2, pp. 447–8). For extended analysis, see Payer, *Bridling of Desire*, pp. 112–15.
[72] *Supplement*, 49.5, p. 155.
[73] *Supplement*, 49.5.ad2, p. 156.
[74] Payer, *Bridling of Desire*, p. 116.

took this view.[75] Peter Lombard, for example, was explicit on the point.[76] Peter the Chanter, Robert of Courson and Thomas of Chobham came to the same conclusion, though Peter the Chanter seems to have had reservations.[77] Such masters were keen to insist that marital sex had to be possible without sin, not least because of their concern to attack and distance themselves from the ideas of dualist heretics who maintained that the created, physical world was the work of an evil deity and therefore entirely sinful. These concerns were clear when Aquinas considered 'whether the marriage act is always sinful':

> If we suppose the corporeal nature to be created by the good God, we cannot hold that those things which pertain to the preservation of the corporeal nature and to which nature inclines, are altogether evil; wherefore, since the inclination to beget an offspring whereby the specific nature is preserved is from nature, it is impossible to maintain that the act of begetting children is altogether unlawful, so that it be impossible to find the mean of virtue therein; unless we suppose, as some are mad enough to assert, that corruptible things were created by the evil God ... wherefore this is a most wicked heresy.[78]

Indeed, for Aquinas, it was possible for marital sex not merely to be without sin, but to have positive value: 'if the motive for the marriage act be a virtue, whether of justice that they may render the debt, or of religion, that they may beget children for the worship of God, it is meritorious'.[79] In this light, sexual pleasure clearly served an important function in ensuring that people were drawn to procreate: 'the end which nature intends in sexual union is the begetting and rearing of the offspring; and that this good might be sought after, it attached pleasure to the union'.[80] It followed that for all its capacity to undermine reason in the individual while having sex, it was neither opposed to reason in the greater scheme of things nor evil itself:

[75] Brundage, *Law, Sex, and Christian Society*, pp. 280, 282, 364–5, 448–50.

[76] Peter Lombard, *Sententiae*, 4.31.8.1 (vol. 2, p. 450). See Baldwin, *Language of Sex*, p. 120.

[77] Baldwin, *Language of Sex*, pp. 121–5. See, however, Brundage, *Law, Sex, and Christian Society*, p. 282, n. 113, where Peter the Chanter is deemed to adhere to the view that sin was always involved.

[78] *Supplement*, 41.3, p. 82. See also SCG 3.126, pp. 121–2; ST 2a2ae.153.2 (vol. 43, p. 193).

[79] *Supplement*, 41.4, p. 85.

[80] *Supplement*, 65.3, p. 339. See also *Supplement*, 49.1, p. 145: 'in order to entice [man] to the act whereby a defect of the species is remedied, divine providence attached pleasure to that act'. See also Noonan, *Contraception*, pp. 293–4. For the view in medicine and natural philosophy that the purpose of sexual pleasure was to ensure that sexual intercourse and therefore procreation occurred, see J. Cadden, *Meanings of Sex Difference in the Middle Ages: Medicine, Science, and Culture* (Cambridge, 1993), pp. 135–7.

the pleasure of copulation in marriage is perfectly in accord with reason; nevertheless, it impedes the exercise of reason because of the physical reactions involved. But this does not mean that it is morally evil, any more than is sleep, when taken in accordance with reason: for reason itself demands that the exercise of reason be sometimes discontinued.[81]

For scholars like Aquinas, there was no sin when a married person had sex with the intention to procreate or to satisfy a partner's demand for payment of the debt, and the pleasure involved was morally unproblematic.

Other scholars, however, though fewer in number, held that there was venial sin even when the intention was procreation or to pay the debt. Hugh of Saint Victor noted that while the good of marriage restrained and limited 'the ardour of immoderate lust', 'Yet it does not effect that evil not exist at all but that it be not damnable; indeed on account of this good that evil is made venial.'[82] Huguccio, the canon lawyer, considered that 'the conjugal act cannot be exercised without sin, although it itself is not a sin, because there is always itching of the flesh and pleasure in the emission of sperm which is always a sin although very minor ... Whence it is that Christ did not wish to be born through coitus because it cannot be exercised without sin, even if it were a saint who was having intercourse.'[83] Pope Innocent III, also a distinguished canon lawyer, wrote: 'Everyone knows that intercourse, even between married persons, is never performed without the itch of the flesh, the heat of passion, and the stench of lust.'[84] Thus there were scholars who argued that all sexual pleasure was sinful even if experienced while trying to have a child or to satisfy one's spouse's lust. These kinds of intercourse were sinless, but not the pleasure that was necessarily felt in the process, and pleasure was bound to be experienced because it was part of ejaculation. Absolutely all sex was therefore at least venially sinful.

This created problems for married couples. If one partner asked for sex, the other was being asked to sin, but was obliged to do it. Huguccio was most worried about the man whose wife demanded payment of the debt; he was obliged to pay, but would experience pleasure in ejaculation and therefore sin: 'I have a wife; she earnestly seeks the debt. If I

[81] ST 1a2ae.34.1 (vol. 20, p. 69).

[82] Hugh of Saint Victor, *On the Sacraments*, 2.11.7, pp. 339–40.

[83] Huguccio, *Summa* on Gratian, *Decretum* C 33.4.7, ad v *nullatenus potest*, as quoted by Payer, *Bridling of Desire*, p. 125, n. 65. For other passages in the *Summa* in which Huguccio makes the same point, see Brundage, *Law, Sex, and Christian Society*, p. 281, n. 112. See also Baldwin, *Language of Sex*, pp. 120–1.

[84] Lothario dei Segni (Pope Innocent III), *On the Misery of the Human Condition*, trans. M. M. Dietz (Indianapolis, 1969), 1.3, p. 8.

refuse, I sin mortally because I act against a precept … if I pay, I sin at least venially because in every act of intercourse there is a certain itching, a certain pleasure which cannot be without sin … and thus I seem to be perplexed.'[85] But Huguccio thought he had found a way out:

> I can pay the debt to my wife and wait until she has fulfilled her pleasure. In fact, in such a case the women is often accustomed to come before the man, and when my wife's pleasure in the carnal act has been fulfilled, I can, if I wish, and free from all sin, withdraw without satisfying my pleasure or emitting the seed of generation.[86]

The husband was thus to wait for his wife's orgasm and withdraw, being careful not to ejaculate at any point, and so not to experience pleasure as Huguccio defined it. This was termed *coitus reservatus* or *amplexus reservatus*, but was not discussed by another canon lawyer or theologian until the fourteenth century.[87]

Although the idea that licit marital sex was rendered sinful by pleasure became less and less common, there were always some theologians and canonists who shared Huguccio's view.[88] It had, however, already received its most withering critique and vigorous rejection from Peter Abelard. He discussed sexual pleasure, along with pleasure in eating, in his *Ethics* when he made the point that sin lay in consent to sin, not in actually doing anything. He was aware that his view was controversial:

> Some people may be more than a little upset because they hear us say that doing the sin doesn't add anything to the guilt or to the damnation before God. For they object that in acting out a sin there follows a kind of pleasure that increases the sin, as in sex or in the eating we talked about. It wouldn't be absurd of them to say this, if they proved that this kind of bodily pleasure is a sin and that no one can commit anything like that without sinning.[89]

But Abelard considered that this position was in fact absurd:

> If they actually accept that, then surely it is illicit for *anyone* to have this bodily pleasure. Hence not even married couples are exempt from sin when they are brought together by this bodily pleasure that is permitted to them, and neither is one who enjoys a delicious meal of his own fruit. All sick people too would be

[85] Huguccio, *Summa* on Gratian, *Decretum* D.13pr. v. *item aduersus*, as quoted by Brundage, *Law, Sex, and Christian Society*, p. 283, n. 117, my translation.

[86] Huguccio, *Summa* on Gratian, *Decretum* D.13pr., as quoted by Brundage, *Law, Sex, and Christian Society*, p. 282, n. 113, my translation. See also U. Ranke-Heinemann, *Eunuchs for the Kingdom of Heaven: The Catholic Church and Sexuality*, trans. P. Heinegg (Harmondsworh, 1990), p. 171, where the same passage is also quoted in translation.

[87] Noonan, *Contraception*, pp. 296–9.

[88] Brundage, *Law, Sex, and Christian Society*, pp. 281, 282 n. 113, 349, 364, 429, 451.

[89] Abelard, *Ethics*, 1.35–6, in *Ethical Writings*, trans. P. V. Spade (Indianapolis, 1995), p. 8.

at fault who favour sweeter foods for refreshment, in order to recuperate from their illness. They surely don't take these foods *without* pleasure; otherwise if they took them they wouldn't help. Finally, even the Lord, the creator of foods as well as of our bodies, wouldn't be without fault if he inserted into those foods flavours such as would necessarily force those who eat them into sin by their pleasure in them. For why would he make such foods for our eating, or permit us to eat them, if it were impossible for us to eat them without sin. And how can sin be said to be committed in doing what is permitted?[90]

Abelard then dismissed the idea that marital sex was only permissible in an impossible fashion:

they say sex in marriage and the eating of delicious food are only permitted in such a way that the pleasure itself is *not* permitted. Rather, they should be done entirely *without* pleasure. But surely if this is so, then they were permitted to be done in a way such that they cannot be done at all. An authorization that permitted their being done in a way that they certainly *cannot* be done is unreasonable.[91]

Abelard concluded: 'In my judgment, it is plain from these considerations that no natural bodily pleasure is to be counted as a sin. It isn't to be regarded as a fault that we take pleasure in what is such that, when it has occurred, pleasure is necessarily felt.'[92] Essentially Abelard's point was that if in doing something that God permits, pleasure cannot be avoided, that pleasure cannot be sinful. He went on to show that key authorities supported his view, including Paul's reference to marriage being granted as an indulgence.[93] There were therefore very different attitudes to sexual pleasure and very different views about sinfulness involved in legitimate sex, and these differences were never resolved.[94]

Reviewing their key ideas about sexuality and gender, the Parisian masters were in many respects consistent in their thinking. They were largely in agreement with each other regarding the greater worth of virginity and celibacy, the purpose of marriage, the need for consent in the making of a marriage, the theory of conjugal debt, the allocation of active and passive roles in sexual intercourse to men and women respectively, and rules about when and how sexual intercourse between husband and wife should be conducted. They were not so consistent in other respects, however, and there could be huge variations in tone even within the work of an individual master. This was especially so with regard to the nature of women. When discussing the nature of women

90 *Ibid.*, 1.36–7, p. 8. 91 *Ibid.*, 1.40, p. 9.
92 *Ibid.*, 1.42, p. 9. 93 *Ibid.*, 1.43–6, pp. 9–10.
94 For differing views and tensions in the treatment of sexual pleasure in medicine and natural philosophy, see Cadden, *Meanings of Sex Difference*, pp. 134–65.

directly, they almost invariably said that she was weak, irrational, lascivious, a temptress and the like. But when they talked about marital affection, other more positive images were produced: she was a companion and friend, she was not a servant, and equality was even mentioned, though astute scholars like Hugh of Saint Victor and Aquinas carefully avoided any formal contradiction. Some scholars contradicted each other, however. For some time this was so with regard to what established a marriage; it was always so with regard to sexual pleasure and sin. Despite a high degree of consensus, the Parisian masters did not offer an entirely consistent view. Were they misogynists? While many people in the twenty-first century are bound to react to their views on women with bemusement and distaste, it is important to remember the images that emerged in discussions of marital affection, and the degree of equality inherent in the theory of the conjugal debt. Furthermore, many of the rules that the scholars generated applied to both sexes, and they were all part of intellectual systems designed to help people achieve salvation. If it is impossible not to have a subjective reaction to medieval intellectual analysis of sexuality and gender, simply to see misogyny is a gross oversimplification.

Marital problems

Having surveyed some of the key ideas about sex and gender that were developed by Parisian scholars, it is important now to consider the impact that scholars expected their ideas to have on the laity. Much of their thinking was conveyed in sermons, some of which were directed specifically to married couples, while confessors' manuals suggest that it was communicated in the course of confession also. Questions asked about marriage in quodlibetal disputations are especially useful in that they indicate specific problems and dilemmas that learned men thought needed resolution. It may be that members of the audience at the disputation simply wanted clarification of basic principles and invented scenarios that would test them out. It is at least as likely, however, that they were seeking to address the perceived needs of ordinary married couples and to get advice on particular problems that cropped up in pastoral work.[95] Moreover, in outlining some of the basic ideas about

95 Some of the same material is used in R. M. Karras, 'Using women to think with in the medieval university', in A. B. Mulder-Bakker (ed.), *Seeing and Knowing: Women and Learning in Medieval Europe 1200–1550* (Turnhout, 2004), pp. 21–33. Karras argues powerfully that Parisian theologians used women to think about more general and abstract issues, treating them as 'non-actors' (p. 30), and displaying misogyny 'in the sense of ignoring women or making them irrelevant' (p. 26). She argues that they

sex and marriage, I have glossed over one of the trickiest aspects of understanding and representing this material. Where an issue concerns both women and men, twenty-first-century sensibilities, at least in western academic culture, demand the use of gender-neutral language. If a felicitous construction eludes the author writing in English, we expect references to 'she or he', 's/he', 'they' used as a neuter singular, or 'she' used to stand for both female and male in a manner that signals disenchantment with past patriarchy. Our expression thus reflects both the nature of the English language and our cultural values. The Latin texts produced by medieval scholars reflect both the nature of Latin, with gendered nouns for example, and their very different cultural values. Hitherto I have tried to sustain gender neutrality in my text where the issues pertained to both sexes, and followed the medieval texts in referring specifically to men and women when an issue was developed in relation to one sex or the other, or a problem was held to concern only one of them. This has the merit of conveying arguments with clarity and brevity, but it does not entirely reflect the complexity of what happens in the medieval texts themselves, and this needs to be tackled directly.

The problems

Quodlibetal questions about marriage focus on problems that arose when one or both parties to a marriage deviated from the norm, either by committing sin or by acting or seeking to act virtuously. Some problems stemmed from actions that could be performed by either the wife or the husband. Thus either could take a vow of chastity before marriage, seek to enter religion after marriage, have illicit sex, commit bigamy or take usury. Questions about these issues were sometimes asked in such a way that they applied to both wives and husbands, and sometimes with specific reference to either wife or husband. Some problems, however, related to the wife only: only she could give alms without her husband's consent; only she could bear a child through fornication or adultery, and be the only person to know the true identity of the father, at least in the opinion of the masters. Other problems were particular to the husband: only he could marry and then become a priest. No straightforwardly sinful action is presented as exclusively male, but

were equally indifferent to the personal needs of men, and that 'masculine scholastic thought ... dehumanized the human' and 'was not primarily concerned with pastoral issues' (p.33). I respectfully disagree for reasons that will become clear.

one other departure from the norm is linked to men: apparently only husbands caused problems by dying and then returning to life.[96]

Discourse/language

Analysing the patterns of questions asked might at first seem promising. Why, for example, are problems that could be caused by either wife or husband sometimes asked in relation to one or the other rather than both? In fact, however, the terms established in the question were not always maintained in the answers, and it is important to grasp the variety of ways in which gender was indicated. First, gender could be signalled by the use of nouns that referred unambiguously to either woman or man. In such cases the male was usually 'vir' or less commonly 'maritus', and the female was 'mulier', 'uxor' or very occasionally 'puella'. This form of gender denotation was explicit and straightforward. Second, an argument could be presented in language that was neutral with regard to the gender of the married person involved. By discussing the nature of, for example, marriage or vows, it was possible to avoid referring to either wife or husband directly. It was also possible to use verbs without a noun or pronoun that would give away the gender of the spouse under discussion. Thus 'dico quod peccat' on its own could be translated 'I say that she sins', 'I say that he sins' or 'I say that she or he sins'. Third, some nouns were gendered themselves but were neutral with respect to the gender of the person signified. The most common was 'homo', a masculine noun which meant 'person'. 'Persona', a feminine noun also meaning 'person', was used less often. 'Coniux', a masculine noun meaning 'spouse', was used less often still. Especially in the case of 'homo', usage might suggest a primarily masculine meaning, though perhaps one which stood in for both sexes, as masculine pronouns such as 'ille' and 'aliquis' might also be thought to do. In discussions where gender difference suddenly emerged as crucial to the argument, however, it is not always safe to make such assumptions. Fourth, a person could be discussed in gender-neutral terms and then be referred to as having a marriage partner of specific gender, implying a specific gender for the original person. Thus a 'homo' with a wife was a definitely a man. Lest, however, this be thought to confirm a predominantly masculine meaning for 'homo' on all occasions, it should be noted that one master first referred to a 'homo' with a wife, and later defined matrimony as that by which 'homo' was joined

96 See, for example, Henry of Ghent, Quodlibet III.27. *Aurea Quodlibeta*, 2 vols. (Venice, 1613), vol. 1, f. 137r.

to 'homo'.[97] This illustrates the dangers of making assumptions about what nouns like 'homo' might denote in terms of gender. Fifth, gendered examples could be introduced to support specific arguments. Feminine examples included a woman who had entered religion then being given in marriage in order to bring about peace, and a religious woman being married to a pagan in order to convert him or stop him persecuting Christians, both of which were used to show how the common good should prevail over vows of chastity. Masculine examples included a man taking orders, which was often cited when the subject of vows came up, and the monk, the nature of whose subjection to his superior was useful as an analogy for the wife's subjection to her husband.

When these various means of denoting gender were deployed, a question that was initially gender-neutral or about either the wife or the husband could develop a very different focus, and indeed the slippage was sometimes considerable. Such slippage did not occur or did not significantly disrupt the focus when the question was specifically about men, even if it could in theory have been asked about women too, or when the question was about women because it was thought applicable only to women. The most striking examples of slippage occurred when the issue applied to both women and men, and the question was either gender-neutral or asked about women.

Problems for wife and husband, asked about both

To give an example of a question equally relevant in theory to both sexes and asked in gender-neutral terms, in 1257 Aquinas was asked whether a simple vow of chastity invalidated a marriage contract.[98] He replied that this was not the case and that only a solemn vow had this effect, a position which he justified by explaining the difference between simple and solemn vows. Although this analysis applied equally to men and to women, Aquinas used masculine pronouns ('aliquis', 'ille'), referred to the vow-maker's wife, and considered the possibility of the vow-maker taking orders. His argument was that a simple vow involved only a promise and this alone could not transfer ownership. So if someone promised a thing to one person and then gave it to another, the donation could not be rescinded because of the initial promise, although the donor did badly in making the donation. Similarly, a man who took a

97 Servais of Mont Saint Eloi, Quodlibetal question 4, B. N. lat. 15350, f. 269vb–270ra.

98 Quodlibet VIII.10. Thomas Aquinas, *Quaestiones de quolibet*, Sancti Thomae de Aquino Opera Omnia 25, 2 vols. (Rome, 1996), vol. 1, pp. 71–2.

simple vow of chastity could subsequently give his body to a wife, and although he sinned in so doing, the marriage was not invalidated by the preceding vow. A solemn vow, on the other hand, involved both a promise and an actual gift. A man therefore took a solemn vow when he both dedicated himself to God with a vow and placed himself in a state of sanctity either by taking orders or by professing a particular rule. In this case he could no longer give his body to a wife, and if he did, the contract would be null. Aquinas thus chose to make his case with reference to a man, but it is extremely difficult to give an account in English that conveys the way in which the text slides away from the gender neutrality of the question as the masculine identity of the vow-maker becomes increasingly explicit. Although at the very end gender-neutral terms were reasserted, 'and thus a marriage is invalidated by a solemn vow, but not by a simple one', no need was felt to state explicitly that the argument applied to women as well as to men.

To give another example, in 1280–1 Henry of Ghent was asked whether a marriage which had been ceremonially and solemnly contracted 'in facie ecclesie' could be dissolved by entry to religion.[99] 'In facie ecclesie' might be translated 'before the church' or 'in front of a church', and this was specified because marriages were perfectly valid without the involvement of a priest to provide nuptial liturgy or a blessing.[100] Throughout his reply, whenever he moved beyond abstract principle Henry assumed that the man was entering religion while the woman remained in the world. First, Henry declared that sacraments must be used according to the manner of their institution by Christ. Then he made a distinction between separation from the marriage bed and complete dissolution of the bond of marriage. With regard to the former, the Bible (Matthew 5.32) provided an explicit ruling from Christ that the church had but to apply as Christ intended. Concerning the latter, however, the Bible offered no direct ruling from Christ, although the custom of the church permitted a man ('vir') who entered religion to dismiss a woman ('mulierem') as long as the marriage was unconsummated, and indeed authorities indicated that this was Christ's intention. This brought Henry to the heart of the problem. In this case, was the marriage dissolved or did the marriage bond persist? Henry argued that

[99] Quodlibet V.39. *Aurea Quodlibeta*, vol.1, f. 322ra–vb.

[100] See P. L. Reynolds, 'Marrying and its documentation in pre-modern Europe', in P. L. Reynolds and J. Witte (eds.), *To Have and To Hold: Marrying and its Documentation in Western Christendom, 1400–1600* (Cambridge, 2007), pp. 1–42 at 16–17. Brooke, *Medieval Idea of Marriage*, p. 139, suggests 'publicly in the Church's view', which from the twelfth century meant 'with a ceremony at the church's door'. See also Biller, *Measure of Multitude*, pp. 22–3.

since marriage derived its force from divine institution and, according to divine institution, marriage was established through mutual consent of souls, it must also be divinely instituted that marriage could be dissolved through discord of souls, as long as it had not been consummated, a rule that had been followed by the church in cases other than entry to religion. In conclusion, Henry stated his belief that the bond of marriage was entirely dissolved by entry to religion rather than persisting in any way, provided that the marriage was unconsummated. Henry did not, however, think it necessary to accept his way of putting things. On the contrary, he acknowledged that the same position could be reached by another argument. Thus it was possible simply to draw a distinction between separation from the marriage bed before and after consummation, with the marriage bond persisting in both cases. The spouse who remained in the world could remarry if the separation occurred before consummation, but not if it happened after consummation. Henry made this last point in terms which could refer to either man or woman, but in exploring it further he envisaged the worldly spouse as a woman. There might seem to be a problem if a second marriage was permitted while the first marriage bond remained, but this was a matter of divine institution according to which there was nothing wrong in one woman having two men in spiritual union, but only one in carnal union. The question had been posed in a manner which applied equally to men and women, and much of Henry's reply was similarly neutral, but whenever he moved beyond generalization to consider the people involved in the marriage, it was the man who entered religion while the woman remained in the world.

The slippage was not always towards a focus on the man, however. In the 1280s Servais of Mont Saint Eloi was asked whether the pope could dispense a vow of chastity that had been solemnized by professing religion.[101] He began in neutral terms, noting that the observance of virginity was voluntary in its origins since no one was bound to it unless they so desired, whereas preserving the faith was a straightforward matter of necessity. Consequently, and here Servais turned to a gendered example, the pope could grant a dispensation for a nun to marry when the faith was in danger, either universally or in a particular country.[102] When, however,

[101] Servais of Mont Saint Eloi, Quodlibetal question 41. B. N. lat. 15350, f. 277vb–278ra. For the date, see P. Glorieux, 'Les quodlibets de Gervais de Mont-Saint-Eloi', *Recherches de théologie ancienne et médiévale* 20 (1953): 129–34 ; T. Sullivan, 'The *quodlibeta* of the canons regular and the monks', in C. Schabel (ed.), *Theological Quodlibeta in the Middle Ages: The Fourteenth Century* (Leiden, 2007), pp. 359–400 at 363–5.

[102] For discussion of this scenario by Hostiensis and its possible significance with regard to the Mongols, see E. Marmursztejn, 'A normative power in the making: theological

the faith was secure, Servais considered martyrdom or some other solution to be preferable. Nevertheless, if the church judged it necessary or useful, he accepted that the pope could grant dispensation because greater utility was to be preferred to lesser. He thus expressed general principles in neutral terms, but applied them to the specifically female example of the religious woman whose marriage would rescue the faith.

The same move, and a clearer sense of what Servais had in mind, can be seen in part of Henry of Ghent's reply to a virtually identical question raised in 1280–1. He was asked whether it was possible to dispense a vow of chastity that had been solemnized by professing and entering religion.[103] His solution proceeded in abstract terms applicable to both women and men, but to make the point that there could be compensation for loss of chastity through the adoption of a greater good, Henry gave two examples concerning religious women. First, he imagined a situation in which neighbouring kings were at war, devastating the community and the church. The daughter of one king could be given to the other as a wife in order to establish peace, even if she were a professed virgin. Second, a professed virgin could be given in marriage to an infidel king if this and this alone would lead to the conversion of the king and his people. In these cases the benefit to the community was obvious, but the individual woman would also receive abundant compensation for the loss of her chastity since she would gain greater merit by obeying a prelate of the church and obediently procuring the common good than by guarding her personal chastity, however devotedly. Indeed, she would lose the merit of chastity if she clung on to it in opposition to the church. This was just part of a much longer analysis mostly presented in gender-neutral terms, but a crucial part was dominated by feminine examples.

Problems for wife and husband, asked about the woman

Significant slippage also occurred in response to questions theoretically applicable to both sexes, but raised with specific reference to women. In 1270, for example, Aquinas was asked about a woman who married

quodlibeta and the authority of the masters at Paris at the end of the thirteenth century', in C. Schabel (ed.), *Theological Quodlibeta in the Middle Ages: The Thirteenth Century* (Leiden, 2006), pp. 345–402 at 371; E. Marmursztejn, *L'autorité des maîtres: scolastique, normes et société au xiiie siècle* (Paris, 2007), p. 122.

103 Henry of Ghent, Quodlibet V.28. *Aurea Quodlibeta*, vol. 1, f. 309v–310v. See Marmursztejn, 'A normative power in the making', pp. 373–4; Marmursztejn, *L'autorité des maîtres*, pp. 123–5.

'in facie ecclesie' after previously taking a vow of chastity. Could she have carnal relations with her husband without sin?[104] Aquinas began his reply in neutral terms, using the distinction between a simple and a solemn vow of chastity. A solemn vow of chastity was an impediment to marriage and invalidated the contract so that a marriage contracted after a solemn vow was in fact no marriage at all. Contracting such a marriage was therefore a sin, even if it was made 'in facie ecclesie' and consummated. A simple vow, on the other hand, was an impediment to marriage but did not invalidate the contract so that a subsequent marriage stood, although entering into it was a mortal sin. Once the marriage was established, however, the woman ('mulier') did not have power over her own body, rather the man ('vir') did, and vice versa. Aquinas then addressed the question directly, using its gender-specific terms. Since no one could deny someone what belonged to them, the wife ('mulier matrimonio iuncta') could not deny her husband ('uiro sui') use of her body, despite her earlier vow. This was especially true after the marriage had been consummated. Furthermore, since no one sinned in doing what they ought, it was universally recognized that a woman who had consummated a marriage contracted after a simple vow of chastity did not sin in rendering the conjugal debt to her husband. Whether she sinned in exacting the debt was less clear. Some maintained that she could also exact the debt without sin, otherwise the burden of marriage might prove intolerable for her, but Aquinas insisted that she sinned because she exercised her own will in exacting the debt and her will remained bound by her earlier vow. Aquinas then explained why solemn and simple vows of chastity were different, and at this point his language changed again. Rather than focusing on the woman in the question, he now referred to the taker of the vow as 'homo', 'aliquis' and 'persona', and to the subsequent marriage partner as 'coniux', while also introducing a purely masculine example, the taking of holy orders. His terms were primarily gender-neutral, with 'homo' used both for the taker of holy orders, necessarily a man, and for someone professing religion, who could be a woman or a man. In giving an account of the argument, I will use masculine pronouns for the sake of brevity, but the Latin terms in brackets indicate the degree of gender neutrality more accurately. Aquinas' point was that a solemn vow involved both a promise and an element of giving. Thus a vow of chastity only became solemn with the taking of holy orders, through which a man ('homo') was actually delivered to divine service, or with profession of a particular rule and the taking of a habit, through which

[104] Quodlibet III.18. Thomas Aquinas, *Quaestiones de quolibet*, vol. 2, pp. 274–5.

a person ('homo') was actually delivered to serve God in religion. A simple vow, on the other hand, involved a promise without any giving. But it was obvious, Aquinas said, that after someone ('aliquis') had not only promised but also given something, he could not then give it away to a different person. If any such attempt were made, the second donation would be invalid. Thus someone ('aliquis') who took a solemn vow of chastity and not only promised but also gave his body to God in order to lead a celibate life could not then give his body to his spouse, binding himself to render the conjugal debt as a matter of necessity. On the other hand, it was quite different if someone promised something without giving it and later actually gave it to a different person. Although he broke his promise, the donation was valid and the recipient could use it as he wished. Thus someone ('persona') who promised his body to God by taking a simple vow of chastity and subsequently gave power over his body to his spouse by a consummated marriage sinned in breaking his vow, but the donation was valid and the spouse ('coniux') had power over his body which meant that he did not sin in rendering the debt. Aquinas had thus moved first from neutral language to a discussion of the woman's position in gendered terms, and then back to primarily neutral language with reference to the masculine example of taking holy orders. Presumably he wanted to answer the question about the woman directly, but also to make it clear that the same principles applied to both men and women, and to cover the taking of orders which applied to men alone.

In the 1280s, however, Servais of Mont Saint Eloi adopted a different strategy in responding to a very similar question. He was asked whether a woman who took a simple vow of chastity and then married sinned mortally every time she had sex with her husband.[105] He declared that she did not sin every time, but only on the first occasion. Like Aquinas, he based his view on the distinction between a simple and a solemn vow of chastity, although he elaborated it in slightly different terms and added further qualifications. Unlike Aquinas, however, he did not discuss the woman at all. Instead he referred to the taker of the vow as 'homo' and identified this person's marriage partner as a wife, 'uxor', or a woman, 'mulier', thus giving 'homo' a clearly masculine meaning. Servais argued that a simple vow only involved a promise so that a man ('homo') remained master of his own body and could therefore give it to his wife ('uxori'). A solemn vow, however, involved giving and thus destroyed any marriage contract. This was not a consequence of scandal, as some claimed, because the public breaking of both simple and

[105] Quodlibetal question 4. B. N. lat. 15350, f. 269vb–270ra.

solemn vows could result in scandal. Nor was it because of ecclesiastical statute since the church could make the same laws for both types of vow. The difference stemmed from the very nature of the solemn vow which, unlike the simple vow, caused a man to lose power over his own body to God when he gave it in perpetual chastity. Turning to the man who took a simple vow of chastity, Servais observed that since he did not give his wife power over his body until after their first sexual union, he still had the power to fulfil his vow up to that moment. Afterwards, however, he did not have this power since he had given his body to his wife and so after this first act he did not sin in rendering the conjugal debt. Servais added a number of qualifications, however. First, he followed Aquinas in arguing that while he did not sin in rendering the debt, he could not demand payment, though he also took the standard line mentioned above that he was still rendering the debt when the woman was ashamed to ask and he took the initiative because he feared that her chastity was in danger. Second, Servais did not think that the husband was simply absolved from his vow; rather, he was excused from carrying it out because of another obligation. To illustrate his point, Servais compared him with someone who had vowed to read out the psalter every day and then became blind; he was excused rather than absolved from his vow since he would have to resume his task if God returned his sight to him. Servais perhaps also wished to suggest that his vow of chastity would come into force again if his wife died. Third, Servais stressed that rendering the debt after his first sexual union with his wife was only free of sin if the fault of that first act had been removed by contrition; it was therefore necessary for him to regret his marriage. Having been asked about a woman, Servais had thus replied in terms of a man. By implication the woman who married after vowing chastity was in exactly the same position, but Servais did not think it necessary to say so.[106]

Why did these slippages take place? In part they may have reflected a desire to cover all aspects of a problem, including those that applied to only one sex. Thus any treatment of solemn vows had to consider the taking of holy orders if it was to address the issues as they pertained to men. Examples may also have been chosen not because of the way they were gendered but because they illustrated a principle. Examples that were well known to embody a particular principle were used as shorthand and their deployment meant that the principle did not have to be

[106] Karras, 'Using women to think with', pp. 30–1, regards this as 'a remarkable example of how women simply fell out of the picture' and interprets it as 'a sign that to [Servais] the masculine was the norm and the feminine insignificant'.

explained at length. We will shortly see the example of the monk's relationship with his superior being brought into discussions about wives giving alms without their husbands' consent, and the point is surely to bring to mind a kind of hierarchical relationship and not to turn discussion away from women. That said, and despite occasional examples to the contrary, it is hard to escape the conclusion that in general masters preferred to solve problems in relation to men. More often than not, slippages went from neutral or feminine language and examples to the masculine. It may be that they preferred to see men taking the active part in the problems they discussed, that the situation for women was always complicated by their subordination to men so that the problem was not entirely theirs, or that they regarded the masculine as more universal. Or it may simply have been the register in which they felt most comfortable.

Problems for wives

Alms This approach did not mean, however, that masters of theology avoided questions that raised issues particular to women, and indeed these questions reveal most about how they believed their ideas to work in practice. A number of questions focused on the wife who wished to give alms. In 1285, for example, Adénulfe of Anagni was asked whether a wife could give alms without her husband's express or presumed consent.[107] Adénulfe replied that a person who was subject to another's power must be ruled by this superior's power because the natural order required that inferiors be ruled by superiors. So when an inferior was subject to a superior in relation to certain things, he could only distribute them when they had been committed to him by the superior, which meant that an inferior could not give alms without the superior's permission. Adénulfe therefore argued that the wife could give alms without her husband's consent if she had property because of her dowry which was meant to sustain the burdens of marriage, or if she made a profit by her own efforts, or if she gained property in any other licit way. Such alms had to be moderate, however, lest her husband be embarrassed by their excess. Otherwise she could not give alms without her husband's express or presumed consent, except in a case of necessity. One of the opening arguments had suggested that the wife could give alms like a man because husband and wife were to be regarded as equals, as indicated by the woman being formed from the man's rib and as his companion. Adénulfe, however, said that while the woman was

[107] Quodlibet I.13. B. N. lat. 14899, f. 147vb–148ra.

equal to the man with regard to the act of marriage, this was not the case with regard to household management of which alms-giving was a part. Adénulfe thus stressed the wife's overall subjection to her husband while allowing her to enjoy limited freedom with regard to her dowry and independent earnings.

In 1286 Godfrey of Fontaines was asked whether a wife could give alms if her husband were unwilling and forbade it.[108] Godfrey replied that no one could give alms unless they had rights of administration over whatever they gave, either because they enjoyed ownership and possession or because the rights had been granted to them. He explained that those who were subject to others with regard to their own persons or external goods could not use either themselves or their goods against their superior's will and command because the superior enjoyed rights of administration and disposition over them. Godfrey explained what this meant by taking the example of a monk. Since he was subject to his superior with regard to both his person and external goods, he could not do anything with either himself or the goods against the will of his superior, or rather he could only act according to his will. Since he did not have any powers of administration over the goods, he could not give anything to the poor without the explicit or implicit permission of his superior. He could only disobey his superior in a case of extreme necessity when the divine precept to love one's neighbour applied and one was bound to obey God rather than any man.

Godfrey then turned to the case of a wife. She was subject to the power of her husband both with regard to her body or person and with regard to external goods and their administration. As an illustration of what this meant, he noted that she could not therefore take a vow of abstinence without her husband's consent, and that he could revoke it if she did. In fact this was not a particularly useful example for the question of alms, because Godfrey had to admit that the woman had equal power over the man in exacting the conjugal debt, so that a husband could not take a vow of chastity against his wife's will. In all other matters, however, the husband was like the head of a body while his wife was a subordinate limb; she was virtually his servant. Thus a wife could not give anything from property she held in common with her husband without his consent. Since the husband had full powers of administration and disposition over temporal goods, even those pertaining to his wife, she could not give alms from any property except with her husband's permission, explicit or implicit. She could not even give alms

[108] Quodlibet III.12. *Les quatres premiers quodlibets de Godefroid de Fontaines*, ed. M. de Wulf and A. Pelzer (Louvain, 1904), pp. 222–5 and 319–20.

from her dowry, which was given to pay for the burdens of marriage and which pertained to her more than other property.

Thus far Godfrey had permitted the wife no independence at all in the giving of alms, but his position softened when he considered the importance of custom. First, he noted that in some places the wife was permitted to own property apart from her dowry, and he said that she could give alms freely from such property even if her husband were unwilling. In other places, however, no such category of property existed and all the wife's possessions were understood to be part of the dowry; here everything which she acquired or earned after the marriage passed into the power and ownership of the husband, just as everything acquired or earned by a monk passed into the ownership of the monastery.[109] Godfrey concluded that the husband alone had the right to administer whatever his wife possessed or acquired, unless a concession were made to the wife by custom or by the husband himself. Second, although the good of any community required that one person should rule and have powers of administration, and the husband was the appropriate head of the household, it was customary to leave management of bread, wine and other household goods to the wife. Godfrey declared that from such goods the wife could and should give alms on behalf of herself and her husband. However, these alms should be moderate according to her husband's resources, the number and need of the poor, and their status. Custom thus led Godfrey to grant wives slightly more freedom in expressing their charitable impulses.

He shifted slightly again when he considered the circumstances in which wives could assume that they had their husbands' implicit consent to give alms. Godfrey noted that some distinguished between wives who worked and made a profit, and wives who did not. They supposed that a wife who earned could give alms without her husband's consent while a wife who did not earn could not do so unless it was customary to allow her goods separate from her dowry. Godfrey, however, considered this distinction to be unnecessary since whatever the wife earned would be subject to her husband's powers of administration. Nevertheless, Godfrey conceded that it ought to be easier for the wife to obtain permission to administer these goods and she could more readily give them as alms without express permission, assuming implicit consent on her husband's part. And even with regard to other goods, the wife could exercise her own judgement based on the condition of the person to whom she wished to give. For example, if the person were very needy

[109] On theologians' awareness of regional variation in marriage practices, see Biller, *Measure of Multitude*, pp. 53–4.

or close to the family, she might well think that her husband would be pleased at the gift of alms, were he present. This, however, was as far as Godfrey was prepared to go and he abruptly resumed the tone with which he had begun his determination. If the wife knew that giving alms was entirely contrary to her husband's wish and command, she should not give anything except in a case of extreme necessity when his command was not binding. Furthermore, she must beware lest strong affection for those to whom she wished to give clouded her judgement in supposing that her husband would have wished to give alms had he known, or in deciding that it was so good to give that her husband ought to wish to give alms and would be evil if he did not. Such judgements, Godfrey remarked, were frequently false. Moreover, it made no difference if her husband would do wrong in refusing alms; she could not give them. Even when a husband did wrong in revoking his wife's vow of chastity, she was bound to obey him. Godfrey thus stressed the wife's subjection to her husband, using the example of the monk to convey its extent. On the other hand, he granted her some practical independence in the light of custom and the circumstances in which she could assume her husband's implicit consent. He differed from Adénulfe, however, in denying her control of her dowry and goods that she earned or acquired independently after her marriage.

In the 1290s a master known only as R. of Arras was asked whether a woman could give alms without her husband's consent from goods which they held in common.[110] The master replied that no one could give something unless they exercised rights of ownership either directly or by grant from their superior. Thus a monk who administered property ought not to give any alms unless this accorded with the explicit or implicit wish of his superior to whose power he was subject. A woman, on the other hand, was subject to the power of her husband who enjoyed rights of ownership and administration over their goods. In these matters the woman was a servant, despite the fact that she enjoyed the same rights over her husband's body as he did over hers. The only exception was that in some places her dowry belonged to her and there she could

[110] 'Collection of Nicholas of Bar', q. 55. B. N. lat. 15850, f. 25vb–26ra. This collection of quodlibetal questions survives in a manuscript that belonged to Nicholas of Bar-le-Duc, bishop of Mâcon, who left it to the Sorbonne where he had studied. Ground-breaking work on the collection was carried out by P. Glorieux, 'Notices sur quelques théologiens de Paris de la fin du xiiie siècle', *Archives d'histoire doctrinale et littéraire du moyen âge* 3 (1928): 201–38. Much of his analysis, especially his dating of the questions, has been substantially revised by S. Piron, 'Nicholas of Bar's collection', in Schabel (ed.), *Theological Quodlibeta in the Middle Ages: The Fourteenth Century*, pp. 333–43. For R. d'Arras, see Glorieux, 'Notices', pp. 222–3; Piron, 'Nicholas of Bar's collection', p. 342.

give alms from her dowry without her husband's consent, but not elsewhere. As for her earnings, they belonged to her husband so that she could not give alms from them without his permission, although R. conceded that she would do better to give alms against her husband's will from these goods than from others. Like other masters, R. used the example of the monk and his superior to illustrate the wife's subjection to her husband. Unlike others, however, he recognized that in some places wives had control of their dowries, while never permitting them control of their earnings.

In the first years of the fourteenth century, Jean Lesage considered alms-giving by sons, servants and wives.[111] He began by outlining the conditions necessary for alms-giving. First, the recipient had to be in distress, otherwise he would receive a gift rather than alms. Second, the giver had to be moved by compassion so that he gave to relieve the recipient's distress; to give for any other reason, such as pleasure, was not to give alms. Third, the giver must give what belonged to him or it would be a case of theft rather than alms-giving. Fourth, he must not give anything which was necessary for his own life and indeed for him to live well, or he would be giving out of love rather than simply to relieve distress. Fifth, all the previous conditions had to be fulfilled for God's sake and not out of vainglory. Jean then turned to the specific issue which he was to consider. It was clear from his general analysis that an alms-giver had to possess whatever was given. Drawing on Roman law and Aristotle, however, Jean argued that sons and servants did not possess anything. On the contrary, the son was possessed by his father and the servant by his master. The woman also possessed nothing. Even if her husband granted possession of something to her, she did not truly possess it because he could legitimately take everything back whenever he wished. Jean concluded that neither the son, the servant, nor the wife could give alms without their lord's express or implicit consent. Furthermore, they should always play safe and seek his consent before giving alms. Indeed, it was really their father, master or husband who gave alms through them. Jean thus completely ignored the question of the wife's dowry and earnings, denying her any independence whatsoever in alms-giving.

The masters were thus in general agreement about the wife's subjection to her husband, and they pursued the implications of this fundamental principle for women. In doing so, they took account of social reality, some masters noting that custom might allow women

[111] Quodlibet I.9. *Jacques de Thérines Quodlibets I et II. Jean Lesage Quodlibet I. Texte critique avec introduction, notes et tables*, ed. P. Glorieux (Paris, 1958), pp. 349–50.

more independence than they possessed in principle. The masters disagreed completely, however, about whether or not the wife was entitled to control of her dowry, her earnings or any other property that she acquired. None of them encouraged the wife to give alms from her husband's property or from property that they held in common without his knowledge, as Thomas of Chobham had done in the early thirteenth century.[112] There was thus no consensus on women and property.

Illicit sex, illegitimate children and telling the truth Another set of questions concerned the woman who bore a child through fornication or adultery. She was believed to be the only person to know that the child had been conceived illicitly and to know the true identity of the father. This knowledge created moral problems for the woman and for those to whom she imparted her knowledge. One problem was her attitude to her illegitimate child. In 1284 Henry of Ghent was asked about a woman who committed fornication and gave birth to a son as a result of the liaison. If she saw him grow up to lead a good life, could she simultaneously wish to have her son and detest the act of fornication by which she had conceived him?[113] Henry replied that she ought to wish that she had not had the child, even if he were holier than John the Baptist, because no one should consent in offending God for the sake of any creature, whether in the past, present or future. Similarly, although a woman was permitted without sin to wish for a good child in marriage, she ought to wish that the child had not been born, however good, and that she had remained a virgin. This was because a small increase in one's own heavenly glory ought to be valued above great heavenly glory for someone else if it were to the detriment of one's own glory. A similar case was put to Eustace of Grandcourt in the early 1300s. A woman had a son by adultery and this son was very good to her. She was not contrite about him, although she was contrite about the act by which he was conceived. Given the manner of her contrition, should and could a priest absolve her?[114] The brief record of Eustace's reply indicates that she could be absolved if she were contrite about the circumstances of the act as well as the act itself.

More complex problems arose when masters considered whether or not a wife should tell others that one of her offspring was illegitimate. In the 1290s, a Franciscan called John, perhaps John of Murrovalle,

112 S. Farmer, 'Persuasive voices: clerical images of medieval wives', *Speculum* 61 (1986): 517–43, esp. 517, 536.

113 Quodlibet VIII.20. *Aurea Quodlibeta*, vol. 2, f. 43ra–rb.

114 'Collection of Nicholas of Bar', q. 146. B. N. lat. 15850, f. 39rb. See Glorieux, 'Notices', pp. 226–9; Piron, 'Nicholas of Bar's collection', p. 341.

was asked about a situation in which a married woman bore a son as a result of adultery and her husband believed the son to be his. If the woman confessed the truth to her priest, should he tell the husband to reject the son and to announce that he must not inherit?[115] John replied that the priest must not instruct the husband in this way lest his reaction was to kill his wife. Furthermore, the wife would gain nothing if her son claimed that she spoke out of hatred for him. John's advice to the wife was that she should wait until her son reached adulthood before informing him of the truth in secret and telling him to leave for foreign parts or to enter religion because he was not the true heir of her husband's property. If he refused, however, he must have the inheritance. John noted the objection that a sin could not be dismissed unless restitution of something wrongly taken had been made, but he held this to be true where restitution was possible. The question displaced the dilemma to the confessor, but in considering the advice to be given addressed the question of what the wife should do. John assumed that she had genuine knowledge of paternity, but that in practice her version of the truth might be challenged or not acted upon. She was to try secret intercession with her son, but if this did not work, her knowledge of paternity was to remain secret.

In the early 1300s Eustace of Grandcourt was asked about a woman whose adultery resulted in a child whom everyone else believed to be her husband's legitimate offspring. The question took the form of a case: a woman had a daughter by an enemy of her husband while this enemy had a son by his wife; the families decided to make peace by means of a marriage between the children who were in fact half-brother and sister; seeing this, ought the woman to remain silent, permitting matters to proceed?[116] Unfortunately Eustace's arguments do not survive, but he concluded that the woman must, if possible, act towards the enemy's son in such a way that her daughter would not accept him. If, however, she could not do this, she must reveal her sin rather than allow the marriage to go ahead. In this case the woman was again held to possess unique knowledge of paternity. It meant that she should seek to influence events in ways that no one else would understand, but if she failed, she was on this occasion to reveal her sin rather than to stand by and let others act upon false knowledge.

Another case was put to Eustace of Grandcourt in the early 1300s. A married woman had a daughter by adultery but her husband believed

115 'Collection of Nicholas of Bar', q. 45. B. N. lat. 15850, f. 23va. See Glorieux, 'Notices', pp. 206–7, 219–22; Piron, 'Nicholas of Bar's collection', pp. 341–2.

116 'Collection of Nicholas of Bar', q. 125. B. N. lat. 15850, f. 37rb–va. See Glorieux, 'Notices', pp. 226–9; Piron, 'Nicholas of Bar's collection', p. 341.

that she was his. On his death the husband left the girl a hundred pounds. Subsequently the mother told her daughter that she was not the daughter of her dead husband, that if he had known this he would never have given her the hundred pounds, and that she should not keep the money. Could the daughter keep her legacy from her supposed father?[117] Eustace replied that if the daughter believed her mother, she ought not to keep the money. If, however, she did not believe her, thinking perhaps that her mother spoke out of levity or because she loved her other children more, and if she was sure that her father would have insisted that he was the true father, she could licitly keep the money. Here Eustace envisaged the adulterous wife seeking to persuade her illegitimate child not to accept an inheritance, thus acting in the manner that John of Murrho had recommended previously. Like John, Eustace imagined the child refusing to believe the mother and keeping the inheritance, only he elaborated on the circumstances in which the child acted properly.

These questions show once again that the masters addressed problems particular to women, and that some of these problems stemmed from women's knowledge of true paternity. Their obligation was not simply to tell the truth, but rather to tell specific people in order to persuade them to behave in ways that would bring about the best possible resolution of the situation that had arisen. It has been noted that theologians who studied in Paris in the late twelfth and early thirteenth centuries, especially Thomas of Chobham, stressed the ability of wives to use spoken language to influence their husbands, persuading them to lead better lives.[118] Parisian quodlibets later in the thirteenth century also sought to harness their 'feminine persuasive power'.[119] Wives were to persuade not only their husbands, however, but also other members of the family, and their responsibility derived in part from their special knowledge of paternity.

Usury Other problems for women related to usury. While both men and women could commit usury, women could find themselves facing particular moral difficulties because of their subjection to their husbands.[120] Many quodlibetal questions were asked about usury, but two examples will illustrate the problems associated with women. Some time after 1256 Guy of l'Aumône was invited to consider the

117 'Collection of Nicholas of Bar', q. 151. B. N. lat. 15850, f. 39vb–40ra. See Glorieux, 'Notices', pp. 226–9; Piron, 'Nicholas of Bar's collection', p. 341.
118 Farmer, 'Persuasive voices', pp. 517–43.
119 The phrase is from *ibid.*, p. 539.
120 For consideration of usurers' wives in the early thirteenth century, see *ibid.*, pp. 526–36.

situation of the wife of a usurer whose property was entirely usurious. If she did not eat, she threatened her own life since she had no other means of sustenance. If, however, she did eat, she was implicated in usury. What was she to do?[121] Guy replied that although the woman was subject to her husband in matters pertaining to the marriage bed, she should not join him in abusing God. So in this case she should either earn food by working with her own hands or beg from good men or her parents. If, however, her husband forced her to live off his ill-gotten gains, she could dismiss him from the marriage bed for the time being, citing spiritual fornication as the cause.

In the early 1300s, Guy of Cluny, or Guy of Pernes, was asked about a woman who possessed money from usury and married a man who believed that her money had been licitly acquired. After they had been married for some time, was the wife obliged to reveal the truth to her husband, and was he obliged to believe her?[122] The point of the last part of the question was presumably that he would have to make restitution if he believed her. According to Guy, if the woman possessed patrimonial goods, she was bound to make restitution, as was her husband in so far as he was aware of the facts. If, however, she did not have goods of this kind, everything depended on the nature of her relationship with her husband and in particular on the extent to which she was dominated by him. If she was not dominated, she perhaps had powers of administration under her husband and could gradually make restitution by giving alms. If, however, she was dominated by her husband and had no administrative authority because he employed a seneschal and furthermore he was very careful with her goods, she must consider whether her husband was an adulterer. If he was, she could leave him and make restitution from her property. If he was not, she had to consider her husband's character. If he was a good and God-fearing man, she must reveal the truth to him and he was bound to make restitution. If he was a hard, greedy man and revelation would achieve nothing, she should keep silent and lament, resolving that if she could find a way of making restitution, she would willingly do it. This left the last part of

[121] *Summa de diversis questionibus theologie*, question 102. B. N. lat. 14891, f. 200va–vb. For the identification of quodlibetal questions within the summa, see I. P. Wei, 'Guy de l'Aumône's "Summa de diversis questionibus theologie"', *Traditio* 44 (1988): 275–323. See also Sullivan, 'The *quodlibeta* of the canons regular and the monks', pp. 387–9.

[122] 'Collection of Nicholas of Bar', q. 164. B. N. lat. 15850, f. 41ra-rb. See Glorieux, 'Notices', pp. 207, 215–17; Piron, 'Nicholas of Bar's collection', p. 341; Sullivan, 'The *quodlibeta* of the canons regular and the monks', pp. 385–6.

the question. If the woman made such a revelation, was her husband obliged to believe her? Guy argued that he must believe her if he saw that she was a good woman, but that he did not have to believe her if he saw that she was bad, hostile to her husband and careless with household goods.

These two questions demonstrate how masters tried to take account of social realities, recognizing that the actual balance of power between husband and wife could vary considerably, depending on character and personality. The wife's proper course of action depended in part on whether she was totally dominated by her husband or enjoyed some freedom of action. Whether or not she should reveal truth to him depended on the likelihood of success in light of his character.

Overall, quodlibetal questions about marriage demonstrate that masters sought to address practical problems facing both sexes. As in all their work on sexuality and gender, their means of denoting gender permitted considerable slippage in terms of focus, most commonly towards the masculine. But while their basic values might now be considered misogynistic, they also recognized the moral problems that these values created for women, and were willing to work through their implications. In doing so, they endeavoured to take account of social realities, especially in so far as both custom and personality diminished the actual significance of their own normative assertions about marriage relationships. They were far from establishing a shared view on the degree of independence that a wife should exercise with regard to property, disagreeing on whether or not she should have control of her dowry, her earnings or any other property licitly acquired after marriage. There was, however, a consensus on the way in which women should seek to exercise power through persuasion. Overwhelmingly, the view was that the wife should seek to influence the behaviour of her husband and her family through talking, above all by selectively revealing and withholding knowledge that she alone possessed.

Parisian theologians were therefore consistent not only in their views of the purpose of marriage, the need for both partners to consent freely to marriage, the theory of conjugal debt, the idea that men were active and women were passive in sexual intercourse, and rules for the conduct of marital sex, but also in seeking to address the moral dilemmas that these views created for women, acknowledging the significance of personality and custom in actual situations, and expecting women to exercise a distinctive kind of power through verbal persuasion, a power derived from specifically feminine knowledge. There were lasting disagreements not only about sexual pleasure and the extent to which marital sex was sinful, but also about the property rights of wives. The complexity of their attitude towards women is evident not only in the contrast between what they said when discussing the nature of women and when treating marital affection, and in the creation of elements of equality within a manifestly patriarchal world view, but also in the unstable nature of their discussions of men and women, with slippages occurring most frequently towards the masculine.

6 Money

When considering the University of Paris in its urban context, it is impossible not to be struck by the way in which the university and the city developed simultaneously. During the twelfth and thirteenth centuries, Paris became a significant centre in both educational and urban terms. With hindsight, signs of early promise might be detected, but at the start of the twelfth century Paris was unexceptional both as a town and in the world of learning. The growth of the schools and the emergence of the university have already been discussed, and the process of urban development was equally rapid. At the beginning of the twelfth century Paris was a small town with a population of fewer than 10,000, concentrated on an island, the Ile de la Cité, in the River Seine. Though Paris was the favourite residence of the Capetian kings, they spent most of their time on the move elsewhere. Not until the middle of the twelfth century were departments of the royal administration permanently based in Paris. At the same time the Capetians built up the market on the Right Bank, granting privileges to the Parisian merchants. The most dramatic transformations occurred during the reign of Philip Augustus (1180–1223), who built the first covered markets of Les Halles, regulated trade, paved the major streets, strengthened royal jurisdiction in the city and constructed new city walls which protected land on both banks of the Seine. By the time of Philip's death, the population probably numbered around 50,000. During the reign of Philip the Fair, Paris became the king's permanent residence, and by 1300 Paris was a major European city, the most important city in the north, a genuine seat of government for the powerful French monarchy and a significant centre for trade.[1]

[1] On the city of Paris and its expansion, see J. W. Baldwin, *The Government of Philip Augustus: Foundations of French Royal Power in the Middle Ages* (Berkeley, 1986), pp. 342–51; R.-H. Bautier, 'Quand et comment Paris devint capitale', *Bulletin de la Société de l'histoire de Paris et de l'Ile de France* 105 (1978): 17–46; J. Boussard, 'Philippe Auguste et Paris', in R.-H. Bautier (ed.), *La France de Philippe Auguste: le temps des mutations. Actes du colloque international organisé par le C.N.R.S. (Paris,*

While developing simultaneously, the university and the city gained a great deal from each other. The university was a source of considerable profit for the townspeople. The masters and students were economically unproductive consumers who brought in money from their families or church livings, at any rate from outside the city, and they spent it on food, wine, clothes and accommodation. These 3,000 to 4,000 consumers were a valuable stimulus to the Parisian economy. The masters and students, on the other hand, needed houses in which to rent accommodation, and markets at which to buy food, drink and clothes. In general, the growth of universities is inconceivable without the growth of towns. Large numbers could not have specialized in intellectual labour without the support of the urban economy, and Paris in particular was renowned for its abundance of food and drink, at reasonable prices.[2] The mutual benefits for the university and the city were therefore considerable. This did not mean, however, that relations between the university men and the townspeople were harmonious. As we have seen, there were serious tensions that sometimes resulted in violent conflict. In general, the university emerged in a position to assert its control over the townspeople. The violent clashes of 1200 led to the grant of a royal charter that subordinated the provost and people of Paris to the university in ways which have already been discussed. Less dramatically, but no less significantly, scholar after scholar complained about the expense of accommodation in Paris, and in the thirteenth century the university gained the privilege of controlling rent.[3] It was also able to regulate some parts of the urban economy that were closely dependent on the university, most notably the production and sale of books.[4]

29 septembre – 4 octobre 1980 (Paris, 1982), pp. 323–40; J. Boussard, *Nouvelle histoire de Paris: De la fin du siège de 885–886 à la mort de Philippe Auguste*, 2nd edn (Paris, 1997); R. Cazelles, *Nouvelle histoire de Paris: De la fin du règne de Philippe Auguste à la mort de Charles V, 1223–1380*, 2nd edn (Paris, 1994); S. C. Ferruolo, '*Parisius-Paradisus*: the city, its schools, and the origins of the University of Paris', in T. Bender (ed.), *The University and the City: From Medieval Origins to the Present* (Oxford, 1988), pp. 22–43, esp. 22, 25–6, 28–9; A. Lombard-Jourdan, *Paris – genèse de la 'ville': la rive droite de la Seine des origines à 1223* (Paris, 1976), esp. 97–121; S. Roux, *Paris in the Middle Ages*, trans. J. A. McNamara (Philadelphia, 2009).

2 Ferruolo, '*Parisius-Paradisus*', pp. 28, 32, 37 ; J. Le Goff, *Intellectuals in the Middle Ages*, trans. T. L. Fagan (Oxford, 1993), pp. xiv–xv, 5–6, 61–3; O. Pedersen, *The First Universities: Studium Generale and the Origins of University Education in Europe* (Cambridge, 1997), pp. 131–2. For judicious comments on attempts to estimate the university population, see W. J. Courtenay, *Parisian Scholars in the Early Fourteenth Century: A Social Portrait* (Cambridge, 1999), pp. 19–22.

3 Ferruolo, '*Parisius-Paradisus*', pp. 27–8; P. Kibre, *Scholarly Privileges in the Middle Ages* (London, 1961), pp. 90, 95, 97–8, 118; Pedersen, *The First Universities*, pp. 223–4.

4 *Ibid.*, pp. 234–5; H. Rashdall, *The Universities of Europe in the Middle Ages*, revised and ed. F. M. Powicke and A. B. Emden, 3 vols. (1936; repr. Oxford, 1997), vol. 1, pp. 421–4; R. H. Rouse and M. A. Rouse, *Manuscripts and their Makers: Commercial*

Given the relationship between the university and the city, it is important to consider the extent to which the university's identity was shaped by its urban context, and how scholars saw themselves in relation to the city. Because the university depended in so many ways upon the town, and in particular because masters charged their students fees, some historians have argued that the town formed a key part of the scholars' self-image. According to Jacques Le Goff, taking fees seemed 'natural' to the masters 'for it conformed the most with the habits of the urban workplace of which they considered themselves to be members. Masters sold their knowledge and instruction the way artisans sold their wares'.[5] Stephen Ferruolo says: 'The urban surroundings also helped the masters to define their own professional identity. It was in the city, by living and working independently and in close quarters with merchants and artisans, that scholars for the first time came to think of teaching as a business (*negotium*).'[6] While Le Goff and Ferruolo have contributed insights of immense value, this view is unconvincing. However much they gained from each other, university men and townspeople were sometimes at war with each other. Moreover, the scholars sought and obtained privileges that set them apart from the townspeople, privileges that marked them out as clerics as opposed to laymen, on the other side of a great divide from merchants and artisans. This very different self-image is borne out by the quodlibetal disputations in which masters of theology were asked about themselves. As we have seen, they claimed to benefit the whole church by teaching others, elucidating the faith and the Bible, and defending the truth against heretics. Their role was to direct ordinary priests and preachers, and they could be compared with prelates. There was nothing of the merchant or the artisan in their self-image. Rather they perceived themselves as leading members of the church. The masters of theology did not identify with the town at all, but set themselves very much apart from it, indeed above it.

Setting themselves apart from and above the town did not, however, mean ignoring it. On the contrary, their view of their function in society implied a responsibility to give moral and spiritual direction to urban dwellers along with the rest of society. Parisian theologians were slow to take this responsibility, showing little interest in economic issues for much of the twelfth century. Peter Lombard's *Sentences* did not offer very much that was relevant.[7] In the 1160s Peter

Book Producers in Medieval Paris 1200–1500, 2 vols. (Turnhout, 2000), vol. 1, pp. 73–97.

5 Le Goff, *Intellectuals in the Middle Ages*, p. 94; see also pp. 62, 126.

6 Ferruolo, '*Parisius-Paradisus*', pp. 37–8.

7 J. T. Noonan, *The Scholastic Analysis of Usury* (Cambridge, MA, 1957), p. 17, n. 22.

of Poitiers considered that usury was a matter for canonists.[8] Indeed, during the twelfth century the Roman and canon lawyers established a substantial body of work in the field, and the theologians had to take account of this subsequently.[9] From the early thirteenth century, however, Parisian theologians took their responsibility to give moral and spiritual direction to townspeople very seriously indeed, scrutinizing every aspect of urban life. The message that the Parisian theologians offered to the city was fundamentally ambivalent. On the one hand, they condemned vital aspects of the urban economy, constantly rehearsing old arguments, and developing new arguments to support traditional conclusions. But at the same time, they began to justify much of what was happening or to play down the seriousness of the moral threat posed by urban activities. The first section of this chapter will look at the ways in which masters maintained a traditional hostility to trade and merchants while also coming up with justifications for mercantile activities, and at their emphasis on the need for justice in exchange. The second section will concern usury, both the grounds for its condemnation and the means by which charging for credit was increasingly justified. Since the process of justification was chiefly based on the scrutiny of particular types of contract, the third section will take quodlibetal disputations about annuities as a case study which reveals how a new consensus could emerge based on new conceptions of an autonomous money economy and of time. The final two sections will show how the masters thought it was possible to live with usury. It was to be tolerated as a lesser evil. Moreover, money was discovered to have properties making it the safest way to do business in a world tainted by usury.

Exchange

Trade and the merchant

Once the theologians began to consider economic matters, their ambivalence was immediately apparent in their assessment of trade and merchants. From the Bible and the Fathers, they inherited a legacy of

[8] J. W. Baldwin, 'The medieval theories of the just price: romanists, canonists, and theologians in the twelfth and thirteenth centuries', *Transactions of the American Philosophical Society* 49 (1959): 1–92, at 58; J. W. Baldwin, *Masters, Princes and Merchants: The Social Views of Peter the Chanter and his Circle*, 2 vols. (Princeton, 1970), vol. 1, p. 262.

[9] Baldwin, 'The medieval theories of the just price', pp. 9, 58; Baldwin, *Masters, Princes and Merchants*, vol. 1, pp. 262, 270–3.

distrust.[10] They were intensely aware of biblical passages which made it seem as if trade was inherently sinful. In Ecclesiasticus they found 'A merchant shall hardly keep himself from doing wrong' (26.29) and 'As a nail sticketh fast between the joinings of the stones; so doth sin stick close between buying and selling' (27.2).[11] A commentary by Augustine drew their attention to a version of Psalm 70.15–16, 'Because I know nothing about business, I shall go in the strength of the Lord.'[12] Most important of all, they turned to Matthew 21.12–13: 'And Jesus went into the temple of God, and cast out all them that sold and bought in the temple, and overthrew the tables of the money-changers, and the seats of them that sold doves, And said unto them, It is written, My house shall be called the house of prayer; but ye have made it a den of thieves.' While this was frequently interpreted as an attack on simoniacal clergy, it was also read as a condemnation of lay merchants.[13] This hostility was to be found in key reference works which theologians consulted or upon which they commented. Texts hostile to trade and merchants were gathered in Gratian's *Decretum*, into which further texts offering the same message were inserted during the twelfth century. Such insertions were known as *paleae*, and one in particular was a commentary on the expulsion from the temple. Known as the *palea Eiciens*, and incorrectly believed to have been written by John Chrysostum, it commented on Matthew, asserting that it was rarely possible for a merchant to please God, and that Christians should not be merchants. It went on to distinguish between craftsmen who did something to the materials that they bought before selling what they had made, and merchants who profited by selling goods that were 'complete and unaltered', in other words, to which they had done nothing, making no improvement. Gratian himself condemned buying cheap and selling dear as 'shameful gain'.[14] While Peter Lombard's *Sentences* contained little of relevance, he still offered the view that merchants, like soldiers, could not perform their activities without committing sin.[15] Unsurprisingly, given its foundation in respected and widely consulted authorities, this negative

[10] Baldwin, 'The medieval theories of the just price', pp. 12–16; Baldwin, *Masters, Princes and Merchants*, vol. 1, p. 262; D. Wood, *Medieval Economic Thought* (Cambridge, 2002), pp. 112–13.

[11] *Ibid.*, p. 112.

[12] O. Langholm, *Economics in the Medieval Schools: Wealth, Exchange, Value, Money and Usury according to the Paris Theological Tradition, 1200–1350* (Leiden, 1992), pp. 128–9; Wood, *Medieval Economic Thought*, p. 113.

[13] Langholm, *Economics in the Medieval Schools*, pp. 101–3.

[14] Baldwin, 'The medieval theories of the just price', pp. 38–9; Baldwin, *Masters, Princes and Merchants*, vol. 1, pp. 262–3; Langholm, *Economics in the Medieval Schools*, pp. 102–3; Wood, *Medieval Economic Thought*, pp. 112–13.

[15] Baldwin, 'The medieval theories of the just price', p. 63.

view was articulated repeatedly. Thus, to give just one example, the author of the first part of the *De Regimine Principum*, possibly Aquinas, observed:

If the citizens themselves are devoted to mercantile transactions, the door to many vices is thrown open. Since the enthusiasm for business especially involves striving for gain, cupidity is led into the citizens' hearts. The result is that all things in the city become venal; when faith is gone the place is thrown open to deceptions; when the public has contempt for the good, everyone is devoted to their own profit and enthusiasm for virtue ceases, and everyone prefers reward to the honor that comes from virtue. It follows that in such a city civil intercourse will necessarily be corrupted.[16]

Taken on their own, however, these expressions of hostility are highly misleading, for the theologians did much to justify trade and the work of the merchant. Crucially they were able to cite Augustine's commentary on Psalm 70.15–16 which was to be found in the *Decretum*:

The businessman consumed by the profit motive blasphemes when he incurs a loss and lies and perjures himself to obtain the highest prices. But such vices belong to men who engage in commerce, they are not intrinsic to commerce as such, which can be conducted without them.[17]

So while individual merchants might well be sinners, the nature of trade was not such that all merchants were bound to sin simply by being merchants. More than this, the theologians emphasized the social utility of trade, arguing that merchants performed a valuable service to the community by transporting goods from places where they were plentiful to places where they were scarce and therefore needed, and by storing goods in the same place until they were needed. Merchants deserved to make a profit in return for their labour, their expenses, their personal expertise and risks that they took. These profits were not sinful provided merchants pursued them with good intentions, aiming to support themselves and their families, to make charitable donations, and to serve the common good by supplying necessities.

While the reception of Aristotle had an impact on their terminology, the arguments remained much the same throughout the thirteenth

[16] Ptolemy of Lucca with portions attributed to Thomas Aquinas, *On the Government of Rulers: De Regimine Principum*, trans. J. M. Blythe (Philadelphia, 1997), 2.3, p. 109. On the authorship of the first part (up to the middle of 2.4), also known as the *De Regno*, often attributed to but not definitely by Aquinas, see J. M. Blythe, 'Introduction' to the above translation, pp. 1–5. See also Langholm, *Economics in the Medieval Schools*, p. 222.

[17] Augustine, *Enarrationes in Psalmos*, on Psalm 70.15; as quoted by Thomas Aquinas, ST 2a2ae.77.4. sed contra (vol. 38, p. 227). See Baldwin, 'The medieval theories of the just price', p. 64; Wood, *Medieval Economic Thought*, pp. 115–16.

century. In the early thirteenth century, addressing the criticism that merchants sold goods to which they had done nothing, Thomas of Chobham wrote:

Commerce is to buy something cheaper for the purpose of selling it dearer. And this is all right for laymen to do, even if they do not add any improvement of the goods which they bought earlier and later sell. For otherwise there would have been great need in many regions, since merchants carry that which is plentiful in one place to another place where the same thing is scarce. Therefore merchants may well charge the value of their labour and transport and expenses in addition to the capital laid out in purchasing the goods.[18]

Towards the middle of the century, the Halesian Summa regarded business as licit if conducted 'for a necessary or pious cause, such as to provide for oneself and one's family in need or to exercise works of mercy'.[19] It also framed its justification of merchants in response to the charge that they did not alter the goods they bought and sold, citing John Chrysostom, the supposed author of the *palea Eiciens*:

Also, if someone with his labour brings some object from one region to another region, the object being in no way impaired, it is indeed transferred complete and unaltered as to substance, but not as to place, and therefore, because he can lawfully demand a reward for his labour, the words of Chrysostom are not meant to apply to such a one. Also, if someone purchases an object under such conditions that storing it is accompanied by risk, because it may be damaged or consumed by fire or removed by a thief, if nevertheless under the said circumstances he may intend to profit by the sale of such an object, then surely, by considering the uncertainty about what may happen in the future, and by undertaking the risk of buying such an object, he does not purchase this object in order to make a profit by selling it complete and unaltered, and therefore what Chrysostom says is not meant to apply to such a one either.[20]

Later in the thirteenth century, Aquinas articulated both the negative and the positive views of trade and merchants, while clearly emphasizing the positive. He did this by using Aristotle to voice the negative view of trade and merchants, before asserting their worth himself in much the same way as other theologians. He began by noting that Aristotle identified two sorts of exchange. The first was 'natural and necessary, and consists in the exchange of commodity for commodity or of commodity for money, for the maintenance of life'. This type of exchange was conducted by 'heads of families or governments, who have to provide the necessities of life for their households or people'.

[18] As quoted by Langholm, *Economics in the Medieval Schools*, pp. 54–5.
[19] As quoted *ibid.*, p. 136.
[20] As quoted *ibid.*, pp. 130–1.

The second was 'of money for money, or even of any commodity for money, though now for the sake of making a profit', and this was the business of merchants. Aquinas then presented Aristotle's assessment of these two types of exchange: 'According to Aristotle, the former sort of exchange is praiseworthy because it supplies natural needs, whereas the second sort is rightly open to criticism since, in itself, it feeds the acquisitive urge which knows no limit but tends to increase to infinity.' From this a conclusion could be drawn: 'It follows that commerce as such, considered in itself, has something shameful about it in so far as it is not intrinsically calculated to fulfil right or necessary requirements.' The longstanding suspicion of trade and merchants was thus expressed, though now attributed entirely to Aristotle. Ordinarily it might be supposed that Aquinas supported a conclusion drawn in this way, but in fact he turned in a different direction by simply declaring that profit itself was 'nevertheless' morally neutral: 'Nevertheless, profit, which is the point of exchange, while it may not carry the notion of anything right or necessary, does not carry the notion of anything vicious or contrary to virtue either.' Profit could therefore be 'subordinated to an activity that is necessary, or even right', and thus trade could be justified. As examples, Aquinas cited 'the man who uses moderate business profits to provide for his household, or to help the poor' and 'the man who conducts his business for the public good in order to ensure that the country does not run short of essential supplies, and who makes a profit as it were to compensate for his work and not for its own sake'.[21] Aquinas had thus presented two opposing views of trade and the merchant, one negative and the other offering justification. Neither view had been explicitly rejected, but he had avoided formal contradiction by attributing hostility to Aristotle, while expressing the supportive view himself. This also had the effect of giving primacy to the view that trade could be licit while never letting it be forgotten that it had sinful associations. This was perhaps emblematic of the theologians' ambivalence: there was always distrust of trade and merchants, but their justification carried greater weight.

[21] ST 2a2ae.77.4 (vol. 38, pp. 226–9). I have made one adjustment to the translation to eliminate unintended ambiguity. The passage in *De Regimine Principum* cited earlier, expressing hostility to merchants, must similarly be set against a passage in which a case is made for 'moderate use of merchants' because of the need for goods to be transported from areas of abundance to areas of scarcity; see Langholm, *Economics in the Medieval Schools*, p. 221.

Justice in exchange

Having settled that trade could be licit, it was important to establish exactly how it ought to be conducted, and all masters of theology agreed on the fundamental requirement that there should be justice in exchange, in other words that a just price should be paid. The term 'just price' was frequently used by theologians like Peter the Chanter and Robert of Courson from the late twelfth century, although they did not elaborate on what it meant beyond indicating that it represented the true value of the goods.[22] During the thirteenth century, the work of Aristotle, especially his *Nichomachean Ethics*, did much to shape the language in which these matters were discussed. Justice was understood in terms of equality between the parties involved in exchange, and equality was established by use of money as a measure. All these elements are apparent in Aquinas' comments on a contract of sale considered 'in itself':

> such a transaction was introduced for the common benefit of both parties, in so far as each one needs something which the other has, as Aristotle explains. But what is equally useful to both should not involve more of a burden for one than for the other and any contract between two parties should, therefore, be based on an equality of material exchange. But the value of consumer products is measured by the price given, which as Aristotle pointed out, is what coinage was invented for. It follows that the balance of justice is upset if either the price exceeds the value of the goods in question or the thing exceeds the price. To sell for more or to buy for less than a thing is worth is, therefore, unjust and illicit in itself.[23]

But what was the just price? Essentially, the just price was taken to mean the current price in a market that was operating freely, without fraud or attempts to create artificial monopolies. Theologians in the late twelfth and early thirteenth centuries did not state this explicitly, but the view was implied by their acceptance that prices differed according to time and place, and by their discussion of particular cases.[24] In the 1240s, however, theologians stated clearly that the just price was the current market price. The Halesian Summa referred to 'a just estimation of the goods, and by trade, just as it is sold commonly in that city or place in which the sale occurs'.[25] Albert the Great said: 'A price is

22 Baldwin, 'The medieval theories of the just price', p. 69; Langholm, *Economics in the Medieval Schools*, p. 44.
23 ST 2a2ae.77.1 (vol. 38, p. 215). For detailed discussion of this passage, see Baldwin, 'The medieval theories of the just price', pp. 73–4.
24 Baldwin, 'The medieval theories of the just price', pp. 70–1; Baldwin, *Masters, Princes and Merchants*, vol. 1, p. 269.
25 As quoted by Baldwin, 'The medieval theories of the just price', p. 71.

just which can equal the value of the goods sold according to the estimation of the market place at that time.'[26] Aquinas was not entirely clear on this point, but nevertheless indicated that he shared this view when he considered a scenario in which a seller brought corn 'to a place where it fetches a high price, but knowing that many others would follow him into the market'. Although the buyers would not have paid such a high price had they known that a period of scarcity was about to end, Aquinas did not require the seller to tell them:

> a seller who sells something according to its market price would not seem to be acting unjustly if he fails to disclose a future contingency. A disclosure or a reduction in price would spell more abounding virtue yet is not required in strict justice.[27]

Furthermore, amongst the reasons why someone might licitly sell something for more than he had paid was 'because prices have gone up in response to local changes or the lapse of time'.[28] Later theologians, including Henry of Ghent, Giles of Lessines and Richard of Middleton, stated clearly that they took the just price to be the current market price.[29]

In part the market price was understood to reflect need or demand. Aristotle had explained that different types of object could not be measured against each other, but that money could measure demand for them.[30] Albert the Great and Aquinas both expounded this view.[31] According to Albert, '[goods] ought to be taken in relation to use, that is, according to their ability in use to supply need, for in that way all are one, and in that way all can be measured by one, which ... is called money'.[32] Aquinas preferred to cite Augustine to make the point: 'It is Augustine who points out that the price of commercial commodities is not assessed in accordance with their relative position on some absolute scale in the natural world, for a horse is sometimes sold for more than a slave, but in accordance with their usefulness to men.'[33] At the

[26] As quoted *ibid.* See also Langholm, *Economics in the Medieval Schools*, p. 179.
[27] ST 2a2ae.77.3 objection 4 and ad 4 (vol. 38, pp. 223, 225).
[28] ST 2a2ae.77.4.ad2 (vol. 38, pp. 229–31). For extended discussion of Aquinas and the just price as the current market price, see Baldwin, 'The medieval theories of the just price', pp. 76–9; J. Kaye, *Economy and Nature in the Fourteenth Century: Money, Market Exchange, and the Emergence of Scientific Thought* (Cambridge, 1998), pp. 96–100 who challenges the view that Aquinas equated the two.
[29] Baldwin, 'The medieval theories of the just price', pp. 75–6.
[30] *Ibid.*, p. 74; Kaye, *Economy and Nature*, pp. 48–9; Wood, *Medieval Economic Thought*, p. 134.
[31] Baldwin, 'The medieval theories of the just price', pp. 74, 77; Kaye, *Economy and Nature*, pp. 66–70; Langholm, *Economics in the Medieval Schools*, pp. 183–7, 229–31.
[32] As quoted *ibid.*, p. 187, and by Wood, *Medieval Economic Thought*, p. 137.
[33] ST 2a2ae.77.2.ad3 (vol. 38, p. 221).

same time, however, masters acknowledged that labour and the cost of production would have an impact on the market price.[34] Thus Robert of Courson acknowledged that 'a merchant should pay attention to the run of sales according to time and place and to the labour expended on the wares; and if his wares are worth ten shillings and he believes by estimation that for his labour he ought to receive twelve pence, then he may sell for eleven shillings without oath or fraud'.[35] Similarly, Aquinas' other reasons why someone might licitly sell something for more than he had paid were 'because he has improved the thing in some fashion' and 'because he has incurred risks in transporting it about or in having it delivered'.[36] It was also recognized that supply would affect the price. That was what Aquinas envisaged when he discussed the obligations of the corn seller who knew that prices would fall when other merchants arrived with their corn to sell. Increasingly the market price was understood to be a common estimate established within a market that was shaped by impersonal forces.[37] The theologians were familiar with the judgement in Roman law that 'the prices of things are determined not by their value and utility to individuals, but by their value determined commonly'.[38] The market price was taken to reflect need as an aggregate rather than the need of any one person.

Increasingly, too, the just price was either considered to be an estimate rather than a specific sum, or prices were permitted to fall within a range on either side of the just price. The canon lawyers were the most forgiving in this regard. As long as the price was within fifty per cent of the just price either way, the sale was valid. If there was a greater discrepancy, the Roman law principle of *laesio enormis*, or 'gross injury', applied and the damaged party was entitled to payment of the balance or to have the sale rescinded.[39] The theologians, however, were much less tolerant.[40] Nevertheless, while not permitting the canonists' fifty per cent deviation from the just price, they came increasingly to think of the just price as an estimate or range of prices. Aquinas, for

34 See Baldwin, 'The medieval theories of the just price', pp. 74–5.
35 As quoted by Langholm, *Economics in the Medieval Schools*, p. 44.
36 ST 2a2ae.77.4.ad2 (vol. 38, pp. 229–31).
37 See Kaye, *Economy and Nature*, pp. 75–6, 152–3, 229–30; Wood, *Medieval Economic Thought*, pp. 136, 138.
38 As quoted by Kaye, *Economy and Nature*, p. 153.
39 Baldwin, 'The medieval theories of the just price', pp. 18–19, 22–7, 42–6; Baldwin, *Masters, Princes and Merchants*, vol. 1, pp. 267–8; Kaye, *Economy and Nature*, p. 91; Wood, *Medieval Economic Thought*, pp. 148–9.
40 Baldwin, 'The medieval theories of the just price', pp. 69–70, 72; Baldwin, *Masters, Princes and Merchants*, vol. 1, p. 268; Kaye, *Economy and Nature*, p. 95; Wood, *Medieval Economic Thought*, p. 149.

example, noted that 'we cannot always fix the just price precisely; we sometimes have to make the best estimate we can, with the result that giving or taking a little here or there does not upset the balance of justice'.[41]

Analysing these changes in detail, Joel Kaye has convincingly demonstrated that towards the end of the thirteenth century different notions of justice and equality were applied to the process of exchange. Aristotle had distinguished between distributive and corrective justice. Distributive justice ensured that goods were distributed amongst people who were unequal in proportion to service or status with the result that people did not receive equal amounts. In mathematical terms, this use of proportion and ratio meant that justice was established according to a geometric mean. Corrective justice concerned relations between people of equal status, and provided strict equality. In this case justice was established according to an arithmetic mean. While Aristotle perhaps had a third type of justice in mind for exchange, although this was not picked up by medieval commentators, he nevertheless understood exchange to function in geometric terms; money established the value of things in proportion to each other, and so justice in exchange was geometrical rather than arithmetical.[42] Kaye shows that medieval theologians initially demanded arithmetical equality in exchange, but that from the late thirteenth century they analysed exchange in terms of geometrical equality. The new approach appeared first in commentaries on Aristotle by Albert the Great and Aquinas, but was then applied in independent analysis of specific financial contracts. In the fourteenth century, as a result of these developments, theologians envisaged a self-ordering market within which self-interested individuals legitimately pursued maximum profit.[43]

In the thirteenth century, however, none of this meant that the individual was allowed to bargain freely to maximize personal advantage. In an attempt to indicate how individuals should behave in negotiation, Aquinas set out how the relative positions of seller and buyer should be taken into account. In his *Summa Theologiae*, having considered a contract of sale 'in itself', he continued:

[41] ST 2a2ae.77.1.ad1 (vol. 38, p. 217).

[42] Baldwin, 'The medieval theories of the just price', pp. 10–12, 62–3, 73; Kaye, *Economy and Nature*, pp. 40–5; Wood, *Medieval Economic Thought*, pp. 133–5.

[43] Kaye goes on to argue brilliantly that this way of thinking about the economy influenced natural philosophy more generally. For summaries of his overall argument, see esp. Kaye, *Economy and Nature*, pp. 2–9, 13–14, 158–62, 163–70. Regarding Albert and Aquinas, see also Baldwin, 'The medieval theories of the just price', pp. 73–4.

> The other way in which we can look at a contract of sale is in so far as it happens to bring benefit to one party at the expense of the other, as in the case where one badly needs to get hold of something and the other is put out by not having it. In such a case the estimation of the just price will have to take into account not merely the commodity to be sold but also the loss which the seller incurs in selling it. The commodity can here be sold for more than it is worth in itself though not for more than it is worth to the possessor. If, on the other hand, a buyer derives great benefit from a transaction without the seller suffering any loss as a result of relinquishing his property, then the latter is not entitled to charge more. This is because the surplus value that accrues to the other is due not to the seller but to the buyer's situation: nobody is entitled to sell another what is not his own though he is justified in charging for any loss he may suffer.[44]

Aquinas thus argued, first, that if the seller would suffer a loss by selling something at the just price, he could sell at a higher price. Second, however, if the seller would not suffer by selling at the just price, but the buyer's need for the thing was especially great, the seller should not exploit the buyer's need by selling above the just price. It is not immediately obvious how this establishes equality between seller and buyer. The second point is confirmed in *De Malo* when Aquinas says it would be unjust 'if one were to sell something to another in need for much more than the value of the thing'.[45] The first part seems to be contradicted in *De Malo* when he says 'the buyer of something justly pays for it as much as it is worth and not as much as the seller is hurt by its privation'.[46] But perhaps the point in the *Summa Theologiae* is that the seller can ask a high price to protect himself against loss, and if a buyer's need is such that he is willing to pay above the just price, the sale is just. Aquinas was setting out the moral imperatives for the seller, which was entirely appropriate since he was addressing the question 'whether someone can licitly sell something for more than it is worth'. He did not explain the equivalent moral imperatives for the buyer, but presumably they would have been, first, that he could seek a low price if he was in need, but that, second, if he was not in need, he should not exploit a seller's need for ready money by forcing him to sell below the just price. Aquinas was typical of the theologians in requiring close scrutiny of the individual merchant's intentions.

[44] ST 2a2ae.77.1 (vol. 38, p. 215). For discussion of this passage, see Baldwin, 'The medieval theories of the just price', pp. 79–80; Langholm, *Economics in the Medieval Schools*, pp. 232–6.

[45] Thomas Aquinas, *On Evil*, trans. R. Regan (Oxford, 2003), 13.4.ad7, p. 402.

[46] *Ibid.*, 13.4.ad14, p. 403.

Usury

Condemnation of usury

In assessing commercial transactions, however, justice in exchange was not the masters' only concern. At least as important, if not more so, was the requirement that usury be avoided. Even as the economy of western Europe came to depend more and more heavily on the extension of credit, the church taught that the sin of usury occurred whenever a loan, or 'mutuum', required the borrower to repay the lender more than had been lent in the first place. Whatever the actual outcome of the transaction, the intention to receive more than had been originally lent made the lender a usurer. Basic definitions were found in quotations from the Fathers gathered in Gratian's *Decretum*. Augustine said that it was usury if the lender expected to received back more than had been given in a loan, whether in the form of money, wheat, wine, oil or anything else.[47] According to Jerome, 'One calls anything whatsoever usury and surplus if one has collected more than one has given.'[48] For Ambrose, 'Usury is whatever exceeds the principal.'[49] Gratian himself defined usury as 'expecting to receive back more than you have given in a loan', and followed Ambrose in declaring that 'Whatsoever exceeds the principal is usury.'[50] These formulations were reinforced by decretals during the twelfth century, most notably Urban III's *Consuluit* of 1187,[51] and reworked with little significant change by theologians who tackled the question of usury subsequently. Thus William of Auxerre in his *Commentary on the Sentences*, written between 1210 and 1220 and known as the *Summa aurea*, defined usury as 'the will to acquire something above the principal of a loan'.[52] A little later Roland of Cremona called it 'the will to steal something in excess of the principal'.[53]

[47] Augustine in Gratian, *Decretum*, 2.14.3.1. See Kaye, *Economy and Nature*, p. 81; Baldwin, *Masters, Princes and Merchants*, vol. 1, p. 271.

[48] Jerome in *Decretum*, 2.14.3.2; as quoted by J. Le Goff, *Your Money or Your Life: Economy and Religion in the Middle Ages*, trans. P. Ranum (New York, 1988), p. 26. See Kaye, *Economy and Nature*, p. 81; Baldwin, *Masters, Princes and Merchants*, vol. 1, p. 271.

[49] Ambrose in Gratian, *Decretum*, 2.14.3.3; as quoted by Kaye, *Economy and Nature*, p. 81. See Baldwin, *Masters, Princes and Merchants*, vol. 1, p. 271.

[50] Gratian, *Decretum*, 2.14.3.1 and 2.14.3.3; as quoted by Wood, *Medieval Economic Thought*, pp. 159–60.

[51] Le Goff, *Your Money*, p. 26; Kaye, *Economy and Nature*, p. 82.

[52] As quoted by Langholm, *Economics in the Medieval Schools*, p. 77; see also Noonan, *Scholastic Analysis of Usury*, p. 42.

[53] As quoted by Langholm, *Economics in the Medieval Schools*, p. 94.

Discussions of usury were underpinned by a keen sense that it posed a potentially devastating threat to Christian society, and this in two respects. First, it was feared that many would abandon their proper roles and responsibilities in pursuit of usurious gain. In 1179 the third Lateran Council took steps against notorious usurers: 'Nearly everywhere the crime of usury has become so firmly rooted that many, omitting other business, practice usury as if it were permitted.'[54] Innocent IV worried that if the rich were allowed to make usurious loans they would not put their money into agriculture, leaving the poor to struggle without animals and tools. Peasants, too, would abandon the land to become usurers, and the result would be famine.[55] Second, usury threatened to engulf society in sin, leading many who were not usurers to damnation. The point was that usurious goods, and above all usurious money, were bound to circulate, and this created moral problems for a whole range of other people. Members of usurers' families might well be in an awkward position because they could hardly avoid living off money or property that had been acquired through usury. So might people who were employed by usurers, including those scholars who were paid to teach the sons of usurers. Others whose spiritual welfare might be endangered by taking money or property from usurers included the recipients of charitable gifts or alms. Spiritual and temporal authorities might also be in trouble because they took usurious money or goods in the form of tax. As usurious money and property passed from the usurers' hands, sin could spread as other people began to live off ill-gotten gains. Matters were made worse because usurers were supposed to make restitution of usurious gains to those from whom they had taken them, and other recipients were in an especially serious position if that obligation passed to them and they failed to meet it.[56]

The condemnation of usury rested on biblical authority in the first instance. All but one of the key passages came from the Old Testament, though the one from the New Testament was vital because it stressed the importance of intention:

Exodus 22.25
If you lend money to any of my people with you who is poor, you shall not be to him as a creditor, and you shall not exact interest from him.

[54] Third Lateran Council, canon 25, *Decrees of the Ecumenical Councils*, ed. N. P. Tanner, 2 vols. (London, 1990), vol. 1, p. 223. See also J. T. Gilchrist, *The Church and Economic Activity in the Middle Ages* (London, 1969), p. 173; Le Goff, *Your Money*, p. 25.
[55] Noonan, *Scholastic Analysis of Usury*, p. 49; Le Goff, *Your Money*, pp. 25–6.
[56] See section on usurious money below.

Leviticus 25.35–7
And if your brother becomes poor, and cannot maintain himself with you, you shall maintain him; as a stranger and as a sojourner he shall live with you. Take no interest from him or increase, but fear your God; that your brother may live beside you. You shall not lend him your money at interest, nor give him your food for profit.

Deuteronomy 23.19–20
You shall not lend upon interest to your brother, interest on money, interest on victuals, interest on anything that is lent for interest. To a foreigner you may lend upon interest, but to your brother you shall not lend upon interest.

Psalm 15(14).1–5
O Lord, who shall sojourn in thy tent? Who shall dwell on thy holy hill? He who walks blamelessly, and does what is right ... who does not put out his money at interest.

Ezekiel 18.5–13
If a man is righteous and does what is lawful and right ... does not lend at interest or take any increase ... he is righteous, he shall surely live, says the Lord God. If he begets a son who ... lends at interest, and takes increase ... shall he then live? He shall not live.

Ezekiel 22.12
You take interest and increase and make gain of your neighbours by extortion; and you have forgotten me, says the Lord God.

Luke 6.34–5
And if you lend to those from whom you hope to receive, what credit is that to you? Even sinners lend to sinners, to receive as much again. But love your enemies, and do good, and lend, expecting nothing in return.

Further authority for the condemnation of usury could be found in the Fathers and early church councils.[57] This did not, however, prevent Parisian theologians from articulating a whole host of arguments to demonstrate that usury was sinful. Some arguments could be stated briefly and were presented simultaneously, often without clear distinction between them. The arguments became increasingly complex, however, and some of the later arguments contradicted earlier ones.

From early in the twelfth century, theologians maintained that usury was theft, a position shared by Anselm, Hugh of Saint Victor, Peter Comestor and Peter Lombard.[58] Canon lawyers developed this approach in the second half of the twelfth century with reference to Roman law according to which a loan involved the transfer of ownership from the lender to the borrower. Roman law also permitted an agreement that

[57] Le Goff, *Your Money*, pp. 23–4.
[58] Noonan, *Scholastic Analysis of Usury*, p. 17; Le Goff, *Your Money*, p. 27.

interest should be paid to be added to the contract, but this was ignored, and it was argued that the lender could not legitimately profit from what now belonged to another.[59] The point about the transfer of ownership was supported by a false etymology: 'a loan [mutuum] is so-called from this, that mine [meum] becomes yours [tuum]'.[60] This argument was taken up by theologians in the late twelfth and early thirteenth centuries. As Thomas of Chobham, for example, explained: 'Where there is a *mutuum*, ownership passes, whence *mutuum* means as it were "yours from mine" [de meo tuum]. Therefore if I have lent you money or also grain or wine, immediately the money is yours, and the grain is yours and the wine is yours. Therefore, if I receive a fee for this, I profit from what is yours, not mine.'[61]

Another reason for condemning usury was that in a loan the borrower bore all the risk: whatever happened to the goods loaned, the borrower remained bound to repay the lender. This argument was closely related to the one concerning transfer of ownership and the two were often presented together. Robert of Courson followed this course, while also explaining the difference between a loan and a lease:

> We distinguish between a lease [*locatio*] and a loan [*mutuum*], for in the case of a lease the object does not pass into the ownership of the receiver but remains his who leases it. The whole risk relating to the object must remain with the lessor because the object remains his entirely. Therefore he may receive a surplus for the damage and use of the object. But it is not like that in the case of a loan. It is called a loan [*mutuum*] because mine [*meum*] becomes yours [*tuum*] or vice versa. As the five shillings which you lend me are mine, ownership to them passes to me from you. It is therefore an iniquity if you should receive something for a thing which is mine, for nothing is due you of my thing.[62]

Underlying this distinction between a loan and a lease was the notion of fungibility which was to play a vital role in discussions of usury. A fungible is something 'that can serve for, or be replaced by, another answering to the same definition',[63] or, as Roman law has it, fungibles 'exist by weight, number or measure'.[64] So if I lend you ten paper-clips, I will be happy to get any ten paper-clips back, not necessarily the very ones that I gave you; paper-clips are fungibles. But if I lend you my house, I expect that particular house back; houses are non-fungibles.

59 Wood, *Medieval Economic Thought*, p. 186; Noonan, *Scholastic Analysis of Usury*, pp. 39–40.
60 Paucapalea, as quoted *ibid.*, p. 39.
61 As quoted by Langholm, *Economics in the Medieval Schools*, p. 56.
62 As quoted *ibid.*, p. 48. See also Noonan, *Scholastic Analysis of Usury*, pp. 41–2.
63 *The Concise Oxford Dictionary*, ed. J. B. Sykes (Oxford, 1976).
64 As quoted by Langholm, *Economics in the Medieval Schools*, p. 48.

Both lawyers and theologians followed Roman law in taking loans to involve fungibles and leases to concern non-fungibles. In a lease where the lender was to receive back a non-fungible, a particular house for example, it was possible that the house would be damaged or destroyed, so it was appropriate that the lender should receive payment for taking this risk. In a loan, however, where the lender was to be repaid a fungible, any five shillings for example, the lender bore no risk and no such payment was justified. It followed that if money were ever treated as a non-fungible, so that the contract required the repayment of exactly the same five shillings, the lender was taking a risk and was therefore entitled to a further payment. This was envisaged in the loan *ad pompam*: if the lender parted with his money so that someone could make a display of wealth, and exactly the same coins were to be returned, the lender now bore a risk and a charge could be made, and Robert of Courson suggested that some princes borrowed for just this reason.[65] The fundamental point about risk, again linked to ownership, was made by many theologians, including Thomas Aquinas who contrasted the loan with investment in partnerships:

> Somebody who lends money hands over the ownership of it to the borrower, and with it the attendant risks and the obligation to make complete restitution, from which it follows that the lender is not entitled to ask for more. Somebody, on the other hand, who entrusts his money to a merchant or a craftsman in a sort of partnership does not hand over the ownership, and so it is still at his risk that the merchant trades or the craftsman works. The lender is, therefore, entitled to ask for a part of the profit of the undertaking in so far as it is also his own.[66]

Yet another argument, again related to ownership, was that the usurer sold time, specifically the time between the grant of the loan and its repayment. Time was not the usurer's to sell because it belonged to God who gave it to all his creatures, making the usurer an especially evil thief. According to Thomas of Chobham, 'the usurer sells the debtor nothing that is his, but only time, which is God's. Therefore, since he sells a thing belonging to another, he ought not to derive any profit from it.'[67] William of Auxerre made the same point, specifically invoking natural law:

> [the usurer] also acts against the universal natural law, because he sells time, which is common to all creatures. Augustine says ... each creature is compelled

[65] Noonan, *Scholastic Analysis of Usury*, pp. 40–1; Langholm, *Economics in the Medieval Schools*, pp. 48–9.

[66] ST 2a2ae.78.2.ad5 (vol. 38, p. 245). I have adjusted the translation.

[67] As quoted by Langholm, *Economics in the Medieval Schools*, p. 56. See also Le Goff, *Your Money*, p. 40; Wood, *Medieval Economic Thought*, p. 174.

to give himself; the sun is compelled to give itself to illuminate; similarly the earth is compelled to give whatever it can, and similarly the water. Nothing, however, so naturally gives itself as time: willy-nilly things have time. Because, therefore, the usurer sells what necessarily belongs to all creatures generally he injures all creatures, even the stones; whence if men were silent against the usurers, the stones would cry out, if they could; and this is one reason why the Church so pursues the usurers. Whence especially against them God says, 'When I shall take up the time, that is, when time will be so in My hand that a usurer cannot sell it, then I will judge justly.'[68]

This argument remained in use throughout the thirteenth century. Giles of Lessines, for example, deployed it in his treatise *De usuris* in 1278: 'But time is common, nor is it the proper possession of anyone, but is given by God equally.'[69] Because of the richness of the imagery with which the point could be embellished, evident in the passage from William of Auxerre, it was especially to be found in material intended for use in sermons.[70] By the end of the thirteenth century and the beginning of the fourteenth, however, theologians like Giles of Rome and Peter John Olivi no longer found it convincing.[71]

A further criticism of usurers, and one which could easily be combined with others, was that they did no work, preferring to exploit the borrower's labour. Thus Thomas of Chobham condemned the usurer because he wished 'to pursue his profit without any labour, even while sleeping, which is contrary to the precept of the Lord, "In labour and the sweat of your face shall you get your bread" [Genesis 3.19].'[72] Later in the thirteenth century, Albert the Great stressed the way in which the usurer took advantage of the borrower who 'accepts the loan from necessity, and in distress … and by hard labour has acquired something as profit on which he could live, and this the usurer, suffering no distress, spending no labour, fearing no loss of capital by misfortune, takes away, and through the distress and labour and changing luck of his neighbour collects and acquires riches for himself'.[73] The absence of risk for the usurer was also brought into play here. Giles of Lessines was

[68] As quoted by Noonan, *Scholastic Analysis of Usury*, pp. 43–4. See also Wood, *Medieval Economic Thought*, p. 175.

[69] As quoted by Noonan, *Scholastic Analysis of Usury*, p. 63.

[70] *Ibid.*, p. 58; Langholm, *Economics in the Medieval Schools*, p. 57.

[71] Noonan, *Scholastic Analysis of Usury*, p. 59; Wood, *Medieval Economic Thought*, pp. 174–5. See also Giles of Rome, Quodlibet V.24, in *B. Aegidii Columnae Romani Quodlibeta* (Louvain, 1646; repr. Frankfurt am Main, 1966), pp. 336–9 (discussed below).

[72] As quoted by Wood, *Medieval Economic Thought*, p. 177. See also Le Goff, *Your Money*, p. 42.

[73] As quoted by Langholm, *Economics in the Medieval Schools*, p. 197. See also Noonan, *Scholastic Analysis of Usury*, pp. 45–6; Wood, *Medieval Economic Thought*, p. 178.

another who complained that the usurer made a profit without working: 'he gains sleeping as working, on feast days as on feriae', the latter being ordinary weekdays.[74]

Usury was also condemned on the grounds that the lender took it against the borrower's will, an argument that could easily be linked with the idea that usury was theft. Critical here was Aristotle's distinction between absolute and conditional or mixed voluntariness to be found in book 3 of the *Nichomachean Ethics*. Aristotle illustrated the distinction with reference to a sea captain who threw his cargo overboard to keep his ship afloat during a storm. In absolute terms the captain did not wish to throw his cargo overboard at all, but in the particular conditions created by the storm there was a sense in which that was what he wanted to do; jettisoning his cargo was therefore an act of conditional or mixed voluntariness.[75] Applied to usury, it was conceded that there was a sense in which the borrower paid willingly for a loan, but only because he needed the loan and could not obtain it freely. It was therefore an act of conditional voluntariness, and in absolute terms the borrower paid against his will. Although the whole of the *Nichomachean Ethics* was not translated from the Greek until the late 1240s, and even translations from Arabic dated from the early 1240s, it would seem that parts were known in Paris earlier. At any rate, Thomas of Chobham deployed the argument in his *Summa confessorum* around 1215:

> however much someone who has agreed to pay usury says that he gives the creditor something voluntarily, all the same he does not give it voluntarily of an absolute will but of a comparative will, because he wishes to give something, better than to be altogether without a loan.[76]

In countering the objection that 'to receive usury is not to take alien goods against the owner's will', William of Auxerre elaborated the argument and concluded that usury was theft:

> it should be recognized that voluntariness is twofold: absolute and conditional or comparative; according to absolute voluntariness the owner of this money does not want the usurer to receive it; but according to comparative voluntariness he wants him to receive and have it, because the usurer will not give the loan for nothing; therefore the usurer takes alien goods against the owner's will, when this expression, 'against the will', is understood as removing his absolute and separate will; and thus it is evident that usury is theft.[77]

[74] As quoted by Noonan, *Scholastic Analysis of Usury*, p. 63.
[75] Aristotle, *The Nichomachean Ethics*, 3.1.
[76] As quoted by Langholm, *Economics in the Medieval Schools*, p. 59.
[77] As quoted *ibid.*, p. 78. See also Noonan, *Scholastic Analysis of Usury*, p. 43; Wood, *Medieval Economic Thought*, p. 165.

Aquinas also deployed the argument, but with much greater emphasis on the forceful way in which the usurer exploited the borrower. First, he had to counter the objection that 'the borrower pays interest knowingly and willingly':

lenders, although not compelling borrowers absolutely, nonetheless compel borrowers in a partially voluntary way, namely, in that the lender imposes a heavy burden on one in need of a loan, namely, that the borrower pay back more than the lender lends. And this is as if one were to sell something to another in need for much more than the value of the thing, for such a sale would be unjust, just as loans at interest are unjust.[78]

A further objection conceded that 'there is partial coercion when a necessity threatens, as is evident in the case of one who jettisons cargo into the sea to save a ship', but pointed out that 'people sometimes borrow at interest without any great need', in which case the lender was not taking advantage of need and was therefore not sinning in charging for the loan. Aquinas, however, identified two forms of necessity, the second of which was experienced even by those who borrowed 'without any great need':

Things are necessary in two ways, as the *Metaphysics* says. Something is indeed necessary in one way if something else cannot exist without it, as, for example, food is necessary for human life. And something is necessary if something else can exist without it but not so well or suitably, and we accordingly call all useful things necessary. And the borrower is under necessity in either the first or the second way.[79]

Aquinas thus maintained that the usurer always exploited need in one way or another, forcing the borrower to act against his own absolute will.

A number of arguments against usury were based on views about the nature of money. One of the earliest stressed that money did not deteriorate. It often cropped up when a contrast was being drawn between loans and leases, and between the proper matter of each contract. When a house was leased, a charge could be made because the house might deteriorate in use. When money was loaned, however, no such charge was justified because money did not deteriorate. The point was generally made very briefly and in conjunction with other arguments, for example by Peter of Tarentaise, John of La Rochelle and Bonaventure.[80]

78 Thomas Aquinas, *On Evil*, 13.4 objection 7 and ad 7, pp. 398, 402. See also ST 2a2ae.78.1.ad7 (vol. 38, p. 241).

79 Thomas Aquinas, *On Evil*, 13.4 objection 8 and ad 8, pp. 398, 402, citing Aristotle, *Metaphysics*, 5.5. See Langholm, *Economics in the Medieval Schools*, pp. 246–8.

80 Langholm, *Economics in the Medieval Schools*, p. 106 (Peter of Tarentaise), p. 139 (John of La Rochelle), pp. 163–5 (Bonaventure); Noonan, *Scholastic Analysis of Usury*, p. 48 (Bonaventure).

Other theologians, however, rejected the argument because it was open to some obvious objections. Albert the Great, for example, pointed out that everyone accepted that a charge could be made when money was lent for display, *ad pompam*, even though money did not then deteriorate in use.[81] Aquinas was equally unconvinced, not least because his most original view of the nature of money ran entirely counter to the idea that it did not deteriorate in use, as we will see.[82]

The sterility of money was also cited in condemnations of usury. The basic point was that when the usurer lent money and received more in return, money was breeding money, or reproducing itself, and this was unnatural. This notion about the nature of money could be found in Roman law and some of the Fathers, and this perhaps influenced scholars in the first part of the thirteenth century.[83] Thus Thomas of Chobham noted that 'money inactive does not of its nature bear any fruit, but a vineyard is naturally fruitbearing'.[84] The idea was significantly reinforced, however, with the reception of the Latin translation of Aristotle's *Politics*. Aristotle approved of trade for the maintenance of the household, but condemned retail trade on the grounds that it was conducted to make money, desire for money was infinite, and acquiring money was an unnatural end. The most unnatural kind of trade, however, was usury because it involved the abuse of money. Money existed to be a means of exchange, but usury made money breed more money without any process of exchange. Aristotle considered it significant that the Greek word for usury, 'tokos', also meant 'offspring'. In the thirteenth century, the word for 'retail trade' was incorrectly translated by William of Moerbeke as 'campsoria', meaning 'money-changing', so Aristotle's general condemnation of trade for profit was missed whereas his attack on usury was welcomed.[85] For some the image of barren metal unnaturally breeding more money became less important than the idea that money was being used contrary to its true purpose. Thus Aquinas used Aristotle's point about the purpose of money without explicit reference to sterility:

[81] Langholm, *Economics in the Medieval Schools*, p. 196; Noonan, *Scholastic Analysis of Usury*, p. 46. Giles of Rome took a similar position; see Noonan, *Scholastic Analysis of Usury*, p. 59.

[82] For Aquinas' explicit rejection of the argument from non-deterioration, see Thomas Aquinas, *On Evil*, 13.4.ad4, pp. 401–2; Langholm, *Economics in the Medieval Schools*, pp. 239, 242.

[83] Wood, *Medieval Economic Thought*, p. 84.

[84] As quoted by Langholm, *Economics in the Medieval Schools*, p. 57. See also Le Goff, *Your Money*, p. 30.

[85] Noonan, *Scholastic Analysis of Usury*, pp. 46–7; Langholm, *Economics in the Medieval Schools*, p. 171, Wood, *Medieval Economic Thought*, pp. 84–5.

money ... according to Aristotle, was invented chiefly for exchanges to be made, so that the prime and proper use of money is its use and disbursement in the way of ordinary transactions. It follows that it is in principle wrong to make a charge for money lent, which is what usury consists in.[86]

Giles of Lessines, on the other hand, preferred to retain the image of unnatural breeding:

Whenever someone uses the transfer of money to make money multiply in kind, a misuse of money and a dishonourable contract take place, and it is called *tokos*, that is, the breeding of a thing.[87]

Thinking further about how money operated as a means of exchange, and still influenced by Aristotle, though now more by his *Ethics*, Aquinas developed yet another argument against usury. He noted that Aristotle had said not only that money was a means of exchange, but that it was a measure:

All other things from themselves have some utility; not so, however, money. But it is the measure of utility of other things, as is clear according to the Philosopher in the *Ethics* V:9. And therefore the use of money does not have the measure of its utility from this money itself, but from the things which are measured by money according to the different persons who exchange money for goods. Whence to receive more money for less seems nothing other than to diversify the measure in giving and receiving, which manifestly contains iniquity.[88]

Aquinas' argument, developed relatively early in his career when he was commenting on the *Sentences*, was that money could not function as a measure if its value was inconstant and it could be sold. By its very nature, therefore, money was non-vendible, a position frequently adopted by other theologians thereafter.[89]

Before long, however, Aquinas produced a much more significant argument against usury based on a different view of the nature of money. The argument depended on classifying money amongst goods that were consumed in their use as opposed to goods that were not:

there are some things whose use consists of consuming the things themselves. For example, the proper use of wine consists of drinking it, and the substance

[86] ST 2a2ae.78.1 (vol. 38, p. 235). For Aquinas' discussion of the imagery of breeding, see Langholm, *Economics in the Medieval Schools*, p. 237.

[87] As quoted by Langholm, *Economics in the Medieval Schools*, p. 309.

[88] *Commentary on the Sentences*, 3.37.1.6; as quoted by Noonan, *Scholastic Analysis of Usury*, p. 52.

[89] Noonan, *Scholastic Analysis of Usury*, pp. 51–3; Wood, *Medieval Economic Thought*, pp. 73–4. For doubts about the argument's distinctiveness and long-term significance, see Langholm, *Economics in the Medieval Schools*, pp. 240–1.

of the wine is thereby consumed, and the proper use of wheat or bread likewise consists of eating it, and this consumes the wheat or bread itself. So also the proper use of money consists of spending it in exchange for other things, since money was devised to facilitate exchange, as the Philosopher says in the Politics.

And there are some things whose use does not consist of consuming the things themselves. For example, the use of a house is as a dwelling, and it does not belong to the nature of inhabitation that the house be razed. And if the house by people dwelling in it should happen to be improved or suffer deterioration, this is incidental. And we should say the same about horses and clothes and the like. Therefore, since use does not consume such things, strictly speaking, the thing itself or its use can be separately leased or sold, or both together can be alienated. For example, one can sell a house while retaining one's use of the house for a time, and one can likewise sell the use of a house while retaining one's title and ownership of the house. But regarding the things whose use consists of consuming them, the use of the thing is only the thing itself, and so whoever is granted the use of such things is also granted the ownership of the things themselves, and vice versa. Therefore, when a person lends money with the stipulation that the entire sum be returned, and the person in addition wants to have a fixed recompense for the use of the money, the person evidently sells separately the use of the money and the very substance of the money. And the use of money is only its substance, as I have said, and so the lender of money at interest sells nothing or sells the same thing twice, namely, the very money whose use consists of its consumption. And this is evidently contrary to the nature of natural justice. And so lending money at interest as such is mortal sin.[90]

So, according to Aquinas, some goods were consumed in their use, and these included wine which was drunk in its use, and wheat or bread which was eaten. Money fell into this category because it was spent when used in exchange. As he went on to explain in his reply to an objection, 'exchange is a use consuming, as it were, the substance of the thing exchanged insofar as the exchange alienates the thing from the one who exchanges it'.[91] In such cases use and substance were identical. But there were other goods whose use did not entail their consumption, and these included houses, horses and clothes. If they deteriorated through use, this was accidental because using a house by living in it, for example, did not necessarily lead to its destruction. In such cases use and substance were distinct and could be treated separately. Granting use of such a thing did not therefore mean transfer of ownership, so a house could be sold and the use retained, or, more significantly, the use could be sold while ownership was retained, as in a lease contract. The situation was entirely different with goods that were consumed in

[90] Thomas Aquinas, *On Evil*, 13.4, pp. 400–1.
[91] *Ibid.*, 13.4.ad15, p. 403.

their use. Because their use and substance were identical, anyone who made a loan expecting the principal (or substance) to be restored plus a further payment for the use of the money was either selling something that did not exist (use distinct from substance) or selling the same thing twice, which was contrary to natural justice and a mortal sin. To put this in terms of ownership, when use of money was granted in a loan, ownership was also transferred because substance was identical with use.[92]

Aquinas clarified the argument when he discussed the loan *ad pompam*, or for display. As we have already seen, it was commonplace to accept this contract as licit, for example on the grounds that, while money was fungible, this particular contract involved treating it as non-fungible. Aquinas was able to justify the loan *ad pompam* in terms of the relationship between consumption and use. He had referred to the 'proper use' of the various goods he had cited, by which he meant their primary or essential use, but it was always possible to use things in other ways, money included:

> the specific and primary use of money is as a means of exchange, since money was instituted for this purpose, and the secondary use of money can be for anything else, for example, as security or for display. And exchange is a use consuming, as it were, the substance of the thing exchanged insofar as the exchange alienates the thing from the one who exchanges it. And so if persons should lend their money to others for use as a means of exchange, which is the specific use of money, and seek a return for this use over and above the principal, this will be contrary to justice. But if persons lend their money to others for another use in which the money is not consumed, there will be the same consideration as regarding the things that are not consumed in their very use, things that are licitly rented and hired out. And so if one gives money sealed in a purse to someone to post it as security and then receives recompense, this is not interest-taking, since it involves a renting or hiring out, not a contract for a loan. And the reasoning is the same if a person gives money to another to use for display.[93]

The point was that in the loan *ad pompam* money was not consumed, which is why it was a secondary use of money. And because the money was not consumed, its substance and its use were no longer identical. Consequently it was licit to lend the substance in the expectation that it would be returned, and to make a charge for its use. When money was

[92] See Noonan, *Scholastic Analysis of Usury*, pp. 53–7; Langholm, *Economics in the Medieval Schools*, pp. 166, 241–4. For canonists' use of this argument, see T. P. McLaughlin, 'The teaching of the canonists on usury (XII, XIII and XIV centuries)', *Mediaeval Studies* 1 (1939): 81–147 at 100–2.

[93] Thomas Aquinas, *On Evil*, 13.4.ad15, pp. 403–4.

used for its primary purpose of exchange, however, it was consumed in use, its use and substance were identical, and it was therefore wrong to lend the substance and make a charge for a use that did not exist separately from the substance. Aquinas did not produce this argument from nowhere; the idea of goods being consumed in use was to be found in Roman law.[94] Nevertheless, it was a new argument against usury. It completely reversed the argument based on the idea that money did not deteriorate in use whereas a house did; now money was entirely consumed in use while the deterioration of a house was purely accidental. This was Aquinas' chief argument against usury, and one which he explored in several works.[95] It was taken up by many theologians subsequently.

Parisian theologians had thus worked diligently to discover rational grounds for the condemnation of usury. Some arguments were valuable chiefly for generating powerful imagery that could be deployed in sermons, but others were sophisticated appeals to natural law. Since the condemnation was based on secure scriptural and patristic authority, it is worth asking why theologians put so much effort into the pursuit of new arguments. The answer perhaps lies in the way in which, while all accepted the general rule, some began to moderate their position quite significantly. Justifications began to be found for charging for credit, and a fundamental ambivalence is again apparent.

Justification of charging for credit

It was generally accepted that someone who granted a loan could licitly receive a gift in return, as an expression of gratitude, provided that it was given entirely freely and was not the result of any kind of demand or prior agreement. As Aquinas put it, as long as the lender accepted something 'not in response to a demand or out of an expressed or tacit sense of obligation, but as a gift, there is no sin; the reason for this is that one would have been entitled to accept a gift before making the loan and one is not worse off through lending'.[96] To make a loan in the hope of a gift, however, was to be guilty of usury by intention. A few scholars, including William of Auxerre and Bonaventure, permitted 'a secondary hope' of a gift.[97] Aquinas also held that the lender was

[94] Noonan, *Scholastic Analysis of Usury*, p. 54; Langholm, *Economics in the Medieval Schools*, p. 241.

[95] See, for example, ST 2a2ae.78.1 (vol. 38, pp. 232–41).

[96] ST 2a2ae.78.2 (vol. 38, p. 243). See also Thomas Aquinas, *On Evil*, 13.4.ad13, p. 403.

[97] Noonan, *Scholastic Analysis of Usury*, p. 105.

'entitled to seek the sort of compensation that cannot be measured in terms of money – things like benevolence and love towards the lender'.[98] In theory, however, this did not represent a great departure from the prohibition of usury.

Of greater significance in the long run was the recognition that lenders might suffer loss as a result of making loans, and that they therefore merited compensation. This brought into play the Roman law concept of 'interest' which referred to damages when a contractual obligation had not been met, and represented that which 'is between' ('inter est'), or the difference between, the injured party's actual position and where that party would have been if the contract had been fulfilled. Canon lawyers adapted 'interest' to mean the difference between the lender's actual position and where he would have been if he had not made the loan. Titles to interest were called 'extrinsic' titles because they were not part of the loan contract itself, but arose from the circumstances that surrounded the loan.[99] Three such extrinsic titles to interest were discussed by theologians as well as canonists.

The first was really a fusion of two ideas. One idea was that there should be a penalty for failure to repay a loan by the agreed date in order to discourage borrowers from defaulting. The other was that lenders deserved compensation for any losses that they actually suffered when a borrower delayed repayment until after the agreed date. The distinction between penalty and compensation was frequently blurred and indeed lost altogether.[100] Thus Thomas of Chobham in the early thirteenth century believed that borrowers who delayed repayment until after the agreed date should pay a penalty, worrying that the lender might otherwise lose his home, be unable to buy goods at market, or find it impossible to pay for his daughter's wedding.[101] Aquinas was clear that 'the lender incurs loss in one way because the borrower does not return the money lent at the specified date, and then the borrower is obliged to pay compensation'.[102] Giles of Lessines agreed that the lender could demand compensation 'for all damage incurred owing to default in repayment'.[103] It was also agreed, however, that it would

[98] ST 2a2ae.78.2 (vol. 38, p. 243).
[99] Noonan, *Scholastic Analysis of Usury*, pp. 105–6; Wood, *Medieval Economic Thought*, pp. 181–2, 187; Kaye, *Economy and Nature*, pp. 183–4; Baldwin, *Masters, Princes and Merchants*, vol. 1, p. 282.
[100] Noonan, *Scholastic Analysis of Usury*, pp. 107–9; Wood, *Medieval Economic Thought*, pp. 188–9.
[101] Langholm, *Economics in the Medieval Schools*, pp. 60–1; Wood, *Medieval Economic Thought*, p. 190.
[102] Thomas Aquinas, *On Evil*, 13.4.ad14, p. 403.
[103] As quoted by Langholm, *Economics in the Medieval Schools*, p. 319.

be usury if the lender intended that the borrower should fail to repay on time and have to pay a penalty. As Duns Scotus put it in the early fourteenth century, 'A manifest sign that a penalty is not in fraud of usury is this: the merchant prefers to have his money returned to him on the agreed day, than to have it tomorrow with the penalty added.'[104] Provided that there was no usurious intention, however, the lender's title to this form of interest was uncontentious.

The other two extrinsic titles caused much more uncertainty. It could be argued that the lender should be compensated for losses or damages that he suffered because he had lent his money, even though the money was repaid on time; interest was justified in terms of 'loss occurring', or *damnum emergens*. It could also be argued that the lender should be compensated for profit that he was not making with the money he had loaned; in this case interest was justified in terms of 'profit ceasing', or *lucrum cessans*. There was, however, extreme reluctance amongst the theologians to countenance payment of interest from the beginning of a loan. Until the second half of the thirteenth century, *damnum emergens* and *lucrum cessans* were barely discussed. Only Robert of Courson envisaged a borrower who worried about the lender not having made profits with the money that he had lent, but Robert dismissed these anxieties and did not permit any compensation to be paid from the start of the loan.[105] In his *Summa Theologiae* Thomas Aquinas apparently allowed compensation for loss from the beginning of a loan: 'Somebody who makes a loan is within his rights to settle terms of compensation for the loss of any advantage which he is entitled to enjoy, for this does not amount to selling the use of money, but is a question of avoiding loss.'[106] But in *De Malo* he clearly condemned this arrangement. As we have seen, he said that the lender might suffer loss in one way if repayment was delayed, and then compensation was due. Aquinas continued: 'The lender incurs loss in a second way when the borrower returns the money lent within the specified time, and then the borrower is not obliged to pay compensation, since the lender ought to have taken precautions against loss to self, and the borrower ought not incur loss regarding the lender's stupidity.'[107] Aquinas thus held that it was the lender's responsibility not to lend if he would thereby lose, and the borrower did not have to compensate him for any misjudgement. In the *Summa Theologiae* he clearly rejected compensation for profit that

[104] As quoted by Noonan, *Scholastic Analysis of Usury*, p. 107.
[105] *Ibid.*, p. 116.
[106] ST 2a2ae.78.2.ad1 (vol. 38, p. 243).
[107] Thomas Aquinas, *On Evil*, 13.4.ad14, p. 403.

the lender might have made: 'One is, however, not entitled to make a contract to secure compensation for the loss that consists in not being able to use the money lent in order to make a profit, because one should not sell something which one has not yet got and which one may be prevented in many ways from getting.'[108] While perhaps creating some confusion about *damnum emergens*, Aquinas did not ultimately envisage payment of interest from the start of a loan.[109] Perhaps the first scholar clearly to envisage payment of interest from the start of a loan as compensation for *lucrum cessans* was the canon lawyer Hostiensis, though he still insisted that the lender's motives must be charitable and that he should not be an established usurer.[110] This stance attracted very little support from the theologians. Only Peter Olivi in the late thirteenth century and Gerald Odonis in the early fourteenth century made cases for *lucrum cessans*, subject to the provision that the lender had had serious plans to use the money to make a profit by trade before he lent it.[111] The overwhelming majority of Parisian masters continued to ignore or condemn extrinsic titles to interest unless repayment had been delayed.[112] It was not until the fifteenth century that interest payments from the start of a loan received substantial academic support.[113] Parisian theologians of the thirteenth and early fourteenth centuries did little to justify charging for credit through analysis of extrinsic titles to interest.

Much more significant in this regard was the way in which they set about scrutinizing a whole host of financial contracts to establish whether or not they were usurious. In part they needed to know how to advise merchants and bankers so that they could avoid sin, but they were also perfectly well aware that some contracts were designed specifically to evade the usury ban, and it was their responsibility to expose usurers. The result, however, was not simply to identify usurious practices but also to establish that some practices were perfectly licit, or that they were licit if conducted in particular ways. The overall effect of their work was to justify and legitimize a significant part of the urban economy.

To give only a few of the main examples, they repeatedly discussed credit sales in which either the buyer paid a higher price in return for

[108] ST 2a2ae.78.2.ad1 (vol. 38, p. 243).

[109] See Noonan, *Scholastic Analysis of Usury*, pp. 117–18; Langholm, *Economics in the Medieval Schools*, pp. 245–6.

[110] Kaye, *Economy and Nature*, pp. 84–5; Noonan, *Scholastic Analysis of Usury*, p. 118; Wood, *Medieval Economic Thought*, p. 191.

[111] Kaye, *Economy and Nature*, p. 119; Langholm, *Economics in the Medieval Schools*, pp. 370, 526–7, but note Langholm's caution.

[112] Noonan, *Scholastic Analysis of Usury*, p. 119.

[113] *Ibid.*, pp. 121–8; Wood, *Medieval Economic Thought*, p. 183.

delayed payment, or the seller accepted a lower price in return for delayed delivery. They analysed many different kinds of partnership in which the parties contributed different proportions of capital and labour on a variety of terms. They considered mortgage contracts in which income-producing property was held as security for a loan, and the lender kept the income produced by the property until the principal was repaid. They debated exchange contracts which often involved not simply the immediate exchange of one type of coinage for another, but rather a delay between an initial payment in one currency in one place and repayment in another currency in another place, or even exchange into a different currency and then back again in the same place (known as 'dry exchange'). All these contracts could be used to extend credit in some way.

So were these various contracts usurious or not? One of the strategies frequently adopted by the masters was to assess them in terms of the bearing of risk. With credit sales, for example, the theologians of the early thirteenth century accepted the view of Pope Alexander III that the contract was usurious if the future price of the goods was so certain that delayed payment was bound to give the seller a profit. If, however, the market was uncertain, and the seller took a risk, the contract was not usurious. The contract could be tested by turning to an expert, a 'good man' who was familiar with fluctuations in the market. If he could predict the future price, there was usury; if he could not, the credit sale was licit.[114] Similarly, profits made by those who invested money in partnerships were more likely to be deemed licit if the investors bore their share of the risk. The decretal *Naviganti* specifically ruled against this, but it was often ignored, not least by Aquinas in the passage quoted above.[115] This is just to scratch the surface of debates about credit sales and partnerships, but it allows us to begin to answer a question posed earlier. Why did the masters of theology devote so much effort to the discovery of arguments against usury when it could be condemned unequivocally on the basis of authority? The explanation is perhaps that the authorities offered no way of establishing whether or not specific contracts were usurious. The arguments against usury, however, could be deployed to differentiate between the licit and the illicit in particular cases. The basic

[114] Baldwin, *Masters, Princes and Merchants*, vol. 1, pp. 274–5; Langholm, *Economics in the Medieval Schools*, pp. 50, 61.

[115] Langholm, *Economics in the Medieval Schools*, pp. 112–13; Wood, *Medieval Economic Thought*, pp. 193–6.

principle was constantly re-examined, not because it was in the slightest doubt, but because ways had to be found to apply the principle. Practical concerns thus lay behind the most abstract and theoretical discussions of basic principles.

Annuities: a case study

In order to grasp the full significance of the masters' work, however, it is necessary to explore their handling of a specific type of contract in detail. Disputations about annuities offer a valuable case study in part because they have received less attention than debates about other contracts. More importantly, it is possible in this case to follow very closely the interaction between masters, both intellectual and emotional, that ultimately resulted in a consensus justifying what was actually happening in contemporary society. Furthermore, tracking this process reveals some fundamental shifts in the ways of thinking that underpinned specific arguments. The masters' intellectual strategies had important social implications.

In the second half of the thirteenth century, the masters of theology at the University of Paris conducted a long-running debate about life annuities and perpetual annuities, which they called life rents (*redditus ad vitam*) and eternal rents (*redditus perpetui*). The buyer of a life rent gave a lump sum of money to the seller in return for annual rent payments for the rest of the buyer's life. In the case of an eternal rent, the seller made annual payments to the buyer and his or her heirs in perpetuity. Sometimes the buyer was the weaker party and purchased a life rent from some corporate body in order to secure a regular income. On other occasions, however, the seller was the weaker party and entered the contract because of an urgent need for ready money. The debate was chiefly played out in the course of quodlibetal disputations held between the mid 1260s and 1290. It saw Henry of Ghent take a lonely stand against a host of other masters, including Matthew of Aquasparta, Servais of Mont Saint Eloi, Richard of Middleton and Godfrey of Fontaines. Henry maintained that such contracts were illicit according to their form, which meant that they were wrong in every case. The other masters argued that they were legitimate in form, so that whether or not a particular contract was acceptable depended on circumstances. Only Giles of Rome offered Henry some belated support.

The matter of annuities was first raised at some point between 1265 and 1269 when Gerard of Abbeville was asked whether it was licit to buy life rents, and whether those who received anything beyond the principal as a result of such purchases were bound to make restitution.[116] Gerard effectively declined to answer the full question, considering only whether a cleric could licitly buy a life rent from a church or a monastery. If the cleric had not yet received a benefice or his benefice was inadequate, Gerard declared that such a purchase was licit for three reasons. First, the sale benefited the church. It received money straightaway which it could put to many good uses. Furthermore, if the buyer died within a short time, the church or monastery stood to make a considerable gain. If, on the other hand, he lived so long that he was receiving more in total than he had originally paid, the church could rescind the contract. Second, the contract was licit because of doubt about when the buyer would die. Gerard's point, although he did not elaborate, was that the buyer could not be sure of the total value of the rent payments he would receive. Gerard cited Alexander III's decretal *Naviganti* to show how usury was removed by this kind of uncertainty. Third, the buyer also gained because he would enjoy the pension for the rest of his life rather than seeing his money entirely consumed through immediate use. Furthermore, if there was any question of sin in this situation, it pertained not to the buyer but to the seller since the seller might benefit from the delay in payment. This brought Gregory IX's decretal *In civitate* into play, although here again doubt would clear the seller of blame. Moreover, if the seller received more than the just price, the buyer could rescind the contract or obtain restitution of part of the price. None of these arguments applied, however, when a cleric enjoyed an adequate income: were such a man to buy a life rent, he would be acting out of cupidity. Gerard did not develop his arguments very fully and only envisaged their application in particular circumstances. Essentially he accepted that an impoverished cleric could licitly buy a life rent from a church or monastery because there was doubt about who would come off best and because the benefits were mutual. Moreover, he did not see equality in exchange as a problem. While the church would gain if the buyer died within a short time, in every other case anyone who lost out could simply

[116] Quodlibet I.15. Ed. F. Veraja, *Le origini della controversia teologica sul contratto di censo nel xiii secolo*, Storia ed economia 7 (Rome, 1960), pp. 199–200. See also *ibid.*, pp. 52–5; Langholm, *Economics in the Medieval Schools*, pp. 281–2; I. P. Wei, 'Intellectuals and money: Parisian disputations about annuities in the thirteenth century', *Bulletin of the John Rylands University Library of Manchester* 83, no. 3 (2001), a special edition further titled P. D. Clarke (ed.), *Owens's Historical Essays in Honour of Jeffrey H. Denton*, pp. 71–94 at 73–4.

rescind the contract. Presumably Gerard did not consider the purchase of life rents to be controversial. Henry of Ghent was soon to change this, at least within the university.

In 1276 Henry of Ghent was asked whether it was licit to buy life rents.[117] He began by investigating the nature of usury. He cited Aristotle's views, condemning usury because it involved money reproducing itself, and stressing that usury was against natural law and not just positive law. He then outlined Thomas Aquinas' natural law argument against usury, adopting his distinction between things whose use and substance were distinct, and things whose use and substance were identical because their use involved the consumption or alienation of their substance. Henry then moved on to the issue of life rents. He pointed out that if someone gave a sum of money in return for an annual payment for the rest of his life, after a certain number of years he would have recovered his principal and received an additional sum. It would, however, be more pious to give the same original sum and to receive it back all at once after the same period of time with the same additional sum, and yet that would be manifest usury. To purchase a life rent in the hope of receiving something beyond the principal if one lived long enough was therefore even more clearly usurious. Henry stressed that what the buyer of the life rent eventually received was irrelevant; usury lay simply in the hope of receiving more than the principal. The form of the life rent contract was therefore flawed. He added, perhaps with Gerard of Abbeville in mind, that this applied equally to pensions bought from churches.

Henry went on to examine arguments previously cited by canonists. In so doing he noted that since usury was against divine and natural law, theologians and philosophers should be consulted about the form of usurious contracts rather than lawyers. It had been argued that life rent contracts were illicit because the seller could so easily come to sin by desiring the buyer's death which would relieve the seller of the burden of making annual payments. But, Henry objected, this did not involve the buyer in any sin. The life rent contract had also been condemned because the buyer made a riskless profit. But Henry did not accept that risk excused usury. In any case, the buyer did take a risk, the risk that he would die early and lose both principal and profit. Yet this did nothing to legitimate the contract which was usurious because

[117] Quodlibet I.39. *Henrici de Gandavo Quodlibet I*, ed. R. Macken (Leuven, 1979), pp. 209–18. See also Kaye, *Economy and Nature*, pp. 108–9; Langholm, *Economics in the Medieval Schools*, pp. 266, 272, 273, 298; E. Marmursztejn, *L'autorité des maîtres: scolastique, normes et société au xiiie siècle* (Paris, 2007), pp. 196–8, 201, 206; Veraja, *Le origini*, pp. 55–62; Wei, 'Intellectuals and money', pp. 74–6.

of the buyer's hope and intention of receiving more than the principal if he lived long enough. If someone lent ten pounds on the understanding that he would receive twelve pounds at the end of the year, adding that nothing at all need be paid to anyone if he died in the meantime, there would still be usury, despite the uncertainty introduced by the last clause, because the lender hoped to live to the end of the year and receive more than he gave. The form of the life rent contract was identical and was therefore straightforwardly usurious. Henry thus condemned the purchase of life rents in all circumstances.

In the following year, 1277, Henry was brought back to the topic of life rents when he was asked whether it was licit to sell them.[118] Clearly there had been criticism of his earlier treatment of the issue and Henry was very much on the defensive. He supposed that the question was put because it was the converse of the question about buying life rents. He had determined buying life rents to be illicit, and he gathered that this had caused displeasure. He called on God to witness that he had simply spoken the truth as he saw it, and not out of favour or hatred for anyone. The truth still appeared to him exactly as he had said. If the church took a different line, he would obey in this matter, as in all others. However, he was a little more certain of his ground than before since 'great men' had told him that they agreed with him. Furthermore, one even claimed to have seen two papal bulls condemning the purchase of life rents and ordering restitution of anything received beyond the principal.

Turning to the question about selling life rents, Henry recalled what he had said the previous year about equality in exchange when asked about buying cheap and selling dear.[119] No one wished genuinely and when fully informed to give more than they received. If they did give more than they received, they either felt now that they were forced by necessity, or would come to feel deceived when they became aware of the imbalance. Yet in a life rent contract the seller intended to repay less than he had received from the buyer, hoping that the buyer would live for a shorter time to make this possible. This was usury, and the contract was therefore illicit for the seller in exactly the same way as it was illicit for the buyer. Henry then considered a case where the seller accepted money and in return granted property to the buyer from which he could take the profits for the rest of his life. This too must be illicit

[118] Quodlibet II.15. *Henrici de Gandavo Quodlibet II*, ed. R. Wielockx (Leuven, 1983), pp. 96–101. See also Kaye, *Economy and Nature*, pp. 109–10; Langholm, *Economics in the Medieval Schools*, p. 273; Marmursztejn, *L'autorité des maîtres*, pp. 197, 206–7; Veraja, *Le origini*, pp. 62–9; Wei, 'Intellectuals and money', pp. 76–7.

[119] Quodlibet I.40. *Henrici de Gandavo Quodlibet I*, pp. 219–30.

because the seller hoped for the buyer's early death, and in entering the contract judged that the buyer's income from the property would be worth less than the money he had given. Henry acknowledged that the seller might initially enter the contract because of an urgent need for ready money and without hoping that the buyer would receive less in the end. But if the buyer died soon and received less than he initially gave, Henry did not see by what title in natural justice the seller could retain what was left of the payment made by the buyer, for which the seller had given nothing in return.

Finally, Henry showed how the criticism of his earlier determination had shaken him. If those with power over human possessions used human positive law to depart from the equality of natural law, he did not wish to discuss it. Statutes of positive law ought to be derived from the first rules of nature and be compatible with them. If written laws seemed to conflict with anything he had inferred from natural law, he believed that proper exposition would reveal that they were in fact concerned with different cases. If the church judged that he had misinterpreted natural law in these questions, he was ready to agree. At the end he did not wish to make any formal determination, but he repeated that it seemed to him equally as illicit to sell life rents in the hope of receiving more as it was to buy them in the same hope. Henry thus maintained his complete rejection of life rents, adding that the seller sinned in much the same way as the buyer.

A very different approach was taken by Matthew of Aquasparta. In the academic year 1277–8, he was asked whether it was licit to buy life rents, with annual rent payments made in either money or fixed measures of corn and wine.[120] Matthew began by noting that both theologians and lawyers held differing opinions on this matter. Some held the contract to be just and licit. Although it involved a certain inequality, this inequality was uncertain. Uncertainty about when the buyer would die meant that the buyer might receive more than the original price if he lived a long time or less if he died soon, and this created a kind of equality. Support for this position could be found in the decretals *In civitate* and *Naviganti*: when payment for goods was to be delayed, they permitted the charging of prices above their current value as long as the future value of the goods was uncertain. But Matthew thought that this left matters too open. If uncertainty alone justified a contract, it would seem to legitimate huge and plainly

[120] Quodlibet I.9. Ed. Veraja, *Le origini*, pp. 201–3. See also *ibid.*, pp. 69–73; Langholm, *Economics in the Medieval Schools*, pp. 325–7; Marmursztejn, *L'autorité des maîtres*, pp. 208–9; Wei, 'Intellectuals and money', pp. 77–9.

unacceptable inequalities; it would even make contracts in games of dice licit, which was definitely not the case. Moreover, the decretals did not apply because they concerned goods of uncertain value whereas the life rent contract specified something definite, either so many measures of wine or corn, or so much money. Others said that the life rent contract was entirely illicit, asserting that there was usury whenever more was expected or required than had been given, and that this contract was usurious in this way. This, however, Matthew considered too strict since few contracts were entirely equal and the whole world would be in danger.

Matthew therefore proposed a 'middle way'. He began by distinguishing three types of contract. The first type was made entirely for the benefit of the receiver. This meant a loan involving things which existed in number, weight and measure. Such a loan had to be entirely free, and to charge anything for the loan was usury. The second type of contract was solely to the advantage of the giver. Thus a deposit contract entailed no benefit for the recipient. The third type of contract was advantageous for both the receiver and the giver. Under this heading Matthew listed leases, sales and barter. In these contracts the 'utility' of both parties had to be considered 'according to a certain equality'. For example, someone could lease a horse, house, field, vineyard, clothing or something of this kind, which would deteriorate but not pass into the recipient's ownership, and then receive something as just compensation for its use. Similarly when goods were bartered or sold, equality should be established. Matthew then considered how the life rent contract was to be placed in this scheme. He clearly considered the second category to be irrelevant since he did not mention it. The problem was that the life rent contract seemed to relate in some way to both the first and the third categories without fitting exactly into either. Most of all, however, it seemed to resemble a sale.

It therefore only remained to apply the notion of equality in the appropriate manner. If everything possible were done to establish equality, due consideration being given to age, health, and infirmity, the contract would be licit. Matthew then gave examples to illustrate what would and would not constitute equality in exchange. This was not a certain equality, but a probable one, based on reasonable expectation in particular cases. This pragmatic approach was very much in line with that taken by Gerard of Abbeville. Doubt about the buyer's death was a factor, but mutual benefit or equality was crucial. However, where Gerard had simply assumed that the contract was a sale, Matthew had to work his way to this conclusion. And whereas Gerard assumed that the contract would be rescinded or adjusted if inequalities emerged,

Matthew required that proper attention be given to the matter when the contract was established. But if Matthew had been much more specific than Gerard about how equality was to be established, his analysis of the form of the life rent contract had culminated in little more than an observation that it most resembled a sale. This hardly countered Henry of Ghent's arguments, and it is not surprising that debate continued.

In the academic year 1284–5 the issue of rent contracts was further considered by two masters, Servais of Mont Saint Eloi and Henry of Ghent. They both explored the idea that rent contracts might involve the selling of the right to receive a rent rather than the rent itself, although they came to very different conclusions. It is impossible to establish the chronological relationship between these two questions, but it has generally been assumed that Servais was earlier.[121] The sole surviving manuscript of his quodlibetal questions simply records that he was asked about the buying and selling of life rents.[122] According to Servais, numerous arguments showed that the life rent contract was fundamentally licit. Canon law texts and the church's current practice could both be cited. Moreover, since it was licit to buy eternal rents, it must be licit to buy life rents. Finally, a life rent did not mean that the buyer received more than he had given, as some seemed to suggest. In fact the buyer received something indeterminate, or rather 'the right to receive a rent for the rest of his life' whose value was therefore indeterminate.

Servais then observed that although the contract was licit it could be abused in many ways and it was perhaps because of this that many worthy men held it to be illicit. They were wrong to argue from specific abuses in this way but it was necessary to examine particular cases to establish the rules. The buyer must not proceed if he estimated that he would probably receive substantially more than he paid out; this would be to do serious harm to his neighbour. An impoverished seller must not be forced by necessity to sell at a loss by a buyer prosperous enough to make him the loan which he really needed. The buyer must not be a cleric with adequate means of support, for clerics should not involve themselves in secular affairs. The contract must not be used to conceal a loan at usury. Rent payments must not be spent on dissolute or extravagant living. They could, however, be spent out of devotion, to permit study or contemplation for example, or on the provision of necessities;

[121] Veraja, *Le origini*, pp. 101, 106, 178; Langholm, *Economics in the Medieval Schools*, p. 288.

[122] Quodlibetal question 25. Ed. Veraja, *Le origini*, pp. 203–4. See also *ibid.*, pp. 101–6; Langholm, *Economics in the Medieval Schools*, pp. 287–8; Marmursztejn, *L'autorité des maîtres*, pp. 209–10; Wei, 'Intellectuals and money', pp. 79–80.

poor scholars and beguines did this, or others did it on their behalf. Similarly, sellers must act out of necessity or out of charity, wishing to help buyers bodily or spiritually. Finally, Servais noted that while it was licit to sell life rents because this involved something good, namely providing for the maintenance of life, it was not licit to sell fixed term rents since this did not involve the same good. The surviving text does little to clarify why Servais took this position. Presumably he objected since what the buyer received was fixed rather than indeterminate, and in practice the buyer invariably received payments which were greater in total than the sum he originally paid.[123] Perhaps he also had in mind the kind of person who bought this kind of contract and the motivation which lay behind it; as he had already indicated, poor scholars and beguines purchased life rents to supply their basic needs, whereas fixed term rents were more likely to be bought by people who wished to make a profit. Servais thus took a similar line to Gerard of Abbeville and Matthew of Aquasparta in that he regarded the life rent contract as a genuine sales contract and he focused attention on the specific circumstances which would determine whether or not the transaction was legitimate. On the other hand, he had a significantly different view of what was sold, namely a right to receive a rent rather than the payments themselves.

Either shortly before or shortly after Servais considered life rents, Henry of Ghent was asked whether it was licit to buy eternal rents.[124] He began by distinguishing between a loan and a sale. A loan must be freely made, without hope of receiving more in return. A sale required equality according to commutative justice. In a sale money was not an 'end' but a 'means'. By this Henry meant that money could not be an object of exchange; it could not be bought or sold. Money was rather the 'means' by which commodities (as 'ends') could be bought or sold.[125] Thus contracts involving money as an 'end' were loans, and hoping to receive something for giving this money was plainly usurious. If therefore money were given without any question of a sale, and it was to be repaid all at once after a certain time along with something beyond the principal, no one doubted that the contract was usurious. If the money were given in the same way in return for annual payments and with the intention that these payments should exceed the original principal,

[123] See Veraja, *Le origini*, p. 105.
[124] Quodlibet VIII.24. *Aurea quodlibeta*, 2 vols. (Venice, 1613), vol. 2, f. 46v–47r. See also Langholm, *Economics in the Medieval Schools*, pp. 271, 274, 298, 339; Marmursztejn, *L'autorité des maîtres*, pp. 209, 212–13; Veraja, *Le origini*, pp. 106–11; Wei, 'Intellectuals and money', pp. 80–2.
[125] See Langholm, *Economics in the Medieval Schools*, p. 271.

Henry did not see how the contract could be anything other than certainly usurious. It made no difference whether the payments were made for life or in perpetuity, unless it was greater cupidity to receive beyond the principal for eternity rather than for the limited period of a life. Henry had apparently answered the original question in so far as it demanded a comparison between life and eternal rents. He continued his analysis, however, because he wished to introduce what was in effect a softening in his hard line against both life and eternal rents.

Those who justified the life rent contract maintained that it was a type of sale. Henry pointed out that life and eternal rents were not really 'bought', although this terminology was used to disguise the offence. In fact the 'ends' of the contract consisted of money, first given in a lump sum and then received in annual payments. It was therefore a pure loan contract. If there were genuinely to be a sale, another contract would have to be involved, or rather two contracts revolving around a legitimate object of exchange, such as a farm. This could work in two ways. In the first way, the so-called buyer of the rent used his money to purchase a farm which he then resold to the so-called seller of the rent (possibly the same person from whom he had just bought the farm) in return for annual monetary payments, either for life or in perpetuity. In the second way, the buyer of the rent purchased it from a seller 'to whom it was owed by right of sale'. This meant that the seller had either sold a farm in return for annual monetary payments in perpetuity, or he had given away ownership of the farm while reserving these payments for his own use. If he then wished to sell this rent and all his rights to it, it was licit for another to buy them. The buyer would not be deemed to be giving money for the rent, but for the seller's right to receive it. Henry tried to clarify this by explaining that with regard to receiving the rent the buyer and the seller would be deemed the same person, and the sale made by one would be deemed to have been made by the other too. In these two ways it was therefore licit to buy a rent, either for life or in perpetuity, without sin. The crucial point was that in these two cases money became a means and not an end of exchange. There was therefore a legitimate sale contract and not a loan.

Henry illustrated the significance of the form of the contract by running through some examples which might seem similar but were in fact very different. As he had already admitted, a farm owner could sell his farm in return for annual payments in perpetuity and then sell the right to receive these payments in return for a lump sum. This was licit in the second way already described. Another owner of a similar farm could not, however, simply create an obligation for annual payments to be made in perpetuity from his farm's income in return for a lump sum. This was illicit because nothing was sold and the farm was just used as security. On the other hand, the person wishing to buy an eternal rent from this owner could secure the same annual income if he bought the farm, so that it was genuinely his, and then sold it back to the original owner in return for annual payments in perpetuity. This was licit in the first way described above.

Henry had thus moved away from his complete rejection of life and eternal rent contracts since he now regarded them as licit in some circumstances when a legitimate object of exchange was involved. His use of a farm to illustrate his arguments suggests that it was also important that the object of exchange should be fruitbearing property, although he did not state this explicitly at any stage.[126] He still insisted, however, that in every other case the contracts constituted loans and not sales, and were therefore illicit according to their form. Like Servais, he accepted that a right to receive a rent could properly be sold, but he had a very restricted view of how such a right could be acquired in the first place. Despite the shift in his position, Henry's view was still fundamentally different from those held by Gerard of Abbeville, Matthew of Aquasparta and Servais of Mont Saint Eloi, and he continued to reject life and eternal rents in most cases.

In 1285 Richard of Middleton joined the opposition to Henry when invited to consider whether it was licit to buy or sell life rents.[127] He began by explaining how profits could justly be made from buying and selling. His crucial point was that goods of equal value in themselves were not of equal use to everyone because they were not everywhere in equal supply. So if a merchant took corn from an area of abundance to an area of scarcity and sold it for more money than he would have received in the area of abundance, the exchange was just because he did not give more than he received in the place where he sold the corn, and because the buyers also profited since they were helped in their need. Richard then defined various different types of contract to which he would refer in his analysis. Most importantly, he said that a loan involved transfer of ownership and that it must be freely given. In a sale, however, something was given for a price.

[126] *Ibid.*, p. 274, considers it to be Henry's point 'that certain kinds of real property are eternally fruitbearing', and that fruitbearing property must be involved in these contracts.

[127] Quodlibet II.23 (II.22 in Glorieux, *La Littérature quodlibétique*, vol. 1, p. 269). *Quolibeta doctoris eximii Ricardi de Mediavilla ordinis minorum* (Brescia, 1591; repr. Frankfurt am Main, 1963), pp. 65–71. See also Langholm, *Economics in the Medieval Schools*, pp. 330–41; Marmursztejn, *L'autorité des maîtres*, pp. 210–11, 213; Veraja, *Le origini*, pp. 111–23; Wei, 'Intellectuals and money', pp. 82–5.

Turning to a case repeatedly condemned by Henry of Ghent, Richard then explained why it was licit to buy or sell land which would belong to the buyer for his lifetime and then revert to the seller. Such a contract was neither usurious nor illicit according to its form, although it could be illicit in particular cases. It was a sale contract, and natural law therefore required equality in the exchange between buyer and seller. A minor inequality could be tolerated, but the contract was invalid according to law if the actual price exceeded or fell short of the just price by more than half that just price, and according to the forum of conscience if either party was obviously injured (even if the price fell within half the just price). In the case of a farm, for example, consideration would have to be given to the size of the farm, the buyer's age and health, risk which might shorten the buyer's life, risk to the farm's yield, and the labour and care required of the buyer to secure the yield. When it was unclear whether the buyer or the seller had the better deal, the contract was licit. If the buyer then died before recovering his money from the fruits of the farm, the seller was not bound to restore anything to the buyer's heirs. If the buyer lived long enough to receive more than he originally paid, he was not bound to make restitution to the seller. On the other hand, when it was obvious from the start that one or other party had the better deal, the contract was illicit.

Next Richard considered whether it was licit to buy monetary life rents. He did not name Henry of Ghent, but he noted his view that the contract was illicit according to its form. Richard rehearsed the argument that there was no genuine sale because money had been invented to be a measure and price of things which were bought and sold, and not to be bought and sold itself. When money was bought, as in the case of life rents, there was in fact a loan. But in a loan contract it was usury to receive anything beyond the principal. Richard, however, took a different view, developing an idea already used by Servais of Mont Saint Eloi and in a more limited way by Henry of Ghent himself. What the buyer bought was not actually money, but the right to receive a certain sum of money annually for life. The right to receive money was not money itself, so money was not bought. The contract therefore embodied not a loan but a proper sale. The contract was therefore not illicit according to its form. Richard noted that someone else (whom he did not name) preferred to put it another way, saying that the buyer bought not money but the seller's obligation to give a certain sum of money annually. Richard, however, felt his own version sounded better.

Richard added that in God's eyes it made no difference whether a life rent were bought directly or indirectly. Those who refused to accept the life rent contract admitted that a man could licitly buy a farm and then sell it for the period of his lifetime in return for annual monetary payments. Having paid out a lump sum, this man would now receive annual payments for the rest of his life. Although Richard did not name him, Henry of Ghent had indeed conceded that this arrangement was acceptable. If, however, it was licit to acquire a life rent in this indirect fashion, Richard argued that it could be done directly. Again he concluded that the life rent contract was not illicit according to its form.

This did not, however, mean that the life rent contract was licit in every case. It was licit when there was equality between buyer and seller as required by natural law, when due weight had been given to the buyer's age and health, risk to his life and other circumstances, when the price had been considered, and when it was not easy to tell who had the better deal. If the buyer then died before recovering the principal, the seller was not obliged to restore any of the price. If the buyer lived long enough to receive more than he paid, he was not obliged to restore anything. But if the buyer clearly had the better of the deal and had paid too little, the contract was illicit and he was bound either to make up the just price or return what he had received beyond the principal. If, on the other hand, the seller clearly enjoyed the better deal, having received too high a price, the contract was again illicit and he was obliged to return what he had received beyond the just price or leave whatever had been bought in the possession of the buyer's heir until he had recovered the principal.

Richard then applied exactly the same sequence of arguments to explain why it was licit to buy either land or a monetary rent not only for a lifetime but also in perpetuity. In a subsequent section in which he explored doubts about his analysis, he recognized concern that when land or rents were purchased in perpetuity an equal exchange was impossible because the buyer or his heirs must inevitably receive more than they originally paid. He pointed out, however, that according to natural law one loved a thing more for oneself than for one's son, and more for one's son than for one's grandson, and so on. The price should be determined with this in mind, up to an agreed point.

In the section exploring doubts, Richard mostly repeated his earlier arguments. He did, however, expand on their practical implications. He noted that one might query his view that buying land or rent for life was illicit when the buyer clearly had the better deal. For it was possible to observe twenty-five-year-old men and women buying life rents at a price which would allow them to recover their principal within eight years. Although they could die within eight years, it was far more probable that they would live twice as long. The buyers plainly had the better deal and the inequality in the contracts seemed blatant. Yet far from being condemned by law, such contracts were tolerated by the church and recommended by many wise men. According to Richard, such contracts might be justified if illness or exposure to danger were so great as to make it unclear whether the buyer would most probably live for eight years or die in the meantime. Alternatively, the contract might be reduced to equality if some danger threatened delivery of whatever had been bought and there was therefore doubt about whether the buyer would enjoy peaceful possession of the rent or land. But Richard insisted that ordinarily such contracts were inexcusable in the forum of conscience. He did not therefore intend to legitimate much current practice as he perceived it. Like Gerard of Abbeville, Matthew of Aquasparta and Servais of Mont Saint Eloi, however, he accepted life rent contracts as a form of sale, so that whether or not particular cases were licit depended on justice in exchange. Moreover, like Servais, he held that a right to receive rent was sold rather than rent itself.

Henry of Ghent was given the opportunity to re-examine this aspect of his own analysis in the academic year 1288–9, when he was asked whether it was licit to obtain a life rent from a church by giving it money to buy land.[128] Henry's determination was brief and in the affirmative. According to canon law, someone who gave his inheritance to a church could licitly retain its usufruct for the rest of his life and receive more again from the church. It was therefore certainly licit to give something to a church while merely retaining its usufruct or receiving an equivalent annual payment from the church. Furthermore, giving the church money to buy land was the same as giving an existing inheritance. It was therefore licit to give money to a church so that it could buy land and to accept a life rent in return. The current practice of the church, cited in one of the opening arguments, was acceptable.

Since the case which Henry had now approved did not fit into either of the two legitimate ways of establishing a life rent which he had outlined in 1284, his overall position was unclear. One of the opening arguments against the legitimacy of the case, however, was simply that the buying of life rents was illicit. In dealing with this, Henry was able to address the fundamental principles once more. He declared that life rents could be acquired in two ways: their acquisition either did or did not stem

[128] Quodlibet XII.21. Henry of Ghent, *Quodlibet XII, quaestiones 1–30*, ed. J. Decorte (Leuven, 1987), pp. 109–15. See also Langholm, *Economics in the Medieval Schools*, pp. 274–5, 293, 298, 340; Marmursztejn, *L'autorité des maîtres*, pp. 213–14; Veraja, *Le origini*, pp. 125–31; Wei, 'Intellectuals and money', pp. 85–6.

from a right. First, Henry considered their acquisition when it stemmed from a right. Someone who transferred his inheritance to another could retain the usufruct for his lifetime and accept a sum of money instead of the usufruct. The key point was that he possessed not only the life rent but also the right to receive the rent, because he had reserved it from his own property. Furthermore, he could licitly sell the life rent because he would be selling not only the annual payments but also the right to receive them which he retained from the property which he had originally sold. Without this right there could not be a legitimate sale. Clearly Henry had now provided a theoretical justification for his answer to the question. He went on to say that the same arguments applied to eternal rents. Someone could equally well give his inheritance to a church and reserve for himself a portion to be paid by the church in perpetual rent, although Henry thought that he should perhaps reserve less than in the case of a life rent. Similarly, both the perpetual rent and the right to receive it could licitly be sold.

There were, however, other ways in which life and perpetual rents could be acquired as a matter of right. Just title could also derive either from performance of service or pure liberality. For example, a king could give someone in return for service or out of generosity a sum of money to be paid annually for life or in perpetuity, thus putting himself, his successors and their property under an obligation. In this case the king did not principally give money, a corporeal thing, but the right to receive money, an incorporeal thing, founded on a corporeal thing upon which an obligation had been placed, and directed towards the receipt of a corporeal thing as a matter of right. Such rents could licitly be sold since the right to receive money was sold rather than money itself.

Henry then turned to the question of life and perpetual rents acquired when no right to receive money had been created. As he had determined elsewhere, these contracts were entirely illicit and their acquisition constituted a type of usury. It was not, for example, licit for someone simply to give money to a community in order to receive a certain sum of money annually for life or in perpetuity. Henry went on to give a series of examples of contracts which might be presented as life or perpetual rent contracts, but which were, as he saw it, plainly usurious. He made his position clear in his concluding remarks. While an incorporeal right to receive a sum of money was different from the money itself and could licitly be bought and sold, such a right could not be bought or sold in direct exchange for money in the first instance. It had to derive initially from a grant made out of generosity or in return for service, or from a farm or something of that kind given by the original recipient of the right. Henry had thus developed his ideas about a right to receive money, multiplying the ways in which such a right could be established. Unlike Servais of Mont Saint Eloi and Richard of Middleton, however, he did not apply this approach to rent contracts which involved money alone. For Henry, life and perpetual rent contracts were still suspect according to their form.

Henry's determination drew an immediate response from Godfrey of Fontaines who was asked whether it was licit to buy life rents and to receive payments beyond the principal.[129] First, he explained that if the rent contract was a loan contract it was illicit because loan contracts had to be made without any gain or any hope of gain on the part of the lender. If, however, the rent contract was a sale contract, with a reasonable equivalence between what was bought and the price paid, it was licit.

Godfrey then explored the view that the rent contract was not a sale contract and was therefore illicit. First, he went through the argument based on the principle that money could not be bought or sold. This meant that when the buyer of a life rent gave money hoping to receive more in return, he did not buy anything. Rather, the buyer made a loan, obliging the seller to return the principal and more, provided that the buyer lived long enough. The same applied even if the rent payments were made in the form of something like corn. Second, Godfrey put an argument to the effect that it was impossible to establish a reasonable equivalence in a life rent contract. Any attempt to do this had to focus on the lifestyle and condition of the buyer. The longer a buyer lived, the more he would receive, so a buyer who was likely to live longer had to pay more than a buyer likely to die sooner. To be licit, however, the contract could not exclude anyone, whatever their age. Godfrey therefore examined an extreme case. He supposed that a young man aged twenty and an old man aged sixty both wished to buy life rents worth ten pounds a year from a monastery. They were in similar condition for their ages and equally likely to reach the usual age of death; for the sake of argument Godfrey suggested seventy. It would seem a fair deal for the old man if he were charged sixty pounds: he would recover his capital in six years and he would probably live for ten years or more, although it was not certain. The young man, on the other hand, should pay more in proportion to the greater period of time before he reached

[129] Quodlibet V.14. *Les quodlibet cinq, six et sept de Godefroid de Fontaines*, ed. M. de Wulf and J. Hoffmans (Louvain, 1914), pp. 63–9. See also Kaye, *Economy and Nature*, pp. 110–15; Langholm, *Economics in the Medieval Schools*, pp. 293–4; Marmursztejn, *L'autorité des maîtres*, pp. 211, 213; Veraja, *Le origini*, pp. 131–43; Wei, 'Intellectuals and money', pp. 86–9.

seventy. Since the old man paid sixty pounds in return for ten pounds a year for ten years, the young man should pay three hundred pounds to receive ten pounds a year for fifty years. But these calculations made no sense given that the young man was more likely to die from various causes in the next fifty years than the old man in the next ten. Furthermore, the young man would be foolish to buy a life rent on these terms since for less than three hundred pounds he could buy property which would yield more than ten pounds a year in perpetuity. Clearly no reasonable equivalence could be established. The life rent contract was irrational and therefore illicit.

Godfrey did not, however, find these arguments acceptable. They would render illicit the purchase of any usufruct and the purchase of an eternal rent without also buying something corporeal like a farm. This ran counter to universal common practice, and Godfrey said that he did not dare to declare all these contracts illicit. He therefore set out to show how the life rent contract was licit. He began by demonstrating that the life rent contract was a true sale contract. He took the line that a life rent was a right to receive money; it was something incorporeal, different from the corporeal thing itself. Although money itself could not be bought or sold, the right to receive money could. Furthermore, it made no difference if the rent payments were made in something other than money. Although rents in, for example, wheat could be changed into money immediately, buying rent in wheat meant buying the right to receive wheat rather than wheat itself. In all rent contracts, therefore, a right rather than money was the 'end' of the sale.

Godfrey then examined the way in which Henry of Ghent had restricted the application of this approach. Although he did not name Henry at any stage, he attacked arguments which Henry had advanced both in the same academic year and previously in 1284. Godfrey had four points to make. First, Henry accepted that someone could base a life or perpetual rent on his property and give it to another person; earlier that year Henry had given the example of a king who made such a grant as a reward for service or out of generosity. Henry also accepted that giving a rent meant giving a right to receive money or some other material thing, rather than giving money itself or whatever. According to Henry, the person to whom the right was given could now sell that right. Godfrey considered it irrational that the recipient of the right could sell it while its originator could not. Moreover, if the originator could give it to the recipient freely, he should also be able to sell it to him for a sum of money. Second, Godfrey turned to Henry's view that the life or eternal rent contract was licit if another contract preceded it. In 1284 Henry had argued that if someone bought a farm from some community for a lump sum and then resold it to the same community in return for a life or perpetual rent, he could then sell the rent to another person. He would be selling the right to receive money rather than money itself. Godfrey held that the person who ended up buying the rent in this way could licitly buy it directly from the community because the second contract made no real difference. Or, to put it the other way round, if a direct purchase from the community was illicit and usurious, then so was the one of which Henry approved. Third, Godfrey argued that whatever could be priced in terms of money could be sold. Life and eternal rents could be priced because whatever could form part of an inheritance, except money, could be priced according to law, and it was clear from Henry's own examples that life and eternal rents could form part of inheritances. Henry was therefore bound to accept that rent could be sold. Fourth, Godfrey returned to Henry's example of a king who granted someone a life rent or an eternal rent. According to Henry, the recipient of this grant could sell the rent. Godfrey maintained that the king could sell the rent directly himself because what could be sold by one person could be sold by another. Evidently, Godfrey was unconvinced by Henry's limited use of the idea of a rent as a right to receive money. For him, the general application of this idea ensured that rent contracts were always genuine sale contracts.

Having established this, Godfrey turned to the question of how a fitting equivalence could be established in the purchase of a life rent or eternal rent. It could not be a question of precise equality because eternal rent payments stretched into infinity and because it was uncertain for how long life rent payments would have to be paid. Nor was it a question of analysing particular cases. The objections he had examined earlier were therefore irrelevant. Rather, it was a question of the prices which buyers and sellers collectively were prepared to accept. In other words, the just price was a common estimate established in the marketplace.

Returning to the original question, Godfrey concluded that if someone bought a life rent and received more than he had paid, he should not be said to receive anything beyond the principal as in the case of usury. Whatever he received after the moment of purchase was 'by reason of the principal and of its nature'. He therefore received what was rightfully his, provided that he had paid the just price when he bought the rent.

In a final flourish, Godfrey dismissed Henry's solution of the specific case put to him earlier that year. Henry had accepted that someone could licitly buy a life rent from a church by giving it money to buy land.

Godfrey observed that the church now had full control of the money and might not use it to buy land at all. Even so, because of the money which it had received, the church gave the buyer the right to receive a monetary rent. This was proper because a genuine sale had taken place without the need for any land to be purchased. Godfrey claimed that this was now accepted by those who had argued to the contrary. Godfrey of Fontaines thus took the same line as Servais of Mont Saint Eloi and Richard of Middleton when he presented the purchase of life and eternal rents as the purchase of the right to receive payment. He also dealt specifically with Henry of Ghent's narrowing of the circumstances in which this approach was valid. However, he also put a new stress on the role of the marketplace in establishing fairness of exchange in the purchase of rent contracts.

In 1290 it emerged that Henry of Ghent did not stand entirely alone when Giles of Rome was asked whether it was licit to buy life rents.[130] First, he explained why usury was illicit. Having considered the etymology of the word, he produced an argument in terms of the relationship between use and substance.[131] Some things could be used without alienation of their substance. It was therefore possible to sell their use while retaining ownership of their substance. Houses and horses, for example, could be leased and a charge could be made for their use while ownership was retained. This was not the case with money. The use of money involved its alienation so it was impossible grant the use of money without granting its substance too. Thus anyone who granted money intending to charge for its use sought to gain from something which did not belong to him. Giles had a taste for homespun wisdom, and he remarked that the usurer was like the proverbial man who wished to sell his garden and eat the cabbages in it. Like others who had taken this approach, Giles acknowledged that while the proper use of money was to alienate or spend it, there were also secondary uses. For example, money might be given so that someone could appear rich. In such cases granting the use of money did not involve granting its substance, so any payment received for the use of the money was not usury.

Giles found other arguments against usury unconvincing because, if valid, they should have undermined various legitimate contracts

[130] Quodlibet V.24. *B. Aegidii Columnae Romani Quodlibeta*, pp. 336–9. See also Langholm, *Economics in the Medieval Schools*, 386–9; Veraja, *Le origini*, pp. 143–5; Wei, 'Intellectuals and money', pp. 89–91.

[131] His argument differed slightly from that advanced by Thomas Aquinas, because he took the use and substance of money to be inseparable rather than identical; see Langholm, *Economics in the Medieval Schools*, p. 388.

as well. Some condemned usury because it involved the sale of time which belonged to everyone. They claimed that when someone lent ten units of some currency in return for twelve units after a year, the lender sold a period of one year. But time could be sold in other situations without sin, for example if someone gave ten horses to another on the understanding that twelve would be returned in a year. Others said that usury was illicit because, while it was legitimate to receive payment for the use of things which deteriorated in use, money did not deteriorate. But silver cups did not deteriorate, and yet one could charge for use. Similarly a book, if properly looked after, did not deteriorate through being read, and yet one could charge for use. As an experienced university teacher, Giles wisely added that a book came into this category because it should be lent on the understanding that if the book were damaged, the borrower was obliged to repair it. Others again argued that usury was illicit because, unlike other transactions, it involved no risk. But it was licit to lend something and receive a payment even if all risk had been eliminated by the taking of security or by some other means. None of these arguments satisfactorily explained the difference between licit and illicit cases. Giles' earlier arguments were therefore the ones to be followed.

Having examined usury in general, Giles explained why buying life rents involved a type of usury. In the purchase of a life rent, money was the beginning and the end of the transaction since the buyer gave money and then received money. Consequently, if the buyer made a profit, he made a profit from the use of money which was impossible without usury. This was not, however, Giles' final word. Next he set out to explain the circumstances in which life rents could be purchased licitly. His argument so far only applied to monetary life rents, and it was indeed his intention to argue in favour of life rent contracts which involved property. He therefore began by disposing of arguments which condemned these too. It had been suggested that life rents were illicit because they encouraged the seller to desire or even work for the buyer's death since this would relieve the seller of the obligation to make payments. But, Giles objected, if this were valid the pope would never grant someone the first or second prebend to become vacant at a particular church lest the man to whom he made this grant desired the death of the current holders. Moreover, one had to weigh things up *per se* rather than *per accidens*. Almost all good things could be badly used. But rhetoric was not condemned because those skilled in rhetoric knew how to pervert justice and were consequently in a position to do many wrongs. Natural intelligence was not condemned although intelligent people, if evil, could perpetrate more crimes than the stupid. So a good contract should not be condemned because someone could use it with cupidity and malice; this was accidental. Considering the matter *per se*, therefore, Giles did not see why it was wrong to buy a life rent when the proceeds from some mill, castle or land were purchased and then given in return for annual payment of a certain sum of money. Such a purchase did not involve money alone; rather, money was used to buy property or the proceeds from property for the rest of the buyer's life, and payments were received out of this. Strangely, Giles ignored recent debate about the sale of rights to receive rent. But essentially he sided with Henry of Ghent in condemning the sale of monetary life rents, while accepting contracts that involved property.

This controversy reveals a great deal about the process of debate that resulted in a consensus that justified an aspect of actual financial practice. An important type of contract was treated again and again over a period of many years. Masters were clearly aware of what their colleagues had said in previous disputations and, while usually declining to name them, engaged directly with their arguments. Views were passionately held and immediately provoked critical responses once formal proceedings were concluded. In his second quodlibet, Henry of Ghent provided a very rare glimpse of the way in which a master's determination might be received, and of the emotional strains that ensued. Clearly, very different views were expressed by the masters. Yet even if we do not entirely believe Godfrey of Fontaines' claim that everyone eventually agreed with him, the majority of masters came to regard life and eternal rents as legitimate contracts: however painfully achieved, a consensus had emerged.

How is the emergence of this consensus to be explained, and what significance should it be granted? Contrasting Godfrey of Fontaines' views with those that Henry of Ghent expressed in his first two quodlibets, Joel Kaye has identified conflicting definitions of economic equality which he takes to be indicative of shifting conceptions of the natural order.[132] According to Kaye, Henry believed that in any sales contract there was an ideal point of equality which both buyer and seller had deliberately to seek. In these terms it was impossible to achieve equality in life and eternal rents, and so they could not be justified. Godfrey, however, redefined equality in terms of the common estimate, 'made not according to any fixed value inherent in the things themselves, but according to the relative *proportions* of the usefulness of the things to the exchangers'.[133] The price was just as long as numbers of people were prepared to buy

[132] Kaye, *Economy and Nature*, pp. 101–15.
[133] *Ibid.*, p. 113 (his emphasis).

and sell at that price. With this view of equality, it was easy to justify life and eternal rents. According to Kaye, Godfrey had ‘expanded his conception of natural equality to bring it into line with the realities of market exchange’.[134] This was part of a new conception of nature that was to have profound consequences for scientific thought in the fourteenth century. While Kaye's overall thesis is very convincing, the general shifts in conceptions of nature that he describes do not underlie or explain the consensus which emerged amongst the masters with regard to life and eternal rents.[135] Godfrey of Fontaines was alone in referring to the common estimate. The other masters either shared Henry of Ghent's notion of equality, or failed to develop their view of equality in sufficient detail to permit classification within Kaye's framework. In order to understand the masters' general approval of life and eternal rents, and the way in which they responded to the money economy of the towns, it is necessary to analyse the strategies which they shared.

At the heart of the emerging consensus was a willingness to restate the problem of life and eternal rents so that it was viewed in terms of the incorporeal. As a corporeal thing, money posed all sorts of problems. The incorporeal right to receive money, however, was another matter entirely. Suddenly the difficulties evaporated: whereas money was a measure which could not properly be sold, a right was indeterminate and a legitimate object of sale. This extra layer of analysis had only to be inserted into the problem for life and eternal rents to be classified as sale contracts, permitting the masters to focus on the issue of equality in exchange. The distinction between a corporeal thing and an incorporeal right had its origins in Roman law and had been developed by canon lawyers before being applied to tithes by theologians in the early thirteenth century: only churchmen could enjoy the right to receive tithes, but the material revenues could nevertheless be granted to laymen.[136] It has also been suggested that theologians of the later thirteenth century became familiar with the notion of the right to use something during debates about voluntary poverty and the friars: arguably friars could not own property, but could have the right to use it.[137] For Henry of Ghent, however, the application of this distinction to life and eternal rents was just convenient intellectual manoeuvring, devoid of any real

134 *Ibid.*, p. 115.

135 It is not Kaye's purpose to explain this consensus, and he does not claim to do so.

136 E. Marmursztejn, ‘A normative power in the making: theological *quodlibeta* and the authority of the masters at Paris at the end of the thirteenth century’, in C. Schabel (ed.), *Theological Quodlibeta in the Middle Ages: The Thirteenth Century* (Leiden, 2006), pp. 345–402 at 400.

137 G. Ceccarelli, ‘“Whatever” economics: economic thought in *quodlibeta*’, in Schabel (ed.), *Theological Quodlibeta in the Middle Ages: The Thirteenth Century*, pp. 503–4.

connection with commercial practice, and he resisted the strategy by carefully scrutinizing the ways in which a right to receive money might be generated. Henry envisaged only two circumstances in which a right to receive money could be created and subsequently sold to establish a life or eternal rent. First, in his eighth quodlibet, he argued that a right to receive money could be created when a farm was sold in return for annual monetary payments, either for life or in perpetuity, and the right thus established could then be sold for a lump sum. Second, in his twelfth quodlibet, he argued that a king could create a right to receive money when he promised annual monetary payments, either for life or in perpetuity, as a reward for service or out of pure generosity, and this right too could be sold subsequently for a lump sum. Henry's analysis had important social implications. In the first case, he tried to retain a link between the right to receive money and corporeal, fruit-bearing property; in effect, he tied legitimation of the money economy to agrarian society. In the second case, Henry bound this same legitimation to traditional forms of authority. Other masters, however, showed no concern about how rights to receive money were created. Servais of Mont Saint Eloi, Richard of Middleton and Godfrey of Fontaines were content simply to redescribe current practices in terms of incorporeal rights, thus making life and eternal rents acceptable within their existing intellectual framework. The social implications of their strategy were, however, far more radical: no longer bound to land or royal authority, the money economy was permitted a kind of autonomy.

Underlying the masters' growing acceptance of life and eternal rents, there were also important conceptions of time and, more specifically, the future.[138] These too were a vital part of their response to a society increasingly dominated by money, merchants and towns. Historians such as Jacques Le Goff and Aron Gurevich have contrasted 'church time' with 'merchant time': 'church time' shaped by liturgy and theology, linked to the process of salvation, easily compatible with agrarian rhythms, and of long standing in medieval society; 'merchant time' linked to profit-making and credit, requiring precise measurement, and emerging in a new urban environment.[139] In discussing life and eternal rents, the masters envisaged a future which stretched on endlessly.

[138] For further discussion of this issue, see I. P. Wei, 'Predicting the future to judge the present: Paris theologians and attitudes to the future', in J. A. Burrow and I. P. Wei (eds.), *Medieval Futures: Attitudes to the Future in the Middle Ages* (Woodbridge, 2000), pp. 19–36.

[139] A. J. Gurevich, *Categories of Medieval Culture*, trans. G. L. Campbell (London, 1985), pp. 141–51; J. Le Goff, 'Merchant's time and church's time in the middle ages', in

Richard of Middleton imagined generation succeeding generation. Godfrey of Fontaines conceived of payments stretching into infinity. Despite their eschatological beliefs, there were no references here to the end of the world. But while this future apparently went on forever, it was measurable in terms of money; indeed, it had to be measured out in this way if fair deals were to be struck. Furthermore, making licit provision in this kind of future required an element of prediction. In order to establish a just price, both Matthew of Aquasparta and Richard of Middleton called for assessments of how long an individual was likely to live, taking age and health into consideration. Richard added the need to weigh the risks involved in the individual's lifestyle. The masters did not expect certain predictions, but they demanded predictions of the probable.[140] Life and eternal rents were legitimate transactions in 'merchant time'.

Living with usury: tolerating a lesser evil

Despite these fundamental shifts in thinking and the consequent discovery that some common financial practices were licit, the masters still regarded many as usurious and sinful. Moreover, these practices were often approved by secular and even ecclesiastical authorities. The masters were well aware that they lived in an imperfect world, and they accepted that usurious practices had to be tolerated as a lesser evil. Aquinas, for example, made the point that many would suffer if usury were entirely eradicated:

> The civil law leaves certain sins unpunished to accommodate imperfect men who would be severely disadvantaged if all sins were strictly prohibited by suitable sanctions. Human law, therefore, allows the taking of usury, not because it deems this to be just but because to do otherwise would impose undue restrictions on many people.[141]

He justified this further by citing the common good, making it clear that usury brought benefits:

> Positive law strives chiefly for the common good of the people. And it sometimes happens that the greatest harm comes to the community if an evil is prevented, and so positive law sometimes permits something as an exception lest

Time, Work, and Culture in the Middle Ages, trans. A. Goldhammer (Chicago, 1980), pp. 29–42.

140 The themes of measurement and probability receive perceptive treatment throughout Kaye, *Economy and Nature*.

141 ST 2a2ae.78.1.ad3 (vol. 38, p. 237). I have adjusted the translation of the final sentence to refer to usury rather than interest, thus following the Latin more closely.

the community suffer greater disadvantage, not because it is just that the thing permitted be done. For example, even God permits that some evils be done in the world so as not to prevent the good deeds that he knows how to elicit from the bad deeds. And it is in this way that positive law permits the taking of usury because of the many advantages that some gain from money lent, albeit lent subject to usury.[142]

Godfrey of Fontaines explained this position in more detail in 1295 when he was asked during a quodlibetal disputation whether secular princes and ecclesiastical prelates sinned in failing to expel usurers from their lands.[143] Godfrey argued that while princes and prelates had to destroy evil and encourage the good, their overriding concern had to be for the common good. In relation to particular evils, they had therefore to remember the weakness of their subjects and consider whether measures of sufficient severity to be effective might not arouse more numerous and greater evils which would be more difficult to extirpate. The good prince should not seek to destroy evils which required measures of this kind. So, for example, prostitution was permitted lest greater evils result from the penalties needed to eradicate it. Thus something which was evil on its own might be good in relation to other things, in so far as through it many goods things might sometimes be preserved and many ills prevented. Turning to the question of usurers, Godfrey argued that those who did such harm that the benefits which they brought did not make up for it were evil both in themselves and in relation to the good of the community, and should be thrown out. This was why the Council of Lyons in 1274 had ordered the expulsion of foreign usurers.[144] Foreign usurers impoverished the land in which they lived because they sent the money which they acquired through usury to their own lands and did not usually make restitution when they died. Princes who protected them sinned gravely because they acted not only against the constitution of the Council but also against natural

142 Thomas Aquinas, *On Evil*, 13.4.ad6, p. 402. I have adjusted the translation of the final sentence to refer to usury rather than interest, thus following the Latin more closely.

143 Quodlibet XII.9. *Les quodlibets onze-quartorze de Godefroid de Fontaines*, ed. J. Hoffmans (Louvain, 1932), pp. 114–18. See also Langholm, *Economics in the Medieval Schools*, p. 295. Especially for examples of kings who had recently expelled foreign usurers and Jews, see Marmursztejn, 'A normative power in the making', pp. 382–5; Marmursztejn, *L'autorité des maîtres*, pp. 145–9.

144 *Liber Sextus Decretalium*, lib. V, tit. V (De Usuris), cap. I (Usurarum voraginem); *Corpus iuris canonici*, ed. E. Friedberg, 2 vols. (Leipzig, 1879–81), vol. 2, p. 1081. See also T. P. McLaughlin, 'The teaching of the canonists on usury (XII, XIII and XIV centuries)', *Mediaeval Studies* 2 (1940): 1–22 at 3; Gilchrist, *Church and Economic Activity*, pp. 109–10.

law, since they neglected the good of their subjects in failing to prohibit the losses which afflicted them. Moreover, since these foreigners could not remain as usurers unless the princes protected them and helped their business by forcing debtors to pay up, such princes were participants in all their evils. It was different with native usurers, however. If they grew rich through taking usury from others' property, they did not impoverish the land because they passed their goods on to their family and friends in that land, and many made restitution to those from whom they had taken usury. Moreover, the princes could not treat them differently from their other subjects and thus they could be said to permit their actions rather than to participate in them. Native usurers could therefore be tolerated if they were not too numerous, did not exact immoderate rates of usury, and appeared to bring many benefits rather than evils to the community. Human laws therefore permitted the taking of usury in this case. Nevertheless, when evils were tolerated for these reasons princes must diligently impose some penalties on those who perpetrated them so that they did less harm to the community. Thus, for example, although prostitutes were tolerated, they were not permitted to stand in respectable places nor treated with reverence or honour. This was why the church, which was more concerned than secular judges with the salvation of souls and the eradication of vices, usually proceeded against such usurers through ecclesiastical censures. Godfrey concluded that the question seemed to refer only to foreign usurers and that they should certainly be expelled. This was required both by the Council of Lyons and by natural law. Those who failed to comply should incur the ecclesiastical penalties decreed by the Council, which Godfrey proceeded to explain.[145]

So, according to Godfrey, usury was rightly tolerated when practised by native usurers because their wealth would remain within the community. This was partly because they were more likely to make restitution, but it was also because they would pass their wealth on to other members of the community. On the face of it, this was an astonishing thing to say because, as has already been remarked, usury was perceived as a threat to the whole community precisely because usurious goods and money were likely to pass from the usurer to others, potentially leading them into sin. The process of accommodation with an imperfect world was, however, more subtle than simply finding reasons to tolerate usury, and involved a quiet and surprising shift in attitudes to

[145] For other views on the toleration of usury as a lesser evil, see Noonan, *Scholastic Analysis of Usury*, pp. 34, 73.

money. Embedded within their arguments, though never highlighted, was the idea that dealing in money had spiritual advantages.

Living with usury: usurious money

A significant number of quodlibetal disputations concerned moral problems arising from the presence of usurious money and other usurious goods in society, a body of material that has hitherto been neglected by historians or treated only in passing.[146] The masters' determinations were long and complex. Deciding what should be done in any particular instance required attention to a range of issues including the intentions of those involved, what exactly they knew about past transactions, their current financial situations, and the nature of their family and business relationships. Once again, however, the arguments against usury, and above all the conceptions of money that were integral to them, were crucial.

A number of problems were solved by using Thomas Aquinas' characterization of money as a good consumed in use. This was the case, for example, when masters considered what usurers were to do with profits made by using usurious money in licit ways. The problem was that usurers did not generally leave their usurious gains lying idle until such time as they felt inclined to make restitution. On the contrary, they put their usurious money to use, quite possibly in ways which were perfectly licit in themselves. The status of the profits made with usurious money therefore required consideration. It was not obvious whether the usurer could legitimately keep them, or whether he ought to give them to the rightful owner of the usurious money which he had used as capital. Most theologians and lawyers in the first half of the thirteenth century had argued that profits made from usurious money grew from a rotten root and were therefore rotten themselves, concluding that the profits should be restored to the original borrower after the original lender had deducted due recompense for his labour.[147] In 1270 Thomas Aquinas was asked whether someone could licitly retain the profits of lawful business which had been financed by usury.[148] He began by presenting

[146] Noonan, *Scholastic Analysis of Usury*, pp. 74–5, 79–81 claims that such matters were first discussed by Bernadine of Siena and Antoninus in the fifteenth century. As will be apparent from subsequent notes, Langholm refers to some of the material.

[147] See Baldwin, *Masters, Princes and Merchants*, vol. 1, pp. 303–4; Langholm, *Economics in the Medieval Schools* pp. 49, 86–7, 110, 114, 244–5; Noonan, *Scholastic Analysis of Usury*, p. 111.

[148] Quodlibet III.19. Thomas Aquinas, *Quaestiones de quolibet*, Sancti Thomae de Aquino Opera Omnia 25, 2 vols. (Rome, 1996), vol. 2, pp. 275–7. See Noonan, *Scholastic Analysis of Usury*, pp. 111–12.

his argument against usury based on the distinction between goods that were consumed in their use and goods that were not. He then turned to the actual question. If usurious money were used in legitimate business, could the ensuing profits be retained or must they be handed over to the original borrower from whom the usurious money had been wrongfully taken? Clearly, the original lender was bound to restore whatever had been taken beyond the principal because it had been taken unjustly. Moreover, he must compensate the original borrower for losses suffered through being deprived of the money he had paid in usury. But, according to Aquinas, this was all that should be paid. Because the use and the substance of the usurious money were identical, one could not give back the substance and then pay something for its use.[149] It was different if one had profited from wrongful possession of someone's house or horse. One was obliged not only to return the house or horse but also to hand over the profits made from them, because the thing and its use could be valued separately. Aquinas had thus applied his theory of money as a good consumed in its use to explain why profit derived from usurious money could be retained by the usurer, while profit derived from other types of usurious property had to be handed over to the original borrower.

In 1291 Giles of Rome addressed the same issue when he considered whether profit made with usurious money should be returned to the original debtor.[150] Giles immediately declared that it was unreasonable to maintain that this was the case, basing his argument on Aquinas' distinction between things which were consumed in use and things which were not. If the usurer took usury in the form of things which were not consumed in use and for whose use a charge could licitly be made, for example a field, vineyard or house, the usurer should return both what he had taken in usury and any profit derived from it. He added just one qualification: if things of this kind were bought with usurious money rather than taken directly as usury, they should be treated like money. Giles then turned to things whose use and consumption were identical, such as money, wine, oil or corn. If the usurer took usury in the form of things like this, he was not bound to restore anything beyond what had been taken as usury. This was the case, for example, if the usurer

[149] Elsewhere Aquinas also argued that the profit made with usurious money was entirely the result of the original lender's industry, which the original borrower could not claim as his own; ST 2a2ae.78.3. See also Langholm, *Economics in the Medieval Schools*, pp. 244–5.

[150] Quodlibet VI.22. *B. Aegidii Columnae Romani Quodlibeta*, pp. 426–8. See Langholm, *Economics in the Medieval Schools*, p. 390.

invested usurious money in trade or if he took wine or corn as usury in places where they were cheap and sold them where they were dearer. Again Giles offered a qualification: the usurer might feel some obligation to compensate the original debtor for losses suffered as a result of paying usury, but this did not mean that the usurer was bound to hand over profits made with usurious money. Having outlined his position, Giles proceeded to justify it in three ways.

First, Giles pointed out that doing business with usurious money might result in loss instead of profit, and whoever enjoyed the profit must bear the loss. If therefore the usurer was obliged to give any profit to the original debtor, it followed that the original debtor must bear any loss. But no one suggested that losses made by a usurer trading with usurious money should be charged to the original debtor, thus releasing the usurer from his obligation to make restitution. It could not therefore be maintained that profits made with usurious money should pass to the original debtor either. If the usurer was in some sense obliged to compensate the debtor for his loss, this had nothing to do with whether or not he had profited from usurious money. In this regard, the debtor who retained the usurer's money for a long time might also have some obligation to compensate the usurer for resulting losses. The usurer's obligation was, however, more compelling because he had sinned in taking usury, unlike the debtor who had been driven into debt by necessity.

Second, Giles noted that if the usurer had to return both usurious money and any profit made with it, the case against usury would be undermined. He recalled that it was wrong to charge simply for the use of money and that this constituted usury. On the other hand, merchants could legitimately invest money in trade because their profits derived from their industry and not the money. If, however, profits made with usurious money had to be given to the original debtor, the debtor received both what he had paid in usury and a charge for its use. The profit could not be said to derive from his industry since he had done nothing. This was therefore a case of usury. But if the payment to him were licit, all other cases of usury were obviously licit too. This was impossible, and it followed that the usurer could retain profits made with usurious money because they derived from his industry.

Third, Giles identified another flaw in the view that usurers had to return profits made with usurious money. If this were the case, the original debtor would be similarly obliged to give the usurer the profits which he had made with the borrowed money. Once more usury would in effect be legitimized, and of course no one maintained this argument. Giles concluded that it was rather the case that just as the debtor did not have to give profits made with borrowed money to the usurer, so the usurer was not obliged to give the debtor profits made with usurious money.

Not all the masters agreed with Thomas Aquinas and Giles of Rome. In the 1280s Servais of Mont Saint Eloi voiced concern that many would be encouraged to make usurious loans if they only had to return the usury and were permitted to keep whatever they made out of it.[151] The prevailing view, however, treated usurious money as different from most other usurious property, and stated specifically that profit derived from usurious gains could be retained if usury had been taken in the form of money or other goods that were consumed in their use. Effectively, most masters did encourage the taking of usury in the form of money since subsequent profits could licitly be kept. In a sense it was safer for the usurer to deal in money rather than other forms of property since less moral danger would surround subsequent transactions.

Classifying money as a fungible was often crucial when deciding whether or not an obligation to make restitution had passed from the usurer to other people. A maxim of canon law declared that 'res transit cum onere suo', 'a thing passes with its burden', and it was important to know when this rule applied.[152] The fungibility of money was brought into play when masters assessed the position of someone who was employed by a usurer. In 1279, for example, Henry of Ghent was asked whether it was licit to accept usurious money in return for the service of instructing a usurer's son.[153] According to Henry, provided the usurer had acquired some of his possessions justly, it was licit to accept money which one knew to be acquired through usury because the usurer could make restitution by other means. The nature of money meant that the usurer could restore an equivalent sum and not necessarily exactly the same money. In this respect unjust possession of money differed from unjust possession of other things like books and horses. Such things, when unjustly possessed, could not licitly be alienated in any way; they could not be given, sold or used to pay a debt, because exactly the

[151] Quodlibetal question 71. B. N. lat. 15350, f. 285rb–vb. See also Langholm, *Economics in the Medieval Schools*, pp. 283, 286–7.

[152] Damasus, *Brocarda correcta per Bartholomeum Brixiensem* (Lyons, 1549), f. 29va. Damasus, a canonist at Bologna, produced his collection of brocards between 1210 and 1215. It was revised by Bartholomew of Brixen in 1234. In discussing this particular maxim, neither Damasus nor Bartholomew made any reference to usurious money or goods. For the maxim, see D. Liebs, *Lateinische Rechtsregeln und Rechtssprichwörter* (Munich, 1982), p. 191. For Damasus' collection, see H. Coing, *Handbuch der Quellen und Literatur der Neueren Europäischen Privatrechtsgeschichte*, vol. 1 (Munich, 1973), p. 375; S. Kuttner, *Repertorium der Kanonistik (1140–1234)*, Studi e Testi 71 (Vatican, 1937), pp. 419–22. I am indebted to Professor Paul Brand and Professor David Seipp for the identification of this brocard.

[153] Quodlibet IV.27. Henry of Ghent, *Aurea quodlibeta*, vol. 1, f. 212r–v.

same thing had to be restored to its rightful owner, not simply its price. Furthermore, no one who knew that the thing was unjustly possessed could licitly buy it or receive it in return for a service or as a gift. Money, however, was only a measure or means of exchange. An unjust possessor of money was not therefore bound to return the same coins, as long as he was capable of making adequate restitution in another way. According to Henry, the fungibility of money thus saved the teacher from implication in usury. In general, although there were other factors to be considered, an employee was less likely to be implicated in usury if he took his pay in the form of money.

The fungibility of money again proved decisive when the masters considered the position of someone who received alms from a usurer. If a usurer took usury in the form of a non-fungible like a horse or a book, he was obliged to restore that item to its rightful owner. If the usurer gave that non-fungible as alms, the recipient was now bound to make restitution. If, however, the usurer took usury in the form of money, its fungibility meant that he did not have to return those exact coins, and nor did someone to whom he gave those coins as alms. This argument was adopted by Henry of Ghent in 1281–2,[154] Giles of Rome in 1287,[155] and Durand of Saint Pourçain in 1312–13.[156] The fungibility of money meant that obligations were not invariably attached to it. It was licit to accept usurious money more often than most other usurious goods.

Once again, it is clear that new arguments against usury did more than back up a condemnation based on authority; they provided the means by which practical questions about the consequences of usury could be solved. Moreover, disputations about usurious money, by stressing money's consumptibility in use or its fungibility, demonstrated that in a sinful world, sullied by usury, it was morally safest to do business in money. Many masters showed that money was less likely than most other things to pass from the usurer to others with an obligation to make restitution attached. In effect, they argued that money was by its nature less likely to transmit sin. While the initial sin of taking usury could never be diminished, it was subsequently safer for both the usurer and others if usury was taken in money, and others took money from the usurer. Historians are more familiar with a general hostility to money

[154] Quodlibet VI.25. *Henrici de Gandavo Quodlibet VI*, ed. G. A. Wilson (Louvain, 1987), pp. 227–32. See Marmursztejn, 'A normative power in the making', p. 393; Marmursztejn, *L'autorité des maîtres*, pp. 172, 174.

[155] Quodlibet II.26. *B. Aegidii Columnae Romani Quodlibeta*, pp. 113–15. See Langholm, *Economics in the Medieval Schools*, p. 389.

[156] Quodlibet I.13. B. N. lat. 14572, f. 6va–vb.

on the part of pious churchmen who associated it with avarice, and reviled it as something filthy and evil.[157] The masters' encouragement to deal in money stands in stark contrast to this demonization of money. They did not, however, present their analyses so as to give prominence to this new view of money; it remained understated or simply implied, built into the conclusions drawn when considering particular scenarios. Perhaps this reflected their pastoral strategy, especially the combination of hope and fear which was fundamental to it. They still wanted people to fear the spiritual consequences of usury, hence the emphatic condemnation of usury which remained upfront. Nevertheless, there had to be hope of salvation, hence their quiet re-conceptualization of money. Overall, the social implications of their thinking were manifest: it was possible, if never easy, to maintain normal social relations with usurers by using money.

Conclusion

The masters of theology repeatedly demonstrated close familiarity with commercial practices. The nature of the medieval town was such that they could not but bear witness to what was going on, and they themselves engaged in financial transactions on their own account and when holding administrative posts within the university.[158] A deep-rooted ambivalence permeated their thinking about the urban economy. They repeated traditional condemnations of trade and merchants, but at the same time justified much of what merchants did. They condemned usury, but decided that many contracts involving credit were licit, that some usury had to be tolerated in practice, and that the properties of money were such that sin originating in usury was most likely to be contained when money was used in transactions.

The impact of their work has been variously assessed. At one extreme, it has been argued that it had no impact because the scholars, both theologians and lawyers, were largely ignored. There was a genuine divergence on moral issues between the scholars and the merchants, and the scholars unwillingly softened their ideas in response to reality without

[157] L. K. Little, *Religious Poverty and the Profit Economy in Medieval Europe* (London, 1978), pp. 34–8, 178; L. K. Little, 'Pride goes before avarice: social change and the vices in Latin Christendom', *American Historical Review* 76 (1971): 16–49; A. Murray, *Reason and Society in the Middle Ages* (Oxford, 1978), pp. 59–80. See also J. Le Goff's comments on the significance of money; Le Goff, *Your Money*, p. 18: 'the status of *money* in medieval ecclesiastical doctrine and thought is the basis for the condemnation of usury' (his emphasis).

[158] Baldwin, *Masters, Princes and Merchants*, vol. 1, p. 261; Kaye, *Economy and Nature*, pp. 6, 19, 28–32, 40, 50, 171–4.

seriously abandoning their hardline position and without having any effect.[159] Their ambivalence was thus the result of a reluctant response to a world in which they made no difference. Other historians have suggested that in order to evade the church's ban on usury, and perhaps in the sincere belief that it made a difference, merchants developed contracts that concealed when a charge was being made for credit. Thus the scholars influenced the nature of contracts and the form of financial activity by unintentionally pushing the financial world into greater inventiveness and sophistication.[160] Yet another approach presents the scholars' work as an effective response to a spiritual crisis in the towns, a crisis stemming from the growth of the money economy and the way in which urban professions seemed to break the moral codes traditionally propounded by the church. In sorting out what was licit and what was illicit in urban life, the scholars, especially those who were friars, helped to create a new morality for the towns and to resolve the spiritual crisis.[161] Ultimately it is impossible to assess the impact of the masters' thinking, but this last approach takes us back to what the masters actually thought they were doing.

Despite disagreements on many specific points, overall there was a high degree of consensus. From the start, theologians agreed that there should be justice in exchange, that the just price was the current market price, that sellers and buyers were not simply free to maximize their profits, and that usury was a grave sin. Most significantly, they developed their thinking so as to legitimate more and more of what was happening in the marketplace, and to make it a morally safer environment. They did this by reappraising specific contracts, such as annuities, and finding them acceptable. They also recognized the benefits of charging for credit when they argued that some usury must be tolerated. Moreover, they diminished the scale of the whole problem by discovering that it was in the nature of money to contain the spread of sin rather than to pass it on. Their ability to make these shifts depended on the application of new arguments against usury. Their desire to develop these arguments when the condemnation of usury was already securely rooted in authority is often explained in terms of a purely intellectual

[159] R. de Roover, 'The scholastic attitude toward trade and entrepreneurship', in *Business, Banking, and Economic Thought in Late Medieval and Early Modern Europe*, ed. J. Kirshner (Chicago, 1974), pp. 336–45.

[160] Gilchrist, *Church and Economic Activity*, pp. 76, 104–15; Noonan, *Scholastic Analysis of Usury*, pp. 191–2, 194–5.

[161] B. H. Rosenwein and L. K. Little, 'Social meaning in the monastic and mendicant spiritualities', *Past and Present* 63 (1974): 4–32; Little, *Religious Poverty and the Profit Economy*, esp. pp. 173–217; Little, 'Pride goes before avarice', pp. 30–1.

response to Aristotle and their obsession with articulating complete intellectual systems. There may be truth in this, but the key point was that they could apply these new arguments to solve practical moral problems that arose from the longstanding condemnation, and thus bring about an accommodation with the burgeoning money economy. This process also depended on new underlying assumptions. As the arguments in favour of annuities reveal, they now accepted the autonomy of the money economy, no longer tying it to agrarian society or traditional forms of authority. Moreover, they assumed that time was 'merchant time'; it was infinite and measurable, and within it predictions of the probable could be made by those with the right expertise. These were profound shifts in thinking, but they were not announced as great new ideas. Traditional prohibitions were strongly maintained, while new ways of thinking were implied or understated. Authority was thus preserved and their pastoral strategies remained intact, even while a new world was granted legitimacy.

7 Anti-intellectual intellectuals in the late thirteenth and early fourteenth centuries: a new context

The identity and authority of Parisian masters of theology in the thirteenth century rested on a number of key ideas and practices. It was possible to know truths with certainty by using reason, and to articulate them clearly in words. This knowledge also depended on living virtuously, and the university's regulations were to ensure that proper behaviour was the norm. Furthermore, the masters were responsible for turning their students into preachers, fulfilling a pastoral function that placed them at the top of a hierarchy of knowledge and justified a status that gave them a measure of independence even from prelates. They also accepted responsibility for the reception of their teaching by a wide audience. In fulfilment of their obligation to save souls by generating and communicating knowledge, they scrutinized sexual and financial behaviour at length and in great detail. While there were always some areas of disagreement, especially with regard to sex, and some of their most important ideas remained implicit, they offered a high degree of consensus. From the late thirteenth century, however, they faced a challenge from women and men operating both inside and outside the university who were intellectually rigorous in attacking the theologians' intellectual practices. Far from straightforwardly anti-intellectual, these anti-intellectual intellectuals produced texts in vernacular languages that circulated outside the university.[1] This chapter will explore Jean de Meun's continuation of the *Romance of the Rose*, Marguerite Porete and *The Mirror of Simple Souls*, and some of the vernacular sermons of Eckhart.

[1] J. Le Goff, *Intellectuals in the Middle Ages*, trans. T. L. Fagan (Oxford, 1993), p. 135 refers to 'anti-intellectualism' and an 'anti-intellectualist current'. By referring to anti-intellectual *intellectuals*, I distance myself from Le Goff's analysis of key figures as simply 'anti-intellectual', and I mimic the way they played with paradox and contradiction.

Jean de Meun and the *Romance of the Rose*

Jean de Meun wrote his continuation of the *Romance of the Rose* in the 1270s, before 1278, about forty years after Guillaume de Lorris had composed the first part. Very little is known about Jean, but he died in 1305 after also translating a number of works from Latin to French: Vegetius' *On Warfare*, Boethius' *Consolation of Philosophy*, and the letters of Abelard and Heloise. The many surviving manuscripts containing both parts of the *Romance of the Rose* are testimony to their huge popularity.[2]

The first part, composed by Guillaume, opens with a young man, usually referred to as 'the lover', recounting a dream in which it is May five or more years earlier. In the dream the young man walks by a river and sees a walled garden with paintings and inscriptions on the walls. He is admitted to the garden by a beautiful girl, Idleness, from whom he learns that this is the garden of Pleasure. He meets Pleasure, Joy, Courtesy, the God of Love, and Pleasant Looks, and joins their dance. Wandering off alone, followed by the God of Love, he comes to the spring of Narcissus in which there are two crystals reflecting the whole garden. Having seen the reflection of the roses, he goes to find them. When he has chosen one more beautiful than the rest, the God of Love shoots him with five arrows. Captured by Love, he does homage to him and receives his commandments. To help the lover cope with the pain of being a lover, Love gives him Hope, Pleasant Thought, Pleasant Conversation and Pleasant Looks. The lover is then left alone, knowing that only the rose-bud can cure his wounds. The roses are enclosed by a hedge through which he passes after meeting Fair Welcome. The roses are guarded, however, by Rebuff, Evil Tongue, Shame and Fear, and the lover flees beyond the hedge. Reason then descends from her tower and advises him to forget his love. This has no effect, and the lover turns to Friend who tells him to plead with Rebuff. He does so and is allowed to love the rose as long as he does not cross the hedge. Generosity of Spirit and Pity then secure him admission to the enclosure, and Venus persuades Fair Welcome to allow him to kiss the rose. Jealousy's response is to enclose the roses within a new wall, and to build a tower in the middle within which he imprisons Fair Welcome, guarded by an old woman. This is the point at which the work of Guillaume de Lorris ends.

[2] C. W. Dunn, 'Introduction', *The Romance of the Rose*, trans. H. W. Robbins (New York, 1962), pp. xiii, xvi–xviii, xxv; S. Kay, *The Romance of the Rose* (London, 1995), pp. 9–10.

At the beginning of Jean's continuation, Reason reappears and lectures the lover on love, advising him to abandon it and to let her be his beloved. The lover refuses, affirming his love for the rose. Friend then appears, recommending strategies that he should adopt as a lover, including concealing his feelings, giving gifts, making empty promises and using force when the opportunity arises. He further advises against marriage, and explains that keeping a woman means letting her be free. The lover decides that he prefers Friend to Reason. Walking away from the castle, he meets Wealth guarding the road to Lavish Giving. The lover wishes to take this road, but Wealth will not permit it, explaining that it leads to poverty, and that he is not rich enough. While the lover endeavours to live according to Friend's advice, Love appears, berates him for wavering, and makes him repeat his commandments. Love then summons his barons to lay siege to the castle and free Fair Welcome. The barons include Constrained Abstinence and False Seeming, and Love asks False Seeming to say where he can be found and how he can be recognized. False Seeming then speaks, explaining that he has many dwellings, but presenting himself chiefly as a mendicant friar. An assault on the castle follows, with False Seeming and Constrained Abstinence killing Evil Tongue. The Old Woman, informed that Evil Tongue is dead, persuades Fair Welcome to accept a chaplet of flowers from the lover. She then offers Fair Welcome the benefit of her experience in love. Her advice includes not to be generous, to have more than one lover, to sell love dearly to the highest bidder, and that a woman should not delay too long before taking her pleasure. The Old Woman lets the lover into the castle, and he is about to take the rose when he is sent packing by Rebuff, Fear and Shame, who lock Fair Welcome in the tower. They attack the lover, who has to be rescued by the barons, and battle ensues. Love's host is losing, so he sends for Venus, his mother, and arranges a truce. Venus joins the army and they all swear to defeat Chastity. Meanwhile, Nature is forging individual creatures to continue the species, but weeps. She confesses to Genius, her priest: God put her in charge of the world that he created, and all things obey her rules, as God desired, except man. God may punish most sins, but Nature shares Love's complaint against those who do not use the 'tools' they have been given by Nature to procreate. Nature sends Genius to the host to excommunicate her opponents and absolve those who work to increase their families. Genius absolves Nature and flies to the host. Love dresses Genius as a bishop, and Genius reads Nature's sentence, condemning those who have neglected to use what she has given them to perpetuate the human race. In his sermon, Genius urges the barons to love and to preach the same message to others, assuring them that they will get to heaven if they do. Using religious imagery, he describes heaven as a park as superior to the garden in which the lover saw pleasure as truth is to fiction. The final assault is led by Venus, who fires a burning arrow through a loophole set between two small pillars in the tower. The whole castle is set alight, causing Rebuff, Fear and Shame to flee. Fair Welcome says that the lover may pluck the rose. The lover, now a pilgrim, penetrates the aperture between the two pillars with his staff and plucks the rose. The lover awakes.

While Jean de Meun's continuation of the *Romance of the Rose* is frequently and rightly analysed in relation to literary genres and other literary texts, it is also clearly a product of the university milieu. More specifically, it seems to offer the perspective of a secular clerk educated in the faculty of arts.[3] Frequent use is made of terms derived from the study of logic, for example. Almost as soon as Jean takes up the story, the lover, on the brink of despair, expresses his frustration with the comfort provided by Hope: 'it is foolish to approach too close to her, for when she constructs a good syllogism, we should be very much afraid that she will draw the negative conclusion'.[4] Reason tells the lover that he is 'not a good logician', and later says that the lover will take his point about Fortune's wheel 'if you know anything of logic, which is a genuine science'.[5] Perhaps Reason might be expected to value logic, but logical jargon is deployed by other figures. False Seeming claims that false religious

> offer to the world a syllogism that has a shameful conclusion: a man wears a religious habit, therefore he is religious. This argument is entirely specious, not worth a privet-knife: the habit does not make the monk. And yet no one can answer it, no matter how high he tonsures his head or shaves it with the razor of Elenchis, which divides fraud into thirteen branches; no one is so good at making distinctions that he dare utter a single word about it.[6]

All scholars would be familiar with logical terminology, but it is noticeable that members of all the faculties except the faculty of arts are

[3] Others to see Jean de Meun as a product of the faculty of arts at Paris include: N. Cohn, *The World-View of a Thirteenth-Century Parisian Intellectual: Jean de Meun and the Roman de la Rose* (Durham, 1961), pp. 7–9; A. Murray, *Reason and Society in the Middle Ages* (Oxford, 1978), p. 350. For placement in the context of the university more generally, see Dunn, 'Introduction', pp. xvii–xviii; G. Paré, *Les idées et les letttres aux XIIIe siècle. Le 'Roman de la Rose'* (Montreal, 1947), pp. 8–10, 346.

[4] *The Romance of the Rose*, trans. F. Horgan (Oxford, 1994), p. 62.

[5] *Ibid.*, pp. 88, 101.

[6] *Ibid.*, pp. 169–70. For other examples, see pp. 181, 187, 197, 317, 331. For extended analysis of Jean's scholarly vocabulary, see Paré, *Les idées et les lettres aux XIIIe siècle*, pp. 15–80.

criticized. Reason likens lawyers, physicians and theologians to merchants because they are always tormented by desire for greater wealth:

Lawyers and physicians are all bound with these bonds, all hanged with this rope, if they sell their knowledge for money. They find gain so sweet and desirable and are so fired with covetousness and trickery that the one would like to have sixty patients for every one he has, and the other thirty cases, or indeed two hundred or two thousand. The same is true of theologians who walk the earth: when they preach in order to acquire honours or favours or wealth, the same anguish tears their hearts.[7]

The theologians in particular receive several digs. Dressed so that Love thinks him 'a holy hermit', False Seeming eats and drinks well 'as a theologian should'.[8] Turning himself into a friar, he compares himself favourably with the secular clergy: 'prelates are not nearly so wise nor so well instructed as me. I have a degree in theology; indeed, by God, I have taught it for a long time. The best men we know have chosen me as their confessor on account of my intelligence and learning.'[9] This was a distorted echo of the claims that we have seen masters of theology making about themselves in their quodlibetal disputations. When Genius wonders how God could either want everyone to be chaste, so that the human race died out, or wish only some to be chaste, so that there was inequality amongst those he loved equally, he concluded: 'Let theologians come and theologize about it: they will never reach a conclusion.'[10]

Several of these attacks on theologians were more specifically aimed at the friars; 'theologians who walk the earth' were presumably friars, for example. Hostility to the friars is expressed at length by False Seeming, who refers explicitly to the controversies that rocked the University of Paris during the thirteenth century. He began by presenting a standard case against begging as a form of voluntary poverty, indicating that this view had prevailed amongst Paris theologians before the friars entered the university:

I can swear forthwith that it is not written in any law, or at least not in ours, that when Jesus Christ and his apostles were on this earth they were ever seeking for bread, for they did not beg (this is what the masters of divinity were formerly accustomed to preach in the city of Paris). They could have demanded, in the fullness of their power, without needing to beg, for they were shepherds in God's name and had the cure of souls. And immediately after their master's death, they even began again to work with their hands, supporting themselves by their work.[11]

7 *Romance of the Rose*, p. 78.
8 *Ibid.*, p. 172. 9 *Ibid.*, p. 190.
10 *Ibid.*, p. 302. 11 *Ibid.*, pp. 173–4.

Emphasizing the importance of work and the very particular circumstances in which begging was permitted, False Seeming recalls the heroic resistance mounted by William of Saint Amour, the master of arts and then theology who 'used to debate and teach and preach on this subject with the Paris theologians', only to be exiled.[12] He also describes how members of the University of Paris responded when the Franciscan Gerard of Borgo San Donnino produced his *Liber introductorius in evangelium aeternum*, or 'Introduction to the Eternal Gospel', which claimed that the writings of Joachim of Fiore were to supersede the Old and New Testaments:

Had it not been for the vigilance of the University, which keeps the keys of Christendom, everything would have been thrown into turmoil when, with evil intent, in the year of our Lord 1255 (and no man living will contradict me) there was released as a model for imitation, and this is true, a book written by the devil, the Eternal Gospel ... The University, which was asleep at the time, raised its head; it awoke at the uproar which the book provoked and scarcely slept afterward but, when it saw the horrible monster, took up arms against it, fully prepared to do battle with it and to hand over the book to the judges.[13]

Gerard's work actually appeared in 1254, and opposition to it was led by William of Saint Amour whose *De periculis novissimorum temporum*, or 'On the Dangers of Most Recent Times', was an attack on the friars in general.[14] These were very much the views of the secular clergy, and especially the secular masters in Paris.

More generally and less dramatically, Jean's continuation also conveys the way in which university men viewed the laity. The idea that learning generated in the university should be widely disseminated is expressed by Genius when he invites Love's army to memorize his sermon:

In this way, wherever you go, to fortress or castle, city or town, in winter or summer, you may recite it to those who were not here. It is good to remember the words that come from a good school, and better to repeat them.[15]

On the other hand, the problems of explaining complex matters to the laity are also mentioned on more than one occasion. Nature notes that 'it is difficult to provide lay people with a solution to the question of

12 *Ibid.*, pp. 174–7; quotation at p. 177.
13 *Ibid.*, p. 182.
14 William of Saint Amour, *De periculis novissimorum temporum*, ed. and trans. G. Geltner (Paris, 2008). For the errors identified by the masters of theology, see *Chartularium*, no. 243, pp. 272–6. On this episode, see M.-M. Dufeil, *Guillaume de Saint-Amour et la polémique universitaire parisienne, 1250–1259* (Paris, 1972); G. Leff, *Heresy in the Later Middle Ages: The Relation of Heterodoxy to Dissent c. 1250–c. 1450*, 2 vols. (Manchester, 1967), vol. 1, 69–83; Paré, *Les idées et les lettres aux XIIIe siècle*, pp. 180–3.
15 *Romance of the Rose*, p. 307.

how predestination and the divine prescience, which knows all things in advance, can coexist with free will'.[16] And Nature will not even attempt to explain the way mirrors work: 'The subject would be too long; it would be hard to explain and very difficult to understand, even if anyone were capable of teaching it, particularly to lay folk, without confining himself to generalities.'[17] And yet the *Romance of the Rose* was written in the vernacular and was therefore at least in part for a lay audience.

Hostility to merchants also emerges at several points. Reason, for example, pities them because they are tortured by their insatiable greed:

> no merchant lives in comfort, for such a war rages in his heart that he burns alive to acquire more goods and will never have enough. He is afraid of losing what he has acquired and chases after what remains to be gained but which he will never possess, for his greatest desire is to acquire the property of others. He has undertaken an extraordinarily difficult task, for he aspires to drink the whole of the Seine but will never be able to do it, because there will always be some left. This is the burning anguish, the everlasting torment, the agonising conflict that tears at his vitals and tortures him with his lack; it is that the more he gains, the more he lacks.[18]

As we have seen, this was very much the lesson that was learned from Aristotle. Usury too meets with Reason's disapproval on familiar grounds: 'Wealth is seriously injured by being robbed of its true nature, which is to help men and go to their aid and not to be loaned at interest.'[19] False Seeming reckons that most who prospered in towns were despoiling the poor:

> But see what quantities of pennies lie in the storehouses of usurers, forgers, money-lenders, bailiffs, beadles, provosts, mayors: all of them practically live by rapine … they all assail the poor and there is none who will not fleece them and clothe himself with the spoils.[20]

This was only part of the learned response to towns and the money economy, but it was articulated in terms that we have seen the theologians also using.

While Reason criticized the townspeople, Nature turned on princes and the nobility:

> But now it has come to this, that there are good men who work at philosophy all their lives, and journey to foreign lands in order to obtain wisdom and worth,

[16] *Ibid.*, p. 264. See also pp. 268, 273.
[17] *Ibid.*, pp. 281–2. [18] *Ibid.*, pp. 77–8.
[19] *Ibid.*, p. 79. [20] *Ibid.*, p. 178.

who endure great poverty as beggars or debtors and who perhaps go barefoot and naked, and who are neither loved nor held in affection. Princes do not care a fig for them, and yet – God preserve me from fevers – they are nobler men than those who hunt hares and those who are accustomed to remain on the family middens.[21]

The complaint that scholars were undervalued was of long standing, and we shall return to the theme of nobility.

In addition to these various contextual references, Jean's continuation was in many respects a summa or encyclopedia of university learning. Especially in Nature's confession to Genius, it contains a considerable body of scientific material, drawing both on the poetic neoplatonism of the twelfth century, above all Alan of Lille, and on Aristotelian science studied in the faculty of arts in the thirteenth century. Theological matters were also included, for example the debate about free will that has already been mentioned, and here Boethius was Jean's chief source.[22] Most criticism of the *Romance of the Rose* stresses the ways in which Jean engages with literary genres and conventions, and in particular his commentary, implicit and explicit, on the first part written by Guillaume de Lorris. To those who study the University of Paris, however, almost every line of Jean's continuation seems to invoke debates that gripped the university or to make reference to some aspect of its basic culture. While it is impossible to be certain that Jean studied in the faculty of arts at the University of Paris, he was certainly familiar with material that was taught there, and gave ready expression to the cultural values of its members, while positioning himself on its margins simply by writing in the vernacular.

Whatever Jean's own relationship with the university, his continuation of the *Romance of the Rose* represented a profound challenge to conceptions of knowledge and authority that were articulated by university scholars, especially the masters of theology. He never presented a clear authorial voice in which an authoritative claim to speak the truth could be made. He produced a text that resists and undermines any interpretation that culminates in a claim to have identified definite meaning. Indeed, his one consistent message seems to be that meaning can never be certain and so knowledge of the truth is unobtainable.[23]

[21] *Ibid.*, p. 289.

[22] Kay, *Romance of the Rose*, pp. 96–100; G. Paré, *Le 'Roman de la Rose' et la scolastique courtoise* (Paris, 1941), pp. 52–86, 88–111, 183–203 ; Paré, *Les idées et les letttres aux XIIIe siècle*, pp. 203–78 ; L. Polak, 'Plato, Nature and Jean de Meun', *Reading Medieval Studies* 3 (1977): 80–103.

[23] For similar conclusions, see Kay, *Romance of the Rose*, passim; J. O. Ward, 'Rhetoric in the faculty of arts at the universities of Paris and Oxford in the middle ages: a

Uncertainty about meaning is generated repeatedly at many levels. From the outset, the lover recounts a dream. Guillaume de Lorris began the *Romance of the Rose* with the claim that dreams can contain truth:

> Some say that there is nothing in dreams but lies and fables; however, one may have dreams which are not in the least deceitful, but which later become clear ... Whoever thinks or says that it is foolish or stupid to believe that a dream may come true, let him think me mad if he likes; for my part I am confident that a dream may signify the good or ill that may befall people, for many people dream many things secretly, at night, which are later seen openly.[24]

Jean de Meun, however, had Nature reject this view, even when dreams were linked with religious fervour:

> Or there are those in whom devout and profound contemplation causes the objects of their meditations to appear in their thoughts, and who truly believe that they see them clearly and objectively. But these are merely lies and deceits, just as in the case of the man who dreams and believes that the spiritual substances he sees are really present.[25]

Nature goes on to list the many things about which people might dream, including the very scenario presented by Guillaume de Lorris: a lover might dream about Jealousy catching him in the act with his sweetheart, because of Evil Tongue. Whatever people dream, however, Nature insists that they are misled:

> Yet they for their part truly believe that these things exist outside themselves, and make of them all an occasion for grief or joy; in fact they carry them all inside their own heads, which, by thus admitting phantoms, deceive the five senses.[26]

Since the *Romance of the Rose* is an account of a dream, Nature seems to indicate that it is deceptive by its very nature.

Jean de Meun thus implanted an idea in the mind of the reader of his text, but it is not possible to say that Jean himself held this to be true because the idea is voiced through Nature. This brings us to another source of uncertainty about meaning. Much of the continuation consists of speeches delivered by allegorical figures who express different points of view. Jean offers no grounds for thinking that one figure speaks with greater authority than another, so a raft of ideas and arguments remain in play, the tensions between them unresolved.[27] To

summary of the evidence', *Bulletin Du Cange (Archivum Latinitatis Medii Aevi)* 54 (1996): 159–231 at 230–1 (citing a thesis by R. Borny).

24 *Romance of the Rose*, p. 3.

25 *Ibid.*, p. 283. 26 *Ibid.*, p. 284.

27 See Kay, *Romance of the Rose*, p. 47.

add to the uncertainty, individual figures subvert their own assertions repeatedly. Nature, for example, having insisted that dreams deceive, claims to be unwilling to consider the nature of dreams or to pronounce upon their veracity: 'Now for my part I do not wish to discuss the truth or falsehood of dreams, nor whether they should all be accepted or all rejected.'[28] The reader might well think that the matter had already been discussed and that Nature had already taken an explicit stance, but apparently not. The idea that dreams deceive has been brought into play, but not even the allegorical figure who expressed it will stick by it. Old Woman, reflecting on the experience of her youth, offers a conventionally negative stereotype of women: they desire many lovers and seek to profit from them. But she goes on to explain that women have to behave like this because men are just the same: 'they are all deceitful traitors, ready to indulge their lusts with everyone, and we should deceive them in our turn'.[29] Examples of women who have suffered at the hands of faithless men are duly provided, and the conventional condemnation of women has been turned against men.[30] Similarly Genius first denounces women for being unable to keep a secret, then illustrates his point with a story in which it is the husband who cannot keep his mouth shut. Once again the gender stereotype is subverted almost as soon as it has been produced.[31] Most strikingly, however, the words of False Seeming generate doubt and uncertainty at every turn. A confessed liar and deceiver, he simultaneously claims to be telling the truth and insists that he will always be true to his duplicitous nature. He assures Love that he is not lying to him, although he would do so if he thought he could get away with it:

> I dare not lie to you, but if I could have felt that you would not have noticed it, I would have served you with a lie: I would certainly have tricked you and would not have refrained, even though it was a sin.[32]

When Love queries his expressions of loyalty, pointing out that loyalty is against his nature, False Seeming does not disagree, inviting him to 'take the risk' because nothing could give him the certainty that he would like:

> Take the risk, for if you require sureties, you will not be any more secure as a result, no indeed, not if I gave you hostages or letters, witnesses or pledges … Do you imagine that I have abandoned trickery and duplicity just because I am

[28] *Romance of the Rose*, p. 285. [29] *Ibid.*, p. 204.
[30] *Ibid.*, pp. 203–4. See Kay, *Romance of the Rose*, pp. 103–4.
[31] *Romance of the Rose*, pp. 252–6. See Kay, *Romance of the Rose*, pp. 104–5.
[32] *Romance of the Rose*, p. 184.

wearing these simple clothes, under whose cover I have performed many great evils? By God, my heart will never change.[33]

Meaning is at its most unstable when the words are spoken by False Seeming.

To further undermine the reader's confidence in the possibility of certain meaning, false signs are repeatedly identified. Nature explains how mirrors alter perception, producing images that magnify, reduce or distort actual objects, so that 'when the observers are thus deceived, having seen such things through the images revealed to them in mirrors or by distance, they go straight to the people, with the false, lying boast that they have seen devils, such are the optical illusions that they experience'.[34] The marks of nobility are, according to Nature, equally misleading. Many look the part, 'they have dogs and birds and therefore look like young noblemen, and they go hunting along rivers and through woods, fields, and heathlands, and indulge in leisurely diversions', but this is just part of the lie by which they 'steal the name of nobility, since they do not resemble their good ancestors'.[35] The world is apparently full of misleading signs. Moreover, if advice dispensed in the course of Jean's continuation were actually followed, it would also be full of people perpetrating deliberate acts of deception. Friend advises men to conceal their true feelings, pretend to offer everything, deceive, make false promises, weep fake tears, lie about their intentions, and mimic their lovers' moods and behaviour.[36] Old Woman would have women cover their true appearance, cry skilfully, hide their thoughts, feign fear and, if necessary, fake their orgasms.[37] The reader of Jean's continuation is invited to suspect deception at every turn.

Even the citation of authorities, the usual guarantee of truthful meaning, fails to generate secure meaning in Jean's continuation. After reporting the harangues of Reason, Friend, False Seeming and Old Woman, the lover expresses concern that he may have caused offence. Women in particular may have found 'words that seem … to be a harsh and savage attack on feminine behaviour'.[38] In his defence, he says that he wrote so that the truth about women would be known, but then he hides behind his authorities:

Moreover, honourable ladies, if it seems to you that I am making things up, do not call me a liar, but blame those authors who have written in their books what I have said, and those in whose company I will speak. I shall tell no lie, unless

[33] *Ibid.*, p. 185.
[34] *Ibid.*, p. 281. Mirrors are discussed at pp. 278–81.
[35] *Ibid.*, p. 291. [36] *Ibid.*, pp. 112–19.
[37] *Ibid.*, pp. 205–22. [38] *Ibid.*, p. 235.

the worthy men who wrote the ancient books also lied … I merely repeat, except for making a few additions on my own account which cost you little.[39]

The lover thus inserts distance between himself and his authorities, refusing to accept responsibility for his words. When he expresses fear that he may be punished by those who feel themselves attacked by the words of False Seeming, he brings the authority of the church into play: 'And if I have said anything that Holy Church judges foolish, I am ready to make any amends she may wish, provided I am capable of doing so.'[40] This was the standard statement of willingness to submit to higher ecclesiastical authority that theologians customarily made, and which generally ensured that they could not be condemned for heresy. Here it serves merely to reinforce the lover's refusal to accept any possible blame.

If the lover who narrates the dream will not take responsibility for the meaning of his words, what about Jean de Meun? Almost the entire continuation is voiced at least through the lover, and generally through other figures as well, denying the apparent security of a strong authorial voice. There are, however, moments of knowing self-reference when the reader is made aware of an author who is not the lover and who has an existence outside the text. Reason refers to the temporary nature of existence in this life, 'as you can learn from the clerks who explain Boethius' *Consolation* and the thoughts contained in it', and she goes on to remark: 'If someone were to translate this book for the laity, he would do them a great service.'[41] Jean de Meun went on to perform just this service, writing a French translation of Boethius' *Consolation of Philosophy*. Friend is so pleased with his advice that he wishes for a wider audience: 'I should like what I want to say to you to become well known: it ought to be in a book for people to read.'[42] Jean has obviously written precisely this book. Most strikingly, Love identifies Guillaume de Lorris as the author of the first part of the *Romance of the Rose*, explaining exactly where he will stop and how the text will be continued by the yet unborn Jean:

Then will come Jean Chopinel, gay in heart and alert in body, who will be born in Meung-sur-Loire and will serve me, feasting and fasting, his whole life long, without avarice or envy … This romance will be so dear to him that he will want to complete it, if he has sufficient time and opportunity, for where Guillaume stops, Jean will continue, more than forty years after his death, and that is no lie.[43]

[39] *Ibid.* [40] *Ibid.*, p. 236. [41] *Ibid.*, p. 77.
[42] *Ibid.*, p. 148. [43] *Ibid.*, p. 162.

Evidently Jean wanted credit for a work which Genius later praises when urging Love and his barons to avoid the vices previously listed by Nature, but which he feels no need to recount: 'The delightful Romance of the Rose gives you a brief account of them: look them up there if you like, the better to avoid them.'[44] Jean is not therefore entirely absent from the text, and his existence outside the text is invoked or implied, but the moments of self-reference simply add another voice to the mix rather than generating a claim to authority that might have pinned down specific meaning. Throughout the continuation different and sometimes contradictory meanings are held in play. Ways of knowing are not placed within a hierarchy in order to reconcile these meanings or privilege some in relation to others.[45] Meaning is therefore left uncertain and disordered.

While meaning is never certain in Jean's continuation, the cacophony of possible meanings is not neutral. On the contrary, it is critically directed, and one of its chief targets was a major weak spot in theological discourse: sexual pleasure. Reason comes closest to expressing the thinking of at least some theologians. She defines the kind of love experienced by the lover as the pursuit of pleasure alone, without concern for procreation:

Love, if my judgement is correct, is a mental illness afflicting two persons of opposite sex in close proximity who are both free agents. It comes upon people through a burning desire, born of disordered perception, to embrace and to kiss and to seek carnal gratification. A lover is concerned with nothing else but is filled with this ardent delight. He attaches no importance to procreation, but strives only for pleasure.[46]

Reason maintains, however, that sex should always be performed with the intention to have children:

But I know well, and this is no conjecture, that anyone who lies with a woman should wish to the best of his ability to perpetuate his divine essence and to preserve himself in a creature like himself (for all men are subject to decay), so that the succession of generations should not fail.[47]

Moreover, sexual pleasure existed to ensure that procreation occurred:

Therefore Nature made the work pleasurable, desiring that it should be so delightful that the workmen should not take to their heels or hate it, for there

[44] *Ibid.*, p. 306.

[45] For the perceptive suggestion that hierarchies of knowledge are run against each other in Jean's continuation, see Kay, *Romance of the Rose*, p. 96.

[46] *Romance of the Rose*, p. 67.

[47] *Ibid.*

are many who would never perform this task unless they were attracted by pleasure.[48]

To seek pleasure for its own sake, however, was wrong:

You should know that no one can love as he ought or with the right intentions if he desires only delight.[49]

According to Reason, this was exactly the lover's problem:

But the love that has ensnared you offers you carnal delight, so that you have no interest in anything else. That is why you want to have the rose, and dream of no other possession.[50]

The kind of love that led to procreation, on the other hand, was experienced by animals as well as men, and it was morally neutral:

There is another, natural, kind of love, which Nature created in the animals and that enables them to produce their young, and to suckle and rear them. If you wish me to define for you the love of which I speak, it is a natural and properly motivated inclination to wish to preserve one's fellow creatures, either by engendering them or by seeing to their rearing. Men and beasts are equally well fitted for this love, which, however profitable it may be, carries with it no praise or blame or merit, and those who love thus deserve neither blame nor praise.[51]

As we have seen, all theologians condemned the pursuit of sexual pleasure for its own sake, and there were certainly many who saw little or no fault in sexual pleasure experienced when the motive for intercourse was procreation. This, however, was always provided that the sex was between husband and wife, whereas Reason simply did not mention marriage. Ideas familiar to and supported by many theologians were thus articulated with a fundamental element missing.

During Friend's great speech, however, the theme of marriage was very much to the fore. He said of husband and wife that 'she ought not to be his lady but his equal and companion, as the law joins them together, and he for his part should be her companion, without making himself her lord and master'.[52] As we have seen, the theme of equality occurred when theologians discussed marital affection. It was, moreover, in the theory of the conjugal debt that each spouse had an equal claim to receive sexual gratification from the other. But Friend's point was rather that lordship was incompatible with love:

no man who wants to be called lord will be loved by his wife, for love must die when lovers assume authority. Love cannot last or survive except in hearts that are free and at liberty.[53]

[48] *Ibid.* [49] *Ibid.* [50] *Ibid.*, p. 70.
[51] *Ibid.*, pp. 88–9. [52] *Ibid.*, p. 144. [53] *Ibid.*

His advice was that marriage was perhaps to be avoided, and that male lovers, whether married or not, should tolerate the indiscretions of their women if they wished to keep them. A brief echo of theological discourse was thus included within a set of ideas utterly inimical to the teaching of all theologians.

Old Woman offered a view of the purpose of marriage that chimed with the theologians' in so far as she thought that women were married to prevent inappropriate behaviour and to ensure that children were brought up properly, but she immediately indicated that women were sure to fight to be free of marital constraints:

> when, in order to prevent dissolute conduct, quarrelling, and killing, and to facilitate the rearing of children, which is their joint responsibility, these ladies and maidens are affianced, taken, and married by law, they still try in every way they can, and whether they be ugly or fair, to regain their freedom.[54]

Whereas some theologians looked to animal behaviour to show that it was natural for couples to stay together to rear their young, Old Woman noted that a caged bird would always struggle to escape back to the woods, and in exactly the same way 'all women, whether maidens or ladies and whatever their origin, are naturally disposed to search willingly for ways and paths by which they might achieve freedom, for they would always like to have it'.[55] Moreover, the freedom they naturally desired was to pursue sexual pleasure:

> Every creature wants to return to its nature, and will not fail to do so, however violent the pressure of force or convention. This should excuse Venus for wishing to make use of her freedom, and all those ladies who take their pleasure although they are bound in marriage, for it is Nature, drawing them towards their freedom, who makes them do this.[56]

Since their appetites are natural, Old Woman contends that they are not to be blamed for giving them full expression. Indeed, lovers had a responsibility to afford each other mutual pleasure, and the woman should pretend to experience pleasure if necessary:

> And when they go to work, they should both exert themselves so conscientiously and to such good effect that both together experience pleasure before the work is finished; they should wait for each other so that they may come to a climax together ... If she feels no pleasure, she should pretend to enjoy the experience and simulate all the signs that she knows are appropriate to pleasure.[57]

[54] *Ibid.*, p. 214. [55] *Ibid.*, p. 215.
[56] *Ibid.*, p. 216. [57] *Ibid.*, p. 220.

Once again an idea that theologians would have acknowledged was a small element within a line of reasoning alien to them.

The importance of procreation is emphasized again by Nature and Genius, and Genius assumes the outward trappings of religion to make the point. Dressed by Love as a bishop, he pronounces sentence on behalf of Nature, condemning those who refuse to have sex, and promising pardon and a place in heaven for those who work to procreate:

> by the authority of Nature, let all those disloyal renegades, great or humble, who scorn those works by which Nature is maintained, be excommunicated and ruthlessly condemned. But if a man strives with all his might to preserve Nature, keeps himself from base thoughts and toils and struggles faithfully to be a true lover, let him go to paradise crowned with flowers. Provided he make a good confession, I will take the whole burden of it upon myself with all the power at my disposal, and he will take away with him no less a pardon than that.[58]

Sexual pleasure is also to be one of the rewards: 'Concentrate on leading a good life; let every man embrace his sweetheart and every lady her lover with kissing, feasting, and pleasure.'[59] Religious imagery is developed as Genius describes heaven as 'the fair and verdant park where the Virgin's son, the white-fleeced lamb, brings the sheep with him, leaping ahead over the grass'.[60] The Trinity is invoked in the healing spring which flows through three channels and contains a three-faceted carbuncle, and the cross is represented by the olive tree standing by the spring.[61] Once again, however, the element of marriage was missing. Moreover, even those theologians who saw no sin in marital sex for procreation did not suggest that married couples won themselves places in heaven by coupling for this reason. The idea that those who were virgins or chaste were thereby excluded from heaven was simply absurd in theological terms. As Jean's continuation reaches its end with the lover plucking the rose, even procreative purpose fades away, and pleasure predominates, although after the lover has scattered his seed, the rosebud 'swelled and expanded'.[62] While meaning is consistently uncertain, Jean's continuation undermines conventional theological thinking about sex and marriage by taking fragments of theological discourse and misplacing them in conjunction with utterly alien notions, forcing them into sequences of thought leading to conclusions that theologians rejected entirely. Elements of their thinking are brought into play in order to be played with. At the heart of almost every move is the refusal to condemn, and frequently the exaltation of, sexual pleasure, the very

[58] *Ibid.*, p. 301. [59] *Ibid.*, p. 306. [60] *Ibid.*, p. 307.
[61] *Ibid.*, pp. 315–16. [62] *Ibid.*, p. 334.

aspect of sexual life on which theologians had most trouble reaching a clear consensus. The very uncertainty of meaning made it possible to challenge the authoritative teaching of theologians in a way that was all the more effective because the challenger could not be clearly identified and refuted.

Jean de Meun had a profound grasp of university learning, but he directed it against the intellectual processes that produced authoritative knowledge in the university. Just as disordered meaning could be used to exploit theological confusion about sexual pleasure, it could be deployed to disparage Reason cumulatively. The naming of sexual organs is a key example. The lover objects to Reason using the word 'testicles': 'I do not think it was courteous of you to pronounce the word "testicles": no well-bred girl should call them by their name.'[63] Reason replies that it cannot be a sin to refer 'in plain and unglossed language' to things God created to perpetuate the human race, prompting the lover to declare that his objection is not to the things but to the vile words that God did not create.[64] This leads Reason to explain that God wanted her to find names 'in order to increase our understanding' and that the words themselves are fine. She suggests that had she 'called testicles relics and relics testicles, then you who thus attack and reproach me would tell me instead that relics was an ugly, base word'.[65] According to Reason, it was only social custom that led women in France to use the names of other things metaphorically: 'purses, harness, things, torches, pricks'.[66] In the rest of Jean's continuation, it is just this custom that prevails, especially as the plucking of the rose becomes imminent. Referring to sexual intercourse, Genius has styluses writing on tablets, hammers beating on the anvil, and the plough ploughing the fertile field.[67] In the end the lover in the guise of a pilgrim thrusts his staff into the aperture between two pillars:

> I knelt without delay, full of agility and vigour, between the two fair pillars ... I wanted to sheathe my staff by putting it into the aperture while the scrip hung outside. I tried to thrust it in at one go, but it came out and I tried again, to no avail because it sprang out every time and nothing I did could make it go in. There was a barrier within, which I could feel but could not see ... when I could not immediately break the barrier, I struggled so hard and with such violence that I was drenched in sweat ... Nothing, however, could have prevented me from sliding my staff all the way in. I did so without delay, but the scrip with its pounding hammers stayed dangling outside.[68]

[63] *Ibid.*, p. 106. [64] *Ibid.* [65] *Ibid.*, p. 108.
[66] *Ibid.*, p. 109. [67] *Ibid.*, pp. 302–3.
[68] *Ibid.*, pp. 332–3.

By not using proper names and developing images in graphic detail, sexual acts are more explicitly portrayed, and Reason's strategy is ignored. More than this, Reason is repeatedly rejected by the other figures. Love does so on Jean's behalf when foretelling the writing of the continuation: 'He [Jean] will be so wise that he will care nothing for Reason.'[69] Just before the rose is finally taken, 'Fear fled, and Shame sprang after her, leaving behind the blazing castle; never again would she set any store by the lessons of Reason.'[70] At the very end, the lover acknowledges his debts, 'But I did not care to thank Reason, who had wasted so much effort upon me.'[71] The status of Reason is thus undermined, another victim of meanings that are uncertain but nevertheless critically directed.

Jean also called into question the kind of social status and recognition that university men should enjoy by entering the longstanding debate about the true nature of nobility.[72] Nature attacks the traditional nobility by arguing that she makes all men alike, and that nobility comes from virtue rather than birth. Those born into noble families therefore have to display virtue to merit the title that their ancestors previously won.

And if anyone, piquing himself on his nobility, dares contradict me and say that noblemen, as the people call them, are superior in condition, by virtue of their noble birth, to those who till the ground or work for their living, then I will reply that no one is noble whose mind is not set on virtue, nor is anyone base except on account of his vices, which make him seem shocking and stupid. Nobility comes from a virtuous heart, for nobility of family is worthless when the heart lacks virtue. Therefore the nobleman must display the prowess of his forebears, who achieved nobility by dint of considerable effort and who, on leaving the world, took all their virtues with them, leaving their possessions to their heirs, who received nothing else from them. They have the possessions but nothing else of theirs, neither nobility nor worth, unless they earn nobility by their deeds, through their own sense or virtue.[73]

Nature further contends that learned clerks are best placed to become noble because they learn how to be virtuous through study:

Now clerks have better opportunities to become noble, courteous, and wise … than do princes or kings who have no scholarship. For, associated in his books with those sciences that are capable of rational proofs and demonstrations, the clerk finds all the evils we should avoid and all the good we can do. He

[69] *Ibid.*, p. 162. [70] *Ibid.*, p. 328.
[71] *Ibid.*, p. 335.
[72] For the classical roots of this debate, see Paré, *Les idées et les lettres aux XIIIe siècle*, p. 108.
[73] *Romance of the Rose*, p. 287.

finds worldly events recorded there, just as they occurred in word and deed; in the lives of the ancients he finds all the baseness of the base and all the deeds of courteous men, the whole of courtesy. In short, he finds everything that we should avoid or cultivate written in a book, as a result of which all clerks, whether masters or disciples, are noble, or should be so.[74]

Study was therefore an alternative to arms as a route to nobility. Knights could win noble status, but 'We ought also to honour the clerk who willingly undertakes mental exertions and concentrates upon pursuing the virtues that he finds written in his book.'[75] This was a bold claim for the status of the learned, but it was also to seek status in terms that had long existed outside the world of learning and did not derive from the university. Scholarly identity was now less distinct because it was conceived in terms that blurred and perhaps even removed boundaries between scholars and the rest of society.

Jean de Meun's continuation of the *Romance of the Rose* undermined the intellectual processes and the distinctive claims to social status that were valued within the university, but by using all the intellectual tools and sophistication that the university had to offer. Theologians in particular were mocked, and the mendicants who played such a strong role in the faculty of theology were bitterly criticized. Theological teaching on sex was subverted, especially with regard to sexual pleasure, the very issue on which theologians failed to establish an agreed view. Parts of learned discourse were knowingly presented in conjunction with alien ideas to produce entertaining distortions. Scholars were to be celebrated not as masters but as nobles, and therefore in terms that applied outside the university. Most threatening of all, the possibility of certain meaning was denied. If meaning was always unstable, neither authoritative texts nor reason could be deployed effectively to generate authoritative knowledge, and the university's goals were unrealizable. Disordered meanings could be deployed critically to subvert apparently authoritative knowledge, but it was not then possible to assert anything else with certainty. Jean was an anti-intellectual intellectual who presented a profound challenge to the university, especially the theologians, and did so in the vernacular for an audience outside the university.

Marguerite Porete and *The Mirror of Simple Souls*

Marguerite Porete wrote *The Mirror of Simple Souls* in Old French around the beginning of the fourteenth century.[76] Very little is known

[74] *Ibid.* [75] *Ibid.*, p. 288.

[76] There are two excellent modern translations: Marguerite Porete, *The Mirror of Simple Souls*, trans. E. L. Babinsky (New York, 1993); Margaret Porette, *The Mirror of Simple*

about her life, and almost all the surviving evidence was generated by her second and final trial for heresy.[77] While the ecclesiastical authorities evidently thought that she disseminated her views to others, nothing is known of the circles in which she moved. She is usually described as a beguine, but she was certainly not typical of such women. Her book was first condemned by Guy of Colmieu, who was bishop of Cambrai between 1296 and 1306, and she had to watch while the book was publicly burned in Valenciennes, from where she perhaps originated. The bishop forbade her to possess or use the book, and made it clear that if she did so or tried to disseminate its contents she would be handed over to secular justice. Evidently she was not daunted, and it was probably now that she added another section to the *Mirror* (chapters 123–39), and then found three theologians willing to evaluate the work. She subsequently added a statement to the *Mirror* indicating that they had given it varying degrees of approval. The first was a Franciscan who judged that the book was inspired by the Holy Spirit, but that few should be allowed to see it, although he also admitted that he did not understand it himself. The second was a Cistercian who stated that the book spoke the truth. The third was the Parisian master of theology, Godfrey of Fontaines, who advised that access to the book should be restricted lest people be led astray, but that it described 'divine practice'.[78] It seems

Souls, trans. E. Colledge, J. C. Marler and J. Grant (Notre Dame, IN, 1999). Reading them in conjunction with the Old French and Latin texts, I sometimes prefer one and sometimes the other. I have quoted from the Babinsky translation simply because I suspect that texts in the Classics of Western Spirituality series are likely to be more widely available. It will be cited henceforth as *Mirror*.

[77] The evidence is gathered in P. Verdeyen, 'Le procès d'inquisition contre Marguerite Porete et Guiard de Cressonessart (1309–1310)', *Revue d'histoire ecclésiastique* 81 (1986): 47–94. For summaries of what is known of her life, see E. Colledge, J. C. Marler and J. Grant, 'Introductory Interpretative Essay', in Margaret Porette, *The Mirror of Simple Souls*, trans. Colledge, Marler and Grant, pp. xxxvi–xliii; R. E. Lerner, *The Heresy of the Free Spirit in the Later Middle Ages* (Berkeley, 1972), pp. 71–2; R. E. Lerner, 'An "Angel of Philadelphia" in the reign of Philip the Fair: the case of Guiard of Cressonessart', in W. C. Jordan, B. McNab and T. F. Ruiz (eds.), *Order and Innovation in the Middle Ages: Essays in Honor of Joseph R. Strayer* (Princeton, 1976), pp. 343–64 at 345–7; R. E. Lerner, 'New light on *The Mirror of Simple Souls*', *Speculum* 85 (2010): 91–116 at 92–5, 107–8; B. McGinn, *The Flowering of Mysticism: Men and Women in the New Mysticism (1200–1350)*, The Presence of God: A History of Western Christian Mysticism 3 (New York, 1998), pp. 244–5; R. A. O'Sullivan, 'The school of love: Marguerite Porete's *Mirror of Simple Souls*', *Journal of Medieval History* 32 (2006): 143–62 at 146–7; M. G. Sargent, 'The annihilation of Marguerite Porete', *Viator* 28 (1997): 253–79 at 256–7, 265.

[78] The approval is translated at *Mirror*, pp. 221–2. The Middle English translation has it at the beginning of the text, while the Latin version has it at the end. For closer analysis, see S. L. Field, 'The Master and Marguerite: Godfrey of Fontaines' praise of *The Mirror of Simple Souls*', *Journal of Medieval History* 35 (2009): 136–49; K. Kerby-Fulton, *Books under Suspicion: Censorship and Tolerance of Revelatory Writing in Late Medieval England* (Notre Dame, IN, 2006), pp. 278–80.

that Marguerite then presented the *Mirror* to John, bishop of Châlons-sur-Marne, presumably in the hope that he too would find it acceptable. This led to her arrest, in late 1308, and she was eventually sent to Paris where the Dominican inquisitor William of Paris took charge of her case. Marguerite, however, refused to answer questions despite excommunication and constant pressure. In April 1310 twenty-one Parisian masters of theology considered fifteen articles extracted from the *Mirror*, and pronounced them to be heretical. A group of four masters of canon law then ruled that she was a relapsed heretic and should be handed over to the secular authorities unless she confessed, in which case she should be imprisoned for life. Marguerite was burned to death on 1 June 1310.

Despite the efforts of the ecclesiastical authorities, the *Mirror* not only survived in Old French, but during the fourteenth and fifteenth centuries was translated into Latin twice, Italian twice and English once, though Marguerite ceased to be known as the author.[79] The text is complex, not least because Marguerite herself made additions and insertions.[80] There are frequent references to the 'hearers' of the book, so presumably it was meant to be read out loud.[81] It consists of an extended conversation between personifications, most of which represent different ways of knowing or levels of understanding. The chief protagonists are Reason, Love and Soul. Reason is supported by Intellect of Reason, and Love by Height of Intellect of Love, while a host of other voices appear as required. Reason is endlessly baffled and confused by Love's teaching, and the conversation is mainly driven by Reason's questions and requests for explanation. As Love puts it in chapter 2, everything will be explained 'through the Intellect of Love and following the questions of Reason'.[82] Marguerite attached great importance to questions, as she made clear at the start of the section she added later: 'by questions one can wander very far, and by questions one is directed to the way'.[83] Wandering is an apt way to describe the book's structure. In the early chapters, Love is pressed to explain the key points for 'Actives', 'Contemplatives'

[79] P. Dronke, *Women Writers of the Middle Ages* (Cambridge, 1984), p. 217; R. Guarnieri, 'Il <<miroir des simples ames>> di Margherita Porete', *Archivio italiano per la storia della pietà* 4 (1965): 501–635 at 504–9; Lerner, *Heresy of the Free Spirit*, pp. 72–4; Sargent, 'The annihilation', p. 261. For a summary of recent scholarship on the translations, see Lerner, 'New light', pp. 91–116.

[80] Sargent, 'The annihilation', pp. 258–9, 264–5.

[81] But see O'Sullivan, 'The school of love', pp. 157–9, for the view that hearing was 'a key metaphor for meditative reading', while granting that the *Mirror* may have been read out.

[82] *Mirror*, 2, p. 81. [83] *Ibid.*, 123, p. 202.

and 'the common folk', but thereafter a clear linear structure is hard to detect. The result, and this was perhaps the intended structure, was a high degree of repetition, with the same issues being treated again and again.[84] Furthermore, Reason frequently asks for explanation of specific passages from earlier in the book, and Love obliges. As a result, the text generates its own internal gloss, as Marguerite acknowledged when she had the Soul refer to 'the glosses of this book' and Love urge the book's audience to 'grasp the gloss'.[85]

While Marguerite did not provide her book with a linear structure, there was such a pattern in her conception of the soul's spiritual progress. At the start of the *Mirror*, Marguerite indicated that she envisaged a movement through seven stages. The first line of the first chapter noted that the soul, 'touched by God and removed from sin at the first stage of grace, is carried by divine graces to the seventh stage of grace'. At the end of the first chapter, Love affirms that there are seven stages and that 'the Soul disposes herself to all the stages before she comes to perfect being'.[86] The *Mirror* is then devoted to consideration of the stage at which the soul is annihilated and unencumbered. That this is the fifth stage is not made clear until chapter 58, and the full seven stages are not set out as an ascent until chapter 118. For the sake of a clarity that Marguerite perhaps deliberately withheld, it is worth briefly setting out the seven stages.[87]

At the first stage, the soul is concerned to obey God's commandments: 'the Soul, who is touched by God through grace and stripped of her power of sin, intends to keep for the rest of her life, that is until death, the commandments of God'. This stage is characterized by fear, 'the Soul regards and considers, through great fear, that God has commanded her to love Him with all her heart, and also her neighbour as herself', and the task seems all-consuming.[88]

The second stage involves going beyond just obeying commandments in order to pursue evangelical perfection:

> the Soul considers that God counsels His special lovers to go beyond what He commands. That one is not a lover who can refrain from accomplishing all that he knows pleases his beloved. But the creature abandons self and strains self

[84] For perceptive comments on structure, see N. Watson, 'Misrepresenting the untranslatable: Marguerite Porete and the *Mirouer des Simples Ames*', *New Comparison* 12 (1991): 124–37 at 126–7.
[85] *Mirror*, 60, p. 138 and 82, p. 158.
[86] *Ibid.*, 1, pp. 80–1.
[87] For discussion of the way in which the seven stages also relate to three types of souls and three types of death, see McGinn, *Flowering of Mysticism*, pp. 257–60.
[88] *Mirror*, 118, p. 189.

above all to do the counsels of men, in the work of mortification of nature, in despising riches, delights and honours, in order to accomplish the perfection of the evangelical counsel of which Jesus Christ is the exemplar. Thus [the Soul] fears neither the loss of possessions, nor people's words, nor the feebleness of the body, for her beloved does not fear them, and so neither can the Soul who is overtaken by Him.[89]

Thus the soul now tries to imitate Christ, fear diminishes, and there is the first sign of loss of self.

At the third stage, the soul abandons good works because they mean so much to her and therefore constitute the most precious thing that she can give up for the sake of her beloved. Thus she realizes that 'she does not love anything except these works of goodness, and for this reason she does not know what to give love if she does not sacrifice this'. Moreover, her will is sustained by the pleasure that she derives from good works, so giving up good works is a significant step in undermining her own will: 'she relinquishes such works from which she has such delights, and she puts the will to death which had life from this'. Thus 'she obliges herself to obey another will, in abstaining from work and from will, in fulfilling another will, in order to destroy her own will'. Marguerite further explained the point of this self-destruction in terms of creating space for love to fill: 'it is necessary to be pulverized in breaking and bruising the self in order to enlarge the place where love would want to be'.[90]

The fourth stage seems to be an intensification of what has been achieved at the third stage. The soul 'is drawn by the height of love into the delight of thought through meditation. And she relinquishes all exterior labours and obedience to another through the height of contemplation.' Marguerite explained that the soul is so intoxicated by love and joy that she cannot imagine a higher state of being. At this stage, however, love is deceiving, and God has still more to give.[91]

It is at the fifth stage that annihilation of the soul occurs as the soul's will dissolves into the will of God:

[the Soul] sees by Light that the will must will the Divine Will alone without any other will, and that for this purpose this will was given. And thus the Soul removes herself from this will, and the will is separated from the Soul and dissolves itself, and [the will] gives and renders itself to God, whence it was first taken, without retaining anything of its own in order to fulfill the perfect Divine Will, which cannot be fulfilled in the Soul without such a gift, so that the Soul might not have warfare or deficiency. Such a gift accomplishes this

[89] *Ibid.*, p. 189. [90] *Ibid.*, p. 190. [91] *Ibid.*, pp. 190–1.

perfection in her and so transforms her into the nature of Love, who delights her with full peace and satisfies her with divine food.[92]

In chapter 58 Marguerite makes clear that after attaining the fifth stage, the soul cannot drop back down again: 'the Soul keeps herself freely at the fifth stage, without falling to the fourth, because at the fourth she has will, and at the fifth she has none'.[93]

The sixth stage was the last that could be experienced in this life, and here the Soul

sees neither God nor herself, but God sees Himself of Himself in her, for her, without her. God shows to her that there is nothing except Him. And thus this Soul understands nothing except Him, and so loves nothing except Him, praises nothing except Him, for there is nothing except Him.[94]

As Marguerite explains in chapter 58, the annihilated soul at the fifth stage ascends momentarily to the sixth stage before returning to the fifth: 'she is often carried up to the sixth, but this is of little duration. For it is an aperture, like a spark, which quickly closes, in which one cannot long remain'.[95] That the sixth stage was a foretaste of the seventh stage was made clear in chapter 61.[96]

The seventh and final stage was 'glorification' and could only be achieved after death. It was impossible to say anything about this stage since 'we will have no understanding until our soul has left our body'.[97]

Although she had not yet set it out in detail, Marguerite commented on the overall shape of this ascent in chapter 61. Her first point was that there was a huge gap between each stage:

there are seven stages, each one of higher intellect than the former and without comparison to each other. As one might compare a drop of water to the total ocean, which is very great, so one might speak of the difference between the first stage of grace and the second, and so on with the rest: there is no comparison.

Her second point, however, was that nonetheless the first four stages had something in common, and the really great divide came with the ascent to the fifth stage:

Even so, of the first four stages, none is so high that the Soul does not still live in some great servitude. But the fifth stage is in the freeness of charity, for this stage is unencumbered from all things.[98]

92 *Ibid.*, pp. 191–2. 93 *Ibid.*, 58, p. 135.
94 *Ibid.*, 118, p. 193. 95 *Ibid.*, 58, p. 135.
96 *Ibid.*, 61, p. 138. 97 *Ibid.*, 118, pp. 193–4.
98 *Ibid.*, 61, p. 138.

So, for Marguerite the greatest jump was between the fourth and fifth stages, and it was decisive because the soul could not fall back down again. From the fifth stage the now annihilated soul would enjoy momentary experiences of the sixth stage which was a glimpse of the seventh stage which awaited after death. The real focus of the *Mirror* as a whole, however, was on the fifth stage.

From the outset, Marguerite stressed that the *Mirror*, and therefore the fifth stage in the ascent, was difficult to understand and that humility was required. The verse prologue began:

> You who would read this book,
> If you indeed wish to grasp it,
> Think about what you say,
> For it is very difficult to comprehend;
> Humility, who is the keeper of the treasury of
> Knowledge
> And the mother of the other Virtues,
> Must overtake you.[99]

Moreover, Marguerite repeatedly stressed that the *Mirror* offered understanding that was beyond even masters of theology. The verse prologue at least implied that with humility they might get somewhere:

> Theologians and other clerks,
> You will not have the intellect for it,
> No matter how brilliant your abilities,
> If you do not proceed humbly.[100]

In chapter 5, however, Love makes it clear that the annihilated soul 'does not seek divine knowledge among the masters of this age'.[101] Moreover, in chapter 9 Love simply declares that learned masters, including theologians, will not be able to make sense of the way in which the annihilated soul no longer possesses will: 'none of the masters of the natural senses, nor any of the masters of Scripture, nor those who remain in the love of the obedience to the Virtues, none perceive this, nor will they perceive what is intended'.[102] Marguerite thus set herself apart from and indeed very much above mere masters of theology.

In large part this was because she held the knowledge with which she was concerned to be shaped by love and not at all by reason. As far as she was concerned, she was therefore operating at a level far above that which could be attained by use of reason. Again, this is made clear in

[99] *Ibid.*, verse prologue, p. 79. See also Love's first speech in chapter 1; 1, p. 80.
[100] *Ibid.*, verse prologue, p. 79.
[101] *Ibid.*, 5, p. 83. [102] *Ibid.*, 9, p. 87.

the verse prologue as she continues to address 'theologians and other clerks':

> And may Love and Faith, together,
> Cause you to rise above Reason,
> [Since] they are the ladies of the house.
> Even Reason witnesses
> In the Thirteenth Chapter of this book,
> And with no shame about it,
> That Love and Faith make her live
> And she does not free herself from them,
> For they have lordship over her,
> Which is why she must humble herself.
> Humble, then, your wisdom
> Which is based on Reason,
> And place all your fidelity
> in those things which are given
> By Love, illuminated through Faith.
> And thus you will understand this book
> Which makes the Soul live by love.[103]

Thereafter Reason is repeatedly belittled. In chapter 12 the Soul mocks Reason for persistently failing to understand:

> Ah, Intellect of Reason, says the Annihilated Soul, how you are so discerning! You take the shell and leave the kernel, for your intellect is too low, hence you cannot perceive so loftily as is necessary for the one who wishes to perceive the being of which we speak.[104]

As indicated in the verse prologue, Reason accepts the superior understanding that Love offers:

> Thus I say to all, that none will grasp this book with my intellect unless they grasp it by the virtue of Faith, and by the power of Love, who are my mistresses because I obey them in all things.[105]

This submission does not, however, bring an end to the denigration of Reason. Love later informs Reason that she 'will always be one-eyed, you and all those who are fed by your doctrine'.[106] The Soul describes those who live by Reason's counsel as 'beasts and donkeys'.[107] As another way of thinking about progress to the fifth stage and annihilation, Marguerite suggested that three deaths were necessary, of sin, of will and finally of reason. Reason in fact dies in chapter 87, but reappears to

[103] *Ibid.*, verse prologue, p. 79.
[104] *Ibid.*, 12, p. 93. [105] *Ibid.*, 13, p. 95.
[106] *Ibid.*, 43, p. 122. [107] *Ibid.*, 68, p. 143.

keep on asking questions.[108] The *Mirror* thus associated reason with the theologians, and expressed nothing but contempt for it, along with an overwhelming sense of superiority.

While Marguerite insisted that reason offered no way of understanding her concept of the annihilation of the soul, her attempts to explain it focused above all on the will. Her key point was that the annihilated soul had lost her own will, and that God now willed through her, and this was articulated repeatedly by Love:

it is no longer her will which wills, but now the will of God wills in her.[109]

she cannot do anything if it is not the will of God, and also she cannot will some other thing.[110]

all that this Soul wills in consent is what God wills that she will, and this she wills in order to accomplish the will of God, no longer for the sake of her own will. And she cannot will this by herself, but it is the will of God which wills it in her.[111]

Now listen and grasp well, hearers of this book, the true intellect by which this book speaks in different places, that the Annihilated Soul neither possesses will, nor is able to possess it, nor is able to will to possess it, and in this the divine will is perfectly accomplished.[112]

the Unencumbered Soul possesses no longer any will to will or not-will, except only to will the will of God, and to accept in peace the divine ordinance.[113]

In essence, what Marguerite was trying to convey was that God's will did not exist in the annihilated soul alongside her own will; the only will operating in the soul was God's will. The result was an unequal union in which the annihilated soul 'loses her name in the One in whom she is melted and dissolved through Himself and in Himself'. Love likened her to the water in a named river, for example the Seine or the Aisne, which then loses that name when it flows into the sea simply to become part of the sea.[114] Love even declares that 'this Soul is God by the condition of Love'.[115]

Attaining this state meant understanding the emptiness and meaninglessness of all human understanding. Love comments that 'the more this Soul has understanding of the divine goodness, the more perfectly she understands that she understands nothing about it, compared to one spark of His goodness, for His goodness is not comprehended except by Himself'.[116] So in one sense the soul has a higher form of understanding, but it is an understanding that she understands nothing, so 'she knows

[108] *Ibid.*, 60, p. 137; 72–3, p. 147; 87, pp. 162–3.
[109] *Ibid.*, 7, p. 85. [110] *Ibid.*, 11, p. 90.
[111] *Ibid.*, p. 92. [112] *Ibid.*, 12, p. 92.
[113] *Ibid.*, 13, p. 96. [114] *Ibid.*, 82, p. 158.
[115] *Ibid.*, 21, p. 104. [116] *Ibid.*, 5, p. 83.

all and she knows nothing'.[117] Or, as Love explains at greater length, 'this Soul is so well established that if she possessed all the understanding of all the creatures who ever were and who are and who are to come, so it would seem to her as nothing, compared to what she loves, which never was understood, is not now, and never will be'.[118] The realization that there could be no genuine understanding of God was accompanied by an intense awareness of the inadequacy of anything that could be said about God. As the Soul says to Love, 'God is none other than the One of whom one can understand nothing perfectly. For He alone is my God, about whom one does not know how to say a word.' The Soul concludes that when she talks about Love, 'I slander because everything I say is nothing but slander about your goodness.'[119] Ultimately, given the annihilated soul's acknowledgment that God was beyond both understanding and words, words were abandoned: 'Such creatures know no longer how to speak of God.'[120] In the end, the annihilated soul must fall silent.

There was, however, an obvious paradox in Marguerite's position. She had to use words to explain the inadequacy of language, and to generate an understanding that true understanding was beyond words. To do this, she pushed language to the limits of meaning, using the apophatic strategies of paradox and contradiction. She referred frequently to the annihilated soul 'who has become nothing, thus possesses everything, and so possesses nothing; she wills everything and she wills nothing; she knows all and she knows nothing'.[121] Similarly, there was Farnearness, 'which we call a spark in the manner of an aperture and quick closure', and which 'receives the Soul at the fifth stage and places her at the sixth'.[122] Reason names this strategy: they are 'double words', and they are difficult to understand.[123] Marguerite did not intend the *Mirror* to be easy reading, and it was through bafflement that her audience might find understanding beyond understanding.

One of the most controversial aspects of Marguerite's approach was her insistence that the annihilated soul took leave of the virtues and 'is saved by faith without works'.[124] Three of the fifteen articles for which she was condemned are known to us, and two of them concern this issue.[125] She made the point repeatedly throughout the *Mirror*. The Soul, for example, tells Love how she takes leave of the virtues:

[117] *Ibid.*, 7, p. 85. [118] *Ibid.*, 11, p. 90. [119] *Ibid.*, p. 91.
[120] *Ibid.*, 18, p. 101. [121] *Ibid.*, 7, p. 85. [122] *Ibid.*, 58, p. 135.
[123] *Ibid.*, 13, p. 94. [124] *Ibid.*, 5, p. 82.
[125] Colledge, Marler and Grant, 'Introductory Interpretative Essay', p. xlv; Lerner, *Heresy of the Free Spirit*, p. 75; McGinn, *Flowering of Mysticism*, p. 245, n. 243; Verdeyen, 'Le procès d'inquisition', pp. 51, 88.

I confess it to you, Lady Love, says this Soul, there was a time when I belonged to them, but now it is another time. Your courtliness has placed me outside their service. And thus to them I can now say and sing: Virtues, I take my leave of you forever.[126]

Love goes on to explain what this means: 'This Soul, says Love, takes account of neither shame nor honour, of neither poverty nor wealth, of neither anxiety nor ease, of neither love nor hate, of neither hell nor of paradise.'[127] And Love elaborates:

Whoever would ask such free Souls, sure and peaceful, if they would want to be in purgatory, they would say no; or if they would want to be certain of their salvation in this life, they would say no; or if they would want to be in paradise, they would say no ... Such a soul neither desires nor despises poverty nor tribulation, neither mass nor sermon, neither fast nor prayer, and gives to Nature all that is necessary, without remorse of conscience.[128]

Marguerite was obviously aware how shocking this sounded because Reason repeatedly expressed dismay at this apparent rejection of fundamental values and practices espoused by the church:

This Soul no longer has any sentiment of grace, nor desire of spirit, since she has taken leave of the Virtues who offer the manner of living well to every good soul, and without these Virtues none can be saved nor come to perfection of life; and whoever possesses them cannot be deceived. Nevertheless, this Soul takes leave of them. Is she not out of her mind, the Soul who speaks thus?[129]

Marguerite agreed that the moral teaching of the church was important for most people. At the start of the *Mirror*, Love acknowledges that the church's commands 'are of necessity for salvation for all: nobody can have grace with a lesser way'.[130] When explaining the annihilated soul's relationship with nature, Love also recognizes that 'one dare not speak overtly about it. And no doubt on account of the simple intellects of other creatures, lest they misapprehend to their damage.'[131] So, on at least one occasion in the *Mirror*, Marguerite showed awareness that some people might be seduced by her words and simply behave in an immoral fashion that she agreed would lead to their damnation. This was not, however, a dominant concern in the *Mirror*. Marguerite was only interested in the annihilated souls, and it is not immediately clear (unsurprisingly) what she had in mind for them.

There was no doubt that despite taking leave of the virtues the annihilated soul continued to have some sort of relationship with them.

[126] *Mirror*, 6, p. 84. [127] *Ibid.*, 7, p. 84.
[128] *Ibid.*, 9, pp. 86–7. [129] *Ibid.*, 8, p. 85.
[130] *Ibid.*, 3, p. 81. [131] *Ibid.*, 17, p. 100.

According to Love, responding to Reason's incredulity, 'such Souls possess better the Virtues than any other creatures, but they do not possess any longer the practice of them, for these Souls no longer belong to the Virtues as they used to'.[132] If this meant that annihilated souls could behave contrary to the virtues and still be saved, this was scarcely reassuring. Marguerite's preferred explanation seems to have been in terms of the virtues and the soul exchanging places in a hierarchy. Love tells an improbable story about a servant becoming wiser and richer than his master, and therefore leaving to serve someone else. His former master then decides to stay with his former servant and to obey him because of his now greater worth. In just this way the soul first obeyed the virtues, at Reason's behest, but then 'gained and learned so much with the Virtues that she is now superior to the Virtues, for she has within her all that the Virtues know how to teach and more, without comparison'. The soul and the virtues were still together, but the soul was now in the superior position.[133] This did not really clarify exactly how an annihilated soul might be expected to behave. There are, however, a number of occasions in the *Mirror* where Marguerite seems to qualify her more provocative statements and make them 'safe'. One has been the subject of much debate. First, as we have seen, Love declares that 'Such a soul neither desires nor despises poverty nor tribulation, neither mass nor sermon, neither fast nor prayer, and gives to Nature all that is necessary, without remorse of conscience.' Then she immediately adds: 'But such Nature is so well ordered through the transformation by unity of Love, to whom the will of this Soul is conjoined, that Nature demands nothing which is prohibited.'[134] On the face of it, Marguerite had first said something outrageous and then pulled back. It has been argued, however, that this second, qualifying statement was a later insertion because it occurs in different places in different versions, and opinions differ as to whether Marguerite was responsible for it.[135] Be that as it may, there are other, textually uncontested, points in the *Mirror* where the same kind of 'safe' interpretation is offered. Once more in response to Reason's anxious questioning, Love explains that the annihilated soul's thought is 'in the Trinity' and 'From this [place] no one falls into sin, and any sin which was ever done ... is as

[132] *Ibid.*, 8, pp. 85–6. [133] *Ibid.*, 21, pp. 103–4. [134] *Ibid.*, 9, p. 87.

[135] E. Colledge and R. Guarnieri, 'The glosses by <<M.N.>> and Richard Methley to <<The Mirror of Simple Souls>>', *Archivio italiano per la storia della pietà* 5 (1968): 357–82 at 362–3; E. Colledge, 'Liberty of spirit: "The Mirror of Simple Souls"', in L. K. Shook (ed.), *Theology of Renewal*, 2 vols. (New York, 1968), vol. 2, pp. 100–17 at 104; Lerner, *Heresy of the Free Spirit*, p. 76; Lerner, 'New light', pp. 110–14; Sargent, 'The annhilation', pp. 258–9.

displeasing to her will as it is to God's. It is His displeasure itself which gives to this Soul such displeasure.' Furthermore, 'if this Soul, who is at rest so high, could help her neighbours, she would aid them with all her power in their need'.[136] There are therefore moments in the *Mirror* when Marguerite's ideas seem straightforwardly compatible with the conventional teaching of the church. But Marguerite's real concern was to work through the consequences of the annihilation of the will:

> This Soul, says Love, does not do any work for God's sake, nor for her own, nor for her neighbours' either ... But God does it, if He wills, [He] who is able to do it. And if He does not will, it does not matter to her one way or the other; she is always in one state.[137]

Having explained that God willed through the annihilated soul which had no will of its own, it simply made no sense to Marguerite to worry about how people in this state would behave. Since God could not be said to sin, how could they? Marguerite made her point, however, in a fashion that was bound to disconcert people and prompt questions.

Even if Marguerite's view of the relationship between the annihilated soul and the virtues was less radical than it might at first seem, her ideas undoubtedly constituted a profound challenge to the role of the priest and the church, and on this matter she not only expressed her thoughts in provocative fashion, but offered no qualifications at all. The annihilated soul was indifferent to masses, sermons, fasts, prayers and the like partly because she had no will of her own, but also because she had a direct relationship with God that left no function for the church. As Love puts it, likening the annihilated soul to the seraphim, 'She no longer wants anything which comes by a mediary.'[138] Throughout the *Mirror*, the church is presented in an unflattering if not disparaging light. Love refers to the church run by the clergy as 'Holy Church the Little', which is governed by Reason, as distinct from 'Holy Church the Great', which is governed by Love.[139] The Soul queries whether those who are not annihilated souls should be able to attain salvation at all since through the church even murderers will be saved if they repent.[140] According to Love, the Soul is 'in the greatest perfection of being, and she is closest to the Farnearness, when she no longer takes Holy Church as exemplar in her life'.[141] It is hardly surprising that John Baconthorpe, who was studying in Paris during Marguerite's trial, called the *Mirror* 'a book against the clergy'.[142]

[136] *Mirror*, 16, p. 99. [137] *Ibid.*, 71, p. 145.
[138] *Ibid.*, 5, p. 83. [139] *Ibid.*, 19, p. 101.
[140] *Ibid.*, 121, p. 197. [141] *Ibid.*, 134, p. 217.
[142] As quoted by Lerner, *Heresy of the Free Spirit*, p. 206; Sargent, 'The annhilation', p. 257.

It is not easy to establish what the *Mirror* meant to Marguerite herself. The Soul is generally held to represent her, and indeed the first time the Soul speaks in chapter 1 she is introduced as 'the Soul who had this book written'.[143] Later, when Love praises the Soul, she refers to the Soul as 'this precious pearl', and 'pearl' is 'marguerite' in Old French.[144] As befits a soul in transformation, however, the question of authorship is not straightforward. In chapter 97, 'this Soul who wrote this book' says: 'I was so foolish at the time when I wrote it; but Love did it for my sake and at my request.'[145] Indeed the process of annihilation raises questions about how Marguerite understood the process of writing. If she thought she was an annihilated soul, how could she write at all when she should have fallen silent? If she did not consider that she had reached that state, how did she think that she knew anything about it? At the start of the *Mirror* Love tells 'a little exemplum of love in the world'. The daughter of a king heard of King Alexander and fell in love with him on the basis of his reputation. Distraught that she could not actually see him, she 'had an image painted which would represent the semblance of the king she loved', and this helped her to dream of him. Similarly, the Soul explains, she learned about a great king, and could find no comfort because of the immense distance between them. Then, 'He gave me this book, which makes present in some fashion His love itself.'[146] The book is thus presented as a kind of devotional aid for Marguerite. More significantly, however, subsequent passages present the writing of the book as part of the process by which Marguerite became an annihilated soul. The Soul says of the book that Love 'tells me that I complete all my enterprises in it'.[147] Later, to quote more of a passage cited earlier, the Soul emphasizes the nature of the task:

> I was so foolish at the time when I wrote [this book]; but Love did it for my sake and at my request, that I might undertake something which one could neither do, nor think, nor say.[148]

Thus Love wanted her to take on the impossible, to try to find words for what was beyond words. Towards what was originally the end of the

[143] *Mirror*, 1, p. 80. For the view that the Soul represents the author, see Sargent, 'The annhilation', p. 258; Watson, 'Misrepresenting the untranslatable', pp. 129–30. But for the suggestion that 'The motive for her putting almost everything in her book in the mouths of projections … might be to intimate that it is not she who is speaking; and this would leave open the possibility that she is, or is becoming, the free soul she aspires to be', see Dronke, *Women Writers*, p. 226. For a judicious assessment, see McGinn, *Flowering of Mysticism*, p. 248.

[144] *Mirror*, 52, p. 129. [145] *Ibid.*, 97, p. 171. [146] *Ibid.*, 1, p. 80.

[147] *Ibid.*, 11, p. 92. [148] *Ibid.*, 97, p. 171.

book, 'the Soul who causes this book to be written' offers an apology to annihilated souls:

I excuse myself ... to all those who remain in nothingness and who are fallen from love into such being. For I have made this book very large through words, [though] it seems to you very small, insofar as I am able to understand you. Now please pardon me by your courtesy, for necessity has no law. I did not know to whom to speak my intention. Now I understand, on account of your peace and on account of the truth, that [this book] is of the lower life. Cowardice has guided [this book], which has given its perception over to Reason through the answers of Love to Reason's petitions. And so [this book] has been created by human knowledge and the human senses; and the human reason and the human senses know nothing about inner love, inner love from divine knowledge. My heart is drawn so high and fallen so low at the same time that I cannot complete [this book] ... I have said, says this Soul, that Love caused [the book] to be written through human knowledge and through willing it by the transformation of my intellect with which I was encumbered, as it appears in this book. For Love made the book in unencumbering my spirit.[149]

Marguerite thus acknowledges that her book, written in words, necessarily belongs to the lower realm of human knowledge and reason. But through the writing of the book, Love has transformed her understanding. In so far as her understanding is expressed in the book, it is still encumbered; now, however, it is unencumbered and she cannot go on writing. The book is inadequate, and she has left it behind.

While Marguerite valued the process of writing for herself, she also had an audience in mind for the book, whatever its unavoidable limitations. She divided that audience into annihilated souls, those who would be annihilated souls in the future, and those who were never going to be annihilated souls. Having written about the momentary experience of the sixth stage of the ascent, the Soul explains that she must also discuss less elevated topics: 'If you have heard in these words a high matter, says this Soul to the hearers of this book, do not be displeased if I speak afterward about little things, for it is necessary for me to do so if I want to accomplish the enterprise of my goal – not, she says, for the sake of those who are this, but for those who are not who yet will be, and will beg continuously as long as they are with themselves.'[150] Here Marguerite's stated purpose is not to transform herself, but to reach out to those who will eventually become annihilated souls. She makes the same point when the Soul says that the book has been made 'so that you little ones might be of this sort without interruption, at least in will, if you still have it', and she adds for those who are already

[149] *Ibid.*, 119, pp. 194–5. [150] *Ibid.*, 59, p. 136.

unencumbered that 'at least you could explain the glosses of this book'.[151] Later the Soul says that she sings 'for those who are not yet unencumbered, so that they might hear something about freeness, and whatever else is necessary until they arrive at this stage'.[152] The fullest analysis of Marguerite's audience and the expected responses, however, is presented by Love:

> You ladies, to whom God has abundantly given this life by His divine goodness without withholding anything, and not only this life which we describe, but also the one of whom no human speaks, you will recognize your practice in this book. And those who are not of this kind, nor were, nor will be, will not feel this being, nor understand it. They cannot do it, nor will they do it. They are not, as you know, of the lineage of which we speak ... But those who are not this now – but they are so in God, which is why they will be so – will understand this being and sense it, through the strength of the lineage from which they are and will be, more strongly indeed than those who have not understood it and sensed it. And such folk of whom we speak, who are this way and will be, will recognize, as soon as they hear it, their lineage from which they come.[153]

So annihilated souls will recognize that the book is about them. Those who are never going to be annihilated souls will not be able to understand or respond to it in any way. Those who will be annihilated souls will understand and respond, indeed they will immediately recognize 'their lineage' so that they come to grasp who they really are. That these future annihilated souls might also have to make a sustained effort, however, was indicated in the section that Marguerite added to the *Mirror*. It began:

> I wish to speak about some considerations for the sad ones who ask the way to the land of freeness, considerations which indeed helped me at the time when I was one of the sad ones, when I lived from milk and pabulum, and when I was still ignorant. And these considerations helped me to suffer and endure during the time when I was off the path, and then helped me to find the path.[154]

In this additional section Marguerite offered the benefit of her experience, giving practical advice on the kind of reflection that would help those who would eventually become annihilated souls. Marguerite therefore wrote the *Mirror* to help future annihilated souls recognize themselves as such, and to explain how they could realize their ultimate goal.[155]

[151] *Ibid.*, 60, p. 138. [152] *Ibid.*, 80, p. 155.
[153] *Ibid.*, 98, p. 172. [154] *Ibid.*, 123, p. 202.
[155] For persuasive analysis of the *Mirror* as a didactic work that must be understood in the context of beguine education and meditative training, see O'Sullivan, 'The school of love', pp. 143–62.

But who were these annihilated souls? They could be anyone and they could be anywhere. Love offers explanations to Actives, Contemplatives and the common folk, but these were not important distinctions because the same message was given to them all. Moreover, it was clearly envisaged that annihilated souls might be found amongst the lower orders since Reason wants annihilated souls to be described to the common folk 'of whom some will be able perchance to come to this stage'.[156] Social hierarchies were therefore irrelevant. It was also difficult, if not impossible, to identify them. Love comments first that 'few people know where these Souls are'.[157] She then goes further, saying that 'a thing which God has created knows not how to find these Souls'.[158] Addressing Faith, Hope and Charity, she explains that 'who they are … is known neither to you nor to them, which is why Holy Church cannot know it'.[159] Annihilated souls were therefore effectively beyond the jurisdiction of the church. The *Mirror* thus challenged notions of social hierarchy and, yet again, the authority of the church.

Notions of social class were, however, extremely important to Marguerite. The *Mirror* is rich in courtly language and imagery, and there are many references to nobility, and occasionally to other social groups. The *exemplum* in the first chapter, for example, features 'a maiden, daughter of a king, of great heart and nobility and also of noble character', and she 'heard tell of the great gentle courtesy and nobility of the king, Alexander'. Here Marguerite was drawing upon the *Roman d'Alexandre*.[160] She frequently associated Love with courtesy. To give just a few examples, Pure Courtesy and Courtesy of the Goodness of Love have brief speaking parts, and the Soul addresses Love as 'overflowing and abundant lover, and courtesy without measure for my sake'.[161] Fine Love is also identified with divine love; thus, to give just one example, the Soul says that the book can only be understood by one 'whom Fine Love rules'.[162] Those who are at the first stage of the ascent are, again according to the Soul, 'saved in an uncourtly way'.[163] Most important of all, the annihilated soul is noble.[164] Love addresses annihilated souls as 'you most noble ones'.[165] She describes the annihilated soul as 'gently

156 *Mirror*, 13, p. 94. 157 *Ibid.*, 17, p. 100.

158 *Ibid.*, 19, p. 101. 159 *Ibid.*, p. 102.

160 O'Sullivan, 'The school of love', p. 159; Sargent, 'The annhilation', p. 267.

161 *Mirror*, 10, p. 88; 15, p. 98; 38, p. 118.

162 *Ibid.*, 53, p. 131. 163 *Ibid.*, 62, p. 139.

164 For extended analysis of Marguerite's treatment of the theme of nobility and lineage, see J. M. Robinson, *Nobility and Annihilation in Marguerite Porete's Mirror of Simple Souls* (New York, 2001), esp. pp. 88–107. See also brief comments from Lerner, *Heresy of the Free Spirit*, p. 233.

165 *Mirror*, 60, p. 137.

noble in prosperity, and supremely noble in adversity, and excellently noble in all places whatever they might be'.[166] The momentary experience of the sixth stage of the ascent is a 'noble' gift.[167] Love exclaims, 'O very high-born one ... it is well that you have entered the only noble manor, where no one enters if he is not of your lineage and without bastardy.'[168] When future annihilated souls read the *Mirror* and recognized their lineage, they were becoming aware of their noble status. Without doubt this vocabulary reflected Marguerite's debt to vernacular literature and in particular the influence of courtly ideas about love.[169] It also gave her an immensely powerful way of representing the enormity of the gap between the annihilated soul and everyone else, and to express her utter contempt for those who lived by the values and religious practices that she associated with the church. At one point the Soul invites Christ not to bother with those who achieve salvation merely by avoiding mortal sin because they are selfish and 'on account of their rudeness'. Love acknowledges their 'crudity', and the Soul continues:

This is the manner, says this Soul, of the merchant folk, who in the world are called crude, for indeed crude they are. For the gentleman does not know how to mingle in the marketplace or how to be selfish. But I will tell you, says this Soul, in what I appease myself concerning such folk. In this, Lady Love, that they are kept outside the court of your secrets, much like a peasant would be kept from the court of a gentleman in the judgment of his peers, where no one can be a part of the court if he is not of correct lineage – and certainly not in the court of a king.[170]

Marguerite's social background is unknown, but she certainly knew how to deploy the noble's disdain for merchants and peasants.[171] She used it to denigrate conventional piety and the church, but it also had implications for the culture of learning. Marguerite was deeply learned and the *Mirror* was a work of great intellect. Yet she adopted a vocabulary that was not from the world of university learning in order to emphasize a

[166] *Ibid.*, 85, p. 160. [167] *Ibid.*, 58, p. 136. [168] *Ibid.*, 52, p. 129.

[169] See E. L. Babinsky, 'The use of courtly language in *Le Mirouer des simples ames anienties* by Marguerite Porete', *Essays in Medieval Studies* 4 (1987): 91–106; McGinn, *Flowering of Mysticism*, pp. 246, 248; B. Newman, '"*La mystique courtoise*": thirteenth-century beguines and the art of love', in *From Virile Woman to WomanChrist: Studies in Medieval Religion and Literature* (Philadelphia, 1995), pp. 137–67; O'Sullivan, 'The school of love', pp. 159–60. For analysis of literary form, see Dronke, *Women Writers*, pp. 218–27.

[170] *Mirror*, 63, p. 140.

[171] Lerner, 'New light', p. 108 suggests that she was 'a woman of means', given how much the parchment for a copy of her work would have cost. At p. 108, note 74, he further comments that 'she most likely came from a wealthy patrician background that had absorbed aristocratic manners and prejudices'.

form of knowing (or unknowing) that she considered superior to anything university theologians had to offer.

Like Jean de Meun, Marguerite Porete attacked reason, undermined the value of knowledge that was based on reason, and called into question the ability of language to convey truth with certainty. To make her point, she used language in ways that made meaning seem uncertain. But whereas Jean did this by holding every idea and way of knowing in play, without hierarchy, Marguerite very definitely had a hierarchy. Parisian theologians were perfectly comfortable with the idea that divinely inspired knowledge was superior to all human knowledge, but Marguerite chose to disparage everything that was below the experience of the annihilated soul. More than this, she attacked the social and institutional embodiments of human knowledge, making withering comments about the church in general and theologians in particular. Furthermore, she did this as a woman, in the vernacular, and outside any institutional framework. There was nothing to guarantee that she would behave with the virtue necessary to know well, and indeed she herself called into question her regard for virtue. Not only was Marguerite herself independent of any institution, but she envisaged that other annihilated souls would be too. They could come from any social background, and there was no way to identify them. To convey their superior status, however, she borrowed the vocabulary of nobility and courtliness. Evidently institutions of learning were irrelevant to the kind of knowing, or unknowing, that Marguerite championed. She had, however, acquired considerable learning by whatever means, and the *Mirror* was no emotional outpouring. Her anti-intellectual stance was therefore a theoretical challenge to the identity and authority of Parisian masters of theology at several levels, and one that had an existence outside the university.[172]

Eckhart

Eckhart was born around 1260 in Thuringia, and he joined the Dominican order in Erfurt. It is possible that he studied the arts in Paris before attending the Dominican school in Cologne. He then read the Sentences in Paris, before leaving in 1294 to become prior

172 For a superb account of the various ways in which Parisian clerics, including theologians, represented beguines in sermons and *exempla*, sometimes explicitly comparing the beguine and the Parisian master, see T. S. Miller, 'What's in a name? Clerical representations of Parisian beguines (1200–1328)', *Journal of Medieval History* 33 (2007): 60–86.

of the Dominican convent in Erfurt and vicar of Thuringia, the latter post involving pastoral responsibility for women's convents. In 1302 he moved to Paris to become a regent master of theology. After one year in this post, he became the first provincial of the newly established Dominican province of Saxonia in northern Germany, a position he held from 1303 to 1311. In 1311 he returned to Paris as a master of theology, this time for two years. From 1313 he spent at least ten years based in Strasburg as vicar-general of the province of Teutonia. During this time, the bishop of Strasburg, John of Zurich, largely supported by the secular clergy, attacked the beguines, demanding that they return to normal lives in their parishes in 1319. Since Eckhart was preaching in women's convents in south Germany, many of which had begun as beguine communities, he is likely to have become involved in these controversies and was probably perceived as a supporter of the beguines by their critics. He also began writing theological works in German at this time. No earlier than 1323 he became head of the Dominican school in Cologne and continued his preaching to popular audiences. In 1325 his work was examined for heresy by Nicholas of Strasburg, who was lector in Eckhart's school and both Dominican and papal visitor to the province of Teutonia. By early 1326, Nicholas had found his work to be entirely orthodox. It has been suggested that this was an attempt to stave off attacks on Eckhart. If so, the attempt failed because later in 1326 inquisitorial proceedings against him were launched by Henry of Virneburg, who had been archbishop of Cologne since 1306. Henry had a long record of hostility to beguines and beghards, considering them to be involved in the heresy of the free spirit. He was a leading figure at the Council of Vienne, where two bulls attacking them were issued, *Cum de quibusdam* and *Ad nostrum*, the latter using some material extracted from Marguerite's *Mirror*.[173] Moreover, he knew the bishop of Strasburg, who was also at the Council of Vienne. Presumably he was therefore well informed about Eckhart's activities in Strasburg, which perhaps explains why he was so relentless in his attack on Eckhart. Several long lists of articles extracted from Eckhart's work were drawn up, and Eckhart composed a response, which survives. In 1327, after preaching in the Dominican church in Cologne, a fellow Dominican read out a statement in Latin upon which Eckhart commented in German, insisting that he was not a heretic and making it clear that he was ready to retract anything that was found to be in error. When

[173] Colledge and Guarnieri, 'The glosses by <<M.N.>>', p. 359; Lerner, *Heresy of the Free Spirit*, pp. 82–3; McGinn, *Flowering of Mysticism*, p. 246; Miller, 'What's in a name?', pp. 61–2.

he appealed to the pope, proceedings shifted to the papal court in Avignon, so Eckhart went there with several leading Dominicans from his region. The lists of articles were examined by a commission of theologians and another of cardinals, and twenty-eight articles were judged heretical. Eckhart died in Avignon in late 1327 or early 1328, but the process continued, perhaps because the pope was heavily dependent on Henry of Virneburg as a key ally against Lewis of Bavaria, with whom he was locked in conflict over control of Italy. It culminated in 1329 with the bull *In agro dominico*, which listed twenty-six articles that Eckhart had accepted that he preached or wrote, and two further articles which Eckhart had denied preaching. The first fifteen and the additional two articles were condemned as heretical, while the other eleven were deemed highly suspect although possibly open to orthodox interpretation.[174]

A significant proportion of Eckhart's works were written or preached in German, many for a female audience, and the following analysis is based on material taken from them. Many of the sermons were preached to women in Strasburg or Cologne. It must be noted, however, that they have come down to us as *reportationes*, so it is impossible to be certain that they are exactly as Eckhart preached them.[175] The treatise *On the Noble Man* was part of the *Liber Benedictus* which was written in Strasburg and dedicated to Agnes, queen of Hungary, perhaps when she entered the religious life.[176] The treatise *On Detachment* has also been used, although its authenticity has been questioned by some experts in the field.[177]

There can be little doubt that Eckhart knew about Marguerite Porete and her work because for two years from 1311 to 1313 both he and William of Paris, who had led the proceedings against Marguerite, were resident in the Dominican house in Paris. Since William had ordered all copies of the *Mirror* to be handed to him or to the Dominican prior in Paris, it is entirely possible that a copy was kept in the house and that Eckhart read it. Whatever the degree of his familiarity with her work, it

174 For accounts of Eckhart's life, see O. Davies, *Meister Eckhart: Mystical Theologian* (London, 1991), pp. 22–45; B. McGinn, *The Harvest of Mysticism in Medieval Germany (1300–1500)*, The Presence of God: A History of Western Christian Mysticism 4 (New York, 2005), pp. 94–107.

175 Davies, *Meister Eckhart*, pp. 72, 127, 239; E. Colledge and B. McGinn, 'Introduction', in Meister Eckhart, *The Essential Sermons, Commentaries, Treatises, and Defense*, trans. E. Colledge and B. McGinn (New York, 1981), pp. 66–7.

176 Davies, *Meister Eckhart*, p. 26.

177 Colledge and McGinn, 'Introduction', in Meister Eckhart, *The Essential Sermons*, p. 68.

has been convincingly argued that he was influenced by her ideas and her language.[178]

Whereas Marguerite wrote about the annihilated or unencumbered soul, however, Eckhart's key term was 'detachment', by which he meant being 'free from all created things'.[179] This definitely included the will, as Eckhart made very clear in his sermon *Beati pauperes spiritu*, 'Blessed are the poor in spirit', where Marguerite's direct influence is most obvious. In this sermon he took poverty as the central theme, stressing from the beginning that he was concerned with internal rather than external poverty. In this sense, according to Eckhart, 'a poor person is someone who desires nothing, knows nothing and possesses nothing'.[180] Treating the first of these characteristics, Eckhart explained that this entailed losing even the will to do God's will:

> as long as it is someone's will to carry out the most precious will of God, such a person does not have the poverty of which we wish to speak. For this person still has a will with which they wish to please God, and this is not true poverty. If we are to have true poverty, then we must be so free of our own created will as we were before we were created. I tell you by the eternal truth that as long as you have the will to perform God's will, and a desire for eternity and for God, you are not yet poor. They alone are poor who will nothing and desire nothing.[181]

Eckhart repeatedly emphasized the need for individuals to return to the state in which they had existed before their creation: 'if we are to be poor in will, then we must will and desire as little as we willed and

[178] E. Colledge and J. C. Marler, '"Poverty of the will": Ruusbroec, Eckhart and *The Mirror of Simple Souls*', in P. Mommaers and N. de Paepe (eds.), *Jan van Ruusbroec: The Sources, Content and Sequels of his Mysticism* (Leuven, 1984), pp. 14–47 at 15, 25–36, 40; Davies, *Meister Eckhart*, pp. 65–8; A. Hollywood, 'Suffering transformed: Marguerite Porete, Meister Eckhart, and the problem of women's spirituality', in B. McGinn (ed), *Meister Eckhart and the Beguine Mystics: Hadewijch of Brabant, Mechthild of Magdeburg, and Marguerite Porete* (New York, 1994), pp. 87–113 at 102–10; Lerner, *Heresy of the Free Spirit*, pp. 1, 183; M. Lichtmann, 'Marguerite Porete and Meister Eckhart: *The Mirror for Simple Souls* mirrored', in McGinn (ed.), *Meister Eckhart and the Beguine Mystics*, pp. 65–86 at 65, 70–1, 82–6; B. McGinn, 'Love, knowledge and *Unio mystica* in the western Christian tradition', in M. Idel and B. McGinn (eds.), *Mystical Union and Monotheistic Faith: An Ecumenical Dialogue* (New York, 1989), pp. 73–8; McGinn, *Harvest of Mysticism*, pp. 99–100; M. Sells, *Mystical Languages of Unsaying* (Chicago, 1994), pp. 180–205; D. Turner, *The Darkness of God: Negativity in Christian Mysticism* (Cambridge, 1995), pp. 138, 179–80. For a critical assessment of these analyses, see Lerner, 'New light', p. 112.

[179] *On Detachment* in Meister Eckhart, *The Essential Sermons*, p. 285.

[180] Meister Eckhart, *Selected Writings*, trans. O. Davies (London, 1994), sermon 22, p. 203.

[181] *Ibid.*, p. 204.

desired before we came into being. It is in this way that someone is poor who wills nothing.'[182]

Similarly Eckhart stressed the importance of knowing nothing. In *Beati pauperes spiritu*, this too was an essential aspect of true inner poverty:

they who are to have this poverty must live in such a way that they do not know that they do not live either for themselves, for truth or for God. They must rather be free of the knowledge that they do not know, understand or sense that God lives in them. More than this: they must be free of all the knowledge that lives in them.[183]

Thus for Eckhart, knowing nothing had to be so complete that there was no knowledge even of not knowing. This absence of knowledge about the self was again represented as a return to the state in which the individual had existed before being created as an individual: 'we say that we should be as free of self-knowledge as we were before we were created'.[184] Eckhart explained further that blessedness did not lie in either knowledge or love, but in 'a something in the soul which is the source of both knowledge and love, although it does not itself know or love'. This something 'does not possess any knowledge of the fact that God acts in it, rather it is itself that which delights in itself just as God delights in himself'. Eckhart therefore advised, 'We should be so solitary and unencumbered that we do not know that it is God who acts in us', and concluded that the genuinely poor must have 'no knowledge of anything, neither of God, nor of creature, nor of themselves'.[185]

Eckhart pursued the theme of not knowing on many occasions. In the treatise *On the Noble Man*, he acknowledged that 'all people have a natural desire for knowledge'. He further recognized that 'when the self, the soul, the spirit sees God, then it knows itself also as knowing subject: that is, it knows that it sees and knows God'.[186] He completely rejected, however, the view that this was to be blessed:

Even if it is true that the soul would not be blessed without this, it does not follow that this is blessedness, for blessedness consists primarily in the fact that the soul sees God in himself. It is in this that the soul receives the whole of her nature and life and all that she is from the ground of God, knowing nothing of knowledge nor of love, nor of anything else at all.[187]

[182] *Ibid.*, p. 205. [183] *Ibid.* [184] *Ibid.*
[185] *Ibid.*, p. 206.
[186] *Ibid.*, *On the Noble Man*, p. 105.
[187] *Ibid.*, p. 106.

So while knowing that one knows God might be a necessary first step, the soul was not truly blessed until it ceased to be aware of itself as knowing.

In another sermon, *Ubi est qui natus est rex judaeorum*, 'Where is he who is born King of the Jews?', Eckhart explained further what he envisaged. Having emphasized the need to 'enter a forgetfulness and an unknowing', he noted the possible objection that this 'sounds like a lack of something' and that 'God created humanity in order that we should know'. This was, however, to misunderstand the nature of unknowing and to attach too much value to the active:

> we must come into a transformed knowing, an unknowing which comes not from ignorance but from knowledge. Then our knowing shall be divine knowledge, and our unknowing shall be ennobled and enriched with supernatural knowing. With respect to this, being passive shall make us more perfect than being active.[188]

Thus to know nothing in Eckhart's sense was to proceed through knowing to unknowing, which meant abandoning all active processes to become passive.

As will already be apparent, willing nothing and knowing nothing involved loss of self. Eckhart discussed 'those who have destroyed themselves as they exist in themselves, in God and in all creatures':

> Such people have taken up the lowest position, and God must pour the whole of himself into them – or he would not be God. I declare the good, eternal and everlasting Truth that God must pour himself according to the whole of his capacity into all those who have abandoned themselves to the very ground of their being, and he must do so so completely that he can hold nothing back of all his life, all his being and nature, even of his divinity, which he must pour fully and in a fructifying way into those who have abandoned themselves for God and have taken up the lowest position.[189]

According to Eckhart, therefore, the process of self-destruction necessarily brought God into those who became detached.

The birth of God within the soul was one of Eckhart's major preoccupations, and he wrote a great deal about that part of the soul which was capable of union with God, deploying a vast array of metaphors.[190] As already noted, he referred to 'a something in the soul which is the source of both knowledge and love, although it does not itself know or love', commenting further: 'It has neither a past nor a future, and it is

[188] *Ibid.*, sermon 24, p. 220.
[189] *Ibid.*, sermon 7, p. 134.
[190] See Davies, *Meister Eckhart*, pp. 149–57; Turner, *Darkness of God*, p. 140.

not something to which anything can be added, for it cannot become larger or smaller.'[191] This 'something' was therefore Godlike in that it existed out of time and was in at least some respects unchangeable. The metaphor of light was even more important to Eckhart:

I have occasionally spoken of a light in the soul which is uncreated and uncreatable. I constantly return in my sermons to this light, which apprehends God without medium, without concealment and nakedly, just as he is in himself. Indeed, it apprehends him in the act of begetting. I can again say truthfully that this light has more unity with God than it does with any of the soul's faculties, although it coexists with these.[192]

A variant on this image was the spark of the soul:

Therefore I say that when we turn away from ourselves and from all created things, to that extent we are united and sanctified in the soul's spark, which is untouched by either space or time. This spark is opposed to all creatures and desires nothing but God, naked, just as he is in himself.[193]

The other metaphor that Eckhart frequently used was the ground of the soul. Preaching on Matthew 2.2, 'Where is he who is born King of the Jews?', he answered:

But I say, as I have often said, that this birth takes place in the soul just as it takes place in eternity, no more and no less. For there is only one birth, and this takes place in the essence and ground of the soul.[194]

In his treatise *On the Noble Man*, he preferred the image of the seed. The inner man is 'the field in which God sows his image and likeness and in which he plants the good seed, which is the root of all wisdom, all skills, all virtues and all goodness: the seed of divine nature', and 'the seed of God grows into God'.[195]

The way in which Eckhart talked about union with God was one of the aspects of his work that was seized upon when he was accused of heresy. The extent to which he presented God and the soul as identical suggested a failure to preserve an adequate distinction between God and those he had created, and thus to constitute a type of pantheism.[196] The notion that there was something uncreated in the soul was also attacked.[197] Eckhart was far from consistent in his use of

[191] Meister Eckhart, *Selected Writings*, sermon 22, p. 206.
[192] *Ibid.*, sermon 7, p. 135. [193] *Ibid.*
[194] *Ibid.*, sermon 24, p. 215. For brilliant analysis of Eckhart's treatment of the ground of the soul, see McGinn, *Harvest of Mysticism*, pp. 83–93, 118–24.
[195] Meister Eckhart, *Selected Writings*, *On the Noble Man*, pp. 100–1.
[196] See the tenth of the twenty-six articles attributed to Eckhart in *In agro dominico*; Meister Eckhart, *The Essential Sermons*, p. 78.
[197] See the first of the two additional articles cited in *In agro dominico*; *ibid.*, p. 80.

metaphors, however, and passages can be found in which he treated these issues in terms that were safely within the bounds of contemporary orthodoxy.[198]

The plethora of metaphors that Eckhart produced, sometimes in seemingly contradictory ways, was at least in part a response to his view of the inadequacy of language when it came to talking about God. In one sermon he observed that 'God is nameless for no one can either speak of him or know him', going on to make his point by subverting the kind of praise conventionally given to God:

> if I say that 'God is good', this is not true. I am good, but God is not good! In fact, I would rather say that I am better than God, for what is good can become better and what can become better can become the best! Now God is not good, and so he cannot become better. Since he cannot become better, he cannot become the best. These three are far from God: 'good', 'better', 'best', for he is wholly transcendent. If I say again that 'God is wise', then this too is not true. I am wiser than he is! Or if I say that 'God exists', this is also not true. He is being beyond being: he is a nothingness beyond being. Therefore St Augustine says: 'The finest thing that we can say of God is to be silent concerning him from the wisdom of inner riches.' Be silent therefore, and do not chatter about God, for by chattering about him, you tell lies and commit a sin.[199]

Eckhart's fundamental point that any statement about God was certain to fall short of the reality of the divine was straightforward, but he chose to make it in a way that was likely to be at least disconcerting if not shocking to his audience. Not only did he deny the validity of conventional statements about God, but he appeared to claim superiority to God, being 'better' and 'wiser' than God, and even to challenge God's very existence. An appreciation that he was doing nothing of the kind depended on grasping the fundamental point which was at least explicitly alluded to when he began by saying that no one could speak of God and again when he referred to God's transcendence.

Eckhart challenged his audience further when, far from falling silent himself, he went beyond the negation involved when he said, for example, that 'God is not good', and added a second negation. Thus when discussing the oneness of God, he defined oneness as 'a negation of negation and a denial of denial', explaining:

> All creatures contain a negation within themselves: one creature denies that it is another. One particular angel denies that he is another. But with God there is a negation of negation: he is one and negates all else, since there is nothing outside God ... By denying something of God – if I were to deny goodness of

[198] Davies, *Meister Eckhart*, pp. 196–8; Turner, *Darkness of God*, pp. 145–8.
[199] Meister Eckhart, *Selected Writings*, sermon 28, p. 236.

God for instance (though I can in truth deny nothing of God) – by denying something of God, I grasp something which he is not. It is precisely this which must be got rid of. God is one; he is the negation of negation.[200]

Eckhart's point was that any particular created thing was not some other created thing. But God was not like that, he was not just another distinct thing, because his being was of a different order altogether. God's being was not divisible in this way, hence his oneness and the need for the second negation. Eckhart frequently argued that there were two types of being: the being of creatures was 'being this or that' or 'distinct being', whereas the being of God was 'being simply', 'absolute being' or 'indistinct being'.[201] Here he made the point by exploiting the limitations of language to set up his sequence of negations.

In *Beati pauperes spiritu* Eckhart again made his basic point about the inadequacy of language and human conception, but he served up a sterner challenge to comprehension because he offered far less by way of explanation. Having described the state of existence from which individuals emerged when they were created, he said:

But when I emerged by free choice and received my created being, I came into the possession of a 'God' for, until creatures came into existence, God was not 'God', but was rather what he was. Then, when creatures emerged and received their created being, God was not 'God' in himself but in creatures.[202]

Later in the sermon, he made a request:

I ask God to make me free of 'God', for my essential being is above 'God' in so far as we conceive of God as the origin of creatures.[203]

He went on to observe:

And if I did not exist, then neither would God have existed as 'God'. I am the cause of God's existence as 'God'.[204]

Once again he was making a straightforward point. The human conception of God and the word 'God' were created by humans and could not remotely measure up to God as he really was. Thus, until humans were created, the conception and the word, indicated in the modern

200 *Ibid.*, sermon 17, p. 182.

201 See Davies, *Meister Eckhart*, pp. 108–9; Hollywood, 'Suffering transformed', p. 105; Turner, *Darkness of God*, pp. 163–5.

202 Meister Eckhart, *Selected Writings*, sermon 22, pp. 204–5. I have added inverted commas on the first occasion that the word 'God' occurs in this passage (I came into the possession of a 'God'). Colledge and McGinn make the same decision in their translation of this sermon; Meister Eckhart, *The Essential Sermons*, p. 200.

203 Meister Eckhart, *Selected Writings*, sermon 22, p. 207.

204 *Ibid.*, p. 208.

translation by inverted commas, did not exist. Eckhart wanted to be free of this human conception of God so that he could engage more closely with the reality of God. Had humans not existed, there would have been no human conception of and word for God; humans could therefore be described as the cause of God being thought to exist in the manner that humans conceived of him. Eckhart did not, however, spell out the key idea that renders these passages relatively easy to unravel. At first sight, or rather on first hearing, 'God was not God' must have seemed like baffling contradiction, and the request to be 'free of God' and the claim to be 'above God' must have come across as deeply shocking. It would be fascinating to know if Eckhart signalled the difference between God (as he really is) and 'God' (the human conception) by altering his voice or using gestures. The insertion of inverted commas is a modern device for indicating this distinction, and modern students discussing these passages almost invariably end up waggling the first two fingers on both hands when referring to God as conceived by humans to recreate the effect when speaking.[205] Whether or not any such performative devices were used, Eckhart posed a tough and provocative test for his audience, and whether or not they understood his ideas, they can have been left in no doubt about the shortcomings of language.

Eckhart deployed the vocabulary of nobility, however, in a straightforward and unproblematic manner. In the treatise *On the Noble Man*, he used it to direct attention to the worth of the inner man:

> The other person in us is the inner man, which Scripture calls the new, the heavenly, the young, the noble man, or the friend. And this is the one which is meant when our Lord says that 'a certain nobleman went away to a distant country to gain a kingdom for himself, and returned'.[206]

He used it more precisely to refer to that part or aspect of the soul which was capable of union with God. Thus the 'light in the soul which is uncreated and uncreatable ... which apprehends God without medium, without concealment and nakedly, just as he is in himself' was just as noble as other faculties of the soul with regard to being, but 'far nobler and more elevated' with regard to function.[207] He also deployed it to describe the process of achieving detachment. When knowing was transformed into unknowing, 'our unknowing shall be ennobled and enriched with supernatural knowing'.[208] The birth of God in the soul

[205] For discussion of the introduction of inverted commas in this way, see Colledge and Marler, '"Poverty of the will"', pp. 16–17.
[206] Meister Eckhart, *Selected Writings*, *On the Noble Man*, p. 99.
[207] *Ibid.*, sermon 7, p. 135. [208] *Ibid.*, sermon 24, p. 220.

was 'the noble birth'.[209] Although Eckhart did not follow Marguerite Porete in using noble contempt for other social orders to convey the gulf between detachment and other forms of religious practice, he made the same decision to eschew the language of learning and the university to explain the highest possible form of knowing.

As with Marguerite Porete's *Mirror of Simple Souls*, however, Eckhart's work was controversial because of what he said about virtue, good works and religious practices. The eighth article of *In agro dominico* attributed to him and condemned the view that 'Those who are not desiring possessions, or honours, or gain, or internal devotion, or holiness, or reward or the kingdom of heaven, but who have renounced all this, even what is theirs, these people pay honour to God.'[210] Certainly there are numerous occasions when Eckhart appears to disparage conventional religious practices, for example in *Beati pauperes spiritu*, when explaining the need to abandon the will:

> In the first place we say that a poor person is someone who desires nothing. Some people do not understand this point correctly. I mean those who cling to their own egos in their penances and external devotions, which such people regard as being of great importance. God have mercy on them, for they know little of the divine truth! These people are called holy because of what they are seen to do, but inside they are asses, for they do not know the real meaning of divine truth. Although such people are happy to say that a poor person is one who desires nothing, they interpret this as meaning that we must live in such a way that we never perform our own will in anything but that we should desire rather to carry out God's most precious will. These people are alright, for they mean well and that is why they deserve our praise. May God in his mercy grant them heaven! But I tell you by the divine truth that such people are not truly poor nor are they like those who are poor. They are greatly esteemed by people who know no better. But I tell you that they are asses, who understand nothing of God's truth. May they attain heaven because of their good intent, but of that poverty, of which we now wish to speak, they know nothing.[211]

Eckhart evidently regarded those who valued and carried out conventional religious practices as well-meaning and perhaps deserving of a place in heaven, but at the same time they were asses who had not grasped higher truths and who were only praised by those who were similarly uninformed. No one could hope to achieve detachment if they were preoccupied with external works. Once detachment had been achieved, however, Eckhart sometimes suggested that standard

[209] *Ibid.*, sermon 25, p. 222.
[210] *In agro dominico*, article 8; Meister Eckhart, *The Essential Sermons*, p. 78.
[211] Meister Eckhart, *Selected Writings*, sermon 22, pp. 203–4.

practices were impossible. Prayer, for example, was a problem because it necessarily involved the will:

> purity in detachment does not know how to pray, because if someone prays he asks God to get something for him, or he asks God to take something away from him. But a heart in detachment asks for nothing, nor has it anything of which it would gladly be free. So it is free of all prayer, and its prayer is nothing else than for uniformity with God.[212]

Lacking any will, those who achieved detachment would no longer pray because they could not. Sometimes Eckhart accepted that such activities were still possible, but pointed to the danger involved. In one sermon he presented a dialogue between himself and a member of his audience:

> Now you could say: sir, if it is necessary that we should be stripped of all things and emptied of them, outside and within, the faculties together with their activity – if all this must be removed, then it is grievous if God allows us to remain without any support ... If we thus enter a state of pure nothingness, is it not better that we should do something in order to drive away the darkness and the dereliction? Should we not pray or read or listen to a sermon or do something else that is virtuous in order to help ourselves?
>
> No, certainly not! The very best thing you can do is to remain still for as long as possible. You cannot turn away from this state to other things without doing yourself harm, that much is sure.[213]

Here Eckhart presented pious and virtuous activities as likely to undermine detachment, recreating the self that had been destroyed in order to bring God into the soul.

There were, however, other sermons in which Eckhart's views seemed much 'safer' in terms of the church's conventional teaching. When discussing the birth of God in the soul in terms of light, he made it clear that this would not happen to someone who sinned: 'But sinners can receive nothing of this, nor are they worthy to do so, since they are filled with sin and evil, which are called "darkness".'[214] And he repeated the point later in the sermon: 'it is impossible for this birth to happen in sinners since this light cannot burn and shine in them. This birth cannot coexist with the darkness of sins.'[215] Detachment did not therefore mean freedom to commit sin. In his treatise *On Detachment*, Eckhart made it clear that he regarded detachment as superior to all other virtues: 'I find no other virtue better than a pure detachment from all things; because all other virtues have some regard for created things, but detachment is free from

212 *On Detachment* in Meister Eckhart, *The Essential Sermons*, p. 292.
213 Meister Eckhart, *Selected Writings*, sermon 25, pp. 225–6.
214 *Ibid.*, sermon 24, p. 216. 215 *Ibid.*, p. 217.

all created things.'[216] He did not, however, deny the existence and validity of other virtues, and indeed he stressed the importance of humility in particular, even while asserting the superiority of detachment: 'I praise detachment above all humility, and that is because, although there may be humility without detachment, there cannot be perfect detachment without perfect humility, because perfect humility proceeds from annihilation of the self.'[217] Thus detachment could not be achieved without the perfect humility that was achieved by destruction of the self. Eckhart therefore advised 'whoever longs to attain to perfect detachment, let him struggle for perfect humility, and so he will come close to the divinity'.[218] In the same treatise, Eckhart discussed prayers and good works, explaining that they did not move God: 'All the prayers and good works that man can accomplish in time move God's detachment as little as if no single prayer or good work were ever performed in time.' But this was because prayers and good works existed in time whereas God saw all things 'in his first everlasting glance', and in that glance he 'saw the smallest prayer and good work that anyone would ever perform, and he took into his regard which prayers and devotion he would or should give ear to'. Prayers and good works were not therefore 'wasted', 'for whoever does well will also be well rewarded, whoever does evil will be rewarded accordingly'.[219] Moreover, in another sermon Eckhart stated explicitly that good works could never be abandoned:

> Now some people want to maintain they have advanced so far that they are free even of good works. But I say again that this cannot be. It was after receiving the Holy Spirit that the disciples first began to practise virtues.[220]

There was apparently no reason to suppose that those who achieved detachment would undermine the pastoral work of the church.

Putting these various passages together, it is entirely possible to attribute to Eckhart a coherent view of virtue, good works and religious practices that did not run counter to contemporary orthodoxy. Prayer, penance and good works should not be ends in themselves, and preoccupation with them should not get in the way of detachment, but detachment did not mean ceasing to behave virtuously. Ordinary believers did not comprehend detachment, but that did not mean that they could not be saved.[221] Undoubtedly, however, there were occasions

[216] *On Detachment*, in Meister Eckhart, *The Essential Sermons*, p. 285.
[217] *Ibid.*, p. 286. [218] *Ibid.*, p. 294. [219] *Ibid.*, pp. 288–9.
[220] Meister Eckhart, *Selected Writings*, sermon 21, p. 202.
[221] For discussion of Eckhart's views on virtue, works and religious practices, see Davies, *Meister Eckhart*, pp. 166–9, 170–2; Turner, *Darkness of God*, pp. 139, 173–4, 179–80.

when he spoke about conventional religious practices in ways that seemed to call their worth into question. It is significant, moreover, that *we* have to bring passages together to propose a consistent view reconstructed out of apparently contradictory statements. Eckhart offered seemingly contradictory views on a great many issues, and those who study Eckhart almost invariably find themselves trying to reconcile these views to establish a consistent underlying set of ideas.[222] Bearing in mind his tendency to expose and exploit the limitations of language and to make statements that were both difficult to comprehend and likely to shock and even mislead unless precisely understood, this raises questions about how he expected to be understood, and what response he looked for in his audience. It may be that he expected his audience to know what he had said on previous occasions. Certainly he referred frequently to earlier sermons, implying that his audience was familiar with his work:

I have occasionally spoken of … I constantly return in my sermons to …[223]
From time to time we have said that … But now we put it differently, going further, and say that …[224]
But I say, as I have often said, that …[225]

Perhaps therefore he expected his audience to be able to interpret whatever he said on one occasion in the light of earlier statements, and to temper his more extreme statements accordingly. On the other hand, he was certainly aware that many who heard him might not understand what he was saying. He alluded to this possibility repeatedly, in *Beati pauperes spiritu* for example:

I ask you to be poor enough to understand what it is that I am saying to you, for I declare by Eternal Wisdom that if you do not yourself become the same as that Wisdom of which we wish to speak, then my words will mean nothing to you … But if you do not understand, then do not worry, for I shall be speaking of a particular kind of truth which only a few good people can grasp … I am the cause of God's existence as 'God'. But it is not necessary for you to know this … Whoever does not understand these words, should not be troubled. For as long as someone is not themselves akin to this truth, they will not understand my words, since this is an unconcealed truth which has come directly from the heart of God.[226]

[222] For summaries of contradictory statements on a range of issues, see Davies, *Meister Eckhart*, pp. 115, 135–6, 196–8; Turner, *Darkness of God*, pp. 140, 144–8. In these works Davies and Turner have offered the most compelling accounts of fundamental consistencies in Eckhart's thought.

[223] Meister Eckhart, *Selected Writings*, sermon 7, p. 135.

[224] *Ibid.*, sermon 22, p. 205. [225] *Ibid.*, sermon 24, p. 215.

[226] *Ibid.*, sermon 22, pp. 203–9.

According to Eckhart, his words would only be understood by those who achieved the state that he was discussing, and they would be few in number. Those who could not follow him, however, need not be concerned. He simply did not countenance the possibility that they might misunderstand and fall into some kind of error.

It has been convincingly suggested that Eckhart chose his words to stimulate a particular response rather than to convey a measured account of his thinking. According to Oliver Davies, he 'uses one device after another in order to shake his listeners free from their assumptions, in order to deliver a "metaphysical shock" ',[227] and he aims 'to use language and imagery not in a descriptive manner but primarily in an expressive way in order to effect a cognitive transformation within his audience'.[228] Bernard McGinn explains how he 'often uses a form of homiletic shock therapy in which he makes outrageous statements that taken at face value are almost blasphemous in character ... The goal of this practice is the deconstruction that leads to silent union.'[229] Denys Turner remarks that he often 'seems careless of the meaning of what he says in its own right', and that 'What appears to matter to him is the meaning which what he says is capable of evoking in the minds of his listeners, as if what mattered to him was not the exactness of *his* meaning, but the exactness with which his language evokes meaning in them.'[230] Perhaps Eckhart considered his audience to be sufficiently well trained to know what was orthodox, and believed that if they tried to make his words fit with orthodox belief they would think in the way that he wanted them to think. If so, he was placing a great deal of confidence in both his audience and his own judgement of them.

Others, however, shared no such confidence, and the terms of *In agro dominico* are revealing in this regard. Eckhart was said to have 'presented many things as dogma that were designed to cloud the true faith in the hearts of many, things which he put forth especially before the uneducated crowd in his sermons and that he also admitted into his writings'.[231] Condemnation was made 'Lest articles of this sort and their contents further infect the hearts of the simple among whom they were preached'.[232] 'The uneducated crowd', 'the simple': the women to whom he preached were not recognized as learned, and they were not

[227] Davies, *Meister Eckhart*, p. 126.
[228] *Ibid.*, p. 196. See also his perceptive comments at pp. 5, 199–201.
[229] McGinn, *Harvest of Mysticism*, p. 142; see also pp. 111, 122.
[230] Turner, *Darkness of God*, p. 149.
[231] *In agro dominico*, in Meister Eckhart, *The Essential Sermons*, p. 77.
[232] *Ibid.*, p. 80.

believed to live in an appropriate institutional setting. The bull further stated that

we have found the first fifteen articles in question as well as the two final ones to contain the error or stain of heresy as much from *the tenor of their words* as from the sequence of their thoughts. The other eleven ... we have found quite *evil-sounding* and very rash and suspect of heresy, though with many explanations and additions they might take on or possess a Catholic meaning.[233]

Quite simply, Eckhart sounded heretical.[234] Even when his words could be given an orthodox interpretation, he struck the wrong note. He deployed his learning and his status irresponsibly.

There was, however, a paradox in Eckhart's own construction of self. He had called for the destruction of the self, insisted that one must know nothing, and drawn attention to the inadequacies of language. But he himself seemed to know everything, speaking always with the authority of the master. Moreover, unlike Marguerite Porete, who fell silent and refused to defend herself, Eckhart defended himself with vigour and a patent sense of outrage. He was dead by the time *In agro dominico* was issued, but he had already stated his case in terms that emphasized his own standing. He was famous, able to claim 'the esteem of the brethren of the whole order and men and women of the entire kingdom and of every nation'. He had produced a vast corpus of writings, which of course his accusers could not understand: 'I am surprised that they do not bring up more objections against what is written in my different works, for it is well known that I have written a hundred things and more that their ignorance neither understands nor grasps.' Moreover, he comforted himself that the masters of theology at Paris had been required to examine the works of Thomas Aquinas and Albert the Great, and that Aquinas in particular had often been accused of error and heresy, only to be 'given approval, both at Paris and also by the Supreme Pontiff and the Roman curia'. He could state curtly to his accusers 'I am not held to respond to you or to anyone except the Pope and the University of Paris', although from his 'own generosity' he 'still wanted to write down and present these things to you so that I do not seem to be avoiding what has been falsely brought against me'.[235] When

[233] *Ibid.* The italics are mine.

[234] It must be noted, however, that 'evil-sounding and very rash and suspect of heresy' was 'a traditional formula'; see B. McGinn, '"Evil-sounding, rash, and suspect of heresy": tensions between mysticism and magisterium in the history of the church', *The Catholic Historical Review* 90 (2004): 193–212 at 193.

[235] Response to the List of Forty-Nine Articles, in Meister Eckhart, *The Essential Sermons*, pp. 71–4.

it came to it, he had been a master of theology at the University of Paris and no one should forget it.

Eckhart was oblivious to the challenge that he had posed to the very authority on which he fell back. While not denigrating reason like Jean de Meun and Marguerite Porete, he implied its relatively low status in the hierarchy of knowledge by directing attention to the kind of knowing that could not be taught in schools and universities because it was a vastly superior unknowing. He evidently expected, moreover, to find it outside the university and amongst women, and he used the language of nobility to express its higher status. Similarly, he challenged the kind of intellectual work performed in the university by exposing the inability of language to convey meaning about the highest truths. Moreover, he did so in the vernacular, frequently to a female audience, in ways that were meant to be hard to follow. He expected only a few to understand because he thought that only those who had achieved detachment could understand. He was unperturbed that most would therefore be left struggling with statements that sometimes seemed shocking in terms of the religious conventions of his day. Like Marguerite, he also talked about the destruction of the will and the self, focusing on that part of the soul where God might be found: a something, a light, a spark, the ground. In so doing he called into question the value of virtue, good works and conventional religious practices. While an overview of his work shows that he did not intend to reject any of these, he often spoke witheringly about conventional piety, suggesting that detachment made it either impossible or dangerous. He thus undermined confidence in the kind of knowing cultivated in the university, and challenged the pastoral strategies by which that knowledge was meant to take effect outside the university.

Conclusion

In the late thirteenth century and more especially the early fourteenth century, it is possible to detect an anti-intellectual challenge to the university and in particular to its theologians. It was provided by highly learned and intellectually sophisticated women and men who were active both inside and outside the university itself, but whose worlds were not unconnected with the university and its theologians. The idea that there was a hierarchy of knowledge was treated in ways that led to the disparagement or rejection of reason and to the insistence that language could not be trusted to convey definite meaning, making truth difficult if not impossible to grasp and communicate. Jean de Meun refused to accept a hierarchy that would generate an ordered relationship between different forms of knowledge, and although Reason was given a voice, other voices repeatedly denigrated what it had to offer, resulting in a cumulative rejection. Marguerite Porete and Eckhart operated with very strong hierarchies of knowledge, but focused on forms of knowing, or rather unknowing, at the top of the hierarchy that could not be taught in a university and indeed required abandonment of what was taught there. Eckhart's emphasis on knowing nothing simply implied the low status of reason, but Marguerite expressed unbridled contempt for everything below annihilation, repeatedly disparaging reason and the kind of understanding that it purported to give. Jean de Meun insisted upon the instability of meaning, holding contradictory ideas constantly in play, declining to use a clear authorial voice to assert any kind of priority, allowing allegorical figures to subvert not only each other but themselves, and always pointing to false signs and strategies of deception. Marguerite and Eckhart both stressed the inadequacy of language when it came to talking about God. Marguerite used paradox and contradiction to make the point, ensuring that meaning was hard to establish, and ultimately falling silent, in life as well as in her text. Eckhart subverted conventional statements about God in provocative fashion, deployed a multitude of metaphors, and turned to negation as a way of exploiting the weakness of language to get beyond words. The value of language and reason, the basic tools used in the university, were therefore called into question.

There was also a challenge to the idea that it was necessary to live virtuously to know correctly, and that virtuous living should be guaranteed by institutional setting. This was the fundamental approach that had been taken from monastic thinking and incorporated into the public discourse justifying the existence of the University of Paris. Now the most radical ideas, calling the power of reason and language into question, were expressed in vernacular languages for audiences outside the university, wholly or partly made up of the laity, and frequently female. Jean de Meun operated outside or on the margins of the university, but with highly partisan insider knowledge derived from the faculty of arts, and in a literary form that implied a lay readership. Marguerite was a woman with no known institutional base, an atypical beguine, so on the margins of a group that was already marginal in the eyes of many, expressly claiming to have written a book that would be beyond most theologians. Eckhart worked with much stronger institutional foundations, invoking the authority of a master of theology at Paris when attacked, and holding offices in the Dominican order that gave him pastoral responsibility for women. Evidently, however, he expected to find the higher forms of unknowing outside the university and amongst women. The boundaries of the university and its function as institutional guarantor of an appropriate context for correct knowing were being ignored both by a master of theology and by those who were outsiders in varying degrees. For some at least, the ways of knowing fostered by the university were losing their status, and the university's contextual role was being undermined.

The pastoral function of the university was also called into question by the same anti-intellectual intellectuals who challenged the university's worth as a producer of knowledge. The public discourse underpinning the authority and standing of the university had stressed the way it turned men into preachers. The theologians had further justified their status in terms of generating knowledge that would be communicated beyond the schools. Now doubt was cast on the pastoral mechanisms of the church that the Paris theologians reckoned to inform. Jean de Meun attacked the friars, mocked theologians, dressed Genius as a bishop to preach in favour of procreative sex, and transformed the lover into a pilgrim just before he finally plucks the rose. He played with ideas about sex and marriage that had been developed by masters of theology, exploiting their lack of consensus about sexual pleasure, sometimes seeming to echo their views, but always omitting a key element, and invariably ending up with the trenchant expression of an idea that ran counter to the pastoral teaching they helped to develop. For Marguerite, the direct relationship between the annihilated soul and God left no role for the church as mediary. Moreover, she expressed no respect for Holy Church the Little, and made it clear that the church would not be able to identify annihilated souls and so would not be able to govern them. She also had the annihilated soul take leave of the virtues and good works, and display indifference to basic religious practices. She briefly acknowledged that these fundamental components of the church's teaching were important if the vast majority of people were to be saved, and she did not imagine that the annihilated soul would behave sinfully, but this was not her real concern. Moreover, she made her points provocatively, using the issues of good works and religious practices chiefly to illuminate her points about the nature of annihilation, thus seeming to cast doubt on the worth of the church's pastoral teaching. While an overview of Eckhart's work might suggest that his views about good works and basic religious practices were essentially conventional, he made his point about the failings of language by subverting customary praise of God; and when explaining the need for abandonment of the will, he appeared to disparage religious practices, suggesting that those who achieved detachment could not or should not perform them.

These anti-intellectual intellectuals showed remarkably little concern about being misunderstood, and little inclination to take responsibility for the wider reception of their works. If Jean de Meun could be pinned down to any definite message, it would be to believe nothing; but the matter was more serious in the cases of Marguerite Porete and Eckhart because they claimed to offer a religious message. According to Marguerite, only annihilated souls – who could be anyone, without regard to social class or education – would understand her. Those who were not and would never be annihilated simply would not grasp her meaning, and she expressed no more than passing concern about how they might be misled. Eckhart offered contradictory statements and made his points in disconcerting ways that were open to misinterpretation unless the basic underlying idea was grasped in full, an idea he did not always opt to spell out. He was fully aware that many would not understand him, expecting only those few who had achieved detachment to see what he meant. While seeking to stimulate particular responses from part of his audience, he showed no concern that those who failed to understand might misunderstand and be led into error. The vision of general pastoral responsibility previously set out by the masters of theology was no longer being respected.

The identity of the university was further challenged by the emphasis that was being placed on nobility in connection with knowing. Two long-standing traditions were brought into play here. Debates about whether noble status should stem from birth or the virtue of the individual could be found in classical texts.[236] Jean de Meun's emphasis on virtue as the basis of noble status therefore had a long history, but he gave it a much newer twist when he claimed noble status for the learned clerk. Another tradition deployed the language of nobility in the context of union between God and the soul.[237] Since love was often the dominant motif describing this union, and this invited the use of courtly imagery, nobility was often attributed to the soul that experienced union with God. With Marguerite and Eckhart, however, this was strongly linked with ideas about abandoning knowledge and reason, so that nobility reinforced the notion that there were superior forms of knowing, or unknowing, that were not to be found in the university. Once the rhetoric of nobility had been deployed both to express the idea that learning should be properly recognized and to refer to the highest forms of knowing, it is not surprising that university men appropriated it for

[236] See Murray, *Reason and Society*, pp. 271–4.
[237] See Robinson, *Nobility and Annihilation*, pp. 9–16, 20–5, 102–4.

themselves, using it to demand actual privileges. In the fourteenth and fifteenth centuries, those who held university degrees came to enjoy noble privileges, asserting their worth by appealing to social categories that originated outside the university.[238]

Some historians of the intellectual culture of the fourteenth century have stressed continuity from the thirteenth century, but most have identified change.[239] Whereas that change used to be characterized in terms of failure and decline, recent work has preferred to emphasize renewal or to avoid that kind of judgement altogether.[240] It has been clearly demonstrated that there were significant changes in the relationship between the masters of theology at Paris and the king of France, with the king consulting the theologians and seeking to use their authority to legitimize his policy.[241] Meanwhile, in the 1320s Pope John XXII summoned theologians to the papal court at Avignon where he set up a central theological school that relieved him of the need to consult theologians based in Paris.[242] Subsequently, the international standing of the university and the faculty of theology was greatly reduced by the Hundred Years War between England and France, which virtually removed English masters and students from the university and made travel difficult for everyone, and by the great Schism, which reduced numbers coming from Germany, Italy and Scandinavia.[243] Increasingly, the university

238 See J. Verger, *Men of Learning in Europe at the End of the Middle Ages*, trans. L. Neal and S. Rendall (Notre Dame, IN, 2000), esp. pp. 31, 69–70, 150–63. On fourteenth- and fifteenth-century students seeking to identify with the aristocracy by copying their behaviour and dress, see R. M. Karras, *From Boys to Men: Formations of Masculinity in Late Medieval Europe* (Philadelphia, 2003), pp. 98–100.

239 The case for continuity is most compellingly made by Verger, *Men of Learning*, pp. 49–56.

240 See the judicious comments of D. Luscombe, *Medieval Thought* (Oxford, 1997), pp. 133–40.

241 W. J. Courtenay, 'The Parisian faculty of theology in the late thirteenth and early fourteenth centuries', in J. A. Aertsen, K. Emery and A. Speer (eds.), *Nach der Verurteilung von 1277. Philosophie und Theologie en der Universität von Paris im letzten Viertel des 13. Jahrhunderts. Studien und Texte / After the Condemnation of 1277. Philosophy and Theology at the University of Paris in the Last Quarter of the Thirteenth Century. Studies and Texts*, Miscellanea Mediaevalia 28 (Berlin, 2001), pp. 235–47; W. J. Courtenay, 'Learned opinion and royal justice: the role of Paris masters of theology during the reign of Philip the Fair', in R. M. Karras, J. Kaye and E. A. Matter (eds.), *Law and the Illicit in Medieval Europe* (Philadelphia, 2008), pp. 149–63. See also I. P. Wei, 'The masters of theology at the university of Paris in the late thirteenth and early fourteenth centuries: an authority beyond the schools', *Bulletin of the John Rylands University Library of Manchester* 75 (1993): 37–63.

242 R. W. Southern, 'The changing role of universities in medieval Europe', *Bulletin of the Institute of Historical Research* 60 (1987): 133–46.

243 W. J. Courtenay, *Parisian Scholars in the Early Fourteenth Century: A Social Portrait* (Cambridge, 1999), pp. 2, 108.

and its theologians maintained their high standing through association with the French monarchy and its political institutions.[244] The dominant intellectual trends are much harder to identify. Historians used to put the emphasis on scepticism about what it was possible to know and doubt about the value of reason in understanding God, as they sought to explain what they perceived as the collapse of great philosophical and theological systems constructed in the thirteenth century.[245] Recent scholarship presents a different picture, demonstrating that sceptical arguments were used to help work out conceptions of knowledge and to refine rather than undermine claims to know truth.[246] Specialist studies, however, offer no clear overall picture, not least because the study of Parisian theologians in the fourteenth century remains patchy, and much work has still to be done.[247] As research continues and historians seek to define and explain the changes that were taking place, new questions need to be asked, and it is important to bear in mind the intellectually sophisticated anti-intellectual challenge that came from women as well as men, from outside the university as well as inside, and in vernacular languages. At the very least the theologians were operating in a new context: they no longer enjoyed a monopoly of high-order theological thinking. More than that, the status of the Paris theologians had rested on their claim to have certain knowledge based partly on the use of reason and language, and partly on virtuous living ensured by an institution that regulated the lives of its members. Their status also depended on their fulfilment of a pastoral function, training men to be preachers, setting out a general framework within which souls could be saved, providing specific advice on fundamental aspects of ordinary life, and fully accepting their responsibility for the wider reception of their teaching. All of this was now called into question. Traditionally, the anti-intellectual intellectuals have been treated separately from the Parisian theologians, and often by different scholars, Jean de Meun as

[244] Le Goff, *Intellectuals in the Middle Ages*, pp. 138–42, 148–50; S. Lusignan, *'Vérité garde le roy': la construction d'une identité universitaire en France (XIIIe-XVe siècle)* (Paris, 1999).

[245] This point is made by almost all outline intellectual histories of the period. See, for example, G. Leff, *Paris and Oxford Universities in the Thirteenth and Fourteenth Centuries: An Institutional and Intellectual History* (New York, 1968), pp. 240–55; Le Goff, *Intellectuals in the Middle Ages*, pp. 130–2, 135–8; Luscombe, *Medieval Thought*, pp. 133–58.

[246] See, for example, D. Perler, 'Skepticism', in R. Pasnau (ed.), *The Cambridge History of Medieval Philosophy*, 2 vols. (Cambridge, 2010), vol. 1, pp. 384–96.

[247] See the comments of J. Marenbon, *Later Medieval Philosophy (1150–1350)* (London, 1987, repr. 1996), p. 188; C. Schabel, *Theology at Paris, 1316–1345: Peter Auriol and the Problem of Divine Foreknowledge and Future Contingents* (Aldershot, 2000), pp. 4, 9.

a literary figure, and Marguerite and Eckhart as 'mystics'. They were dealing with many of the same themes and ideas as the theologians, however, and their worlds were not unconnected. In seeking to understand how the masters of theology at Paris sustained their authority in a changing world, future research must consider the extent to which they responded to the challenge posed by anti-intellectual intellectuals. By thus rethinking the boundaries that frame our own scholarship, we may achieve a better understanding of the social and intellectual pressures that shaped fourteenth-century intellectual culture, and the fourteenth century will perhaps emerge as a period of reinvention.

Bibliography

MANUSCRIPT SOURCES

Paris, Bibliothèque Nationale, latin 14572
Paris, Bibliothèque Nationale, latin 14891
Paris, Bibliothèque Nationale, latin 14899
Paris, Bibliothèque Nationale, latin 15350
Paris, Bibliothèque Nationale, latin 15850

PRINTED SOURCES

Adelard of Bath, *Conversations with his Nephew: On the Same and the Different, Questions on Natural Science and On Birds*, ed. and trans. C. Burnett (Cambridge, 1998)

Alan of Lille, *Anticlaudianus or The Good and Perfect Man*, trans. J. J. Sheridan (Toronto, 1973)

The Art of Preaching, trans. G. R. Evans (Kalamazoo, MI, 1981)

The Plaint of Nature, trans. J. J. Sheridan (Toronto, 1980)

Anselm, *The Prayers and Meditations of Saint Anselm with the Proslogion*, trans. B. Ward (Harmondsworth, 1973)

St Anselm's Proslogion, trans. M. J. Charlesworth (Oxford, 1965)

Anselm of Canterbury, *The Major Works*, ed. B. Davies and G. R. Evans (Oxford, 1998)

Aristotle, *The Basic Works of Aristotle*, ed. R. McKeon (New York, 1941, repr. 2001)

Beati Gosvini Vita celeberrimi Aquicinctensis monasterii abbatis septimi a duobus diversis eiusdem coenobii monachis separatim exarata, e veteribus ms, ed. R. Gibbons (Duaci, 1620)

Bernard of Clairvaux, *Five Books on Consideration: Advice to a Pope*, trans. J. D. Anderson and E. T. Kennan (Kalamazoo, MI, 1976)

The Letters of St Bernard of Clairvaux, trans. B. S. James (Stroud, repr. 1998)

On the Song of Songs I, trans. K. Walsh (Kalamazoo, MI, 1971)

On the Song of Songs II, trans. K. Walsh (Kalamazoo, MI, 1976)

Bernard Silvestris, *The Cosmographia of Bernardus Silvestris*, trans. W. Wetherbee (New York, 1973)

Bonaventure, *Breviloquium*, trans. D. V. Monti (New York, 2005)

Breviloquium, trans. E. E. Nemmers (St Louis, 1946)

De Reductione Artium ad Theologiam, trans. Sister Emma Thérèse Healy (New York, 1955), reprinted in A. Hyman and J. J. Walsh (eds.), *Philosophy in the Middle Ages: The Christian, Islamic, and Jewish Traditions* (Indianapolis, 1973, repr. 1978)

Commentaria in quatuor libros sententiarum magistri Petri Lombardi, 1; *Opera Omnia*, 1 (Quaracchi, 1882)

Commentaria in quatuor libros sententiarum magistri Petri Lombardi, 2; *Opera Omnia*, 2 (Quaracchi, 1885)

The Journey of the Mind to God, trans. P. Boehner, ed. with introduction and notes by S. F. Brown (Indianapolis, 1993)

The Soul's Journey into God; The Tree of Life; The Life of St Francis, trans. E. Cousins (New York, 1978)

Chartularium Universitatis Parisiensis, ed. H. Denifle and E. Chatelain, 4 vols. (Paris, 1889–97)

Corpus iuris canonici, ed. E. Friedberg, 2 vols. (Leipzig, 1879–81)

Damasus, *Brocarda correcta per Bartholomeum Brixiensem* (Lyons, 1549)

Decrees of the Ecumenical Councils, ed. N. P. Tanner, 2 vols. (London, 1990)

Eadmer, *The Life of St Anselm*, trans. R. W. Southern (London, 1962)

'Ex Vita B. Gosvini Aquicinctensis Abbatis', ed. M.-J.-J. Brial, in *Recueil des Historiens des Gaules et de la France* 14 (1806)

Meister Eckhart, *The Essential Sermons, Commentaries, Treatises, and Defense*, trans. E. Colledge and B. McGinn (New York, 1981)

Selected Writings, trans. O. Davies (London, 1994)

Gardiner, E. (ed.), *Visions of Heaven and Hell before Dante* (New York, 1989)

Giles of Rome, *B. Aegidii Columnae Romani Quodlibeta* (Louvain, 1646; repr. Frankfurt am Main, 1966)

Godfrey of Fontaines, *Le dixième quodlibet de Godefroid de Fontaines*, ed. J. Hoffmans (Louvain, 1931)

Les quatres premiers quodlibets de Godefroid de Fontaines, ed. M. de Wulf and A. Pelzer (Louvain, 1904)

Les quodlibet cinq, six et sept de Godefroid de Fontaines, ed. M. de Wulf and J. Hoffmans (Louvain, 1914)

Les quodlibets onze-quartorze de Godefroid de Fontaines, ed. J. Hoffmans (Louvain, 1932)

Gregory the Great, *Moralia in Iob Libri I–X*, ed. M. Adriaen, Corpus Christianorum Series Latina 143 (Turnhout, 1979)

Moralia in Iob Libri XI–XXII, ed. M. Adriaen, Corpus Christianorum Series Latina 143A, (Turnhout, 1979)

S. Gregory the Great, *Morals on the Book of Job*, ed. C. Marriott, 3 vols. (Oxford, 1844–7)

Henry of Ghent, *Aurea Quodlibeta*, 2 vols. (Venice, 1613)

Henrici de Gandavo Quodlibet I, ed. R. Macken (Louvain, 1979)

Henrici de Gandavo Quodlibet II, ed. R. Wielockx (Leuven, 1983)

Henrici de Gandavo Quodlibet VI, ed. G. A. Wilson (Louvain, 1987)

Henrici de Gandavo Quodlibet XV, ed. G. Etzkorn and G. A. Wilson (Leuven, 2007)

Quodlibet XII, quaestiones 1–30, ed. J. Decorte (Leuven, 1987)

Hildegard of Bingen, *Hildegard of Bingen: An Anthology*, ed. F. Bowie and O. Davies (London, 1990)

The Letters of Hildegard of Bingen, vol. 1, trans. J. L. Baird and R. K. Ehrman (Oxford, 1994)

Scivias, trans. C. Hart and J. Bishop (New York, 1990)

Hugh of Saint Victor, *The Didascalicon: A Medieval Guide to the Arts*, trans. J. Taylor (New York, 1961)

On the Sacraments of the Christian Faith (De Sacramentis), trans. R. J. Deferrari (Cambridge, MA, 1951)

Hyman, A. and J. J. Walsh (eds.), *Philosophy in the Middle Ages: The Christian, Islamic, and Jewish Traditions* (Indianapolis, 1973, repr. 1978)

Jacques de Thérines Quodlibets I et II. Jean Lesage Quodlibet I. Texte critique avec introduction, notes et tables, ed. P. Glorieux (Paris, 1958)

Jacques de Vitry, *Historia occidentalis*, ed. J. F. Hinnebusch, Spicilegium Friburgense 17 (Fribourg, 1972)

John of Salisbury, *The Historia Pontificalis of John of Salisbury*, trans. M. Chibnall (London, 1956)

The Metalogicon of John of Salisbury: A Twelfth-Century Defense of the Verbal and Logical Arts of the Trivium, trans. D. D. McGarry (Berkeley, 1955)

Lothario dei Segni (Pope Innocent III), *On the Misery of the Human Condition*, trans. M. M. Dietz (Indianapolis, 1969)

Marguerite Porete, *The Mirror of Simple Souls*, trans. E. L. Babinsky (New York, 1993)

Margaret Porette, *The Mirror of Simple Souls*, trans. E. Colledge, J. C. Marler and J. Grant (Notre Dame, IN, 1999)

Peter Abelard, *Dialogue between a Philosopher, a Jew and a Christian*, in *Ethical Writings*, trans. P. V. Spade (Indianapolis, 1995)

Ethics, in Ethical Writings, trans. P. V. Spade (Indianapolis, 1995)

'The glosses of Peter Abailard on Porphyry', in R. McKeon (ed. and trans.), *Selections from Medieval Philosophers*, 2 vols. (New York, 1929), vol. 1, pp. 208–58

Historia Calamitatum, in *The Letters of Abelard and Heloise*, trans. B. Radice, revised M. T. Clanchy (London, 2003)

Peter Lombard, *The Sentences. Book 2: On Creation*, trans. G. Silano (Toronto, 2008)

Sententiae in IV libris distinctae, Spicilegium Bonaventurianum 4 and 5 (Grottaferrata, 1971 and 1981)

[Peter the Chanter] Pierre le Chantre, *Summa de sacramentis et animae consiliis*, deuxième partie, ed. J.-A. Dugauquier, Analecta Mediaevalia Namuracensia 7 (Louvain, 1957)

Summa de sacramentis et animae consiliis, troisième partie, (III, 2a) *Liber casuum conscientiae*, ed. J.-A. Dugauquier, Analecta Mediaevalia Namurcensia 16 (Louvain, 1963)

Peter the Chanter, *Petri Cantoris Parisiensis Verbum Adbreviatum*, Textus Conflatus, ed. M. Boutry, Corpus Christianorum Continuatio Medievalis 196 (Turnhout, 2004)

[Peter Comestor] Pierre le Mangeur, *De Sacramentis*, ed. R. M. Martin, Spicilegium Sacrum Lovaniense 17 (Louvain, 1937)

Philip the Chancellor, *Philippi Cancellarii Parisiensis Summa de Bono*, ed. N. Wicki (Bern, 1985)

Porphyry the Phoenician, *Isagoge*, trans. E. D. Warren (Toronto, 1975)

Ptolemy of Lucca with portions attributed to Thomas Aquinas, *On the Government of Rulers: De Regimine Principum*, trans. J. M. Blythe (Philadelphia, 1997)

Les Registres de Grégoire IX, ed. L. Auvray, 4 vols. (Paris, 1896–1955)

Richard of Middleton, *Quolibeta doctoris eximii Ricardi de Mediavilla ordinis minorum* (Brescia, 1591; repr. Frankfurt am Main, 1963)

The Romance of the Rose, trans. H. W. Robbins (New York, 1962)

The Romance of the Rose, trans. F. Horgan (Oxford, 1994)

Rupert of Deutz, *Apologia* [*Super quaedam capitula regulae Benedicti*, book 1], PL vol. 170, cols. 477–98

Commentaria in Canticum Canticorum, ed. H. Haacke, Corpus Christianorum Continuatio Medievalis 26 (Turnhout, 1974)

De Gloria et Honore Filii Hominis Super Mattheum, ed. H. Haacke, Corpus Christianorum Continuatio Mediaevalis 29 (Turnhout, 1979)

De Sancta Trinitate et Operibus Eius Libri I–IX, ed. H. Haacke, Corpus Christianorum Continuatio Medievalis 21 (Turnhout, 1971)

De Sancta Trinitate et Operibus Eius Libri X–XXVI, ed. H. Haacke, Corpus Christianorum Continuatio Medievalis 22 (Turnhout, 1972)

McKeon, R., (ed. and trans.), *Selections from Medieval Philosophers*, 2 vols. (New York, 1929)

Pullan, B., *Sources for the History of Medieval Europe from the Mid-Eighth Century to the Mid-Thirteenth Century* (Oxford, 1966)

Sigmund, P. E. (trans. and ed.), *St. Thomas Aquinas on Politics and Ethics* (New York, 1988)

Spade, P. V., (trans. and ed.), *Five Texts on the Mediaeval Problem of Universals* (Indianapolis, 1994)

Thomas Aquinas, *On Evil*, trans. R. Regan (Oxford, 2003)

On the Truth of the Catholic Faith. Summa Contra Gentiles, trans. A. C. Pegis, 5 vols. (New York, 1955–7)

On the Unity of the Intellect against the Averroists (De Unitate Intellectus Contra Averroistas), trans. B. H. Zedler (Milwaukee, 1968)

Quaestiones de quolibet, Sancti Thomae de Aquino Opera Omnia 25, 2 vols. (Rome, 1996)

Quodlibetal Questions 1 and 2, trans. S. Edwards (Toronto, 1983)

The Summa Contra Gentiles of Saint Thomas Aquinas: The Third Book (Part II – Chapters LXXXIV–CLXIII), trans. The English Dominican Fathers (London, 1928)

Summa Theologiae: Latin Text and English Translation, ed. T. Gilby *et al.* 61 vols. (London, 1964–80)

Summa Theologica. First Complete American Edition, trans. Fathers of the English Dominican Province, 3 vols. (New York, 1947–8)

The 'Summa Theologica' of St. Thomas Aquinas: Second Part of the Second Part QQ. CLXXI–CLXXXIX, trans. Fathers of the English Dominican Province (London, 1934)

The 'Summa Theologica' of St. Thomas Aquinas: Third Part (Supplement) QQ. XXXIV–LXVIII, trans. Fathers of the English Dominican Province (London, 1922)

St Thomas Aquinas, Siger of Brabant, St Bonaventure, *On the Eternity of the World (De Aeternitate Mundi)*, trans. C. Vollert, L. H. Kendzierski, P. M. Byrne (Milwaukee, 1964)

Thorndike, L., *University Records and Life in the Middle Ages* (New York, 1944)

William of Auvergne, *Guilielmi Alverni ... Opera Omnia*, 2 vols. (Paris, 1674; repr. Frankfurt am Main, 1963)

William of Saint Amour, *De periculis novissimorum temporum*, ed. and trans. G. Geltner (Paris, 2008)

William of Saint Thierry, *The Enigma of Faith*, trans. J. D. Anderson (Washington, DC, 1974)

The Golden Epistle: A Letter to the Brethren at Mont Dieu, trans. T. Berkeley (Kalamazoo, MI, 1980)

SECONDARY WORKS

Aertsen, J. A., K. Emery and A. Speer (eds.), *Nach der Verurteilung von 1277. Philosophie und Theologie en der Universität von Paris im letzten Viertel des 13. Jahrhunderts. Studien und Texte / After the Condemnation of 1277. Philosophy and Theology at the University of Paris in the Last Quarter of the Thirteenth Century. Studies and Texts*, Miscellanea Mediaevalia 28 (Berlin, 2001)

Allen, P., *The Concept of Woman: The Aristotelian Revolution, 750 B.C.–A.D. 1250*, 2nd edn (Grand Rapids, MI, 1997)

Anciaux, P., *La théologie du sacrement de pénitence au xiie siècle* (Louvain, 1949)

Arnold, J. H., *Belief and Unbelief in Medieval Europe* (London, 2005)

Avi-Yonah, R., 'Career trends of Parisian masters of theology, 1200–1320', *History of Universities* 6 (1986–7): 47–64

Babinsky, E. L., 'The use of courtly language in *Le Mirouer des simples ames anienties* by Marguerite Porete', *Essays in Medieval Studies* 4 (1987): 91–106

Baldwin, J. W., *The Government of Philip Augustus: Foundations of French Royal Power in the Middle Ages* (Berkeley, 1986)

The Language of Sex: Five Voices from Northern France around 1200 (Chicago, 1994)

'Masters at Paris from 1179 to 1215: a social perspective', in R. L. Benson and G. Constable (eds.), *Renaissance and Renewal in the Twelfth Century* (Oxford, 1982), pp. 138–72

Masters, Princes and Merchants: The Social Views of Peter the Chanter and his Circle, 2 vols. (Princeton, 1970)

'The medieval theories of the just price: romanists, canonists, and theologians in the twelfth and thirteenth centuries', *Transactions of the American Philosophical Society* 49 (1959): 1–92

'Studium et Regnum: the penetration of university personnel into French and English administration at the turn of the twelfth and thirteenth centuries', *Revue des études islamiques* 44 (1976): 199–215

Baschet, J., *Les justices de l'au-delà: les représentations de l'enfer en France et en Italie (XIIe–XVe siècle)* (Rome, 1993)

Bautier, R.-H., 'Les origines et les premiers développements de l'abbaye Saint-Victor de Paris', in J. Longère (ed.), *L'abbaye parisienne de Saint-Victor au moyen âge: communications présentées au XIIIe colloque d'humanisme médiéval de Paris (1986–1988)* (Paris, 1991), pp. 23–52

'Paris au temps Abélard', in J. Jolivet (ed.), *Abélard en sons temps. Actes du colloque international organisé à l'occasion du 9e centenaire de la naissance de Pierre Abélard (14–19 mai 1979)* (Paris, 1981), pp. 21–77

'Quand et comment Paris devint capitale', *Bulletin de la Société de l'histoire de Paris et de l'Ile de France* 105 (1978): 17–46

Bautier, R.-H., (ed.), *La France de Philippe Auguste: le temps des mutations. Actes du colloque international organisé par le C.N.R.S. (Paris, 29 septembre–4 octobre 1980* (Paris, 1982)

Begley, R. B. and J. W. Koterski (eds.), *Medieval Education* (New York, 2005)

Bell, D. N., *The Image and Likeness: The Augustinian Spirituality of William of St Thierry*, Cistercian Studies Series 78 (Kalamazoo, MI, 1984)

Bellomo, M., *The Common Legal Past of Europe 1000–1800*, trans. L. G. Cochrane, (Washington, DC, 1995)

Bender, T. (ed.), *The University and the City: From Medieval Origins to the Present* (Oxford, 1988)

Benson, R. L. and G. Constable (eds.), *Renaissance and Renewal in the Twelfth Century* (Oxford, 1982)

Bériou, N., *L'avènement des maîtres de la parole. La prédication à Paris au XIIIe siècle*, 2 vols. (Paris, 1998)

'La prédication au béguinage de Paris pendant l'année liturgique 1272–1273', *Recherches Augustiniennes* 13 (1978): 105–229

La prédication de Ranulphe de la Houblonnière: sermons aux clercs et aux simples gens à Paris au xiiie siècle, 2 vols. (Paris, 1987)

Bernstein, A. E., 'Esoteric theology: William of Auvergne on the fires of hell and purgatory', *Speculum* 57 (1982): 509–31

'Heaven, hell and purgatory: 1100–1500', in M. Rubin and W. Simons (eds.), *The Cambridge History of Christianity. Vol. 4: Christianity in Western Europe c. 1100–c. 1500* (Cambridge, 2009), pp. 200–16

'The invocation of hell in thirteenth-century Paris', in J. Hankins, J. Monfasani and F. Purnell (eds.), *Supplementum Festivum: Studies in Honor of Paul Oskar Kristeller*, Medieval and Renaissance Texts and Studies 49 (Binghamton, New York, 1987), pp. 13–54

'Teaching and preaching confession in thirteenth-century Paris', in A. Ferreiro (ed.), *The Devil, Heresy and Witchcraft in the Middle Ages: Essays in Honor of Jeffrey B. Russell* (Leiden, 1998), pp. 111–30

'Theology between heresy and folklore: William of Auvergne on punishment after death', *Studies in Medieval and Renaissance History* 5 (1982): 5–44

Bianchi, L., 'Aristotle as a captive bride: notes on Gregory IX's attitude towards Aristotelianism', in L. Honnefelder, R. Wood, M. Dreyer and M.-A. Aris (eds.), *Albertus Magnus und die Anfänge der Aristoteles-Rezeption im lateinischen Mittelalter: Von Richardis Rufus bis zu Franciscus de Mayronis, Albertus Magnus and the Beginnings of the Medieval Reception of Aristotle in the Latin West: From Richardus Rufus to Franciscus de Mayronis* (Münster, 2005), pp. 777–94

Censure et liberté intellectuelle à l'université de Paris (xiiie–xive siècles) (Paris, 1999)

Biller, P., 'Confession in the middle ages: introduction', in P. Biller and A. J. Minnis (eds.), *Handling Sin: Confession in the Middle Ages* (York, 1998)

The Measure of Multitude: Population in Medieval Thought (Oxford, 2000)

Biller, P. and A. J. Minnis (eds.), *Handling Sin: Confession in the Middle Ages* (York, 1998)

Bochenski, I. M., *A History of Formal Logic*, trans. I. Thomas (Notre Dame, IN, 1961)

Bouchard, C., *Holy Entrepreneurs: Cistercians, Knights, and Economic Exchange in Twelfth-Century Burgundy* (Ithaca, NY, 1991)

Bourdieu, P., *Homo Academicus*, trans. P. Collier (Cambridge, 1988)

Boussard, J., *Nouvelle histoire de Paris: De la fin du siège de 885–886 à la mort de Philippe Auguste*, 2nd edn (Paris, 1997)

'Philippe Auguste et Paris', in R.-H. Bautier (ed.), *La France de Philippe Auguste: le temps des mutations. Actes du colloque international organisé par le C.N.R.S. (Paris, 29 septembre–4 octobre 1980* (Paris, 1982), pp. 323–40

Boyle, L. E., *Pastoral Care, Clerical Education and Canon Law, 1200–1400* (London, 1981)

'The quodlibets of St. Thomas and pastoral care', *The Thomist* 38 (1974): 232–56, reprinted in L. E. Boyle, *Pastoral Care, Clerical Education and Canon Law, 1200–1400* (London, 1981), second item, same pagination

The Setting of the Summa Theologiae of Saint Thomas, The Etienne Gilson Series 5 (Toronto, 1982)

'*Summae confessorum*', in *Les genres littéraires dans les sources théologiques et philosophiques médiévales: definition, critique et exploitation. Actes du colloque international de Louvain-la-Neuve 25–27 mai 1981* (Louvain-la-Neuve, 1982), pp. 227–37

'The *Summa confessorum* of John of Freiburg and the popularization of the moral teaching of St. Thomas and of some of his contemporaries', in A. A. Maurer *et al.* (eds.), *St. Thomas Aquinas, 1274–1974: Commemorative Studies* (Toronto, 1974), vol. 2, pp. 245–68, reprinted in L. E. Boyle, *Pastoral Care, Clerical Education and Canon Law, 1200–1400* (London, 1981), third item, same pagination

Bredero, A. H., *Bernard of Clairvaux: Between Cult and History* (Edinburgh, 1996)

Broadie, A., *Introduction to Medieval Logic*, 2nd edn (Oxford, 1993)

Brooke, C. N. L., *The Medieval Idea of Marriage* (Oxford, 1989)

Brower, J. E., 'Trinity', in J. E. Brower and K. Guilfoy (eds.), *The Cambridge Companion to Abelard* (Cambridge, 2004), pp. 223–57

Brower, J. E. and K. Guilfoy (eds.), *The Cambridge Companion to Abelard* (Cambridge, 2004)

Brundage, J. A., *Law, Sex, and Christian Society in Medieval Europe* (Chicago, 1987)

Medieval Canon Law (London, 1995)

The Medieval Origins of the Legal Profession: Canonists, Civilians, and Courts (Chicago, 2008)

Bullough, V. L. and J. A. Brundage (eds.), *Handbook of Medieval Sexuality* (New York, 1996)
Sexual Practices and the Medieval Church (Buffalo, 1982)
Burrow, J. A. and I. P. Wei (eds.), *Medieval Futures: Attitudes to the Future in the Middle Ages* (Woodbridge, 2000)
Bynum, C. W., 'Did the twelfth century discover the individual?', *Journal of Ecclesiastical History* 31 (1980): 1–17
Jesus as Mother: Studies in the Spirituality of the High Middle Ages (Berkeley, 1982)
Cadden, J., *Meanings of Sex Difference in the Middle Ages: Medicine, Science, and Culture* (Cambridge, 1993)
Carfantan, J. (trans.), *William, Abbot of St Thierry: A Colloquium at the Abbey of St Thierry* (Kalamazoo, MI, 1987)
Cazelles, R., *Nouvelle histoire de Paris: De la fin du règne de Philippe Auguste à la mort de Charles V, 1223–1380*, 2nd edn (Paris, 1994)
Ceccarelli, G., '"Whatever" economics: economic thought in *quodlibeta*', in C. Schabel (ed.), *Theological Quodlibeta in the Middle Ages: The Thirteenth Century* (Leiden, 2006), pp. 475–505
Chenu, M.-D., *La théologie comme science au xiiie siècle* (Paris, 1957)
La théologie au douzième siècle (Paris, 1957)
Clanchy, M. T., *Abelard: A Medieval Life* (Oxford, 1997)
'Abelard's mockery of St. Anselm', *Journal of Ecclesiastical History* 41 (1990): 1–23
Cobban, A. B., 'Medieval student power', *Past and Present* 53 (1971): 28–66
The Medieval Universities: Their Development and Organization (London, 1975)
'The role of colleges in the medieval universities of northern Europe, with special reference to France and England', *Bulletin of the John Rylands University Library of Manchester* 71 (1989): 49–70
Cochrane, L., *Adelard of Bath: The First English Scientist* (London, 1994)
Cocking, J. M., *Imagination: A Study in the History of Ideas* (London, 1991)
Cohn, N., *The World-View of a Thirteenth-Century Parisian Intellectual: Jean de Meun and the Roman de la Rose* (Durham, 1961)
Coing, H., *Handbuch der Quellen und Literatur der Neueren Europäischen Privatrechtsgeschichte*, vol. 1 (Munich, 1973)
Colish, M. L., *Peter Lombard*, 2 vols. (Leiden, 1994)
Colledge, E., 'Liberty of spirit: "The Mirror of Simple Souls"', in L. K. Shook (ed.), *Theology of Renewal*, 2 vols. (New York, 1968), vol. 2, pp. 100–17
Colledge, E. and R. Guarnieri, 'The glosses by <<M.N.>> and Richard Methley to <<The Mirror of Simple Souls>>', *Archivio italiano per la storia della pietà* 5 (1968): 357–82
Colledge E. and J. C. Marler, '"Poverty of the will": Ruusbroec, Eckhart and *The Mirror of Simple Souls*', in P. Mommaers and N de Paepe (eds.), *Jan van Ruusbroec: The Sources, Content and Sequels of his Mysticism* (Leuven, 1984), pp. 14–47
The Concise Oxford Dictionary, ed. J. B. Sykes (Oxford, 1976)

Constable, G., *Monks, Hermits and Crusaders in Medieval Europe* (London, 1988)
'Renewal and reform in religious life: concepts and realities', in R. L. Benson and G. Constable (eds.), *Renaissance and Renewal in the Twelfth Century* (Oxford, 1982), pp. 37–67
Three Studies in Medieval Religious and Social Thought: The Interpretation of Mary and Martha; The Ideal of the Imitation of Christ; The Orders of Society (Cambridge, 1995)
Coolman, B. T., *The Theology of Hugh of St. Victor: An Interpretation* (Cambridge, 2010)
Copleston, F. C., *A History of Medieval Philosophy* (London, 1972)
Coulter, D. M., *Per Visibilia ad Invisibilia: Theological Method in Richard of St. Victor (d. 1173)* (Turnhout, 2006)
Courtenay, W. J., 'Dominicans and suspect opinion in the thirteenth century: the cases of Stephen of Venizy, Peter of Tarentaise, and the articles of 1270 and 1271', *Vivarium* 32 (1994): 186–95
'Inquiry and inquisition: academic freedom in medieval universities', *Church History* 58 (1989): 168–81
'Learned opinion and royal justice: the role of Paris masters of theology during the reign of Philip the Fair', in R. M. Karras, J. Kaye and E. A. Matter (eds.), *Law and the Illicit in Medieval Europe* (Philadelphia, 2008), pp. 149–63
'The Parisian faculty of theology in the late thirteenth and early fourteenth centuries', in J. A. Aertsen, K. Emery and A. Speer (eds.), *Nach der Verurteilung von 1277. Philosophie und Theologie en der Universität von Paris im letzten Viertel des 13. Jahrhunderts. Studien und Texte / After the Condemnation of 1277. Philosophy and Theology at the University of Paris in the Last Quarter of the Thirteenth Century. Studies and Texts*, Miscellanea Mediaevalia 28 (Berlin, 2001), pp. 235–47
Parisian Scholars in the Early Fourteenth Century: A Social Portrait (Cambridge, 1999)
Teaching Careers at the University of Paris in the Thirteenth and Fourteenth Centuries (Notre Dame, IN, 1988)
Courtenay, W. J. and J. Miethke (eds.), *Universities and Schooling in Medieval Society* (Leiden, 2000)
Cousins, E. H., *Bonaventure and the Coincidence of Opposites* (Chicago, 1978)
Cullen, C. M., *Bonaventure* (Oxford, 2006)
Daly, S. R., 'Peter Comestor: Master of Histories', *Speculum* 32 (1957): 62–73
Dautrey, P., 'Croissance et adaptation chez les cisterciens au treizième siècle: les débuts du collège des Bernadins de Paris', *Analecta Cisterciensia* 32 (1976): 122–215
Davies, B., *The Thought of Thomas Aquinas* (Oxford, 1992)
Davies, O., *Meister Eckhart: Mystical Theologian* (London, 1991)
d'Avray, D. L., *The Preaching of the Friars: Sermons diffused from Paris before 1300* (Oxford, 1985)
d'Avray, D. L. and M. Tausche, 'Marriage sermons in *ad status* collections of the central middle ages', *Archives d'histoire doctrinale et littéraire du moyen âge* 47 (1980): 71–119

Davy, M. M., *Les sermons universitaires parisiens de 1230–1231* (Paris, 1931)

Déchanet, J.-M., 'Amor ipse intellectus est: la doctrine de l'amour-intellection chez Guillaume de Saint-Thierry', *Revue du Moyen Age Latin* 1 (1945): 349–74

Delhaye, P., 'L'enseignement de la philosophie morale au xiie siècle', *Mediaeval Studies* 11 (1949): 77–99, reprinted in *Enseignement et Morale au XIIe Siècle* (Fribourg, 1988), pp. 59–81

'<<Grammatica>> et <<Ethica>> au xiie siècle', *Recherches de théologie ancienne et médiévale* 25 (1958): 59–110, reprinted in *Enseignement et Morale au XIIe Siècle* (Fribourg, 1988), pp. 83–134

'L'organisation scolaire au xiie siècle', *Traditio* 5 (1947): 211–68

Denley, P., 'Communes, despots and universities: structures and trends of Italian *studi* to 1500', in J. E. Law and B. Paton (eds.), *Communes and Despots in Medieval and Renaissance Italy* (Aldershot, 2010), pp. 295–306

'Communities within communities: student identity and student groups in late medieval Italian universities', in F. Piovan and L. S. Rea (eds.), *Studenti, università, città nella storia padovana: atti del convegno Padova 6–8 febbraio 1998* (Trieste, 2001), pp. 723–44

de Roover, R., *Business, Banking, and Economic Thought in Late Medieval and Early Modern Europe*, ed. J. Kirshner (Chicago, 1974)

Dronke, P., *Women Writers of the Middle Ages* (Cambridge, 1984)

Duby, G., *The Knight, the Lady, and the Priest: The Making of Modern Marriage in Medieval France*, trans. B. Bray (New York, 1983)

Medieval Marriage: Two Models from Twelfth-Century France, trans. E. Forster (Baltimore, 1978)

Dufeil, M.-M., *Guillaume de Saint-Amour et la polémique universitaire parisienne, 1250–1259* (Paris, 1972)

Dunbabin, J., *A Hound of God: Pierre de la Palud and the Fourteenth-Century Church* (Oxford, 1991)

'Meeting the costs of university education in northern France, *c*. 1240–*c*. 1340', *History of Universities*, 10 (1991): 1–27

'The reception and interpretation of Aristotle's *Politics*', in N. Kretzmann, A. Kenny and J. Pinborg (eds.), *The Cambridge History of Later Medieval Philosophy* (Cambridge, 1982), pp. 723–37

Edwards, R. R. and S. Spector (eds.), *The Olde Daunce: Love, Friendship, Sex and Marriage in the Medieval World* (New York, 1991)

Elliott, D., *Spiritual Marriage: Sexual Abstinence in Medieval Wedlock* (Princeton, 1993)

Evans, G. R., *Alan of Lille: The Frontiers of Theology in the Later Twelfth Century* (Cambridge, 1983)

Anselm (London, 1989)

Bernard of Clairvaux (Oxford, 2000)

The Mind of St Bernard of Clairvaux (Oxford, 1983)

Old Arts and New Theology: The Beginnings of Theology as an Academic Discipline (Oxford, 1980)

Farmer, S., 'Persuasive voices: clerical images of medieval wives', *Speculum* 61 (1986): 517–43

Ferreiro, A. (ed.), *The Devil, Heresy and Witchcraft in the Middle Ages: Essays in Honor of Jeffrey B. Russell* (Leiden, 1998)

Ferruolo, S. C., *The Origins of the University: The Schools of Paris and their Critics, 1100–1215* (Stanford, 1985)

'The Paris statutes of 1215 reconsidered', *History of Universities* 5 (1985): 1–14

'*Parisius-Paradisus*: the city, its schools, and the origins of the University of Paris', in *T. Bender* (ed.), *The University and the City: From Medieval Origins to the Present* (Oxford, 1988), pp. 22–43

Field, S. L., 'The Master and Marguerite: Godfrey of Fontaines' praise of *The Mirror of Simple Souls*', *Journal of Medieval History* 35 (2009): 136–49

Flanagan, S., *Hildegard of Bingen: A Visionary Life* (London, 1989)

Fried, J. (ed.), *Schulen und Studium im Sozialen Wandel des hohen und späten Mittelalters*, Vorträge und Forschungen 30 (Sigmaringen, 1986)

Gabriel, A. L., 'The ideal master of the medieval university', *Catholic Historical Review* 60 (1974): 1–40

Les genres littéraires dans les sources théologiques et philosophiques médiévales: definition, critique et exploitation. Actes du colloque international de Louvain-la-Neuve 25–27 mai 1981 (Louvain-la-Neuve, 1982)

Gieysztot, A., 'Management and resources', in H. de Ridder-Symoens (ed.), *A History of the University in Europe. Vol. 1: Universities in the Middle Ages* (Cambridge, 1992), pp. 108–43

Gilchrist, J. T., *The Church and Economic Activity in the Middle Ages* (London, 1969)

Gilson, E., *History of Christian Philosophy in the Middle Ages* (New York, 1955)

The Mystical Theology of Saint Bernard, trans. A. H. C. Downes (London, 1940)

The Philosophy of Bonaventure, trans. I. Trethowan and F. J. Sheed (London, 1938)

Glorieux, P., 'L'enseignement au moyen âge: techniques et méthodes en usage à la faculté de théologie de Paris au xiiie siècle', *Archives d'histoire doctrinale et littéraire du moyen âge* 35 (1968): 65–186

La littérature quodlibétique de 1260 à 1320, 2 vols. (Paris, 1925 and 1935)

'Notices sur quelques théologiens de Paris de la fin du xiiie siècle', *Archives d'histoire doctrinale et littéraire du moyen âge* 3 (1928): 201–38

Les Origines du Collège de Sorbonne (Notre Dame, IN, 1959)

'Les quodlibets de Gervais de Mont-Saint-Eloi', *Recherches de théologie ancienne et médiévale* 20 (1953): 129–34

Godman, P., *The Silent Masters: Latin Literature and Its Censors in the High Middle Ages* (Princeton, 2000)

Gold, P. S., *The Lady and the Virgin: Image, Attitude and Experience in Twelfth-Century France* (Chicago, 1985)

'The marriage of Mary and Joseph in the twelfth-century ideology of marriage', in V. L. Bullough and J. A. Brundage (eds.), *Sexual Practices and the Medieval Church* (Buffalo, 1982), pp. 102–17

Guarnieri, R., 'Il <<miroir des simples ames>> di Margherita Porete', *Archivio italiano per la storia della pietà* 4 (1965): 501–635

Gurevich, A., *Medieval Popular Culture: Problems of Belief and Perception*, trans. J. M. Bak and P. A. Hollingsworth (Cambridge, 1988)

Gurevich, A. J., *Categories of Medieval Culture*, trans. G. L. Campbell (London, 1985)

‘Popular and scholarly medieval cultural traditions: notes in the margin of Jacques Le Goff’s book’, *Journal of Medieval History* 9 (1983): 71–90

Hamesse, J., ‘Theological quaestiones quodlibetales’, in C. Schabel (ed.), *Theological Quodlibeta in the Middle Ages: The Thirteenth Century* (Leiden, 2006), pp. 17–48

Hamesse, J., B. M. Kienzle, D. L. Stoudt, A. T. Thayer (eds.), *Medieval Sermons and Society: Cloister, City, University* (Louvain-la-Neuve, 1998)

Haren, M., *Medieval Thought: The Western Intellectual Tradition from Antiquity to the Thirteenth Century*, 2nd edn (Toronto, 1992)

Häring, N. M., ‘Alan of Lille, <<De Planctu naturae>>’, *Studi Medievali*, third series, 19 (1978): 797–897

Harkins, F. T., *Reading and the Work of Restoration: History and Scripture in the Theology of Hugh of St Victor* (Toronto, 2009)

Haseldine, J., ‘Friendship and rivalry: the role of *amicitia* in twelfth-century monastic relations’, *Journal of Ecclesiastical History* 44 (1993): 390–414

Haskins, C. H., ‘The life of mediaeval students as illustrated by their letters’, in *Studies in Mediaeval Culture* (Oxford, 1929), pp. 1–35, as revised and expanded from *American Historical Review*, 3 (1898): 203–29

Studies in Mediaeval Culture (Oxford, 1929)

Hayes, Z., *Bonaventure: Mystical Writings* (New York, 1999)

Hissette, R., *Enquête sur les 219 articles condamnes a Paris le 7 mars 1277* (Louvain, 1977)

‘Une question quodlibétique de Servais du Mont-Saint-Eloi sur le pouvoir doctrinal de l’évêque’, *Recherches de théologie ancienne et médiévale* 49 (1982): 234–42

Hollywood, A., ‘Suffering transformed: Marguerite Porete, Meister Eckhart, and the problem of women’s spirituality’, in B. McGinn (ed), *Meister Eckhart and the Beguine Mystics: Hadewijch of Brabant, Mechthild of Magdeburg, and Marguerite Porete* (New York, 1994), pp. 87–113

Idel, M., and B. McGinn (eds.), *Mystical Union and Monotheistic Faith: An Ecumenical Dialogue* (New York, 1989)

Illich, I., *In the Vineyard of the Text: A Commentary to Hugh’s Didascalicon* (Chicago, 1993)

Jacobi, K., ‘Philosophy of language’, in J. E. Brower and K. Guilfoy (eds.), *The Cambridge Companion to Abelard* (Cambridge, 2004), pp. 126–57

Jaeger, C. S., *The Envy of Angels: Cathedral Schools and Social Ideals in Medieval Europe, 950–1200* (Philadelphia, 1994)

James, B. S., *Saint Bernard of Clairvaux: An Essay in Biography* (London, 1957)

Johnson, P. D., *Equal in Monastic Profession: Religious Women in Medieval France* (Chicago, 1991)

Jolivet, J. (ed.), *Abélard en sons temps. Actes du colloque international organisé à l’occasion du 9e centenaire de la naissance de Pierre Abélard (14–19 mai 1979)* (Paris, 1981)

Jordan, W. C., *Unceasing Strife, Unending Fear: Jacques de Thérines and the Freedom of the Church in the Age of the Last Capetians* (Princeton, 2005)

Jordan, W. C., B. McNab and T. F. Ruiz (eds.), *Order and Innovation in the Middle Ages: Essays in Honor of Joseph R. Strayer* (Princeton, 1976)

Karras, R. M., *From Boys to Men: Formations of Masculinity in Late Medieval Europe* (Philadelphia, 2003)

'Using women to think with in the medieval university', in A. B. Mulder-Bakker (ed.), *Seeing and Knowing: Women and Learning in Medieval Europe 1200–1550* (Turnhout, 2004), pp. 21–33

Karras, R. M., J. Kaye and E. A. Matter (eds.), *Law and the Illicit in Medieval Europe* (Philadelphia, 2008)

Kay, S., *The Romance of the Rose* (London, 1995)

Kaye, J., *Economy and Nature in the Fourteenth Century: Money, Market Exchange, and the Emergence of Scientific Thought* (Cambridge, 1998)

Keats-Rohan, K. S. B., 'John of Salisbury and education in twelfth century Paris from the account of his *Metalogicon*', *History of Universities* 6 (1986–7): 1–45

Kerby-Fulton, K., *Books under Suspicion: Censorship and Tolerance of Revelatory Writing in Late Medieval England* (Notre Dame, IN, 2006)

Kibre, P., 'Academic oaths at the university of Paris in the middle ages', in J. H. Mundy, R. W. Emery and B. N. Nelson (eds.), *Essays in Medieval Life and Thought: presented in Honor of Austin Patterson Evans* (New York, 1955), pp. 123–37

The Nations in the Mediaeval Universities (Cambridge, MA, 1948)

Scholarly Privileges in the Middle Ages (London, 1961)

Kooper, E., 'Loving the unequal equal: medieval theologians and marital affection', in R. R. Edwards and S. Spector (eds.), *The Olde Daunce: Love, Friendship, Sex and Marriage in the Medieval World* (New York, 1991), pp. 44–56

Kretzmann, N., A. Kenny and J. Pinborg (eds.), *The Cambridge History of Later Medieval Philosophy* (Cambridge, 1982)

Kuttner, S., *Repertorium der Kanonistik (1140–1234)*, Studi e Testi 71 (Vatican, 1937)

Kwanten, F. E., 'Le Collège Saint-Bernard à Paris: Sa fondation et ses débuts', *Revue d'histoire ecclésiastique* 43 (1948): 443–72

Lagerlund, H., *Modal Syllogistics in the Middle Ages* (Leiden, 2000)

Langholm, O., *Economics in the Medieval Schools: Wealth, Exchange, Value, Money and Usury according to the Paris Theological Tradition, 1200–1350* (Leiden, 1992)

Lawrence, C. H., *Medieval Monasticism: Forms of Religious Life in Western Europe in the Middle Ages*, 3rd edn (Harlow, 2001)

'Stephen of Lexington and Cistercian university studies in the thirteenth century', *Journal of Ecclesiastical History* 11 (1960): 164–78

Leclercq, J., *Bernard of Clairvaux and the Cistercian Spirit* (Kalamazoo, MI, 1976)

'L'idéal du théologien au moyen âge: textes inédites', *Revue des sciences religieuses* 21 (1947): 121–48

The Love of Learning and the Desire for God: A Study of Monastic Culture, trans. C. Misrahi (London, 1978)
'Le magistère du prédicateur au xiiie siècle', *Archives d'histoire doctrinale et littéraire du moyen âge* 15 (1946): 105–47
'The renewal of theology', in R. L. Benson and G. Constable (eds.), *Renaissance and Renewal in the Twelfth Century* (Oxford, 1982), pp. 68–87
Leff, G., *Heresy in the Later Middle Ages: The Relation of Heterodoxy to Dissent c. 1250–c. 1450*, 2 vols. (Manchester, 1967)
Paris and Oxford Universities in the Thirteenth and Fourteenth Centuries: An Institutional and Intellectual History (New York, 1968)
'The *Trivium* and the three philosophies', in H. de Ridder-Symoens (ed.), *A History of the University in Europe. Vol. 1: Universities in the Middle Ages* (Cambridge, 1992), pp. 307–36
Le Goff, J., *The Birth of Purgatory*, trans. A. Goldhammer (London, 1984)
Intellectuals in the Middle Ages, trans. T. L. Fagan (Oxford, 1993)
Time, Work and Culture in the Middle Ages, trans. A. Goldhammer (Chicago, 1980)
Your Money or Your Life: Economy and Religion in the Middle Ages, trans. P. Ranum (New York, 1988)
Lerner, R. E., 'An "Angel of Philadelphia" in the reign of Philip the Fair: the case of Guiard of Cressonessart', in W. C. Jordan, B. McNab and T. F. Ruiz (eds.), *Order and Innovation in the Middle Ages: Essays in Honor of Joseph R. Strayer* (Princeton, 1976), pp. 343–64
The Heresy of the Free Spirit in the Later Middle Ages (Berkeley, 1972)
'New light on *The Mirror of Simple Souls*', *Speculum* 85 (2010): 91–116
Lichtmann, M., 'Marguerite Porete and Meister Eckhart: *The Mirror for Simple Souls* mirrored', in B. McGinn (ed.), *Meister Eckhart and the Beguine Mystics: Hadewijch of Brabant, Mechthild of Magdeburg, and Marguerite Porete* (New York, 1994), pp. 65–86
Liebs, D., *Lateinische Rechtsregeln und Rechtssprichwörter* (Munich, 1982)
Little, L. K., 'Pride goes before avarice: social change and the vices in Latin Christendom', *American Historical Review* 76 (1971): 16–49
Religious Poverty and the Profit Economy in Medieval Europe (London, 1978)
Lombard-Jourdan, A., *Paris – genèse de la 'ville': la rive droite de la Seine des origines à 1223* (Paris, 1976)
Longère, J., *Oeuvres oratoires de maîtres parisiens au xiie siècle: étude historique et doctrinale*, 2 vols. (Paris, 1975)
Longère, J. (ed.), *L'abbaye parisienne de Saint-Victor au moyen âge: communications présentées au XIIIe colloque d'humanisme médiéval de Paris (1986–1988)* (Paris, 1991)
Luscombe, D., 'Peter Comestor', in K. Walsh and D. Wood (eds.), *The Bible in the Medieval World: Essays in Memory of Beryl Smalley* (Oxford, 1985), pp. 109–29
Luscombe, D. E. 'From Paris to the Paraclete. The correspondence of Abelard and Heloise', *Proceedings of the British Academy* 74 (1988): 247–83
Medieval Thought (Oxford, 1997)
The School of Peter Abelard: The Influence of Abelard's Thought in the Early Scholastic Period (Cambridge, 1969)

Lusignan, S., *'Vérité garde le roy': la construction d'une identité universitaire en France (XIIIe-XVe siècle)* (Paris, 1999)
Maddocks, F., *Hildegard of Bingen: The Woman of her Age* (New York, 2003)
Marenbon, J., *Early Medieval Philosophy (480–1150)* (London, 1983)
Later Medieval Philosophy (1150–1350) (London, 1987, repr. 1996)
The Philosophy of Peter Abelard (Cambridge, 1997)
Marmursztejn, E., *L'autorité des maîtres: scolastique, normes et société au xiiie siècle* (Paris, 2007)
'A normative power in the making: theological *quodlibeta* and the authority of the masters at Paris at the end of the thirteenth century', in C. Schabel (ed.), *Theological Quodlibeta in the Middle Ages: The Thirteenth Century* (Leiden, 2006), pp. 345–402
Matter, E. A., *The Voice of My Beloved: The Song of Songs in Western Medieval Christianity* (Philadelphia, 1990)
Maurer, A. A. *et al.* (eds.), *St. Thomas Aquinas, 1274–1974: Commemorative Studies* (Toronto, 1974)
McGinn, B., '"Evil-sounding, rash, and suspect of heresy": tensions between mysticism and magisterium in the history of the church', *The Catholic Historical Review* 90 (2004): 193–212
The Flowering of Mysticism: Men and Women in the New Mysticism (1200–1350), The Presence of God: A History of Western Christian Mysticism 3 (New York, 1998)
The Growth of Mysticism, The Presence of God: A History of Western Mysticism 2 (London, 1994)
The Harvest of Mysticism in Medieval Germany (1300–1500), The Presence of God: A History of Western Christian Mysticism 4 (New York, 2005)
'Love, knowledge and *Unio mystica* in the western Christian tradition', in M. Idel and B. McGinn (eds.), *Mystical Union and Monotheistic Faith: An Ecumenical Dialogue* (New York, 1989), pp. 73–8
McGinn, B. (ed), *Meister Eckhart and the Beguine Mystics: Hadewijch of Brabant, Mechthild of Magdeburg, and Marguerite Porete* (New York, 1994)
McKeon, P. R., 'The status of the university of Paris as *Parens Scientiarum*: an episode in the development of its autonomy', *Speculum* 39 (1964): 651–75
McLaughlin, M. M., *Intellectual Freedom and its Limitations in the University of Paris in the Thirteenth and Fourteenth Centuries* (New York, 1977)
McLaughlin, T. P., 'The teaching of the canonists on usury (XII, XIII and XIV centuries)', *Mediaeval Studies* 1 (1939): 81–147 and 2 (1940): 1–22
Mews, C. J., *The Lost Love Letters of Heloise and Abelard: Perceptions of Dialogue in Twelfth-Century France* (New York, 1999)
'Orality, literacy, and authority in the twelfth-century schools', *Exemplaria* 2 (1990): 475–500
Peter Abelard (Aldershot, 1995)
Michaud-Quantin, P., 'Les catégories sociales dans le vocabulaire des canonistes et moralistes au xiiie siècle', in *Etudes sur le vocabulaire philosophique du moyen âge* (Rome, 1970), pp. 163–86
Sommes de casuistique et manuels de confession au moyen âge (XII–XVI siècles) (Louvain, 1962)

Universitas. Expressions du mouvement communautaire dans le moyen-âge latin (Paris, 1970)

'Le vocabulaire des catégories sociales chez les canonistes et les moralistes du xiiie siècle', in D. Roche and C. E. Labrousse (eds.), *Ordres et Classes. Colloque d'Histoire Sociale. Saint-Cloud 24–25 mai 1967* (Paris, 1973), pp. 73–86

Milis, L., 'William of Saint Thierry, his birth, his formation and his first monastic experiences', in J. Carfantan (trans.), *William, Abbot of St Thierry: A Colloquium at the Abbey of St Thierry* (Kalamazoo, MI, 1987), pp. 9–33

Miller, T. S., 'What's in a name? Clerical representations of Parisian beguines (1200–1328), *Journal of Medieval History* 33 (2007): 60–86

Mommaers, P. and N de Paepe (eds.), *Jan van Ruusbroec: The Sources, Content and Sequels of his Mysticism* (Leuven, 1984)

Moore, R., *Jews and Christians in the Life and Thought of Hugh of St. Victor* (Atlanta, 1998)

Moore, R. I., *The Formation of a Persecuting Society: Power and Deviance in Western Europe, 950–1250* (Oxford, 1987)

Morey, J. H., 'Peter Comestor, biblical paraphrase, and the medieval popular Bible', *Speculum* 68 (1993): 6–35

Mowbray, D., *Pain and Suffering in Medieval Theology: Academic Debates at the University of Paris in the Thirteenth Century* (Woodbridge, 2009)

Muessig, C., 'Audience and preacher: *ad status* sermons and social classification', in C. Muessig (ed.), *Preacher, Sermon and Audience in the Middle Ages* (Leiden, 2002), pp. 255–76

Muessig, C. (ed.), *Preacher, Sermon and Audience in the Middle Ages* (Leiden, 2002)

Mulchahey, M. M., *'First the Bow is Bent': Dominican Education before 1350* (Toronto, 1998)

Mulder-Bakker, A. B., (ed.), *Seeing and Knowing: Women and Learning in Medieval Europe 1200–1550* (Turnhout, 2004)

Mundy, J. H., R. W. Emery and B. N. Nelson (eds.), *Essays in Medieval Life and Thought: presented in Honor of Austin Patterson Evans* (New York, 1955)

Murphy, J. J., *Rhetoric in the Middle Ages: A History of Rhetorical Theory from St Augustine to the Renaissance* (Berkeley, 1974)

Murray, A., *Reason and Society in the Middle Ages* (Oxford, 1978)

Murray, A. V., *Abelard and St Bernard: A Study in Twelfth Century 'Modernism'* (Manchester, 1967)

Newman, B., 'Authority, authenticity and the repression of Heloise', *Journal of Medieval and Renaissance Studies* 22 (1992): 121–57

From Virile Woman to WomanChrist: Studies in Medieval Religion and Literature (Philadelphia, 1995)

'Hildegard of Bingen: visions and validation', *Church History* 54 (1985): 163–75

Sister of Wisdom: St. Hildegard's Theology of the Feminine (Aldershot, 1987)

Newman, M. G., *The Boundaries of Charity: Cistercian Culture and Ecclesiastical Reform, 1098–1180* (Stanford, 1996)

Noonan, J. T., *Contraception: A History of its Treatment by the Catholic Theologians and Canonists*, enlarged edn (Cambridge, MA, 1986)

The Scholastic Analysis of Usury (Cambridge, MA, 1957)

O'Sullivan, R. A., 'The school of love: Marguerite Porete's *Mirror of Simple Souls*', *Journal of Medieval History* 32 (2006): 143–62

Paquet, J., 'Coût des études, pauvreté et labeur: fonctions et métiers d'étudiants au moyen âge', *History of Universities*, 2 (1982): 15–52

Paré, G., *Les idées et les letttres aux XIIIe siècle. Le 'Roman de la Rose'* (Montreal, 1947)

Le 'Roman de la Rose' et la scolastique courtoise (Paris, 1941)

Pasnau, R. (ed.), *The Cambridge History of Medieval Philosophy*, 2 vols. (Cambridge, 2010)

Payer, P. J., *The Bridling of Desire: Views of Sex in the Later middle ages* (Toronto, 1993)

'Confession and the study of sex in the middle ages', in V. L. Bullough and J. A. Brundage (eds.), *Handbook of Medieval Sexuality* (New York, 1996), pp. 3–31

Sex and the New Medieval Literature of Confession, 1150–1300 (Toronto, 2009)

Pedersen, O., *The First Universities: Studium Generale and the Origins of University Education in Europe* (Cambridge, 1997)

Pegues, F., 'Ecclesiastical provisions for the support of students in the thirteenth century', *Church History* 26 (1957): 307–18

'Royal support of students in the thirteenth century', *Speculum* 31 (1956): 454–62

Perler, D., 'Skepticism', in R. Pasnau (ed.), *The Cambridge History of Medieval Philosophy*, 2 vols. (Cambridge, 2010), vol. 1, pp. 384–96

Piron, S., 'Nicholas of Bar's collection', in C. Schabel (ed.), *Theological Quodlibeta in the Middle Ages: The Fourteenth Century* (Leiden, 2007), pp. 333–43

Poirel, D., *Hugues de Saint-Victor* (Paris, 1998)

Polak, L., 'Plato, Nature and Jean de Meun', *Reading Medieval Studies* 3 (1977): 80–103

Poole, R. L., 'The masters of the schools of Paris and Chartres in John of Salisbury's time', *English Historical Review* 35 (1920): 321–42

Quinn, J. F., *The Historical Constitution of St Bonaventure's Philosophy* (Toronto, 1973)

Ranke-Heinemann, U., *Eunuchs for the Kingdom of Heaven: The Catholic Church and Sexuality*, trans. P. Heinegg (Harmondsworh, 1990)

Rashdall, H., *The Universities of Europe in the Middle Ages*, revised and ed. F. M. Powicke and A. B. Emden, 3 vols. (1936; repr. Oxford, 1997)

Rexroth, F., 'Ritual and the creation of social knowledge: the opening celebrations of medieval German universities', in W. J. Courtenay and J. Miethke (eds.), *Universities and Schooling in Medieval Society* (Leiden, 2000), pp. 65–80

Reynolds, P. L., 'Marrying and its documentation in pre-modern Europe', in P. L. Reynolds and J. Witte (eds.), *To Have and To Hold: Marrying and its Documentation in Western Christendom, 1400–1600* (Cambridge, 2007), pp. 1–42

Reynolds, P. L. and J. Witte (eds.), *To Have and To Hold: Marrying and its Documentation in Western Christendom, 1400–1600* (Cambridge, 2007)

Riché, P., 'Jean de Salisbury et le monde scolaire du xiie siècle', in M. Wilks (ed.), *The World of John of Salisbury* (1984, repr. Oxford, 1994), pp. 39–61
Ridder-Symoens, H. de, 'Mobility', in H. de Ridder-Symoens (ed.), *A History of the University in Europe. Vol. 1: Universities in the Middle Ages* (Cambridge, 1992), pp. 280–304
Ridder-Symoens, H. de (ed.), *A History of the University in Europe. Vol. 1: Universities in the Middle Ages* (Cambridge, 1992)
Roberts, G. R., 'Purgatory: "birth" or evolution?', *Journal of Ecclesiastical History* 36 (1985): 634–46
Roberts, P. B., 'Sermons and preaching in/and the medieval university', in R. B. Begley and J. W. Koterski (eds.), *Medieval Education* (New York, 2005), pp. 83–98
Robinson, J. M., *Nobility and Annihilation in Marguerite Porete's Mirror of Simple Souls* (New York, 2001)
Roche, D. and C. E. Labrousse (eds.), *Ordres et Classes. Colloque d'Histoire Sociale. Saint-Cloud 24–25 mai 1967* (Paris, 1973)
Roest, B., *A History of Franciscan Education (c. 1210–1517)* (Leiden, 2000)
Rorem, P., *Hugh of Saint Victor* (Oxford, 2009)
Rosemann, P. W., *Peter Lombard* (Oxford, 2004)
Rosenwein, B. H. and L. K. Little, 'Social meaning in the monastic and mendicant spiritualities', *Past and Present* 63 (1974): 4–32
Rouse, R. H. and M. A. Rouse, *Manuscripts and their Makers: Commercial Book Producers in Medieval Paris 1200–1500*, 2 vols. (Turnhout, 2000)
Preachers, Florilegia and Sermons: Studies on the Manipulus florum of Thomas of Ireland (Toronto, 1979)
'*Statim invenire*: schools, preachers, and new attitudes to the page', in R. L. Benson and G. Constable (eds.), *Renaissance and Renewal in the Twelfth Century* (Cambridge, MA, 1982), pp. 201–25
Roux, S., *Paris in the Middle Ages*, trans. J. A. McNamara (Philadelphia, 2009)
Rubin, M. and W. Simons (eds.), *The Cambridge History of Christianity. Vol. 4: Christianity in Western Europe c. 1100–c.1500* (Cambridge, 2009)
Russell, J. B., *Lucifer: The Devil in the Middle Ages* (Ithaca, NY, 1984)
Sargent, M. G., 'The annihilation of Marguerite Porete', *Viator* 28 (1997): 253–79
Schabel, C., *Theology at Paris, 1316–1345: Peter Auriol and the Problem of Divine Foreknowledge and Future Contingents* (Aldershot, 2000)
Schabel, C. (ed.), *Theological Quodlibeta in the Middle Ages: The Fourteenth Century* (Leiden, 2007)
Theological Quodlibeta in the Middle Ages: The Thirteenth Century (Leiden, 2006)
Schneyer, J., *Die Sittenkritik in den Predigten Philipps des Kanzlers*, Beiträge zur Geschichte der Philosophie und Theologie des Mittelalters 39/4 (Münster, 1962)
Schwinges, R. C., 'Student education, student life', in H. de Ridder-Symoens (ed.), *A History of the University in Europe. Vol. 1: Universities in the Middle Ages* (Cambridge, 1992), pp. 195–243
Sells, M., *Mystical Languages of Unsaying* (Chicago, 1994)

Shook, L. K. (ed.), *Theology of Renewal*, 2 vols. (New York, 1968)
Shriver, G. H. (ed.), *Contemporary Reflections on the Medieval Christian Tradition: Essays in Honor of Ray C. Petry* (Durham, NC, 1974)
Sicard, P., *Hugues de Saint-Victor et son Ecole* (Turnhout, 1991)
Singer, C., *From Magic to Science: Essays on the Scientific Twilight* (New York, 1958)
Studies in the History and Method of Science, 2 vols. (Oxford, 1917 and 1921)
Siraisi, N., 'The faculty of medicine', in H. de Ridder-Symoens (ed.), *A History of the University in Europe. Vol. 1: Universities in the Middle Ages* (Cambridge, 1992), pp. 360–87
Smalley, B., *The Becket Conflict and the Schools: A Study of Intellectuals in Politics* (Oxford, 1973)
English Friars and Antiquity in the Early Fourteenth Century (Oxford, 1960)
'Studies on the Commentaries of Cardinal Stephen Langton (part II)', *Archives d'histoire doctrinale et littéraire du moyen âge* 5 (1930): 152–82
The Study of the Bible in the Middle Ages (Oxford, 1952)
Smith, L., *The Glossa Ordinaria: The Making of a Medieval Bible Commentary* (Leiden, 2009)
'William of Auvergne and confession', in P. Biller and A. J. Minnis (eds.), *Handling Sin: Confession in the Middle Ages* (York, 1998), pp. 95–107
Southern, R. W., 'The changing role of universities in medieval Europe', *Bulletin of the Institute of Historical Research* 60 (1987): 133–46
'Humanism and the school of Chartres', in *Medieval Humanism and Other Studies* (Oxford, 1970), pp. 61–85
'The letters of Abelard and Heloise', in *Medieval Humanism and Other Studies* (Oxford, 1970), pp. 86–104
Saint Anselm: A Portrait in a Landscape (Cambridge, 1990)
Saint Anselm and his Biographer: A Study of Monastic Life and Thought 1059–c. 1130 (Cambridge, 1963)
Spade, P. V., *Thought, Words and Things: An Introduction to Late Mediaeval Logic and Semantic Theory* (Version 1.1, 2002; http://pvspade.com/Logic/docs/thoughts1_1a.pdf)
Spatz, N., 'Approaches and attitudes to a new theology textbook: the *Sentences* of Peter Lombard', in N. van Deusen (ed.), *The Intellectual Climate of the Early University: Essays in Honor of Otto Gründler* (Kalamazoo, MI, 1997), pp. 27–52
Spatz, N. K., 'Imagery in university inception sermons', in J. Hamesse, B. M. Kienzle, D. L. Stoudt, A. T. Thayer (eds.), *Medieval Sermons and Society: Cloister, City, University* (Louvain-la-Neuve, 1998), pp. 329–42
Stelling-Michaud, S., *L'université de Bologne et la pénétration des droits romain et canonique en Suisse aux xiiie et xive siècles* (Geneva, 1955)
Stock, B., *The Implications of Literacy: Written Language and Models of Interpretation in the Eleventh and Twelfth Centuries* (Princeton, 1983)
Myth and Science in the Twelfth Century: A Study of Bernard Silvester (Princeton, 1972)
Sullivan, T., 'The *quodlibeta* of the canons regular and the monks', in C. Schabel (ed.), *Theological Quodlibeta in the Middle Ages: The Fourteenth Century* (Leiden, 2007), pp. 359–400

Tentler, T. N., *Sin and Confession on the Eve of the Reformation* (Princeton, 1977)

'The summa for confessors as an instrument of social control', in C. Trinkaus and H. A. Oberman (eds.), *The Pursuit of Holiness in Late Medieval and Renaissance Religion* (Leiden, 1974), pp. 103–37

Thijssen, J. M. M. H., *Censure and Heresy at the University of Paris 1200–1400* (Philadelphia, 1998)

Traver, A. G., 'Rewriting history? The Parisian secular masters' *Apologia* of 1254', *History of Universities* 15 (1997–9): 9–45

Trinkaus, C. and H. A. Oberman (eds.), *The Pursuit of Holiness in Late Medieval and Renaissance Religion* (Leiden, 1974)

Trio, P., 'Financing of university students in the middle ages: a new orientation', *History of Universities* 4 (1984): 1–24

Turner, D., *The Darkness of God: Negativity in Christian Mysticism* (Cambridge, 1995)

Eros and Allegory: Medieval Exegesis of the Song of Songs (Kalamazoo, MI, 1995)

Turner, G., 'St Thomas Aquinas on the "scientific" nature of theology', *New Blackfriars* 78 (1997): 464–76

Tweedale, M. M., *Abailard on Universals* (Amsterdam, 1976).

Van Deusen, N. (ed.), *The Intellectual Climate of the Early University: Essays in Honor of Otto Gründler* (Kalamazoo, MI, 1997)

Van Engen, J. H., *Rupert of Deutz* (Berkeley, 1983)

Van Steenberghen, F., *Aristotle in the West: The Origins of Latin Aristotelianism*, trans. L. Johnston (Louvain, 1955)

van't Spijker, I., *Fictions of the Inner Life: Religious Literature and Formation of the Self in the Eleventh and Twelfth Centuries* (Turnhout, 2004)

Venarde, B. L., *Women's Monasticism and Medieval Society: Nunneries in France and England, 890–1215* (Ithaca, NY, 1997)

Veraja, F., *Le origini della controversia teologica sul contratto di censo nel xiii secolo*, Storia ed economia 7 (Rome, 1960)

Verdeyen, P., *La Théologie Mystique de Guillaume de Saint-Thierry* (Paris, 1990)

'Le procès d'inquisition contre Marguerite Porete et Guiard de Cressonessart (1309–1310)', *Revue d'histoire ecclésiastique* 81 (1986): 47–94

Verger, J., 'A propos de la naissance de l'université de Paris: contexte social, enjeu politique, portée intellectuelle', in J. Fried (ed.), *Schulen und Studium im Sozialen Wandel des hohen und späten Mittelalters*, Vorträge und Forschungen 30 (Sigmaringen, 1986), pp. 69–96

Men of Learning in Europe at the End of the Middle Ages, trans. L. Neal and S. Rendall (Notre Dame, IN, 2000)

'Patterns', in H. de Ridder-Symoens (ed.), *A History of the University in Europe. Vol. 1: Universities in the Middle Ages* (Cambridge, 1992), pp. 35–74

'Teachers', in H. de Ridder-Symoens (ed.), *A History of the University in Europe. Vol. 1: Universities in the Middle Ages* (Cambridge, 1992), pp. 144–68

Walsh, K. and D. Wood (eds.), *The Bible in the Medieval World: Essays in Memory of Beryl Smalley* (Oxford, 1985)

Ward, J. O. 'Rhetoric in the faculty of arts at the universities of Paris and Oxford in the middle ages: a summary of the evidence', *Bulletin Du Cange (Archivum Latinitatis Medii Aevi)* 54 (1996): 159–231

Watson, N., 'Misrepresenting the untranslatable: Marguerite Porete and the *Mirouer des Simples Ames*', *New Comparison* 12 (1991): 124–37

Weber, C. F., '*Ces grands privilèges*: the symbolic use of written documents in the foundation and institutionalization processes of medieval universities', *History of Universities* 19 (2004): 12–62

Wei, I. P., 'From twelfth-century schools to thirteenth-century universities: the disappearance of biographical and autobiographical representations of scholars', *Speculum* 86 (2011): 42–78

'Gender and sexuality in medieval academic discourse: marriage problems in Parisian quodlibets', *Mediaevalia* 31 (2010): 5–34

'Guy de l'Aumône's "Summa de diversis questionibus theologiae"', *Traditio* 44 (1988): 275–323

'Intellectuals and money: Parisian disputations about annuities in the thirteenth century', *Bulletin of the John Rylands University Library of Manchester* 83, no. 3 (2001), a special edition further titled P. D. Clarke (ed.), *Owens's Historical Essays in Honour of Jeffrey H. Denton*, pp. 71–94

'The masters of theology at the university of Paris in the late thirteenth and early fourteenth centuries: an authority beyond the schools', *Bulletin of the John Rylands University Library of Manchester* 75 (1993): 37–63

'Predicting the future to judge the present: Paris theologians and attitudes to the future', in J. A. Burrow and I. P. Wei (eds.), *Medieval Futures: Attitudes to the Future in the Middle Ages* (Woodbridge, 2000), pp. 19–36

'Scholars and travel in the twelfth and thirteenth centuries', in P. Horden (ed.), *Freedom of Movement in the Middle Ages: People, Ideas, Goods* (Donington, 2007), pp. 73–85

'The self-image of the masters of theology at the university of Paris in the late thirteenth and early fourteenth centuries', *Journal of Ecclesiastical History* 46 (1995): 398–431

Weijers, O., 'The chronology of John of Salisbury's studies in France (Metalogicon, II.10)', in M. Wilks (ed.), *The World of John of Salisbury* (1984, repr. Oxford, 1994), pp. 109–16

Terminologie des universités au xiiie siècle (Rome, 1987)

Weisheipl, J. A., *Friar Thomas d'Aquino: His Life, Thought and Works* (New York, 1974)

Wetherbee, W., *Platonism and Poetry in the Twelfth Century: The Literary Influence of the School of Chartres* (Princeton, 1972)

Wieland, G., 'The reception and interpretation of Aristotle's *Ethics*', in N. Kretzmann, A. Kenny and J. Pinborg (eds.), *The Cambridge History of Later Medieval Philosophy* (Cambridge, 1982), pp. 657–72

Wilks, M. (ed.), *The World of John of Salisbury* (1984, repr. Oxford, 1994)

Wilshire, L. E., 'The condemnations of 1277 and the intellectual climate of the medieval university', in N. Van Deusen (ed.), *The Intellectual Climate of the Early University: Essays in Honor of Otto Gründler* (Kalamazoo, MI, 1997), pp. 151–93

Winroth, A., *The Making of Gratian's Decretum* (Cambridge, 2000)

Wippel, J. F., 'The quodlibetal question as a distinctive literary genre', in *Les genres littéraires dans les sources théologiques et philosophiques médiévales: definition, critique et exploitation. Actes du colloque international de Louvain-la-Neuve 25–27 mai 1981* (Louvain-la-Neuve, 1982), pp. 67–84

'Quodlibetal questions, chiefly in theology faculties', in *Les questions disputées et les questions quodlibétiques dans les facultés de théologie, de droit et de médecine*, Typologie des sources du moyen âge occidental 44–45 (Turnhout, 1985), pp. 151–222

Wood, D., *Medieval Economic Thought* (Cambridge, 2002)

Wood, M. M., *The Spirit of Protest in Old French Literature* (New York, 1917)

Young, S. E., '"Consilio hominum nostrorum": a comparative study of royal responses to crisis at the University of Paris, 1200–1231', *History of Universities* 22 (2007): 1–20

Zinn, G. A., '*Historia fundamentum est*: the role of history in the contemplative life according to Hugh of St. Victor', in G. H. Shriver (ed.), *Contemporary Reflections on the Medieval Christian Tradition: Essays in Honor of Ray C. Petry* (Durham, NC, 1974), pp. 135–58

Ziolkowski, J., *Alan of Lille's Grammar of Sex: The Meaning of Grammar to a Twelfth-Century Intellectual* (Cambridge, MA, 1985)

Index

Abelard, Peter *see* Peter Abelard
academic careers 87
accidents 18, 21
Adelard of Bath 37–40
  on philosophy 41–2
Adénulfe of Anagni 282–3
agent intellect 146–50
aids, preaching 237, 238, 244–5
Alan of Lille 42–3, 45–7
  on contrition 240
  works
    Anticlaudianus 42–3
    Art of Preaching, The 230, 232–3, 237, 245
    Liber poenitentialis 243
    Plaint of Nature 45–7
Alberic 33
Albert the Great 301–2, 304
  on usury 311, 314
Alexander of Hales 115
Alexander III 49, 322
  Naviganti 322, 324, 327
Alexander IV 116–17, 125
allegory 40–4
alms 203, 282–7
Ambrose 306
angels 193, 226
  see also demons
Angers (university) 89
annihilated souls 383–92, 410–11
annuities 323–45, 354–5
Anselm of Bec and Canterbury 3, 53–9, 72
  on the devil 224–7
  works
    Cur Deus Homo ('Why God Became Man') 224–7
    De Grammatico 54
    Proslogion 54–9
Anselm of Laon 14–15, 35
  and Abelard 30
  glosses 48
anti-intellectual intellectuals 6–7, 356–7, 408–14
Anticlaudianus or the Good and Perfect Man (Alan of Lille) 42–3
Apologia (Rupert of Deutz) 12–13
apparitions of souls 205–6
Aquinas, Thomas *see* Thomas Aquinas
argument 22–7
  see also disputation
Aristotle 18, 123–4
  Adelard on 39
  Aquinas on 153, 154, 160, 252
  as part of university curriculum 94, 95, 110
  on science 172
  on syllogism 23–7
  on trade and merchants 299–300, 302
  works
    De Sophisticis 18
    Nichomachean Ethics 301, 312
    On Interpretation 18
    Politics 314
    Posterior Analytics 18
    Prior Analytics 18, 23–4
    see also Bonaventure; Thomas Aquinas
Art of Preaching, The (Alan of Lille) 230, 232–3, 237, 245
arts/sciences, Hugh of Saint Victor on 79–80
ascent to God
  Bonaventure 126–43
  in *Mirror* 377–83
audience 236–7, 244–5
  Aquinas on 160
  Eckhart's 394
  of *Mirror* 388–9
  Romance of the Rose 362
Augustine 131–2
  on purgatory 196
  on trade and merchants 297, 298
  on usury 306

Authentica Habita (Frederick I) 49
Averroes 162

bachelors 96, 235–6
barbarisms 46
Barbarismus (Donatus) 95
Baschet, Jérome 205
Beati pauperes spiritu (Eckhart) 395–6, 402, 405
beghards 393
beguines 375, 393
Being, God as 127, 137–9
benefices 118
Bernard of Chartres 16–17
Bernard of Clairvaux 3, 53, 59–65, 72
  and conflict with schoolmen 73–8
  Five books on Consideration 62–3
  letter from Hildegard of Bingen 71
  sermons
    on 2 Kings 5 63–4
    on Solomon's Song of Songs 59–63
  on visions of Hildegard of Bingen 68
  and William of Saint Thierry 65
Bernard Silvestris 40–1
Bernstein, Alan 204–5, 208, 210–11
Bible
  Bonaventure on study of 165–6
  concordances 237
  on men and women 248
  and *Parens scientiarum* 104–5
  and purgatory 185
  Song of Songs 59–63
  textual interpretation of 35, 80–1
  on trade and merchants 296–7
  on usury 307–8
  see also Bernard of Clairvaux, sermons
Blanche of Castille 101
Boethius 18
  on *Isagoge* 28
  and *Romance of the Rose* 363
Boethius of Dacia 162, 167
Bologna 36–7, 50, 89–91
Bonaventure 124–43
  Aristotelian conflict 161, 162, 164–6
  biography 124–5
  on purgatory 217–18
  works
    Breviloquium 126–7, 217–18
    Commentary on the Sentences 127, 128
    Conferences on the Hexaemeron 165–6
    Retracing the Arts to Theology (*De reductione artium ad theologiam*) 142–3
    Soul's Journey into God, The 125–43
Book of Divine Works (Hildegard of Bingen) 68–9
Book of Life's Merits, The (Hildegard of Bingen) 68
Boso 226
Breviloquium (Bonaventure) 126–7, 217–18

Cambridge (university) 89
canon law 37, 108, 182–3, 247–8
  on annuities 329, 335
  justice in exchange 303–4
  on usury 308, 319, 351
  see also Huguccio
careers, academic 87
Categories (Aristotle) 18
  see also Isagoge
cathedral schools 8–9
Causes and Cures (Hildegard of Bingen) 69
Chartres, School of 40
chastity 275–6, 277–81, 283, 285
children
  illegitimate 287–9
  purpose of marriage 252–3
church
  defined by Godfrey of Fontaines 183–4
  and *Mirror* 386
Cicero 23
Cistercian order 100
classes, in Porphyry's *Isagoge* 19–20
classical texts 8, 11, 43, 173, 411
Collège de Sorbonne 114, 117
Collège des Dix-Huit 113–14
College of the Treasurer 114
colleges 113–14
Comestor, Peter *see* Peter Comestor
Commentary on the Benedictine Rule (Rupert of Deutz) 12
Commentary on the Sentences (Bonaventure) 127, 128
communication, means of 228
  confession 239–44
  preaching 229–38
  quodlibetal disputations 174–5, 228–9
  target audiences 244–5
concordances, Bible 237
Concordia discordantium canonum ('A Harmony of Conflicting Canons') (Gratian) 36–7
condemnation of 1277 167–8
conduct, statutes of 95–100
  see also Parens scientiarum
Conferences on the Hexaemeron (Bonaventure) 165–6
confession 239–44

conflict 123
between Paris and university 92, 294
religious orders and university
in the 1250s 116–18, 168
in the 1280s 120–1
in twelfth-century schools 44–7
conjugal debt 260–3
consent, to marriage 254–8
Consuluit (Urban III) 306
consummation of marriage 254–8
contrition 198–9, 213, 239–41, 287
control, social 246
Cosmographia (Bernard Silvestris) 40–1
Council of Lyons (1274) 125, 346–7
Council of Rheims (1148) 73–5, 77–8
Council of Sens (1140) 73
Council of Soissons (1121) 10, 16
Council of Vienne 393
credit *see* usury
crisis of 1200 92
crisis of 1229 101, 115
Cuno (abbot of Siegburg) 12
Cur Deus Homo ('Why God Became Man') (Anselm of Bec and Canterbury) 224–7
curiositas 158–9, 161
curiosity 99
curriculum 94, 95
in *Parens scientiarum* 109–10
see also degrees

Davies, Oliver 406
De Grammatico (Anselm of Bec and Canterbury) 54
De Malo (Thomas Aquinas) 320
De periculis novissimorum temporum ('On the Dangers of Most Recent Times') (William of Saint Amour) 117, 361
De Regimine Principum (Aquinas?) 298
De sacramentis (Hugh of Saint Victor) 189–95
De sacramentis (Peter Comestor) 198–9
De Sophisticis (Aristotle) 18
De universo (William of Auvergne) 204
De usuris (Giles of Lessines) 311
debt, conjugal 260–3
Decretum (Gratian) 36–7, 47, 251, 266, 297
usury 306
'Defence of Logic' (*Metalogicon*) (John of Salisbury) 16–17, 44–5, 171
degrees 121–2
demons 215
see also angels

detachment 394–6, 401–4
devil 224–8
dialectic *see* logic
Dialogue between a Philosopher, a Jew and a Christian (Abelard) 170–1
Didascalicon ('On the Study of Reading') (Hugh of Saint Victor) 79, 83–4
differences 18, 20–1
disputations, quodlibetal 174–5, 228–9, 230–2, 242–3
on annuities 323–45
questioning masters 295
Dominican order 114–18, 143–243
and Aquinas 143
Donatus 95
dreams 209, 210, 364–7
Drythelm 187–9
Duns Scotus, John 241, 320
Durand of Saint Pourçain 266, 267, 352

Eadmer, on Anselm of Bec and Canterbury 54, 57
Eckhart 392–408, 409–10, 411–14
biography 392–4
and Marguerite Porete 394–5
works
Beati pauperes spiritu 395–6, 402, 405
In agro dominico 402, 406–7
On Detachment 403–4
On the Noble Man 396, 398
Ubi est qui natus est rex judaeorum 397
Eliseus 64
England (nation) 111
Esti animarum (Innocent IV) 116
Eternal Art 132, 134
eternity of the world 4
Ethics (Peter Abelard) 270–1
Eugenius III 68
Eustace of Grandcourt 287, 288–9
evil, and God 14, 15
Ex litteris vestre (Innocent III) 92–3
exchange, justice in 301–5
excommunication
of the Dominicans 116–17
masters disagreeing with the church 179–81
of scholars at Rheims 49
of university 100–1

faculty of arts 111, 112–13
fear 192, 219
Ferruolo, Stephen 295
financial support 49–50, 118–19

fire, hell/purgatorial
  Aquinas on 213, 214
  Bonaventure on 217
  Peter Comestor on 199
  William of Auvergne on 204–5, 207–12
Five books on Consideration (Bernard of Clairvaux) 62–3
flying scholarships (*bursae volantes*) 119
Foulques de Neuilly 238
Four Books of the Sentences (Peter Lombard) 36, 47–8, 195–7, 251, 295, 297
France (nation) 111
Francis, Saint 124, 125, 166
Franciscan order 114–18, 234
  and Bonaventure 124
Frederick I, Holy Roman Emperor 49
free will 227–8
French solution 256
funerary practices, in the statutes 96
fungibles 309–10, 317
  money as 351–2

Gaunilo 56
gender-neutral language 272–3
genera 18–20, 22–3, 28
Gerald Odonis 321
Gerard of Abbeville 323–5
Gerard of Borgo San Donnino 117, 361
Gervais/Gervase *see* Servais of Mont Saint Eloi
Gilbert of Poitiers 73–5, 77–8
Giles of Lessines 302
  on money 315
  on time 311
  on usury 311–12
    interest 319
Giles of Rome 311, 323, 340–2
  usurious money 349–51, 352
God
  Being 127, 137–9
  Bonaventure on 126–43
  Eckhart on 400–1
  and evil 14, 15
  Good 127, 139
  Hugh of Saint Victor on 83–4
  knowledge/existence of
    Anselm of Bec and Canterbury 54–9
    Bernard of Clairvaux 62–3
    Thomas Aquinas 150–7
Godfrey of Fontaines 179–81, 323
  on annuities 337–40, 342–3, 345
  on law 183–4
  on marital problems 283–5
  on *Mirror* 375
  on usury 346–7
Good, God as 127, 139
good works 203, 378, 402, 404, 408
Goswin, Saint 15–16
grace
  Aquinas on 145, 154–5, 160
  Bonaventure on 136–7
  Marguerite Porete on 377
grammatical metaphors 46–7
Gratian
  Decretum 36–7, 47, 297, 306
  on marriage 251, 256, 266
great dispersion 101–2, 123
Gregory the Great, *Moralia in Job* 104–7, 198
Gregory IX
  In civitate 324, 327
  and *Parens scientiarum* 3–4, 92, 102–11
Gregory X 125
ground of the soul, metaphor of Eckhart 398
Gurevich, Aaron 186–7, 344
Guy of Cluny (or Guy of Pernes) 290–1
Guy of Colmieu 375
Guy de l'Aumône 100, 289–90

Halesian Summa 299, 301
hell
  fire 204–5, 208, 213
  Hugh of Saint Victor on 195
  Peter the Chanter on 202
  William of Auvergne on 204–5, 208, 211–12
Heloise 10, 357
Henry of Ghent 176–9
  on annuities 323, 325–7, 330–2, 333–4, 335–7, 338–9, 342–4
  on conflict with the church 181–2
  just price 302
  on marital problems 276–7, 278, 287
  on usurious money 351–2
Henry III, of England 118
Henry of Virneburg 393, 394
heresy
  Abelard 10, 16
  Eckhart 393–4, 407–8
  Marguerite Porete 375–6
  Rupert of Deutz 14
hierarchy of knowledge 179, 184
  Abelard on 35
Hildebert of Lavardin 199, 199n.84
Hildegard of Bingen 53, 68–72
  works
    Book of Divine Works 68–9
    Book of Life's Merits, The 68

Causes and Cures 69
Scivias 68, 69–70
Historia Calamitatum ('History of My Misfortunes') (Abelard) 9, 31, 34
Historia occidentalis (Jacques de Vitry) 238
Historia Scholastica (Peter Comestor) 48
homosexuality, Alan of Lille on 45–7
Honorius III 91, 115, 118
Hugh of Saint Victor 3, 53, 78–86
on contrition 240–1
on marriage 251, 253, 254–6, 257, 258–9
sexual pleasure 269
on men and women 248
on purgatory 191–5, 219
and visions 189–91
works
De sacramentis 189–95
Didascalicon ('On the Study of Reading') 79, 83–4
Huguccio 256, 266, 269–70
humility 62, 81–3, 240–1, 380, 404

imagination 209, 211
In agro dominico (Eckhart) 394, 402, 406–7
In civitate (Gregory IX) 324, 327
inception 96, 236
Innocent III 269
Innocent IV 116
on usury 307
intellect
agent 146–50
Aquinas on 145–6
Bonaventure on 133–5, 138
see also knowledge
intellectuals, anti-intellectual 6–7
intelligible species 146–8, 156–7
intention 147
in masters' conflict with the church 181–2
and sexual pleasure 265, 266–7
of sin 220–4
interest (monetary) 307, 308, 309, 313, 316, 319–21
interpretation, textual 33–7
Isagoge (Porphyry) 18–23, 28
Italian solution 256
Ivo of Chartres 36

Jacques de Vitry, *Historia occidentalis* 238
James, Saint 172
Jean de Barastre 115
Jean de Meun 6–7, 357–74, 408–9, 410, 411–14
in *Romance of the Rose* 367–8
Jean Lesage 286
Jerome 306
Jesus Christ, Bonaventure on 129–30, 140
Joachim of Fiore 117, 125, 361
Jocius of London 113–14
John, Bishop of Châlons-sur-Marne 376
John of Candeilles 94–5
John Chrysostom 297, 299
John of Freiburg, *Summa confessorum* 243–4
John (of Murrovalle?) 287–8
John of Parma 125
John of Saint Giles 115
John of Salisbury 16–17
on the conflict between the monasteries and the schoolmen 73–5, 77–8
on logic 27, 44–5
universals 28
Metalogicon ('Defence of Logic') 16–17, 44–5, 171
moral philosophy 171
John XXI 167
John XXII 412
John of Zurich 393
justice in exchange 301–5, 354
Jutta of Sponheim 68, 70

Kaye, Joel 304, 342–3
keys of St Peter 241–2
knowledge
Bernard of Clairvaux on 61
Bonaventure on 130–2
Eckhart on 396–8
hierarchies of 35, 179, 184, 408–9
Hugh of Saint Victor on 79–80
and Marguerite Porete 392

Lanfranc 53
Langton, Stephen 230
language
Aquinas on use of 154
and conflict between monasteries and schoolmen 75
in consent of marriage 255–6
Eckhart's use of 405–7, 409
gender in 272–5, 278–82
grammatical metaphors 46–7
and logic 27
in *Mirror* 391, 392, 409
and textual interpretation 34
and universals 27–30, 45
use in *Romance of the Rose* 372–3

law
  Bologna 36–7, 50
  canon 37, 108, 182–3, 247–8
    on annuities 329, 335, 351
    justice in exchange 303–4
    on usury 308, 319
  Roman
    trade 303
    on usury 308–9, 314, 318, 319, 343
lawyers, and conflict with masters 182–4
Le Goff, Jacques 186, 200, 203, 205, 295, 344
learning, Bonaventure on 135, 142–3
legal corporation, of the university 108–9
Lewis of Bavaria 394
Liber introductorius in evangelium aeternum ('Introduction to the Eternal Gospel') (Gerard of Borgo San Donnino) 117, 361
Liber poenitentialis (Alan of Lille) 243
Liber poenitentialis (Robert of Flamborough) 243
licences to teach 108, 116
light, metaphor of Eckhart 398, 401, 403
loans *see* usury
logic 3, 17–33
  discussed in *Romance of the Rose* 359
  Hugh of Saint Victor on 80
  old 18
  and use of language 27
Lombard, Peter *see* Peter Lombard
Louis IX 102, 114

McGinn, Bernard 406
Marguerite Porete 6–7, 374–92, 409, 410, 411–14
  and Eckhart 394–5
  on writing *Mirror* 387–8
marriage 5
  consent and consummation 254–8
  marital affection 258–60
  marital problems 272–92
  purpose of 250–4
  in *Romance of the Rose* 369–70, 371
  sex in 260–72, 371
masters 8, 120–1
  about conflict with the church 179–84
  collective organization 91–3
  and conflict with lawyers 182–4
  crisis of 1200 92
  financial support 49–50, 118–19
  regulation of in Bologna 91
  self-image of 174–84
  setting up schools 12
  statutes of conduct 95–100
  of theology 4
    in *Romance of the Rose* 360–1
  on trade 296
Matthew of Aquasparta 323, 327–9, 345
meaning 6, 374, 409
memory
  Abelard definition of 30–1
  Bonaventure on 132–3, 134–5
men/women, nature of 248–50
merchants and trade 296–306, 353–5
messengers (*nuntii volantes*) 112
Metalogicon ('Defence of Logic') (John of Salisbury) 16–17, 44–5, 171
metaplasms 46–7
Mirror of Simple Souls, The (Marguerite Porete) 374–92
misogyny 247–8
monasteries 87
  and schoolmen 52–3, 72–8, 85–6
  schools in the 8
money, nature of and usury 313–18, 348–53
mood 25–7
Moore, R.I. 184–5
moral philosophy 170–4
Moralia in Job (Gregory the Great) 104–7, 198
Mystical Theology (Denys) 141
myth 3, 40–4

nations 111–13
Natural History (Hildegard of Bingen) 69
natural reason 145, 153, 164, 252–3
natural world
  and myth and poetry 40–4
  sense perception 2–3, 37–40
Naviganti (Alexander III) 322, 324, 327
Nicholas of Strasburg 393
Nichomachean Ethics (Aristotle) 301, 312
nobility
  Eckhart on 401, 402
  in *Romance of the Rose* 362–3, 373–4
Normandy (nation) 111
numbers 132

old logic 18
Olivi, Peter *see* Peter Olivi
'On the Dangers of Most Recent Times' (*De periculis novissimorum temporum*) (William of Saint Amour) 117, 361
On Detachment (Eckhart) 403–4
On Interpretation (Aristotle) 18
On the Noble Man (Eckhart) 396, 398

On the Unity of the Intellect against the Averroists (Aquinas) 162–3
Orléans (university) 89
Oxford (university) 235

Padua (university) 89
pain 219–20
Aquinas on purgatorial 214
William of Auvergne on 219–20
paleae 297
Panormia (Ivo of Chartres) 36
Parens scientiarum (Parent of Sciences) 3–4, 92, 102–11, 121, 122
Paris
city development 293–6
pastoral revolution 174
patronage, financial support for students 118–19
Paul, Saint, on marriage 251
penances
and confession 239–40
interior 206–7
and purgatory 185, 188, 198–9, 201, 202, 211–12, 217–18, 219–20
supplementary 207
unequal 215
penitents, and purgatory 196–7
persuasion 291
Peter Abelard 9–12
and Anselm of Laon 30
and the conflict with monasteries 73, 75–7
on contrition 240
and Goswin 15–16
and Heloise 10
on intention 220–4
and John of Salisbury 17
on marriage, and sexual pleasure 270–1
on Porphyry 21–2, 23
on priests 242
and textual interpretation 33–6
theological work 33
on William of Champeaux 29–30
works
Dialogue between a Philosopher, a Jew and a Christian 170–1
Ethics 270–1
Historia Calamitatum ('History of My Misfortunes') 9, 31, 34
Sic et Non 33–6
Peter the Chanter
and Foulques de Neuilly 238
on just price in trade 301
on marriage 268
on preaching 230–1
on priests 242
on purgatory 201–4
works
Summa de Sacramentis et animae consiliis 201–3
Verbum Adbreviatum 203–4
Peter Comestor (Pierre le Mangeur) 48
De sacramentis 198–9
on purgatory 198–201
Peter Lombard
on contrition 240
Four Books of the Sentences 36, 47–8, 195–7, 251, 295, 297
on marriage 255, 256, 257, 259
conjugal debt 262
and sexual pleasure 265–6, 267, 268
on priests 241–2
on purgatory 195–8
on trade 297
Peter of Nemours 94
Peter Olivi 321
Peter of Poitiers
Summa de confessione 243
on usury 295–6
Peter the Venerable 73
phantasms 146–7, 149–50, 156–7, 209
Philip Augustus 92, 293
Philip the Chancellor 123
Philip the Fair 293
Philip IV, of France 118–19
philosophy
Adelard of Bath on 41–2
Bonaventure on 135, 165–6
moral 170–4
Picardy (nation) 111
Plaint of Nature (Alan of Lille) 45–7
Plato 19, 20, 28, 39, 40, 41
pleasure, sexual 265–72, 368–9, 370–2
poetry 3, 40–4
Politics (Aristotle) 314
Porphyry
Isagoge 18–23, 28
tree 20
positions, sexual 263–4
Posterior Analytics (Aristotle) 18
prayer
Anselm of Bec and Canterbury 58
Bonaventure on 129
Eckhart on 404
preaching 103–4, 105–8, 229–38, 244–5
predestined souls 202–3
pride 61, 99, 105, 240–1
Prior Analytics (Aristotle) 18, 23–4
property 18, 21

prophecy 155–6
Proslogion (Anselm of Bec and Canterbury) 54–9
Pseudo-Denys, *Mystical Theology* 141
Ptolemy of Lucca 298n.16
punishment *see* hell; purgatory
purgatory 185–91, 218–20
  Hugh of Saint Victor on 189–95
  Peter the Chanter on 201–4
  Peter Comestor (Pierre le Mangeur) on 198–201
  Peter Lombard on 195–8
  William of Auvergne on 204–12

quadrivium 17–18
Quasi lignum vitae (Alexander IV) 116–17
Questiones Naturales ('Natural Questions') (Adelard) 37–40
quiddity *see* intelligible species
quodlibetal disputations 174–5, 228–9, 230–2, 242–3
  annuities 323–45
  questioning masters 295
  see also marital problems

R. of Arras 285–6
ransom theory 224–6
rapture 156–7
Raymund of Pennaforte 143
reading
  Didascalicon ('On the Study of Reading') (Hugh of Saint Victor) 79
  William of Saint Thierry on 67
reason
  Anselm of Bec and 58–9
  and faith 75
  natural 145, 153, 164, 252–3
  and sex 265
religious orders
  teaching 159–60
  and the university 114–18
rents, life/eternal *see* annuities
retail trade 314
Retracing the Arts to Theology (*De reductione artium ad theologiam*) (Bonaventure) 142–3
Richard of Middleton 302, 323
  on annuities 332–5, 345
Robert of Courson 92, 93, 121, 242, 268
  on just price in trade 301, 303
  on usury 309, 310, 320
Robert de Sorbon 114, 259
Robert of Flamborough, *Liber poenitentialis* 243
Roland of Cremona 115, 306
Roman d'Alexandre 390
Roman law
  trade 303
  on usury 308–9, 314, 318, 319, 343
Romance of the Rose (Guillaume de Lorris and Jean de Meun) 357–74
  story 357–9
Romano, cardinal of Saint Angelo 101
Roscelin of Compiegne 28–9
Rue du Fouarre 111
Rupert of Deutz 12–15, 104, 105
Rutebeuf 100

satisfaction theory 226–7
schoolmen, and monasteries 52–3, 72–8, 85–6, 87
schools 8–9, 12
  cathedral 8–9
  conflict with monasteries 72–8
  as stable institutions of learning 47–51
  see also monasteries
sciences/arts
  Bonaventure on 165
  Hugh of Saint Victor on 79–80
Scivias (Hildegard of Bingen) 68, 69–70
Scriptures *see* Bible
seed, metaphor in Eckhart 398
self, Eckhart on 407–8
self-image, of masters 174–84
self-knowledge 62, 82
sense perception 2–3, 37–40
sense-based knowledge
  Adelard on 39
  Aquinas and 145–54, 156, 160–1
  Bonaventure and 130–2, 143
sermons *see* preaching
Servais of Mont Saint Eloi 231–2, 233–4, 323
  on annuities 329–30
  on marital problems 277–8, 280–1
  on usurious money 351
sex 5, 252–3
  and consent to marry 256–7
  consummation of marriage 254–8
  homosexuality 45–7
  marital 252, 253–4, 260–72
  non-marital 252
  pleasure in 265–72, 368–9, 370–2
  positions in 263–4
  and *Romance of the Rose* 371, 372–3
Sextus the Pythagorean 265
sexual pleasure 265–72, 368–9, 370–2
Sic et Non (Abelard) 33–6
Siger of Brabant 162, 167
similitude 126–8
sin
  and intention 220–4

and sexual pleasure 265–72
venial 201–4, 205, 213, 215, 219
see also confession; sexual pleasure
social class
and Marguerite Porete 390–2
nobility 362–3, 373–4, 401, 402
Song of Songs (Bible) 59–63, 104
Sorbonne, Collège de 114, 117
souls
after death 218
Hugh of Saint Victor on 192–4
Peter Comestor on 201
William of Auvergne on 205
annihilated 383–92
spark of 398
Soul's Journey into God, The (Bonaventure) 125–43, 164–5
spark of the soul, metaphor of Eckhart 398
species 18–20, 22–3, 28
spiritual elite 60, 61, 65–8, 72
statutes of conduct for masters and students 93–100, 122, 235
Stephen of Garlande 10
strikes, 1229 101, 115
students 87
collective organizations 89–91
financial support 118–19
and the schools 49–51
statutes of conduct 95–100
studia generalia 88–90
studiositas 158, 161
substance, in *Categories* 18
suffrages 219
Bonaventure on 218
Hugh of Saint Victor on 195
Peter the Chanter on 204
Peter Lombard on 197–8
Thomas Aquinas on 215–17
William of Auvergne on 206
Summa aurea (William of Auxerre) 306
Summa confessorum (John of Freiburg) 243–4
Summa confessorum (Thomas of Chobham) 243, 312
Summa Contra Gentiles (Aquinas) 143–4, 145, 250
Summa de confessione (Peter of Poitiers) 243
Summa de Sacramentis et animae consiliis (Peter the Chanter) 201–3
Summa Theologiae (Aquinas) 144, 145, 212–16, 243, 250
on trade 304–6
on usury 310, 314–15, 318–19, 320–1, 345
interest 320–1
Super speculam (Honorius III) 118
syllogism 22–7

teaching, Aquinas on 157–61
Tempier, Stephen 167
textbooks 47–8
textual interpretation 33–7, 80–1
theft, usury as 312–13
theology 171–4
defining 48–9
masters of 4, 115–16
Parens scientiarum 110
statutes for the conduct of 97–8
Thomas Aquinas 124, 143–61
Aristotelian conflict 161–4
biography 143–4, 167
on contrition 241
on the devil 227–8
on marriage 252–3, 254, 256, 257–8, 259–60
and conjugal debt 261–2, 263
problems 275–6, 278–80
sexual pleasure 265, 266, 267, 268–9
on money 314–18
on nature of men and women 248–50
on purgatory 212–17
on theology 171–3, 175
on trade and merchants 299–300
just price 301, 302, 303, 304–6
on usury 310, 313, 314, 318–19, 345–6, 348–9
interest 319, 320–1
works
De Malo 320, 345–6
On the Unity of the Intellect against the Averroists 162–3
Summa Contra Gentiles 143–4, 145, 250
Summa Theologiae 144, 145, 212–16, 227–8, 243, 250, 304–6
usury 310, 314–15, 318–19, 320–1, 345
see also De Regimine Principum
Thomas of Chobham 268, 287, 289
on money 314
Summa confessorum 243, 312
on trade and merchants 299
on usury 309, 310, 311, 312
interest 319
time
and purgatory 219
and usury 310–11

times, acceptable for sex 264–5
Topics (Aristotle) 18, 95
trade and merchants 5–6, 296–306, 353–5, 362
transformation 105–8
translation of texts 2
Trinity
  Abelard on 32–3
  Bonaventure on 139–40
triple vision 127
trivium 17
truth 4
  and *Romance of the Rose* 363–6
Turner, Denys 406

Ubi est qui natus est rex judaeorum ('Where is he who is born King of the Jews?') (Eckhart) 397
uncertainty 192
unity ('unicity') of the intellect 4, 162–3
universals 27–30, 44–5
universities 411–12
  development of 87–91
  life after 119–21
  Paris 3–4
urban culture 5–6
Urban III 306
Urban IV 117
  Peter of Poitiers on 295–6
usury 6, 289–92, 296, 306–23, 345–8, 353, 354–5
  and money from 348–53
  Peter of Poitiers on 295–6
  in *Romance of the Rose* 362
  see also annuities

venial sins 201–4, 205, 213, 215, 219
Verbum Adbreviatum (Peter the Chanter) 203–4
virtue 3
  Hugh of Saint Victor on 82–3
visions
  of Hildegard of Bingen 68, 69–72
  and purgatory 186–91
Volmar 70
voluntariness of punishment 214–15

'Where is he who is born King of the Jews?' (*Ubi est qui natus est rex judaeorum*) (Eckhart) 397
'Why God Became Man' (*Cur Deus Homo*) (Anselm of Bec and Canterbury) 224–7
will, the
  Bonaventure on 134–5
  Eckhart on 403
  in *Mirror* 386
  Thomas Aquinas on 227–8
William of Auvergne
  De universo 204
  on purgatory 204–12
William of Auxerre 306, 310–11, 312
William of Champeaux 11–12, 14–15, 29–30, 78
William of Moerbeke 314
William of Paris 376, 394
William of Saint Thierry 3, 53, 65–7, 72
  and the conflict with the schoolmen 73
William of Saint Amour 117, 361
wills 110, 119
women
  and marriage 5, 271–2
  nature of 248–50
  and *Romance of the Rose* 365, 366–7

Lightning Source UK Ltd.
Milton Keynes UK
UKOW06f2201261115

263570UK00007B/160/P

9 781107 460362